大学英语四级
考试一本通

王江涛 编著

西安交通大学出版社
XI`AN JIAOTONG UNIVERSITY PRESS

图书在版编目(CIP)数据

大学英语四级考试一本通 / 王江涛编著. —西安：
西安交通大学出版社，2013.8

ISBN 978-7-5605-5533-1

Ⅰ.①大…　Ⅱ.①王…　Ⅲ.①大学英语水平考试—自
学参考资料　Ⅳ.①H310.42

中国版本图书馆 CIP 数据核字（2013）第 189384 号

书　　　名	大学英语四级考试一本通	
编　　　著	王江涛	
责 任 编 辑	黄科丰　孙　岩	
封 面 设 计	贾臻臻	
出 版 发 行	西安交通大学出版社	
地　　　址	西安市兴庆南路 10 号（邮编：710049）	
电　　　话	(010)62605588　62605019(发行部)	
	(029)82668315(总编室)	
读 者 信 箱	bj62605588@163.com	
印　　　刷	北京慧美印刷有限公司	
字　　　数	420 千	
开　　　本	880mm×1230mm　1/32	
印　　　张	13.75	
版　　　次	2013 年 8 月第 1 版　2013 年 8 月第 1 次印刷	
书　　　号	ISBN 978-7-5605-5533-1/H · 1551	
定　　　价	25.00 元	

前　言

自 2006 年开始，全国大学英语四级考试统一采用新题型。与旧的四级考试题型相比，新题型在听力理解、阅读理解等部分均出现了较大的变化，使得很多考生不知所措。本书旨在帮助四级考生迅速掌握新四级的学习方法和考试技巧，在短期内攻克四级考试。

一、本书内容

本书是为即将参加四级考试的广大考生量身定做的，共七章。它根据《大学英语四级考试大纲》，按照试卷的题型顺序分为写作、快速阅读、听力理解、仔细阅读、完形填空和翻译六章，每章又分为高分攻略、真题选析和强化训练三大部分。第七章倾力推出两套专家预测试卷，以便考生在考前模考。

前六章的"高分攻略"部分权威透视了各大题型的复习方法与应试技巧，帮助考生迅速攻克各题型。"写作"一章详细分析了最新大纲对于写作的要求，推荐了写作常用的钻石句型，同时详尽讲解了书信、告示等常考应用文的写作方法。"快速阅读"一章具体分析了最新大纲要求，透彻讲解了应试技巧、解题顺序和技巧。"听力理解"一章详细分析了短对话的四大解题技巧、九大必考场景；长对话的三大解题技巧、两大解题原则和三大必考场景；短文理解的三大常考题材和三大解题技巧；以及复合式听写的题型概述、评分标准与三大解题技巧。"仔细阅读"一章提供了选词填空的题型介绍、选项特点和三大解题技巧，以及篇章阅读理解的八大出题规律和五大题型的题型分类、题干形式、解题技巧、正误选项特征等。"完形填空"一章分析了五大应试技巧和四大核心考点。"翻译"一章讲解了十大考点与三大选词技巧。

前六章的"真题选析"部分详尽解析了几套新四级考试经典真题。"强化训练"部分则精心编写了几套权威预测试题，帮助考生迅速进入实战状态。以"写作"章节为例，编者精选了十篇经典真题作文，并在"强化训练"部分提供了二十大必背范文以及十大万能框架；入选的每篇作文都提供了优秀范文及其译文，便于考生理解和背诵。

二、本书特色

与市面上其他同类书相比，本书具有以下特色：

1. 本书囊括了四级所有题型，集真题分析与模拟预测于一体。新东方作为四级考试培训的权威机构，在四级培训方面积累了丰富的经验，总结了独特的答题技巧。本书详细讲解了这些答题技巧，将语言基础与应试技能较好地融合在一起，能够帮助考生在短期内提高英语综合运用能力。

2. 本书由多年奋战在四级培训第一线的资深教师编著。编者自 2003 年在新东方授课以来，先后主讲过四级各项课程，充分了解四级考生在复习备考和临场答题时面临的实际问题，总结出了一套行之有效的四级复习方法与应试技巧，成功辅导数万考生以理想的成绩顺利通过四级考试。

3. 本书按照试卷的题型顺序编写，帮助考生迅速进入实战状态，短期内提高应试技能，冲击高分。

三、使用方法

为了更好地利用本书，建议考生采用如下使用方法：

说明：这只是一种推荐的使用方法，请读者结合自身的实际情况进行合理安排。某种题型较薄弱的同学可以在该题型上多投入时间，进行重点巩固。

本书自 2008 年出版以来，得到了全国考生及新东方学员的厚爱与支持，再次表示由衷的感谢！根据最新命题规律，新版图书在第四版的基础上替换了三分之一的内容，主要修订如下：第一章第二节"真题选析"部分替换了七套最新写作真题，附有精彩范文及参考译文；第三节"强化训练"部分增加了十篇最新热点话题精彩范文及参考译文；第三章第一节增添了最新四级真题复合式听写部分的核心词汇与句型；第六章第一节增加了三套四级翻译真题、答案及解析。

四级没有大家想象的那么可怕，只要掌握方法、认真准备，就可以轻松过关！祝天下有志者终过四级！

北京新东方学校

王江涛

附表　四级考试试卷构成及时间分配

一、试卷构成

试卷构成	测试内容		测试题型	分值
听力理解	听力对话 （15%）	短对话 （8个短对话）	多项选择 （8题,8%）	35% （35分钟, 249分）
		长对话 （2个长对话）	多项选择 （7题,7%）	
	听力短文 （20%）	短文理解 （3篇短文）	多项选择 （10题,10%）	
		短文听写 （1篇短文）	复合式听写(8词3句,共10%, 每词0.5%,每句2%)	
阅读理解	快速阅读理解10% （15分钟）		多项选择或是非判断(7题) +句子填空或其他(3题)	35% （40分钟, 249分）
	仔细阅读理解 25% （25分钟）	选词填空或简答题 （1篇文章）	选词填空(15词选10 词)或简答(8题)(5%)	
		篇章阅读理解 （2篇文章）	多项选择(10题,共20%, 每题2%)	
完形填空	完形填空(1篇文章)		多项选择 （20题,共10%,每题0.5%）	10%(15分 钟,70分)
写作和 翻译	写作15%（30分钟）		短文写作（1篇短文）	20%(35分 钟,142分)
	翻译5%（5分钟）		汉译英(5个句子)	

四级考试成绩采用满分 710 分的计分体制，不设及格线；成绩以成绩报告单的形式报告，内容包括：总分及听力理解、阅读理解、完形填空、写作和翻译四部分的单项分。

二、时间分配(共 125 分钟)

08：45　　　　验证入场(身份证、准考证、学生证缺一不可)

09：00　　　　发答题卡(答题卡 1 正面为作文题，背面写作文)，
　　　　　　　9：00 之后禁止入场。

09：10~09：40　　写作(09：35 发试题册)

09：40~09：55　　快速阅读理解(在答题卡 1 背面作答)

09：55~10：00　　收答题卡 1，建议快速浏览听力选项

10：00~10：35　　听力理解(以下在答题卡 2 上作答)

10：35~11：00　　仔细阅读理解(选词填空或简答＋篇章阅读理解)

11：00~11：15　　完形填空(11：05 监考教师提醒 15 分钟后交卷)

11：15~11：20　　翻译

在答题过程中，考生必须在答题卡上作答，在试题册上作答无效。所有
选择性试题务必用 2B 铅笔画线作答；所有非选择性试题（即写作、填空等）
务必用黑色签字笔作答。

目　录

第一章 写 作

最新大纲

根据全国大学英语四、六级考试委员会2006年11月公布的《大学英语四级考试大纲》，写作(Writing)和翻译(Translation)部分测试学生用英语进行书面表达的能力，所占分值比例为20%，其中写作15%，翻译5%，考试时间35分钟。

写作选取考生熟悉的题材。考生需根据规定的题目和提供的提纲、情景、图片或图表等，写出一篇不少于120词的短文。写作要求是思想表达正确、意义连贯、无严重语言错误。考试时间30分钟。

大学英语四级考试写作部分要求考生达到教育部高等教育司最新《大学英语课程教学要求》(教学大纲)中的一般要求，即"能完成一般性写作任务；能描述个人经历、观感、情感和发生的事件等；能写常见的应用文；能就一般性话题或提纲在半小时内写出120个词的短文，内容基本完整，用词恰当，语意连贯。能掌握基本的写作技能"。

考核技能

写作部分考核的技能是：

A. 思想表达

1. 表达中心思想

2. 表达重要信息和特定信息

3. 表达观点、态度等

B. 篇章组织

4. 围绕所给的题目叙述、议论或描述，突出重点

5. 连贯地组句成段、组段成篇

C. 语言运用

6. 运用恰当的词汇

7. 运用正确的语法

8. 运用合适的句子结构

9. 使用正确的标点符号

10. 运用衔接手段表达句子之间和段落之间的关系（如对比、原因、结果、程度、目的等）

D. 写作格式

11. 运用正确的、符合英语表达习惯的写作格式

评分原则

1. CET用以检查考生是否达到大学英语教学大纲规定的四级教学要求，对作文的评判应以此要求为准则。

2. CET作文题采用总体评分（Global Scoring）方法。阅卷人员就总的印象给出奖励分（Reward Scores），而不是按语言点的错误数目扣分。

3. 从内容和语言两个方面对作文进行综合评判。内容和语言是一个统一体。作文应表达题目所规定的内容，而内容要通过语言来表达。要考虑作文是否切题，是否充分表达思想，也要考虑是否用英语清楚而合适地表达思想，也就是要考虑语言上的错误是否造成理解上的障碍。

4. 避免趋中倾向。该给高分的给高分，包括满分；该给低分的给低分，包括零分。一名阅卷人员在所评阅的全部作文卷中不应只给中间的几种分数。

评分标准

1. 本题满分为15分。

2. 阅卷标准共分五等：2分、5分、8分、11分及14分。各有标准样卷一至二份。

3. 阅卷人员根据阅卷标准，对照样卷评分，若认为考卷与某一分数（如8分）相似，即定为该分数（即8分）；若认为稍优或稍劣于该分数则可加一分（即9分）或减一分（即7分），但不得加或减半分。

4. 评分标准：

   2分——条理不清，思路紊乱，语言支离破碎或大部分句子均有错误，且多数为严重错误。

   5分——基本切题。表达思想不清楚，连贯性差。有较多的严重语言错误。

   8分——基本切题。有些地方表达思想不清楚，文字勉强连贯，语言错误相当多，其中有一些是严重错误。

   11分——切题。表达思想清楚，文字连贯，但有少量语言错误。

   14分——切题。表达思想清楚，文字通顺、连贯，基本无语言错误，仅有个别小差错。

（注：白卷、作文与题目毫不相关，或只有几个孤立的词而无法表达思想，则给0分。）

5. 词数不足应酌情扣分：

词数	110~119	100~109	90~99	80~89	70~79	60~69	50~59	<49
扣分	1	2	3	4	5	6	7	9

（注：①题目中给出的主题句、起始句、结束句等，均不得记入所写词数。②规定的内容未写全者，按比例扣分。③如果扣为0分，要慎重处理。）

6. 为了便于掌握评分标准，现将各档作文分对应的得分率列于下表。其中9分的得分率为60（相当于百分制的60分）。

作文分	15	14	13	12	11	10	9	8	7	6	5	4	3	2	1
得分率	100	94	87	80	74	67	60	54	47	40	34	27	20	14	7

具体要求

根据教育部高等教育司2004年出版的最新《大学英语课程教学要求》（教学大纲），四级写作的具体要求如下：

能填写常见表格，如注册表、申请表、问卷调查表等；

能写给或回复他人祝贺卡、生日卡、邀请信、便条、短信、通知等；

能写出简单的指示语、个人广告、社团海报、个人简历等；

能简要地描述个人经历、发生的事件、读过的故事、观看的电影、喜怒哀乐等情感，写出或回答个人或公司的信函、电子邮件、传真等；

能就一定话题或提纲在30分钟内写出120个词左右的短文，内容完整、用词恰当、语意连贯；

能在一般写作或应用文写作中使用恰当的写作技能。

第一节　高分攻略

一、权威解析

（一）印象原则：书写工整、卷面整洁、字迹清晰

在人际交往过程中，第一印象至关重要，四级写作也不例外。阅卷老师要在

短时间内批阅上千份试卷，平均在每份试卷上停留的时间很短，同时，还要接受大量不良英语的强烈冲击，其难度不言而喻。试想让你每天批阅几千份外国人写的不伦不类的中文作文并进行评分会是什么情况。考生应该进行换位思考，为阅卷老师，也为自己的分数着想，尽量把字写工整，谨慎涂改。

通常，阅卷老师看三点即可打分。以2012年6月四级作文"过度包装"为例：

第一点看你是否把答题纸写满12行，基本写满则词数合格，否则扣分；同时看文章是否是三段（四级写作一般以三段为宜），是否两头小、中间大（第一、三段较短，第二段较长，这是英文的写作规范）。

第二点看第一段是否说明现状，是否有"目前许多商品存在过度包装的现象"之类的话；第二段是否陈述观点，第一句是否有"出现这一现象的原因"之类的话；第三段是否提出自己的建议，是否有"我对这一现象的看法和建议"之类的话。如果文章符合上述要求，则没有跑题。

第三点是扫描和查看，主要看是否有"刺眼"的地方，即文章中是否有很多错误。同时，老师会随意读一两句，敲定最后分数。使用得当的经典句型，会给阅卷老师留下极好的印象，有助于取得高分。

（二）语言第一位

四级写作主要包括三大层面：语言、结构和内容。阅卷老师也是从这三大层面进行评分的。很多考生之所以会觉得四级写作较难，也是因为这三方面。有的同学语法较差，下笔全是语言错误；有的同学逻辑思维能力较差，想到什么写什么；有的同学表达能力较差，中文作文都写不出来。

四级写作重点考查考生的英语表达能力。阅卷老师最重视的是语言，考生最需要提高的也是语言。有的同学以为使用一些高难词汇就能取得高分，其实不然。中英文写作都讲究"平淡如水"、"简洁就是美"、"绚烂之极，归于平淡"。美国作家海明威经常使用小学词汇，但他是诺贝尔文学奖的得主，可见语言的好坏不在于辞藻华丽与否，而在于使用是否得当。中学词汇用好了，完全可以取得各种英语写作考试的满分。当然，基础较好的同学适当使用高难词汇有助于提高分数。但是不要盲目追求难度，"与其写一个错误的复杂句，不如写一个正确的简单句"。

四级写作的话题、观点和词数都有严格限制，它只是一个展示你英语书面表达能力的平台。因此，考生应该把构思的时间减到最少，把主要精力放在推敲语言上，力争将语法、拼写、标点等低级错误减至最少，力求用词、用句准确恰当，表达地道。这样，即便没有使用高难词汇和复杂句式，也可以保证稳得及格分数。考生切记作文不是口语，语言永远是第一位的，它决定了得分的高低。

阅卷老师在语言方面主要从两个方面进行评判：

1. 基本正确

四级考生的最大问题不是作文写得太简单，而是作文中严重错误太多。基础一般的同学即使使用小学或中学词汇和句型，只要使用得基本正确，也可以得到及格分数。考生最常犯的语言错误有三类：语法、拼写、标点。最常犯的语法错误包括：时态错误、冠词错误、主谓不一致等。

●时态

四级写作以现在时为主，尤其是一般现在时。图表描述段和举例论证段会用到过去时，即描述过去的年代和数据或列举自己经历过的小事时，须用过去时。文章结尾在展望未来时可使用将来时。

●冠词

冠词有a, an, the，考生应通过范文学习其用法，不要死抠语法书。

●主谓一致

主语和谓语应该保持一致。如果主语是单数第三人称或单数名词时，谓语动词后面应加"-s"。这些错误看似很小，但都属于严重的语法错误。

另外，考生还应掌握常见单词的拼写，谨慎使用标点。建议考生只使用两种标点：逗号和句号。但不要一逗到底，独立的句子应该用句号断开。

2. 丰富多变

基础较好的同学，要想取得四级写作高分，应做到丰富多变。丰富多变体现在词汇和句型两方面。同一词语在一句话、一个段落乃至一篇文章中最好不要重复出现，应尽量使用同义词或近义词替换（无法替换的关键词除外）。例如：think可以替换为reckon, assume, argue等词。如果想不到同义词或近义词，可以使用上义词进行替换。此外，句型也应富于变化，不要拘泥于主谓宾句型，可以使用主系表、过去分词和现在分词短语作状语、不定式短语作状语、状语从句等多种句型。

四级作文如果量化成句数，只需写10句左右。全文应以短句为主，长短句相结合。所谓短句是指10个词左右的句子，不能全篇都是5、6个词的短句。同时，全文应有一定数量的长句，一般15～20词即可，太长则易冗赘。有的同学以为，只写长句不写短句就能取得高分。实际上，老师看长句会觉得很累，以为你不会写短句,通常不会给高分。如果一篇中文作文每句都30多个字,定然晦涩难懂,英文作文也不例外。精炼的短句可以放在段首表示强调;复杂的长句可以进行具体的论证、举例或描述。考生可以每段单数句使用短句,双数句使用长句,长短结合,这样阅卷老师看起来也比较舒服。

英语句型分为简单句和复杂句,基本句型有五种:

1)主+谓:I succeed. 我成功了。

2)主+谓+宾:I like Lin Daiyu. 我喜欢林黛玉。

3)主+系+表:Kim Heesum is beautiful. 金喜善很漂亮。

4)主+谓+间宾+直宾:Wei Xiaobao gives Ake an English dictionary.
   韦小宝给了阿珂一本英文字典。

5)主+谓+宾+宾补:Dragon Saber makes many people selfish.
   屠龙刀使很多人变得自私。

在词汇使用方面,英文中充当主语、宾语的一般是名词、代词和非谓语动词,充当谓语的一般是动词,其余动词均使用非谓语动词形式。判断简单句和复杂句的方法就是看谓语动词。只有一个谓语动词的句子是简单句;有一个以上谓语动词的句子分为两种情况:一是并列谓语,在第二个或最后一个谓语动词前有并列连词and, or, but等;一是从句,标志为从句引导词(有时可以省略)。

英语句子中的修饰语一般有三种:

1)定语:形容词、名词、动词或定语从句。修饰名词,短定语放在前面,长定语放在后面,非限定性定语用逗号隔开。一句可有多个定语。

2)状语:修饰形容词、副词、动词或整句,副词在前,介词短语和状语从句在后。一句可有多个状语。

3)插入语:名词(短语)、从句。非必要成分,一般用逗号、括号或破折号分开。

复杂句一般包括三种:

1)并列句:and, or, but等并列连词连接的句子,可将同义、近义、反义的句子连接成并列句。

2)复合句:即从句,常见的有主语从句、宾语从句、表语从句、定语从句、状语从句、同位语从句等。

3)非谓语动词:包括动名词、不定式、分词(过去分词、现在分词)、独立主格结构等。

我们在写作时,应充分利用已有的句法知识,采用各种句法结构,使作文句式多样、生动活泼。

(三)结构第二位

结构是文章的框架。英文文章和段落的内部逻辑严谨,无论是整个篇章还是各个段落,通常都是"总—分—总"结构。四级作文一般需写成三段:第一段一般进行总论,第二段进行分论,第三段再次进行总论。每段内部也是"总—分—总"结构:第一句一般是主题句,进行总体论述;中间是论证部分;最后一句是小结。如果不写小结,就是"总—分"结构。

除了大的框架外,阅卷老师还会从以下三个方面衡量文章的结构,它们都是文章连贯衔接的手段。

1. 关联词

四级写作类似于中国古代的八股文,文章结构无非起承转合,而关联词的运用往往直接影响作文结构,需要引起充分重视。关联词的使用应适度,过犹不及。四级作文使用3~5个即可。很多考生关联词使用过多,以致文章啰嗦冗长。

1)起:启动观点,开篇点题。

第一段和每段第一句话是起,作用在于启动整篇文章或整个段落。如:nowadays, at present 等。

2)承:观点承接,正面论证。

第二段和每段中间是承。如:

(1)分类论证:

first(ly), in the first place, first and foremost, above all, to begin with, on the one hand, for one thing

second(ly), in the second place, besides, furthermore, moreover, in addition, what's more, on the other hand, for another

last(ly), (the) last but not (the) least, even worse, more importantly

(2)举例论证:for example, for instance, a case in point is

(3)解释论证:indeed, in fact, certainly, obviously, truly, in other words

3)转:观点转折,反面论证。

第二段和每段中间部分既可以承,又可以转。基础好的同学可以进行反面论证,对问题进行逆向思维。but, however太过普通,可以选择使用 yet, instead, whereas, otherwise, by contrast, in comparison, conversely, nevertheless, unfortunately, on the contrary等精彩表达。

4）合：文章结尾，合并归纳。

第三段以及每段最后一句话是合，用以总结整篇文章或整个段落。在论说文中，表示合的关联词可以使用三次，分别用在第三段首句和第二、三段的尾句。

（1）因此：thus, hence, therefore, accordingly, consequently, as a result/consequence

（2）总之：in conclusion, in general, generally speaking, by and large, on the whole

（3）简言之：in short/brief, briefly speaking, in a word, to sum up

2. 同义替换

同义替换包括词汇和句型，类似于语言的第二个评分标准——丰富多变。

3. 代词替换

中文多名词，英文多代词。英文中名词太多容易造成文章冗长，因此应尽量使用代词替换名词。其中，I, you等代词比较主观，it, that, they等代词比较客观。英文写作讲究客观性、以理服人，应避免主观臆断，多使用客观性的代词。

(四)内容第三位

内容就是你的观点或思维。四级写作是语言考试，不是思维考试。你的观点不需要是原创的，只要不跑题即可。四级英语写作也不是高考语文作文，千万不要别出心裁写什么诗歌、散文。你的第一个反应是什么就写什么，99％的同学怎么写你就怎么写，你会什么就写什么。有的同学题目越看越亲切，就是不知道如何下笔，这是缺乏思维训练的表现，是中文写作的问题，而不是英文写作的问题。平时多分析本书中精彩范文的观点，多看中英文报刊，能积累观点，扩大知识面。

(五)写作时间分配

四级写作30分钟，可分为三个阶段：

1. 审题：3分钟

一定要审题。很多英语基础较好的同学四级写作未能取得高分，就是因为没有仔细审题。有些同学担心时间不够，草草浏览题目，动笔就写，而写完发现跑题了，写得再好也是零分。审题时确定文章的中心思想和每段的主题句，可以列出简短的中英文提纲。

2. 写作：25分钟

应该把大部分时间用于写作。多数同学没有时间打草稿，因此，动笔之前把句子考虑成熟，尽量少作改动。建议考生考前按照时间要求写几篇文章，以便了解时间分配。考试时，必须使用黑色签字笔，不要使用蓝色笔，更不要使用铅笔，最好也不要使用涂改液。另外，一定要把作文写在答题纸的指定区域内，千万不要写在试卷或草稿纸上。

3. 检查：2分钟

要想在写作中取得理想分数，还要花一两分钟时间检查，看文中是否有常见的语法、拼写、标点等错误。修改时最好不要划掉一句或一段重新写。考生平时写完作文后也应养成检查的好习惯。

1）语法

基础不太好的同学需简单补充一些语法常识。虽然语法在四级中不再作为单独的考查点，但如果语法太薄弱，很难在写作部分取得理想分数。要取得写作及格分数，文中不应有太多严重的语法、拼写和标点错误。

2）拼写

四级词汇量为4500，但常见的写作词汇只有1000～2000。只要拼写正确、运用得当，完全可以得满分。

3）标点

建议基础一般的同学只使用两种标点——逗号和句号，以免犯标点错误。但不要一逗到底，独立的句子应该用句号断开。基础较好的同学可以使用较复杂的标点，如：

（1）分号表示并列，可以连接两个同义或反义的句子；

（2）冒号表示解释，冒号后面是对前面进行解释；

（3）破折号表示解释或转折；

（4）英文直接引语用逗号引出，不要用冒号；

（5）英文书名使用下划线，而不要用书名号。

二、高分真经

(一)背诵

背诵是提高英语综合能力的法宝，可分为以下5个层次：(1)精彩词汇；(2)精彩句型；(3)精彩句子；(4)万能框架；(5)经典范文。注意句子和句型不一样，精彩句子应像单词那样背诵。背诵前，确保自己已充分理解所有内容。

语言学习有两个关键词——输入(Input)和输出(Output)。听力和阅读属于输入，考生处于被动状态，只需在考场上将听到和看到的东西弄懂。应对这种题目的技巧很多，容易在短期内提高。但口语和写作属于输出，要求考生必须变被动为主动，所以很难在短期内突破。考生如果没有大量的输入，很难进行自由输出。

四级写作需要在30分钟内完成一篇短文，共计120余词，很多同学叫苦不迭。但若将其改为中文作文，大家就会觉得易如反掌。原因何在？俗话说："熟读唐诗三百首，不会吟诗也会吟。"同学们从小到大背诵了大量中文佳作，可以随意组合，自由输出。然而，在英语学习中，多数同学只沉溺于背单词、抠语法、做阅读，很少有人背诵英文文章。正因为没有大量输入，写作才始终处于"挤牙膏"的状态，想一句说一句，说一句翻译一句。

提高英语写作水平要做到多读、多背、多写、多改。多读、多背是首要任务，是积累输入的关键。本书附有大量经典英文句型、表达和范文，希望大家平时勤于背诵。

有的同学对我说，自己背过很多英文文章，但上了考场还是大脑一片空白，什么都想不起来。其实这种情况很常见，主要有两个原因：一是没有进行造句的练习，只是盲目背诵。二是背得不够熟练。学习任何东西都讲究先求质，再求量。大家学了很多年英语，文章看了很多，为什么还是写不好？关键是量铺开了，但质没有上去。一篇文章应背到脱口而出的程度，才能在考场上自由发挥。

(二)默写

背完经典范文后，进行默写。然后对照原文纠错，搞清楚错在什么地方。多数同学在写的时候都会犯小错误，如在拼写、单复数、大小写等方面犯错。这些就是你在写作中的弱点，也是阅卷老师最不能容忍的地方。培根说过："Writing makes an exact man.(写作使人精确。)"只有默写下来你才会发现自己常犯哪些错误。

(三)中译英

中译英也是提高写作的好方法。根据范文的中文译文,按自己的理解将其译成英文。译完后,你就会发现自己的翻译和原文有很大差距,这些差距就是取得写作高分的关键。这时,对照范文,看看原作者是怎么写的,思考为什么这样写。同样一句中文,范文中使用了哪些词汇和句型?你使用了哪些词汇和句型?学习范文中使用的词汇和句型。通过不断练习,你的写作水平不知不觉就提高了。

(四)写作

模仿范文写作新的文章,套用范文的精彩词汇、句型、句子和框架。最初套用时可能比较生硬,但随着不断的积累,组合起来会越来越顺手。

上述的高分策略是提高四级英语写作水平最有效的方法。在练习写作的初始阶段,可勤查语法书和词典等工具书,背记常用词和短语,以扩大词汇量,拓展知识面。背单词时要深刻理解所背词语的内在含义,并了解其使用环境。备考时,认真阅读本书关于写作方面的论述,熟记一些关联词、句型和范文,并进行仿写。考试时,使用学习过的、熟悉而有把握的词汇和句型,对于没有把握的句子,要尽量采取"回避政策",切忌自编自造汉语式的英语词组和句型。

三、钻 石 句 型

第 一 段

(一)现状说明

1. When asked about..., most people believe that..., but other people consider it differently.

   当谈论到……的时候,大多数人认为……但其他人看法不同。

2. When it comes to..., people's opinions differ. Some hold the opinion that..., while others claim that...

   当谈论到……的时候,人们的观点不同。有些人认为……,而其他人认为……

3. There is no consensus of opinions among people as to the role of... Some people claim that..., while others believe that...

   人们对于……的作用没有一致意见。有些人认为……,而其他人认为……

4. There is a general discussion today about the issue of... Those who criticize... argue that... They believe that... But people who advocate..., on the other hand, argue that...

现在关于……的问题有广泛的讨论。那些反对……的人认为……他们认为……但另一方面，那些支持……的人认为……

5. Most are of the opinion that... But I personally believe that...

大多数人赞成……但我个人认为……

6. Now people in growing numbers are beginning to realize that...

现在越来越多的人开始认识到……

7. Now, it is generally acknowledged that..., but I doubt whether...

现在，公认……但我怀疑是否……

(二)图表描述

1. In 1990, it increased/decreased from... to...

1990年，从……增加/下降到……

2. By comparison with 1998, it increased/decreased by...

和1998年相比，它增加/下降了……

3. The figure has nearly doubled, compared with that of last year.

和去年相比，数据几乎翻倍。

4. It has increased almost three times, compared with...

和……相比，它几乎增加了三倍。

5. The number is twice as much as that of 1990.

数字是1990年的两倍。

6. It accounts for... percent of the total.

它占总数的百分之……

7. The number was..., less/more than a half/third/quarter of the 1990 total.

数字是……，少于/多于1990年总数的二/三/四分之一。

第二段

(一) 原因列举

1. The phenomenon/change in... mainly results/arises from the fact that...

   ……方面的现象/变化主要源于……的事实。

2. One may regard the phenomenon as a sign of/response to...

   人们可能把这个现象当做……的一种表示/反应。

3. There are many causes/reasons for the dramatic growth/decrease. Firstly, ... Secondly, ... Finally, ...

   这种急剧的增长/下降有很多原因。首先，……其次，……最后，……

4. A number of factors can account for the change in...

   有很多原因可以解释……方面的变化。

5. Another contributory factor of... is...

   另一个起作用的因素是……

6. Why are/do/did...? For one thing, ... For another, ... Perhaps the primary reason is...

   为什么……首先，……其次，……也许最主要的原因是……

7. ...is also responsible for the rise/decrease in...

   ……也是造成……增加/下降的原因。

(二) 观点陈述

1. The advantages of A outweigh any benefit we gain from B.

   A的优点超过我们从B当中获得的任何优点。

2. Good as A is, it has its own disadvantages. For one thing, it...; for another, it...

   尽管A很好，但它也有自己的缺点。首先，它……；其次，它……

3. Although A has enormous/substantial/considerable advantage over B, it cannot compete with B in...

   尽管与B相比，A有很大的优势，但在……方面，它无法与B媲美。

4. A's advantage sounds ridiculous/means nothing when B's advantage is considered.

   当我们考虑B的优点时，A的优点听起来很荒谬/一无是处。

（三）利弊说明

1. Although a lot of people believe that..., I doubt/wonder whether the argument bears much analysis/close examination.

   尽管很多人认为……我怀疑这种论点是否经得起仔细分析。

2. As opposed to widely held ideas, I argue that...

   我反对公认的观点，认为……

3. Although the popular belief/idea is that..., a current study/survey indicates that...

   尽管普遍认为……目前的一项研究/调查显示……

4. They may be right about..., but they seem to neglect/fail to mention the fact that...

   他们关于……也许是正确的，但他们似乎忽视了/没能注意到……的事实。

5. Although it is widely accepted that..., it is unlikely to be true that...

   尽管公认……但是……不太可能正确。

6. It is true that..., but this is not to say that...

   ……确实……但这并不是说……

7. There is absolutely no reason for us to accept/resist that...

   我们毫无理由认为/否定……

8. What these people fail to understand/consider/mention is that...

   这些人没能理解/考虑/涉及的是……

9. You may say that... It probably will. But...

   你可能会说……事实可能如此，但是……

10. It is one thing to believe that..., but it is quite another to say that....

    认为……是一回事，但是认为……是另外一回事。

（四）举例论证

1. Numerous examples can be given, but this/these will suffice.

   可以给出无数的例子，但这个/这些就足够了。

2. I can think of no better illustration than the following one(s).

   我想不出比下面这个/这些更好的例子了。

3. This case effectively clarifies the fact that...

   这个例子清楚证明了……的事实。

4. This story tells that...

   这个故事告诉我们……

第三段

(一)归纳结论

1. From what has been discussed above, we may safely draw the conclusion that...
   通过上面讨论的内容，我们确实可以得出结论：……

2. All the evidence supports an unshakable conclusion that...
   所有这些论据都支持一个不可动摇的结论：……

3. It is high time that we placed great emphasis on...
   我们早就该重视……了。

4. It is high time that we put an end to the undesirable phenomenon of...
   我们早就该阻止……这一不良现象了。

5. There is no denying that further attention must be paid to the problem of...
   毫无疑问，我们应该对……问题给予进一步的关注。

(二)建议措施

1. It is necessary that effective actions should be taken to prevent the situation.
   我们很有必要采取有效措施制止这种状况。

2. Hence, it is imperative for us to take drastic measures/steps.
   因此，我们很有必要采取严厉措施。

3. We should appeal to the authorities to make strict laws to control this problem.
   我们应该呼吁政府制定严格的法律来控制这个问题。

4. We should enhance/cultivate the awareness of people that this issue is vital for us.
   我们应该提高/培养人们的意识：这个问题对我们很重要。

5. Only in this way can we solve the problem.
   只有这样，我们才能解决这个问题。

6. I believe we humans can overcome this difficulty and we will have a brighter future.
   我相信人类能够克服这个问题，拥有更美好的未来。

四、书信写作

　　不同的应用文有不同的格式要求，一般来说，书信类写作格式大致相同，告示类写作格式基本相同。书信是重要的交际工具，通常分为私人信函和公务信函两大类。私人信函一般写给亲人、朋友或同学；公务信函一般谈论或处理重要事务，可能是推荐信、求职信、求学信、邀请信、询问信、回复信、投诉信。总之，凡是不属于"私人"的信函，一律称为"公务"信函。

信函的格式和语气多种多样，私人信函不同于公务信函。一般来说，前者的格式和语气比较随便，而后者则正式得多。不过，两种信函中使用的语言都应清楚明确、直截了当。公务信函的措辞应讲究礼貌，还要注意用词准确、行文简洁。

公务信函的段落通常较短。首段和末段一般只包含一句话。开头的段落用一句话说明事由。必要时，可以再加一句话提及以前的书信联系。回复公务信函时，最好说明何时收到关于何事的信函。特别提示：写公务信函的开头和结尾时，要注意礼貌用词。

四级写作一般需从称呼写起，根据题目要求写出正文和结尾客套语，签名一般用"李明"。

（一）称呼

称呼是书信的开头部分，一般用dear开头，注意头衔的使用。英式英语称呼后用逗号，美式英语称呼后用冒号。在写给亲友的私人信函中可以直呼收信人的名字，但在公务信函里一定要写出收信人的姓氏。特别注意：四级英语写作一般要求称呼后使用逗号，而不用冒号。

称呼一般分为两种情况：

1. 写给机构：

1）不认识负责人：Dear Sir or Madam, To Whom It May Concern

2）认识负责人：Dear Mr. President, Dear Mr.（Michael）Wang
  （使用全名或姓氏）

2. 写给个人：

1）关系不亲密：Dear Mr. President, Dear Mr.（Michael）Wang
  （使用全名或姓氏）

2）关系亲密：Dear Michael（直呼其名）

（二）正文

正文是书信中最重要的内容，也是得分的关键。书信一般有三点提纲，即三个内容要点。因此，考生应严格按照大纲要求写成三点式文章，每点表达一个提纲要点，顺序不要打乱，做到条理清晰，简洁准确。书信作文首尾两段可套用一些固定句型。下面介绍常见的两种正文写法。

● **写法一**

基础一般的同学，首尾两段可以使用自我介绍、表示感谢、期待回信等套话，只需在第二段将三点提纲改写成六句。

1. **首段**：1～2句，私人信函不用作自我介绍。也可先阐明写作目的，再作自我介绍。

   1）自我介绍：1句

   I am a freshman/sophomore/junior/senior/undergraduate from the Department of Chinese Language and Literature of Beijing University.

   我是北京大学中文系的一名大一学生/大二学生/大三学生/大四学生/本科生。

   2）写作目的：1句

   （1）I am writing the letter in purpose of placing an order of some books.

   我写这封信是为了订购一些图书。

   （2）I am writing to inform you that I wish to resign from my current post/position.

   我写这封信是告诉您我想辞职。

2. **二段**：6句

   1）改写提纲一：2句

   2）改写提纲二：2句

   3）改写提纲三：2句

3. **尾段**：1～2句，也可先写期待回信，再表示感谢。

   1）表示感谢：1句，个人建议信通常不用表示感谢。

   （1）My thanks for you to your generous help are beyond words.

   我对您慷慨帮助的感谢无以言表。

   （2）Words fail me when I want to express my sincere gratitude to you.

   感激之情，无以言表。

   （3）I take this opportunity to show my heartfelt appreciation to the kind assistance you render me.

   我想借此机会对您的热心帮助表示衷心的感谢。

   2）期待回信：1句

   （1）I look forward to hearing from you soon.

   我期待着尽快得到您的回信。/ 盼即赐复。

   （2）I am looking forward to your favorable reply at your earliest convenience.

盼即赐复。/ 我期待着尽快得到您的答复。

（3）Your prompt attention to my inquiry would be highly appreciated.

十分感谢您对我的询问予以迅速关注。

● **写法二**

基础较好的同学，若想取得四级写作高分，关键是少用套话。因此，自我介绍、期待回信等套话可以不写。

1. **首段**：3句
   1）改写提纲一：1句
   2）两点原因或情况：2句

2. **二段**：4句
   1）改写提纲二：1句
   2）两点原因或情况：2句
   3）小结：1句

3. **尾段**：3句
   1）改写提纲三：1句
   2）两点原因或情况：2句

（三）结尾客套

结尾客套是表示礼节的套语，第一个字母要大写，后面要加逗号。可通用"Yours sincerely,"。

（四）签名

书信类应用文最后一部分是签名，一般用"Li Ming"，切勿写上自己的真实姓名。

五、告示写作

告示类应用文写法各不相同，但大致也有统一的格式和要求，一般要求下列格式：

（一）标题

书信类应用文不用写标题，但告示类应用文必须写标题，这点非常重要。标题需要说明告示的主旨，一般为词组性短语，实词（有实际意义的词，如名词、动词、形容词等）第一个字母需要大写，虚词（没有实际意义的词，如介词、冠词、连词等)第一个字母需要小写。

(二)日期

书信类应用文不要求写日期，但告示类应用文一般需要注明日期，写在标题下一行的右下方，右端与右边线对齐，常见写法为June 18, 2010等。

(三)正文

根据题目要求，写1~3段。

1. 常用时态

一般采用现在时或将来时，可以使用现在进行时表示近期即将发生的事情，如is organizing；也可使用动词不定式，如to be held；或will/shall do, may/can do结构，如will be invited, may sign up等。

2. 开头句型

1）Your attention, please...

2）It has been decided that...

3）May I have your attention please? ...

4）...is requested to note that...

5）...has/have the honor to announce...

6）...takes the pleasure in announcing that...

7）...has/have the pleasure to notice/announce（that）...

8）This is to note/notice/notify/announce that...

9）It is hereby noted/announced/proclaimed/made public that...

10）...is/are authorized to invite/announce/declare that...

11）Under the auspices of... , a report/lecture/seminar on... will be given by... on...

12）Owing to/due to/because of/in order to... , we beg to inform... that...

13）Under the auspices of..., ...will organize/hold a... match/competition/contest between... and... on...

(四)署名

　　书信类应用文签名一般是个人，但告示类应用文的签名可以是个人或公告单位，实词第一个字母大写，虚词第一个字母小写，右端与右边线对齐。

第二节　真题选析

一、论说文

(一)2009年12月

真　题

Directions: *For this part, you are allowed 30 minutes to write a short essay entitled* ***Creating a Green Campus.*** *You should write at least 120 words following the outline given below in Chinese:*

1．建设绿色校园十分重要，
2．绿色校园不仅指绿色环境，
3．为了建设绿色校园我们应该……

范　文

Creating a Green Campus

　　In recent years, extravagance and waste **have become increasingly serious in some parts of our university campus. We can see that** paper, bottles and cans are thrown away, that food is wasted just because it tastes bad, and that clothes are discarded simply because they are out of fashion. **As a consequence, large numbers of people have put great emphasis on** creating a green campus.

　　There are at least two ways to identify a green campus. **One is that** natural resources must be conserved and made full use of, for example, we college students making wiser use of paper and second-hand textbooks. **The other is that educators promote habits of** thrift **among various departments and professionals.**

　　Accordingly, we must take effective steps. On one hand, university leaders **should act by demanding stricter conservation of** our resources, such as water, electricity, and so forth. **On the other hand, we should increase awareness among college students of the significance of** creating a green campus **for both our society and ourselves.**

译 文

建设绿色校园

近年来，在大学校园的一些地方，奢侈浪费已经变得日益严重。我们可以看到纸张、瓶子和易拉罐被丢弃，食物由于味道不好而被浪费，衣服仅仅因为过时了而被扔掉。因此，很多人已经开始充分重视创建绿色校园。

至少有两种方法可以辨别绿色校园。一是自然资源必须被保护并充分利用，例如，我们大学生更加充分地利用纸张和二手课本。二是教育者在各个院系和专业人员中倡导节约的习惯。

因此，我们必须采取有效措施。一方面，大学领导应该行动起来，更严格地要求节约水、电等资源。另一方面，我们应该提高大学生的意识，让他们认识到建设绿色校园对我们的社会和我们自己都非常重要。

(二)2010年6月

真 题

Directions: *For this part, you are allowed 30 minutes to write a short essay on the topic of **Due Attention Should Be given to Spelling**. You should write at least 120 words following the outline given below.*

1. 如今不少学生在英语学习中不重视拼写
2. 出现这种现象的原因是……
3. 为改变这种状况，我认为……

范 文

Due Attention Should Be given to Spelling

A large number of students now neglect spelling in English study. Take a simple word "modern" **for instance. Only a few students can** spell "modern" without trouble—others may spell it as "morden", "mordern" or something else.

For various causes, spelling **is now becoming a** neglected art. **To begin with, a great many students don't care about** spelling. **Some say they are going to** have a secretary when they get a job, and he or she will correct their spelling. **What is more, the majority of** word processors and email programs come with a built-in spell checker, **which discourages students to** spell well. **The last but not the least,** teachers **appear not to be extremely concerned about** students' spelling errors.

To change this situation, I maintain that both students and teachers should

exert every effort. **For one thing, utmost significance has to be attached to** spelling. **For another, to make better** spellers of students, every teacher, especially the one who teaches English, **should be concerned about** students' poor spelling.

译 文

拼写应被给予应有的重视

现在很多学生在英语学习中忽视拼写。以一个简单的单词"modern"为例，只有一些学生能够轻松地拼写出"modern"，其他人则可能将其拼作"morden"、"mordern"或其他形式。

由于各种原因，现在拼写成了一种被忽视的艺术。首先，很多学生不关心拼写。有些人认为，他们找到工作后会有一位秘书，而秘书将改正他们的拼写。此外，大多数文字处理软件和电子邮件程序都内设拼写检查，这不利于学生认真拼写。最后一点，也是非常重要的一点，老师们似乎并不特别关注学生们的拼写错误。

为了改变这一状况，我认为学生和老师都应该努力。一方面，我们应该充分重视拼写。另一方面，为了使学生能更认真地拼写，每位教师，尤其是英语教师应该关注学生拼写较差的状况。

(三)2010年12月

真 题

Directions: *For this part, you are allowed 30 minutes to write a short essay entitled* ***How Should Parents Help Children to Be Independent?*** *You should write at least 120 words following the outline given below.*

1. 目前不少父母为孩子包办一切
2. 为了让孩子独立，父母应该……

范 文

How Should Parents Help Children to Be Independent?

At present, a good many parents are overdoing in taking care of their children. **From** doing laundry **to** job hunting, **they have made every effort**. **Unfortunately, instead of** making life easier for the next generation, **such deeds deprive the youth of opportunities to** grow independent.

For purpose of cultivating a sense of self-dependence in their children, parents **are supposed to** first stop doing what the youngsters are able to do for themselves. **In addition, it is advisable that** parents expose their children to more difficulties and failures on purpose, **helping them to learn valuable lessons from setbacks. Last but not least**, parents should help their children **develop a sense of responsibility.**

It is hopeful that all parents realize an independent soul dies in a bed of roses and find a more sensible way to love their kids.

译 文

父母应怎样帮助孩子变得独立?

如今,很多家长都照顾自己的孩子照顾得过头。从洗衣服到求职,他们都为孩子竭尽所能。令人遗憾的是,这样的行为非但不会使下一代的生活变得更轻松,反而剥夺了年轻人独立的机会。

为了培养子女的独立意识,首先,家长们不应该继续帮青少年做他们力所能及的事情。此外,建议家长可以故意让孩子面对更多困难和失败,以帮助他们从挫折中获得宝贵的经验教训。最后还有重要的一点,家长应帮助孩子培养责任感。

希望所有的家长都能意识到"独立的精神死于安乐窝中",并能找到一种更合理的方式来爱孩子。

(四)2011年6月

真 题

Directions: *For this part, you are allowed 30 minutes to write a short essay entitled* **Online Shopping**. *You should write at least 120 words following the outline given below.*

1. 现在网上购物已成为一种时尚
2. 网上购物有很多好处,但也有不少问题
3. 我的建议

范 文

Online Shopping

Nowadays, can we find a person who has not heard of online shopping? **It may be a little difficult.** Online shopping **is coming into fashion in most cities due to the rapid development of** Internet technology.

Online shopping **is welcomed by the majority of people owing to its obvious advantages: it's convenient and** people can do it 24 hours. You can shop whenever you want—if you want to buy a mobile phone at 2 a.m., you can. **Unfortunately,** shopping online **has its own disadvantages too:** you can't touch the item, let alone try it on. The material of the dress that you see on the screen may be flimsier than what you have expected, and the dress will probably look much better on the model than it does on you.

Personally, I find buying online **to be an excellent way to** shop for certain items. **Nevertheless,** for other items, such as clothes, **I reckon it is better to** shop at a regular store. In a regular store, you can see the real color, feel the material, and try it on.

译 文

网上购物

现在，我们能够找到从未听说过网上购物的人吗？恐怕有点困难。由于互联网技术的飞速发展，网购在大多数城市都已成为时尚。

由于网购具有明显的优势，即其方便性以及随时性，大多数人都喜欢网购。只要喜欢，你可以随时购物——如果你想半夜两点买部手机，没问题。可惜的是，网购也有缺点：你无法接触商品，更别说试穿了。你在屏幕上看到的衣服面料可能比你预期的要更薄，而且衣服很可能穿在模特身上比穿在你身上更好看。

就我个人而言，我认为网购对于购买某些商品来说是一种很好的方式。然而，对于诸如服装等其他商品，我认为最好在传统商店购买。在传统商店，你可以看到真正的颜色，感受面料，并且试穿。

（五）2011年12月

真 题

Directions: *For this part, you are allowed 30 minutes to write a short essay entitled* **Nothing Succeeds Without a Strong Will** *by commenting on the humorous saying,* "*Quitting smoking is the easiest thing in the world. I've done it hundreds of times.*" *You should write at least* **120** *words but no more than* **180** *words.*

范 文

Nothing Succeeds Without a Strong Will

Maybe the majority of us have heard of the humorous saying, "Quitting smoking is the easiest thing in the world. I've done it hundreds of times." **But have you ever thought about its implication? Undoubtedly**, nothing succeeds without a strong will.

Those who claim to have practiced smoking-quitting for hundreds of times do not have a strong will. **Without** a strong will, **one can never give up** smoking **once and for all, not to mention** being successful in other endeavors. **It is** a strong will **that contributes to the success of** the Olympic winners, **that results in the spectacular victory of** the 2010 World Expo, **and that leads to the successful** exploration of the moon.

Where there is a will, there is a way. **Only when** the will is strong enough **will the way lead us to success.**

译 文

没有坚强的意志，任何事情都无法取得成功

或许我们大多数人都听过这个幽默的说法，"戒烟是世界上最容易的事情，我已经戒了几百次了。"但你可曾想过它的言外之意？毫无疑问，没有坚强的意志，任何事情都无法取得成功。

那些声称戒烟数百次的人没有坚强的意志。若没有坚强的意志，人们永远不能彻底戒烟，更不用说在其他方面取得成功。正是坚强的意志促成了奥运会冠军的成功，促成了2010年世博会的伟大胜利，也使得探索月球取得成功。

有志者事竟成。只有意志足够坚强时，我们才能迈向成功。

(六)2012年6月

真 题

Directions: *For this part, you are allowed 30 minutes to write a short essay entitled **On Excessive Packaging** following the outline given below. You should write at least **120** words but no more than **180** words.*

1. 目前许多商品存在过度包装的现象
2. 出现这一现象的原因
3. 我对这一现象的看法和建议

范 文

On Excessive Packaging

In today's commercial society, excessive packaging seems to be part of our daily life. It's not rare for us to see a variety of commodities with colorful wrappings in the market. And most of us may have the experience of having to open several boxes or wrappers before finally seeing the product we have bought.

The following two reasons account for the prevalence of excessive packaging. In the first place, a great many consumers are willing to buy those delicately packaged commodities as presents for others. In the second place, so as to make commodities look decent and attractive, commercial enterprises prefer to pay more for the fine packaging.

Considering its side effects, it is imperative for us to take drastic measures to reduce it. To begin with, the authorities should impose restrictions on excessive packaging. In addition, it is necessary to arouse customers' awareness that packaging doesn't equal to quality, and to let them know the bad impact of excessive packaging.

译 文

过度包装

在如今的商业社会，过度包装似乎是我们日常生活的一部分。我们经常可以看到市场上有很多商品都拥有五颜六色的包装。大多数人可能都经历过不得不打开几个盒子或几层包装纸，才能最终看到购买的商品。

下面两点原因造成了过度包装的盛行。首先，很多消费者愿意购买那些包装精美的商品作为送给别人的礼物。其次，为了使商品看起来更加雅观和诱人，商家更愿意为精美的包装花费更多。

考虑到其负面影响，我们急需采取严厉措施来减少过度包装。首先，政府应该限制过度包装。其次，有必要唤醒消费者的意识：包装并不等于质量，并且要让他们了解过度包装的负面影响。

(七)2012年12月

 真 题

Directions: *For this part, you are allowed 30 minutes to write a short essay entitled "**Education Pays**" based on the statistics provided in the chart below (Weekly earnings of 2010).*

*Please give a brief description of the chart first and then make comments on it. You should write at least **120** words but no more than **180** words.*

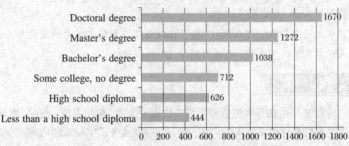

Education: A Worthy Investment

Source: US Bureau of Labor Statistics

 范 文

Education Pays

The column chart above clearly illustrates the statistics of the weekly earnings of people with different educational backgrounds in the United States in 2010. **According to the data from** U.S. Bureau of Labor Statistics, **there was a steady increase from** $444 for people with less than a high school diploma to $1670 for those with Doctoral degree.

The reasons for this trend are as follows. In the first place, it has long been an accepted fact that higher degree **is a pre-requisite for** a promising career, or finding a good job. **In the second place, in our highly competitive society, whether one is in China or the U.S., it can be said that it is impossible for a person to find a good job with a promising future without** at least a college degree.

From the analysis given above, we may predict that in order to remain competitive in the workplace as well as in salary, people in mounting numbers will return back to school to continue their higher education, even though they already have their college or university degree.

译 文

教育有回报

上述柱状图清晰地展示了美国2010年不同教育背景人群的周薪数据。根据美国劳工统计局的数据，周薪从拥有高中以下文凭人群的444美元稳步提升到博士学位拥有者的1670美元。

形成上述趋势的原因如下。首先，只有拥有更高的学位，才能找到一份好工作并拥有光明的职业前景，这是长期以来大家公认的事实。其次，无论在中国还是美国，当今社会竞争极其激烈，一个人如果连大学文凭都没有，可以说就不可能找到好工作，前途黯淡。

从上述分析我们可以预计：为了保持在工作和薪水方面的竞争力，越来越多的人就算有了大学文凭，也将回到学校继续深造。

二、应用文

应用文是指在日常生活和工作中使用的文体，包括书信、告示、致辞等。由于考生平时对这类文体不太关注，这部分可能是考试中较难的内容，希望大家在复习中多注意这类文体的写作格式和方法，掌握其特点，为在考试中取得高分奠定良好的基础。

(一)2005年1月

真 题

Directions: *For this part, you are allowed to write A **Campaign Speech** in support of your election to the post of chairman of the Student Union. You should write at least 120 words following the outline given below in Chinese:*

1. 你认为自己具备了什么条件(能力、性格、爱好等)可以胜任学生会主席的工作?
2. 如果当选你将会为本校同学做什么?

范 文

A Campaign Speech

Today I am very glad to run for the chairperson of the Student Union. **I am junior in the Department of Chinese Language and Literature.**

I am sure that I am qualified for this position. First, I am good at communicating and organizing. By the way, with my outstanding leadership, I

have been elected president of our department **several times. Second, I am warm-hearted and easygoing. Not only do my qualifications and work experience make me a perfect candidate, my cheerful personality is well suited for the position. Last, my hobbies include sports and music.**

If I am elected, I will exert all my efforts. **Firstly, I will** organize suitable activities. **Secondly**, I will try to reach your demands as well. **Therefore, I do not hesitate to** recommend myself as an ideal candidate. **I am sure you will make a wise decision in** voting for me.

译 文

竞选演说

今天，我很高兴来竞选学生会主席。我是中文系大三的学生。

我确信自己胜任这个职位。首先，我善于与人沟通和组织活动。顺便说一句，由于我的杰出领导能力，我多次当选我们系的学生会主席。其次，我热心、随和。不但我的条件和工作经历使我成为最合适的人选，我令人愉快的性格也非常适合这个职位。最后，我的爱好包括运动和音乐。

如果我当选，我将竭尽全力。第一，我将组织大量合适的活动。第二，我将努力满足大家的需求。因此，我毫不犹豫地推荐自己为理想人选。我确信你们会作出明智的选择投票选我。

(二)2006年6月17日

真 题

Directions: *For this part, you are allowed 30 minutes to write a poster recruiting volunteers. You should write at least 120 words following the outline given below:*

1. 校学生会将组织一次暑假志愿者活动，现招募志愿者，
2. 本次志愿者活动的目的、内容、安排等，
3. 报名条件及联系方式。

范 文

Volunteers Needed

June 17, 2006

The Students' Union **is organizing a school-wide** voluntary program **during** this summer vacation. **Now** volunteers **are wanted**.

The following is the introduction to this program. **First, the purpose of it is to improve students' ability and enrich after-class activities. Second,** the Students' Union will open free English classes for primary school students in a remote village in Sichuan Province. **Last,** the classes **will last for a week. Currently, we will recruit** 5 volunteers **to work as** English teachers.

Those who are interested in taking part in the activity, please send your resume to the e-mail address studentunion@pku.edu.cn **before** June 20th. The Students' Union **will contact the chosen candidates for an interview before July 1st. Everybody is welcome to be present at the program.**

The Students' Union

译 文

招募志愿者

学生会将在今年暑假组织一次志愿者活动。现招募志愿者。

下面是对这次活动的介绍。首先,活动的目的是提高同学们的能力,丰富课外活动。其次,学生会将在四川省的一个偏远山村为小学生开办免费的英语课程。最后,课程将持续一周。目前,我们将招募五名志愿者作为英语教师。

有兴趣参加此活动的同学,请在6月20日前将简历发至studentunion@pku.edu.cn。学生会将在7月1日前联系选中的候选人进行面试。欢迎大家参加此项活动。

学生会

2007年6月17日

(三)2007年6月

真 题

Directions: *For this part, you are allowed 30 minutes to write an announcement to welcome students to join to a club. You should write at least 120 words following the outline given below:*

1. 本社团的主要活动内容,
2. 参加本社团的好处,
3. 如何加入本社团。

范 文

Welcome to Our Club

June 23, 2007

The Speech Club is organizing school-wide speech training and contests to be held on each Saturday at the Students' Recreational Center. Five prestigious experts and professors will be invited to be speech lecturers and contest judges. For each speech contest, the first six winners will be given awards.

Attending our club has substantial advantages. Firstly, it can improve your ability to deliver a speech which is of utmost significance to your future career and development. Secondly, it can help you to possess self-confidence, enrich your extra-curricular activities and make your campus life dimensional, colorful and vigorous. To sum up, the experiences in our club will be extraordinarily unforgettable throughout your life.

Students who are interested in taking part in it may sign up with the monitor of their classes before Tuesday next week (June 26). Everybody is welcome to attend our club.

Speech Club

译 文

欢迎加入我们的社团

演讲社将于每周六在学生活动中心举办全校性的演讲培训与比赛。我们将邀请五名资深专家及教授作为演讲教师与评委。每次比赛的前六名将得到奖励。

参加我们的社团好处多多。首先，它能提高你发表演讲的能力，这对你未来的职业和发展都非常重要。其次，它能帮助你拥有自信，丰富你的课外活动，并且使你的校园生活丰富多彩、充满活力。总之，参加我们的社团将是你一生中非常难忘的经历。

有兴趣参加的同学们请在下周二(6月26日)之前在你们的班长那里报名。欢迎大家加入我们的社团。

演讲社
2007年6月23日

第三节 强化训练

一、二十大必背范文

(一)出国留学

Directions: *For this part, you are allowed 30 minutes to write a short essay on the topic* ***Studying Abroad****. You should write at least 120 words following the outline given below:*

1. 目前很多中国学生出国留学，
2. 出国留学的好处，
3. 我的看法。

范 文

Studying Abroad

　　Nowadays, going abroad for studies **is enjoying a striking popularity among adolescents. Importance should be attached to** studying abroad.

　　There are a great many advantages of studying overseas. First and foremost, living and studying abroad offers students a different perspective of the world. On a university campus, international students are likely to encounter their counterparts from various countries and areas and are exposed to diverse ideas and values. **What is more,** overseas experience is the best opportunity for the real-life use of foreign languages. There is no better opportunity to improve second-language skills than living in the country in which it is spoken.

　　Generally speaking, it is my view that although going abroad is expensive and perhaps painful, the payoff is worthwhile. **In the first place**, in addition to knowledge, overseas students can gain precious experiences that those who stay at home will never have. **Furthermore**, overseas experience, frustrating and painful as it may be, is conducive to the growth of adolescents.

译 文

出国留学

　　目前，出国留学在青少年中非常流行。我们应该充分重视留学问题。

出国留学有很多好处。首先，在国外生活和学习可为学生提供一个看待世界的不同视角。在大学校园中，国际学生很可能遇到来自不同国家和地区的同伴，并且面临迥异的想法和价值观。此外，海外经历是在实际生活中运用外语的最佳时机。没有什么比住在母语国家提高第二外语技能更好的机会了。

总之，我认为尽管出国留学费用很昂贵，并且过程可能会让人痛苦，但这种付出是值得的。首先，除了知识之外，留学生可以获得留在国内的学生永远无法获得的宝贵经验。其次，尽管留学经历可能使人沮丧、痛苦，然而这对青少年的成长是有益的。

(二)就业

Directions: *For this part you are allowed 30 minutes to write a composition on the topic **Jobs for Graduates**. You should write at least 120 words and base your composition on the outline below:*

1. 大学生找工作难，
2. 原因有很多，
3. 解决的办法。

 范　文

Jobs for Graduates

Job hunting **has always been a headache for college students. Though many** graduates are employed right after graduation, **some are not. Most serious of all, some still have no idea where to** go working even a long time after graduation.

The reasons for this phenomenon are various. On the one hand, a few years ago colleges and universities enrolled so many students in popular majors, such as economy, finance and so on that the number of graduates was greater than the need in the market. **On the other hand**, most graduates would rather stay in large cities without suitable job to do than go to the country.

I reckon this problem can be solved if both colleges and students take measures. First, they should research the market and develop special skills to suit its need. **Second**, students' **attitude towards** employment **should be changed**. They should go to small cities and country. There they can also give full play to their professional knowledge. **In a word, if we pay much attention, the situation can be improved.**

译 文

毕业生就业

找工作对大学毕业生来说已经变成了一个非常头疼的问题。尽管多数毕业生一毕业就找到了工作，但还是有些人没有找到。最为严重的是，有些人在毕业很长时间之后，还不知道去哪儿工作。

产生这一现象的原因有很多。首先，前些年各大学院和大学录取了很多经济、金融等热门专业的学生，以至于毕业生的数量大大超过了市场需求。其次，大多数大学生宁愿待在大城市，找不到合适的工作，也不愿去乡镇。

我认为如果大学和学生都采取有效措施，这个难题是可以解决的。首先，大学应该进行市场调查，培养学生的特殊技能以适应需求。其次，学生的就业观念应该转变。他们应该去小城市和乡镇，在那里他们可以充分发挥自己的专业知识。总而言之，如果我们更加重视，这种状况可以得到改进。

(三)互联网

Directions: *For this part you are allowed 30 minutes to write a composition on the topic* **Internet**. *You should write at least 120 words and base your composition on the outline below:*

1. 互联网使用的现状，
2. 对于大学生是否应该使用互联网，人们的看法不同，
3. 我的看法。

范 文

Internet

In recent years, people are developing an inseparable relationship with Internet. **As is known to all, it is** convenient **for us to** click the mouse when surfing on line, either to entertain ourselves or to meet the work's needs.

On the one hand, no one denies that Internet **is currently one of the most** useful media **in our daily life**. **As a college student, I** get on line every day to exchange information through e-mails with my net friends. **But on the other hand, a good many people admit that** they are too much addicted to Internet to maintain a regular and wholesome lifestyle.

Thus, it is necessary for us to use Internet **in a reasonable way and restrain**

from overindulgence. After all, Internet is invented to enrich our life, and to improve the efficiency of our work rather than shackle us with a chain.

译 文

互联网

近年来,人们与互联网之间的关系变得越来越不可分割。众所周知,无论是为了自我娱乐还是适应工作的需求,对我们来说,在网上冲浪时点击鼠标非常方便。

一方面,不可否认互联网是我们现在日常生活中最有用的媒体之一。作为一名大学生,我每天上网借助电子邮件和我的网友交流信息。但另一方面,很多人承认他们过于沉迷网络,以至于无法保持一种正常和健康的生活方式。

因此,我们很有必要以一种合理的方式使用互联网,避免过度沉迷。毕竟,人们发明互联网是为了丰富我们的生活,提高我们的工作效率,而不是让它像锁链一样来束缚我们。

(四)考试

Directions: *For this part you are allowed 30 minutes to write a composition on the topic **My Views on Examinations**. You should write at least 120 words and base your composition on the outline below:*

1. 大学都用考试来衡量学生的成绩,
2. 考生可能带来的副作用,
3. 我对考试的看法。

范 文

My Views on Examinations

In most colleges and universities the examination is used as a chief means of deciding whether a student succeeds or fails in mastering a particular subject. **Although it does the job quite efficiently, its side effects are also enormous.**

To begin with, examinations lower the standards of teaching. Since teachers are often judged by examination results, they are reduced to training their students in exam techniques. No subjects can be taught successfully merely through being approached with intent to take examinations. **In addition, the most undesirable effect is that** examinations encourage bad study habits. As the examination score is the only criterion for his academic performance, a student is driven to memorize mechanically rather than to think creatively.

In fact, few of us admit that examinations **can contribute anything really important to the students'** academic development. **If that is the case, why cannot we make a change** and devise something more efficient and reliable than examinations?

译 文

我看考试

在绝大多数大学里,考试是用来衡量学生是否掌握某一课程的主要手段。虽然考试这一方法比较有效,但其副作用也相当大。

首先,考试造成教学水平下降。由于教师的好坏往往根据学生的考试成绩来判断,所以教师被迫训练学生应试技巧。而几乎没有什么课程是仅仅通过教授应试技巧就可以教好的。其次,考试最糟糕的副作用是使学生养成不良的学习习惯。由于考试成绩是衡量学生学习好坏的唯一标准,学生只能被迫机械地死记硬背,而不去进行创造性的思考。

实际上,很少有人承认考试对学生的学习起到重要作用。如果确实如此,我们为什么不进行改革,设计出比考试更有效、更可靠的评估方法呢?

(五)节日

Directions: *For this part you are allowed 30 minutes to write a composition on the topic* **Which to Celebrate—the Western or Eastern Festivals**? *You should write at least 120 words and base your composition on the outline below:*

1. 年轻人日益喜欢西方节日,
2. 关于西方节日与东方节日,人们的看法不同,
3. 我的看法。

范 文

Which to Celebrate—the Western or Eastern Festivals?

Nowadays, the majority of young people are willing to celebrate western festivals. **As a result, importance should be attached to the issue of** festival celebration.

For one thing, western festival celebrations **are so colorful that especially**

the youth cannot resist all the temptation of having one. Just imagine the romantic atmosphere on St. Valentine's Day, the fun on All Fool's Day and the ecstasy brought by gifts and games at Christmas. For another, Chinese festivals have their own attractions. Think about the comfort of family reunion during Spring Festival and the delicacy of national feelings on many occasions.

As for me, some fashionable western festivals are no doubt days to set aside as special. Meanwhile, I cannot afford to be absent from family gathering during many Chinese festivals. My celebration would be a combined one, some for western festivals, some for Chinese ones.

译 文

过西方节日还是东方节日？

现在，大多数年轻人喜欢过西方的节日。因此，我们应该重视庆祝节日的问题。

一方面，西方节日如此丰富多彩以至于年轻人尤其难以抵挡其诱惑，设想一下情人节的浪漫气氛、愚人节的乐趣以及圣诞节礼物和游戏带来的惊喜。另一方面，中国的节日也有其魅力。想想春节期间全家团圆的温馨以及很多节日中民族情感的慰藉。

对我而言，一些时尚的西方节日无疑是要特别度过的。同时，我也无法在很多中国节日中缺席家庭聚会。我的节日庆祝是中西结合的。

(六)网上交友

Directions: *For this part you are allowed 30 minutes to write a composition on the topic* Internet Friendship. *You should write at least 120 words and base your composition on the outline below:*

1. 网上交友的现状，
2. 我所了解的一个例子，
3. 我对于网上交友的看法。

范 文

Internet Friendship

According to the recent survey by CCTV, 80% of people who surf online are there in search of social interaction. As a consequence, the voice speaking through the other side of the line can be used to disguise aspects of a user's personality. **And this might bring an unpleasant or even damaging outcome.**

Numerous examples can be given, but this will suffice. One of my closest friend, Helen, started a net relationship with a man she knew as "Prince Charming". The physical contact, **however**, reveals that her beloved idol was a husband with wife.

In my view, first and foremost, it is true that people may gain community on the net, but this exists only in cyberspace. **Furthermore, although** Internet friendship **can give** users companionship and even romance, **it often ends with failure and even disaster. It is high time that we placed great emphasis on this phenomenon.**

译 文

网上交友

根据中央电视台的最新调查，80％的人在网上冲浪是在寻找社交。其结果是，网线另一端发出的声音可以用来掩盖一名用户性格的方方面面。而这可能带来不良的甚至是破坏性的后果。

关于此问题，可以列举无数的例子，下面这个便具有足够的代表性。我最好的一个朋友海伦，和一位网名叫"白马王子"的男子开始了一场网恋。而亲身接触证明她所深爱的偶像原来是一个有妇之夫。

在我看来，首先人们确实可以在网上获得社交，但这只存在于网络空间中。此外，尽管网络友谊可以给用户带来友情甚至爱情，但它也经常以失败和灾难告终。我们该高度重视这一现象了。

(七)青少年犯罪

Directions: *For this part you are allowed 30 minutes to write a composition on the topic* **Juvenile Delinquency**. *You should write at least 120 words and base your composition on the outline below:*

1. 青少年犯罪的现状，
2. 这个问题的原因，
3. 我的建议。

范文

Juvenile Delinquency

Recently, juvenile delinquency **is increasingly** lower than normal age. **Careful deliberation of this problem has given me several ideas as to why this should be so.**

To begin with, with the rising divorce rate, some children are not properly taken care of, and are easily led astray by evildoers. **What is more, inexperienced and gullible young people plunge into** the illusory world of electric games, on-line chat or even pornography. Such alienation from proper social values is the slippery slope to crime.

It is my view that, first of all, the whole of society should attach great importance to the sound growth of youngsters. Furthermore, proper guidance and protection of adults and schools are vital to teenagers. To sum up, if we exert every effort, the juvenile crime rate **will undoubtedly be brought down and effectively controlled in a short while.**

译文

青少年犯罪

目前,青少年犯罪正在越来越趋于低龄化。认真思考这个问题后,我得出了出现该问题的几点原因。

首先,随着离婚率的上升,有些孩子没有得到适当的照顾,他们很容易被坏人带入歧途。其次,无知、轻信的年轻人陷入电子游戏、网络聊天甚至色情的虚幻世界中不能自拔。这种偏离的社会价值观很容易导致犯罪。

在我看来,首先,整个社会应该高度重视青少年的健康成长。其次,成人和学校的正确引导和保护对青少年至关重要。总而言之,如果我们竭尽全力,短期之内青少年犯罪率无疑会下降并得到有效控制。

(八)求学信

Directions: *For this part, you are allowed 30 minutes to write a letter applying for admission into a college or university. You should write at least 120 words according to the outline given below in Chinese:*

1. 入学条件,

2.　学费和奖学金，

3.　住宿情况。

范　文

Dear Sir or Madam,

　　I am a Chinese student who wishes to apply for admission into your prestigious university. My plan is to start my course next term, and I would be grateful if you would be kind enough to provide me with certain essential information.

　　First, what qualifications do I need to follow a course of study at your university? I already have a bachelor's degree from Beijing University, but I wonder if there are any further academic requirements. Second, how much are the tuition fees? Although I intend to be self-supporting, I would be interested to hear if there are any scholarships available for international students. Third, what is the situation regarding accommodation?

　　I look forward to your reply, and to attending your esteemed institution.

Yours sincerely,

Li Ming

译　文

尊敬的先生或女士：

　　我是一名中国学生，想申请您这所著名大学。我计划下学期开始我的课程，如果您能好心提供一些基本信息，我将非常感谢。

　　首先，我在您的大学听课需要什么条件？我已经从北京大学获得了学士学位，但我想知道是否有进一步的学术要求。其次，学费是多少？尽管我打算自费留学，但我想了解一下国外学生是否可以获得奖学金。最后，住宿情况怎么样？

　　我期待着您的答复，并且希望能进入贵校学习。

您真诚的，

李明

(九)致辞

Directions: *Write a speech on the opening of a conference in no less than 120 words. In your speech, you should:*

1. 进行自我介绍，
2. 详细介绍大会内容，
3. 结束语。

范 文

> **Good morning, ladies and gentlemen, welcome to** Beijing! **To begin with, I would like to make a brief introduction to myself. I am** the president of Motorola（China）Electronics Ltd.
>
> **The following is my introduction to the** conference. **First, it is my great honor to be here with all of you and** declare open the Conference of International Trade Cooperation. **Second, on behalf of** our company, **I would like to express my heartfelt welcome to all the guests and delegates. Last, I believe our cooperative efforts are sure to be productive.**
>
> **I wish all of you enjoy yourselves during this** conference **and hope the above information will help you. If you have any question for me, please feel free to ask at any time. Thank you for your attention.**

译 文

　　女士们、先生们，早上好！欢迎来到北京！首先，我想做一个简单的自我介绍。我是摩托罗拉(中国)电子有限公司的总裁。

　　下面是我对这次大会的介绍。首先，我很荣幸和大家聚在一起，并且宣布国际贸易合作大会的开幕。其次，我谨代表我们公司，表达对所有贵宾和代表的衷心欢迎。最后，我相信我们的齐心协力一定会富有成果。

　　我希望大家在这次大会中愉快，并希望上述信息能对您有所帮助。如果您还有任何问题要问我，请随时提问。感谢您的关注。

（十）告示

Directions: *The Students' Union of your department is planning a Chinese Speaking Contest. Write an announcement which covers the following information:*

1. 比赛目的、时间、地点，
2. 参赛者的要求，
3. 裁判和奖励的细节。

You should write about 120 words. Do not sign your own name at the end of the letter. Use Department of Chinese Language and Literature at the end of the announcement.

范　文

Chinese Speaking Contest

February 3, 2007

　　To improve students' ability to speak Chinese **and enrich after-class activities, the Students' Union of** Department of Chinese Language and Literature **is organizing a school-wide** Chinese speaking contest **to be held on next Saturday（10 February）at the Students' Auditorium. Those who are interested in taking part in it may sign up with the monitor of their classes before Tuesday next week.** Five professors will be invited to be judges. The first six winners will be given awards. **Everybody is welcome to be present at the** contest.

The Students' Union

Department of Chinese Language and Literature

译　文

中文演讲比赛

　　为提高同学们的中文演讲能力，丰富同学们的课外活动，中文系学生会将于下周六（2月10日）在学生大礼堂组织一场全校中文演讲比赛。有兴趣参加的同学请于下周二之前到本班班长处报名。我们将邀请五位教授担任评委，并将给前六名获奖者颁奖。欢迎大家积极参与。

中文系学生会

2007年2月3日

（十一）网络游戏

Directions: *For this part, you are allowed 30 minutes to write a composition on the topic **Online Games**. You should write at least 120 words, and base your composition on the outline below:*

1. 现在有些大学生沉迷于网络游戏，家长和学校对此忧心忡忡，
2. 但有人认为网络游戏并非一无是处，
3. 你的看法。

范 文

Online Games

As a product of modern computer and the Internet, online games **have become very popular among college students. A great many students have enjoyed great pleasure and satisfaction from** these games. **But as we see, some students lacking self-discipline are too much indulged in** these games so that **their health and academic performances are affected. This phenomenon has caused much worry from the teachers and parents.**

However, some others argue that online games **are not always harmful. They can train the ability of youngsters to respond to things quickly. Moreover, they can stimulate their imagination and their interest in computer science. More importantly, it does bring college students much pleasure and release their pressure greatly.**

From my point of view, online games **are a wonderful entertainment if you play them in a reasonable way. When they interfere too much with your study, it is better for you to give them up at once. Yet if you have enough self-control over them, you can certainly obtain real pleasure and benefit a lot from them.**

译 文

网络游戏

作为现代电脑与网络的产物,网络游戏在大学生中已经变得非常流行。很多学生喜欢从这些游戏中获得的极大快乐与满足。但是正如我们所看到的那样,一些缺乏自律的学生太沉迷于这些游戏,以至于影响了他们的健康和学习成绩。这种现象已经引起了教师和家长的极大忧虑。

然而,有人认为网络游戏并不总是有害的。它们可以训练年轻人对事物做出快速反应的能力。此外,它们可以激发年轻人的想象力和对电脑的兴趣。更为重要的是,它确实给大学生带来了很多快乐并极大地减轻了他们的压力。

在我看来,如果以适当的方式玩网络游戏,这是一种极好的娱乐方式。当它们过于影响学习的时候,则最好立即放弃。然而如果对它们有足够的自制力,你当然可以从中获得真正的快乐并受益匪浅。

（十二）考证热

Directions: *For this part, you are allowed 30 minutes to write a composition on the topic* **Certificate Craze on Campus**. *You should write at least 120 words, and base your composition on the outline below:*

1. 近几年大学校园内出现"考证热"，
2. 产生这一现象的原因，
3. 你的看法。

范 文

Certificate Craze on Campus

In recent years, to get a certificate has become a new craze among college students. Just randomly ask a student on campus what he is busy doing, quite possibly, you may get the answer that he is preparing for a certificate of some kind. Why does this craze appear?

There are mainly two reasons behind this phenomenon. To begin with, it is the employment pressure that forces college students to get more certificates. With the admission expansion of colleges, a lot more graduates have to face the fierce competition in the job market. How can one make himself more competitive? More certificates at hand, maybe. Furthermore, diploma and certificates are still vital standards by which a good many employers measure a person's ability. In order to increase the qualifications for a job, the students compel themselves to run from one exam to another.

From my point of view, we should be more rational when it comes to certificates, since certificates do not necessarily prove one's ability. Being crazy in getting certificates blindly is nothing but wasting time. To conclude, we should focus on improving our ability but not getting a certificate of no practical value.

译 文

校园考证热

近年来，考证在大学生中已经变成一种新的热潮。只要在校园中随机询问一名学生他在忙什么，你很可能就会得到这样的答案：他正在准备考取某种证书。为何会出现这种热潮呢？

出现这种现象主要有两点原因。首先，就业的压力迫使大学生去考取更多证书。随着大学扩招，有更多的毕业生不得不面对就业市场的激烈竞争。一个人如何使自己更具竞争力？可能就是有更多证书在手。此外，学位和证书仍是很多雇主衡量一个人的能力的重要标准。为了给求职增加资历证明，学生们迫使自己不断参加考试。

在我看来，由于证书并不一定能证明某人的能力，我们应该更加理性地对待证书。盲目地热衷于获得证书只是浪费时间。总之，我们应该重视提升自身能力，而不是获得没有实用价值的证书。

(十三)节俭

Directions: *For this part, you are allowed 30 minutes to write a composition on the topic **Extravagant Spending on College Campus**. You should write at least 120 words, and base your composition on the outline below:*

1. 很多大学生每月的花销越来越高，根本没有节俭的概念，
2. 分析产生这一现象的原因，
3. 我的看法。

范 文

Extravagant Spending on College Campus

According to a survey, in recent years the monthly expenditure of a college student has been on the sharp rise. Many college students have no concept of thrift in their mind. They take it for granted that they spend money from their parents before they enter into society. This extravagant spending is primarily caused by the following factors.

First of all, nowadays most of the students are the only children of their families. They are the apple in their family's eyes and naturally get more care and pocket money. In addition, with the improvement of living standards, parents can afford higher expenditure of their children. Moreover, some students like to pursue fashion and trends, which tend to need more money. Finally, campus love is also a possible factor causing extravagant spending.

From my point of view, a college student, as a pure consumer, should learn to be thrifty. We should limit our expenditure on daily necessities but not buy whatever we want regardless of their prices. **The habit of** thrift **can help us form right values and is favorable to our future development.**

译 文

大学校园内的奢侈消费

根据一项调查,近年来大学生每月的花销已经急剧增加。很多大学生脑中根本没有节俭的概念。在步入社会之前,他们想当然地花父母给的钱。这种奢侈消费的现象主要由以下原因引起。

首先,现在大多数学生是家里的独生子女。他们是父母眼中的宝贝,自然会得到更多的关心和零用钱。其次,随着生活水平的提高,父母能够承担孩子更高的消费。此外,一些学生喜欢追求时尚和潮流,这往往也需要更多钱。最后,校园恋爱可能也是造成奢侈消费的另一个原因。

在我看来,一名大学生作为纯消费者,应该学会节俭。我们的支出应该限制在日常必需品上,而不是不顾价格购买我们想要的一切。节俭的习惯能帮助我们树立正确的价值观,并有利于我们未来的发展。

(十四)挫折教育

Directions: *For this part, you are allowed 30 minutes to write a composition on the topic* ***Frustration Education should be Strengthened among College Students.*** *You should write at least 120 words, and base your composition on the outline*:

1. 加强挫折教育十分重要,
2. 举例说明你的观点,
3. 为了加强挫折教育,我们应该……

范 文

Frustration Education should be Strengthened among College Students

It is universally acknowledged that college students should be guided correctly to face frustrations in life. Frustration **is inevitable during our life, and** frustration education **should be carried out among colleges and universities. The truth of it is deep and profound.**

A great many remarkable illustrations contribute to this argument. A case in point is that there are an increasing number of college students committing

suicide each year when confronted with some kind of frustration. This is close to suggest that strengthening frustration education **allows of no delay. As a matter of fact, it seems that successful people tend to be good at dealing with** frustrations. **Moreover, most of the students are often annoyed and discouraged** by frustrations **instead of drawing lessons.**

Judging from the evidence offered, we might safely draw the conclusion that frustration education **is essential to the college students. But what is worth noting is colleges should also provide psychological service for the students while** giving frustration education. **To conclude, college students should be guided in the right path when facing setbacks in life.**

译 文

应给大学生加强挫折教育

人们普遍认为,我们应该正确引导大学生面对生活中的挫折。挫折在我们生活中必不可少,而挫折教育应该在大学中展开。其中的道理既深刻又意义深远。

有很多值得注意的例子支持上述论证。一个恰当的例子就是当面对某种挫折的时候,每年自杀的大学生越来越多。这充分证明了加强挫折教育刻不容缓。事实上,成功人士似乎往往擅长面对挫折。此外,大多数学生经常因挫折而烦恼和感到沮丧,而并非吸取教训。

根据上述论证,我们可以确定地得出结论:挫折教育对大学生十分重要。但值得注意的是,在进行挫折教育的同时,大学也应该为学生提供心理服务。总之,在面对生活中的挫折时,我们应给予大学生正确的引导。

(十五)公务员热

Directions: *For this part, you are allowed 30 minutes to write a composition on the topic **Test for Civil Servants***. *You should write at least 120 words, and base your composition on the outline below:*

1. 近几年兴起了一股报考公务员的热潮,
2. 分析产生这一现象的原因,
3. 你的看法。

范文

Test for Civil Servants

In recent years, there are people in expanding numbers who have participated in the test for civil servants. Millions of students choose civil servant as their most ideal occupation after graduation. And among them, the high-educated, like masters and doctors, take quite a large percentage. The craze in civil servant test has attracted widespread attention.

The following fundamental causes can account for this kind of craze. First and foremost, nowadays college students face great employment pressure. Civil servant, as one of the most stable professions in today's China, becomes their preferable choice. Moreover, recently, the welfare and salary of civil servants have been improved greatly, which undoubtedly attracts many people. Last but not least, the high social position of civil servants is a crucial factor drawing many people to take part in the civil servant test.

In my opinion, this craze in civil servant test will continue in the following years. However, from the long run, it does not do good to the development of our nation. If most high quality talents gather in the government departments, it might lead to a waste of resources. Accordingly, both the individuals and the government should have a more objective recognition of the civil servant test craze.

译 文

公务员考试

近年来，有越来越多的人参加公务员考试。数以百万的学生选择公务员作为他们毕业后最理想的职业。在他们中间，硕士和博士等受过高等教育者占相当大的比例。报考公务员的热潮已经引起了广泛的关注。

下面几点主要原因可以解释这种热潮。首先，最重要的一点是，现在的大学生面对巨大的就业压力。公务员作为当今中国最稳定的职业之一，成为他们的首选。其次，近年来公务员的福利和工资已有极大地改善和提高，这无疑吸引了很多人。最后还有重要的一点，公务员较高的社会地位也是吸引很多人报考公务员的一个重要原因。

在我看来，报考公务员的热潮在未来几年中仍将继续。然而，从长远来看，这对我们国家的发展并没有好处。如果大多数高素质人才聚集于政府部门，这可能会导致一种资源浪费。因此，个人和政府都应对报考公务员的热潮有更客观的认识。

（十六）电视选秀

Directions: *For this part, you are allowed 30 minutes to write a composition on the topic **Attending TV PK Shows Does（or Does no）good to Young People**. You should write at least 120 words, and base your composition on the outline below:*

1. 现在各种各样的电视选秀节目吸引了许多年轻人，
2. 为了实现明星梦，一些年轻人甚至放弃了学业，
3. 你的看法。

Attending TV PK Shows Does No Good to Young People

Nowadays, TV PK shows **are great hits in China and have attracted a large number of adolescents.** Some youngsters even give up their studies to attend these shows **in the hope of winning their fame overnight. Some people argue that** these shows **provide young people more chance to show talents, while others assume that** attending these shows **does no good to the juvenile. As for me, I prefer to the latter opinion.**

It should be admitted that some young people like Li Yuchun has stood out from the numerous attendants in the PK show, **but that doesn't mean** attending the PK shows **is a good way to become successful for teenagers. The following reasons can support my view. First and foremost, TV PK shows breed restlessness and induce young people to hunt after fame at whatever cost. Furthermore, TV PK shows can subvert the youngsters' values. They cling to the idea that** attending the PK shows **is a shortcut to success, so they may despise the way of achieving success by hard work. Finally, if the young fail in these shows, they will suffer a psychological unbalance.**

In a word, entering for TV PK shows **is not a good way for young people to achieve success. I hold the opinion that young people should think twice before deciding to** attend PK shows.

译 文

参加电视选秀节目对年轻人没有好处

现在，电视选秀节目是中国的一大热点，已经吸引了很多年轻人。为了一夜成名，有些年轻人甚至放弃了他们的学业来参加这些节目。有人认为这些节目为年轻人提供了更多展示才能的机会，而其他人认为参加这些节目对年轻人没有好处。就我而言，我支持后者的观点。

不可否认，像李宇春等一些年轻人确实在选秀节目的无数参与者中脱颖而出，但这并不意味着参加选秀节目是年轻人成功的好途径。下述原因可以支持我的观点。首先且是最重要的一点，电视选秀节目引起了不安，并诱使年轻人不惜一切代价追逐名声。此外，选秀节目可能扭曲年轻人的价值观。他们认为参加选秀节目是成功的一条捷径，因而或许会轻视通过努力工作获得成功的方式。最后，如果年轻人在这些节目中失败，他们将遭受心理失衡。

总之，参加电视选秀节目不是年轻人获得成功的好途径。我认为年轻人在决定参加之前应该慎重。

（十七）图画作文

Directions:

A. Study the following two pictures carefully and write an essay in at least 120 words.

B. Your essay must be written neatly on the ANSWER SHEET 2.

C. Your essay should meet the requirements below:

1. Describe the pictures.

2. Deduce the purpose of the painter of the pictures.

3. Suggest counter measures.

A Brief History of World Commercial Fishing

范 文

　　As is shown in the pictures, we can see clearly that with the increase of commercial fishing, **the number of** fishes **sharply decreased. In one picture, there were** various kinds of fish and only one fishing-boat in 1900. **On the contrary,** in 1995 **there was** only one fish, but many fishing-boats.

　　The purpose of these pictures is to show us that due attention has to be paid to the decrease of ocean resources. **Owing to** over-fishing, **the number of** fishes **has obviously decreased. If we let this situation go as it is, we won't know where** fish **is in the future. By that time, our** environment **will suffer a great destruction.**

　　Therefore, it is imperative for us to take drastic measures. For one thing, we should appeal to our authorities to make strict laws to control commercial fishing. **For another, we should enhance the awareness of people that** the ocean resources **are very vital to us. I believe that we human beings can overcome this difficulty, and we will have a bright future.**

译 文

　　如图所示,我们可以清楚地看到,随着商业捕鱼的增加,鱼的数量明显下降。在一幅图中,1900年有很多种鱼,只有一艘捕鱼船。相反,在1995年,只有一条鱼,但是渔船很多。

　　这两幅图的目的是告诉我们应该充分重视海洋资源的减少。由于过度捕捞,鱼的数量明显下降。如果我们对这种情况听之任之,我们在将来会不知道哪里有鱼。到那个时候,我们的环境将遭受巨大的破坏。

　　因此,我们很有必要采取严厉措施。一方面,我们应该呼吁政府制定严格的法律来控制商业捕鱼。另一方面,我们应该增强人们的意识:海洋资源对我们非常重要。我认为我们人类能够克服这个困难,并将拥有美好的未来。

(十八)情景作文

Directions: *For this part, you are allowed 30 minutes to write an essay entitled **Man and Computer** by commenting on the saying, "The real danger is not that the computer will begin to think like man, that man will begin to think like the computer." You should write at least 120 words but no less than 180 words.*

范 文

Man and Computer

The computer **has become an indispensable part in man's life. While it has brought great convenience to us, its rapid development has also aroused much concern about whether it will one day** think like man, **or even worse,** whether man will think like the computer.

In my judgment, although the computer may have incredible intelligence, **it is unlikely that it will** take the place of man someday. **Unfortunately, with the increasing reliance on the computer, there is indeed a danger that some people may** think and act the same way as the computer which is programmed. **They may lose the ability to** think critically and reactively, **and eventually develop** some "programmed routine" in their behavior, neglecting the rich subtleties of human feelings.

Accordingly, while making good use of the computer, **we should always bear in mind that** it is only a useful tool for us, and that we can always think of better and more humane ways of coping with our problems.

译 文

人和电脑

电脑已经成为人们生活中不可缺少的一部分。在电脑为我们带来巨大便利的同时，它的快速发展也引起了很多人的担心：电脑有天是否会像人类一样思考，或更糟糕的是，人类是否会像电脑一样思考。

在我看来，虽然电脑可能拥有令人难以置信的智慧，但是它不可能在某天取代人类。可惜的是，随着人们对电脑的依赖感逐渐增强，确实有这样的危险：有些人可能会像电脑一样程序化地思考和行事。他们可能会失去自己的批判性思维和应变思维能力，最终发展成行为举止遵照某些"程序化的常规"，而忽略丰富、微妙的人类感觉。

因此，在我们好好利用电脑的同时，我们应该始终牢记：电脑只是一个对我们有用的工具，而我们总能想出更好、更人性化的方法来应对自己的难题。

(十九)图表作文

Directions: *In this section, you are asked to write an essay based on the following diagram. Describe the diagram and analyze the possible causes. You should write at least 150 words.*

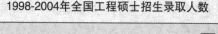

1998-2004年全国工程硕士招生录取人数

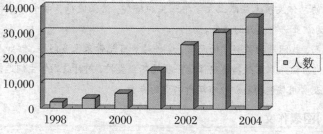

工程硕士：Master of Engineering

范 文

　　The diagram clearly illustrates that dramatic elevation has occurred in the recruitment of Master of Engineering（ME）**in the past seven years. In 1998, the number was at a low level, only about 2,500. Surprisingly, it reached to more than 35,000 in 2004 within no more than seven years.**

　　Some driving factors that contribute to the above-mentioned changes may be summarized as follows. First and foremost, China has become particularly active in manufacturing, **which leads to the increasing demand of qualified** engineers. **In addition, the development of job market on the whole cannot keep pace with the expansion of college graduates, which obliges a large number of students to stay on campus for another three years to get better prepared for their career.**

　　On the other side of the coin, however, this tendency may bring about a good many problems, such as the waste of talent. **We should take effective measures to ensure this situation doesn't get out of hand, and encourage students to** choose majors in which theoretical knowledge and practical skills will be demanded in the job market.

译 文

　　这幅图表清楚地表明，在过去七年里，工程硕士的招生数量出现了急剧增长。在1998年，招生人数较少，只有大约2500人。令人惊讶的是，在不到七年的时间里，2004年招生人数达到了35000多人。

　　促成上述变化的一些主要原因可以概括如下。首先，最重要的一点是，中国在制造业方面已经变得尤为活跃，这导致对高素质工程师的需求增加。此外，就业市场的总体发展无法跟上大学毕业生的增加，这促使很多学生继续待在校园三年，为就业进行更好的准备。

　　然而，就问题的另一方面而言，这种趋势可能带来很多问题，例如人才的浪费。我们应该采取有效措施确保这一状况不会失控，同时鼓励学生们选择那些理论知识及实用技能均被就业市场所需要的专业。

(二十)图表作文

Directions: *Write an essay based on the following chart in your writing, you should*

（1）*interpret the chart, and*

（2）*give your comments.*

You should write about 150 words.

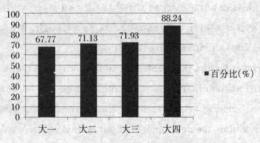

某高校学生兼职情况

范 文

　　The column chart clearly reveals the statistics of students taking part-time jobs **in a certain** university. **According to the survey, there has been a steady increase from** 67.77% **to** 71.93% for students holding temporary jobs from freshmen to juniors, **while the percentage of** seniors working part-time **jumped markedly to** 88.24%.

The most obvious way that having a part-time job **can adversely affect** students' studies **is by becoming a drain on the their time. Another way that** part time employment **can be detrimental to** students **is by reducing the perceived incentive to** study. **Despite presenting certain pitfalls,** working part-time during one's college years **also offer several potential benefits. For one, it can help** students **to better understand their preferences or to "test out" a possible career direction. Additionally, companies seeking to recruit recent grads will give preference to those with real-world experience.**

In the end, the impact of a part-time job on student's academic career **depends on the** student's **ability to maintain focus and balance his or her own time.**

译 文

这幅柱状图清晰地显示了某高校学生兼职情况的数据。根据调查，从大一到大三，兼职学生的百分比从67.77%稳步上升到71.93%，而大四兼职学生的百分比则急剧上升到88.24%。

兼职对学生学业造成的不利影响最明显表现在耽误时间。不利影响的另一方面是，做兼职会减少学生已有的学习动力。尽管前面列出了某些弊端，但在大学阶段做兼职还是有很多好处的。首先，兼职能帮助学生更好地了解自己的喜好或"检验"可能的职业方向。其次，那些招聘新近毕业生的公司都会偏爱有实际社会经验的大学生。

总之，兼职对大学生的学业是否有影响取决于他们能否分清重点以及平衡自己的时间。

二、十大万能框架

特别提示

下列框架仅供参考，切勿照搬原文。使用时稍加修改，以免留下背模板的痕迹。要想取得四级写作高分，考生还需扎扎实实提高实力，背诵、默写、互译、模仿经典范文和句型，多读、多背、多写、多改！

(一)

Although a lot of people believe that _____, I doubt/wonder whether the argument bears much analysis/close examination.

Undoubtedly, this issue conveys the meaning that _____. Owing to _____, _____. Once a person _____, scarcely can he or she _____. Just as _____ put it, "_____". No matter how _____, we will definitely _____. In general, _____.

Hence, it is vital for us to derive positive implications. On the one hand, we should frequently use it to enlighten the youth to _____. On the other hand, we should be sensible enough to _____. Only by doing so can we become winners in the competitive world.

译 文

尽管很多人认为 _____，我怀疑这种论证是否经得起检验。

毫无疑问，这个问题说明 _____。因为 _____，所以 _____。一旦一个人 _____，他(她)很难 _____。正如 _____ 所说："_____。"无论 _____，我们无疑都需要 _____。总而言之，_____。

因此，我们很有必要得出积极含义。一方面，我们应该经常利用它来启发年轻人 _____。另一方面，我们应该充满理智 _____。只有这样我们才能成为竞争世界的强者。

(二)

When asked about _____, most people believe that _____, but other people consider it differently.

Importance has to be attached to the issue of _____. First and foremost, _____. In addition, _____. The last but not the least, _____. Generally speaking, _____.

To overcome this difficulty, it is necessary to take effective steps to reverse the disturbing trend. One measure would be _____. But more importantly, _____. Although the drive to fight against it is a long-standing and tremendous one, our joint efforts will eventually pay off. I assume that a happy and brilliant future is awaiting us if we exert every effort to it.

译 文

当谈论到 _____ 的时候，大多数人认为 _____，但其他人却看法不同。

对于 _____ 的问题应该给予重视。首先，_____。其次，_____。最后，_____。总之，_____。

为了克服这个困难，我们很有必要采取有效措施扭转这个不好的趋势。一种措施是 _____。但更为重要的是，_____。尽管抵制这个问题是个长期而艰巨的过程，我们的齐心协力最终是会有所回报的。我认为如果我们竭尽全力，等待着我们的将是一个美好而光明的未来。

（三）

There is no consensus of opinions among people as to the role of _____. Some people claim that _____, while others believe that _____.

To begin with, this issue is to show us that _____, yet the profound meanings subtly conveyed should be taken more seriously. First and foremost, _____. What is more, _____. Generally speaking, _____.

Numerous examples can be given, but these will suffice. A case in point is _____. Another illustration is closely related to us, the examinees. If we _____, we will _____. On the whole, these examples effectively clarify the saying that "_____".

译 文

关于 _____ 的作用，人们没有一致意见。有些人认为 _____，而其他人认为 _____。

首先，这个问题告诉我们 _____，然而它微妙传达的深刻含义应该被认真对待。首先，_____。其次，_____。总之，_____。

关于此问题，可以列举无数例子，但这些就足以说明问题了。一个恰当的例子是 _____。另一个例子和我们考生密切相关。如果我们 _____，我们将 _____。总而言之，这些例子清楚地证明了这一说法："_____。"

（四）

When we use the word "_____", we do not simply mean _____, which is a very narrow definition of the word. In fact, throughout history people of many different cultures have regarded _____ as _____.

The fact that _____ indicates that _____. In the first place, as an example of _____, we should remember _____. In the second place, although _____ by international standards, people all over the country do not hesitate to _____. Moreover, _____. In a word, _____.

To crack this hard nut, it is crucial for us to take effective actions. Above all, relevant laws and regulations should be made to severely punish those who _____. Furthermore, we should enhance the awareness of people that _____ is of great significance to us. Only in this way can we curb the current evil phenomenon.

译 文

当我们使用 _____ 这个词的时候，我们不仅仅指 _____，这只是这个词的狭义定义。事实上，在整个历史当中，不同文化的人们都把 _____ 当做 _____。

_____ 的事实证明了 _____。首先，作为 _____ 的一个例子，我们应该记得 _____。其次，尽管按照国际标准 _____，全国各族人民毫不犹豫 _____。此外，_____。简而言之，_____。

为了解决这个难题，我们很有必要采取有效措施。首先，我们应该制定相关的法律法规来严惩那些 _____ 的人。其次，我们应该提高人们的意识：_____ 对我们很重要。只有这样我们才能制止当前的这一不良现象的发生。

（五）

There is a general discussion today about the issue of _____. Those who criticize _____ argue that _____. They believe that _____. But people who advocate _____, on the other hand, argue that _____.

We can deduce that this issue is trying to attract our attention to the tragedy of _____, which is part of the threat to humans. In my opinion, _____ is a symbol of humans, and we too will be left homeless if we allow the destruction of the environment to continue.

This simple issue is a wake-up call for the whole of the human race. If this vivid image of the grim future of our planet is not to become a reality, we must take positive steps right now to put an end to the plundering of the Earth's natural resources.

译 文

现在,关于 _____ 的问题有广泛的讨论。那些反对 _____ 的人认为 _____。他们认为 _____。但另一方面,那些支持 _____ 的人认为 _____。

我们可以推断这个问题正在吸引我们注意 _____ 的悲剧,这也是对人类威胁的一部分。在我看来,_____ 是人类的一种象征,如果我们让这种环境破坏继续下去的话,我们将无家可归。

这个简单的问题向整个人类敲响了警钟。如果不想让我们星球的这个可怕未来成为现实,我们必须采取积极措施制止掠夺地球自然资源的行为。

(六)

Because of the rapid social development, the number of people who _____ has greatly increased/decreased. It is generally believed that _____ plays an important role in modern society.

Due attention has to be paid to the issue of _____. With the reform and opening-up in recent years, people in increasing numbers have come to realize the importance of _____. If we let this situation go as it is, we do not know where humans will be in the near future.

Therefore, it is necessary for us to take drastic measures. To begin with, we should appeal to the authorities to make strict laws to control _____. In addition, we should enhance the awareness of people that _____ is vital to us. Only in this way can we solve this problem.

译 文

由于社会的迅速发展,_____ 的人数急剧上升/下降。人们普遍认为 _____ 在现代社会中发挥着重要作用。

我们应该对 _____ 问题给予充分重视。随着近年来的改革开放政策,越来越多的人开始认识到 _____ 的重要性。如果我们对这种情况听之任之,我们不知道在不远的将来人类会在哪里。

因此,我们急需采取严厉措施,首先,我们应该呼吁各级政府制定严格的法律来控制 _____。另外,我们应该提高人们的意识:_____ 对我们很重要。只有这样,我们才能解决这个问题。

（七）

Nowadays, there exists a very common phenomenon in our society that _____.

Why does this phenomenon appear/take place/arise? I assume there are several possible factors. The first is that _____. Another major reason is due to _____. Current studies show that another primary cause is _____. In general, _____.

Having considered the above argument, I have come to the conclusion that the benefits of _____ outweigh the disadvantages. On the one hand, _____. On the other hand, _____. From this we can conclude that _____.

译文

现在，在我们社会中有一个非常普遍的现象：_____。

为什么会出现这种现象？我认为有几个可能的原因。第一个原因是_____。另外一个重要原因是_____。目前研究显示另一个主要原因是_____。总之，_____。

考虑到上述论证，我得出以下结论：_____问题的优点多于缺点。一方面，_____。另一方面，_____。由此我们得出结论_____。

（八）

There has been significant changes in _____ in the past _____ years.

There is no denying that _____ is the indication of civilization, progress and development. Nevertheless, it causes the serious problem of _____. Experts have warned that unless effective measures are taken, the problem of _____ will eventually get out of hand. Actually, people are showing a real concern over the problem. For example, people _____ so as to prevent it from happening.

Indeed, the earth is our home and we have the duty to take care of it for ourselves and our descendents. In my opinion, we should work out concrete solutions to the problem of _____. On the one hand, _____. On the other hand, _____. Only in this way can we really crack this hard nut.

译文

在过去_____年中，在_____方面已经发生了急剧的变化。

毫无疑问，_____是文明、进步和发展的标志。然而，它也造成了_____的严重问题。专家已经警告人们：除非采取有效措施，否则这个问题最终将难以控制。

事实上，人们正在对这个问题予以真正的关注。例如，人们_____以便阻止其发生。

实际上，地球是我们的家园，我们有责任为自己和我们的后代爱护好它。在我看来，我们对_____的问题应该制定具体的措施。一方面，_____。另一方面，_____。只有这样，我们才能真正解决这个难题。

（九）

When it comes to _____, people's opinions differ. Some hold the opinion that _____, while others claim that _____.

It seems that I am sending a message about the significance of _____ and the need of everyone to fight against the danger of this issue. In fact, what I am saying is if we do not exert our efforts to it, _____. If we let this situation go as it is, our _____ will suffer a great destruction.

To improve this situation, the best way to _____ is to _____. First and foremost, we should always be ready to _____, no matter whether we are college students or staff members. More importantly, _____. Only by doing so can we help to make the world a better place.

译文

当谈论到_____的时候，人们的观点有所不同。有些人认为_____，而其他人认为_____。

似乎我在发表关于_____重要性的信息，需要大家与这个问题所带来的危害作斗争。实际上，我所要表达的是：如果我们不竭尽全力，那么_____。如果我们对这种情况听之任之，我们的_____将遭受巨大的破坏。

为了改善这种状况，_____最好的方式是_____。首先，无论我们是大学生还是职员，我们都应该时刻准备好_____。更重要的是，_____。只有这样，我们才能使这个世界变得更加美好。

（十）

Dear Sir or Madam,

I am senior from the Department of Chinese Language and Literature of Beijing University. As I am planning to _____, I have decided to _____ with due consideration of _____.

Would you be so kind as to furnish me with some related information? First of all, _____. Secondly, _____. Lastly, _____.

I would like to express my sincere gratitude for your kind consideration of my requests. I look forward to hearing from you soon.

Yours sincerely,

Li Ming

译 文

尊敬的先生或女士：

我是北京大学中文系大四的学生。由于我计划 _____，充分考虑到 _____，我决定 _____。

您可否好心提供一些相关信息？首先，_____。其次，_____。最后，_____。

对于您好心考虑我的请求，在此向您表示我真诚的感谢。期待着尽快收到您的回信。

您真诚的，

李明

第二章　快速阅读

最新大纲

　　根据全国大学英语四、六级考试委员会出版的《大学英语四级考试大纲》，快速阅读部分"采用1～2篇较长篇幅的文章或多篇短文，总长度约为1000词。要求考生运用略读和查读的技能从篇章中获取信息。略读考核学生通过快速阅读获取文章主旨大意或中心思想的能力，阅读速度约每分钟100词。查读考核学生利用各种提示，如数字、大写单词、段首句或句首词等快速查找特定信息的能力。快速阅读理解部分采用的题型有多项选择、是非判断、句子填空、完成句子等"。

第一节　高分攻略

一、应试技巧

1. 试题考查内容与文章内容的出现顺序一致，自始至终均有考点，但并非平均分布。

2. 共10题，通常前7题为多项选择（四选一）或是非判断，后3题为句子填空或完成句子。

3. 是非判断分三种情况：正确（Y）、错误（N）、原文未提及（NG）。题目一般是陈述句，要求考生根据文中信息，对陈述句进行判断。

4. 第8～10题是对原文的转述，答案一般是文中原词，长度为2～4个，所填内容通常是名词短语，空格多在句尾。

5. 重视文章前两段、最后一段及每段首尾句，掌握文章的主题句、结论句与主旨，通常一半以上的题目答案在段落的首尾句。

6. 重视逻辑关系。逻辑关系位于文章的段落之间、句子之间以及句子内部，包括：因果关系（因为：because, in that, since, as, for, because of, due to, owing to；所以：therefore, hence, accordingly, as a result, consequently等）；并列和递进关系（and, or, not only... but also, then, moreover, in addition, in other words等）；转折关系（but, however, yet, instead, nevertheless等）。例如，并列和递进关系反映了前后句子主旨的相似性，对此类关系只阅读其中一半内容即可。

7. 重视特殊标点：冒号、括号、破折号，这些标点后的内容都是对前面信息的进一步解释，同样只读其中一半即可。

二、解题顺序

（一）先读题目，后看文章，预测文章内容，定位大写字母、时间、地点、数字、比较级、最高级等关键词

以2009年12月的真题为例：

2）What did Allegheny College in Meadville do three years ago?

关键词：Allegheny College in Meadville

4）Monica Inzer, dean of admission and financial aid at Hamilton, believes

_____.

关键词：Monica Inzer, at Hamilton

（二）同时运用略读、查读

1. 略读（Skimming）

亦称跳跃式阅读，重点在于快速了解文章的中心思想，即以尽可能快的速度有选择地进行阅读，跳过某些细节，迅速掌握文章的主旨。略读主要解决主旨大意题，这类题比例不大。

例：大纲样题

The passage gives a general description of the structure and use of a landfill.

本题要求使用略读方法解决，迅速浏览文章的小标题及首尾段，进行归纳总结。

2. 查读（Scanning）

亦称寻读，重点在于有目的地查询特定信息，即从大量资料中迅速查找某一特定信息或具体事实，略去无关的部分。方法是：快速扫描文章，明确要查询信息的特征，确定查询范围，如：日期、数目重点查询具体数字，人名、地名查询大写字母，事件、观点查询相关关键词。

（三）仔细阅读得出答案

仔细阅读文章的某一特定部分，深入理解该部分，进行归纳、总结、判断，此种方法适于推断型试题。

三、是非判断技巧

自2007年12月起，四级快速阅读的题型从是非判断改为多项选择（四选一），

但大纲中并未明确提及是非判断题型以后不再考查，故考生须掌握这一题型的解题方法，做好两手准备。

（一）Y（for Yes，= agree with，正确）

1. 使用同义词或同义结构替换原文。

例：2006年6月24日真题

2. General Eisenhower felt that the broad German motorways made more sense than the two-lane highways of America.

原文：The old convoy had started me thinking about good, two-lane highways, but Germany's Autobahn or motorway had made me see the wisdom of broader ribbons across the land.

解析：原文中的made me see the wisdom of broader ribbons across the land被替换为made more sense。

2. 归纳并推断原文中的几句话。

例：2006年12月真题

3. Laura Hillenbrand is an example cited to show how emotional energy can contribute to one's success in life.

原文：Consider Laura Hillenbrand, who despite an extremely weak body wrote the best-seller *Seabiscuit*. ...It was emotional energy that helped her succeed.

解析：原文中的helped her succeed被替换为contribute to one's success。

（二）N（for No，= contradict，错误）

1. 使用反义词、反义结构，与原文意思相反。

例：2006年12月真题

2. People these days tend to lack physical energy.

原文：But it's not physical energy that most of us lack.

2. 使用表示不同范围、频率、可能性的词汇。

常用all（全部），usually（通常），always（总是），impossible（完全不可能）替换原文中的many（很多），sometimes（有时），unlikely（不太可能）等。

例：大纲样题

3. Compared with other major industrialized countries, America buries a much higher percentage of its solid waste in landfills.

原文：The United States ranks somewhere in the middle of the major countries （United Kingdom, Canada, Germany, France and Japan）in landfill disposal.

解析：题目中以a much higher percentage替换了原文的in the middle of。

3. 两种不同条件替换

must, only等一种条件替换both... and..., or, also等多种条件。

例：大纲样题

6. In the United States the building of landfills is the job of both federal and local governments.

原文：In the United States, taking care of trash and building landfills are local government responsibilities.

（三）NG（for Not Given, =Not Given, 原文未提及）

题目中的部分内容在原文中没有提及或找不到依据。

例：2006年12月真题

7. The real-estate broker the author knows is talented in home redecoration.

原文：A real estate broker I know keeps herself amused on the job by mentally redecorating the houses she shows to clients. "I love imagining what even the most run-down house could look like with a little tender loving care," she says. "It's a challenge—and the least desirable properties are usually the most fun."

解析：由题干中的real-estate broker定位到第三个建议下首段第三句，此处指出"我认识的一位房产经纪人喜欢在想象中装修她给客户展示的房子，这样使她觉得这份工作很有趣"，并未提及"作者认识的这位房产经纪人对室内装修很有天赋"。

第二节　真题选析

Part II　　　**Reading Comprehension（Skimming and Scanning）**　　（**15 minutes**）

Directions: *In this part, you will have 15 minutes to go over the passage quickly and answer the questions on **Answer Sheet 1**. For questions 1-7, choose the best answer from the four choices marked [A], [B], [C] and [D]. For questions 8-10, complete the sentences with the information given in the passage.*

That's enough, kids

It was a lovely day at the park and Stella Bianchi was enjoying the sunshine with her two children when a young boy, aged about four, approached her two-year-old son and pushed him to the ground.

"I'd watched him for a little while and my son was the fourth or fifth child he'd shoved," she says. "I went over to them, picked up my son, turned to the boy and said, firmly, 'No, we don't push.'" What happened next was unexpected.

"The boy's mother ran toward me from across the park," Stella says. "I thought she was coming over to apologise, but instead she started shouting at me for 'disciplining her child'. All I did was let him know his behaviour was unacceptable. Was I supposed to sit back while her kid did whatever he wanted, hurting other children in the process?"

Getting your own children to play nice is difficult enough. Dealing with other people's children has become a minefield.

In my house, jumping on the sofa is not allowed. In my sister's house it's encouraged. For her it's about kids being kids: "If you can't do it at three, when can you do it?"

Each of these philosophies is valid and, it has to be said, my son loves visiting his aunt's house. But I find myself saying "no" a lot when her kids are over at mine. That's OK between sisters but becomes dangerous territory when you're talking to the children of friends or acquaintances.

"Kids aren't all raised the same," agrees Professor Naomi White of Monash University. "But there's still an idea that they're the property of the parents. We see our children as an extension of ourselves, so if you're saying that my child is behaving inappropriately, then that's somehow a criticism of me."

In those circumstances, it's difficult to know whether to approach the child directly or the parent first. There are two schools of thought.

"I'd go to the child first," says Andrew Fuller, author of *Tricky Kids*. "Usually a quiet reminder that 'we don't do that here' is enough. Kids have finely tuned *antennae* (直觉) for how to behave in different settings."

He points out that bringing it up with the parent first may make them feel neglectful, which could cause problems. Of course, approaching the child first can bring its own headaches, too.

This is why White recommends that you approach the parents first. "Raise your concerns with the parents if they're there and ask them to deal with it," she says.

Asked how to approach a parent in this situation, psychologist Meredith Fuller answers: "Explain your needs as well as stressing the importance of the friendship. Preface your remarks with something like: 'I know you will think I'm silly but in my house I don't want...'"

When it comes to situations where you're caring for another child, White is straightforward: "Common sense must prevail. If things don't go well then have a chat."

There're a couple of new grey areas. Physical punishment, once accepted from any adult, is no longer appropriate. "Now you can't do it without feeling uneasy about it," White says.

Men might also feel uneasy about dealing with other people's children. "Men feel nervous," White says. "A new set of considerations has come to the fore as part of the debate about how we handle children."

For Andrew Fuller, the child-centric nature of our society has affected everyone. "The rules are different now from when today's parents were growing up," he says. "Adults are scared of saying, 'Don't swear', or asking a child to stand up on a bus. They're worried that there will be conflict if they point these things out—either from older children, or their parents."

He sees it as a loss of the sense of common public good and public *courtesy*(礼貌), and says that adults suffer from it as much as children.

Meredith Fuller agrees. "A code of conduct is hard to create when you're living in a world in which everyone is exhausted from overwork and lack of sleep, and a world in which nice people are perceived to finish last."

"It's about what I'm doing and what I need," Andrew Fuller says. "The days when a kid came home from school and said, 'I got into trouble', and dad said, 'You probably deserved it', are over. Now the parents are charging up to the school to have a go at teachers."

This jumping to our children's defence is part of what fuels the "walking on eggshells" feeling that surrounds our dealings with other people's children. You know that if you *remonstrate*(劝诫) with the child, you're going to have to deal with the parent. It's admirable to be protective of our kids, but is it good?

"Children have to learn to negotiate the world on their own, within reasonable boundaries," White says. "I suspect that it's only certain sectors of the population doing the running to the school—better-educated parents are probably more likely to be too involved."

White believes our notions of a more child-centred society should be challenged. "Today we have a situation where, in many families, both parents work, so the amount of time children get from parents has diminished," she says.

"Also, sometimes when we talk about being child-centred, it's a way of talking about treating our children like *commodities*(商品). We're centred on them but in ways that reflect positively on us. We treat them as objects whose appearance and achievements are something we can be proud of, rather than serve the best interests of the children."

One way over-worked, under-resourced parents show commitment to their children is to leap to their defence. Back at the park, Bianchi's *intervention*(干预) on her son's behalf ended in an undignified exchange of insulting words with the other boy's mother.

As Bianchi approached the park bench where she'd been sitting, other mums came up to her and congratulated her on taking a stand. "Apparently the boy had a longstanding reputation for bad behaviour and his mum for even worse behaviour if he was challenged."

Andrew Fuller doesn't believe that we should be afraid of dealing with other people's kids. "Look at kids that aren't your own as a potential minefield," he says. He recommends that we don't stay silent over inappropriate behaviour, particularly with regular visitors.

注意：此部分试题请在**答题卡1**上作答。

1. What did Stella Bianchi expect the young boy's mother to do when she talked to him?

   [A] Make an apology.　　　　　[C] Discipline her own boy.

   [B] Come over to intervene.　　　[D] Take her own boy away.

2. What does the author say about dealing with other people's children?

   [A] It's important not to hurt them in any way.

   [B] It's no use trying to stop their wrongdoing.

   [C] It's advisable to treat them as one's own kids.

   [D] It's possible for one to get into lots of trouble.

3. According to Professor Naomi White of Monash University, when one's kids are criticised, their parents will probably feel _____.

   [A] discouraged　　　　　　　[C] puzzled

   [B] hurt　　　　　　　　　　[D] overwhelmed

4. What should one do when seeing other people's kids misbehave according to Andrew Fuller?

   [A] Talk to them directly in a mild way. [C] Simply leave them alone.

   [B] Complain to their parents politely.　[D] Punish them lightly.

5. Due to the child-centric nature of our society, _____.

   [A] parents are worried when their kids swear at them

   [B] people think it improper to criticise kids in public

   [C] people are reluctant to point out kids' wrongdoings

   [D] many conflicts arise between parents and their kids

6. In a world where everyone is exhausted from overwork and lack of sleep, _____.

   [A] it's easy for people to become impatient

   [B] it's different to create a code of conduct

   [C] it's important to be friendly to everybody

   [D] it's hard for people to admire each other

7. How did people use to respond when their kids got into trouble at school?

[A] They'd question the teachers.　　[C] They'd tell the kids to calm down.

[B] They'd charge up to the school.　　[D] They'd put the blame on their kids.

8. Professor White believes that the notions of a more child-centred society should be

　_____.

9. According to Professor White, today's parents treat their children as something they _____.

10. Andrew Fuller suggests that, when kids behave inappropriately, people should not

　_____.

试题详解

　　本文是一篇问题解决型的议论文，主要讨论管教别人的孩子这一问题。文章首先叙述了一位家长的经历，说明管教别人的孩子会招来麻烦。其次指出在发现别人的孩子言行不当时，人们对于先找家长还是先找孩子持有不同看法。接着分析了在对待孩子的问题上的其他灰色地带和因素。最后指出如何解决这一问题。

1. A　根据关键词Stella和boy's mother定位到第三段第二句：I thought she was coming over to apologise.（我以为她是来道歉的），将apologise同义替换为make an apology，故选A。

2. D　根据关键词dealing with other people's children定位到第四段第二句：Dealing with other people's children has become a minefield.（管教别人的孩子更是变成了雷区），将minefield同义替换为lots of trouble，故选D。

3. B　根据关键词Professor Naomi White of Monash University定位到第七段第三句：...if you're saying that my child is behaving inappropriately, then that's somehow a criticism of me.（如果你说我的孩子表现不好，你在某种程度上就是在批评我），故选B。

4. A　根据关键词Andrew Fuller定位到第九段："I'd go to the child first," says Andrew Fuller, author of *Tricky Kids*. "Usually a quiet reminder that 'we don't do that here' is enough."（"我会先接触孩子，"《棘手的孩子们》的作者安德鲁·福勒说。"通常一个温和的提醒'我们不这样做'就足够了"），将go to the child和a quiet reminder同义替换为talk to them directly in a mild way，故选A。

5. C 根据关键词the child-centric nature of our society定位到第十六段第三句："Adults are scared of saying, 'Don't swear', or asking a child to stand up on a bus. They're worried that there will be conflict if they point these things out—either from older children, or their parents."（"成年人害怕说'不要骂人'，或者害怕让小孩子在公交车上站着。他们担心如果自己指出这些会引起矛盾——或者来自年龄较大的小孩，或者来自他们的父母"），故选C。

6. B 根据关键词in a world where everyone is exhausted from overwork and lack of sleep定位到倒数第九段第二句：A code of conduct is hard to create when you're living in a world in which everyone is exhausted from overwork and lack of sleep...（当你生活在一个人人都因工作过度和缺乏睡眠而变得疲惫不堪的世界，……很难创造一种行为规范），故选B。

7. D 根据关键词kids got into trouble at school定位到倒数第八段第二句：The days when a kid came home from school and said, 'I got into trouble', and dad said, 'You probably deserved it', are over.（"孩子放学回家说'我有麻烦了'，而父亲说'你活该'的日子已经一去不复返了"），故选D。

8. challenged
根据关键词notions of a more child-centred society should be定位到倒数第五段第一句：White believes our notions of a more child-centred society should be challenged.（怀特认为我们更以孩子为中心的社会观点应该受到质疑），故填challenged。

9. can be proud of
根据关键词treat, as something定位到倒数第四段尾句：We treat them as objects whose appearance and achievements are something we can be proud of, rather than serve the best interests of the children.（我们把孩子看成了物品，以其外表和成就为自豪，而不是为了孩子的最大利益去做），故填can be proud of。

10. stay silent
根据关键词Andrew Fuller和behave inappropriately定位到文章尾句：He recommends that we don't stay silent over inappropriate behaviour, particularly with regular visitors.（他建议我们不应该对不恰当的行为坐视不管，尤其是对常客），故填stay silent。

二、经典真题二

Part II　　　**Reading Comprehension**（**Skimming and Scanning**）　　（**15 minutes**）

Directions: *In this part, you will have 15 minutes to go over the passage quickly and answer the questions on* **Answer Sheet 1***. For questions 1-7, choose the best answer from the four choices marked* [A], [B], [C] *and* [D]*. For questions 8-10, complete the sentences with the information given in the passage.*

How Do You See Diversity?

As a manager, Tiffany is responsible for interviewing applicants for some of the positions with her company. During one interview, she noticed that the candidate never made direct eye contact. She was puzzled and somewhat disappointed because she liked the individual otherwise.

He had a perfect résumé and gave good responses to her questions, but the fact that he never looked her in the eye said "untrustworthy," so she decided to offer the job to her second choice.

"It wasn't until I attended a diversity workshop that I realized the person we passed over was the perfect person," Tiffany confesses. What she hadn't known at the time of the interview was that the candidate's "different" behavior was simply a cultural misunderstanding. He was an Asian-American raised in a household where respect for those in authority was shown by *averting*（避开）your eyes.

"I was just thrown off by the lack of eye contact; not realizing it was cultural," Tiffany says. "I missed out, but will not miss that opportunity again."

Many of us have had similar encounters with behaviors we perceive as different. As the world becomes smaller and our workplaces more diverse, it is becoming essential to expand our understanding of others and to reexamine some of our false assumption.

Hire Advantage

At a time when hiring qualified people is becoming more difficult, employers who can eliminate invalid *biases*（偏见）from the process have a distinct advantage. My company, Mindsets LLC, helps organizations and individuals see their own blind spots. A real estate recruiter we worked with illustrates the positive difference such training can make.

"During my Mindsets coaching session, I was taught how to recruit a diversified workforce. I recruited people from different cultures and skill sets. The agents were able to utilize their full potential and experiences to build up the company. When the real estate market began to change, it was because we had a diverse agent pool that we were able to stay in the real estate market much longer than others in the same profession."

Blinded by Gender

Dale is an account executive who attended one of my workshops on supervising a diverse workforce. "Through one of the sessions, I discovered my personal bias," he recalls. "I learned I had not been looking at a person as a whole person, and being open to differences." In his case, the blindness was not about culture but rather gender.

"I had a management position open in my department; and the two finalists were a man and a woman. Had I not attended this workshop, I would have automatically assumed the man was the best candidate because the position required quite a bit of extensive travel. My reasoning would have been that even though both candidates were great and could have been successful in the position, I assumed the woman would have wanted to be home with her children and not travel." Dale's assumptions are another example of the well-intentioned but incorrect thinking that limits an organization's ability to tap into the full potential of a diverse workforce.

"I learned from the class that instead of imposing my gender biases into the situation, I needed to present the full range of duties, responsibilities and expectations to all candidates and allow them to make an informed decision." Dale credits the workshop, "because it helped me make decisions based on fairness."

Year of the Know-It-All

Doug is another supervisor who attended one of my workshops. He recalls a major lesson learned from his own employee.

"One of my most embarrassing moments was when I had a Chinese-American employee put in a request to take time off to celebrate Chinese New Year. In my ignorance, I assumed he had his dates wrong, as the first of January had just passed. When I advised him of this, I gave him a long talking-to about turning in requests early with the proper dates.

"He patiently waited, then when I was done, he said he would like Chinese New

Year off, not the Western New Year. He explained politely that in his culture the new year did not begin January first, and that Chinese New Year, which is tied to the lunar cycle, is one of the most celebrated holidays on the Chinese calendar. Needless to say, I felt very embarrassed in assuming he had his dates mixed up. But I learned a great deal about assumptions, and that the timing of holidays varies considerably from culture to culture.

"Attending the diversity workshop helped me realize how much I could learn by simply asking questions and creating dialogues with my employees, rather than making assumptions and trying to be a know-it-all," Doug admits. "The biggest thing I took away from the workshop is learning how to be more 'inclusive' to differences."

A Better Bottom Line

An open mind about diversity not only improves organizations internally, it is profitable as well. These comments from a customer service representative show how an inclusive attitude can improve sales. "Most of my customers speak English as a second language. One of the best things my company has done is to contract with a language service that offers translations over the phone. It wasn't until my boss received Mindsets' training that she was able to understand how important inclusiveness was to customer service. As a result, our customer base has increased."

Once we start to see people as individuals, and discard the stereotypes, we can move positively toward inclusiveness for everyone. Diversity is about coming together and taking advantage of our differences and similarities. It is about building better communities and organizations that enhance us as individuals and reinforce our shared humanity.

When we begin to question our assumptions and challenge what we think we have learned from our past, from the media, peers, family, friends, etc., we begin to realize that some of our conclusions are *flawed*(有缺陷的) or contrary to our fundamental values. We need to train ourselves to think differently, shift our mindsets and realize that diversity opens doors for all of us, creating opportunities in organizations and communities that benefit everyone.

注意：此部分试题请在**答题卡1**上作答。

1. What bothered Tiffany during an interview with her candidate?

　[A] He just wouldn't look her in the eye.

　[B] He was slow in answering her questions.

　[C] His résumé didn't provide the necessary information.

　[D] His answers to some of her questions were irrelevant.

2. Tiffany's misjudgment about the candidate stemmed from _____.

　[A] racial stereotypes　　　　　　　[C] cultural ignorance

　[B] invalid personal bias　　　　　　[D] emphasis on physical appearance

3. What is becoming essential in the course of economic globalization according to the author?

　[A] Hiring qualified technical and management personnel.

　[B] Increasing understanding of people of other cultures.

　[C] Constantly updating knowledge and equipment.

　[D] Expanding domestic and international markets.

4. What kind of organization is Mindsets LLC?

　[A] A real estate agency.　　　　　　[C] A cultural exchange organization.

　[B] A personnel training company.　　[D] A hi-tech company.

5. After one of the workshops, account executive Dale realized that _____.

　[A] he had hired the wrong person

　[B] he could have done more for his company

　[C] he had not managed his workforce well

　[D] he must get rid of his gender bias

6. What did Dale think of Mindsets LLC's workshop?

　[A] It was well-intentioned but poorly conducted.

　[B] It tapped into the executives' full potential.

　[C] It helped him make fair decisions.

　[D] It met participants' diverse needs.

7. How did Doug, a supervisor, respond to a Chinese-American employee's request for leave?

　[A] He told him to get the dates right.　　[C] He flatly turned it down.

　[B] He demanded an explanation.　　　　[D] He readily approved it.

8. Doug felt _____ when he realized that his assumption was wrong.

9. After attending Mindsets' workshops, the participants came to know the importance of _____ to their business.

10. When we view people as individuals and get rid of stereotypes, we can achieve diversity and benefit from the _____ between us.

试题详解

　　本文是一篇说明文，"分—总"结构，详细介绍了了解多元化的好处。文章首先通过五个案例说明人力资源主管参加思维公司多元化培训的成果，接着总结如何包容多元化。

1. A　根据题干中的Tiffany和during an interview将答案定位到首段第二、三句。原文中的puzzled and somewhat disappointed被替换为题干中的bothered，A选项同义替换了原文中的the candidate never made direct eye contact（应试者一直没和她进行直接的目光交流）。后文的he never looked at her in the eye也与A选项呼应。

2. C　根据题干中的misjudgment和the candidate将答案定位到本文第三段第二句：What she hadn't known at the time of the interview was that the candidate's "different" behavior was simply a cultural misunderstanding.（那时候，她没有意识到她认为那位应试者表现得"不同"，其实不过是一种文化误解），即她对那位应试者的误解是由于她忽视了文化因素，故选C。原文中的hadn't known 被替换为选项中的ignorance，后文的not realizing it was cultural也与C选项呼应。

3. B　根据题干中的is becoming essential定位到原文第五段第二句：As the world becomes smaller and our workplaces more diverse, it is becoming essential to expand our understanding of others and to reexamine some of our false assumption.（随着世界变小，我们的工作环境变得更多元化，我们很有必要增加对他人的了解，再度审视我们的一些错误假设）。前文提到的应试者是亚裔美国人，来自不同文化，由此可知此处的"他人"即来自其他文化的人，故选B。原文中的expand our understanding of被替换为选项中的increasing understanding of，others被替换为people of other cultures。

4. B　根据题干中的Mindsets LLC定位到Hire Advantage下面的首段第二、三句：My company, Mindsets LLC, helps organizations and individuals see their own

blind spots. A real estate recruiter we worked with illustrates the positive difference such training can make.（我的公司——思维有限责任公司，帮助企业和个人看到自己的盲点。一个与我们合作的地产公司招聘人员说明了这种培训能够带来的积极影响），由此可知，Mindsets是一个人力资源培训公司，故选B。原文中的recruiter被替换为选项中的personnel。

5. D　根据题干中的account executive Dale定位到Blind by Gender下的第一段：Dale is an account executive who attended one of my workshops on supervising a diverse workforce. "Through one of the sessions, I discovered my personal bias," he recalls...In his case, the blindness was not about culture but rather gender.（Dale是位业务经理，他参加了我们关于多元化员工管理的讲习班。"通过其中一次培训，我发现了自己的个人偏见"，他回忆说……就他而言，他的盲点不在于文化，而在于性别）。Dale发现了自己在性别上的偏见，由此推断他认识到自己应该消除性别偏见，故选D。后文的I learned from the class that instead of imposing my gender biases into the situation...也与D选项呼应。

6. C　根据关键词Dale和workshop定位到Blinded by Gender下的末段尾句：...Dale credits the workshop, "because it helped me make decisions based on fairness（Dale认为是讲习班的功劳："因为讲习班让我在公平的基础上作出决定"）。原文中的make decisions based on fairness被替换为选项中的make fair decisions，故选C。

7. A　根据关键词Doug和a Chinese-American employee's request定位到Year of the Know-It-All下面的前两段。文章提到，Doug是参加讲习班的另外一位管理人员。他回忆了自己从员工那里吸取的一大教训。"让我感到最尴尬的时刻之一就是我的一位美籍华裔员工向我请假去庆祝中国新年的时候。我无知地认为他把日期搞错了，因为1月1日刚刚过去。当我向他提出这点时，我跟他说了半天应该在正确的日期前递交申请。原文中的request to take time off被替换为题干中的request for leave；文中的I gave him a long talking-to about turning in requests early with proper dates被同义替换为选项A。

8. very embarrassed

空格前的felt暗示，空格处应填表示某种感觉的形容词或短语。根据关键词Doug, felt和assumption定位到Year of Know-It-All下的第三段第三句：Needless to say, I felt very embarrassed in assuming he had his dates mixed up.（毋庸赘言，

我因为错误地认为他把日期弄混了而感到十分尴尬）。原文中的说话人I被替换为题干中的Doug，文中的felt在题干中原词重现，故答案为very embarrassed。

9. inclusiveness

空格前的the importance of暗示，此处应填一个名词或名词短语。根据关键词Mindsets和importance定位到A Better Bottom Line下的首段第五句：It wasn't until my boss received Mindsets' training that she was able to understand how important inclusiveness was to customer service.（我们的老板参加了思维公司的培训之后才认识到包容对于客服的重要性）。文中的It wasn't until...training被替换为题干中的After...workshops，文中的understand how important被替换为题干中的know the importance，to customer service被替换为题干中的to their business，故填inclusiveness。

10. differences and similarities

空格前的the和空格后的between us暗示，此处应填一个复数名词或名词短语。根据关键词people as individuals 和stereotypes定位到本文倒数第二段前两句：Once we start to see people as individuals, and discard the stereotypes, we can move positively toward inclusiveness for everyone. Diversity is about coming together and taking advantage of our differences and similarities.（一旦我们把人看作个体，抛弃旧有的思维定势，我们就一定能做到对每个人都包容。多元化就是大家聚到一起，充分利用彼此之间的不同之处和相似之处）。文中的once被替换为题干中的when，see被替换为view，discard被替换为get rid of，move...for everyone被替换为achieve diversity，taking advantage of被替换为benefit from，our被替换为between us，故填differences and similarities。

三、经典真题三

Part II　　**Reading Comprehension**（Skimming and Scanning）　　(15 minutes)

Directions: *In this part, you will have 15 minutes to go over the passage quickly and answer the questions on **Answer Sheet 1**. For questions 1-7, choose the best answer from the four choices marked* [A], [B], [C] *and* [D]. *For questions 8-10, complete the sentences with the information given in the passage.*

Colleges taking another look at value of merit-based aid*

Good grades and high test scores still matter—a lot—to many colleges as they award financial aid.

But with low-income students projected to make up an ever-larger share of the college-bound population in coming years, some schools are re-examining whether that aid, typically known as "merit aid", is the most effective use of precious institutional dollars.

George Washington University in Washington, D.C., for example, said last week that it would cut the value of its average merit scholarships by about one-third and reduce the number of *recipients*(接受者), pouring the savings, about $2.5 million, into need-based aid. Allegheny College in Meadville, Pa., made a similar decision three years ago.

Now, Hamilton College in Clinton, N.Y., says it will phase out merit scholarship altogether. No current merit-aid recipients will lose their scholarships, but need-based aid alone will be awarded beginning with students entering in fall 2008.

Not all colleges offer merit aid; generally, the more selective a school, the less likely it is to do so. Harvard and Princeton, for example, offer generous need-based packages, but many families who don't meet need *eligibility*(资格) have been willing to pay whatever they must for a big-name school.

For small regional colleges that struggle just to fill seats, merit aid can be an important revenue-builder because many recipients still pay enough tuition dollars over and above the scholarship amount to keep the institution running.

But for rankings-conscious schools in between, merit aid has served primarily as a tool to recruit top students and to improve their academic profiles. "They're trying to buy students," says Skidmore College economist Sandy Baum.

Studies show merit aid also tends to benefit disproportionately students who could afford to enroll without it.

"As we look to the future, we see a more pressing need to invest in need-based aid," says Monica Inzer, dean of admission and financial aid at Hamilton, which has offered merit scholarships for 10 years. During that time, it rose in US News & World Report's ranking of the best liberal arts colleges, from 25 to 17.

Merit aid, which benefited about 75 students a year, or about 4% of its student body, at a cost of about $1 million a year, "served us well," Inzer says, but "to be discounting the price for families that don't need financial aid doesn't feel right any more."

Need-based aid remains by far the largest share of all student aid, which includes state, federal and institutional grants. But merit aid, offered primarily by schools and states, is growing faster, both overall and at the institutional level.

Between 1995-96 and 2003-04, institutional merit aid alone increased 212%, compared with 47% for need-based grants. At least 15 states also offer merit aid, typically in a bid to enroll top students in the state's public institutions.

But in recent years, a growing *chorus*(异口同声) of critics has begun pressuring schools to drop the practice. Recent decisions by Hamilton and others may be "a sign that people are starting to realize that there's this destructive competition going on," says Baum, co-author of a recent College Report that raises concerns about the role of institutional aid not based on need.

David Laird, president of the Minnesota Private College Council, says many of his schools would like to reduce their merit aid but fear that in doing so, they would lose top students to their competitors.

"No one can take one-sided action," says Laird, who is exploring whether to seek an *exemption*(豁免) from federal anti-trust laws so member colleges can discuss how they could jointly reduce merit aid. "This is a merry-go-round that's going very fast, and none of the institutions believe they can sustain the risks of trying to break away by themselves."

A complicating factor is that merit aid has become so popular with middle-income families, who don't qualify for need-based aid, that many have come to depend on it. And, as tuitions continue to increase, the line between merit and need blurs.

That is one reason Allegheny College doesn't plan to drop merit aid entirely.

"We still believe in rewarding superior achievements and know that these top students truly value the scholarship," says Scott Friedhoff, Allegheny's vice president for enrollment.

Emory University in Atlanta, which boasts a \$4.7 billion *endowment*(捐赠), meanwhile, is taking another approach. This year, it announced it would eliminate loans for needy students and cap them for middle-income families. At the same time, it would expand its 28-year-old merit program.

"Yeah, we're playing the merit game," acknowledges Tom Lancaster, associate dean for undergraduate education. But it has its strong points, too, he says. "The fact of the matter is, it's not just about the lowest-income people. It's the average American middle-class family who's being priced out of the market."

*A few words about merit-based aid:

Merit-based aid is aid offered to students who achieve excellence in a given area, and is generally known as academic, athletic and artistic merit scholarships.

Academic merit scholarships are based on students' grades, GPA and overall academic performance during high school. They are typically meant for students going straight to college right after high school. However, there are scholarships for current college students with exceptional grades as well. These merit scholarships usually help students pay tuition bills, and they can be renewed each year as long as the recipients continue to qualify. In some cases, students may need to be recommended by their school or a teacher as part of the qualification process.

Athletic merit scholarships are meant for students that *excel*(突出) in sports of any kind, from football to track and field events. Recommendation for these scholarships is required, since exceptional athletic performance has to be recognized by a coach or a *referee*(裁判). Applicants need to send in a tape containing their best performance.

Artistic merit scholarships require that applicants excel in a given artistic area. This generally includes any creative field such as art, design, fashion, music, dance or writing. Applying for artistic merit scholarships usually requires that students submit a *portfolio*(选辑) of some sort, whether that includes a collection of artwork, a recording of a musical performance or a video of them dancing.

注意：此部分试题请在**答题卡1**上作答。

1. With more and more low-income students pursuing higher education, a number of colleges are _____.

   [A] offering students more merit-based aid

   [B] revising their financial aid policies

   [C] increasing the amount of financial aid

   [D] changing their admission processes

2. What did Allegheny College in Meadville do three years ago?

   [A] It tried to implement a novel financial aid program.

   [B] It added $2.5 million to its need-based aid program.

   [C] It phased out its merit-based scholarships altogether.

   [D] It cut its merit-based aid to help the needy students.

3. The chief purpose of rankings-conscious colleges in offering merit aid is to
   _____.

   [A] improve teaching quality   [C] attract good students

   [B] boost their enrollments   [D] increase their revenues

4. Monica Inzer, dean of admission and financial aid at Hamilton, believes _____.

   [A] it doesn't pay to spend $1million a year to raise its ranking

   [B] it gives students motivation to award academic achievements

   [C] it's illogical to use so much money on only 4% of its students

   [D] it's not right to give aid to those who can afford the tuition

5. In recent years, merit-based aid has increased much faster than need-based aid due
   to _____.

   [A] more government funding to colleges

   [B] fierce competition among institutions

   [C] the increasing number of top students

   [D] schools' improved financial situations

6. What is the attitude of many private colleges toward merit aid, according to David
   Laird?

   [A] They would like to see it reduced.

   [B] They regard it as a necessary evil.

   [C] They think it does more harm than good.

   [D] They consider it unfair to middle-class families.

7. Why doesn't Allegheny College plan to drop merit aid entirely?

   [A] Rising tuitions have made college unaffordable for middle-class families.

   [B] With rising incomes, fewer students are applying for need-based aid.

   [C] Many students from middle-income families have come to rely on it.

   [D] Rising incomes have disqualified many students for need-based aid.

8. Annual renewal of academic merit scholarships depends on whether the recipients
   remain _____.

9. Applicants for athletic merit scholarships need a recommendation from a coach or
   a referee who _____ their exceptional athletic performance.

10. Applicants for artistic merit scholarships must produce evidence to show their
    _____ in a particular artistic field.

试题详解

本文是一篇议论文，介绍了大学奖学金政策的演变。文章首先指出了一些大学改变了奖学金政策，其次列举原因，最后说明了其他大学对此的看法。

1. B 根据关键词 low-income students 定位到第二段：But with low-income students projected to make up an ever-larger share of the college-bound population in coming years, some schools are re-examining whether that aid, typically known as "merit aid", is the most effective use of precious institutional dollars.(但在未来几年，随着来自低收入家庭的大学新生比例不断增大，一些学校开始重新审视被大家称为"奖学金"的学生资助措施是否使大学里的宝贵资金得到了最有效的利用)，故选B"修改其资金援助政策"。

2. D 根据关键词 Allegheny College in Meadville 定位到第三段：George Washington University in Washington, D.C., for example, said last week that it would cut the value of its average merit scholarships by about one-third and reduce the number of recipient, pouring the savings, about $2.5 million, into need-based aid. Allegheny College in Meadville, Pa., made a similar decision three years ago.(例如，位于华盛顿的乔治华盛顿大学上周称，他们将把奖学金的平均额下调大概三分之一，并减少获得者的数量，这样就可以将节约下来的总数约250万美元的资金投放到贫困助学金上。宾夕法尼亚州米德维尔士的Allegheny学院三年前就作出了类似的决定)，故选D"减少奖学金来帮助贫困学生"。

3. C 根据关键词 rankings-conscious 定位到第七段：But for rankings-conscious schools in between, merit aid has served primarily as a tool to recruit top students and to improve their academic profiles. "They're trying to buy students," says Skidmore College economist Sandy Baum.(但是对于介于上述两种学校之间的关注自身排名的学校而言，奖学金一直是招揽优秀学生并提高学校声誉的主要工具。Skidmore学院的经济学者Sandy Baum说："他们在购买学生。")，故选C"吸引好学生"。

4. D 根据关键词 Monica Inzer 和 at Hamilton 定位到第十段："Merit aid, which benefited about 75 students a year, or about 4% of its student body, at a cost of about $1 million a year, "served us well," Inzer says, but "to be discounting the price for families that don't need financial aid doesn't feel right any more."(每

年100万美元的奖学金能够资助75名学生，约占学生总数的4%，Inzer说，这"取得了良好的效果"，但"给不需要经济援助的家庭打折已不再被认为是合适的事情"），故选D"不应该给那些能够负担学费的人提供资助"。原文中的discounting the price被替换为选项中的give aid(给予资助)。

5. B　根据关键词merit-based aid和increased定位到第十二段：Between 1995-96 and 2003-04, institutional merit aid alone increased 212%, compared with 47% for need-based grants. At least 15 states also offer merit aid, typically in a bid to enroll top students in the state's public institutions.（1995至1996学年和2003至2004学年，学校提供的奖学金增长了212%。相比之下，贫困助学金增长了47%。至少有15个州还在提供奖学金，尤其在州立公立学校展开的争夺优秀生的竞争之中），故选B"学校之间的激烈竞争"。原文中的in a bid暗示出竞争的激烈，下段中的this destructive competition也指代in a bid...institutions。

6. A　根据关键词David Laird定位到第十四段：David Laird, president of the Minnesota Private College Council, says many of his schools would like to reduce their merit aid but fear that in doing so, they would lose top students to their competitors.（明尼苏达私立学院理会主席David Laird认为，他那里的很多学校都想减少奖学金，但担心这样做会把优秀生拱手让给竞争对手），故选A"他们愿意看到奖学金减少"。

7. C　根据题干doesn't Allegheny College plan to drop merit aid entirely定位到第十六段首句：A complicating factor is that merit aid has become so popular with middle-income families, who don't qualify for need-based aid, that many have come to depend on it.（中等收入家庭不具备贫困助学金的申请资格，但奖学金在他们中间已很普遍，以至于他们已经开始依靠奖学金了，这是个复杂的因素），故选C"很多来自中等收入家庭的学生已经开始依靠奖学金了"。

8. qualified
根据关键词renewal和recipients定位到原文注释部分第二段倒数第二句：These merit scholarships usually help students pay tuition bills, and they can be renewed each year as long as the recipients continue to qualify.（这些奖学金通常能够帮助学生支付学费，只要获得者可以保持获奖资格，每年均可领到奖学金），故填

qualified。需要注意的是，原文中的continue to被替换为空格前的remain，remain是系动词，后接表语，应将原文中的qualify改为形容词形式qualified。

9. recognizes

根据关键词recommendation和coach or a referee定位到原文注释部分第三段第二句：Recommendation for these scholarships is required, since exceptional athletic performance has to be recognized by a coach or a referee（要获得这些奖学金需要得到推荐，因为突出的运动表现必须得到教练或者裁判的认可），故填recognizes。需要注意的是，题干将原文的被动语态改为主动语态，主语a coach or a referee是单数，时态是一般现在时，故谓语动词recognize后应加-s。

10. excellence

根据关键词applicants for artistic merit scholarships定位到原文注释部分末段首句：Artistic merit scholarships require that applicants excel in a given artistic area.（艺术类奖学金要求申请人在某一艺术领域有上佳表现）以及尾句：Applying for artistic merit scholarships usually requires that students submit a portfolio of some sort, whether that includes a collection of artwork, a recording of a musical performance or a video of them dancing.（申请艺术类奖学金一般要求学生上交一份某艺术门类的选辑，作品选、音乐录音或舞蹈录像均可），故填excellence。需要注意的是，题干将上述两句整合，原文末句的submit a portfolio被替换为题干中的produce evidence，答案应为in之前的excel，但由于their后应接名词或名词短语，因此将excel改为excellence。另外，原文中的portfolio已被替换为题干中的evidence，故不应填portfolios。

第三节 强化训练

强化训练一

Directions: *In this part, you will have 15 minutes to go over the passage quickly and answer the questions on **Answer Sheet 1**. For questions 1-7, choose the best answer from the four choices marked [A], [B], [C] and [D]. For questions 8-10, complete the sentences with the information given in the passage.*

Education Study Finds U.S. Falling Behind

Teachers in the United States earn less relative to national income than their counterparts in many industrialized countries, yet they spend far more hours in front of the classroom, according to a major new international study.

The salary differentials are part of a pattern of relatively low public investment in education in the United States compared with other member nations of the Organization for Economic Cooperation and Development, a group in Paris that compile the report. Total government spending on educational institutions in the United States slipped to 4.8 percent of gross domestic product in 2008, falling under the international average—5 percent—for the first time.

"The whole economy has grown faster than the education system," Andreas Schleicher, one of the reports' authors, explained. "The economy has done very well, but teachers have not fully benifited." The report, due out today, is the sixth on education published since 2001 by the organizations of 30 nations, founded in 1960, and now covering much of Europe, North America, Japan, South Korea, Australia and New Zealand.

In addition to the teacher pay gap, the report shows the other countries have begun to catch up with the United States in higher education: college enrollment has grown by 20 percent since 2005 across the group, with one in four young people now earning degrees. For the first time, the United State's college graduation rate, now at 33 percent, is not the world's highest. Finland, the Netherlands, New Zealand and Britain have surpassed it.

The United States is also producing a greater boost in income here while the lack of a high school diploma imposes a bigger income penalty. "The number of graduates is increasing, but that stimulates even more of a demand—there is no end in sight," Mr. Schleicher said. "The demand for skill, clearly, is growing faster than the supply that is coming from schools and colleges."

The report lists the salary for a high school teacher in the United States with 15 years experience as ＄36,219, above the international average of ＄31,887 but behind seven other countries and less than 60 percent of Switzerland's ＄62,052. Because teachers in the United States have a heavier classroom load—teaching almost a third more hours than their counterparts abroad—their salary per hour of actual teaching is ＄35, less than the international average of ＄41(Denmark, Spain and Germany pay more than ＄50 per teaching hour, South Korea ＄77). In 2004, such a veteran teacher in the United States earned 1.2 times the average per capita income whereas in 2009 the salary was just under the national average. Only the Czech Republic, Hungary, Iceland and Norway pay their teachers less relative to national income; in South Korea, teachers earn 2.5 times the national average. Teacher pay accounts for 56 percent of what the United States spends on education, well below the 67 percent average among the group of countries.

The new data come as the United States faces a shortage of two million teachers over the next decade, with questions of training, professionalism and salaries being debated by politicians local and national. Joost Yff, an international expert at American Association of Colleges of Teacher Education, said training of teachers is comparable among most of the nations in the study, and that they are all dealing with similar issues of raising standards and increasing professionalism.

Though the United States lags behind in scores on standardized tests in science and mathematics, students here get more instruction in those subjects, the report shows. The average 14-year-old American spent 295 hours in math and science classes in 2009, far more than the 229 international average; only Australia (370 hours), Mexico (367) and New Zealand(320) have more instruction in those subjects.

Middle-schoolers here spend less time than their international counterparts studying foreign languages and technology, but far more hours on physical education and vocational skills. High School students in the United States are far more likely to have part-time jobs: 64 percent of Americans ages 15 to 19 worked while in school, compared with an international average of 31 percent（only Canada and the Netherlands, with 69 percent, and Denmark, with 75 percent, were higher）.

One place the United States spends more money is on special services for the disabled and the poor. More than one in four children here are in programs based on physical or mental handicaps, twice or three times the rate in other countries.

The report shows a continuing shift in which the United States is losing its status as the most highly educated among the nations. The United States has the highest level of high school graduates ages 55 to 64, but falls to the sixth, behind Norway, Japan, South Korea, the Czech Republic and Switzerland, among ages 25 to 34. Among college graduates, it leads in the older generation but is third behind Canada and Japan in the younger *cohort*（一群）. While the portion of Americans with high school diplomas remains at 88 percent across age groups, the average age among member countries is rising. It has gone from 58 percent of those ages 45 to 54, to 66 percent of those ages 35 to 44 and 72 percent of those ages 25 to 34. A higher percentages of young people in Norway, Japan, South Korea, the Czech Republic and Switzerland have degrees than in the United States.

"The U.S. has led the development in college education and making education sort of accessible for everyone," Mr. Schleicher said. "It's becoming the norm."

注意：此部分试题请在**答题卡1**上作答。

1. Compared with their counterparts in many industrialized countries, the U.S. teachers _____.

   ［A］earn more   ［C］are younger

   ［B］work longer   ［D］are smarter

2. The U.S. government spent _____ of its GDP on education in 2008.

   ［A］4.8%   ［C］less than 4.8%

   ［B］5%   ［D］more than 5%

3. What do we learn about Finland education from the passage?

   ［A］It enjoys the highest college rate.

   ［B］It surpasses the U.S. in college graduation rate.

   ［C］It enjoys a 20% increase in college enrollment.

   ［D］It has more young people earning degrees than British does.

4. When the number of graduates in the U.S. increases, _____.

    [A] there are not enough jobs for them to do

    [B] they suffer a drop in initial salaries

    [C] the demand for their ability is rising

    [D] more college students drop their study

5. The new study shows that the actual teaching salary per hour in the U.S. is _____.

    [A] $ 35   [C] $ 50

    [B] $ 41   [D] $ 77

6. What does the report say about the U.S. students' study of science and mathematics?

    [A] They score higher on tests in those subjects than other subjects.

    [B] They are not smart in those subjects.

    [C] They get the most instruction in those subjects in the OECD.

    [D] They spend more time in those subjects than international average.

7. Compared with other countries in OECD, high school students in the U.S. spend more time in _____.

    [A] doing part-time jobs

    [B] foreign languages and technology

    [C] physical education and vocational skills

    [D] science and mathematics

8. It is for the special services for _____ that the United States pays more money than other OECD countries.

9. Those who have high school diplomas in the U.S. account for _____ of the Americans of all ages.

10. According to Mr. Schleicher, the U.S. is becoming the norm of _____ _____ and has made education accessible for everyone.

试题详解

本文为一篇说明性报道，作者通过经济合作与发展组织的一份报告引出美国教育滞后的问题，并将美国的教师收入、国家教育资金投入水平、美国毕业生比例等与其他国家作比较，从而说明美国教育已经丧失了其领先地位。

1. B　根据关键词their counterparts in many industrialized countries定位到首段：
Teachers in the United States earn less relative to national income than their
counterparts in many industrialized countries, yet they spend far more hours in
front of the classroom, according to a major new international study.（根据一项
最新的国际研究，从国民收入来说，美国教师的工资收入低于很多其他工
业化国家的同行，但在教室里工作的时间却更长），故选B"工作时间更长"。
原文中的spend far more hours被替换为选项中的work longer。

2. A　根据关键词U.S.与GDP on education in 2008定位到第二段尾句：Total
government spending on educational institutions in the United States slipped to
4.8 percent of gross domestic product in 2008, falling under the international
average—5 percent—for the first time.（2008年，美国政府在教育机构方面的
总体投入下降到国内生产总值的4.8%，首次跌到5%的国际平均水平之下），
故选A。原文中的gross domestic product即题干中的GDP（国内生产总值）。

3. B　根据关键词Finland定位到第四段最后两句：For the first time, the United
State's college graduation rate, now at 33 percent, is not the world's highest.
Finland, the Netherlands, New Zealand and Britain have surpassed it.（美国33%
的大学毕业率首次不再是世界第一。芬兰、荷兰、新西兰和英国已经超过美
国），故选B"在大学毕业率方面超过美国"。

4. C　根据关键词the number of graduates与increases定位到第五段尾句："The
number of graduates is increasing, but that stimulates even more of a demand—
there is no end in sight," Mr. Schleicher said. "The demand for skill, clearly, is
growing faster than the supply that is coming from schools and colleges."
（Schleicher先生说："毕业生数量的不断增加会刺激对大学毕业生更高的要
求——这是一个长期问题。对技能要求的增长速度显然比大学毕业生供应
量的增长速度更快。"），故选C"对他们的能力要求也在增长"。

5. A　根据关键词actual teaching salary per hour in the U.S.定位到第六段第二句：
Because teachers in the United States have a heavier classroom load—teaching
almost a third more hours than their counterparts abroad—their salary per hour
of actual teaching is $35, less than the international average of $41（Denmark,
Spain and Germany pay more than $50 per teaching hour, South Korea $77）.
（由于美国教师的课业负担较重——美国教师的工作时间要比其国外同行

多三分之一——他们每小时的实际课时费是35美元，低于每小时41美元的国际平均水平，其中丹麦、西班牙、德国教师每小时工资在50美元以上，韩国是77美元），故选A。

6. D 根据关键词report和students' study of science and mathematics定位到第八段。该段指出尽管美国在科学与数学的标准化考试成绩方面落后，但学生在那些科目上得到了更多的指导，接着举例说明，虽然14岁的美国学生在这些方面得到的指导远远超过平均水平，但却低于澳大利亚、墨西哥等国家，故选D"他们花在这些科目上的时间高于平均水平"。

7. C 根据关键词high school students和spend more time定位到第九段首句：Middle-schoolers here spend less time than their international counterparts studying foreign languages and technology, but far more hours on physical education and vocational skills. (美国中学生在外语和科技方面的学习时间少于其他国家，但在体育和职业技能方面的学习时间却远远超过其他国家)，故选C"在体育和职业技能方面"。原文中的middle-schoolers被替换为题干中的high school students, far more hours被替换为spend more time。

8. the disabled and the poor

根据关键词special services, the United States和pays more money定位到倒数第三段首句：One place the United States spends more money is on special services for the disabled and the poor. (美国投入资金较多的一个方面是为残疾人和穷人提供特殊服务)，故填the disabled and the poor。题干使用了It is... that... 强调句型。

9. 88 percent

根据关键词high school diplomas定位到倒数第二段倒数第三句：While the portion of Americans with high school diplomas remains at 88 percent across age groups, the average age among member countries is rising. (当美国各年龄段具有高中文凭的比例仍停留在88%时，其他国家具有高中文凭的平均年龄却在上升)，故填88 percent。原文中的remain被替换为题干中的account for, across age groups(各年龄段)被替换为all ages。

10. college education

根据关键词Mr. Schleicher, the U.S., becoming the norm, accessible for everyone定位到尾段："The U.S. has led the development in college education and making education sort of accessible for everyone," Mr. Schleicher said. "It's becoming the norm."(Schleicher先生说："美国引领了大学教育的发展，使教育成为每个人的权利，美国教育正在成为一种典范。")，故填college education。原文尾句的it指代美国的教育情况。

强化训练二

Directions: *In this part, you will have 15 minutes to go over the passage quickly and answer the questions on **Answer Sheet 1**. For questions 1-7, choose the best answer from the four choices marked* [A], [B], [C] *and* [D]. *For questions 8-10, complete the sentences with the information given in the passage.*

Raising Wise Consumers

Almost anyone with a profit motive is marketing to innocents. Help your kids understand it's OK not to have it all. Here are five strategies for raising wise consumers.

1. Lead by example

While you may know that TV commercials stimulate desire for consumer goods, you'll have a hard time selling your kids on the virtues of turning off the tube if you structure your own days around the latest sitcom or reality show.

The same principle applies to money matters. It does no good to lecture your kids about spending, saving and sharing when doing out their pocket money if you spend every free weekend afternoon at the mall. If you suspect your own spending habits are *out of whack*(有毛病), consider what financial advisor Nathan Dungan says in his book *Wasteful Sons and Material Girls: How Not to Be Your Child's ATM*. "In teaching your child about money, few issues are so critical as your own regular consumer decisions," he writes. "In the coming weeks, challenge yourself to say no to your own wants and to opt for less expensive options."

2. Encourage critical thinking

With children under six, start by telling them, "Don't believe everything you see," says Linda Millar, vice-president of Education for Concerned Children's Advertisers, a non-profit group of 26 Canadian companies helping children and their families to be wise consumers. "Show them examples of false or exaggerated advertising claims, such as a breakfast cereal making you bigger or stronger."

Shari Graydon, a media educator and past president of Media Watch, suggests introducing children to the "marketing that doesn't show"—the *mascots*(吉祥物) and websites that strengthen brand loyalty, the trading toys that cause must-have-it fever and the celebrity *endorsements*(代言). "Explain that advertisers pay millions of dollars for celebrities to endorse a product, and that the people who buy the product end up sharing the cost," she says.

3. Supervise with sensitivity

According to a survey conducted by the Media Awareness Network in 2001, nearly 70 percent of children say parents never sit with them while they surf the Net and more than half say parents never check where they've been online. The states for TV habits paint a similar picture. A 2003 Canadian Teachers' Federation study of children's media habits found that roughly 30 percent of children in Years Three to Six claims that no adult has input into their selection of TV shows; by Year Eight, the figure rises to about 60 percent.

"Research suggests that kids benefit more from having parents watch with them than having their viewing time limited," says Graydon, noting that many children have TV sets in their bedrooms, which effectively free them from parental supervision. And what exactly does "supervision" mean? "Rather than ridiculing your child's favorite show, which will only create distance between you, you can explain why certain media messages conflict with the values you'd like to develop in your child," Grandon says.

If you're put off by coarse language in a TV show, tell your child that hearing such language sends the (false) message that this is the way most people communicate when under stress. If violence in a computer game disturbs you, point out that a steady diet of onscreen violence can weaken sensitivity towards real-life violence. "And when you do watch a show together," adds Graydon, "discuss some of the hidden messages, both good and bad."

4. Say no without guilt

I'm not proud to admit it, but when Tara asked me if I could take her shopping, I ended up saying yes. More precisely, I told her that if she continued to work hard and do well in school, I would take her over the school holidays. The holidays have now passed and I still haven't taken her, but I have no doubt she'll remind me of it soon enough. When I do take her, I intend to set firm limits (both on the price and the clothing items) before we walk into the store.

Still, I wonder why I gave in so quickly to Tara's request. Author Thompson says that my status as a baby boomer may provide a clue. "We boomer parents spring from a consumer culture in which having the right stuff helps you fit in," she explains. "Our research has shown that even parents in poor homes will buy Game Boys over necessities." In fact, 68 percent of parents routinely give in to their kid's requests.

To counteract this tendency, Graydon says parents have to "learn, or relearn, how to say no." And what if the child calls you a miser or reminds you that her best friend has four Barbies and she doesn't even have one? Graydon suggests practicing this *mantra*(祷文): "We create our own family rules according to our own family values. We create our own family rules according to our own family values. We create..."

5. Offer alternatives

As parents know, saying "You can't have that" only intensifies a kid's desire for whatever "that" is. Rather than arbitrarily restricting their TV or computer time to protect them from media influence, Jeff Derevensky, a professor of applied child psychology at McGill University, suggests creating a list of mutually acceptable alternatives. "If you want to encourage your children to build towers or play board games, be prepared to participate," he says. "Many kids will do these activities with their parents but not with other kids."

Miranda Hughes, a part-time physician and mother of four, fills her home with such basics as colored pencils and paints, craft materials, board and card games, building toys, a piano with the lid permanently open, sheet music and books of all kinds. "I also offer my own time whenever possible," she says. Although Hughes has a television in her house, "complete with 150 channels," she says her kids watch only about an hour a week. "I haven't had to implement any rules about TV or computer use," she says. "There's usually something else my kids would rather be doing."

注意：此部分试题请在**答题卡1**上作答。

1. According to Nathan Dungan, the most important issue in teaching your child about money is _____.

[A] the way you spend your money

[B] suspecting your own habits of spending

[C] the way your child spends his or her money

[D] the amount of money at the child's disposal

2. From the passage we know that Linda Millar _____.

[A] suggests believing nothing but what we see and hear

[B] believes a cereal can make us bigger and stronger

[C] is a mother of six children and directs a non-profit organization

[D] warns us to keep away from false or exaggerated advertising claims

3. Shari Graydon suggests that children should be aware of _____.

[A] brand loyalty

[B] invisible marketing

[C] the must-have-it fever

[D] exaggerated advertisements

4. According to the study of children's media habits, how many of children in Year Eight claim to have their selected TV shows without parental supervision?

[A] Roughly 30 percent.

[B] About 60 percent.

[C] Nearly 70 percent.

[D] Approximately 70 percent.

5. Shari Graydon noted that children benefit more when _____.

[A] parents watch TV shows with them

[B] parents effectively limit their TV viewing time

[C] media messages don't conflict with their values

[D] there is a TV set in their own bedrooms

6. When parents watch TV shows with their children, they should _____.

[A] leap over violent programs which can lead to real-life violence

[B] avoid communicating with each other using coarse language

[C] discuss some of the good and bad invisible messages

[D] supervise each other with sensitivity

7. Graydon suggests that to avoid having the tendency to routinely give in to their child's requests parents should _____.

［A］create their family rules according to their family values

［B］set firm limits to whatever he or she requests

［C］satisfy his or her needs as little as possible

［D］learn to say no to their child without guilt

8. Author Thompson says that boomer parents, who were born in a ＿＿＿＿＿＿＿＿＿＿, believe that having the right stuff helps one fit in.

9. Jeff Derevensky suggests that to protect children from media influence, parents may as well create a list of ＿＿＿＿＿＿＿＿＿＿.

10. The passage is intended to teach parents how to raise their kids to be ＿＿＿＿＿＿＿＿＿＿.

试题详解

本文介绍了帮助父母教育孩子不受电视与网络等的诱惑，成为理性消费者的五大策略。

1. A 根据关键词Nathan Dungan定位到第一个小标题下的第二段，第四句提到："In teaching your child about money, few issues are so critical as your own regular consumer decisions," he writes.（他写道："在教导孩子关于花钱的问题时，没有什么比你自己的消费习惯更加重要了。"），故选A"你花钱的方式"。原文中的few issues are so critical被替换为题干中的the most important issue，选项A替换了原文的your own regular consumer decisions。

2. D 根据关键词Linda Millar定位到第二个小标题下的首段，尾句提到：Show them examples of false or exaggerated advertising claims, such as a breakfast cereal making you bigger or stronger.（告诉他们虚假或夸大的广告宣传的例子，例如一种谷类早餐宣称可以使你更高大、更强壮），故选D"警告我们远离虚假或夸大的广告宣传"。

3. B 根据关键词Shari Graydon定位到第二个小标题下的第二段首句前半句：Shari Graydon, a media educator and past president of Media Watch, suggests introducing children to the "marketing that doesn't show".（媒体教育者、Watch媒体公司的前总裁Shari Graydon建议向孩子们介绍"那些没有显现出来的营销手段"），故选B"看不见的营销活动"，原文中的marketing that doesn't show被替换为选项中的invisible marketing。

4. B 根据关键词children in Year Eight定位到第三个小标题下的首段末句：A 2003 Canadian Teachers' Federation study of children's media habits found that roughly 30 percent of children in Years Three to Six claims that no adult has input into their selection of TV shows; by Year Eight, the figure rises to about 60 percent.（2003年加拿大教师联合会关于儿童媒体习惯的一项研究发现，大约30%的三至六岁儿童声称没有大人干预他们选择电视节目；到了八岁，这一数字上升到大约60%），故选B。

5. A 根据关键词Shari Graydon及benefit more定位到第三个小标题下的第二段首句前半句："Research suggests that kids benefit more from having parents watch with them than having their viewing time limited," says Graydon.（Graydon说："研究显示，与限制孩子看电视的时间相比，父母与孩子一起看电视益处更多。"），故选A"父母和他们一起看电视节目"。

6. C 根据关键词when及watch TV shows with their children定位到第三个小标题下的末段尾句："And when you do watch a show together," adds Graydon, "discuss some of the hidden messages, both good and bad."（Graydon接着说："当你们一起看电视的时候，讨论一些隐含信息，不管是好的还是坏的。"），故选C"讨论一些好的和坏的隐含信息"。原文中的hidden被替换为选项中的invisible。

7. D 根据关键词Graydon及tendency定位到第四个小标题下的末段首句：To counteract this tendency, Graydon says parents have to "learn, or relearn, how to say no."（为了抵制这一趋势，Graydon认为父母必须"学习或再学习如何说不"），故选D"学习毫不愧疚地拒绝孩子"。

8. consumer culture
根据关键词Author Thompson定位到第四个小标题下的第二段第三句："We boomer parents spring from a consumer culture in which having the right stuff helps you fit in," she explains.（她解释说："我们婴儿潮出生的父母成长于一种消费文化之中，认为拥有一定的物质产品有助于适应这种文化。"），故填consumer culture。

9. mutually acceptable alternatives
根据关键词Jeff Derevensky定位到第五个小标题下的首段第二句：Rather than arbitrarily restricting their TV or computer time to protect them from media influence, Jeff Derevensky, a professor of applied child psychology at McGill University, suggests creating a list of mutually acceptable alternatives.（McGill大学的应用儿童心理学教授Jeff Derevensky认为，不应该为了保护孩子不受媒体

的影响而任意地限制他们看电视或使用电脑的时间，而应该创造出一些双方都能认可的替代物），故填mutually acceptable alternatives。

10. wise consumers

根据题干可知本题为主旨题，应关注全文标题、各小标题及首段。根据关键词raise定位到全文标题：*Raising Wise Consumers*（培养明智的消费者），故填wise consumers。

强化训练三

Directions: *In this part, you will have 15 minutes to go over the passage quickly and answer the questions on **Answer Sheet 1**. For questions 1-7, choose the best answer from the four choices marked* [A], [B], [C] *and* [D]. *For questions 8-10, complete the sentences with the information given in the passage.*

Belief in the Value of a College Degree

A new national survey of young adults age 18 to 25 from the nonprofit, nonpartisan opinion research organization Public Agenda finds that the vast majority of today's young adults—the African American, Hispanic or Latino, Asian American or white—strongly believe in the value of higher education. Most of the young adults surveyed in Life After High School: Young People Talk about Their Hopes and Prospects report that their parents inspired the goal of going to college and most had a teacher in high school who took a strong personal interest in them and encouraged them to go on to college.

Young People Have Strong Belief in College Education

Across racial and ethnic lines, young Americans see going to college as a positive thing to do. Three in four（74%）young adults agree that college helps prepare you for the real world. 77% of African Americans, 81% of Hispanics, 85% of Asian Americans and 81% of whites said that "people respect you more when they know you've graduated from college."

These findings counter the belief of some that large numbers of minority youth despise academic success. Only 7% of young African Americans and 3% young Hispanics surveyed say that graduating from college is something their circle of friends looks down on.

But the survey confirms what national data shows—going to college is still not commonplace for most African Americans and Hispanics. The African Americans and Hispanics(8% each) surveyed were less likely to have earned a bachelor's degree than their Asian American(25%) and white(16%) peers.

Substantial numbers believe their high school teachers and classes should have done a lot more to prepare them for college level work(51% African American, 48% Hispanic, 44% Asian American and 39% white). But they also hold themselves accountable for preparation. 69% of African Americans, 75% of Hispanics, 70% of Asian Americans and 65% of whites admit that they themselves "could have paid a lot more attention and worked harder" in high school.

Positive Views Encouraged the Kids to Go to College

Parents seem to be prime movers for getting kids to go to college. About 6 to 10 said that their parents strongly expected them to go to college (61% of African Americans, 59% of Hispanics, 86% of Asian Americans and 63% of whites). Majorities of all groups point to a parent as the one person who has been the most important influence on their decisions on issues like work and college.

In terms of inspiration, teachers, coaches and other adult mentors also come in for some high marks. 74% of African Americans, 69% of Hispanics, 63% of Asian Americans and 66% whites said they had a high school teacher who took a personal interest in them and encouraged them to go to college. Similar majorities said they had a teacher or coach who really inspired them to do their best.

As for high school counselors, the young people across all demographic groups surveyed indicated that counseling resources were stretched thin, with 53% saying there were not enough counselors in their high school. About half (52%) said their school counselors usually made an effort to get to know them, while 47% said they usually felt like "just another face in the crowd."

Different Views

Almost 9 in 10 (89%) agree that "college is not for everyone" and a solid majority (57%) agreed that "earning money instead of sitting in a classroom" can be an advantage. But Life After High School raises serious questions about the future of young adults with no college degree. Compared to those with either a 2- or 4-year degree, this group is less happy with their work situation and less focused on planning a future. Just 1 in 5 of these less educated young adults said they love their job, compared with 31% of those with degrees. 7 in 10 with limited education said they are in their current job more by chance than by design, compared to 56% of young workers with degrees. Lack of parental encouragement seems to play a big role. By a 30-point margin, young workers with less education are less likely than the more educated to say their parents strongly expected them to go to college (32% vs. 67%). By a 22-point margin they are less likely to point to a parent as their number one source of guidance (47% vs. 69%).

Those without college degrees are more likely to say they could have worked harder in school (78% of the less educated said this compared to 62% with degrees). While conventional wisdom may hold that those without college degrees didn't have mentors in high school, majorities said they did, in fact, have a high school teacher or coach who took an interest and inspired them.

Differences about Education Related to Men and Women

This research suggests that young women have internalized the worth of post-secondary education more than young men have. Young men are more likely to say they didn't attend or complete college because they "had enough of school" (32% vs. 22% of young women), and were more likely to say they didn't complete additional education because they preferred to work and make money (56% vs. 42%). In contrast, 7 in 10 (69%) young women who went to college said they "really enjoy being in school", whereas a significantly smaller majority of young men (58%) who went to college said the same thing.

Summary: Hopes, Inspiration and Trade-offs

Perhaps the most heartening message from Life After High School is that the vast majority of today's young adults—across racial and ethnic lines—believe that higher education is a way to earn both society's respects and insure the career advancement and financial security they yearn for.

According to the young adults themselves, parents are the most important adults who inspire them to get a higher education. Pointedly, those young people who don't continue on after high school are much less likely to say their parents expected them to go to college or that their parents are their most important source of guidance.

The findings indicate that African American and Hispanic young people are far more likely than their white peers to say they had to compromise on their choice of college due to financial constraints.

Finally, the report states "few would deny that many individuals shape constructive, honorable and satisfying lives without higher education, and there is a useful debate about whether all young people need or will even tolerate more schooling after high school. Even so, it is worth asking how comfortable we are with the haphazard, let-the-chips-fall-where-they-may career path so many young people who aren't in college seem to be pursuing."

注意：此部分试题请在**答题卡1**上作答。

1. What does the survey conducted by Public Agenda find?

    [A] Less and less young adults enjoy receiving higher education.

    [B] Most young adults regret wasting too much time in school.

    [C] Higher education doesn't necessarily ensure financial return.

    [D] Parents and teachers are important in inspiring young adults to go to college.

2. According to the passage, what does the national data show?

    [A] Many African Americans and Hispanics fail to receive college education.

    [B] Higher education guarantees one's career advancement and financial security.

    [C] Majorities of young people follow their parents' will on career selection.

    [D] The tuition in college is too high for most minorities in America.

3. 51% African American young adults think that _____.

    [A] it's their own fault that they didn't get college education

    [B] their high school didn't prepare them successfully for college level work

    [C] they were not given equal opportunities for higher education

    [D] most of them meet prejudices in college

4. What can we know about high school counselors according to the research?

    [A] They show no interests in students.

    [B] They do not play a great role in inspiring students to get to college.

    [C] They cannot help students solve difficult problems.

    [D] They are not willing to offer professional advice to students.

5. The author points out that just 1 in 5 of the less educated young adults _____.

　[A] are satisfied with their current job

　[B] respect their parents' opinion

　[C] have a good chance of success

　[D] consider college education valuable

6. 78% of less educated people admit that _____.

　[A] they did not have mentors to inspire them in school

　[B] they earn less than those with college education

　[C] they did not study as hard as they should in school

　[D] they regret giving up studying too early

7. Compared with young men, young women who go to college are more likely to _____.

　[A] prefer arts

　[B] get good grades

　[C] study hard

　[D] enjoy being in school

8. 57% young adults agreed that compared with studying in school, it is more advantageous to _____.

9. Many today's young adults have a common agreement that higher education can help them _____ as well as insure the career advancement and financial security.

10. African American and Hispanics young people say they had to compromise on their choice of college because of the _____.

试题详解

　　本文主要介绍了美国各种族年轻人对大学文凭的看法。调查结果显示，美国绝大多数年轻人都认为大学文凭不但能为他们赢得社会尊重，还能确保他们的职业发展与经济安全。然而，仍有少数人认为赚钱比读书更重要。

1. D　根据关键词Public Agenda定位到首段尾句：Most of the young adults surveyed in Life After High School: Young People Talk about Their Hopes and Prospects report that their parents inspired the goal of going to college and most had a teacher in high school who took a strong personal interest in them and

encouraged them to go on to college.(参与"高中后的生活：年轻人谈论希望与前途"这一调查的大多数年轻人都认为他们的父母激励他们设定上大学的目标，而且大多在高中时都有一位老师对他们非常关注，并且鼓励他们继续读大学)，故选D"家长和老师在激励年轻人上大学方面非常重要"。

2. A 根据关键词national data定位到第一个小标题下的第三段首句：But the survey confirms what national data shows—going to college is still not commonplace for most African Americans and Hispanics.(但是调查证实了全国数据所反应的情况：对大多数非裔美国人和拉美裔美国人而言，上大学并不普遍)，故选A"很多非裔美国人和拉美裔美国人无法接受大学教育"。原文中的most被替换为选项中的many，is still not commonplace被替换为fail to receive college education。

3. B 根据关键词51% African American定位到第一个小标题下的第四段首句：Substantial numbers believe their high school teachers and classes should have done a lot more to prepare them for college level work.(大多数人都认为他们的高中老师和高中课程并未很好地为他们的大学教育做准备)，故选B"他们在高中的学习并没有为他们的大学学业做好准备"。原文中的should have done a lot more(本应做更多)被替换为选项中的didn't prepare them successfully(并未成功准备)。

4. B 根据关键词high school counselors定位到第二个小标题下的第三段首句：As for high school counselors, the young people across all demographic groups surveyed indicated that counseling resources were stretched thin, with 53% saying there were not enough counselors in their high school.(至于高中顾问，所有受访的年轻人都认为，顾问资源十分短缺，53%的人说他们的高中里并没有足够的顾问)，故选B"他们在激励学生上大学方面并未发挥很大作用"。原文中的stretched thin(十分短缺)被替换为选项中的do not play a great role(并未发挥很大作用)。

5. A 根据关键词1 in 5定位到第三个小标题下的首段第四句：Just 1 in 5 of these less educated young adults said they love their job, compared with 31% of those with degrees.(在未受过良好教育的青年人中只有五分之一说他们热爱自己的工作，而在有大学学历的人中，此项数据是31%)，故选A"满意他们现在的工作"。原文中的love(热爱)被替换为选项中的be satisfied with(对……满意)。

6. C 根据关键词78% of less educated people定位到第三个小标题下的第二段首句：Those without college degrees are more likely to say they could have worked harder in school（78% of the less educated said this compared to 62% with degrees).(那些没有大学学历的人更有可能认为他们在学校时应该更刻苦一些。拥有大学学历的人此项数据为62%，与之相比，受教育水平不高的人的数据是78%），故选C "他们在学校没有像他们应该做的那样刻苦学习"。原文中的could have worked harder(本应更加刻苦)被替换为选项中的did not study as hard as they should(并未像他们应该的那样刻苦学习)。

7. D 根据关键词young men, young women以及"题目与原文顺序基本一致"原则定位到第四个小标题下的内容，尾句提到：In contrast, 7 in 10（69%）young women who went to college said they "really enjoy being in school", whereas a significantly smaller majority of young men（58%）who went to college said the same thing.(相反，在上过大学的年轻女性中，有十分之七认为她们"确实喜欢待在学校"，而在上过大学的年轻男性中，持此观点的人数要少得多），故选D"喜欢待在学校"。

8. earn money
根据关键词57% young adults定位到第三个小标题下的首段首句：Almost 9 in 10（89%）agree that "college is not for everyone" and a solid majority（57%）agreed that "earning money instead of sitting in a classroom" can be an advantage.(大约十分之九的人认为"大学并不适合所有人"，同时，大多数人认为 "挣钱而不是坐在教室里"更具优势），故填earn money。原文中的sitting in a classroom被替换为题干中的studying in school, advantage被替换为advantageous。

9. earn society's respect
根据关键词today's young adults及insure the career advancement and financial security定位到最后一个小标题下的首段：Perhaps the most heartening message from Life After High School is that the vast majority of today's young adults—across racial and ethnic lines—believe that higher education is a way to earn both society's respects and insure the career advancement and financial security they yearn for.(也许"高中后的生活"这项调查中最振奋人心的信息就是现在绝大多数的年轻人，不论种族与民族，都认为接受高等教育是赢得社会尊重与确保他们渴求的职业发展和经济稳定的方式），故填earn society's respect。原文中的the vast majority of（绝大多数）被替换为题干中的have a common agreement(拥有共识)，and被替换为as well as。

10. financial constraints

根据关键词compromise及their choice of college定位到最后一个小标题下的第三段：The findings indicate that African American and Hispanic young people are far more likely than their white peers to say they had to compromise on their choice of college due to financial constraints.（研究发现，非裔美国人和拉美裔年轻人比他们的白人同龄人更有可能说由于经济所限，他们不得不在选择大学方面进行妥协），故填financial constraints。原文中的due to（由于）被替换为题干中的because of。

强化训练四

Directions: *In this part, you will have 15 minutes to go over the passage quickly and answer the questions on **Answer Sheet 1**. For questions 1-7, choose the best answer from the four choices marked* [A], [B], [C] *and* [D]. *For questions 8-10, complete the sentences with the information given in the passage.*

Stress Pains Many in College

Most students in US colleges are just plain stressed out, from everyday worries about grades and relationships to darker thoughts of suicide, according to a poll of undergraduates from coast to coast. The survey was conducted for the Associated Press and mtvU, a television network available at many colleges and universities.

Students' Stress Problems

Four in ten students say they endure stress often. Nearly one in five say they feel it all or most of the time. But most are bearing it. Nearly two-thirds in the survey say they enjoy life.

The majority cite classic stress symptoms including trouble concentrating, sleeping and finding motivation. Most say they have also been disturbed, worried, too tired to work. "Everything is being piled on at once," said Chris Curran, a junior at the Albany College of Pharmacy in Albany, N.Y. He said he has learned to cope better since starting school. "You just get really disturbed and anxious. Then you start procrastinating and it all piles up." Many cite eating problems and say they have felt lonely, depressed, like they are failures. Substantial numbers are even concerned about spring break, chiefly not having enough money or being in good physical shape.

More than a quarter of the students sometimes think they should cut down on drinking or going out. A third says they sometimes want to use drugs or alcohol to relax. About 15% say they're at least somewhat concerned about drinking too much on spring break. One in five say they have felt too stressed to do schoolwork or be with friends. About the same number say things have been so bad in the past three months that they have seriously considered dropping out of school. Darker still, about one in six say they have friends who in the past years have discussed committing suicide, and about one in ten say they have seriously considered it themselves. Friends have actually tried to end their lives in that time, one in ten say.

In this ocean of campus anxiety, 13% say they have been diagnosed with a mental health condition such as depression or an anxiety disorder. Of that group, two-thirds say they always or usually follow their treatment, one-tenth say they have been unable to stick to it, and the rest are not on a plan. The *perils*(危险) of halting treatment were highlighted last month when police said the girlfriend of Steven Kazmierczak, who fatally shot five people and then himself at Northern Illinois University, told them he had stopped taking medication.

All is not doom and gloom for today's students. Six in ten in the survey say they are usually hopeful and enjoy life. Half even concede they feel understood by their families.

What Causes the Stress Problem

The survey shows plenty of sources of stress, led by the seven in ten students who attribute it to school work and grades. Financial problems are close behind, while relationships and dating, family problems and extracurricular activities all are named by half as adding pressure.

College women have a more stressful existence than men, with 45% of females and 34% of males saying they face pressure often. The youngest students cite frequent stress most often. Whites report more stress than blacks and Hispanics. From schoolwork to dating, women are more possible than men to say they experience pressure from virtually every potential source of distress in the survey. Six in ten women and just four in ten men say family issues cause problems, though the differences between the sexes in most areas are slimmer. Besides balancing her approaching graduation with the 20-hour-per-week job that helps finances school, Jeanette Devereaux-Weber said she has a new pressure: beginning her post-college life. She has not decided what to do. "It doesn't feel like looking for a summer job anymore, it's looking for a career, it's things that will shape everything to come," she said. "Sometimes it feels like you have to make the right choice away or you will behind everyone else."

How to Solve the Stress Problem

The poll shows a spotty sense among students of how to find assistance handling pressure. Just over half say they are sure whom they would turn to for help. Only one in seven say they were very familiar with the counseling offered at their schools. Overall, 26% of students say they have considered talking to a counselor or getting other professional help. Just 15% say they have actually done so. Professional help, though, is not atop students' list when they need help. Three-quarters say they would be most likely to turn to friends; nearly two-thirds cite their parents and half say they would talk to brothers or sisters. Only one in five say they would seek out school counselors.

Of the 9% who said they had considered suicide in the past year, only half said they had considered talking to a counselor or professional and four in ten had actually received such help. While 11% said they had friends who had tried committing suicide in the past year, that doesn't mean there have been many attempts because many people often know each individual who has tried. According to the most recent figures from the Federal Centers for Disease Control and Prevention, far less than one of every 100 people aged 18 to 24 tried to injure himself in 2006. However, there were fewer than 3,500 suicides out of 29 million people of that age in 2005.

How is the Survey Conducted?

The survey was conducted by Edison Media Research from Feb 28 to March 6 by having 2,253 undergraduate students fill out confidential forms. The margin of sampling error was plus or minus 3 percentage points. The students, aged 18-24, were handed the questionnaires at 40 randomly chosen four-year schools around the country. To protect privacy, the schools where the poll was conducted are not being identified and the students who responded were not asked for their names. Those mentioned in this story were not among those polled and did not necessarily attend schools involved in the survey.

　　MtvU's sponsorship of the poll is related to its work on "Half of Us", which it runs with the Jed Foundation, a non-profit group that works to reduce suicide among young people. "Half of Us" is a program designed to raise awareness about emotional problems faced by college students.

注意：此部分试题请在**答题卡1**上作答。

1. According to the survey, how many of the college students in the US say they enjoy their life?

　　[A] Nearly 20%.　　　　　　　　[C] About 30%.

　　[B] More than 25%.　　　　　　　[D] Nearly 66.7%.

2. The classic symptom of stress mentioned by the majority of students includes

　　_____.

　　[A] money problems　　　　　　　[C] concentrating problems

　　[B] eating problems　　　　　　　[D] physical problems

3. How many of the college students in the US say they have considered dropping out of school seriously?

　　[A] About 10%.　　　　　　　　[C] About 16.6%.

　　[B] About 15%.　　　　　　　　[D] About 20%.

4. How many of the college students diagnosed with a mental health condition have been unable to follow their treatment?

　　[A] 7%.　　　　　　　　　　　[C] 50%.

　　[B] 10%.　　　　　　　　　　[D] 66.6%.

5. The leading cause of college students' stress problem is _____.

　　[A] school work and grades　　　　[C] relationships and dating

　　[B] financial problems　　　　　　[D] family problems

6. Who may face the least pressure according to the survey?

　　[A] College women.

　　[B] White female college students.

　　[C] The youngest female college students.

　　[D] Black and Hispanic male college students.

7. The examples of Jeanette Devereaux-Weber in the passage revealed the new pressure of _____.

　　[A] approaching graduation　　　[C] solving family issues

　　[B] starting post-college life　　　[D] financing school

8. When facing stress problem, only 20% of the college students would turn to _____.

9. Because of stress problem the rate of students aged 18 to 24 trying to injure themselves in 2006 is _____ than that in 2005.

10. The schools where the poll was conducted are not being identified in order to _____.

试题详解

　　本文主要介绍了一项调查所反应出的美国大学生在压力方面的现状，包括面临压力的大致情况、压力的来源及解决方法，最后介绍了调查是如何开展的。

1. D　根据关键词enjoy their life定位到第一个小标题下的首段尾句：Nearly two-thirds in the survey say they enjoy life.（调查中有将近三分之二的人说他们享受生活），故选D。

2. C　根据关键词classic symptom of stress及majority of students定位到第一个小标题下的第二段首句：The majority cite classic stress symptoms including trouble concentrating, sleeping and finding motivation（大多数提到的典型压力症状包括难以集中注意力、失眠及缺乏动力），故选C"注意力问题"。

3. D　根据关键词considered dropping out of school定位到第一个小标题下的第三段第四、五两句：One in five say they have felt too stressed to do schoolwork or be with friends. About the same number say things have been so bad in the past three months that they have seriously considered dropping out of school.（五分之一的人说他们已经感觉到家庭作业或与朋友相处的压力太大。大约同样数量的人认为过去三个月情况变得特别糟糕，以至于他们已经认真考虑过辍学的问题），故选D。

4. B　根据关键词unable to follow their treatment定位到第一个小标题下的第四段前两句：In this ocean of campus anxiety, 13% say they have been diagnosed with a mental health condition such as depression or an anxiety disorder. Of that group, two-thirds say they always or usually follow their treatment, one-tenth say

they have been unable to stick to it, and the rest are not on a plan.(在有焦虑症状的校园人群中，13%的人说他们已被诊断出抑郁症或焦虑症等心理问题。在这一群体中，三分之二的人说他们一直或经常能坚持治疗，十分之一的人说他们已无法坚持治疗，其他人还没有治疗计划)，故选B。原文中的stick to it被替换为题干中的follow their treatment。

5. A 根据关键词leading cause定位到第二个小标题下的首段首句：The survey shows plenty of sources of stress, led by the seven in ten students who attribute it to school work and grades.(调查显示了众多的压力来源，其中排在首位的是学业和分数，十分之七的学生将压力归结于此)，故选A"学业与分数"。原文中的led by被替换为题干中的leading cause。

6. D 根据关键词face the least pressure定位到第二个小标题下的第二段前三句：College women have a more stressful existence than men, with 45% of females and 34% of males saying they face pressure often. The youngest students cite frequent stress most often. Whites report more stress than blacks and Hispanics. (女大学生比男生感觉到的压力更大，45%的女生和34%的男生说他们经常面对压力。年龄最小的学生最常提到压力。白人比黑人和拉美裔美国人感觉到的压力更大)，故选D"黑人和拉美裔的男性大学生"。

7. B 根据关键词Jeanette Devereaux-Weber定位到第二个小标题下的第二段倒数第四句：Besides balancing her approaching graduation with the 20-hour-per-week job that helps finances school, Jeanette Devereaux-Weber said she has a new pressure: beginning her post-college life.(在平衡即将面临的毕业和她为了完成学业必须去做的每周20小时的工作之外，Jeanette Devereaux-Weber说她有个新的压力：开始大学毕业后的生活)，故选B"大学毕业后的生活"。原文中的beginning被替换为选项中的starting。

8. school counselors
根据关键词facing stress problems定位到第三个小标题How to Solve the Stress Problem(如何解决压力问题)，再根据关键词20%定位到该小标题下的首段尾句：Only one in five says they would seek out school counselors.(只有五分之一的人说他们会去找学校的顾问)，故填school counselors。原文中的solve被替换为facing，one in five被替换为题干中的20%，seek out被替换为turn to。

9. much higher
根据关键词students aged 18 to 24定位到第三个小标题下的第二段最后两句：

According to the most recent figures from the Federal Centers for Disease Control and Prevention, far less than one of every 100 people aged 18 to 24 tried to injure himself in 2006. However, there were fewer than 3,500 suicides out of 29 million people of that age in 2005.（根据联邦疾病控制与预防中心的最新数据，2006年，在18至24岁的人中间，不到百分之一的人试图伤害自己。然而，在2005年，在2900万该年龄段的人群中，只有不到3500个自杀案例），经过简单计算可知，2006年的比例比2005年高很多，故填much higher。

10. protect privacy

根据关键词the schools where the poll was conducted定位到最后一个小标题下的首段倒数第二句: To protect privacy, the schools where the poll was conducted are not being identified and the students who responded were not asked for their names.（为了保护隐私，未公开进行调查的学校，也未要求回答问卷的学生提供姓名），故填protect privacy。原文中的to被替换为in order to。

第三章　听力理解

最新大纲

　　根据《大学英语四级考试大纲》，听力理解部分测试学生获取口头信息的能力。录音材料用标准的英式或美式英语朗读，语速约为每分钟130词。听力部分分值比例为35%，其中对话占15%，短文占20%。考试时间为35分钟。

　　对话部分(Listening Conversations)包括短对话和长对话，均采用多项选择题的形式进行考核。短对话约有7～8段，每段为一轮对话和一个问题；长对话有两段，每段为5～8轮对话和3～4个问题；对话部分共15题。每段对话均朗读一遍，每个问题后留有15秒的答题时间。

　　短文部分包括短文理解(Listening Passages)和复合式听写(Compound Dictation)。短文有3篇，每篇文章的长度为200～250词，朗读一遍；题目形式为多项选择，每篇3～4题，共10题，每个问题后留有15秒的作答时间。复合式听写测试考生在不同层面上（从词汇到语篇）的听力理解能力。这部分测试采用一篇200～250词的短文，并从中删去若干个单词和句子，要求考生根据听到的内容填写所缺信息，全文朗读三遍。需要注意的是，所缺单词必须填写原词，所缺句子信息既可按原文填写，也可用自己的语言表达。

考核能力

　　根据《大学英语四级考试大纲》，听力理解部分考核学生获取口头信息的能力，包括理解主旨大意、重要事实和细节、隐含意义、判断话语的交际功能、说话人的观点和态度等。听力理解部分考核的技能是：

A. 理解中心思想和重要细节

　　1. 理解中心思想

　　2. 听懂重要或特定的细节

　　3. 判断说话人的观点、态度等

B. 理解隐含的意思

　　4. 推断隐含的意义

　　5. 判断话语的交际功能

C. 借助语言特征理解听力材料

6. 辨别语音特征，如从连续的话语中辨别语音、理解重音和语音语调等

7. 理解句间关系，如比较、原因、结果、程度、目的等

大学英语四级听力理解部分要求考生达到《教学要求》中的一般要求，即"能听懂英语授课，能听懂日常英语谈话和一般性题材讲座，能基本听懂慢速英语节目，语速为每分钟130词左右，能掌握其中心大意，抓住要点。能运用基本的听力技巧理解"。

选材原则

命题的语料均来自英文原版材料，包括日常生活中的对话、讲座、广播电视节目等。选材的原则是：

1. 题材广泛，包括人文科学、社会科学、自然科学等领域，但所涉及的背景应为学生所了解或已在文章中提供；

2. 体裁多样，包括叙述文、说明文、议论文等；

3. 听力的篇章难度略低。

第一节　高分攻略

一、短对话

（一）解题技巧

1. 重视对立关系的选项：其中之一可能为正确选项

例1：2009年6月真题

15. [A] **He is pleased with his exciting new job.**

[B] He finds the huge workload unbearable.

[C] He finds his office much too big for him.

[D] **He is not so excited about his new position.**

听力原文： M: I heard about your promotion, you must be thrilled.

W: Not really, the new office is huge, but the workload has doubled.

Q: What do we learn about the man from the conversation?

试题解析： 选项A、D意思截然相反，正确答案为D。

2. 重视结构相似的选项

如果两个选项中相似的东西极多, 只有个别地方不一样, 则其中之一为正确选项的几率较大。

例1: 2006年6月24日真题

17. [A] The man has never seen the woman before.

[B] **The two speakers work** for **the same** company.

[C] **The two speakers work** on **the same** floor.

[D] The woman is interested in market research.

听力原文: M: Nice weather, isn't it? I've seen you around the office but I don't think we've met. I am Henry Smith. I work in the market research section.

W: Nice to meet to you, Henry. I am Helen Grant. I am in the advertising section on the 9th floor.

Q: What can we infer from the conversation?

试题解析: 选项B、C结构相似, 正确答案为B。

例2: 2006年12月真题

17. [A] The tickets are more expensive than expected.

[B] The tickets are sold in advance at half price.

[C] **It's** difficult **to buy the tickets** on the spot.

[D] **It's** better **to buy the tickets** beforehand.

听力原文: M: Do we have to get the opera tickets in advance?

W: Certainly. Tickets at the door are usually sold at a higher price.

Q: What does the woman imply?

试题解析: 选项C、D结构相似, 正确答案为D。

3. 听到什么, 不选什么

该原则适用于简单的短对话。短对话相对而言难度不大, 命题者必然在选项上做文章, 常利用对话中的原词作为干扰, 用与原文"貌合神离"的选项来诱骗未听懂原文、只听到只言片语的考生上当。正确选项往往并未使用太多对话中的原词, 而是原文的同义替换。

例：2009年12月真题

14. [A] He moved to **Baltimore** when he was **young**.

   [B] He can provide little useful information.

   [C] He will show the woman around **Baltimore**.

   [D] He will ask **someone** else to help the woman.

听力原文：M: I need to talk to **someone** who knows **Baltimore** well. I'm told
      you lived there.

      W: Oh, but I was really **young** at the time.

      Q: What does the man mean?

试题解析：选项A中出现了原文中的Baltimore和young，选项C中出现了原文
      中的Baltimore，选项D中出现了原文中的someone，而正确答案是
      未出现任何对话原词的选项B。

4. 排除不符合四级考试内容的选项

从考试常见话题出发，适当发挥自己的想象力，排除那些和四级考试正常
思路相背离的选项。四级听力短对话只考与大学校园生活相关的温馨话题，一
贯宣扬积极向上的人文精神。牢记这一原则，将对提高你的四级听力成绩大有
帮助。

四级听力一般不考以下话题，诸如：politics（政治），religion（宗教），campus
violence（校园暴力），democracy（民主），sexual discrimination（性别歧视），racial
discrimination（种族歧视），human rights（人权）。

例：2009年12月真题

15. [A] He is rather disappointed.

   [B] He is highly ambitious.

   [C] He can't face up to the situation.

   [D] He knows his own limitations.

听力原文：M: Aren't you disappointed that you didn't get the promotion?

      W: Maybe a little, but I know I need more experience before I'm
      ready for that kind of responsibility.

      Q: What do we learn about the man from this conversation?

试题解析：选项A为"他相当失望"，B为"他很有野心"，C为"他无法面对这
      一状况"，均为消极选项，只有D"他知道自己的局限"是积极向上
      的选项，正确答案为D。

（二）必考场景

1. 住宿场景

1）场景规律

学生图便宜，合租来分担，清静不可少，宁可来搬家。

2）必背词汇

advertise 做广告	expensive 昂贵的	housekeeper 管家
expenses 费用	safe 安全	apartment 公寓
rent 出租	noise 噪音	tolerate 忍受
missing 找不到的	housing developer 房屋开发商	
house for sale 在售房屋	buy a home 购买房屋	
poor quality 质量低劣	potential buyer 潜在购买者	
get along 相处	make a mess 一团糟	
clean up 打扫		

经典考题：2006年6月24日真题

12. [A] The woman does her own housework.

[B] The woman needs a housekeeper.

[C] The woman's house is in a mess.

[D] The woman works as a housekeeper.

听力原文：M: Are you telling me you don't have a housekeeper?

W: No, we don't. If you make a mess, you clean it up yourself.

Q: What do we learn from this conversation?

试题解析：选项中的housework, housekeeper表明对话与家务劳动及管家相关，正确答案为A。

2. 人际关系场景

1）场景规律

生活有难题，帮忙不可少，女士求实用，更会过日子。

2）必背词汇

lend/borrow 借	return 归还	missing 找不到的
personality 性格	emotional 感情的	behavior 行为
well-off 富裕的	talkative 健谈的	temper 脾气
feel better 感觉好一点	get upset 不高兴	in bad mood 情绪不好

经典考题：2009年6月真题

11. [A] She expected more people at her party.

    [B] She enjoys entertaining small children.

    [C] She threw a surprise party for her friend.

    [D] She has always enjoyed great popularity.

听力原文： M: There were more than a hundred people at Kate's birthday party. How come she's got so many friends?

W: It's really no surprise. You know she was popular even when she was a child.

Q: What does the man imply about Kate?

试题解析： 根据女士所说的There were more than a hundred people at Kate's birthday party. (凯特的生日聚会上有一百多人)和男士所说的she was popular even when she was a child(甚至还是个孩子的时候，她就很受欢迎)，故选D"她一直很受欢迎"。

3. 天气场景

必背词汇

warm 温暖的	sensitive 敏感的	unreliable 不可靠的
freeze to death 冷得要命	put on 穿衣	
nice weather 好天气	weather forecast 天气预报	

经典考题：2006年6月24日真题

14. [A] The woman didn't expect it to be so warm at noon.

    [B] The woman is sensitive to weather changes.

    [C] The weather forecast was unreliable.

    [D] The weather turned cold all of a sudden.

听力原文： M: You look like you're freezing to death. Why don't you put this on?

W: Thank you, it was so warm at noon. I didn't expect the weather to turn so quickly.

Q: What do we learn from the conversation?

试题解析： 根据选项，对话与天气变化和女士的反应有关，正确答案为D。

4. 购物场景

1）场景规律

学生自然穷，购物打折店，贵物买不起，花钱要节省。

买票总卖光，订票订不到，货品常卖完，万事难如意。

2）必背词汇

Christmas 圣诞节	gift/present 礼物	girlfriend 女朋友
boyfriend 男朋友	budget 预算	supermarket 超市
restaurant 饭店	bookstore 书店	

经典考题：2009年12月真题

12. [A] Shopping with his son.

　　[B] Buying a gift for a child.

　　[C] Promoting a new product.

　　[D] Bargaining with a salesgirl.

听力原文： M: Can you recommend something that a school boy of 7 or 8 will really like?

　　　　　　W: I'd suggest this toy train, sir. It's an excellent brand, very popular all over the world these days.

　　　　　　Q: What is the man doing?

试题解析： 根据男士所说的Can you recommend something that a school boy of 7 or 8 will really like?(你能为我推荐一些七八岁的学龄男孩确实喜欢的东西吗?)，故选B"给一个小孩买礼物"。

5. 就餐场景

1）场景规律

妻子不做饭，不在食堂吃，请客去饭店，服务有缺陷。

2）必背词汇

dinner 正餐，晚餐	steak 烤肉，烤鱼	chocolate 巧克力
cake 蛋糕	dessert 餐后甜点	fat 脂肪
sugar 糖	order 点菜	menu 菜单
vegetable 蔬菜	fruit 水果	picnic 野餐
French Fries 炸薯条	ice cream 冰淇淋	apple pie 苹果派
watch weight 注意身材	look great 看起来不错	

经典考题：2006年12真题

12. [A] She'll have some chocolate cake.

　　[B] She'll take a look at the menu.

　　[C] She'll go without dessert.

　　[D] She'll prepare the dinner.

听力原文：M: What would you like for dessert? I think I'll have apple pie and ice cream.

　　　W: The chocolate cake looks great, but I have to watch my weight. You go ahead and get yours.

　　　Q: What would the woman most probably do?

试题解析：本题在but转折处命题，女士为保持身材会抵制巧克力等甜点的诱惑，故选C。

6. 学习场景

1）场景规律

学习永远难，教授永远严，论文写不完，无法延期交。

考试不简单，男生易失败，女生来安慰，再难不放弃。

借书借不到，买书不好买，多去图书馆，笔记借来看。

2）必背词汇

paper 论文	computer 计算机	informative 信息量大的
professor 教授	seminar 研讨会	schedule 日程
available 可获得的	psychology 心理学	textbook 教材
semester 学期	request form 申请表	
get information 获得信息	go to office 去办公室	
after class 课后	at the library 在图书馆	
leave a note 留个便条	take the course 听课	

经典考题：2009年12月真题

17. [A] Female students are unfit for studying physics.

　　[B] He can serve as the woman's tutor.

　　[C] Physics is an important course at school.

　　[D] The professor's suggestion is constructive.

听力原文：M: Professor Clark suggested I get a tutor for advanced physics.

W: Well, that might help. Advanced physics is a pretty difficult course.

Q: What does the man mean?

试题解析： 根据男士所说的that might help（那也许会有帮助），故选D"教授的建议是有帮助的"。constructive意为"有帮助的，建设性的"，tutor意为"家教，导师"，advanced physics意为"高等物理"。

7. 约会场景

1）场景规律

约会易失败，从来不准时，吃饭总成功，从来都请客。

2）必背词汇

opera 歌剧	ticket 票	hostess 女主人
in advance / beforehand 提前	at a higher price 高价	
on the spot 现场	attend the party 参加晚会	
go out of one's way 竭尽全力	make the party a success 使晚会成功	

经典考题：2006年12月真题

14. [A] Go to the library.

　　[B] Meet the woman.

　　[C] See Professor Smith.

　　[D] Have a drink in the bar.

听力原文： M: Professor Smith asked me to go to his office after class. So it's impossible for me to make it to the bar at ten.

W: Then it seems that we'll have to meet an hour later at the library.

Q: What will the man do first after class?

试题解析： 男士说的so it is impossible...和女士说的then it seems...，均以史密斯教授让男士下课后去办公室为前提，故选C。

8. 交通场景

1）场景规律

火车总迟到，飞机易晚点，车祸能生还，轻伤很常见。

2）必背词汇

Seattle 西雅图	railway 地铁	Japanese 日语
taxi 出租车	driver 司机	speed 超速

crash 撞车   truck 卡车

New York 纽约   turn suddenly 突然转弯

经典考题：2009年6月真题

16. [A] The woman is going to hold a big party tomorrow.

[B] The man has no idea what the right thing to do is.

[C] The woman doesn't know how to get to the party.

[D] The man offers to drive the woman to the party.

听力原文：M: I can't decide what to do about the party tomorrow.

W: You don't have to go if you don't want to, but I'll be glad to give you a ride if you do.

Q: What do we learn from the conversation?

试题解析：根据男士所说的I'll be glad to give you a ride if you do.（如果你想去，我很乐意送你），故选D"男士提出开车送女士去晚会"。give sb. a ride意为"送某人一程"。

9. 工作场景

1）场景规律

工作总迟到，老是编理由，繁忙又枯燥，上司难讨好。

写好求职信，自信来求职，整洁又准时，还是会紧张。

2）必背词汇

chair 主持	conference 会议	appointment 预约
company 公司	patient 病人	customer 客户
manager 经理	dentist 牙医	physician 医生
agreeable 使人愉快的	promote 提升	thoroughness 周到
occasion 场合	colleague 同事	club 俱乐部
lawyer 律师	cancel 取消	fire 解雇
boss 老板	researcher 研究员	active 活跃的
sociable 好交际的	deliver lecture/speech 发表演讲	

market research section 市场调研部   advertising section 广告部

high position 高层职位   travel agent 旅行社代理人

office worker 办公室职员   board meeting 董事会

marketing director 市场主管

经典考题：2009年12月真题

18. [A] Indifferent.

　[B] Doubtful.

　[C] Pleased.

　[D] Surprised.

听力原文： W: Bill, have you heard the latest news? It appears we two won't be laid off after all.

　　　　 M: Oh, I'm somewhat tired of working here. I've been wondering whether I should resign. Anyway, the news seems to be good for you.

　　　　 Q: How does the man feel about the news?

试题解析： 根据男士所说的Anyway, the news seems to be good for you.（不管怎么说，这个消息对你来说不错），由男士说话的口吻可知，他对这则消息漠不关心，故选A"漠不关心的"。对话中的laid off意为"解雇，下岗"，wonder意为"考虑"，resign意为"辞职"。

二、长 对 话

(一)解题技巧

1. 开头必考

在长对话中，寒暄过后的第一句话很可能是对话的主题，也是破解全文的关键所在，务必引起高度重视。首句中的核心词汇、结论或对首句的同义替换，往往就是答案。

例：2009年12月真题，Conversation One

听力原文：

W: Hello, Clarkson College. May I help you?

M: Yes, I'm looking for information on courses in computer programming. I would need it for the fall semester.

W: Do you want a day or evening course?

M: Well, **it would have to be an evening course, since I work during the day.**

19. [A] He prefers the smaller evening classes.

    [B] He has signed up for a day course.

    [C] He has to work during the day.

    [D] He finds the evening course cheaper.

解析：根据长对话"开头必考"原则，开头提到：it would have to be an evening course, since I work during the day.（由于我白天上班，所以只能选晚上的课程），故选C"他白天必须上班"。注意：since经常引出原因，为出题点之一。

2. 听到什么选什么

与短对话不同，长对话由于篇幅较长、难度较高，因此解题的基本原则是"听到什么选什么"。正确选项往往是原文的原词重现或语义再现，很少使用同音词或音近词作为干扰选项。在长对话中，含有实际意义的问答内容（尤其是特殊疑问句）往往是细节题考查的重点。

例：2009年12月真题，Conversation Two

听力原文：

M: I very rarely do anything work-related. So it's easy to escape the markets. I generally go to the gym or go for a run, especially if I've had a bad day. I always **cook** a meal, rather than have a take-away, to do something my brain would regard as **creative.**

Q24: Why does the man prefer to cook a meal rather than have a take-away?

24. [A] He can save on living expenses.

    [B] He considers **cooking creative.**

    [C] He can enjoy healthier food.

    [D] He thinks take-away is tasteless.

解析：根据长对话"听到什么选什么"原则，原文提到：I always cook a meal, rather than have a take-away, to do something my brain would regard as creative.（我总自己做饭，而不是叫外卖，去做一些我认为有创意的事情），故选B"他认为做饭有创意"。

3. 结尾必考

长对话最后一题的答案往往在对话结尾。长对话结尾处一般是提出建议、指出下一步行动或总结对话主题，核心词往往令人印象深刻，是答题的关键。解答长对话和短文听力题目时，要相信自己的第一感觉，若无确切把握，不要轻易改动答案。

例：**2009年12月真题，Conversation One**

听力原文

M: Oh, I know how to get there. **Is there anything that I should bring with me?**

W: No, just your check book.

M: Well, thank you so much.

W: You're very welcome. Bye.

M: Bye.

Q22：What does the man want to know at the end of the conversation?

22. [A] What to bring for registration.

　　[B] Where to attend the class.

　　[C] How he can get to Frost Hall.

　　[D] Whether he can use a check.

解析：根据长对话"结尾必考"原则，结尾提到：Is there anything that I should bring with me?(我还要随身带点什么吗?)，故选A"注册时带什么"。

(二)两大原则

1. 积极向上和符合生活常识的选项一般是正确答案

例：**2006年6月24日真题，Conversation One**

21. [A] The woman thinks Mr. Saunders is asking for more than they can offer.

　　[B] Mr. Saunders will share one third of the woman's responsibilities.

　　[C] Mr. Saunders believes that he deserves more paid vacations.

　　[D] The woman seems to be satisfied with Mr. Saunders' past experience.

解析：A为"女士认为桑德斯先生要求过分"，C为"桑德斯先生认为他应该得到更多的带薪假期"，A、C两个选项含义消极，为干扰选项。B、D选项含义积极向上，B为"桑德斯先生将分担女士三分之一的责任"，D为"女士似乎对桑德斯先生以往的经历感到满意"。正确答案为D。

2. 关于对话主题的题目，正确答案可能是概括性强的选项

例：大纲样题，Passage One

19. [A] The benefits of strong business competition.

    [B] A proposal to lower the cost of production.

    [C] Complaints about the expense of modernization.

    [D] Suggestions concerning new business strategies.

    Q: What are the two speakers talking about?

解析： 选项说明该题涉及文章的主题。根据规律"概括性强的可能是答案"，
B概括性最差，故排除。根据常识，激烈的市场竞争对企业一般无益，
故排除A。再根据"积极向上"的原则，抱怨的内容不大可能是答案，
故选D。

（三）必考场景

1. 学习场景

1）图书馆

online 在线	catalogue 检索	Hollywood 好莱坞
studio 制片厂	magazine 杂志	controversial 矛盾的
outdated 过时的	Golden Age 鼎盛时期，黄金时代	
periodical literature 期刊文学	*Los Angeles Times*《洛杉矶时报》	
Reference Desk 信息查询台	reference material 参考资料	
practical value 实用价值	cope with 处理	

2）选课

Dickens 狄更斯	philosophy 哲学	lecturer 老师
plus 另外	degree 学位	allowance 补助，津贴
quit 放弃	boring 枯燥的	prefer 更喜欢
literature 文学	transfer 转变	
get through 读完	drift away 渐渐离开	
hold interest 保持兴趣	bother with 为……烦恼	
to be honest 坦率地说	labor of labor 麻烦的工作	
labor of love 兴趣所在	job prospect 工作前景	

2. 工作场景

1）面试

impressed 印象深刻的	trade 交易	bond 债券
reputation 声誉	international 国际的	team 团队
broker 经纪人	client 客户	candidate 候选人
position 职位	account 账户	handle 处理
offer 提供	employment 雇用	application 申请
colleague 同事	interview 面试	exchange 交换
resign 辞职	insurance 保险	deserve 应得

receive job resume 收到工作简历　　financial company 财务公司

stock market 股票市场　　present job 目前的工作

in charge of 负责　　head broker 经纪人经理

on the daily bases 每天　　report to 汇报

benefit package 福利待遇　　paid vacation 带薪假期

be entitled to 有权，有资格　　personnel department 人事部

business report 业务报告　　public relations 公关

past experience 过去的经历　　share responsibility 分担责任

be satisfied with 对……满意

2）公司

proposal 方案	production 生产	advertising 广告
strategy 战略	modernize 使现代化	factory 工厂
equipment 设备	install 安装	option 选择
finance 财务	staff 员工	engineer 工程师
paper 报纸	aggressive 进取的	competitor 竞争者
afford 承担	justify 值得	investment 投资
figure 数据	up-to-date 最近的	inefficiency 无效率
restrain 抑制	go over 仔细检查	

stay competitive 保持竞争性　　range from 从……到……

all the way up to 直到　　human resource 人力资源

television commercial 电视广告　　keep ahead of 领先

result in 导致　　high profit 高额利润

draw up a budget 草拟预算　　　　business strategy 商业策略

expense of modernization 现代化的代价　better-educated 受到更好教育的

lower the cost of production 降低生产成本

3. 生活场景

1）旅游

Quebec 魁北克	Montreal 蒙特利尔	wedding 婚礼
sightseeing 观光	province 省	French 法语
fantastic 极好的	historical 历史性的	
capital city 首都	old building 老建筑	
brush up 复习	local custom 当地风俗	

2）访谈

author 作家	lucky 幸运的	achieve 获得
adult 成人	grab 抓住	spoil 损坏
invisible 看不见的	platform 站台	character 人物
saint 圣人	resourceful 资源丰富的	originate 起源
Harry Potter《哈利·波特》	target audience 目标受众	
fairy tale 童话故事	best seller 畅销书	

三、短文理解

（一）常考题材

1. **记叙文**

1）人物传记：多考政治家、科学家、文艺家的生平和成就，也考普通人的特殊经历和业绩。注意生卒年月、地点、成就及社会评价。

2）幽默故事：频率最高，浅显易懂，注意5W1H（who, when, where, why, what, how）。

2. **说明文**

1）科普知识：频率最高。

2）风土人情：多考英美等西方国家的机构介绍，以及西方文学艺术。如著名作家作品、吉卜赛人历史、美洲作物历史、英国监狱、伦敦出租车司机等。

3）学校教育：英美教育体系介绍，如美国学校教育制度、英语学习与教育情况、图书馆使用说明等。

4）日常生活：日常生活用品，如书籍、电脑、服饰等。

3. 议论文

常讨论话题，如税收、子女、家庭生活等。

(二)解题技巧

1. 重视开头

四级听力短文理解中75%的考题答案在文章的首尾，一般首尾各有一道考题，有时开头甚至会有两道考题，需要引起高度重视。

> **例：2009年12月真题，Passage One**
>
> **开头：**
>
> Since early times, people have been fascinated with the idea of life existing somewhere else besides earth. **Until recently, scientists believed that life on other planets was just a hopeful dream.**
>
> 26. What did scientists once believe according to the passage?
>
> [A] There were no planets without moons.
>
> [B] There was no air or water on Jupiter.
>
> [C] Life was not possible in outer space.
>
> [D] The mystery of life could not be resolved.
>
> **试题解析：**根据"重视开头"原则，开头提到：Until recently, scientists believed that life on other planets was just a hopeful dream.（直到近来，科学家一直认为其他行星上的生命只是一个充满希望的梦），故选C"外太空不可能存在生命"。

2. 听到什么选什么

> **例：2009年12月真题，Passage Two**
>
> **原文：She asks them to** tell her **what** they think **they are supposed to do.**
>
> 30. What does Dr. Myer do to ensure her patients understand her instructions?
>
> [A] She encourages them to ask questions when in doubt.
>
> [B] She makes them write down all her instructions.
>
> [C] She has them act out what they are to do at home.
>
> [D] She **asks them** to repeat **what they are supposed to do.**

解析：根据"听到什么选什么"原则，原文提到：She asks them to tell her what they think they are supposed to do.(她请他们说出应该做什么)，故选D "她请他们复述应该做的事情"。

3. 关注结尾

例：2009年12月真题，Passage Two

结尾：

When new or difficult material is presented, almost all listeners are faced with the challenge **because human speech lacks the stability and permanence of the printed word.** Oral communication is fast-moving and impermanent.

31. What does the speaker say about human speech?

[A] It lacks the stability of the printed word.

[B] It contains many grammatical errors.

[C] It is heavily dependent on the context.

[D] It facilitates interpersonal communication.

试题解析：根据"关注结尾"原则，结尾提到：because human speech lacks the stability and permanence of the printed word(因为人们的谈话缺少书面文字所具有的稳定性与持久性)，故选A"它(人们的谈话)缺乏书面文字的稳定性"。

四、复合式听写

(一)题型概述

复合式听写测试考生在不同层面上(从词汇到语篇)的听力理解能力。这部分测试采用一篇200～250词的短文，并从中删去若干个单词和句子，全文朗读三遍。要求考生根据听到的内容填写所缺信息，所缺单词必须填写原词，所缺句子信息既可按原文填写，也可用自己的语言表达。

1. 第一遍：全文朗读，没有停顿，听懂大致内容；

2. 第二遍：

    1) 单词听写部分每个空格后略有停顿，边听边填所需单词；

    2) 句子听写部分有较长时间的停顿，根据所听内容写出大意；

3. 第三遍：与第一遍相同，没有停顿，供检查核对。

(二)评分标准

1. 给分标准

1）S1～S8每题0.5分。拼写完全正确的单词给0.5分,凡有错不给分,大小写错误忽略不计;

2）S9满分为2分,答出第一和第二部分内容且语言正确各得1分;

3）S10满分为2分,答出第一和第二部分内容且语言正确各得1分;

4）S11满分为2分,答出第一部分内容且语言正确得0.5分,答出第二部分内容且语言正确得0.5分,答出第三部分内容且语言正确得1分;

5）没有答对问题得0分。

2. 扣分标准

1）S9至S11题中有语言错误扣0.5分,每题语言错误扣分不超过0.5分,凡不得分部分如有语言错误不再重复扣分;

2）S9至S11题中凡有与问题无关的内容扣0.5分;

3）S9至S11题中如出现明显属于笔误造成的拼写错误和大小写、标点符号错误,不扣分;

4）用汉语回答问题不给分。

(三)解题技巧

1. 预读全文, 预测空格

1）预读全文: 利用考前间隙和播放考试指令的时间,迅速预读全文,尤其是主题句。文章第一句一般是主题句,没有空格。

例: 2009年12月真题

第一句:

In the humanities, authors write to inform you in many ways.

通过预读第一句"在人文学科中,作者以多种方式写作来告知读者",可知本文与人文学科中的写作有关。

2）预测空格: 根据主题句预测文章发展脉络和大意,同时预测空格内容。

(1)篇章结构:多考说明文,开头或段首多为主题句,然后进一步说明、扩展、论证,由此推断逻辑关系。如:furthermore为递进,therefore为结果,however为转折等。

（2）语法结构：

　　A. 判断词性：名词、动词、形容词等；

　　B. 判断形式：单复数、原形或分词、比较级、最高级等。

例：2009年12月真题

In the humanities, authors write to inform you in many ways. These methods can be（36）_____ into three types of informational writing: factual, descriptive, and process.

Factual writing provides（37）_____ information on an author, composer, or artist or on a type of music, literature, or art. Examples of factual writing include notes on a book jacket or（38）_____ cover and longer pieces, such as an article describing a style of music which you might read in a music（39）_____ course. This kind of writing provides a（40）_____ for your study of the humanities.

As its name（41）_____, descriptive writing simply describes, or provides an（42）_____ of, a piece of music, art, or literature. For example, descriptive writing might list the colors an artist used in a painting or the（43）_____ a composer included in a musical composition, so as to make pictures or sounds in the reader's mind by calling up specific details of the work.（44）_____

_____.

Process writing explains a series of actions that bring about a result.（45）_____

_____. This kind of writing is often found in art, where understanding how an artist created a certain effect is important.（46）_____.

通过预读，可知下列信息：

36. 空格前的助动词be暗示应填动词的过去分词形式，且能与之后的介词 into搭配。

37. 空格前的动词provides及之后的名词information暗示应填形容词或名词，修饰information。

38. 空格前的连词or暗示所填词应与cover一起组成名词短语，与book jacket 形成并列结构，故应填名词作定语。

39. 所填词应与空前的music和空后的course组成名词短语，体现前后两词的具体关系。

40. 空格前的冠词a和空格后的介词for暗示应填以辅音因素开头的单数名词。

41. 空格前的as引导定语从句，因此所填词应为name的谓语动词。根据空格后主句的时态可知应填第三人称单数形式的动词。

42. 空格前的冠词an和空格后的介词of暗示应填以元音音素开头的单数名词，并与空格后的piece并列。

43. 根据句子结构，空格后应是定语从句，修饰所填词，因此应填一个名词，与冠词the共同构成从句谓语动词concluded的宾语。

2. 听写单词务必准确

以下是复合式听写的核心词汇，涵盖所有四级听写考查过的词汇，请务必熟练拼写。

1) 名词(214个)

action 行为	boarder 边界	competitor 竞争者
adult 成人	building 建筑	concept 观念
agency 代表处	burden 负担	concerts 音乐会
agreement 协议	calculator 计算器	congress 国会
agriculture 农业	cancer 癌症	context 背景；上下文
album 影集；专辑	capital 首都	control 控制
America 美国(2考)	card 卡片	copyright 版权
American 美国人	career 职业	copy 副本
answer 答案	case 案件	country 国家
anybody 任何人	chat 聊天	crime 犯罪
anything 任何事	children [pl.] 孩子	culture 文化
appointment 约会	choice 选择	customer 顾客
appreciation 欣赏	cities 城市	damaging 损坏
areas 地区	climate 气候	decision 决定
arrival 到达	clock 钟	define 定义
atmosphere 大气	colleague 同事	definition 定义
author 作者	college 学院	department 部
average 平均数	company 陪伴；公司(2考)	detail 细节
awkwardness 笨拙,不雅观	comparison 比较	development 发展
background 背景	competition 竞争(2考)	dinner 正餐

diversity 多样性

effort 努力

electricity 电

emergency 紧急事件

energy 能量

essay 文章

everything 一切

evidence 证据

example 例子(2考)

exception 例外

explosion 爆炸

failure 失败

fast food 快餐

favorite 最爱(的)

figure 数据(2考)

film 胶卷;电影(2考)

fishing 捕捞

food 食品

friend 朋友

fruit 成果

fund 资金

future 未来

gas 气体

generation 一代

government 政府

grandparent 祖父,祖母

greenhouse 温室

growth 增长(2考)

handbag 手提包

heat 热量

history 历史

home 家庭

households 家庭

house 房子

humanities 人文学科

humanity 人类

idea 观念

image 图像

independence 独立

indication 暗示

individual 个人

industry 产业(3考)

information 信息

ingredient 要素

instrument 设施;乐器(2考)

inter-dependence 相互依赖

item 东西

joke 笑话

journey 旅程

knowledge 知识

labor 劳动;劳动力(2考)

lack 缺乏

language 语言

learning 学习

library 图书馆

lifestyle 生活方式

light 光

literature 文学

material 材料

meaning 意义

member 成员

microwave 微波

minute 分钟

model 样式

money 金钱

motion 运动

murder 谋杀(2考)

mystery 奥秘

nation 国家

note 笔记

offence 冒犯

official 官员

oven 炉

parents 父母

part 部分

passport 护照

past 过去

path 道路

people 人们

percentage 百分比(2考)

percent 百分之一

phenomenon 现象(2考)

phrase 短语

piece 一篇

pocket 口袋

practice 行为

presentation 呈现

print 印刷品

problem 问题(3考)

procedures 程序

process 进程

productivity 生产力

product 产品

property 财产

proportion 比例

protection 保护

protocol 议定书

purpose 目的

quality 质量(2考)

quarter 四分之一

rates 价格

reader 读者

record 记录

red meat 红肉

reference 提到;涉及(2考)

retirement 退休

reverse 相反的情况

reward 收益

row 一排

rule 规则

Russia 俄罗斯

sales 销售

satisfaction 满意

scene 场景

schedule 日程

selection 选择

semester 学期

skill 技能

society 社会

something 某事

sort 种类

species 物种

speed 速度

stack 一叠

standard 标准

statistics 数据

stranger 陌生人

street 街道

survive 幸存,活下来

symbol 象征

technique 技巧(2考)

technology 技术

The United States 美国(2考)

theft 偷窃

things 东西

thoughts 思想

town 城镇

trade 贸易

train 培训

trend 趋势

type 种类

underemployment 未就业

unemployment 失业

usage 用法

US 美国

value 价值

variety 多样性

vegetable 蔬菜

vocabulary 词汇

way 方式

word 词

workforce 劳动力

writing 写作(4考)

WTO (World Trade Organization) 世界贸易组织

2）动词(93个)

accomplish 完成

accustom 使习惯于

acquire 获得

adjust 适应

admire 钦佩

appreciate 欣赏;感激

approve 批准;赞成

associate 联系

belong 属于

blame 责备

bring 带来

build 建造

change 改变

classify 分类

clear 清除

collect 收集

communicate 沟通

concentrate 关注

consider 认为

controll 控制

couple 结合

depend 取决于

destroy 破坏

determine 决定(2考)

discover 发现

enable 使能够

engage 从事

enjoy 享受

ensure 确保

establish 创建,建立

exchange 交流

exist 生存；存在

expect 期待

explain 解释

face 面对

figure 想出，弄明白

fit 适合

focus 关注

generate 产生

handle 处理

imply 暗示

include 包括

increase 增加

inquire 询问

interact 相互影响

introduce 提出

investigate 调查

keep 保留

learn 学习（2考）

load 装载

might 可能

mix 结合

move 运动

negotiate 谈判

occur 发生

permit 允许

plan 计划

predict 预测

preserve 保存

produce 制造

provide 提供（2考）

purchase 购买

reach 达成

realize 认识到

receive 收到

recognize 认识

recommend 推荐

refine 改善

remember 记得

represent 代表

reproduce 繁殖

require 要求

respond 做出反应

ruin 毁灭

rush 匆忙做

sewn 缝纫

share 分享

shoot 拍摄

solve 解决

spend 花费

spread 传播

study 学习

submit 提交

suspect 怀疑

teach 教授

tell 告诉

threaten 威胁

transmit 传播

trap 困住

understand 理解

use 使用（4考）

value 重视

view 看待

3) 形容词(78个)

abstract 抽象的

accepted 被接受的

accurate 精确的

additional 额外的

adequate 足够的

alarming 惊人的

American 美国的

aware 明白的

balanced 平衡的

better 更好的（3考）

bound 必定的

careful 小心的

changing 变化的

common 普遍的

considerate 体贴的

convenient 方便的

critical 至关重要的

cultural 文化的

curious 好奇的

deliberate 故意的

descriptive 描述性的

difficult 困难的

distant 遥远的

disturbing 烦扰的

easy 容易的

economic 经济的

enough 足够的

environmental 环境的

equivalent 相同的

experimental 实验的

familiar 熟悉的

foreign 外国的(2考)

formal 正式的

German 德国的

given 特定的

greater 更快的;更大的(2考)

hand-written 手写的

healthier 更健康的

higher 更高的

historical 有历史意义的

important 重要的

improved 改进的

independent 独立的

informal 非正式的

informational 提供信息的

interesting 有趣的

interpersonal 人际的

late 迟到的

limited 有限的

major 主要的

mysterious 神秘的

national 国家的

natural 自然的

own 自己的

particular 特殊的

personal 个人的

polite 礼貌的

popular 流行的(2考)

preventive 预防性的

productive 多产的

proportional 成比例的

public 公共的

rational 合理的

right 正确的

rude 粗鲁的

scientific 科学的

second 第二的

serious 严重的

sheer 绝对的

single 单一的

slight 轻微的

social 社会的

stolen 被窃的

unusual 不平常的,与众不同的

unwatched 无人看管的

vital 重要的(2考)

worst 最坏的

wrong 错误的

4) 副词(27个)

abruptly 突然地

actually 实际上

almost 几乎

appropriately 适当地

backward 后退

briefly 简短地

carefully 认真地

completely 完全地

currently 目前(2考)

efficiently 高效地

emotionally 情绪上地

even 即使

extremely 非常

gradually 逐渐地

highly 高度地

increasingly 日益地

necessarily 必然地

often 经常(2考)

particularly 尤其(2考)

partly 部分地

perhaps 也许

probably 可能

rarely 很少地

rather 相当

similarly 同样地

straight 直接

usually 通常

5) 介词(1个)

across 穿过

6）词组（37个）

a single day 仅仅一天	lead to 导致
a wide selection of 种类繁多的	let alone 更别提
all of us 我们大家	lie around 到处都是
as a consequence of 由于	make sense 有意义
as long as 只要	more than 多于
as well as 以及	no longer 不再
at a later time 稍后	on vacation 度假
bank account 银行账户	philosophy of life 人生哲学
be responsible for 对……负责（2考）	regardless of 无论
believe in 信任	seem to 似乎
cross one's mind 出现，闪现	serve as 作为
cut off 切断，断绝	space out 分隔，隔开
deal with 解决	sports event 运动会
family member 家庭成员	take responsibility for 负责任
find out 发现	tend to 倾向于
half of 一半的	try out 尝试
hundreds of 成百上千的	try to 努力
is measured by 被……衡量	used to 曾经
keep up with 跟上	

3. 听记要点、扩充成句

句子听写无需使用原句，简化即可。

1） **使用缩略词语和各种符号：**完整写下较短单词，长难单词使用缩写，自己能看懂即可，最后补充完整。

2） **选择性记笔记：**重点记下名词、动词、形容词等实词，省略定语、状语。先记下句子主干，最后补全句子。

3） **简化句子**

（1）词汇替换：使用同义词或近义词替换写不出的单词，不涉及句子结构的改变，主要为名词、动词、形容词替换。

例：I've got to **go over my notes** for tomorrow's midterm.

I've got to **study** for tomorrow's midterm.

（2）口语替换：把原文中婉转、曲折的句型转换成更加口语化的表达。

例：I should bring the book to you, but it completely **slipped my mind**.

I had **forgotten** to bring the book.

（3）肯定和否定替换：肯定句和否定句可以相互替换，用自己熟悉的句型重新搭建句子结构。

例：Although she won the English speech contest, **she didn't think it's such a big deal.**

She is modest about her success in the contest.

（4）句子和短语替换：句子和短语可以相互替换，用自己熟悉的表达进行改写。

例：The banana pie is incredible but **Mike doesn't care much for dessert.**

The banana pie doesn't appeal to Mike.

4）重点句型研读

（1）原句：What **we may find** interesting is that it **usually** takes more words to be polite.

简化：What is interesting is that it takes more words to be polite.

（2）原句：But to a stranger, I **probably would** say "would you mind closing the door?"

简化：But to a stranger, I **will** say "would you mind closing the door?"

（3）原句：There are **bound to be** some words and phrases that belong in formal language and others **that are** informal.

简化：There are some words and phrases that belong in formal language and others informal.

（4）原句：something **that is simply there** around them, not something they can use

简化：something around them, not something they can use

（5）原句：The fast food industry can be seen as **a clear** example of American **cultural product**

简化：The fast food industry can be seen as **an** example of American **culture**

（6）原句：...**spread** around the world, they **have been viewed** as symbols of **American society and culture**

简化：...**are** around the world, they **are seen** as symbols of **America**

(7) 原句: These "**greenhouse gases**" trap heat in the **atmosphere** and are blamed for changing the world's **climate**.

简化: These **gases** trap heat in the **air** and are blamed for changing the world's **weather.**

(8) 原句: But **currently**, nations producing **only 44 percent have approved the Protocol**. Russia produces **17 percent** of the world's greenhouse gases.

简化: But **now**, nations producing **44% approve it**. Russia produces **17%** of the world's greenhouse gases.

(9) 原句: To join **the WTO**, a country must reach **trade** agreements with **major** trading countries that are **also WTO** members.

简化: To join **it**, a country must reach agreements with **main** trading countries that are members.

(10)原句: the **equivalent** German models **tend to be** heavier and slightly less easy to use

简化: the **similar** German models **are** heavier and **difficult** to use

(11)原句: **Similarly**, it is smaller than most **of its competitors, thus** fitting **easily** into a pocket or a handbag.

简化: **Also**, it is smaller than most **others, and** fitting into a pocket or a handbag.

(12)原句: The **only** problem was the **slight awkwardness** in loading the film.

简化: The problem was the **little difficulty** in loading the film.

(13)原句: In 1897, **the library** moved into its **own** building across the street from the capital.

简化: In 1897, **it** moved into its building across the street from the capital.

(14)原句: **The library** provides books **and materials** to the U.S. Congress and **also** lends books to **other American libraries, government agencies and foreign libraries.**

简化: **It** provides books to the U.S. Congress and lends books to **other libraries and government agencies.**

(15)原句: Anyone who wants copyright protection for a **publication** in the U.S. must send two copies to **the library**.

简化：Anyone who wants copyright protection for a **book** in the U.S. must send two copies to **it**.

(16) 原句：If you **realize that means a quarter** of world catch, you will **understand** that the problem is serious.

简化：If you **know it is one fourth** of world catch, you will **know** that the problem is serious.

(17) 原句：Some countries **are beginning** to **deal with** this problem, but it's **vital** we find a **rational** way of fishing.

简化：Some countries **begin** to **solve** it, but it's **important** we find a **right** way of fishing.

(18) 原句：It **would make sense** to give the fish enough time to recover, **grow to full size** and reproduce.

简化：It **is right** to give the fish enough time to recover, **grow up** and reproduce.

(19) 原句：Regardless of your age, you can make **a number of important** changes in your **current** lifestyle.

简化：Regardless of your age, you can make **many** changes in your lifestyle.

(20) 原句：We know **much** more about preventive health **today** than our parents and grandparents **did in the past**.

简化：We know more about preventive health than our parents and grandparents.

(21) 原句：And this **new knowledge** can be **transmitted** to our children to help them **become** healthier than **our generation**.

简化：And this can be **taught** to our children to help them **be** healthier than us.

(22) 原句：he has found out how it works and learned to use it **appropriately**

简化：he has found out how it works and learnt to use it **properly**

(23) 原句：by trying it out and seeing **whether** it works, by gradually changing it and refining it

简化：by trying it out and seeing **if** it works, by gradually changing it and refining it

(24)原句：introducing **many of the concepts** that the schools think only they can teach them

简化：introducing **many concepts** that the schools think only they can teach them

(25)原句：They **are** also **sharing information about** concerts **and** sports events, **as well as** jokes and **their philosophies** of life.

简化：They also **share info on** concerts, sports events, jokes and **views** of life.

(26)原句：**A hand-written** note to a friend or a family member is the best way to **communicate** important **thoughts**.

简化：**Writing a** note to a friend or a family member is the best way to **convey** important **ideas**.

(27)原句：This writing practice brings rewards that **can't be seen in bank accounts**.

简化：This writing practice brings rewards that **not in money**.

(28)原句：that move at a speed greater than light, and **therefore**, might serve as our passports to the past

简化：that move at a speed greater than light, and **thus**, might serve as our passports to the past

(29)原句：seems to **have been** part of humanity **for as long as** humans have existed

简化：seems to **be** part of humanity since humans have existed

(30)原句：used **a definition of time** for experimental purposes, as that which is measured by a clock

简化：used "**time**" for experimental purposes, as that which is measured by a clock

(31)原句：I remember being **carefully taught** that independence, not **interdependence**, was everything.

简化：I remember being **told** that independence, not **dependence,** was everything.

(32)原句：**what** my parents were **trying** to teach me **was** to **take responsibility for** my actions and my choices

简化：my parents **tried** to teach me to **be responsible for** my actions and my choices

（33）原句：I would **do almost anything** not to be a burden, and not **require** any help from **anybody**.

简化：I would **try** not to be a burden, and not **ask** any help from **others**.

（34）原句：there have been hundreds of thefts and cases of **deliberate** damaging **of** public property

简化：there have been hundreds of thefts and cases of damaging public property **on purpose**

（35）原句：Things **get** stolen when **it is** easy to steal them because they are left **lying around** unwatched.

简化：Things **are** stolen when **they are** easy to steal because they are left unwatched.

（36）原句：A better way to solve this problem **might be for all of us to be** more careful with our things.

简化：A better way to solve this problem **may be that we becoming** more careful with our things.

（37）原句：Partly as a **consequence** of this limited time, over **half** of all American homes now have microwave ovens.

简化：Partly as a **result** of this limited time, over **50%** of all American homes now have microwave ovens.

（38）原句：The United States Departments of Agriculture and the food industry collect sales **statistics** and keep **accurate** records.

简化：The United States Departments of Agriculture and the food industry collect sales **data** and keep **precise** records.

（39）原句：Red meat, **which used to be** the most popular choice for dinner, is no longer an American favorite.

简化：Red meat, the most popular choice for dinner **before**, is no longer an American favorite.

（40）原句：It's **considered** very rude to be late—even by 10 minutes—for an appointment in **America**.

简化：It's very rude to be late—even by 10 minutes—for an appointment in **U.S.**

（41）原句：It has enabled Americans to be **extremely** productivity, and productivity **itself** is highly valued in **America**.

简化：It has enabled Americans to be **very** productive, and productivity is highly valued in **U.S.**

（42）原句：Americans believe in spending their time and energy today so that the fruits of their labor may be enjoyed **at a later time**.

简化：Americans believe in spending their time and energy today so that the fruits of their labor may be enjoyed **later**.

第二节 真题选析

一、经典真题

Section A

Directions: *In this section, you will hear 8 short conversations and 2 long conversations. At the end of each conversation, one or more questions will be asked about what was said. Both the conversation and the questions will be spoken only once. After each question there will be a pause. During the pause, you must read the four choices marked [A], [B], [C] and [D], and decide which is the best answer. Then mark the corresponding letter on **Answer Sheet 2** with a single line through the centre.*

11. [A] Only true friendship can last long.

    [B] Letter writing is going out of style.

    [C] She keeps in regular touch with her classmates.

    [D] She has lost contact with most of her old friends.

12. [A] A painter.   [C] A porter.

    [B] A mechanic.   [D] A carpenter.

13. [A] Look for a place near her office.   [C] Make inquiries elsewhere.

    [B] Find a new job down the street.   [D] Rent the $600 apartment.

14. [A] He prefers to wear jeans with a larger waist.

    [B] He has been extremely busy recently.

    [C] He has gained some weight lately.

    [D] He enjoyed going shopping with Jane yesterday.

15. [A] The woman possesses a natural talent for art.

    [B] Women have a better artistic taste than men.

    [C] He isn't good at abstract thinking.

    [D] He doesn't like abstract paintings.

16. [A] She couldn't have left her notebook in the library.

    [B] She may have put her notebook amid the journals.

    [C] She should have made careful notes while doing reading.

    [D] She shouldn't have read his notes without his knowing it.

17. ［A］She wants to get some sleep.　　［C］She has a literature class to attend.

　　［B］She needs time to write a paper.　　［D］She is troubled by her sleep problem.

18. ［A］He is confident he will get the job.

　　［B］His chance of getting the job is slim.

　　［C］It isn't easy to find a qualified sales manager.

　　［D］The interview didn't go as well as he expected.

Questions 19 to 21 are based on the conversation you have just heard.

19. ［A］He can manage his time more flexibly.

　　［B］He can renew contact with his old friends.

　　［C］He can concentrate on his own projects.

　　［D］He can learn to do administrative work.

20. ［A］Reading its ads in the newspapers.　　［C］Contacting its manager.

　　［B］Calling its personnel department.　　［D］Searching its website.

21. ［A］To cut down its production expenses.

　　［B］To solve the problem of staff shortage.

　　［C］To improve its administrative efficiency.

　　［D］To utilize its retired employees' resources.

Questions 22 to 25 are based on the conversation you have just heard.

22. ［A］Buy a tractor.　　［C］See a piece of property.

　　［B］Fix a house.　　［D］Sign a business contract.

23. ［A］It is only forty miles from where they live.

　　［B］It is a small one with a two-bedroom house.

　　［C］It was bought at a price lower than expected.

　　［D］It has a large garden with fresh vegetables.

24. ［A］Growing potatoes will involve less labor.

　　［B］Its soil may not be very suitable for corn.

　　［C］It may not be big enough for raising corn.

　　［D］Raising potatoes will be more profitable.

25. ［A］Finances.　　［C］Equipment.

　　［B］Labor.　　［D］Profits.

Section B

Directions: *In this section, you will hear 3 short passages. At the end of each passage, you will hear some questions. Both the passage and the questions will be spoken only once. After you hear a question, you must choose the best answer from the four choices marked [A], [B], [C] and [D]. Then mark the corresponding letter on **Answer Sheet 2** with a single line through the centre.*

Passage One

Questions 26 to 29 are based on the passage you have just heard.

26. [A] To introduce the chief of the city's police force.

   [B] To comment on a talk by a distinguished guest.

   [C] To address the issue of community security.

   [D] To explain the functions of the city council.

27. [A] He has distinguished himself in city management.

   [B] He is head of the International Police Force.

   [C] He completed his higher education abroad.

   [D] He holds a master's degree in criminology.

28. [A] To coordinate work among police departments.

   [B] To get police officers closer to the local people.

   [C] To help the residents in times of emergency.

   [D] To enable the police to take prompt action.

29. [A] Popular.   [C] Effective.

   [B] Discouraging.   [D] Controversial.

Passage Two

Questions 30 to 32 are based on the passage you have just heard.

30. [A] People differ greatly in their ability to communicate.

   [B] There are numerous languages in existence.

   [C] Most public languages are inherently vague.

   [D] Big gaps exist between private and public languages.

31. [A] It is a sign of human intelligence.   [C] It is something we are born with.

   [B] It improves with constant practice.   [D] It varies from person to person.

32. ［A］How private languages are developed.

    ［B］How different languages are related.

    ［C］How people create their languages.

    ［D］How children learn to use language.

Passage Three

Questions 33 to 35 are based on the passage you have just heard.

33. ［A］She was a tailor.　　　　　　［C］She was an educator.

    ［B］She was an engineer.　　　　　［D］She was a public speaker.

34. ［A］Basing them on science-fiction movies.

    ［B］Including interesting examples in them.

    ［C］Adjusting them to different audiences.

    ［D］Focusing on the latest progress in space science.

35. ［A］Whether spacemen carry weapons.　［C］How NASA trains its spacemen.

    ［B］How spacesuits protect spacemen.　［D］What spacemen eat and drink.

Section C

Directions: *In this section, you will hear a passage three times. When the passage is read for the first time, you should listen carefully for its general idea. When the passage is read for the second time, you are required to fill in the blanks numbered from 36 to 43 with the exact words you have just heard. For blanks numbered from 44 to 46 you are required to fill in the missing information. For these blanks, you can either use the exact words you have just heard or write down the main points in your own words. Finally, when the passage is read for the third time, you should check what you have written.*

　　Crime is increasing worldwide. There is every reason to believe the (36)_____ will continue through the next few decades.

　　Crime rates have always been high in multicultural, industrialized societies such as the United States, but a new (37)_____ has appeared on the world (38)_____ —rapidly rising crime rates in nations that previously reported few (39)_____ . Street crimes such as robbery, rape, (40)_____ , and auto theft are clearly rising, (41)_____ in eastern European countries such as Hungary and in western European nations such as the United Kingdom.

　　What is driving this crime (42)_____ ? There are no simple answers. Still, there're certain conditions (43)_____ with rising crime: increasing *heterogeneity*

148

（混杂）of populations, greater cultural pluralism, higher immigration, democratization of governments, （44）_____.

These conditions are increasingly observable around the world. For instance, cultures that were previously isolated and *homogeneous*（同种类的）such as Japan, Denmark, and Greece, （45）_____

_____.

Multiculturalism can be a rewarding, enriching experience, but it can also lead to a clash of values. Heterogeneity in societies will be the rule in the twenty-first century, and （46）_____.

试题详解

11. D　生活场景

听力原文：M：I just received an email from one of my former classmates. I was surprised, I hadn't heard from him for ages.

W：Well, I've been out of touch with most of my old friends, only one or two still drop me a line occasionally.

Q：What does the woman mean?

试题解析：根据女士所说的I've been out of touch with most of my old friends（我已和大部分老朋友失去联系），故选D。

12. A　工作场景

听力原文：M：If you can make up your mind about the color, I can start on the outside of your house early next week.

W：Well, right now I think I want white for the window frames and yellow for the walls. But I'll let you know tomorrow.

Q：Who is the woman talking to?

试题解析：根据对话中的color, house, window frames, walls, 可知男士为油漆工, 故选A。

13. C　租房场景

听力原文：W：Excuse me. Do you have any apartments available for under 500 dollars a month? I need to move in next week when my new job starts.

M：The only vacant one I have is 600 dollars. Have you inquired the apartment complex down the street?

Q：What does the man suggest the woman do?

试题解析：根据男士说的Have you inquired the apartment complex down the street, 故选C"去别处问问"。

14. C 生活场景

听力原文：W:You bought a pair of jeans yesterday, didn't you? What are they like?

M:Oh, they are pretty much like my other ones except with a larger waist. I guess I haven't spent much time exercising lately.

Q:What can we infer from the conversation about the man?

试题解析：根据男士说的with a larger waist. I guess I haven't spent much time exercising lately(腰围大一些。我想我最近没有好好运动)，故选C"他最近有些增肥"。

15. D 生活场景

听力原文：W:I really like those abstract paintings we saw yesterday. What do you think?

M:I guess it's something I haven't acquired a taste for yet.

Q:What does the man imply?

试题解析：根据男士说的I guess it's something I haven't acquired a taste for yet.（我想我还不具备欣赏这种油画的品位），故选D"他不喜欢抽象画"。

16. B 学习场景

听力原文：W:You haven't seen a blue notebook, have you? I hope I didn't leave it in the reading room.

M:Did you check that pile of journals you've borrowed from the library the other day?

Q:What is the man trying to say to the woman?

试题解析：根据男士所说的Did you check that pile of journals you've borrowed from the library the other day?（你有没有检查前几天从图书馆借回来的那堆学术期刊?），故选B"她可能把笔记本放在期刊中了"。

17. A 论文场景

听力原文：M:How about joining me for a cup of coffee?

W:I'd love to, but I'm exhausted. I was up till 3 this morning writing a paper for my literature class.

Q:Why does the woman decline the man's invitation?

试题解析：根据女士说的 I was up till 3 this morning writing a paper for my literature class.(为了写我的文学课的论文，我一直熬到凌晨3点)，故选A"她想睡一会儿"。

18. B 求职场景

听力原文：W：You had a job interview yesterday, didn't you? How did it go?

M：Not too bad, I guess. There were about twenty candidates competing for the sales manager's job. And finally it was down to three of us, but the other two seemed better qualified.

Q：What does the man imply?

试题解析：根据男士说的 And finally it was down to three of us, but the other two seemed better qualified.(最后只剩下我们三个人，但他俩都比我更胜任这份工作)，选B"他得到这份工作的机会很渺茫"。

Conversation One(工作场景)

本对话共七个回合，是关于退休后的生活与工作的。

W：Simon, how does it feel to be retired?

M：Well, not so bad.

W：How have you been spending your time?

M：**I've been spending more time with my family. I've also travelled a bit,**(**19**) you know, off season when everywhere is less crowded and hotels cost less.

W：Great.

M：You know I haven't stopped work completely.

W：Yes, could you tell us more about this?

M：I'm on a scheme that's called phased retirement. I had a six-month break from work. After that I could apply for project work with the company I used to work for.

W：How does the scheme work?

M：Well, it's a trial at the moment. **Instead of hiring temporary staff, the company advertises posts on its website that retired employees like myself can access.** (**20**)

W：What sort of works advertised?

M：Well, all sorts of things, really. Administrative work and more specialized work, the sort of thing I can do. Some of the projects can last five or six months, and others can just be a couple of days. I can decide more or less when to work, so I can manage my own time.

W: I can see it's good for you. What does your company get out of this?

M: Well, **I still have all my old contacts at work, so I know who to contact to get something done.**(**21**)The company gets flexibility, too. Once the job's over, that's it. I'm not on their books any more.

Questions 19 to 21 are based on the conversation you have just heard.

19. Why does Simon find his retired life enjoyable?

正确答案：A

试题解析：根据长对话"开头必考"原则，对话开头提到：I've been spending more time with my family. I've also travelled a bit(我可以拿出更多的时间跟家人在一起。我也旅行了一阵)，故选A"他能更灵活地安排自己的时间"。

20. How does Simon get to know about the company's available posts?

正确答案：D

试题解析：根据长对话"听到什么选什么"原则，原文提到：Instead of hiring temporary staff, the company advertises posts on its website that retired employees like myself can access.(公司不再雇用临时员工，而是在公司网站上刊登针对退休员工的职位招聘信息)，故选D"搜索公司网站"。

21. Why does the company adopt the phased retirement scheme?

正确答案：D

试题解析：根据长对话"结尾必考"原则，结尾提到：I still have all my old contacts at work, so I know who to contact to get something done.(在工作上，我的老熟人都在，所以我知道该找谁来解决问题)，故选D "利用公司退休员工的资源")。phased retirement scheme意为"阶段退休计划"。

Conversation Two(生活场景)

本文共九个回合，是关于购买农场的对话。

W: Oh, where are we going?

M: I want to show you something.

W: I know, but what is it?

M: **A farm. It's just down this road. It's a small place, but at least it would be our own.**(**22**)

W: A farm? How can we afford to buy a farm?

M: It isn't very large, only 40 acres. We wouldn't have to pay very much right now.

W: Is there a house on the place?

M: **A small one, two bedrooms,（23）** but it needs to be fixed up a little. I can do the job myself.

W: OK. Is there enough space for a kitchen garden?

M: There is about half an acre around the house. That's plenty of space.

W: Then we can grow our own fresh vegetables. And maybe keep a few chickens, couldn't we?

M: Yes, and we can probably grow a lot of our own food.

W: What are you thinking about growing, if we do take this place?

M: **Well, it really isn't big enough for corn. I thought we might try to raise a crop of potatoes.（24）**

W: Potatoes? There are a lot of work.

M: We are used to hard work, aren't we?

W: **Yes, we are, but the money. Do we have enough to get started? It seems like a dream.（25）**

M: I think we've saved enough. We can pay a little on the farm and maybe put a few dollars down on the tractor, too.

Questions 22 to 25 are based on the conversation you have just heard.

22. What are the speakers going to do at the time of the conversation?

正确答案：C

试题解析：根据长对话"开头必考"原则，对话开头提到：A farm. It's just down this road. It's a small place, but at least it would be our own.(一个农场。就在这条路的尽头。虽然比较小，但至少它将属于我们)，故选C"看一块地"。

23. What does the man say about the farm?

正确答案：B

试题解析：根据长对话"听到什么选什么"原则，原文提到：A small one, two bedrooms(有一个两居室的小房子)，故选B。

24. Why does the man intend to grow potatoes rather than corn on the farm?

正确答案：C

试题解析：根据长对话"听到什么选什么"原则，原文提到：Well, it really isn't

big enough for corn. I thought we might try to raise a crop of potatoes.(这个农场的面积确实不够种植玉米，我想我们只能种土豆了)，故选C "它的大小不够种植玉米"。

25. What is the woman's greatest concern about the man's plan?

正确答案：A

试题解析：根据长对话 "结尾必考" 原则，结尾提到：Yes, we are, but the money. Do we have enough to get started? It seems like a dream.(是啊，我们可以辛勤工作，但问题在于钱。我们有足够的钱开始运作吗？这听起来像是一场梦)，故选A。

Section B

Passage One(介绍类：警察局局长)

本文介绍了一位警察局局长的杰出工作，开头一题、中间二题、结尾一题，分别考查了开头、however、first和结尾四个考点。

Members of the city council and distinguished guests, **it is my privilege to introduce to you today—Mr. Robert Washington—chief of our city's police force.** (26) He'll address us on the subject of the Community Policing Program. Most of you know that Mr. Washington has a distinguished record as head of our police force for more than ten years. **However, you may not know that he also holds a master's degree in criminology**(27) and studied abroad for a year with the international police force, which deals with crimes around the world. **Mr. Washington first introduced the Community Policing Program eight years ago. The idea behind the program is to get police officers out of their cars and into our neighborhoods where they can talk directly to merchants and residents about the real dynamics of our city.**(28) These officers do more than make arrests. They try to find ways to help solve the problems that contribute to crime in the first place. Often, that means hooking people up with services offered by other city agencies such as schools, hospitals, housing, drug treatment centers. **And the program seems to be working. Crime is down and our citizens report that they feel more secure.**(29) Today, Mr. Washington is going to tell us more about this program. Now let's welcome Mr. Robert Washington.

Questions 26 to 29 are based on the passage you have just heard.

26. What is the purpose of the speaker's remarks?

正确答案：A

试题解析：根据"重视开头"原则，开头提及：it is my privilege to introduce to you today—Mr. Robert Washington—chief of our city's police force（今天，我很荣幸向大家介绍市警察局局长罗伯特·华盛顿先生），故选A。

27. What does the speaker say about Mr. Robert Washington?

正确答案：D

试题解析：根据"听到什么选什么"原则，原文提及：However, you may not know that he also holds a master's degree in criminology（然而大家可能不知道，华盛顿先生还取得了犯罪学硕士学位），故选D。

28. What is the idea behind the Community Policing Program?

正确答案：B

试题解析：根据"听到什么选什么"原则，原文提及：Mr. Washington first introduced the Community Policing Program eight years ago. The idea behind the program is to get police officers out of their cars and into our neighborhoods where they can talk directly to merchants and residents about the real dynamics of our city.（华盛顿先生早在八年前就引入了社区警务项目，这个项目是为了让警察们从车里出来走入社区，与商人、居民直接沟通），故选B"要求警察接近民众"。

29. How has the Community Policing Program turned out to be?

正确答案：C

试题解析：根据"关注结尾"原则，结尾提及：And the program seems to be working. Crime is down and our citizens report that they feel more secure.（看上去社区警务项目起到了一定作用，城市的犯罪率降低并且市民们反映他们更有安全感），故选C"有效的"。

Passage Two

本文介绍了语言习得理论，开头、中间、结尾各有一题，分别考查了开头、because和but三个考点。

There are between 3,000 and 6,000 public languages in the world. And we must add approximately 6 billion private languages since each one of us necessarily has one. Considering these facts, the possibilities for breakdowns in communication seem infinite in number.（30）However, we do communicate successfully from time to time. And we do learn to speak languages. But learning to speak languages seems to be a very mysterious process. For a long time, people thought that we learned language only by imitation and association. For example, a baby touches a hot pot and starts to cry. The mother says, "Hot! Hot!" And the baby, when it stops crying, imitates the mother and says "Hot! Hot!" However, Noam Chomsky, a famous expert in language, pointed out that although children do learn some words by imitation and association, they also combine words to make meaningful sentences in ways that are unique, unlearned and creative. Because young children can make sentences they have never heard before, **Chomsky suggested that human infants are born with the ability to learn language.**(**31**) Chomsky meant that underneath all the differences between public and private languages, there is a universal language mechanism that makes it possible for us as infants to learn any language in the world. **This theory explains the potential that human infants have for learning language, but it does not really explain how children come to use language in particular ways.**(**32**)

Questions 30 to 32 are based on the passage you have just heard.

30. Why does the speaker say there are great possibilities for communication breakdowns?

    正确答案: B

    试题解析: 根据 "重视开头" 原则, 开头提及: There are between 3,000 and 6,000 public languages in the world. And we must add approximately 6 billion private languages since each one of us necessarily has one. Considering these facts, the possibilities for breakdowns in communication seem infinite in number. (全世界有3000到6000种公共语言。由于每人都有属于自己的一种语言, 所以还需要增加60亿种个人语言。考虑到这些因素, 我们沟通的障碍将会永无止境), 故选B"存在大量的语言"。

31. What is Chomsky's viewpoint on the ability to learn language?

    正确答案: C

    试题解析: 根据 "听到什么选什么" 原则, 原文提及: Because young children can make sentences they have never heard before, Chomsky suggested that human infants are born with the ability to learn language. (由于小孩可以独立使用单词造句, 乔姆斯基指出婴儿天生具备学习语言的能力), 故选C "它是我们生来

就具备的"。

32. What does Chomsky's theory fail to explain according to the speaker?

正确答案：D

试题解析：根据"关注结尾"原则，结尾提及：This theory explains the potential that human infants have for learning language, but it does not really explain how children come to use language in particular ways.(这个理论阐明了婴儿有学习语言的潜能，但没有解释婴儿是通过何种方式掌握语言的)，故选D"婴儿如何学习使用语言"。

Passage Three(工作类：演讲准备)

本文介绍了一位女宇航员根据不同听众准备演讲的情况，开头、中间、结尾各一题，分别考查了开头、because及结尾考点。

When US spacewoman Joan Higginbotham is not flying and working in space, she might be found somewhere on earth giving a speech. **Higginbotham, who grew up in Chicago, and became an engineer before joining NASA,** (33) that is, the National Air and Space Administration, gives about a dozen speeches a year. **Each speech is different, because she tailors her remarks to each audience.** (34) Through interviews and emails, she finds out in advance her listeners' educational level and what information they want to know. On the subject of space walks, for example, audiences vary in their interests and how much complexity they can comprehend. To elementary school children, Higginbotham may discuss a problem that many kids want to know about. "How do spacemen in a spacesuit eat, drink and go to the bathroom?" Her answer is, "The spacesuit is really a small spacecraft with room for food and water containers and a waste collection system." To a high school audience, she might satisfy a curiosity that often arises in her pre-speech interviews with students who obviously have seen many science fiction movies. "**Do spacemen carry weapons in case they encounter enemies in space?**" (35)Her answer is, "No!" To scientists, she might provide technical details on such topics as the design of spacesuit that protects spacemen from the deadly temperature extremes of space. Just as elaborate preparation is required for success in space, Higginbotham says that it's important for speakers to learn as much as possible about their listeners before a speech because every audience is different.

Questions 33 to 35 are based on the passage you have just heard.

33. What did Joan Higginbotham do before joining NASA?

正确答案：B

试题解析：根据"重视开头"原则，开头提及：Higginbotham, who grew up in Chicago, and became an engineer before joining NASA（希金博特姆出生于芝加哥，在进入美国国家航空航天局之前是一名工程师），故选B。

34. How does Higginbotham prepare her speeches on space walks?

正确答案：C

试题解析：根据"听到什么选什么"原则，文中提及：Each speech is different, because she tailors her remarks to each audience（因为希金博特姆对每次的听众都能做到"量体裁衣"，因此她的每一次演讲均不相同），故选C"根据不同听众调整演讲稿"。

35. What does the high school audience want to know about space travel?

正确答案：A

试题解析：根据"关注结尾"原则，结尾提及：Do spacemen carry weapons in case they encounter enemies in space?（宇航员是否需要为抵御太空中的敌人而佩带武器），故选A。

Section C

36. trend
37. phenomenon
38. scene
39. offenses
40. murder
41. particularly
42. explosion
43. associated

44. changing national boarders, greater economic growth, and the lack of accepted social ideas of right and wrong

45. are now facing the sort of cultural variety that has been common in America for most of its history

46. failure to recognize and plan for such diversity can lead to serious crime problems

二、经典真题二

Section A

Directions: *In this section, you will hear 8 short conversations and 2 long*

conversations. At the end of each conversation, one or more questions will be asked about what was said. Both the conversation and the questions will be spoken only once. After each question there will be a pause. During the pause, you must read the four choices marked [A], [B], [C] *and* [D], *and decide which is the best answer. Then mark the corresponding letter on* **Answer Sheet 2** *with a single line through the centre.*

注意：此部分试题请在**答题卡2**上作答。

11. [A] She expected more people at her party.

    [B] She enjoys entertaining small children.

    [C] She threw a surprise party for her friend.

    [D] She has always enjoyed great popularity.

12. [A] They are not used to living in a cold place.

    [B] They feel lucky to live in Florida.

    [C] They are going to have a holiday.

    [D] They have not booked their air tickets yet.

13. [A] He was pleased to get the medal.   [C] He used to be a firefighter.

    [B] He was very courageous.   [D] He was accused of causing a fire.

14. [A] Make a profitable investment.

    [B] Buy a new washing machine.

    [C] Get parts for the machine from Japan.

    [D] Have the old washing machine fixed.

15. [A] He is pleased with his exciting new job.

    [B] He finds the huge workload unbearable.

    [C] He finds his office much too big for him.

    [D] He is not so excited about his new position.

16. [A] The woman is going to hold a big party tomorrow.

    [B] The man has no idea what the right thing to do is.

    [C] The woman doesn't know how to get to the party.

    [D] The man offers to drive the woman to the party.

17. [A] Drawing up a business plan.   [C] Finalizing a contract.

    [B] Discussing a term paper.   [D] Reviewing a co-authored article.

18. [A] She ordered some paper.   [C] She chatted online with a friend.

    [B] She had the printer repaired.   [D] She filled in an application form.

Questions 19 to 22 are based on the conversation you have just heard.

19. [A] His health is getting worse.

    [B] He can no longer work at sea.

    [C] His past life upsets him a good deal.

    [D] He has not got the expected pension.

20. [A] She passed away years ago.　　　　[C] She has been working at a clinic.

    [B] She used to work as a model.　　　　[D] She has been seriously ill for years.

21. [A] She has made lots of money as a doctor.

    [B] She is going to take care of her old dad.

    [C] She has never got on with her father.

    [D] She is kind and generous by nature.

22. [A] He dines out with his wife every weekend.

    [B] He is excellent but looks bad-tempered.

    [C] He does not care about his appearance.

    [D] He is not quite popular with his patients.

Questions 23 to 25 are based on the conversation you have just heard.

23. [A] The man has sent the order to the woman by mistake.

    [B] Some of the telephone systems don't work properly.

    [C] Some of the packs do not contain any manuals.

    [D] The quality of the goods is not up to the standard.

24. [A] Send a service engineer to do the repairs.

    [B] Consult her boss about the best solution.

    [C] Pass the man's order to the right person.

    [D] Solve the problem at her company's cost.

25. [A] Ideal.　　　　　　　　　　　　　[C] Partial.

    [B] Temporary.　　　　　　　　　　　[D] Creative.

Section B

Directions: *In this section, you will hear 3 short passages. At the end of each passage, you will hear some questions. Both the passage and the questions will be spoken only once. After you hear a question, you must choose the best answer from the four choices marked [A], [B], [C] and [D]. Then mark the corresponding* *letter on **Answer Sheet 2** with a single line through the centre.*

注意：此部分试题请在**答题卡2**上作答。

Passage One

Questions 26 to 28 are based on the passage you have just heard.

26. ［A］It is entertaining.   ［C］It takes lots of time.
    ［B］It is a costly hobby.   ［D］It requires training.

27. ［A］They can harm nearby plants.   ［C］They fight each other for food.
    ［B］They may catch some disease.   ［D］They may pollute the environment.

28. ［A］Place the food on warmer spots.   ［C］Avoid using any contaminated food.
    ［B］Use prepared feed mixtures only.   ［D］Continue the feeding till it gets warm.

Passage Two

Questions 29 to 31 are based on the passage you have just heard.

29. ［A］He will betray even his best friends.
    ［B］He is able to make up good excuses.
    ［C］He will lie whenever he wants.
    ［D］He tries to achieve his goal at any cost.

30. ［A］She made him apologize.   ［C］She broke up with him.
    ［B］She readily forgave him.   ［D］She refused to answer his calls.

31. ［A］Buy her a new set of tires.   ［C］Lend her his batteries.
    ［B］Help clean her apartment.   ［D］Move furniture for her.

Passage Three

Questions 32 to 35 are based on the passage you have just heard.

32. ［A］The atmosphere they live in is rather unreal.
    ［B］Their parents put too much pressure on them.
    ［C］It's hard for them to get along with other kids.
    ［D］They have to live in the shadow of their parents.

33. ［A］He always boasts about his rich father.
    ［B］He will grow up to be good for nothing.
    ［C］He has too much to know the value of things.
    ［D］He is too young to manage his inherited property.

34. [A] She wants Amanda to get professional care.

    [B] She has no experience in raising children.

    [C] She wants to show off her wealth.

    [D] She has no time to do it herself.

35. [A] The lifestyle depicted in Hollywood movies.

    [B] The worship of money, beauty and pleasure.

    [C] The attention the media focuses on them.

    [D] The pursuing of perfection in performance.

Section C

Directions: *In this section, you will hear a passage three times. When the passage is read for the first time, you should listen carefully for its general idea. When the passage is read for the second time, you are required to fill in the blanks numbered from 36 to 43 with the exact words you have just heard. For blanks numbered from 44 to 46 you are required to fill in the missing information. For these blanks, you can either use the exact words you have just heard or write down the main points in your own words. Finally, when the passage is read for the third time, you should check what you have written.*

注意: 此部分试题请在**答题卡2**上作答。

Around 120 years ago, Ebbinghaus began his study of memory. He (36) _____ on studying how quickly the human mind can remember (37) _____. One result of his research is known as the total time *hypothesis* (假设), which simply means the amount you learn (38) _____ on the time you spend trying to learn it. This can be taken as our first rule of learning.

Although it is usually true that studying for four hours is better than studying for one, there is still the question of how we should use the four hours. For example, is it better to study for four hours (39) _____ or to study for one hour a day for four days in a (40) _____? The answer, as you may have (41) _____, is that it is better to spread out the study times. This (42) _____, through which we can learn more (43) _____ by dividing our practice time, is known as the distribution of practice effect. Thus, (44) _____.

But we're not finished yet. We haven't considered how we should study over very

short periods of time.（45）_____.
Should you look at the same word in rapid succession, or look at the word and then
have some delay before you look at it again?（46）_____

_____.

试题详解

11. D　生活场景

　　听力原文：W: There were more than a hundred people at Kate's birthday party.
　　　　　　　　　How come she's got so many friends?

　　　　　　　M: It's really no surprise. You know she was popular even when she
　　　　　　　　　was a child.

　　　　　　　Q: What does the man imply about Kate?

　　听力解析：根据女士所说的more than a hundred people at Kate's birthday party
　　　　　　　（凯特的生日聚会上有一百多人）和男士所说的she was popular
　　　　　　　even when she was a child（甚至还是个孩子的时候，她就很受欢
　　　　　　　迎），可知选D"她一直很受欢迎"。

12. C　旅行场景

　　听力原文：M: They say there'll be a snowstorm tonight, and the cold weather
　　　　　　　　　will last quite a few days.

　　　　　　　W: Oh! We're so lucky. We'll be getting away for a while, and having
　　　　　　　　　a holiday in Florida. But let's call right now to confirm our flight.

　　　　　　　Q: What do we learn about the two speakers?

　　试题解析：根据女士所说的We are so lucky. We'll be getting away for a while,
　　　　　　　and having a holiday in Florida.（我们真幸运。我们将离开一段时
　　　　　　　间，去佛罗里达度假），可知选C"他们要去度假"。

13. B　工作场景

　　听力原文：W: Tony was awarded a medal for rescuing several families from the
　　　　　　　　　forest fire.

　　　　　　　M: I really admire his courage.

　　　　　　　Q: What do we learn about Tony from the conversation?

　　试题解析：根据男士所说的I really admire his courage.（我确实佩服他的勇
　　　　　　　气），可知选B"他非常勇敢"。

14. B 生活场景

听力原文：M: My washing machine is more than fifteen years old and it had worked just fine until last night.

W: You'll never be able to get parts for it, even from Japan. So it might be time to invest a more recent model.

Q: What does the woman suggest the man do?

试题解析：根据女士所说的it might be time to invest a more recent model(或许是该买台新款了)，可知选B"买一台新洗衣机"。It might be time to do something是提建议的委婉表达方式。

15. D 工作场景

听力原文：W: I heard about your promotion. You must be thrilled.

M: Not really, the new office is huge, but the workload has doubled.

Q: What do we learn about the man from the conversation?

试题解析：根据男士所说的Not really, the new office is huge, but the workload has doubled.(没有，新办公室很大，但工作量加倍了)，可知选D"他对新职位并不太激动"。

16. D 交通场景

听力原文：W: I can't decide what to do about the party tomorrow.

M: You don't have to go if you don't want to, but I'll be glad to give you a ride if you do.

Q: What do we learn from the conversation?

试题解析：根据男士所说的I'll be glad to give you a ride if you do(如果你想去，我很乐意送你)，可知选D "男士提出开车送女士去晚会"。give sb. a ride意为"送某人一程"。

17. C 工作场景

听力原文：M: Now if you have any questions about the contract, I'll be happy to answer them.

W: Nothing comes to mind right now, but I'd like to go over all the articles of the contract once more before signing it.

Q: What are the speakers doing right now?

试题解析：根据女士所说的I'd like to go over all the articles of the contract once more before signing it(我想在签合同之前再看一遍所有的条款)，可知选C"完成一项合同"。

18. A　工作场景

听力原文：M: We are out of paper for the printer. Can you please order some?

W: I completed the order from online yesterday and it will be here by noon. I'll let you know when it comes in.

Q: What did the woman do?

试题解析：根据男士所说的 We are out of paper for the printer.（我们的打印机没纸了）和女士所说的 I completed the order from online yesterday（我昨天在网上完成了订购），可知选 A"她订购了一些纸张"。

Conversation One（工作场景）

本对话共5个半回合，内容是关于 old Jake 与 Doctor Johnson 两个家庭的。

W: Bob, do you know who I saw the other day? Old Jake, looking terribly depressed. Did he get pensioned off at last?

M: Yes. **They made him retire after 50 years at sea. He is pretty upset about it,** （19）but what can you do? He really is pasted.

W: He is all alone, isn't he?

M: Yes, **his wife's been dead for years.**（20）They had one daughter, Doris. But she went off to town as soon as she left school. And he hasn't heard from her since. I hear she is making good money as a model.

W: Maybe someone could get in touch with her. Get her to come back for a while to help?

M: I don't suppose she come. **She never got on with her father.**（21）He is bit of a tough character and she is rather selfish. Oh, I expect old Jake will get by. He's healthy at least; comes into a clinic for a check regularly.

W: Are you his doctor?

M: No, my partner Doctor Johnson is.

W: That bad-tempered old thing?

M: Oh, **he isn't really bad-tempered. He just looks it. He is an excellent doctor,** （22）taught me a lot, and he has a very nice family. His wife invites me over there to supper every week. Very pleasant.

W: Yes. I teach their daughter Pen at school. She is a bit careless and lazy about her school work, but a bright little thing and very popular with her age group.

Questions 19 to 22 are based on the conversation you have just heard.

19. Why does old Jake look terribly depressed?

    正确答案：B

    试题解析：根据长对话"开头必考"的原则，对话开头提到：They've made him retire after 50 years at sea. He is pretty upset about it.（在海上工作了50年后，他们让他退休了。他对此相当失落），故选B"他不能在海上工作了"。

20. What do we learn about Jake's wife?

    正确答案：A

    试题解析：根据长对话"听到什么选什么"原则，原文提到his wife's been dead for years（他的妻子去世很多年了），故选A"她多年前去世了"。

21. What does the man say about Jake's daughter?

    正确答案：C

    试题解析：根据长对话"听到什么选什么"原则，原文提到She never got on with her father.（她和父亲相处得一直不好），故选C"她和父亲相处得一直不好"。

22. What does the man say about Jake's doctor?

    正确答案：B

    试题解析：根据长对话"结尾必考"原则，结尾提到：he isn't really bad-tempered. He just looks it. He is an excellent doctor（他并不是脾气不好。他只是看起来那样。他是一个优秀的医生），故选B"他很优秀但是看起来脾气不好"。

Conversation Two(工作场景)

本对话共7个半回合，是关于要求补寄电话说明书的谈话。

W: Hello, Mr. Summerfield. How are you today?

M: Very well. Thank you, Ms. Green.

W: What can I do for you?

M: Well, unfortunately, there is a problem with the order we received from you yesterday. **It seems we've not received the right quantity of manuals to support the telephone system.**(23)

W: Oh, dear, that's bad news. I'm very sorry to hear that, and you don't know how many packs are without manuals?

M: No, because we haven't opened every pack. But in several of those that have been opened there are none, no manuals.

W: I'm very sorry about this inconvenience, Mr. Summerfield. **We'll send out the manuals this afternoon by express mail entirely at our cost,**（24）and the manuals should arrive tomorrow or the day after at the latest.

M: All of them, right?

W: Yes. It may be that some have them already, but we cannot be sure. So the best thing is to send out the manual for every pack.

M: Yes. Yes, I see. That would be great.

W: Please accept our apologies for this mix-up. I assure you we will do everything possible to find out why the mistake happened.

M: **Right. Thanks for your swift action.**

W: Not at all. Thank you and goodbye for now. Do call if there is anything else.

M: **All right. Thank you.**（25）Goodbye, Ms. Green.

W: Goodbye.

Questions 23 to 25 are based on the conversation you have just heard.

23. What problems are the speakers discussing?

正确答案：C

试题解析：根据长对话"开头必考"原则，开头提到：It seems we've not received the right quantity of manuals to support the telephone system.（似乎我们没有收到足够的支持电话系统的说明书），故选C"一些包装盒里没有包含任何说明书"。

24. What does the woman promise to do?

正确答案：D

试题解析：根据长对话"听到什么选什么"原则，原文提到：We'll send out the manuals this afternoon by express mail entirely at our cost（今天下午我们将自己付费通过特快专递将说明书寄出去），故选D"由她的公司付费来解决问题"。

25. What does the man think of the solution?

正确答案：A

试题解析：根据长对话"结尾必考"原则，结尾男士连连真诚致谢：Right.

Thanks for your swift action.(好的。感谢您迅速的解决措施)和All right. Thank you.(好的。谢谢),故选A"很满意"。

Section B
Passage One(科普类：喂鸟)

本文简要说明了喂鸟的一些注意事项以及冬季喂鸟的有关事宜。出题工整：开头一题，中间两题，结尾一题。

Attracting and feeding wild birds are entertaining activities that have long been enjoyed by people all over the world. Feeding birds has become so popular that prepared feed mixtures are readily available. We feed birds for many reasons. **Many pleasant hours can come from watching birds.**(26) A hobby often develops into a serious study of their habits. Accurate identification of birds is usually the first goal. But observations that an amateur bird-watcher can make are really limitless. **There is, however, responsibility associated with bird feeding, including a disease hazard. Attracting numbers of birds continually to the same spot can be harmful to them, particularly species that pick food from the ground contaminated by the droppings of other birds.**(27) In winter feeding efforts are most satisfying to people and are of greatest benefit to birds. During this time when fewer natural foods are available and air temperatures are lower, extra feeding can keep a bird warm and well. Once begun, feeding should never stop during these lean months. If you start a local increase of birds, be prepared to do what may be required to eliminate hazards to those you want to be friend. **A constant supply of food should be given until the cold is over and spring has come.**(28) If feeding is stopped during severe weather, birds used to relying upon the feeders might starve.

Questions 26 to 28 are based on the passage you have just heard.

26. What does the speaker say about bird watching?

正确答案：A

试题解析：根据"重视开头"原则，开头提到：Attracting and feeding birds are entertaining activities.(吸引并给鸟类喂食是令人愉悦的活动) 以及Many pleasant hours can come from watching birds.(很多快乐时光来自观察鸟类)，故选A"它(观察鸟类)是令人愉悦的"。

27. What does the speaker say about birds fed continually on the same spot?

正确答案：B

试题解析：根据"听到什么选什么"原则，原文提到：There is, however, responsibility associated with bird feeding, including a disease hazard. Attracting numbers of birds continually to the same spot can be harmful to them, particularly species that pick food from the ground contaminated by the droppings of other birds.（然而，还有与喂鸟相关的责任，包括疾病危害。不断吸引大量鸟类到同一地点对它们是有害的，尤其是对那些从被其他鸟类的粪便污染的地面捡拾食物的鸟来说），故选B"它们可能会得病"。

28. What does the speaker suggest we do when feeding birds in winter?

正确答案：D

试题解析：根据"关注结尾"原则，结尾提到：A constant supply of food should be given until the cold is over and spring has come.（食物的持续供应应该坚持到寒冷的天气过去，春天来临），故选D"继续喂食直到天气转暖"。

Passage Two(故事类：借口)

本文是一篇记叙文，讲述了说话者的一位朋友总是找借口推脱的三个小故事。

My friend Leo makes up weak and poor excuses whenever there is something he doesn't want to do.（29）Just two weeks ago, he was at my house when he decided he didn't want to go into work. He called his boss and said he had to get a new set of tires put on his truck. Then he sat down and watched TV with me. Not only had he lied but his excuse wasn't a very convincing one. Another time, he cancelled a date with his girlfriend at the last minute telling her he had to get a new battery for his truck. **She was angry and refused to go out with him again until he apologized.**（30）Last weekend, Leo offered the poorest excuse yet. **He'd promised he'd help me move some furniture,**（31）from my parents' house to my new apartment. He was supposed to bring his truck over about 8 o'clock Saturday morning. I waited, and then called and left a message on his machine. About 11:30, he called and said he was sorry but he'd been getting a new set of tires put on his truck. I guess he'd forgotten he used the same excuse when he called his boss from my house. I think I need a new set of friends. I'm beginning to get tired of Leo's excuses.

Questions 29 to 31 are based on the passage you have just heard.

29. What does the speaker tell us about her friend Leo?

    正确答案：C

    试题解析：根据"重视开头"原则，开头提到：My friend Leo makes up weak and poor excuses whenever there is something he doesn't want to do.（只要我的朋友Leo有不想做的事情，他就开始编造不可信的借口），故选C"只要他愿意，他就撒谎"。

30. What did his girlfriend do when Leo canceled a date with her at the last minute?

    正确答案：A

    试题解析：根据"听到什么选什么"原则，原文提到：She was angry and refused to go out with him again until he apologized.（她生气了，拒绝和他一起出去，直到他道歉），故选A"她迫使他道歉"。

31. What favor did the speaker ask Leo to do last weekend?

    正确答案：D

    试题解析：根据"关注结尾"原则，结尾提到：He'd promised he'd help me move some furniture（他答应帮我搬一些家具），故选D"为她搬一些家具"。

Passage Three（生活类：好莱坞的孩子们）

本文介绍了好莱坞的孩子们追逐金钱、美貌与享乐的生活。出题工整：开头一题，中间两题，结尾一题。

In Hollywood, everybody wants to be rich, famous and beautiful. Nobody wants to be old, unknown and poor. **For Hollywood kids, life can be difficult because they grow up in such an unreal atmosphere.**（32）Their parents are ambitious and the children are part of the parents' ambitions. Parents pay for wasteful grand parties, expensive cars and designer clothes. **When every dream can come true, kids don't learn the value of anything because they have everything. A thirteen-year-old boy, Trent Maguire, has a driver, credit cards and unlimited cash to do what he wants when he wants to.**（33）"One day, I'll earn more than my dad!" he boasts. **Parents buy care and attention for their children because they have no time to give it themselves. Amanda's mother employs a personal trainer, a bodyguard, a singing coach and a councilor to look after all her fifteen-year-old daughter's needs.**（34）Often, there is no parent at home most days, so children decide whether to make their own meals or go out to restaurants, when to watch television or do homework. They organize their own social lives. They play no childhood games. They become adults before they're ready. Hollywood has always been the city of dreams. **The kids there live unreal lives where money, beauty and pleasure are the only gods.**（35）Will children around the world soon start to think the same? Or do they already?

Questions 32 to 35 are based on the passage you have just heard.

32. Why is life said to be difficult for Hollywood kids?

正确答案：A

试题解析：根据"重视开头"原则，开头提到：For Hollywood kids, life can be difficult because they grow up in such an unreal atmosphere.（对于好莱坞的孩子们来说，由于他们生长在这样一种不真实的环境中，生活并不容易），故选A "他们生活的环境非常不真实"。

33. What does the speaker say about Trent Maguire, a thirteen-year-old boy?

正确答案：C

试题解析：根据"听到什么选什么"原则，原文提到：When every dream can come true, kids don't learn the value of anything because they have everything. A thirteen-year-old boy, Trent Maguire, has a driver, credit cards and unlimited cash to do what he wants when he wants to.（当每个梦想都能成真时，由于孩子们拥有一切，所以他们不知道东西的价值。一个13岁的男孩Trent Maguire有一名司机、很多信用卡和花不完的现金，想干什么干什么），故选C"他拥有的太多了，以至于他并不知道东西的价值）。

34. Why does Amender's mother employ other people to look after her needs?

正确答案：D

试题解析：根据"听到什么选什么"原则，原文提到：Parents buy care and attention for their children because they have no time to give it themselves. Amanda's mother employs a personal trainer, a bodyguard, a singing coach and a councilor to look after all her fifteen-year-old daughter's needs.（由于父母们没有时间亲自照顾孩子，他们给自己的孩子购买关心与关注。Amanda的母亲雇了一个私人教练、一个保镖、一个声乐老师和一个顾问来满足她15岁女儿的所有需求），故选D"她没有时间自己做"。

35. What will probably have negative effects on the lives of Hollywood kids?

正确答案：B

试题解析：根据"关注结尾"原则，原文提到：The kids there live unreal lives where money, beauty and pleasure are the only gods.（孩子们过着不真实的生活，在那里金钱、美貌与享乐是唯一的神灵），故选B"对于金钱、美貌、享乐的崇拜"。

Section C

36. concentrated

37. information

38. depends

39. straight

40. row

41. suspected

42. phenomenon

43. efficiently

44. our second rule of learning is this: it is better to study fairly briefly but often

45. Let's say you are trying to learn some new and rather difficult English vocabulary using a stack of cards

46. The answer is it is better to space out the presentations of the word you are to learn

三、经典真题三

Section A

Directions: *In this section, you will hear 8 short conversations and 2 long conversations. At the end of each conversation, one or more questions will be asked about what was said. Both the conversation and the questions will be spoken only once. After each question there will be a pause. During the pause, you must read the four choices marked [A], [B], [C] and [D], and decide which is the best answer. Then mark the corresponding letter on **Answer Sheet 2** with a single line through the centre.*

注意：此部分试题请在**答题卡2**上作答。

11. [A] Get some small change.　[C] Cash a check at a bank.
　　[B] Find a shopping center.　[D] Find a parking meter.

12. [A] Shopping with his son.　[C] Promoting a new product.
　　[B] Buying a gift for a child.　[D] Bargaining with a salesgirl.

13. [A] Taking photographs.　[C] Mending cameras.
　　[B] Enhancing images.　[D] Painting pictures.

14. 〔A〕He moved to Baltimore when he was young.

 〔B〕He can provide little useful information.

 〔C〕He will show the woman around Baltimore.

 〔D〕He will ask someone else to help the woman.

15. 〔A〕He is rather disappointed.　　〔C〕He can't face up to the situation.

 〔B〕He is highly ambitious.　　〔D〕He knows his own limitations.

16. 〔A〕She must have paid a lot for the gym.

 〔B〕She is known to have a terrific figure.

 〔C〕Her gym exercise has yielded good results.

 〔D〕Her effort to keep fit is really praiseworthy.

17. 〔A〕Female students are unfit for studying physics.

 〔B〕He can serve as the woman's tutor.

 〔C〕Physics is an important course at school.

 〔D〕The professor's suggestion is constructive.

18. 〔A〕Indifferent.　　〔C〕Pleased.

 〔B〕Doubtful.　　〔D〕Surprised.

Questions 19 to 22 are based on the conversation you have just heard.

19. 〔A〕He prefers the smaller evening classes.

 〔B〕He has signed up for a day course.

 〔C〕He has to work during the day.

 〔D〕He finds the evening course cheaper.

20. 〔A〕Learn a computer language.　　〔C〕Buy some computer software.

 〔B〕Learn data processing.　　〔D〕Buy a few coursebooks.

21. 〔A〕Thursday evening, from 7:00 to 9:45.

 〔B〕From September 1 to New Year's eve.

 〔C〕Every Monday, lasting for 12 weeks.

 〔D〕Three hours a week, 45 hours in total.

22. 〔A〕What to bring for registration.　　〔C〕How he can get to Frost Hall.

 〔B〕Where to attend the class.　　〔D〕Whether he can use a check.

Questions 23 to 25 are based on the conversation you have just heard.

23. 〔A〕A training coach.　　〔C〕A professional manager.

 〔B〕A trading adviser.　　〔D〕A financial trader.

24. [A] He can save on living expenses. [C] He can enjoy healthier food.
    [B] He considers cooking creative. [D] He thinks take-away is tasteless.

25. [A] It is something inevitable. [C] It takes patience to manage.
    [B] It is frustrating sometimes. [D] It can be a good thing.

Section B

Directions: *In this section, you will hear 3 short passages. At the end of each passage, you will hear some questions. Both the passage and the questions will be spoken only once. After you hear a question, you must choose the best answer from the four choices marked [A], [B], [C] and [D]. Then mark the corresponding letter on **Answer Sheet 2** with a single line through the centre.*

注意: 此部分试题请在**答题卡2**上作答。

Passage One

Questions 26 to 28 are based on the passage you have just heard.

26. [A] There were no planets without moons.
    [B] There was no air or water on Jupiter.
    [C] Life was not possible in outer space.
    [D] The mystery of life could not be resolved.

27. [A] It has a number of active volcanoes.
    [B] It has an atmosphere like the earth's.
    [C] It has a large ocean under its surface.
    [D] It has deep caves several miles long.

28. [A] Light is not an essential element to it.
    [B] Life can form in very hot temperatures.
    [C] Every form of life undergoes evolution.
    [D] Oxygen is not needed for some life forms.

Passage Two

Questions 29 to 31 are based on the passage you have just heard.

29. [A] Whether they should take the child home.
    [B] What Dr. Meyer's instructions exactly were.
    [C] Who should take care of the child at home.
    [D] When the child would completely recover.

30. ［A］She encourages them to ask questions when in doubt.

　　［B］She makes them write down all her instructions.

　　［C］She has them act out what they are to do at home.

　　［D］She asks them to repeat what they are supposed to do.

31. ［A］It lacks the stability of the printed word.

　　［B］It contains many grammatical errors.

　　［C］It is heavily dependent on the context.

　　［D］It facilitates interpersonal communication.

Passage Three

Questions 32 to 35 are based on the passage you have just heard.

32. ［A］Job security.　　　　　　　　　［C］Challenging work.

　　［B］Good labour relations.　　　　　［D］Attractive wages and benefits.

33. ［A］Many tedious jobs continue to be done manually.

　　［B］More and more unskilled workers will lose jobs.

　　［C］Computers will change the nature of many jobs.

　　［D］Boring jobs will gradually be made enjoyable.

34. ［A］Offer them chances of promotion.

　　［B］Improve their working conditions.

　　［C］Encourage them to compete with each other.

　　［D］Give them responsibilities as part of a team.

35. ［A］They will not bring real benefits to the staff.

　　［B］They concern a small number of people only.

　　［C］They are arbitrarily set by the administrators.

　　［D］They are beyond the control of ordinary workers.

Section C

Directions: *In this section, you will hear a passage three times. When the passage is read for the first time, you should listen carefully for its general idea. When the passage is read for the second time, you are required to fill in the blanks numbered from 36 to 43 with the exact words you have just heard. For blanks numbered from 44 to 46 you are required to fill in the missing information. For these blanks, you* *can either use the exact words you have just heard or write down the main points in your own words. Finally, when the passage is read for the third time, you should check what you have written.*

注意：此部分试题请在**答题卡2**上作答。

In the humanities, authors write to inform you in many ways. These methods can be （36）＿＿＿＿＿ into three types of informational writing: factual, descriptive, and process.

Factual writing provides （37）＿＿＿＿＿ information on an author, composer, or artist or on a type of music, literature, or art. Examples of factual writing include notes on a book jacket or （38）＿＿＿＿＿ cover and longer pieces, such as an article describing a style of music which you might read in a music （39）＿＿＿＿＿ course. This kind of writing provides a （40）＿＿＿＿＿ for your study of the humanities.

As its name （41）＿＿＿＿＿, descriptive writing simply describes, or provides an （42）＿＿＿＿＿ of, a piece of music, art, or literature. For example, descriptive writing might list the colors an artist used in a painting or the （43）＿＿＿＿＿ a composer included in a musical composition, so as to make pictures or sounds in the reader's mind by calling up specific details of the work. （44）＿＿＿＿＿

＿＿＿＿＿＿＿＿＿＿＿＿＿＿＿＿＿＿＿.

Process writing explains a series of actions that bring about a result. （45）＿＿＿＿

＿＿＿＿＿＿＿＿＿＿＿＿＿＿＿＿＿. This kind of writing is often found in art, where understanding how an artist created a certain effect is important.

（46）＿＿＿＿＿＿＿＿＿＿＿＿＿＿＿＿＿＿＿＿＿＿.

试题详解

11. A　生活场景

听力原文：M: Excuse me, do you have change for a ten-dollar note? I need to pay the parking meter.

W: I'm sorry, but I think you can get it through the money changer in the shopping center across the street.

Q: What is the man trying to do?

试题解析：根据男士所说的do you have change for a ten-dollar note（你有10美元的零钱吗？），可知选A"换一些零钱"。

12. B 购物场景

听力原文：M: Can you recommend something that a school boy of 7 or 8 will really like?

W: I'd suggest this toy train, sir. It's an excellent brand, very popular all over the world these days.

Q: What is the man doing?

试题解析：根据男士所说的Can you recommend something that a school boy of 7 or 8 will really like?（你能为我推荐一些七八岁的学龄男孩确实喜欢的东西吗？），可知选B"给一个小孩买礼物"。

13. A 生活场景

听力原文：W: Do you let people know when you're taking pictures of them?

M: I try not to. You know any picture of a person who poses for the camera would look dull and unnatural.

Q: What are the speakers talking about?

试题解析：根据女士所说的Do you let people know when you're taking pictures of them?（当你为人们拍照的时候，你让他们知道吗？），可知选A"拍照片"。

14. B 生活场景

听力原文：W: I need to talk to someone who knows Baltimore well. I'm told you lived there.

M: Oh, but I was really young at the time.

Q: What does the man mean?

试题解析：根据男士所说的but I was really young at the time(但是我那时年纪很小)，可知他对现在的巴尔的摩市并不了解，故选B"他能提供的有用信息很少"。

15. D 工作场景

听力原文：W: Aren't you disappointed that you didn't get the promotion?

M: Maybe a little, but I know I need more experience before I'm ready for that kind of responsibility.

Q: What do we learn about the man from this conversation?

试题解析：根据男士所说的but I know I need more experience before I'm ready for that kind of responsibility(但我知道自己需要更多经验才能承

177

担那种责任），可知选D"他知道自己的局限"。选项C中的face up
to意为"勇敢地面对"。

16. C 生活场景

听力原文：W: I've been working out the gym since January. I was a bit out of
　　　　　 shape.

　　　　　 M: You look terrific. It seems that your effort has paid off.

　　　　　 Q: What does the man imply about the woman?

试题解析：根据女士所说的working out the gym(做体操来健身)和男士所说
　　　　　 的You look terrific. It seems that your effort has paid off.(你看上去
　　　　　 棒极了。看来你的努力有了回报)，可知选C"她的健身锻炼已经
　　　　　 产生了良好的结果"。

17. D 学习场景

听力原文：W: Professor Clark suggested I get a tutor for advanced physics.

　　　　　 M: Well, that might help. Advanced physics is a pretty difficult
　　　　　 　 course.

　　　　　 Q: What does the man mean?

试题解析：根据男士所说的that might help(那也许会有帮助)，可知选D"教
　　　　　 授的建议是有帮助的"。constructive意为"有帮助的，建设性的"，
　　　　　 tutor意为"家教，导师"，advanced physics意为"高等物理"。

18. A 工作场景

听力原文：W: Bill, have you heard the latest news? It appears we two won't be
　　　　　 laid off after all.

　　　　　 M: Oh, I'm somewhat tired of working here. I've been wondering
　　　　　 　 whether I should resign. Anyway, the news seems to be good for
　　　　　 　 you.

　　　　　 Q: How does the man feel about the news?

试题解析：根据男士所说的Anyway, the news seems to be good for you.(不管
　　　　　 怎么说，这个消息对你来说不错)，由男士说话的口吻可知，他对
　　　　　 这则消息漠不关心，故选A"漠不关心的"。对话中的laid off意为
　　　　　 "解雇，下岗"，wonder意为"考虑"，resign意为"辞职"。

Conversation One（选课场景）

本对话共12个回合，内容是关于一位男士上夜校学习计算机课程的。

W: Hello, Clarkson College. May I help you?

M: Yes, I'm looking for information on courses in computer programming. I would need it for the fall semester.

W: Do you want a day or evening course?

M: Well, **it would have to be an evening course, since I work during the day.**（19）

W: Uh-huh, have you taken any courses in data processing?

M: No.

W: Oh, well, **data processing is a course you have to take before you can take computer programming.**（20）

M: Oh, I see. Well, when is it given? I hope it's not on Thursdays.

W: **Well, there's a class that meets on Monday evenings at 7:00.**（21）

M: Just once a week?

W: Yes, but that's almost 3 hours from 7:00 to 9:45.

M: Oh, well, that's alright. I could manage that. How many weeks does the course last?

W: En...Let me see. **12 weeks.**（21）You start the first week in September, and finish... oh, just before Christmas, December 21st.

M: And how much is the course?

W: That's 300 dollars including the necessary computer time.

M: Uh-huh, OK, en...where do I go to register?

W: Registration is on the second and third of September, between 6:00 and 9:00 in Frost Hall.

M: Is that the round building behind the parking lot?

W: Yes. That's the one.

M: Oh, I know how to get there. **Is there anything that I should bring with me?**（22）

W: No, just your check book.

M: Well, thank you so much.

W: You're very welcome. Bye.

M: Bye.

Questions 19 to 22 are based on the conversation you have just heard.

19. Why does the man choose to take an evening course?

正确答案：C

试题解析：根据长对话"开头必考"原则，开头提到：it would have to be an evening course, since I work during the day（我白天上班，所以只能选晚上的课程），故选C"他白天必须上班"。注意：since经常引出原因，为出题点之一。

20. What does the man have to do before taking the course of computer programming?

正确答案：B

试题解析：根据长对话"听到什么选什么"原则，原文提到：data processing is a course you have to take before you can take computer programmin（在你学习电脑编程之前，必须先学习数据处理课程），故选B"学习数据处理"。

21. What do we learn about the schedule of the evening course?

正确答案：C

试题解析：根据长对话"听到什么选什么"原则，原文提到：there's a class that meets on Monday evenings at 7:00（有一个班每周一晚上七点上课），后文又提到课程会持续12 weeks（12周），故选C"每周一，连续12周"。

22. What does the man want to know at the end of the conversation?

正确答案：A

试题解析：根据长对话"结尾必考"原则，结尾提到：Is there anything that I should bring with me?（我需要带些什么吗？），故选A"注册时带什么"。

Conversation Two(工作场景)

本对话共五个回合，对话中的男士是一位金融市场从业人员。对话中的人就其工作压力展开了讨论。

W: **So why exactly does your job have a reputation for being stressful?(23)**

M: Stress is generally driven by the feeling of being out of control of a situation, and a feeling of a situation controlling you. **Trading in financial markets combines both.(23)**

W: How do you relax in the evening?

M: I very rarely do anything work-related. So it's easy to escape the markets. I generally go to the gym or go for a run, especially if I've had a bad day. **I always**

cook a meal, rather than have a take-away, to do something my brain would regard as creative.(24)

W: Do you think what you do to relax is an effective way to beat stress?

M: I don't think there's a specific rule about how to beat stress. I generally find that what I do is effective for me.

W: Would you consider changing your job because of the high-stress factor?

W: I have considered leaving my job due to stress-related factors. **However, I do think that an element of stress is a good thing,**(25) and if used the right way, can actually be a positive thing.

W: What do you enjoy about the stressful aspects of your job?

M: Having said all that, I do actually enjoy an element of uncertainty. I enjoy a mental challenge. Trading generates a wide range of emotions second by second. How you deal with and manage those emotions dictates short, medium, and long term trading performance and success.

Questions 23 to 25 are based on the conversation you have just heard.

23. What is the man's job?

正确答案：D

试题解析：根据长对话"开头必考"原则，开头女士问So why exactly does your job have a reputation for being stressful?（为什么你的工作被认为压力很大？），男士回答Trading in financial markets combines both.（金融市场中，这两方面的压力都有），故选D"金融交易员"。

24. Why does the man prefer to cook a meal rather than have a take-away?

正确答案：B

试题解析：根据长对话"听到什么选什么"原则，原文提到：I always cook a meal, rather than have a take-away, to do something my brain would regard as creative.（我总是自己做饭，而不是叫外卖，去做一些我认为有创意的事情），故选B"他认为做饭有创意"。

25. What does the man say about an element of stress in his job?

正确答案：D

试题解析：根据长对话"结尾必考"原则，结尾提到：However, I do think that an element of stress is a good thing（然而，我认为有一点压力是件好事），故选

D"它是件好事"。注意：however, but等强转折之后的内容极易成为出题点，应特别关注。

Section B

Passage One(科普类：外星生命)

本文介绍了木星的一颗卫星上可能存在生命的一些科研情况。出题工整：开头一题，中间一题，结尾一题，在开头和结尾两次出现了until recently这一重要考点。

Since early times, people have been fascinated with the idea of life existing somewhere else besides earth. **Until recently, scientists believed that life on other planets was just a hopeful dream.**(26) But now they are beginning to locate places where life could form. In 1997, they saw evidence of planets near other stars like the sun. But scientists now think that life could be even nearer in our own solar system. One place scientists are studying very closely is Europa, a moon of Jupiter. **Space probes have provided evidence that Europa has a large ocean under its surface.** (27) The probes have also made scientists think that under its surface Europa has a rocky core giving off volcanic heat. Water and heat from volcanic activity are two basic conditions needed for life to form. A third is certain basic chemicals such as carbon, oxygen and nitrogen. Scientists believe there might be such chemicals lying at the bottom of Europa's ocean. They may have already created life or may be about to. You may wonder if light is also needed for life to form. **Until recently, scientists thought that light was essential.** (28) But now, places have been found on earth that are in total blackness such as caves several miles beneath the surface. And bacteria, primitive forms of life, have been seen there. So the lack of light in Europa's sub-surface ocean doesn't automatically rule out life forming.

Questions 26 to 28 are based on the passage you have just heard.

26. What did scientists once believe according to the passage?

正确答案：C

试题解析：根据"重视开头"原则，开头提到：Until recently, scientists believed that life on other planets was just a hopeful dream.(直到近来，科学家一直认为其他行星上的生命只是一个充满希望的梦)，故选C "外太空不可能存在生命"。注意：时间副词until recently后面一般都是对之前情况的回顾，暗示最近情况发生了变化。本文中两次出题考查，需要引起高度重视。

27. What have scientists found about Europa, a moon of Jupiter?

正确答案：C

试题解析：根据"听到什么选什么"原则，原文提到：Space probes have provided evidence that Europa has a large ocean under its surface.（太空探测卫星已经找到了Europa地表下存在一个巨大海洋的证据），故选C"它的地表下存在巨大海洋"。

28. What have scientists come to know recently about the formation of life?

正确答案：A

试题解析：根据"关注结尾"原则，结尾提到：Until recently, scientists thought that light was essential.（直到近来，科学家一直认为光对于生命的形成非常重要）。until recently再次暗示科学家现在不这样认为了，故选A"光并非生命形成的重要因素"。

Passage Two（故事类：看病）

　　本文讲述了一位医生发现书面指示比口头指示更准确的故事。出题工整：开头一题，中间一题，结尾一题，分别考查了开头、中间和because三个考点。

　　In her early days as an emergency room physician, Doctor Joanna Myer treated a child who had suffered a second degree burn. After the child had been treated and was being prepared for discharge, Doctor Myer talked to the parents about how they should care for the child at home. Also listening to her were a half a dozen other family members. A few hours later, when she came to say goodbye, **the family asked her to settle an argument they'd been having over exactly what advice she had given.** （**29**）"As I talked to them, I was amazed." she said, "All of them had heard the simple instructions I had given just a few hours before, but they had three or four different versions. The most basic details were unclear and confusing. I was surprised, because these were intelligent people." This episode gave Doctor Myer her first clue to something every doctor learns sooner or later—most people just don't listen very well. Nowadays, she says, she repeats her instructions, and even conducts a reality check with some patients. **She asks them to tell her what they think they are supposed to do.** （**30**）She also provides take-home sheets which are computer print-outs tailored to the patients' situation. Dr. Myer's listeners arc not unusual. Whcn new or difficult material is presented, almost all listeners are faced with the challenge **because human speech lacks the stability and permanence of the printed word.（31）** Oral communication is fast-moving and impermanent.

Questions 29 to 31 are based on the passage you have just heard.

29. What did the child's family members argue about in the hospital?

正确答案：B

试题解析：根据"重视开头"原则，开头提到：the family asked her to settle an argument they'd been having over exactly what advice she had given（关于她刚刚给出的建议，这家人有个争论请她解决），故选B"Myer医生的指示究竟是什么"。注意：over之后经常引出某种活动的内容。

30. What does Dr. Myer do to ensure her patients understand her instructions?

正确答案：D

试题解析：根据"听到什么选什么"原则，原文提到：She asks them to tell her what they think they are supposed to do.（她请他们说出他们认为自己应该做什么），故选D"她请他们复述应该做的事情"。

31. What does the speaker say about human speech?

正确答案：A

试题解析：根据"关注结尾"原则，结尾提到：because human speech lacks the stability and permanence of the printed word（因为人们的谈话缺少书面文字所具有的稳定性与持久性），故选A "它缺乏书面文字的稳定性"。注意：because, since, as, for, in that等引导原因的连词之后经常出现考点，需要特别关注。

Passage Three(管理类：员工激励)

本文介绍了激励员工的一些方法，出题工整：开头一题，中间两题，结尾一题，分别考查了in contrast, however, but和比较结构四个考点。

It is logical to suppose that things like good labor relations, good working conditions, good wages and benefits, and job security motivate workers, but one expert, Frederick Hertzberg argued that such conditions do not motivate workers. They are merely satisfiers. **Motivators, in contrast, include things such as having a challenging and interesting job, recognition and responsibility.（32）However, even** with the development of computers and robotics, there're always plenty of boring, repetitive and mechanical jobs, and lots of unskilled people who have to do them. （33）So how do mangers motivate people in such jobs? **One solution is to give them some responsibilities, not as individuals, but as part of a team.**（34）For example, some supermarkets combine office staff, the people who fill the shelves, and the people who work at the check-out into a team, and let them decide what product lines to stock, how to display them and so on. Many people now talk about the importance of a company's shared values or culture with which all the staff can identify, for example, being the best hotel chain, or making the best, the most user-friendly or the most reliable products in a particular field. **Such values are more likely to motivate workers than financial targets which ultimately only concern a few people.**（34）Unfortunately, there is only a limited number of such goals to go around. And by definition, not all the competing companies in an industry can seriously claim to be the best.

Questions 32 to 35 are based on the passage you have just heard.

32. What can actually motivate workers according to Frederick Hertzberg?

    正确答案：C

    试题解析：根据"重视开头"原则，开头提到：Motivators, in contrast, include things such as having a challenging and interesting job, recognition and responsibility.（相反，激励因素包括诸如拥有一个富有挑战性而且有趣的工作、认可及责任），故选C "有挑战性的工作"。注意：in contrast, by contrast, but, however等强转折连词之后极易出现考点，需引起特别关注，以下两题分别考查了however和but考点。

33. What does the speaker say about jobs in the computer era?

    正确答案：A

    试题解析：根据"听到什么选什么"原则，原文提到：However, even with the development of computers and robotics, there're always plenty of boring, repetitive and mechanical jobs, and lots of unskilled people who have to do them.（然而，即使随着电脑和机器人技术的发展，仍然有很多枯燥、重复、机械的工作，以及很多做这些工作的没有技术的工人），故选A "很多沉闷的工作仍需人工来做）。

34. What do some supermarkets do to motivate their employees?

正确答案：D

试题解析：根据"听到什么选什么"原则，原文提到：One solution is to give them some responsibilities, not as individuals, but as part of a team.（一种解决方法就是赋予他们一些责任，不是作为个体，而是作为团队的一部分），故选D"作为团队的一部分，给他们一些责任"。

35. Why does the speaker say financial targets are less likely to motivate workers?

正确答案：B

试题解析：根据"关注结尾"原则，结尾提到：Such values are more likely to motivate workers than financial targets which ultimately only concern a few people.（这些价值比经济指标更有可能激励员工，后者最终只与少数人相关），故选B"它们只涉及少数人"。注意：than, as...as 等比较结构也是四级听力经常考查的考点之一。

Section C

36. classified   37. background

38. album   39. appreciation

40. context   41. implies

42. image   43. instruments

44. Descriptive writing in the humanities, particularly in literature, is often mixed with critical writing

45. It tells the reader how to do something, for example, explaining the technique used to shoot a film

46. Authors may actually use more than one type of technique in a given piece of informational writing

第三节 强 化 训 练

强化训练一

Section A

Directions: *In this section, you will hear 8 short conversations and 2 long conversations. At the end of each conversation, one or more questions will be asked about what was said. Both the conversation and the questions will be spoken only once. After each question there will be a pause. During the pause, you must read the four choices marked* [A], [B], [C] *and* [D], *and decide which is the best answer. Then mark the corresponding letter on* **Answer Sheet 2** *with a single line through the centre.*

11. [A] If he can help her fill out a job application.

　　[B] If he can introduce her to the campus counselor.

　　[C] If he knows of any job openings with his former employer.

　　[D] If he'll be returning to the campus where he worked last year.

12. [A] The doctor is not available until late the next morning.

　　[B] If the man wants the best doctor he should try Dr. Noon.

　　[C] If the man wants a suitable doctor he should wait until 12 o'clock.

　　[D] The doctor who usually handles these things is not in the mornings.

13. [A] He will allow the woman to miss the class.

　　[B] He will reconsider the woman's excuse.

　　[C] He suggests that the student try to reschedule the operation.

　　[D] He won't let the students leave unless they have medical excuses.

14. [A] Ask Johnson one more time.

　　[B] Ask Johnson to extend the deadline.

　　[C] Ask Johnson to clarify the submission date.

　　[D] Ask Johnson to spend more time explain.

15. [A] Dave will never listen.　　　　　[C] She thinks Dave is insane.

　　[B] She doesn't know Dave.　　　　 [D] She thinks Dave will listen one day.

16. [A] At a tailor's.   [C] At a photographer's.

    [B] At a butcher's.   [D] At a hairdresser's.

17. [A] She didn't go to the game.

    [B] She also left the game before it was over.

    [C] She's also curious about who won the game.

    [D] She was sitting right behind the man at the game.

18. [A] His suit is too old to wear.

    [B] He is just looking forward to a new suit.

    [C] Both of them need to buy new clothes.

    [D] He doesn't want to buy new clothes.

Questions 19 to 21 are based on the conversation you have just heard.

19. [A] More work as an instructor.   [C] A longer vacation period.

    [B] A higher salary.   [D] A research assignment.

20. [A] He'll start next week.   [C] He would like time to decide.

    [B] He wouldn't enjoy it.   [D] He wants his advisor's opinion.

21. [A] Tom's talent for teaching.

    [B] Tom's interesting approach to research.

    [C] A present he received for graduation.

    [D] A congratulatory letter from the department.

Questions 22 to 25 are based on the conversation you have just heard.

22. [A] She wants him to recommend books.

    [B] She wants to apply to graduate schools.

    [C] She wants to take an advanced course.

    [D] She wants him to give her a good grade.

23. [A] He does not intend to offer the course.

    [B] He does not think the course will interest her.

    [C] He never accepts undergraduates in his course.

    [D] He thinks the course will be too difficult for her.

24. [A] She is unusually prepared.

    [B] She wants to take an easy course.

    [C] She needs additional credits in the subject.

    [D] She wants to read a book in this field.

25. ［A］Pick out some books for her.

　　［B］Tutor her himself.

　　［C］Let her enroll in an easier course.

　　［D］Ask another professor for his opinion.

Section B

Directions: *In this section, you will hear 3 short passages. At the end of each passage, you will hear some questions. Both the passage and the questions will be spoken only once. After you hear a question, you must choose the best answer from the four choices marked ［A］, ［B］, ［C］ and ［D］. Then mark the corresponding letter on **Answer Sheet 2** with a single line through the centre.*

Passage One

Questions 26 to 28 are based on the passage you have just heard.

26. ［A］He was a friend of Bernstein's.　　［C］He won a contest.

　　［B］His family vacationed there.　　［D］He went to college nearby.

27. ［A］The audience might get wet.　　［C］The lawn is usually very crowded.

　　［B］The setting isn't very pretty.　　［D］It is very noisy outside.

28. ［A］It has been going on for a long time.　［C］All the seats are indoors.

　　［B］It is not well-known.　　［D］It is held in Boston.

Passage Two

Questions 29 to 32 are based on the passage you have just heard.

29. ［A］The role of the print media.

　　［B］Television's effect on the movie industry.

　　［C］The relations between different media.

　　［D］Radio news as a substitute for newspaper.

30. ［A］Many newspaper reporters also work in the radio industry.

　　［B］Radio is a substitute for newspaper in people's homes.

　　［C］Newspapers discourage people from listening to the radio.

　　［D］People who listen to the radio also buy newspapers.

31. ［A］The number of movie goers declined.

　　［B］Television had no effect on movie attendance.

[C] Old motion pictures were often broadcast on television.

[D] Movie attendance increased due to advertising on TV.

32. [A] To provide an example of something motion pictures can't present.

[B] To illustrate another effect of television.

[C] To demonstrate the importance of televised sports.

[D] To explain why television replaced radio broadcasting.

Passage Three

Questions 33 to 35 are based on the passage you have just heard.

33. [A] To convince local merchants to hire college students.

[B] To inform students of a university program.

[C] To recruit counselors to work in the placement office.

[D] To interest students in a career in counseling.

34. [A] Their salary requirements.　　　　[C] A resume.

[B] A permission.　　　　　　　　　[D] A job.

35. [A] Write cover letters.　　　　　　　[C] Arrange their work schedules.

[B] Select appropriate courses.　　　[D] Refine their interviewing techniques.

Section C

Directions: *In this section, you will hear a passage three times. When the passage is read for the first time, you should listen carefully for its general idea. When the passage is read for the second time, you are required to fill in the blanks numbered from 36 to 43 with the exact words you have just heard. For blanks numbered from 44 to 46 you are required to fill in the missing information. For these blanks, you can either use the exact words you have just heard or write down the main points in your own words. Finally, when the passage is read for the third time, you should check what you have written.*

The last heart-pounding race of the Summer Olympics ended Sunday in a white marble arena in the heart of Athens. That brings the modern Olympics a full circle—back to the precise spot where they were (36)_____ 108 years ago.

These games broke many records. Athens hosted 11,099 athletes, the largest number ever and also the most women athletes ever. (37)_____ of 202 countries and areas took part, more than any other sporting event. The Olympic Games traveled for the first time to all (38)_____ . Shot Put was held in Olympia and women competed there for the first time. It also（39）_____ records as the most expensive and most fortified international sporting event ever（40）_____.

In the 2004 Athens Games, the runners, jumpers and（41）_____ may not have set world records, but at least they outdid their（42）_____ predecessors. For only the second time since 1988, the average gold-medal（43）_____ in track and field improved, though slightly.（44）_____

_____. The improvements offer comfort to both sides in a scientific debate over the recent stagnation of Olympic performances and world records.

（45）_____.

China's Liu Xiang became the first Asian in history to win the men's 110m hurdles at the Olympic Games.（46）_____

_____.

试题详解

11. C 求职场景

选项分析：A、B、C选项表明对话可能与女士请求男士帮助找工作相关，D仅是男士的个人情况，与其他选项明显不同，故排除。

听音重点：女士的话。

听力原文：M: I heard you were thinking of **applying for a job** as a campus counselor.

W: **Yeah.** Do you know if they need anyone at that place where you worked last summer?

Q: What does the woman ask the man?

12. C 看病场景

选项分析：A、C、D均与见到某位医生的时间相关，只有B未涉及，故排除B。

听音重点：12 o'clock同义替换noon。D为强干扰项，对话中的She's usually not in so early，表示医生常晚到，而D表示整个上午均不在。

听力原文：M: Hello, can you tell me which doctor might be suitable for my problem?

W: Dr. Renfrew's the one you need. **But she's usually not in so early. How about noon?**

Q: What does the woman mean?

13. A 请假场景

选项分析：选项表明对话可能与请假有关。C不符合常理，故排除。根据原文"看病是我允许请假的少数例外之一"，可知除了看病之外，教授还允许使用其他理由请假，故排除选项D"除非学生们以看病为理由，否则教授不许请假"。

听音重点：medical excuses包含foot surgery。

听力原文：W: Prof. Smith, I know your course has a "no absence" policy. But I have to have **foot surgery** next Friday and can't be here.

M: **Medical excuses** are one of the few exceptions I make.

Q: What does Prof. Smith mean?

14. B 论文场景

选项分析：B、C、D中的deadline（最后期限）、date（日期）、more time（更多时间）均属时间范畴，而A中的one more time 指"再一次"，与其他选项明显不同，故排除A。

听音重点：ask Johnson to extend the deadline同义替换ask him for more time。

听力原文：M: About my section of **report**, it's unlikely I can e-mail it over to you by Monday. This class of Johnson just kills me.

W: Well, **we could ask him for more time.**

Q: What does the woman suggest they do?

15. A 建议场景

选项分析：选项中的she, thinks, Dave表明本题考查女士对Dave的看法，因此女士不可能不认识Dave，故排除B。

听音重点：由女士对话可知，Dave不听任何人的话，故选A。insane意为"精神失常的，疯狂的"，one day意为"总有一天"，表将来。

听力原文：M: Why don't you suggest to Dave that he at least improve his habits for showing up late to class?

W: **When do you think he'll listen to someone?**

Q: What does the woman imply?

16. D 理发场景

选项分析：选项表明考查对话发生地点。

听音重点：the same cut, a bit longer over the ears and in the back.

听力原文：M: Do you want the same **cut** as last time?

W: **The same on top**, but I'd like it **a bit longer over the ears and in the back.**

Q: Where does this conversation probably take place?

17. B 比赛场景

选项分析：选项中的go to, left, won, at the game表明对话与看比赛或比赛的结果相关。

听音重点：I was just a few minutes behind you.

听力原文：M: You know I had to leave the basketball game halfway through last night, so I never found out who won.

W: Well, don't look at me. **I was just a few minutes behind you.**

Q: What does the woman mean?

18. D 购物场景

选项分析：选项中的suit, buy, clothes表明对话与买衣服相关, A未提及买衣服, 故排除。

听音重点：通过You know how I feel about shopping可知, 男士不想购物。

听力原文：W: I'm thinking of getting a new pantsuit to wear to James' wedding.

M: I just hope that my old suit still fits. **You know how I feel about shopping.**

Q: What does the man imply?

Conversation One(兼职场景)

M: Hello, Professor Miller. You wanted to see me?

W: Oh yes, Tom. Thanks for coming. It's about your work as a teaching assistant. I've just read your evaluations, the ones the students filled out towards the end of the semester.

M: Yes? Well, how were they?

W: Would you like to take a look? Out of a possible score of five, you got a four-point-eight. That's very high, Tom.

M: Well, what a pleasant surprise!

W: When we see such a high score, we generally try to keep the T.A. on a little longer and perhaps even ask them to cover more classes. What do you say, Tom? **Would you like to handle a double load in the fall?** (**19**)

M: I'm sure I would, but I don't know if I can. Next fall will be my last semester of coursework for my master's and I'll be very busy doing research on my thesis. **Could I have a few days to think about it?** (**20**)

W: Certainly. I wouldn't want you to fall behind in your coursework, but **I do think you should consider getting more experience in the classroom. You seem to have a real gift.** (**21**)

M: Thanks for the compliment, Professor.

W: Let me know by the beginning of next week, will you?

M: Sure. I'll drop by again on Monday or Tuesday.

Questions 19 to 21 are based on the conversation you have just heard.

19. What does Professor Miller offer Tom?

正确答案: A

选项分析: 选项A为"作为讲师的更多工作",选项D为"一个研究任务",两项均与工作有关,意思相近,故其一可能为正确答案。

听音重点: 根据原文Would you like to handle a double load in the fall,女士建议Tom在秋季从事更多的助教工作。

20. What's Tom's answer to Professor Miller's offer?

正确答案: C

选项分析: 选项C为"他需要时间来作决定",选项D为"他需要导师的意见",两项均与作决定相关,故其一可能为正确答案。

听音重点: 根据原文Could I have a few days to think about it,可知他需要几天时间考虑。

21. What is the gift the professor refers to?

正确答案: A

选项分析: 选项A为"汤姆教学的才能",选项B为"汤姆进行研究的有趣方法",两项均与工作有关,故其一可能为正确答案。

听音重点: 根据原文I do think you should consider getting more experience in the classroom. You seem to have a real gift,可知教授认为Tom拥有教学的才能。

Conversation Two（选课场景）

M: Come in, come in! What can I do for you?

W: Professor Donner, are you giving your Advanced Geology course again next semester?

M: Yes, I'm planning on it.

W: **I wonder if I could enroll in it. I know it's a graduate course and I'm only a junior, but...**（22）

M: Aren't you a bit young? **I've allowed qualified seniors to take the course and they usually have a hard time keeping up.**（23）

W: I know, but the geology of the American West is my major interest and **I've done a lot of reading in the field.**（24）Last semester I took Prof. Burma's course and I didn't find it nearly challenging enough.

M: I see. You certainly aren't one of those students who are out for easy grades.

W: I would say not. I really want to learn something.

M: **Well, I'll speak to Prof. Burma. If he thinks you're ready, I'll let you enroll.**（25）

W: Oh, thank you, Professor Donner. It's really very nice of you.

Questions 22 to 25 are based on the conversation you have just heard.

22. Why does the woman talk to the professor?

正确答案：C

选项分析：四个选项句子结构相同，可知女士希望教授做某事，选项D与常理不符，故排除。

听音重点：根据原文I wonder if I could enroll in it. I know it's a graduate course and I'm only a junior，but...，可知女士希望参加一门高级课程。

23. What is the professor's first reply to the woman's request?

正确答案：D

选项分析：选项B为"他认为这门课程不会使她有兴趣"，选项D为"他认为这门课程对她来说太难"，两项均说明课程不适合她，故其一可能为正确答案。

听音重点：根据原文I've allowed qualified seniors to take the course and they usually have a hard time keeping up，可知教授认为这门课程很难。

24. What does the woman say to persuade the professor to help her?

正确答案：A

选项分析：选项B与四级听力积极向上的原则不符，故排除。

听音重点：根据原文I've done a lot of reading in the field，可知女士认为自己准备得很充分。

25. What does the professor promise to do?

正确答案：D

选项分析：选项C为"让她学习一门更容易的课程"，与其他三选项明显不同，故排除。

听音重点：根据原文I'll speak to Prof. Burma. If he thinks you're ready, I'll let you enroll，可知教授准备征求另一位教授的意见。

Section B

Passage One(大学经历)

　　本文叙述了一位音乐教授读大学时参加音乐节的回忆，描述了当时音乐节的盛况以及该音乐节产生和发展的历程。

　　When I was in college, I won a music competition and the prize was a week at the Tangle wood Music Festival.(26) Anyway it is one of the world's most famous music festivals and the summer home of Boston Symphony Orchestra. This is located in the beautiful hills in New England. The summer musical season consists of about fifty concerts given over about nine weeks: from July 1st to the first week in September. The biggest stars on the music scene appear here. The year I went I was lucky enough to see Bernstein conducting. I know it is sometimes hard to get tickets but, of course, mine were a part of the prize. If you want to sit inside, the tickets are expensive. It's much cheaper to sit outside on the lawn. **But it might rain, or some nights are really cool even in the summer.**(27) Either way the sound system is excellent. So it doesn't matter where you sit. **I seem to recall that the festival got started in the 1930s.** Some residents invited a band to perform a few outdoor concerts. The concerts were so successful that after a couple of years, somebody donated a house as permanent home. **After that, things really took off. And the festival has gotten bigger and better every year.**(28) Attending was such a wonderful experience. I'd love to be able to go again.

Questions 26 to 28 are based on the passage you have just heard.

26. Why did the speaker go to Tangle wood?

四级短文听力的第一题通常考查开头，根据首句"读大学时，我赢得了一场音乐比赛，所获的奖励是参与Tangle wood音乐节一周"，故选C"他赢得了一场比赛"。

27. According to the speaker, what is the disadvantage of sitting on the lawn?

根据四级短文听力"听到什么选什么"的原则，原文为"但是可能会下雨，而且有些夏日的夜晚也很凉"，故选A"观众可能被淋湿"。

28. What does the speaker imply about the festival?

四级短文听力的最后一题一般考查段落结尾，根据倒数第二、三句"后来，一切取得了飞速发展。这个音乐节逐年发展壮大、越办越好"，故选A。

Passage Two(媒体关系)

本文介绍了随着广播的流行，报业所面临的挑战和机遇，并说明了不同的媒体之间是如何相互影响的。

With the introduction of radio, newspaper publishers wondered how broadcasting would affect them.(29) Many feared that radio as a quick and easy means of keeping people informed would replace the newspaper industry altogether. Others hoped that the brief newscast heard on the air would stimulate listeners' interests in the story so they'd buy the paper to get more information. This second idea turned out to be closer to the truth. Radio and print were not substitutes for each other but actually supported each other. **You can see the relationship between different media is not always one of displacement but can be one of reinforcement.(30)** However, this is not always the case. Take television and motion pictures for example, with the popularization of TV, the motion picture industry suffered greatly. **Movie attendance dropped when the audience chose to stay at home and be entertained.(31) Likewise, when a football game was shown on the air, the stands were often empty because fans chose to watch the game at home.(32)**

Question 29 to 32 are based on the passage you have just heard.

29. What is the main topic of the talk?

根据"重视开头"原则，首句为"随着广播的引入，报纸发行者需要了解广播将如何影响他们"，故选C"不同媒体之间的关系"。

30. According to the speaker, what is the relationship between radio and the newspaper industry?

根据"听到什么选什么"原则，原文提到"可以看出，不同媒体之间并非总是替代关系，而可以相互增援"，故选D"听广播的人也买报纸"。

31. According to the speaker, how did the introduction of television affect motion pictures?

根据"听到什么选什么"原则，原文为"当观众选择待在家里享受娱乐时，电影院的观众就减少了"，故选A"去电影院看电影的人少了"。

32. Why does the speaker mention a football game?

根据"关注结尾"原则，尾句为"同样，当电视上转播一场足球赛时，由于球迷选择在家观看比赛，看台上常常空着"，故选B "举例说明电视的另一种影响"。

Passage Three（工作介绍）

本文是大学就业服务处一位教师的讲话，他向学生们介绍了可以选择兼职工作的具体情况及注意事项。

As a result of rising university cost, many students are finding it necessary to take on part-time jobs. **To make finding those jobs easier, the placement services put together a listing of what is available.**（33）For some students, these part-time jobs could lead to full-time work after graduation as they may offer experience in their own fields, such as finance, marketing or even management. For example, National Saving Bank offers work on a half-time basis: that's twenty hours a week. Shops and restaurants have positions requiring fewer hours, even less time as expected of those providing child care. We have a number of families registered with us who were looking for baby-sitters for as few as four hours a week. For students who prefer outdoor work, there are seasonal positions right on campus working on gardening. These often require the most time and are the least flexible in terms of scheduling. To see a complete list of these and other available jobs, including the salary offered and the hours required, stop by our office. **Oh, and be sure to bring a resume with you.**（34）When you find something that interests you, we'll put you in touch with the person offering it. **In addition, our counselors will give you advice on successful interviewing.**（35）

Questions 33 to 35 are based on the passage you have just heard.

33. What is the purpose of the speaker?

    正确答案：B

    选项分析：选项B、D意思相近，故其一可能为答案。

    听音重点：根据"重视开头"原则，第二句为"为了使学生更容易找工作，就业服务处列出了所有可用信息"，可见发言者的目的是通知学生们学校的一个项目，故选B。

34. What should students bring with them to the office?

    正确答案：C

    选项分析：选项D与常理不符，故排除。

    听音重点：根据"听到什么选什么"的原则，原文为be sure to bring a resume with you，即建议学生们带着简历，故选C。

35. What will the counselors at the office help students do?

    正确答案：D

    选项分析：选项A、D意思相近，故其一可能为正确答案。

    听音重点：根据"关注结尾"原则，尾句为"此外，我们的顾问还会为学生提供成功面试的建议"，故选D"改善面试技巧"。

Section C

36. revived   37. Representatives

38. continents   39. broke

40. staged   41. throwers

42. immediate   43. performance

44. Swimming times were also faster in Athens than in Sydney in 2000, but by an even slimmer margin than track performances

45. China finished second in the gold medal count, its best ever show since it started competing in the Olympics in 1984

46. His gold medal is said to be "the heaviest", or most significant, of the 32 that China won in the Athens Olympics

强化训练二

Section A

Directions: *In this section, you will hear 8 short conversations and 2 long conversations. At the end of each conversation, one or more questions will be asked about what was said. Both the conversation and the questions will be spoken only once. After each question there will be a pause. During the pause, you must read the four choices marked* [A], [B], [C] *and* [D], *and decide which is the best answer. Then mark the corresponding letter on **Answer Sheet 2** with a single line through the centre.*

11. [A] Ordering a typing machine.　　[C] Making an appointment.

　　[B] Sitting for a contest.　　[D] Applying for a secretary's post.

12. [A] Her project is due this Thursday.

　　[B] She needs to work on her project this Thursday.

　　[C] She doesn't like the trip.

　　[D] She needs to get an A in the class.

13. [A] The woman has decided to quit her job.

　　[B] Jobs are easier to find in the city.

　　[C] The woman works in the city.

　　[D] The woman lives in the suburbs.

14. [A] She was delayed.　　[C] She had a car accident.

　　[B] She had a bad cold.　　[D] She got home before 9 o'clock.

15. [A] He arrives at the subway station late.

　　[B] The subway is not on time.

　　[C] The subway left an hour ago.

　　[D] The woman keeps him from boarding the subway.

16. [A] Brother and sister.　　[C] Teacher and student.

　　[B] Doctor and patient.　　[D] Interviewer and interviewee.

17. [A] Someone else should make the introduction.

　　[B] Dan isn't a very good violinist.

　　[C] There will be other musicians to introduce.

　　[D] It's rather late to ask Dan to make the introduction now.

18. [A] He makes a fool of himself by eating too much.

   [B] He likes to eat something other than beef.

   [C] He wants to eat more roast beef.

   [D] He couldn't eat any more roast beef.

Questions 19 to 21 are based on the conversation you have just heard.

19. [A] On television.   [C] In class.

   [B] At registration.   [D] At work.

20. [A] It allows them to meet students from other universities.

   [B] It promotes the concept of self-learning.

   [C] It allows more flexibility in students' schedules.

   [D] It doesn't require any examinations.

21. [A] It's a requirement for psychology majors.

   [B] She wasn't able to get into the traditional course.

   [C] She lives far from the university.

   [D] She has to work a lot of hours this semester.

Questions 22 to 25 are based on the conversation you have just heard.

22. [A] In a library.   [C] In a bookstore.

   [B] In a school.   [D] In a publisher's office.

23. [A] A photograph.   [C] An old envelop.

   [B] An inscription.   [D] A list of prices.

24. [A] Talk to some politicians.   [C] Sell some of her books.

   [B] Sign her name in the book.   [D] Do some research.

25. [A] She might be wasting her time.

   [B] He can help her locate the name.

   [C] She had better get two poetry books instead.

   [D] She should wait and check the book out of the library.

Section B

Directions: *In this section, you will hear 3 short passages. At the end of each passage, you will hear some questions. Both the passage and the questions will be spoken only once. After you hear a question, you must choose the best answer from the four choices marked* [A], [B], [C] *and* [D]. *Then mark the corresponding letter on* **Answer Sheet 2** *with a single line through the centre.*

201

Passage One

Questions 26 to 28 are based on the passage you have just heard.

26. 〔A〕Keep vegetables fresher for a longer period.

　　〔B〕Grow crops in nontraditional climates.

　　〔C〕Transport produce more quickly.

　　〔D〕Produce larger vegetables.

27. 〔A〕To adjust the soil temperature.

　　〔B〕To bring nutrients to the soil.

　　〔C〕To provide air-conditioning.

　　〔D〕To transport water to higher elevations.

28. 〔A〕It's the main use for electricity in the United States.

　　〔B〕It's used to cool water used for irrigation.

　　〔C〕It's necessary for growing vegetables in hot climates.

　　〔D〕It's another possible use for sea water.

Passage Two

Questions 29 to 32 are based on the passage you have just heard.

29. 〔A〕The development of individual watches.

　　〔B〕The industrialization of the United States.

　　〔C〕How wrist watches are manufactured.

　　〔D〕Reasons for increased popularity.

30. 〔A〕They were not very accurate.

　　〔B〕People considered them essential.

　　〔C〕Only a few people had them.

　　〔D〕They were common in the United States, but not in Europe.

31. 〔A〕They were inexpensive.　　　　〔C〕It was important to be on time.

　　〔B〕It was fashionable to wear them.　〔D〕They were a sign of wealth.

32. 〔A〕Watches became less important because factories had clocks.

　　〔B〕The availability of watches increased.

　　〔C〕More clocks were manufactured than watches.

　　〔D〕Watches were of higher quality than ever before.

Passage Three

Questions 33 to 35 are based on the passage you have just heard.

33. [A] The advertising of a new product.

    [B] A new trend in the United States.

    [C] The role of supermarkets in the coffee business.

    [D] The coffee market in Boston.

34. [A] Gourmet coffee is grown in the United States.

    [B] Gourmet coffee tastes better.

    [C] Regular brands of coffee have too much caffeine.

    [D] Gourmet coffee is less expensive.

35. [A] They will lose some coffee business.

    [B] They will introduce new regular brands of coffee.

    [C] They will successfully compete with gourmet coffee sellers.

    [D] They will run out of coffee.

Section C

Directions: *In this section, you will hear a passage three times. When the passage is read for the first time, you should listen carefully for its general idea. When the passage is read for the second time, you are required to fill in the blanks numbered from 36 to 43 with the exact words you have just heard. For blanks numbered from 44 to 46 you are required to fill in the missing information. For these blanks, you can either use the exact words you have just heard or write down the main points in your own words. Finally, when the passage is read for the third time, you should check what you have written.*

Emily Dickinson is one of the greatest American (36)_____. She was born in a (37)_____ New England village in Massachusetts on December 10, 1830. She was the second child of the family. She died in the same house fifty-six years later. During her lifetime she never left her native land. She left her home state only once. She left her village very few times. And after 1872 she (38)_____ left her house and yard. In the last years of her life she (39)_____ to a smaller and smaller circle of family and friends. In those later years she dressed in white, avoided strangers, and communicated (40)_____ through notes and poems even with (41)_____. The

doctor who (42)_____ her illness was allowed to "examine" her in another room, seeing her walk by an open door. She was thought of as a "strange" figure in her home village. When she died on May 15, 1886, she was unknown to the rest of the world. Only seven of her poems had appeared in print. But to think Emily Dickinson only as a strange (43)_____ is a serious mistake. (44)_____
_____. According to Henry James, a famous American novelist, she was one of those on whom nothing was lost. Only by thus living could Dickinson manage (45)_____
_____. She read only a few books but knew them deeply. Her poems are simple but remarkably rich. (46)_____
_____.

试题详解

11. D 求职场景

选项分析：选项表明本题考查行为动作。

听音重点：通过resume, references, certificate, secretarial, typing可知对话内容为求职。

听力原文：W: I have got a **certificate** from a **secretarial** school, and I also won a medal at a **typing** contest.

M: OK, please leave your **references** and **resume** here, and I will give you a reply as soon as possible.

Q: What is the woman most probably doing?

12. B 作业场景

选项分析：由选项中的project, due(到期)可知本题考查作业。

听音重点：加强对but的敏感度。but后面一般表示对前面的否定。make it意为"成功做某事"。

听力原文：M: You should go on the trip on Thursday. We are going to see many different places.

W: **I originally planned to go, but** then my professor assigned this project due on Friday. I'm afraid that I won't be able to make it.

Q: What does the woman mean?

13. C 住房场景

选项分析：通过选项中的woman, work, live可知对话与女士的工作与住房有关。

听音重点：I would like to表示虚拟语气，but后表示对前面内容的否定。

听力原文：M: Have you decided where you are going to live when you get married?

W: **I would like to live in the city near my work, but** my husband wants a home in the suburbs to save on expenses.

Q: What can we infer from the conversation?

14. A 天气场景

选项分析：四个选项主语一致，其他信息分别为：耽误了、感冒、车祸和几点到家，可知某种不好的原因致使某事发生。

听音重点：If it hadn't been snowing so hard, ... 表示虚拟语气，指雪很大，导致迟到。

听力原文：W: **If it hadn't been snowing so hard, I might have been home** by 9 o'clock.

M: It's too bad you didn't make it. Jane was here and she wanted to see you.

Q: What happened to the woman?

15. B 交通场景

选项分析：各项中均含有subway（地铁），可见对话围绕地铁展开。

听音重点：I'm disgusted by / with...（对……厌烦）。

听力原文：M: **I'm disgusted by** the way the subway is running. I've been waiting for an hour.

W: Well, so have I. But I think the subway will be coming soon.

Q: What can we learn from the conversation?

16. C 作业场景

选项分析：选项表明考查人物关系。

听音重点：assignment, chapter, textbook, discuss。

听力原文：M: Could you please explain the **assignment** for Monday, Ms. Smith?

W: Certainly. Read the next **chapter** in your **textbook** and come to **class** prepared to **discuss** what you've read.

Q: What is the probable relationship between the two speakers?

17. A 演出场景

选项分析：选项中的violinist, musician表明对话与演出有关。

听音重点：He'll be playing the violin. 选项D暗示正在演奏，故不选。

听力原文：M: Let's ask Dan to introduce the **musicians** to the **audience** at the beginning of the **concert.**

W: Ask Dan? **He'll be playing the violin!**

Q: What does the woman mean?

18. D 饮食场景

选项分析：选项中的eat, roast beef表明对话与饮食有关。

听音重点：...but I've really had enough. 表示已经吃饱了，委婉拒绝。

听力原文：W: Please help yourself. Today's **roast beef** is very good. We've **ordered** enough for five people.

M: Thank you very much. The beef is really **delicious, but I've really had enough.**

Q: What does the man mean?

Conversation One（选课场景）

M: Hi, Lynn. **I saw you at registration yesterday.**（19）I sailed right through. But you were standing in a line.

W: Yeah, I waited an hour to sign up for a distance learning course.

M: Distance learning? Never heard of it.

W: Well, it's new this semester. It's only open to psychology majors. But I bet it'll catch on else where. Yesterday over a hundred students signed up.

M: Well, what is it?

W: It's an experimental course. I registered for Child Psychology. All I have to do is to watch a twelve-week series of televised lessons. The department shows them several different times a day and in several different locations.

M: Don't you ever have to meet with your professor?

W: Yeah. After each part of the series, I have to talk to her and the other students on the phone, you know, about our ideas. Then we'll meet on campus three times for reviews and exams.

M: It sounds pretty non-traditional to me. But I guess it makes sense considering how

many students have jobs. **It must really help with their schedules.**（20）Not to
mention how it'll cut down on traffic.

W: You know, last year my department did a survey and they found out that 80% of
all psychology majors were employed. That's why they came up with the program.
**Look, I'll be working three days a week next semester and it was either cut
back on my classes or try this out.**（21）

M: The only thing is, doesn't it seem impersonal though? I mean, I miss having class
discussions and hearing what other people think.

W: Well, I guess that's why phone contacts are important. Anyway it's an experiment.
Maybe I'll end up hating it.

M: Maybe. But I'll be curious to see how it works out.

Questions 19 to 21 are based on the conversation you have just heard.

19. Where did the man see the woman yesterday?

正确答案：B

选项分析：选项B为"在报到处"，选项C为"在教室"，二者均为校园场景，其
一可能为正确答案。

听音重点：根据原文I saw you at registration yesterday, 可知男士见到女士的地
点是报到处。

20. What did the speakers agree is the major advantage of the distance learning course?

正确答案：C

选项分析：选项A、C结构相近，其一可能为正确答案。

听音重点：根据原文It must really help with their schedules, 可知远程教学使课
程安排更加灵活。

21. Why did the woman decide to enroll in the distance learning course?

正确答案：D

选项分析：选项B、C、D结构相近，其一可能为正确答案。

听音重点：根据原文Look, I'll be working three days a week next semester and it
was either cut back on my classes or try this out, 可知女士本学期不
得不工作很长时间。

Conversation Two(书店场景)

W: **I enjoy going through secondhand bookstores, don't you?**(**22**) It's interesting to see what people used to enjoy reading. Did you see this old book of children's stories?

M: Some of these books aren't so old, though. See. This mystery was published only six years ago. It cost seventy-five cents. You can't beat that.

W: Hey! Look at this!

M: What? Are you getting interested in nineteenth-century poetry all of a sudden?

W: No. **Look at the inscription.**(**23**) Someone gave this book as a present and wrote a note on the inside of the front cover. It's dated 1893. Maybe it's worth something.

M: Everything on that shelf is worth fifty cents.

W: But if this is the signature of someone who is well-known, it might bring a lot more. I hear William Shakespeare's signature is worth about a million dollars.

M: Oh? I can hardly read what that one says. Who wrote it?

W: The name looks like "Harold Dobson". Maybe "Dobbins"? Wasn't he a politician or something? **I'm going to buy this book and see if I can find a name like that in the library.**(**24**)

M: **Good luck. Your poetry book may make you rich, but I'll bet my seventy-five-cent mystery is a better buy.**(**25**)

Questions 22 to 25 are based on the conversation you have just heard.

22. Where is this conversation taking place?

正确答案: C

选项分析: 选项C为"在书店", 选项D为"在一家出版社办公室", 意思相近, 其一可能为正确答案。

听音重点: 根据原文 I enjoy going through secondhand bookstores, don't you, 可知对话发生在书店。

23. What did the woman find in her book?

正确答案: B

选项分析: 选项均为物体, 选项A"一张照片"和选项B"一幅题字"意思相近, 其一可能为正确答案。

听音重点: 根据原文 Look at the inscription, 可知为题字。

24. What does the woman intend to do later on?

正确答案：D

选项分析：选项A为"和一些政客交谈"，与对话主题明显不符，故排除。

听音重点：根据原文I'm going to buy this book and see if I can find a name like that in the library，可知女士打算进行一些调查研究。

25. What does the man think of the woman's plan?

正确答案：A

选项分析：选项A为"她可能在浪费时间"，选项B为"他能帮她查找姓名"，二者意思相反，其一可能为答案。

听音重点：根据原文Good luck. Your poetry book may make you rich，but I'll bet my seventy-five-cent mystery is a better buy，可知男士认为女士可能在浪费时间。

Section B

Passage One(科普知识：农业技术)

本文介绍了在热带地区使用新技术种植温带蔬菜的情况，并以夏威夷的农业工程师使用冰冷的海水浇灌温带植物为例。文章最后还提到了使用冰冷的海水为楼宇降温。

Did you know that vegetables can be tricked into growing in the climates they are not used to?(26) Cool climate vegetables are now able to be grown in places as hot as Hawaii. In Hawaii, engineers have been able to convince such vegetables that they are living in cooler climate. That way they grow faster and taste better. What these engineers have been using is cold sea water. How did they use it? **They place pipes in the soil and cold water flowed through them cooling the earth.**(27) This helps plant growth and enables gardeners in hot climates to grow crops from cooler climates. Also some of the pipes are exposed to the air and thus irrigate the gardens. What is special about this process is that nothing damaging to the natural environment is used. **Another use for cold sea water is to cool buildings. People believe that, for example, the entire west coast of the United States could be air-conditioned using sea water.**(28)

Questions 26 to 28 are based on the passage you have just heard.

26. What does the new system enable farmers to do?

根据"重视开头"原则，首句为"你知道人们可以在不适宜的气候下种植蔬菜吗?"故选B"在非传统的气候中种植蔬菜"。

27. How were the pipes used in Hawaii?

根据"听到什么选什么"原则,原文为"他们在地下铺设管道,让冷海水流过管道,为土壤降温",故选A"调节土壤温度"。

28. Why does the speaker mention air-conditioning?

根据"关注结尾"原则,最后两句为"冷海水的另一用途是为楼宇降温。例如,人们认为使用海水可以为整个美国西海岸降温",故选D "这是海水的另一用途"。

Passage Two(钟表发展史)

本文介绍了19世纪末20世纪初钟表在美国和欧洲普及的历史。随着西方工业化进程的推进,人们开始关注时间的准确性,钟表走进了千家万户。

Watches and clocks seem as much part of our life as breathing or eating.(29) **And yet did you know that watches and clocks were scarce in the United States until the 1850s?**(30) In the late 1700s, people didn't know the exact time unless they were near a clock. Those delightful clocks in the squares of European towns were built for the public. After all, most citizens simply couldn't afford a personal time piece. **Well into the 1800s in Europe and United States, the main purpose of a watch with a gold chain, was to show others how wealthy you were.**(31) The word "wrist watch" didn't even enter the English language until nearly 1900s. By then the rapid pace of industrialization in the United States meant that measuring time had become essential. How could the factory worker get to work on time unless he or she knew exactly what time it was? Since the efficiency was now measured by how fast the job was done, everyone was interested in time. **And since industrialization made possible the manufacture of large quantities of goods, watches became fairly inexpensive.** (32) Furthermore, electric lights kept factories going around the clock. Being "on time" had entered the language and life of every citizen.

Questions 29 to 32 are based on the passages you have just heard.

29. What does the essay mainly discuss?

根据"重视开头"原则,首句为"手表和时钟似乎与呼吸和吃饭一样,是我们生活的一部分",结合后文,选A"个人手表的发展"。

30. What was true of watches before the 1850s?

根据"听到什么选什么"原则，第二句为"你知道手表和时钟在19世纪50年代前在美国都很稀有的吗？"，故选C"只有少数人拥有它们"。

31. According to the essay, why did some people wear watches in the 1800s?

根据"听到什么选什么"原则，原文为"到了19世纪初期的欧洲和美国，人们戴黄金链条的手表主要是为了显示自己如何富有"，故选D "它们是财富的象征"。

32. What effect did industrialization have on watch-making?

根据"关注结尾"原则，文章倒数第二句为"工业化使得大规模制造物品成为可能，所以手表变得相当便宜"，故选B"拥有手表的可能性增加了"。

Passage Three(新式咖啡)

　　本文介绍了美国近年来出现的一种新式咖啡的市场发展情况。由于新式咖啡的盛行，主要的咖啡商在波士顿展开了一场咖啡市场大战。文章最后预测了新式咖啡的发展前景。

　　A lot of people in the United States are coffee drinkers. Over the last few years, a trend has been developing to introduce special coffee called gourmet coffee into the American market. **Boston seems to have been the birthplace of this trend.** (33) In fact, major gourmet coffee merchants from other cities came to Boston where today they are in a kind of coffee war with Boston merchants. They are all competing for an important share of gourmet coffee market. Surprisingly, the competition among these businesses will not hurt any of them. Experts say that the gourmet coffee market in the United States is growing and will continue to grow to the point of eight million dollar market by 1999. **Studies have shown that gourmet coffee drinkers seldom go back to the regular brands in supermarkets since it tastes better.** (34) **As a result, these regular brands will be real losers in the competition.** (35)

Questions 33 to 35 are based on the passages you have just heard.

33. What is the main topic of this story?

根据"重视开头"原则，文章第三句为"波士顿似乎已经成为这种潮流的发源地"，故选B"美国的一种新潮流"。

34. What probably leads people to choose gourmet coffee over regular brands?

根据"听到什么选什么"原则，原文为"研究发现，由于新式咖啡味道更佳，其饮用者很少再回去选择超市中的常规品牌"，故选B"新式咖啡味道更佳"。

35. What will probably happen in the future to stores that sell regular brands of coffee?

根据"关注结尾"原则，尾句为"因此，这些常规品牌将成为竞争中名副其实的失败者"，故选A"它们将失去一些咖啡生意"。

Section C

36. poets
37. typical
38. rarely
39. retreated
40. chiefly
41. intimates
42. attended
43. figure

44. She lived simply and deliberately. She faced the essential facts of life

45. both to fulfill her obligations as a daughter, a sister, and a housekeeper and to write on the average one poem a day

46. Not until the 1950s was she recognized as one of the greatest American poets

强化训练三

Section A

Directions: *In this section, you will hear 8 short conversations and 2 long conversations. At the end of each conversation, one or more questions will be asked about what was said. Both the conversation and the questions will be spoken only once. After each question there will be a pause. During the pause, you must read the four choices marked [A], [B], [C] and [D], and decide which is the best answer. Then mark the corresponding letter on **Answer Sheet 2** with a single line through the centre.*

11. [A] The interview was easier than the previous one.

    [B] Joe is sure that he will do better in the next interview.

    [C] Joe probably failed in the interview.

    [D] The oral part of the interview was easier than the written part.

12. [A] She is too busy to go.   [C] She doesn't want to wait long.

    [B] She is willing to go.   [D] She enjoys the wonderful weather.

13. [A] She didn't get the film.

    [B] She had no idea where the film was.

    [C] The supermarket closed after she left.

    [D] She went to see a film.

14. [A] A bus station.　　　　　　[C] A railway station.

　　[B] A highway.　　　　　　　　[D] An airport.

15. [A] Her back hurt during the meeting.

　　[B] She agreed that it was a good meeting.

　　[C] She will take back what she has said.

　　[D] His support would have helped this morning.

16. [A] Someone has taken away her luggage.

　　[B] Her flight is 50 minutes late.

　　[C] Her luggage has been delayed.

　　[D] She can't find the man she's been waiting for.

17. [A] Boss and secretary.　　　　[C] Father and son.

　　[B] Teacher and student.　　　　[D] Lawyer and client.

18. [A] Her salary will be raised.

　　[B] She will look after all his money.

　　[C] She will become a manager.

　　[D] She will have as much money as the man.

Questions 19 to 21 are based on the conversation you have just heard.

19. [A] To improve his skating techniques. [C] To take a course.

　　[B] To take a vacation.　　　　　　　[D] To learn to ski.

20. [A] Her sister lives there.　　　　　[C] She lives thirty minutes from there.

　　[B] She attended college there.　　　[D] She visited there last year.

21. [A] The low humidity.　　　　　　　[C] The high altitude.

　　[B] The changing climate.　　　　　[D] The extreme temperatures.

Questions 22 to 25 are based on the conversation you have just heard.

22. [A] American literature.　　　　[C] Art history.

　　[B] Elementary education.　　　[D] Medicine.

23. [A] They are professional story tellers.

　　[B] They are parents of young children.

　　[C] The stories will help them improve their vocabulary.

　　[D] The stories are required for a course.

24. [A] It uses an extensive vocabulary.

    [B] It's useful as a teaching tool.

    [C] Its author is unknown.

    [D] Children find it repetitive and boring.

25. [A] At the beginning of a semester.   [C] At the end of a semester.

    [B] During midterm week.   [D] In the middle of summer vacation.

Section B

Directions: *In this section, you will hear 3 short passages. At the end of each passage, you will hear some questions. Both the passage and the questions will be spoken only once. After you hear a question, you must choose the best answer from the four choices marked [A], [B], [C] and [D]. Then mark the corresponding letter on **Answer Sheet 2** with a single line through the centre.*

Passage One

Questions 26 to 28 are based on the passage you have just heard.

26. [A] They devote a lot of time to theoretical problems.

    [B] They often live near observatories.

    [C] They are constantly analyzing data.

    [D] They spend most of their time looking through telescopes.

27. [A] The natural colors of astronomical objects can be captured.

    [B] The images can be studied by different astronomers.

    [C] Fewer data need to be analyzed.

    [D] The cost of equipment needed is reduced.

28. [A] To photograph objects without using a telescope.

    [B] To take more photographs.

    [C] To solve the problem of weak light.

    [D] To spend less time at their telescopes.

Passage Two

Questions 29 to 32 are based on the passage you have just heard.

29. [A] The development of the railway industry.

    [B] The financing of railroad construction.

    [C] The reasons railroad regulations were changed.

    [D] The safety record of the railroad industry.

30. ［A］The high cost of meeting environmental regulations.

  ［B］The growth of auto industry.

  ［C］Safety problems with railroad tracks.

  ［D］The use of oversized freight containers.

31. ［A］It creates personal fortunes for investors.

  ［B］It keeps a traditional way of doing business.

  ［C］Its competitors are inconsiderate of customers.

  ［D］It contributes less to air pollution than other kinds of transportation.

32. ［A］The repair of public roads.

  ［B］The construction of new tunnels.

  ［C］The creation of government agencies.

  ［D］The hiring of extra traffic patrollers.

Passage Three

Questions 33 to 35 are based on the passage you have just heard.

33. ［A］To give an assignment for the next class.

  ［B］To point out an example of good writing.

  ［C］To change students' methods of writing.

  ［D］To review material covered in an earlier lecture.

34. ［A］To improve overall effectiveness.

  ［B］To add more specific details and examples.

  ［C］To make smooth transitions between ideas.

  ［D］To correct spelling and grammar.

35. ［A］They will become inspired to write poetry.

  ［B］They will make a habit of revising their papers.

  ［C］They will become more interested in keeping diaries.

  ［D］They will develop a negative attitude toward long papers.

Section C

Directions: *In this section, you will hear a passage three times. When the passage is read for the first time, you should listen carefully for its general idea. When the passage is read for the second time, you are required to fill in the blanks numbered from 36 to 43 with the exact words you have just heard. For blanks numbered from 44*

215

to 46 you are required to fill in the missing information. For these blanks, you can either use the exact words you have just heard or write down the main points in your own words. Finally, when the passage is read for the third time, you should check what you have written.

What we consider to be writing today, that is words made up of letters or (36)_____ that make up sentences, began to be developed around 3000 years BC in (37)_____ Egypt, about 2000 BC in Greece, in (38)_____ Europe, and about 1500 years BC in China. The system that developed in Greece, however, (39)_____ developed into alphabet form used in most languages, although the ancient form of writing is still used in China today.

The Western alphabet was developed by the ancient Greeks nearly 3000 years ago. The alphabet, as it is called, is (40)_____ after the first two Greek letters, Alpha and Beta, and is believed to be highly (41)_____. In fact, the Greeks are the only (42)_____ that has ever invented an (43)_____ language for writing. And (44)_____, especially when communicating *verbally*（口头地）using a telephone. Indeed, (45)_____. For example, (46)_____.

试题详解

11. C 面试场景

选项分析：四个选项中均出现了interview，可知对话与面试相关。

听音重点：That's easier said than done.（说时容易做时难。）

听力原文：W: Listen to me, Joe. The interview is already a thing of the past. Just forget about it.

M: **That's easier said than done.**

Q: What can we infer from the conversation?

12. B 约会场景

选项分析：A、B正好相反，故其一可能为正确选项。

听音重点：If you don't mind while I get prepared（如果你不介意等我准备好）表

示已接受邀请。条件句一般表示接受或有条件接受。当一个人提出邀请或建议时，另一个人的回答往往不是YES或NO。

听力原文：M: Wonderful day, isn't it? Want to join me for a ride?

W: If you don't mind while I get prepared.

Q: What does the woman mean?

13. A 购物场景

选项分析：A、B意思相近，故其一可能为正确选项。

听音重点：It was closed before I got there.

听力原文：M: Did you get the film for your camera in the supermarket?

W: **It was closed before I got there.** I had no idea that it closes so early in the evening.

Q: What does the woman mean?

14. D 住房场景

选项分析：选项表明本题考查动作发生地点。

听音重点：表示地点的名词。

听力原文：M: How do Jane and Bill like their new house?

W: It's really comfortable, **but** they're tired of having to hear the **jets** go over their house at all hours.

Q: What is located close to Jane and Bill's new house?

15. D 会议场景

选项分析：选项中的meeting表明对话为会议场景。

听音重点：虚拟语气you should have backed me up then, when I needed it（我最需要支持的时候，你应该支持我），选项D为虚拟语气的内部替换。

听力原文：M: I agree with what you said at the meeting this morning. It was very good.

W: **You should have backed me up then, when I needed it.**

Q: What does the woman mean?

16. C 机场场景

选项分析：A、B、C表明对话与机场及行李有关，只有D与此无关，故排除D。

听音重点：找行李还是找人。

听力原文：W: Could you help me, sir? My flight got in 15 minutes ago. **Everyone else has picked up the luggage but mine hasn't come through.**

M: I'm sorry, Madam. I'll go and find out if there is any more to come.

Q: What's the woman's problem?

17. B 学习场景

选项分析：选项表明对话考查情景中的人物关系。

听音重点：情景关键词。

听力原文：M: The **essays** you have done this **term** have been weak, and your **attendance** at the **lectures** has been poor.

W: I'm sorry. I've been busy with my **union activities**.

Q: What is the probable relationship between the two speakers?

18. A 工作场景

选项分析：A、B、D均与金钱相关，只有C例外，故排除C。

听音重点：give sb. a raise意为"给某人加薪"，no problem给出肯定答复，反问句加强语气。

听力原文：W: If you are **promoted to manager**, will you **give us a raise**?

M: **No problem.** What else would I do with all the money that will come pouring in?

Q: What will happen to the woman if the man is promoted?

Conversation One（旅游场景）

M: **I have been studying too much and need a change. So I've just made plans to go away during January break.（19）**

W: Really? Where are you going?

M: I'm planning to visit New Mexico.

W: **My sister and I vacationed there last year and we had a great time.（20）**

M: Did you get into Albuquerque?

W: Sure. Whenever we were skiing.

M: Is it far from the mountains?

W: Not at all. See even though Albuquerque is on a high flat plateau. There are even higher mountains near it. Just half an hour away from the city, there are snow-covered slopes.

M: Well. As the mountains are just thirty minutes away, I guess I should take my ice skates and my ski's.

W: Definitely.

M: I heard that the weather there is great.

W: It is. **No humidity, moderate temperatures, but you do need to be careful about high altitude.（21）**

M: What should I do about that?

W: Oh, just take it easy for a few days. Don't go hiking up the mountains or exercise too vigorously. Just do everything gradually.

M: I'm sure I will be fine. And I will let you know all about my trip when I come back.

Questions 19 to 21 are based on the conversation you have just heard.

19. What's the main purpose of the man's trip?

正确答案：B

选项分析：选项均表示动作，可知该题考查具体行为。

听音重点：根据原文So I've just made plans to go away during January break，可知男士计划去度假。

20. Why does the woman know so much about Albuquerque?

正确答案：D

选项分析：选项B、C、D均说的是女士和某一地点的关系，结构相近，其一可能为正确答案，而选项A说的是女士的姐姐，与其他三项明显不同，故排除。

听音重点：根据原文My sister and I vacationed there last year and we had a great time，可知女士和她姐姐去年曾经去那里度过假。

21. According to the woman, what may cause the man the most problems in the Albuquerque?

正确答案：C

选项分析：选项均表示气候环境，可知该题考查具体环境。

听音重点：根据原文but you do need to be careful about high altitude，可知答案是海拔较高。

Conversation Two（课堂场景）

M: Hi, Helen. What do you think of our class in children's literature?

W: It looks pretty good. I was surprised to see you in there. **Are you also majoring in elementary education?（22）**

219

M: No. I'm not. But as a Psychology major, I can use this to fulfill the requirement in Developmentary Psychology.

W: **Have you finished the first assignment yet?(23)**

M: Not yet. I just bought the books today. How about you?

W: I started this afternoon. It's great fun reading those wonderful children's stories by Dr. Sues.

M: Dr. Sues? I don't remember seeing his name on the reading list.

W: His full name is Theodore Sues Gysel. That's how he is listed in the bibliography. Dr. Sues is his pen name.

M: I loved reading those stories as a child. It'll be interesting to read them now from a different perspective. I guess they'll give me a good idea of how children think.

W: Those stories are also great for classroom use.

M: How's that?

W: Well, take a typical Dr. Sues' book like *The Cat in the Hat*. It has a controlled vocabulary of only 200 words.

M: **So that means the children get a lot of practice using a small number of words over and over.(24)**

W: Exactly. In fact, *The Cat in the Hat* was written primarily to show how a controlled vocabulary reader could also be interesting and fun.

M: **Well, it sounds as though this course is also going to be interesting and fun.** **(25)** I think I'll get started on those readings tonight.

Questions 22 to 25 are based on the conversation you have just heard.

22. What is Helen's major field of study?

   正确答案：B

   选项分析：根据23、24题中反复出现的children，stories等词，可知对话可能与儿童教育相关。

   听音重点：根据原文Are you also majoring in elementary education，可知女士的专业为小学教育。

23. Why will the speakers be reading children's stories?

   正确答案：D

   选项分析：根据25题各选项，可知对话者为学生，故排除选项A、B，答案在C、D之间。

听音重点：根据原文Have you finished the first assignment yet，可知这是一门课程的要求。

24. What is true about the book called *The Cat in the Hat*?

正确答案：B

选项分析：根据对话的主题——儿童教育，排除选项A"它需要庞大的词汇量"。根据四级听力"积极向上"的原则，排除选项D。答案在选项B、C之间。

听音重点：根据原文So that means the children get a lot of practice using a small number of words over and over，可知此书可用作教学工具。

25. When does the conversation probably take place?

正确答案：A

选项分析：根据各题选项中大量关于学习的表达，排除选项D"在暑假期间"。

听音重点：根据原文Well, it sounds as though this course is also going to be interesting and fun，可知对话可能发生在一个学期的开始。

Section B

Passage One(科普知识：天文学家)

多数人认为天文学家的工作就是通过望远镜观测，本文指出，真正的天文学家其实很少使用望远镜，他们大部分时间都在分析数据。本文同时介绍了如何通过望远镜拍摄遥远的天体。

　　Most people think that astronomers are people who spend their time looking through telescopes every night.(26) In fact, a real astronomer spends most of his or her life analyzing data and may only be at the telescope a few weeks of the year. Some work on purely theoretical problems and never use a telescope at all. You might not know how rarely images are viewed directly through telescopes. The most common way to observe the skies is to photograph them. The process is very simple. First a plate is coated with light sensitive material. The plate is put so that the image received by the telescope is recorded on it. **Then the image can be developed, enlarged and published so that many people can study it.**(27) **Because most objects are very remote, the light we receive from them is very weak.**(28) But by using a telescope as camera, long time exposures can be made. In this way, objects can be photographed that are a hundred times too weak to be seen by just looking through a telescope.

Questions 26 to 28 are based on the passage you have just heard.

26. According to the speaker, what do people often think about astronomers?

根据"重视开头"原则，首句为"大多数人认为天文学家是每天夜里用望远镜进行观测的人"，故选D"他们花费大部分时间用望远镜观测"。

27. What is one advantage of photographing the skies?

根据"听到什么选什么"原则，原文为"图像可以被冲洗、放大并发表，这样很多人可以研究它"，故选B"不同的天文学家可以研究这些图像"。

28. What is one reason astronomers make long time exposures?

根据"关注结尾"原则，倒数第三句为"由于大部分物体极其遥远，从它们发来的光线非常微弱"，故选C"为了解决光线微弱的问题"。

Passage Two(铁路发展)

本文介绍了铁路货运在20世纪的发展历程。20世纪初期，铁路大规模地用于运输货物。然而到了1970年，铁路行业被大量问题困扰，从而被小汽车和卡车取代。1980年，由于政府和铁路公司采取了一系列措施，铁路开始占有越来越多的市场份额。

At the beginning of the 20th century, the railroads were used to transport everything.(29) Powerful railroad barons made fortunes without having to be accountable to the public or considerable to the customers. **But cars and trucks changed all of that.**(30) And by 1970, the rail industry was beset with problems. Trucks were taking all the new business. And even so the rail industry remained cold to customers. Also, many regulations kept the rail industry from adjusting to shifting market. But in 1980, the rail industry entered the modern era when a law was passed that allowed railroad companies to make quick adjustments to practices. Companies reduced their lines by 1/3 and used fewer employees. They also took steps to minimize damage to product. And also increase their shipping capacity by stacking freight containers on railroad cars. The image of rail industry has changed dramatically. Today, companies are very responsive to customers and are gaining increasing market shares in the shipping industry. **The railroad safety record is also strong. Trains also come out ahead of the trucks on environmental grounds because they give off only 1/10 to 1/3 the pollution that is emitted by trucks.**(31) **And railroad does not wear out highways as trucks do.**(32)

Questions 29 to 32 are based on the passage you have just heard.

29. What does the speaker mainly discuss?

   根据"重视开头"原则，首句为"在20世纪初期，铁路被用来运输一切"，结合后文可知本文与铁路行业的发展相关，故选A。

30. What is one reason of the decline in the use of railroads?

   根据"听到什么选什么"原则，原文为"但是小汽车和卡车改变了一切"，故选B"汽车行业的发展"。

31. What is one reason why the railroad industry is gaining public support?

   根据"听到什么选什么"原则，原文为"火车排放的污染物只是卡车的十分之一到三分之一，因此，它在环保方面优于卡车"，故选D"它比其他的运输工具造成的空气污染更少"。

32. According to the speaker, what expenses does trucking create for the public?

   根据"关注结尾"原则，尾句为"火车不像卡车那样磨损公路"，故选A"公共道路的维修"。

Passage Three(英文写作)

　　本文是一位教授关于英文写作的讲座。教授要求学生了解正式写作(formal writing）需要认真修改，并指出修改不只是改正拼写和语法错误，而是要全面修订，以提高论文的整体水平。

　　By the end of the term, I hope you'll be convinced that formal writing always requires revision.(**33**) Sometimes it requires a fairly major rewriting of the paper. Some students may have the mistaken idea that revision means simply making corrections in spelling and grammar. I call that proofreading. **What I expect you to do is to improve the overall effectiveness of your paper.**(**34**) But how can you tell if your paper is effective? Well, for example, start by asking yourself these questions: Is the topic restricted enough to be fully discussed within the given links? Are the main ideas clear? Are they supported by the specific details in the examples? Do they move smoothly from one idea to the next? You'll need enough time for a possible main revision, that is, you have to make a lot of changes before your paper becomes really clear to the reader. So I'll expect a draft of each paper two weeks before the final date. In that way I can criticize it and get it back in time for you to revise it. Then you can hand in a final draft for grading. This process may seem like a great deal of trouble at first, but I think you will find it valuable. **In fact, after you finish this course, you will hand in a term paper with first revising it carefully.**（35）

Questions 33 to 35 are based on the passage you have just heard.

33. What is the purpose of the talk?

根据"重视开头"原则，首句为"到学期末，我希望你们了解正式写作需要修改"，故选C"改变学生的写作方式"。

34. What should be the students' main goal as they revise their work?

根据"听到什么选什么"原则，原文为"我希望你们做的是提高你们论文的整体效力"，故选A"提高整体效力"。

35. What effect does the speaker think the class will have on the students?

根据"关注结尾"原则，尾句为"实际上，在你们完成这个课程之后，你们要经过仔细修改后上交一篇学期论文"，故选B"他们将养成修改论文的习惯"。

Section C

36. characters   37. ancient

38. southern   39. gradually

40. named   41. unique

42. civilization   43. alphabet-based

44. what makes this form of writing so important in modern societies is that words can be spelled out, to avoid confusion or misunderstanding

45. if we consider how the Greek alphabet makes communication possible we realize just how fascinating a development it was

46. consider how much more difficult it would be to use a computer keyboard without the use of an alphabet

强化训练四

Section A

Directions: *In this section, you will hear 8 short conversations and 2 long conversations. At the end of each conversation, one or more questions will be asked about what was said. Both the conversation and the questions will be spoken only once. After each question there will be a pause. During the pause, you must read the four choices marked* [A], [B], [C] *and* [D], *and decide which is the best answer. Then mark the corresponding letter on* **Answer Sheet 2** *with a single line through the centre.*

11. [A] Spanish.   [C] Japanese.

    [B] Arabic.   [D] Chinese.

12. [A] Because he lost the pen.

    [B] Because he had bought the wrong pen.

    [C] Because he had forgotten to bring the pen.

    [D] Because he was not able to bring the pen.

13. [A] Go out with his wife.   [C] Stay at home with his wife.

    [B] Work for extra time.   [D] Go out with his boss.

14. [A] The woman shouldn't be anxious.

    [B] She's already one hour late.

    [C] The woman shouldn't wait to be interviewed.

    [D] She's too nervous to calm down.

15. [A] Teacher and student.   [C] Patient and doctor.

    [B] Customer and saleswoman.   [D] Employee and manager.

16. [A] The film was too long to see.   [C] She slept through the film.

    [B] The film was not interesting.   [D] She turned to another channel.

17. [A] The problem may have been a very complicated one.

    [B] The woman can't solve the problem.

    [C] The problem may have been a very easy one.

    [D] The man can solve the problem himself.

18. [A] Most people killed in the traffic accident are heavy drinkers.

    [B] She doesn't agree with the man.

    [C] Drunk drivers are not guilty.

    [D] People should pay more attention to the danger of drunk driving.

Questions 19 to 21 are based on the conversation you have just heard.

19. [A] At the beginning of the semester.   [C] At the end of the semester.

    [B] At the middle of the semester.   [D] During vacation.

20. [A] The woman won.   [C] The man lost his ball.

    [B] The man won.   [D] The woman lost her ball.

21. [A] To get his things.   [C] To instruct the class.

    [B] Run to the dorm.   [D] To reserve a court.

Questions 22 to 25 are based on the conversation you have just heard.

22. [A] In a classroom.　　　　　　[C] In the dormitory.

　　[B] In a snack bar.　　　　　　[D] In a camera shop.

23. [A] The man's brother.　　　　　[C] A neighbor.

　　[B] The man's roommate.　　　　[D] A photographer.

24. [A] He's noisy.　　　　　　　　[B] He's messy.

　　[C] He doesn't tell the truth.　　[D] He doesn't close the door.

25. [A] He worked for a radio station.　[C] He took a long trip.

　　[B] He lived in a dormitory.　　　[D] He visited the man's family.

Section B

Directions: *In this section, you will hear 3 short passages. At the end of each passage, you will hear some questions. Both the passage and the questions will be spoken only once. After you hear a question, you must choose the best answer from the four choices marked [A], [B], [C] and [D]. Then mark the corresponding letter on **Answer Sheet 2** with a single line through the centre.*

Passage One

Questions 26 to 28 are based on the passage you have just heard.

26. [A] He teaches a course on finance.　[C] He's a Lincoln scholar.

　　[B] He does it as a hobby.　　　　[D] He works for a museum.

27. [A] He needed the money.　　　　[C] Cents were cheap to collect.

　　[B] Someone gave him a rare penny.　[D] All of his friends collected them.

28. [A] Discuss the life of Lincoln.　　[C] Show the audience his coins.

　　[B] Explain how the cent is made.　[D] Trade coins with club members.

Passage Two

Questions 29 to 32 are based on the passage you have just heard.

29. [A] The training of modern dance.

　　[B] Pioneer modern dancers.

　　[C] The influence of modern dance of ballet.

　　[D] The origins and characteristics of modern dance.

30. [A] The tickets were overpriced.　　[C] They were conventional.

　　[B] The theatres were crowded.　　[D] They were created in Europe.

31. ［A］Pop music.　　　　　　　　　　［C］Elaborate scenery.

　　［B］Free expression.　　　　　　　　［D］Lightness of movement.

32. ［A］They weren't formally trained.

　　［B］They performed to classical music.

　　［C］They imitated the techniques of ballet.

　　［D］They performed mainly in Europe.

Passage Three

Questions 33 to 35 are based on the passage you have just heard.

33. ［A］Farmer's loss of independence.

　　［B］Improvements in farm machinery in the United States.

　　［C］International trade in the nineteenth century.

　　［D］Jefferson's views about commercialized agriculture.

34. ［A］The United States increased its agricultural imports.

　　［B］New banking laws made it easy to buy farmland.

　　［C］Economic depressions lowered the prices of farm products.

　　［D］Crop production became surprisedly increased.

35. ［A］It decreased the power of the railroads to control farm prices.

　　［B］It affected the prices of their crops.

　　［C］It made farmers less dependent on local bankers.

　　［D］It provided evidence that Jefferson's ideal could be achieved.

Section C

Directions: *In this section, you will hear a passage three times. When the passage is read for the first time, you should listen carefully for its general idea. When the passage is read for the second time, you are required to fill in the blanks numbered from 36 to 43 with the exact words you have just heard. For blanks numbered from 44 to 46 you are required to fill in the missing information. For these blanks, you can either use the exact words you have just heard or write down the main points in your own words. Finally, when the passage is read for the third time, you should check what you have written.*

Why do we cry? Can you imagine life without tears? Not only do tears keep your eyes lubricated, they also（36）_____ a substance that kills certain（37）_____ so they can't infect your eyes. Give up your tears and you'll lose this on-the-spot （38）_____. Nobody wants to give up the flood of （39）_____ tears you produce when you get something （40）_____ or chemical in your eyes. Tears are very good at washing this （41）_____ stuff out . Another thing you couldn't do without your tears is cry from joy, anger or （42）_____. Humans are the only animals that produce tears in response to （43）_____, and most people say a good cry makes them feel better. （44）_____ . Tear researcher, Winifred, is trying to figure out how it happens. One possibility he says is that tears discharge certain chemicals from your body, chemicals that build up during stress. When people talk about crying it out, "I think that might actually be what they are doing", he says. （45）_____? Boys, for example , cry only about a quarter as often as girls once they reach teenage years, and we all cry a lot less now than we did as babies. Could it possibly be that we face less stress? （46）_____.

试题详解

11. A 学习场景

选项分析：选项均为语言，故对话与语言学习相关。

听音重点：语言。

听力原文：M: Mr. Black is **fluent in Spanish** and now he's beginning to study Arabic.

W: He also knows a few words in Japanese and Chinese.

Q: Which language does Mr. Black speak well?

12. C 借物场景

选项分析：选项均为原因，故问题涉及某事的原因。

听音重点：原因。

听力原文：W: Did you remember to bring the pen which I lent you?

M: I'm sorry. It completely **slipped my mind**. I promise I'll bring it at the same time tomorrow.

Q: Why did the man apologize to the woman?

13. B 加班场景

选项分析：选项均为动作且出现代词his，可知对话考查男士的行为。

听音重点：男士的具体行为。

听力原文：W: Honey, I think we should go out and relax this weekend.

M: Yes, darling. But **my boss asked me to work over the weekend.**
You know, **time is really pressing for us.**

Q: What will the man do this weekend?

14. D 面试场景

选项分析：A、D为相反选项，故其一可能为正确选项。

听音重点：女士是否焦急。

听力原文：M: You still have one hour to wait, please take it easy.

W: Take it easy! How can I take it easy when **I'm so anxious about
the interview.**

Q: What does the woman mean?

15. B 购物场景

选项分析：选项均为人物关系，可知对话考查对话中的人物关系。

听音重点：动作发生地点及人物关系。

听力原文：M: **The shoes are so expensive**, but they fit me well.

W: **They are fashionable and not so expensive** if the quality is
considered.

Q: What's the relationship between the man and woman?

16. C 虚拟语气

选项分析：A、B、C都提到了film，故对话应与电影有关。

听音重点：女士对电影的态度。

听力原文：M: What do you think of the film on Channel 5 last night? It was about
how a couple went through the hardships in their life.

W: **I wish I'd stayed awake long enough to see the whole thing.**

Q: What does the woman mean?

17. A 生活场景

选项分析：A、C正好相反，故其一可能为正确选项。

听音重点：问题是否容易解决。

听力原文：M: **It's really a complicated problem.** I wonder if a problem like this can be solved by Linda.

W: Well, **if she can't solve it, no one can.**

Q: What can be concluded from the conversation?

18. D 交通场景

选项分析：C与生活常识明显不符，故排除。

听音重点：对话者对于酒后驾车的态度。

听力原文：M: I think it's high time we turned our attention to the danger of drunk driving now.

W: I can't agree with you more. You see, **countless innocent people are killed by drunk drivers each year.**

Q: What does the woman mean?

Conversation One(体育场景)

M: **I can't wait until this week is over, all these final exams are driving me crazy.(19)**

W: Well, why don't you take a break and do something that will take your mind off your test?

M: Like what?

W: I don't know. Tennis?

M: That's not a bad idea, except that my racket is still in the shop getting restrung.

W: Well, then how about a game of racket ball. You did promise me we play again before vacation.

M: I know, but it's embarrassing to lose all the time, especially to a beginner.

W: **Oh, come on, I beat you once, and it was just beginner's luck.(20)**

M: Fine, I'll accept. Where do you want to play now, at Harf or Canny?

W: I like Harf. But I think most of the racket ball courts are reserved for class instruction now. We might have a better chance to find a place at Canny.

M: You are probably right. **Let me call and see if I can reserve a court.(21)**Is 2:30 a good time for you?

W: Sure. Let me just run to the dorm and get my things. I'll be right back.

Questions 19 to 21 are based on the conversation you have just heard.

19. When does this conversation probably take place?

正确答案：C

选项分析：选项A为"在学期开始"，选项C为"在学期末"，二者意思相反，其一可能为正确答案。

听音重点：根据原文I can't wait until this week is over, all these final exams are driving me crazy, 可知对话发生在学期末。

20. What was the result of their last game?

正确答案：A

选项分析：选项A为"女士赢"，选项B为"男士赢"，二者意思相反，其一可能为答案。

听音重点：根据原文Oh, come on, I beat you once, and it was just beginner's luck, 可知女士赢了。选项C、D所答非所问。

21. What will the man do while the woman is gone?

正确答案：D

选项分析：根据20题各选项，可知对话与打球相关，选项D为"去预订球场"，可能为正确答案。选项C"去教课"明显与对话内容不符，故排除。

听音重点：根据原文Let me call and see if I can reserve a court, 可知男士将预订球场。

Conversation Two(住房场景)

W: **Let's go in here and order some coffee while we look at your pictures.**（22）

M: Good idea. We'd both like coffee, please. **Okay, here's one of Ed, my roommate.**（23）I took this picture right after we arrived at school this fall. We had just met in fact. And this was our room in the dormitory while we were unpacking all of our things. What a mess!

W: You certainly had a lot of boxes. How did you ever find room for everything?

M: In the beginning we thought we'd never get all things arranged, but now we're very comfortable. Lucky for me, Ed keeps his things neat.

W: Do you like living in the dormitory?

M: It's not bad. **Sometimes Ed turns his radio up too loud or makes too much noise. Then I get angry.**（24）Sometimes I leave my books and clothes lying around and he gets angry. **But usually we get along. Here's a picture of him taken when we went to visit my family during vacation.**（25）

W: And this last one?

M: That's my dog, Spot.

Questions 22 to 25 are based on the conversation you have just heard.

22. Where does this conversation most probably take place?

正确答案：B

选项分析：选项均为地点，可知本题考查对话发生的地点。

听音重点：根据原文Let's go in here and order some coffee while we look at your pictures，可知对话可能发生在小吃店。

23. Who is Ed?

正确答案：B

选项分析：选项A为"男士的兄弟"，选项B为"男士的室友"，二者结构相近，其一可能为答案。

听音重点：根据原文Okay，here's one of Ed，my roommate，可知Ed是男士的室友。

24. Why does the man sometimes get angry with Ed?

正确答案：A

选项分析：选项A为"他很吵闹"，选项B为"他很脏乱"，二者结构相近，其一可能为答案。选项D"他不关门"与常识不符，故排除。

听音重点：根据原文Sometimes Ed turns his radio up too loud or makes too much noise. Then I get angry，可知Ed很吵闹。

25. What did Ed do during vacation?

正确答案：D

选项分析：选项均表示行为，可知本题可能提问某人在某段时间做了什么。

听音重点：根据原文Here's a picture of him taken when we went to visit my family during vacation，可知Ed假期去了男士家。

Section B

Passage One(硬币收藏)

　　本文是一位硬币收藏者受某一社团邀请，就硬币收藏所做的讲座。收藏者主要叙述了自己收藏硬币的经历，同时详细介绍了一种珍贵硬币——林肯便士的具体情况。

　　I was really glad when your club invited me to share my coin collection. **It has been my hobby since I c ollected my first Lincoln cent in 1971.（26）**That is the current cent with Abraham Lincoln's image. Just a little history before I started my own collection. Lincoln cents are made of copper, and they were the first United States coins to bear the likeness of the president. It was back in 1909 when the country was celebrating the centennial of Lincoln's birth in 1809. Before that, the penny had an American Indian head on it. The new cent was designed by artist Victor David Braner. This is interesting because he put his initials VDB on the reverse side of the coin as the original design. There was a general discussion when the initials were discovered. And only a limited number of coins were made with the initials on them. Today a cent with the initials is called the 1909s' VDB. It's worth 500 dollars. Now when I started my coin collection, I began with cent for several reasons. There were a lot of them. Several hundred billion were made and there were a lot of people collecting them. So I have plenty of people to trade with and talk to about my collection. **Also it was the coin I could afford to collect as a young teenager.**(27) In the twenty five years since then, I have managed to acquire over three hundred coins. Some of them are very rare. **Next, I will be sharing with you today some of my rare collection.**(28)

Questions 26 to 28 are based on the passage you have just heard.

26. Why does the man collect coins?

   根据"重视开头"原则，第二句为"自从1971年我收藏第一枚林肯美分开始，收藏硬币便一直是我的爱好"，故选B"他把它作为兴趣"。

27. What was one of the reasons the speaker collected coins as a teenager?

   根据"听到什么选什么"原则，原文为"而且硬币是我作为一个年轻人能够收藏的东西"，故选C"美分收藏起来很便宜"。

28. What will the speaker do next?

   根据"关注结尾"原则，尾句为"接下来，今天我将和你们分享我的一些稀有收藏"，故选C"给听众展示他的硬币"。

Passage Two（现代舞蹈）

   本文介绍了现代舞蹈的起源及其特点。19世纪末，古典芭蕾不再盛行，美国人期望有自己的现代舞蹈形式。1900年前后，美国的舞蹈家创造了一种自由表现的新型舞蹈。

   Why did modern dance begin in the United States? To begin to answer this question, we need to look back a little bit and talk about classical ballet.(29) By the late 1800s, ballet had lost a lot of its popularity. Most of the ballet dancers who performed in the United States were brought over from Europe. **They performed using strict techniques that had been passed down through the centuries.**（30）Audiences and dancers in the United States were eager for their own modern dance form and so around 1900 dancers created one. How was this modern dance so different from classical ballet? Most importantly, it wasn't carefully designed. **Instead, the dance depended on the free expression of the dancers.**（31）Music and scenery were of little importance to the modern dance. And lightness of movement wasn't important either. In fact, modern dancers made no attempt to hide the effort in the dance step. But even if free expressions attract audiences, many dance critics were less enthusiastic about the performances. **They doubt the art of dancers who were not formally trained.**（32）Yet the free personal expression of the pioneer dancers is the basis of the controlled freedom of modern dance today.

Questions 29 to 32 are based on the passage you have just heard.

29. What does the essay mainly discuss?

根据"重视开头"原则，前两句为"为什么现代舞蹈起源于美国？为了回答这个问题，我们需要稍微回顾并讨论一下古典芭蕾"，故选D"现代舞的起源和特点"。

30. Why were ballet performances unpopular in the United States in the early 1900s?

根据"听到什么选什么"原则，原文为"他们使用数百年来流传下的严格技巧进行表演"，故选C"它们是传统的"。

31. What is the outstanding feature of the modern dance performances?

根据"听到什么选什么"原则，原文为"反之，这种舞蹈取决于舞蹈者的自由表现"，故选B"自由表现"。

32. Why were early modern dancers criticized by dance critics?

根据"关注结尾"原则，倒数第二句为"他们质疑舞蹈者的技巧，因为他们没有经过正规的训练"，故选A"他们没有受过正规训练"。

Passage Three(美国历史)

本文介绍了美国农民的发展史。19世纪初期，他们过着自由、简单的生活。19世纪中期，农民开始专业化生产，农业由此发生了巨变。19世纪末，机械化革命加速了专业化进程，美国农民已经和世界市场紧密相关。

One of the most popular myths about the United States in the 19th century was that of the free and simple life of the farmer. (33) It was said that the farmers worked hard on their own land to produce whatever their families needed. They might sometimes trade with their neighbors, but in general they could get along just fine by depending on themselves, not on commercial ties with others. This is how Thomas Jefferson idealized the farmer at the beginning of the 19th century. And at that time, this may have been close to the truth especially on the frontier. But by the mid 19th century, great changes in agriculture were going on as farmers began to specialize in the raising of crops such as cotton or corn. (34) By late in the century, revolution in farm machinery had greatly increased production of specialized crops. And big network of railroads had linked farmers all over the country to markets in the east and even overseas. By raising and selling specialized crops, farmers could afford more and better goods and achieved a much higher standard of living but at a price. Now farmers were no longer dependent just on weather and their own efforts. Their life was increasingly controlled by banks, which had power to grant or deny loans for new machinery. Their life was also controlled by the railroads which set the rates for shipping their crops to market. As businessmen, farmers now had to worry about world market because it affected the prices of their crops. (35) So by the end of the 19th century, the period of Jefferson's independent farmer had come to a close.

Questions 33 to 35 are based on the passage you have just heard.

33. What is the main topic of the talk?

根据"重视开头"和"关注结尾"原则, 首句为"19世纪美国最流行的故事就是农民自由、简单的生活", 尾句为"因此, 到了19世纪末期, 美国总统杰弗逊所谓的独立农民的阶段寿终正寝"。故选A"农民们独立性的丧失"。

34. According to the speaker, what was the major change in the agriculture during the 19th century?

根据"听到什么选什么"原则, 原文为"到19世纪中期, 随着农民开始专业化种植棉花和玉米等农作物, 农业发生了巨变", 故选D "农作物产量增长速度惊人"。

35. According to the speaker, why was the world market important for the United States agriculture?

根据"关注结尾"原则，倒数第二句为"由于世界市场影响了农作物的价格，作为商人，农民们现在不得不担心世界市场"，故选B"它影响了农作物的价格"。

Section C

36. contain

37. bacteria

38. defense

39. extra

40. physical

41. irritating

42. sadness

43. emotions

44. Many scientists, therefore, believe that crying somehow helps us cope with emotional situations

45. If Winifred is right, what do you think will happen to people who restrain their tears

46. Maybe we found another ways to deal with it, or maybe we just feel embarrassed

第四章 仔细阅读

最新大纲

根据《大学英语四级考试大纲》，阅读理解部分包括仔细阅读（Reading in Depth）和快速阅读（Skimming and Scanning），测试学生通过阅读获取书面信息的能力；所占分值比例为35%，其中仔细阅读理解部分25%，快速阅读理解部分10%。考试时间40分钟。

仔细阅读部分要求考生阅读三篇短文。两篇为多项选择题，每篇长度为300～350词，一篇为选词填空（Blanked Cloze），文章长度为200～250词。仔细阅读部分测试考生在不同层面上的阅读理解能力，包括理解主旨大意和重要细节、综合分析、推测判断以及根据上下文推测词义等。多项选择题型的短文后有若干问题，考生根据对文章的理解，从每题的四个选项中选择最佳答案。选词填空测试考生对篇章语境中词汇的理解和运用能力，要求考生阅读一篇删去若干词汇的短文，然后从所给的选项中选择正确的词汇填空，使短文复原。

考核技能

根据《大学英语四级考试大纲》，阅读理解部分考核考生通过阅读获取书面信息的能力，包括理解主旨大意、重要事实和细节、隐含意义，判断作者的观点、态度等。阅读部分考核的技能是：

A. 辨别和理解中心思想和重要细节

1. 理解明确表达的概念或细节

2. 理解隐含表达的概念或细节（如总结、判断、推论等）；通过判断句子的交际功能（如请求、拒绝、命令等）来理解文章意思

3. 理解文章的中心思想（如找出能概括全文的要点等）

4. 理解作者的观点和态度

B. 运用语言技能理解文章

5. 理解词语（如根据上下文猜测词和短语的意思）

6. 理解句间关系（如原因、结果、目的、比较等）

7. 理解篇章（如运用词汇及语法承接手段来理解篇章各部分之间的关系）

C. 运用专门的阅读技能

8. 略读文章,获取文章大意

9. 查读文章,获取特定信息

大学英语四级考试阅读理解部分要求考生达到《教学要求》中的一般要求,即"能基本读懂一般性题材的英文文章,阅读速度达到每分钟70词。在快速阅读篇章较长、难度略低的材料时,阅读速度达到每分钟100词。能基本读懂国内英文报刊,掌握中心意思,理解主要事实和有关细节。能读懂工作、生活中常见的应用文体的材料。能在阅读中使用有效的阅读方法"。

选材原则

命题的语料均来自英文原版材料,包括日常生活中的报刊、书籍等。选材的原则是:

1) 题材广泛,涉及人文科学、社会科学、自然科学等领域,但材料的背景应为学生所了解的或已在文章中提供;

2) 体裁多样,包括叙述文、说明文、议论文等;

3) 仔细阅读篇章难度适中,快速阅读、选词填空的篇章难度略低;

4) 词汇范围不超出《教学要求》中一般要求的词汇,超出该范围的关键词汇若影响理解,则以汉语或英语释义。

第一节 高分攻略

一、选词填空

(一)题型介绍

选词填空(Blanked Cloze)是四级考试改革之后出现的新题型,解题时间5～10分钟,分值为5%,每个选项分值0.5%。测试考生对篇章语境中词汇的理解和运用能力,要求考生阅读一篇删去10个词的记叙、说明或议论性短文,全文200～250词(一般没有超纲词汇),然后从所给的15个选项中选择正确的词填空,使短文复原,同时要求表达正确,语意连贯。

选词填空主要考查考生对连贯性、一致性、逻辑性等语篇整体特征以及单词在实际语境中的理解，即要求考生在理解全文的基础上，弄清文章的宏观结构并细化到每个单词的微观理解。新题型和原来的词汇题相比，更注重实际运用。

(二)选项特点

1. 一般首句不设空，一句中不设两空。

2. 选项一般为实词，含2～4个名词、2～3个动词、2～4个形容词、1～2个副词。一般不考查介词、冠词等虚词。

3. 每个正确选项均有干扰选项，一般名词、动词、形容词、副词各一个，或为同词性干扰选项，或为多余选项干扰。在选项表中，正确选项与干扰项一般不在一起。

4. 选项的词性、词形、时态、语态不作任何变化。

5. 如选项中出现一组近义词或反义词，往往有一个是干扰选项。

(三)解题技巧

1.速读全文，了解大意

考生首先应通读全文，弄清文章的大意和结构，掌握准确的背景知识，为正式填空做好准备。一般情况下，文章开头和结尾的句子都能表达完整的信息，揭示文章的背景和主题思想，在阅读时要仔细，争取迅速把握文章的主题。

例：2009年12月真题

Directions: *In this section, there is a passage with ten blanks. You are required to select one word for each blank from a list of choices given in a word bank following the passage. Read the passage through carefully before making your choices. Each choice in the bank is identified by a letter. Please mark the corresponding letter for each item on **Answer Sheet 2** with a single line through the centre. **You may not use any of the words in the bank more than once.***

Questions 47 to 56 are based on the following passage.

In families with two working parents, fathers may have more impact on a child's language development than mothers, a new study suggests.

Researchers __47__ 92 families from 11 child care centers before their children were a year old, interviewing each to establish income, level of education and child care arrangements. Overall, it was a group of well-educated middle-class families, with married parents both living in the home.

When the children were 2, researchers videotaped them at home in free-play sessions with both parents, __48__ all of their speech. The study will appear in the November issue of *The Journal of Applied Developmental Psychology*.

The scientists measured the __49__ number of *utterances*（话语）of the parents, the number of different words they used, the complexity of their sentences and other __50__ of their speech. On average, fathers spoke less than mothers did, but they did not differ in the length of utterances or proportion of questions asked.

Finally, the researchers __51__ the children's speech at age 3, using a standardized language test. The only predictors of high scores on the test were the mother's level of education, the __52__ of child care and the number of different words the father used.

The researchers are __53__ why the father's speech, and not the mother's, had an effect.

"It's well __54__ that the mother's language does have an impact," said Nadya Pancsofar, the lead author of the study. It could be that the high-functioning mothers in the study had __55__ had a strong influence on their children's speech development, Ms. Pancsofar said, "or it may be that mothers are __56__ in a way we didn't measure in the study."

通过速读全文，可知本文是一篇说明文，"总—分"结构，介绍了一个实验，实验结果证明父亲在孩子的语言发展方面所起的作用似乎超过母亲。

2. 浏览选项，分析词性

由于选项中的单词只能用一次，而且不要求改写，因此将选项词汇按词性分类能大大缩小选择范围。比如空格前面若为冠词，则该处必须填入一个名词。另外，在判断词性时可以重点分析动词的时态，即哪几个是动词原形，哪几个是动词过去式或过去分词等，根据上下文时态对应的原则，进一步缩小选择范围。

例：2009年12月真题

[A] already	[F] describing	[K] recruited
[B] analyzed	[G] established	[L] total
[C] aspects	[H] quality	[M] unconscious
[D] characters	[I] quoted	[N] unsure
[E] contributing	[J] recording	[O] yet

名词	aspects	方面	characters	人物；字
	quality	质量；性质	recording	录音
动词	analyzed	分析	contributing	贡献，起作用
	describing	描述	established	建立，制定
	quoted	引用	recruited	招募，吸纳
	total	总计，共计		
形容词	contributing	贡献的，起作用的	established	确定的
	recording	记录的	total	总的，全体的
	unconscious	无意识的；无知觉的	unsure	不确定的，不肯定的
副词	already	已经	yet	还，仍然

3. 积极思考，谨慎选择

在文章大意基本确定之后，就可以根据空格中应填的词性、常识以及上下文的内在逻辑关系，选择合适的选项填空。但务必要注意通篇考虑，寻找线索，以确保文章连贯，语言顺畅，上下文感情色彩一致。在选择的过程中不必按顺序做题，可先选出最有把握的词，然后删除该选项，进而缩小范围。

1）空格前为冠词(a, an, the)、形容词或及物动词，应填名词；

2）空格前为have/has/had，应填过去分词；

3）空格前为be动词，应填过去分词、现在分词或形容词；

4）空格前为副词，应填形容词；

5）空格前为介词，应填名词或动名词；

6）空格后为形容词或从句，应填副词；

7）空格前后为名词，应填动词或形容词；

8）空格前后为动词，应填名词或副词。

例：2009年12月真题

名词

50. C 空前的other和空后的介词of提示所填词应为名词。number of utterances, the number of different words, the complexity of their sentences 和 other 50 ，都是空后their speech的不同方面，由此可知答案应为[C]aspects（方面）。

动词

47. K 分析句子结构可知，所填词作该句的谓语动词。本段主要讲的是研究对象的构成，故填[K]recruited(招募，吸纳)最符合文意。

形容词

49. L 由空前的the和空后的名词number可知，所填词应为形容词。由空后number of utterances和the number of different words的关系推测，本句的逻辑可能是先说utterances的总数，然后是different words(不同单词)各自的数目，故答案为[L]total(全体的，总的)。

副词

55. A 分析句子结构，由空前的had及空后的had a strong influence可知，本句句子成分完整，故应填副词。由于Nadya Pancsofar肯定了母亲在孩子语言发展中的作用，故选[A]already(已经)。选项[O]yet(还，尚，仍然)常用于否定句或疑问句中，故排除。

4. 复查全文，验证答案

填空完成后，利用一分钟的时间再次复查全文，根据语感来验证答案。

二、篇章阅读理解

(一)八大出题规律

1. 主题句

四级阅读整篇文章的主题句往往在文章首段的段首、段尾，或尾段的段尾，而每段的主题句一般位于段首或段尾。主题句的特点是：观点明确、形式简洁、语义完整。在演绎类的文章中，文章的主题句往往位于篇首；在归纳类文章中，则常位于篇尾；有时，主题句也在文章中间。通常，找到主题句就找到了答案。

例：2009年12月真题，Passage Two

Hamilton isn't the only educator crossing the Atlantic. Schools in France, Egypt, Singapore, etc. have also recently made top-level hires from abroad. Higher education has become a big and competitive business nowadays, and like so many businesses, it's gone global. Yet the talent flow isn't universal. **High-level personnel tend to head in only one direction: outward from America.**

62. What is the current trend in higher education discussed in the passage?

　　[A] Institutions worldwide are hiring administrators from the U.S.

　　[B] A lot of political activists are being recruited as administrators.

　　[C] American universities are enrolling more international students.

　　[D] University presidents are paying more attention to fund-raising.

解析：　由题干中的discussed in the passage可知，本题考查全文主旨。本段是文章的第二段，尾句是全文的主题句，故选A。

2. 强转折、强对比

1）强转折

转折句和转折关系往往是文章表达重要观点或陈述关键事物的标志。作者一般使用转折连词引出全文或段落的主旨。but，yet一般出现在段首或陈述完某一理论和现象后，however一般出现在语义转折之处，这些词前后的内容差别很大，其后往往是作者真正的写作目的或基本观点和态度。常考转折连词还有in fact，nevertheless，nonetheless，though，although等。

例：2009年12月真题，Passage One

Throughout this long, tense election, everyone has focused on the presidential candidates and how they'll change America. Rightly so. **But selfishly, I'm more fascinated by Michelle Obama and what she might be able to do, not just for this country, but for me as an African-American woman.** As the potential First Lady, she would have the world's attention. And that means that for the first time people will have a chance to get up close and personal with the type of African-American woman they so rarely see.

57. Why does Michelle Obama hold a strong fascination for the author?

　　[A] She serves as a role model for African-American women.

　　[B] She possesses many admirable qualities becoming a First Lady.

[C] She will present to the world a new image of African-American women.

[D] She will pay closer attention to the interests of African-American women.

解析： 根据关键词fascination定位到首段第二句：But selfishly, I'm more fascinated by Michelle Obama and what she might be able to do, not just for this country, but for me as an African-American woman. (但平心而论，我对米歇尔·奥巴马以及她能做些什么更加着迷，不仅对她能为美国做什么着迷，更对她能为同为非裔女性的我做什么着迷)，以及首段尾句：And that means that for the first time people will have a chance to get up close and personal with the type of African-American woman they so rarely see. (这就意味着人们将有机会靠近并接触他们极少见到的这一类非裔美国女性)。故选B"她将向世界展示非裔美国女性的崭新形象"。

2）强对比

四级阅读中的对比往往是正误观念或新旧观点对比。通常先提出错误观念或旧观点，然后提出正确观念或新观点进行驳斥。转折连词之后的正确观念或新观点是出题重点，需要引起高度重视。常考对比连词有on the other hand, on the contrary, in/by contrast/comparison, in opposition (to), not...but..., while, rather than等。

例：2006年12月真题

Even people who have a physical disease or *handicap* (缺陷) may be "well" in this new sense, if they make an effort to maintain the best possible health they can in the face of their physical limitations. "Wellness" may perhaps best be viewed **not** as a state that people can achieve, **but** as an ideal that people can strive for. People who are well are likely to be better able to resist disease and to fight disease when it strikes. And by focusing attention on healthy ways of living, the concept of wellness can have a beneficial impact on the ways in which people face the challenges of daily life.

65. According to the author, the true meaning of "wellness" is for people _____.

   [A] to best satisfy their body's special needs

   [B] to strive to maintain the best possible health

   [C] to meet the strictest standards of bodily health

   [D] to keep a proper balance between work and leisure

解析： 根据第二句："wellness" may perhaps best be viewed not as..., but as..., wellness 应被视为一种人们可为之努力的理想 (an ideal that people can strive for)，

结合前句可知，这种理想的具体内容是指maintain the best possible health，故选B。

3. 列举、举例

1) 列举

列举指使用表示顺承关系的连词列举事实，这些连词包括first(ly), second(ly), third(ly), last(ly), finally, on the one hand, on the other hand, above all, moreover, furthermore, in addition, what is more, not only..., but also...等。列举处往往是事实细节题的主要出题点，考生需要根据题干中的关键词找到文中列举处，然后对照原文与选项进行作答。如果从正面出题，与原文内容一致的选项为正确选项；如果从反面出题，则与原文内容相反的选项为正确选项。

例：2006年6月17日真题

The following list is a good place to start.

● Educational requirements differ from country to country. In almost every case of "cross-boarder" job hunting, just stating the title of your degree will not be an adequate description. Provide the reader with details about your studies and related experience.

34. When writing about qualifications, applicants are advised to _____.

　[A] provide a detailed description of their study and work experiences

　[B] give the title of the university degree they have earned at home

　[C] highlight their keen interest in pursuing a "cross-boarder" career

　[D] stress their academic potential to impress the decision maker

解析：　根据列举处的尾句，第一点注意事项是不能只简单提到学位名称，而要对自己的教育背景和相关工作经历进行详细描述，故选A。

2) 举例

四级阅读经常通过举例论证使作者的观点更有说服力，这也是命题重点之一。常见的表示举例的引导词有：for example, for instance, as, just as, take...as an example, a case in point is等。举例经常与文章或段落的中心密切相关，而对于和中心关联不明显的例证，可通过上下文进行理解。四级阅读中出现的任何一个例子，都可在上下文中找到总结说明，这些总结说明可以作为解题依据。

例：2009年12月真题，Passage Two

In the past few years, prominent schools around the world have joined the trend. **In 2003, when Cambridge University appointed Alison Richard, another former Yale provost, as its vice-chancellor, the university publicly stressed that in her previous job she had overseen（监督）"a major strengthening of Yale's financial position."**

65. Cambridge University appointed Alison Richard as its vice-chancellor chiefly because _____.

　　［A］she was known to be good at raising money

　　［B］she could help strengthen its ties with Yale

　　［C］she knew how to attract students overseas

　　［D］she had boosted Yale's academic status

解析：根据关键词Cambridge University和Alison Richard定位到第五段第二句：In 2003, when Cambridge University appointed Alison Richard, another former Yale provost, as its vice-chancellor, the university publicly stressed that in her previous job she had overseen "a major strengthening of Yale's financial position."（2003年，英国剑桥大学任命另一位美国耶鲁大学前教务长Alison Richard为副校长时曾公开声称：在之前的职位上，她的监管使得"耶鲁的财政地位得到了极大的巩固"），故选A "她因擅长筹集资金而闻名"。选项中的"擅长筹集资金"是对原文"使财政地位得到了极大的巩固"的提炼和同义转述。

4. 因果

　　两个事件的内在因果关系往往是出题重点，出题方式有两种：给出原因找结果或给出结果找原因。表示因果关系的词汇和短语如下：

　　1）表原因

　　　　（1）连词：because, since, as, for, in that

　　　　（2）介词短语：because of, owing to, due to

　　　　（3）动词短语：result from, arise from, originate from, owe to, attribute to

　　　　（4）名词：basis, cause

2）表结果

（1）连词：so, therefore, hence, accordingly, consequently, as a result, as a consequence

（2）动词/动词短语：cause, result in

（3）名词：result, consequence

例：2008年12月真题，Passage One

There are **many reasons** for this—typically, men take more risks than women and are more likely to drink and smoke—but perhaps **more importantly**, men don't go to the doctor.

58. What does the author state is the most important reason men die five years earlier on average than women?

[A] Men drink and smoke much more than women

[B] Men don't seek medical care as often as women.

[C] Men aren't as cautious as women in face of danger.

[D] Men are more likely to suffer from fatal diseases.

解析：本题考查作者认为男性比女性平均寿命少五年的最重要的原因是什么，答案在第二段，选B。

5. 引言、专有名词

四级阅读文章中，作者为正确表达自己的观点或使论点更有说服力，常引用权威人士的论断或重要发现，这里往往是命题之处，考查引言得出的结论。此外，文中出现专有名词（人名、地名或其他专有名词）时，通常也会考查细节或推断题。

例：2009年6月真题，Passage One

The designers who undertake green fashion still face many challenges. Scott Hahn, cofounder with Gregory of Rogan and Loomstate, which uses all-organic cotton, says high-quality sustainable materials can still be tough to find. "**Most designers with existing labels are finding there aren't comparable fabrics that can just replace what you're doing and what your customers are used to,**" he says. For example, organic cotton and non-organic cotton are virtually indistinguishable once woven into a dress. But some popular synthetics, like stretch nylon, still have few eco-friendly equivalents.

58. According to Scott Hahn, one big challenge to designers who will go organic is that _____.

    [A] much more time is needed to finish a dress using sustainable materials

    [B] they have to create new brands for clothes made of organic materials

    [C] customers have difficulty telling organic from non-organic materials

    [D] quality organic replacements for synthetics are not readily available

解析：根据关键词 Scott Hahn 和 challenge to designers 定位到第二段。该段指出，Scott Hahn 认为高质量的环保面料很难找到，没有匹配的面料替代设计师和顾客已经适应的面料，很难找到与合成材料相媲美的环保面料，故选 D "没有高质量的有机的合成面料替代品"。

6. 特殊标点

特殊标点一般表示进一步的解释说明，包括：冒号、分号、括号、破折号等。其中，引号既表示引用，又可表特殊含义。段首的特殊标点所引出的内容，通常表达作者的观点或说明文章的主题。在主题段或主题句中，特殊标点往往是理解中心思想的关键。

例：2009年12月真题

Just as she will have her critics, she will also have millions of fans who usually have little interest in the First Lady. Many African-American blogs have written about what they'd like to see Michelle bring to the White House—mainly showing the world that a black woman can support her man and raise a strong black family. **Michelle will have to work to please everyone—an impossible task.**

60. What does the author say about Michelle Obama as a First Lady?

    [A] However many fans she has, she should remain modest.

    [B] She shouldn't disappoint the African-American community.

    [C] However hard she tries, she can't expect to please everybody.

    [D] She will give priority to African-American women's concerns.

解析：四级阅读命题一般依照文章顺序，故将答案定位到59题出处(末段第二句)之后的末段第三句：Michelle will have to work to please everyone—an impossible task.(米歇尔必须努力取悦每个人——这是不可能完成的任务)，故选C"无论她如何努力，她也不可能指望取悦每个人"。四个选项中，只有C是原文的同义转述。

7. 复杂句、特殊句型

四级常考的复杂句包括长句、从句(尤其需要注意定语从句和同位语从句)、不定式、插入语、同位语等,注重考查全文段落和句间关系的理解,需要搞清复杂句的逻辑关系。同时,表示条件或让步的复杂句,以及虚拟语气、特殊句型(如not...but)等,一般暗示着作者的观点和态度,也是出题点。

例:2009年12月真题

The chief reason is that American schools don't tend to seriously consider looking abroad. For example, when the board of the University of Colorado searched for new president, it wanted a leader familiar with the state government, a major source of the university's budget. "We didn't do any global consideration," says Patricia Hayes, the board's chair. **The board ultimately picked Bruce Benson, a 69-year-old Colorado businessman and political** *activist*(活动家) **who is likely to do well in the main task of modern university presidents: fund-raising.** Fund-raising is a distinctively American thing, since U.S. schools rely heavily on donations. The fund-raising ability is largely a product of experience and necessity.

63. What is the chief consideration of American universities when hiring top-level administrators?

　　[A] Their political correctness.

　　[B] Their ability to raise funds.

　　[C] Their fame in academic circles.

　　[D] Their administrative experience.

解析:　根据关键词American universities和hiring top-level administrators定位到第三段,该段倒数第三句指出The board ultimately picked Bruce Benson, a 69-year-old Colorado businessman and political activist who is likely to do well in the main task of modern university presidents: fund-raising.(董事会最终选中了69岁的科罗拉多州商人兼政治活动家Bruce Benson,这是因为他可以圆满完成现代大学校长的主要任务——筹募资金),故选B "他们筹集资金的能力"。

8. 生词及一词多义

包含生词辨义和熟词僻义,推测词义有以下两种方法:

1) 根据上下文的因果、转折、对比等逻辑关系;

2）根据上下文的定义或解释说明，标志有：

(1)定语从句；

(2)破折号、括号、冒号；

(3)or, namely, that is, in other words等词汇或短语。

例：2006年12月真题

The field of medicine has not traditionally distinguished between someone who is merely "not ill" and someone who is in excellent health and pays attention to the body's special needs. **Both types have simply been called "well."**

64. Traditionally, a person is considered "well" if he _____.

[A] does not have any unhealthy living habits

[B] does not have any physical handicaps

[C] is able to handle his daily routines

[D] is free from any kind of disease

解析：根据原文，传统医学把not ill和excellent health两种状态都称为well，由此可知传统医学认为的well就是远离疾病，故选D。

(二)五大题型

四级阅读一般分为五大题型：细节题、主旨题、推理题、态度题和语义题。细节题考查把握事实和细节的能力，包括人物、地点、原因、数字等具体内容；主旨题考查把握主题及中心思想的能力；推理题考查根据表层含义推测隐含意义的能力；态度题考查领会、理解作者观点、态度、感情倾向的能力；语义题考查理解关键词句的能力。

1. 细节题：四级阅读最常考题型

1）题型分类

(1) 词语细节题：答案直接来自原文，只需按照题干中的关键词返回原文定位，找到对应表达，即可在上下文中找到答案。

(2) 隐含细节题：从题干中很难找到直接对应原文的表达，或答案间接隐含在原文中，或答案是原文中某一事实的原因、前提或结果等。

2）题干形式

(1) According to the passage, ...may...

(2) Those against...argue that...

（3）According to the passage, why... ?

（4）According to the author, ...

（5）According to the passage, why is...?

（6）In the first paragraph, people are reminded that...

3）解题技巧

（1）如针对某段内容提问，只读该段即可解题；

（2）如针对引言、举例或特殊标点（冒号、引号、破折号等）后的内容出题，只读该部分内容即可解题。

4）正确选项特征

（1）如有两个含义相近或相反选项，其一可能是正确选项。

例：2009年12月真题，Passage One

58. What is the common stereotype of African-American women according to the author?

　　[A] They are victims of family violence.

　　[B] They are of an inferior social group.

　　[C] They use quite a lot of body language.

　　[D] They live on charity and social welfare.

解析： A、B两选项含义相近，A为"她们是家庭暴力的受害者"，B为"她们属于地位低下的社会群体"，正确选项为B。

（2）正确选项一般不是照抄原文，而是进行同义替换。

例：2009年12月真题，Passage One

Many African-American blogs have written about what they'd like to see Michelle bring to the White House—mainly showing the world that a black woman can support her man and raise a strong black family.

59. What do many African-Americans write about in their blogs?

　　[A] Whether Michelle can live up to the high expectations of her fans.

　　[B] How Michelle should behave as a public figure.

　　[C] How proud they are to have a black woman in the White House.

　　[D] What Michelle should do as wife and mother in the White House.

解析: 根据关键词write about和blogs定位到末段第二句"很多非裔美国人在博客中写出他们希望看到米歇尔带给白宫的东西——主要是向世界展示一位黑人女性能够支持她的丈夫，并且支撑一个稳固的黑人家庭"，故选D"作为妻子和母亲，米歇尔在白宫应该做什么"。原文破折号后的support her man被替换为as wife，raise a strong black family被替换为(as) mother。

(3) 排除式题型中，含有模糊性概括词的一般是正确选项，而含绝对意义词的一般是错误选项。

A. 模糊概括词：some, certain, someone, sometimes, less, (not) as...as..., more...than...

B. 绝对含义词：all, any, everyone, everything, no, none, never, must, have to, always, too, so, alone, absolutely, mainly, entirely, completely, very, the most, hardly, scarcely

5) 错误选项特征

(1) 含有原文未涉及的内容；
(2) 更换原文关键词造成意义改变；
(3) 将原文内容过度绝对化；
(4) 与原文矛盾。

例：2009年12月真题，Passage Two

Many European universities, meanwhile, are still mostly dependent on government funding. But government support has failed to keep pace with rising student numbers. The decline in government support has made fund-raising an increasingly necessary ability among administrators, and has hiring committees hungry for Americans.

64. What do we learn about European universities from the passage?

[A] The tuitions they charge have been rising considerably.

[B] Their operation is under strict government supervision.

[C] They are strengthening their position by globalization.

[D] Most of their revenues come from the government.

解析: A、C两选项符合错误选项的第一个特征，故排除；B选项符合错误选项的第三个特征，是对原文的过度推断，故排除。

2. 主旨题

1）题型分类： 标题型、目的型、大意型

2）题干形式

（1）标题型：

A. Which of the following titles best summarize the main idea of the passage?

B. The best title for the passage would be...

（2）目的型：

A. The author's main purpose in writing the passage is to...

B. What's the author's purpose in writing this article?

（3）大意型：

A. The passage is mainly about...

B. The passage mainly discusses...

3）解题技巧

（1）主旨题答案一般在文章首尾段；

（2）文章中出现频率较高的词一般就是关键词，暗含中心思想。可能是同词复现，也可能是同类词复现；

（3）文章或段落的主题句一般具有概括性，结构简洁明了，一般不用长难句；

（4）文章或段落的其他句子都是对主题句的进一步论证、解释或说明。

4）正确选项特征

（1）正确选项一般内容全面、含义深刻、概括全文。

例：2005年1月真题

30. What is the author's purpose in writing this article?

[A] To justify the study of the Boston University Medical Center.

[B] To stress the importance of maintaining proper weight.

[C] To support the statement made by York Onnen.

[D] To show the most effective way to lose weight.

解析：选项D内容全面、含义深刻、概括全文。综合文章第一句、第三段第二句以及文章最后一段，可以看出作者主要强调减肥的最有效途径是锻炼，故选D。

（2）如果出现内容相近或相反的两个选项，其一可能是正确选项。

例：2006年6月17日真题

25. The passage mainly discusses _____.

　　[A] unequal treatment of boys and girls in developing countries

　　[B] the major contributions of educated women to society

　　[C] the economic and social benefits of educating women

　　[D] the potential earning power of well-educated women

解析：B、C两个选项内容相近，其一可能为正确选项。在本文第一段论点部分，作者提到enhancing women's contribution to development is actually as much an economic as a social issue；最后一段结论部分中，作者又强调...educating women has great social benefits. But it has enormous economic advantages as well。综上所述，本文所讨论的是女性接受教育所带来的经济和社会效益，故选C。B选项虽与C选项内容相近，但文中只提到了enhancing women's contribution to development的意义，未提到受教育女性对社会的具体贡献，故排除。

（3）正确选项一般含有概括性词语或抽象名词，如：way, benefit, importance, necessity, necessary, chance, opportunity, concept, approach, difficulty, many, both, various等。

例：2005年12月真题

31. The passage is mainly about _____.

　　[A] the benefits of manageable stress

　　[B] how to avoid stressful situations

　　[C] how to cope with stress effectively

　　[D] the effect of stress hormones on memory

解析：A选项出现了抽象名词benefit。文章首段末句宾语从句中的内容为全文主旨。选项中A的stress替换主旨句中的challenging situations；manageable替换原文中的in which you are able to rise to the occasion；benefits替换be good，故选A。

5) 错误选项特征

（1）含有原文未提及的信息；

（2）将原文内容过于一般化或没有具体信息；

（3）以偏概全。

例：2006年6月17日真题

25. The passage mainly discusses _____.

[A] unequal treatment of boys and girls in developing countries

[B] the major contributions of educated women to society

[C] the economic and social benefits of educating women

[D] the potential earning power of well-educated women

解析：A选项符合错误选项的第一特征，未体现文章的中心内容"教育"，故排除；B选项符合错误选项的第二特征，文中未提到受教育女性对社会的具体贡献，故排除；D选项符合错误选项的第三特征，只是文章论据部分的内容，故排除。

---

3. 语义题

1）题型分类

（1）单词短语题：一词多义、生僻词汇

（2）句子含义题：不能孤立判断，必须结合上下文

2）题干形式

（1）What do...mean by saying "..."?

（2）By saying "...", ...means "...".

（3）By saying "...", ...wants to convey the message that ...

（4）The "..."refers to...

（5）Traditionally, a person is considered "..." if he...

（6）According to the author, the true meaning of "..." is for people...

3）解题技巧

（1）定冠词the+被考词汇，前一句有解释；

（2）选项与被考单词字面意义相近的一般不是答案；

（3）符合全文主题、关系紧密的一般是正确答案，反之不是。

4）正确选项特征

（1）如果考查句意，正确选项往往语气不肯定或意义解释深刻。

例：大纲样题

65. What do the environmentalists mean by saying "Not so fast"?

　　[A] Don't be too optimistic.

　　[B] Don't expect fast returns.

　　[C] The oil drilling should be delayed.

　　[D] Oil exploitation takes a long time.

解析：A选项含有不肯定含义，意义解释深刻，故选A。

（2）如果考查熟词僻义，与上下文意义一致的解释往往是正确答案。

例：2006年12月真题

　　The field of medicine has not traditionally distinguished between someone who is merely "not ill" and someone who is in excellent health and pays attention to the body's special needs. Both types have simply been called "well."

64. Traditionally, a person is considered "well" if he _____.

　　[A] does not have any unhealthy living habits

　　[B] does not have any physical handicaps

　　[C] is able to handle his daily routines

　　[D] is free from any kind of disease

解析：本题考查的well是熟词，根据该段前两句，传统医学把not ill和excellent health两种状态都称为well，可知传统医学认为的well就是远离疾病，D选项的解释与上下文意义一致，故选D。

（3）正确选项往往同义替换所考词汇或句子。

例：2006年12月真题

　　As diners thirst for leading brands, bottlers and restaurateurs *salivate*（垂涎）over the profits. A restaurant's typical mark-up on wine is 100 to 150 percent, whereas on bottled water it's often 300 to 500 percent. But since water is much cheaper than wine, and many of the fancier brands aren't available in stores, most diners don't notice or care.

59. The "fancier brands" (Line 4) refers to _____.

　　[A] tap water from the Thames River

　　[B] famous wines not sold in ordinary stores

［C］PepsiCo's Aquafina and Coca-Cola's Dasani

［D］expensive bottled water with impressive names

解析：　根据本段尾句细节推断选D。D选项中的expensive同义替换题干中的
fancier(fancy的比较级，意为"昂贵的，高档的")和原文首句的leading。D
选项中的something with impressive names同义替换题干的brands(品牌)。

5）错误选项特征

（1）对句子的解释太宽或太窄。

例：2006年12月真题

58. By saying "My dog could tell the difference between bottled and tap water", von
Wiesenberger wants to convey the message that _____.

［A］plain tap water is certainly unfit for drinking

［B］bottled water is clearly superior to tap water

［C］bottled water often appeals more to dogs' taste

［D］dogs can usually detect a fine difference in taste

解析：　A对句子的解释太宽，C、D对句子的解释太窄，故排除。

（2）与该词含义无关或相反，或含有被考查词汇的常规含义。

例：2006年12月真题

65. According to the author, the true meaning of "wellness" is for people _____.

［A］to best satisfy their body's special needs

［B］to strive to maintain the best possible health

［C］to meet the strictest standards of bodily health

［D］to keep a proper balance between work and leisure

解析：　选项A为"最大地满足他们身体的特殊需求"，D为"在工作和娱乐之间保
持适当的平衡"，均与wellness的含义无关，故排除。正确选项为B"努力保
持最可能的健康状态"。

4. 观点题

1）题型分类： 作者观点题、作者态度题

2）题干形式

（1）What is the author's attitude toward...

（2）The author's attitude toward...could be described as...

（3）It's the author's view that...

（4）Which of the following statements best expresses the author's view?

（5）The author hopes to have the current situation on...improved by...

3）解题技巧

（1）作者观点常用personally, I think/hold, in my opinion/view, it is my view that等词引出，尤其是观点句中的must, should, ought to；

（2）与作者相反的观点常用suppose, claimed/ranked/considered/perceived as引出；直接或间接引语中一般不是作者观点，而是引用的观点；

（3）必背褒义词；

optimistic	乐观的	supporting	支持的
positive/favorable	赞成的	praising	赞扬的
approving	满意的	admiring	羡慕的
sober	冷静的	enthusiastic	热情的
concerned	关切的	polite	礼貌的
pleasant	愉快的	serious	严肃的
interesting	有趣的	humorous	幽默的
sympathetic	同情的	cautious	审慎的

（4）必背贬义词；

negative	否定的	critical	批评的
contradictory	反对的	suspicious/doubtful	怀疑的
disgusted	厌恶的	worried	担忧的
disappointed	失望的	pessimistic	悲观的
depressed	沮丧的	ironic	讽刺的
sarcastic	挖苦的	cynical	玩世不恭的
sentimental	伤感的	emotional	激动的
arbitrary	武断的		

（5）议论文的中心句暗示作者观点；说明文较客观，作者往往中立；描述性文章中，作者观点一般比较间接，但带有倾向性。

4）正确选项特征

（1）议论文中，意义深刻、富有哲理、符合一般规律的选项一般是正确选项。

例：大纲样题

57. Which of the following statements best expresses the author's view?

　　[A] The words people use can influence their behavior.

　　[B] Unpleasant words in sports are often used by foreign athletes.

　　[C] Aggressive behavior in sports can have serious consequences.

　　[D] Unfair judgments by referees will lead to violence on the sports field.

解析：　本文是议论文，选项A含义最深刻、富有哲理、符合一般规律，故选A。B、
　　　　C、D较具体，故排除。

（2）正确选项的态度常常与文章中的褒贬态度保持一致。

例：大纲样题

　　In the heat of battle, players have been observed to throw themselves across the court without considering the consequences that such a move might have on anyone in their way. I have also witnessed a player reacting to his opponent's intentional and illegal blocking by deliberately hitting him with the ball as hard as he could during the course of play. Off the court, they are good friends. Does that make any sense? **It certainly gives proof of a court attitude which departs from normal behavior.**

61. The author hopes to have the current situation on sports improved by ＿＿＿＿.

　　[A] regulating the relationship between players and referees

　　[B] calling on players to use clean language in the court

　　[C] raising the referee's sense of responsibility

　　[D] changing the attitude of players on the sports field

解析：　通过本段尾句，可知如今运动员在赛场上的态度背离了行为标准；通过
　　　　尾段第二句You may soon see and possibly feel the difference in your reaction
　　　　to the term "associate" rather than "opponent"，可知作者试图通过自己的建
　　　　议改变运动员在赛场上的态度，综合推断，故选D。

5）错误选项特征

（1）中性词选项一般为错误选项，如：indifferent（冷淡的），neutral（中立的），
　　　impassive（冷漠的），disinterested/uninterested（不关心的），apathetic（不关

心的), ambivalent（矛盾的）, impersonal（不带个人感情的）, subjective（主观的）, objective（客观的）, impartial（不偏袒的）, informative（提供信息的）, descriptive（描述性的）, matter-of-fact（事实的）等。作者一般持支持或反对态度。

例：2003年1月真题

21. What is the author's attitude toward high-tech communications equipment?

　　[A] Critical.　　　　　　　　　　[C] Indifferent.

　　[B] Prejudiced.　　　　　　　　　[D] Positive.

解析：　选项C为中性词，故排除。根据文章首段尾句中的benefit, enhanced等褒义词汇，可知作者持肯定态度，故正确选项为D。A"批评的"和B"带偏见的"不符合文章原意。

　（2）错误选项一般混淆两个事物或作者与别人的两种观点。

例：大纲样题

57. Which of the following statements best expresses the author's view?

　　[A] The words people use can influence their behavior.

　　[B] Unpleasant words in sports are often used by foreign athletes.

　　[C] Aggressive behavior in sports can have serious consequences.

　　[D] Unfair judgments by referees will lead to violence on the sports field.

解析：　选项B、C、D分别将"外国运动员"、"进攻行为"、"不公正裁判"与本文的主题"人们的语言影响行为"相混淆，故为错误选项，因此排除。

5. 推理题

1）题型分类

（1）局部推理题：多考

（2）篇章推理题：少考

2）题干形式

（1）We learn from the second paragraph that...

（2）It can be learned from the passage that...

（3）It can be inferred from the passage that...

（2）What do we learn about...from the last paragraph?

（3）What do we know about...from the passage?

3）解题技巧

（1）针对局部推理题，根据题干关键词在文中定位，按照上下文推理即可；

（2）针对篇章推理题，根据篇章或段落首尾的主题句解题。

4）正确选项特征

（1）如果所有选项均可凭常识判断，含义最深刻的是正确选项；或唯一不是常识的是正确选项。

例：2006年6月24日真题

61. It can be inferred from the passage that _____.

[A] honesty should be encouraged in interpersonal communications

[B] more employers will use emails to communicate with their employees

[C] suitable media should be chosen for different communication purposes

[D] email is now the dominant medium of communication within a company

解析：四个选项均可使用常识进行判断，选项C含义最深刻，故选C。根据尾段首句，Hancock的研究可以帮助公司为其雇员设计最好的交流方式，后又举例：销售产品时最好采用电话方式，评估工作时采用电子邮件。由此可知，交流目的不同，所适用的交流媒介各异，相应的选择也不同。

（2）正确选项一般较主观、不合理、不肯定或有新意，如：

A. 主观词汇： believe, suggest, expect, suspect, like, dislike, discuss, ignore, overlook

B. 不肯定词汇：can, could, should, may, might, be likely to, some, most, more or less, often, usually, possible, dubious, relatively, not necessarily, whether...or...

例：大纲样题

The oil industry goes with the high end of the range, which could equal as much as 10% of U.S. consumption for as long as six years.

63. We learn from the second paragraph that the American oil industry _____.

[A] shows little interest in tapping oil in ANWR

[B] expects to stop oil imports from Saudi Arabia

[C] tends to exaggerate America's reliance on foreign oil

[D] believes that drilling for ANWR will produce high yields

解析： D选项含有主观词汇believe，通过细节推断本句，故选D。believes替换原
文的goes with（同意），等于to accept an idea or a plan。the range指from 3
billion to 16 billion barrels，the high end指16 billion barrels。

5）错误选项特征

（1）推理过度，主次不分。

例：大纲样题

66. It can be learned from the passage that oil exploitation beneath ANWR's frozen
earth _____.

   [A] involves a lot of technological problems

   [B] remains a controversial issue

   [C] is expected to get under way soon

   [D] will enable the U.S. to be oil independent

解析： 选项A主次不分，选项D推理过度，选项C缺乏依据，故排除。根据原文，
由于much bargaining over leases和environmental permits and regulatory
review并非技术问题，故排除A。D对布什的看法过于绝对化，would...
provide a major boost to the country's energy independence不等于will enable
the U.S. to be oil independent，故排除D。

（2）以假乱真，编造信息。

例：2006年12月真题

57. What do we know about Iceberg Water from the passage?

   [A] It is a kind of iced water.　　　　[C] It is a kind of bottled water.

   [B] It is just plain tap water.　　　　[D] It is a kind of mineral water.

解析： A、B、D全为编造信息。选项A是根据iceberg设置的干扰选项，iced water
指"冰镇的水"。B是根据第四段尾句中的Pepsico's Aquafina and Coca-
Cola's Dasani are both purified tap water设置的干扰选项，如果Iceberg
Water是自来水的话，那么文章首句Reaching new peaks of popularity...is
Iceberg Water与第三段第一句前后矛盾，故排除B。D文中未提及。

第二节 真题选析

一、经典真题

Section A

Directions: *In this section, there is a passage with ten blanks. You are required to select one word for each blank from a list of choices given in a word bank following the passage. Read the passage through carefully before making your choices. Each choice in the bank is identified by a letter. Please mark the corresponding letter for each item on* **Answer Sheet 2** *with a single line through the centre.* ***You may not use any of the words in the bank more than once.***

Questions 47 to 56 are based on the following passage.

A bookless life is an incomplete life. Books influence the depth and breadth of life. They meet the natural __47__ for freedom, for expression, for creativity and beauty of life. Learners, therefore, must have books, and the right type of book, for the satisfaction of their need. Readers turn __48__ to books because their curiosity concerning all manners of things, their eagerness to share in the experiences of others and their need to __49__ from their own limited environment lead them to find in books food for the mind and the spirit. Through their reading they find a deeper significance to life as books acquaint them with life in the world as it was and it is now. They are presented with a __50__ of human experiences and come to __51__ other ways of thought and living. And while __52__ their own relationships and responses to life, the readers often find that the __53__ in their stories are going through similar adjustments, which help to clarify and give significance to their own.

Books provide __54__ material for readers' imagination to grow. Imagination is a valuable quality and a motivating power, and stimulates achievement. While enriching their imagination, books __55__ their outlooks, develop a fact-finding attitude and train them to use leisure __56__. The social and educational significance of the readers' books cannot be overestimated in an academic library.

[A] abundant	[I] establishing
[B] characters	[J] narrow
[C] communicating	[K] naturally
[D] completely	[L] personnel
[E] derive	[M] properly
[F] desire	[N] respect
[G] diversity	[O] widen
[H] escape	

Section B

Directions: *There are 2 passages in this section. Each passage is followed by some questions or unfinished statements. For each of them there are four choices marked [A], [B], [C] and [D]. You should decide on the best choice and mark the corresponding letter on **Answer Sheet 2** with a single line through the centre.*

Passage One

Questions 57 to 61 are based on the following passage.

If you're a male and you're reading this, congratulations: you're a survivor. According to statistics, you're more than twice as likely to die of skin cancer than a woman, and nine times more likely to die of AIDS. Assuming you make it to the end of your natural term, about 78 years for men in Australia, you'll die on average five years before a woman.

There're many reasons for this—typically, men take more risks than women and are more likely to drink and smoke—but perhaps more importantly, men don't go to the doctor.

"Men aren't seeing doctors as often as they should," says Dr. Gullotta. "This is particularly so for the over-40s, when diseases tend to strike."

Gullotta says a healthy man should visit the doctor every year or two. For those over 45, it should be at least once a year.

Two months ago Gullotta saw a 50-year-old man who had delayed doing anything about his smoker's cough for a year.

"When I finally saw him it had already spread and he has since died from lung cancer," he says. "Earlier detection and treatment may not have cured him, but it would have *prolonged*(延长) his life."

According to a recent survey, 95% of women aged between 15 and early 40s see a doctor once a year, compared to 70% of men in the same age group.

"A lot of men think they're *invincible*(不可战胜的)," Gullotta says. "They only come in when a friend drops dead on the golf course and they think, 'Geez, if it could happen to him, ...'"

Then there's the ostrich approach. "Some men are scared of what might be there and would rather not know," says Dr. Ross Cartmill.

"Most men get their cars serviced more regularly than they service their bodies," Cartmill says. He believes most diseases that commonly affect men could be addressed by preventive check-ups.

Regular check-ups for men would inevitably place strain on the public purse, Cartmill says. "But prevention is cheaper in the long run than having to treat the diseases. Besides, the ultimate cost is far greater; it's called premature death."

57. Why does the author congratulate his male readers at the beginning of the passage?

　　[A] They are more likely to survive serious diseases today.

　　[B] Their average life span has been considerably extended.

　　[C] They have lived long enough to read this article.

　　[D] They are sure to enjoy a longer and happier life.

58. What does the author state is the most important reason men die five years earlier on average than women?

　　[A] Men drink and smoke much more than women.

　　[B] Men don't seek medical care as often as women.

　　[C] Men aren't as cautious as women in face of danger.

　　[D] Men are more likely to suffer from fatal diseases.

59. Which of the following best completes the sentence "Geez, if it could happen to him, ..."(Lines 2-3, Para. 8)?

　　[A] it could happen to me, too 　　　[C] I should consider myself lucky

　　[B] I should avoid playing golf 　　　[D] it would be a big misfortune

60. What does Dr. Ross Cartmill mean by "the ostrich approach"(Line 1, Para. 9)?

　　[A] A casual attitude towards one's health conditions.

　　[B] A new therapy for certain psychological problems.

　　[C] Refusal to get medical treatment for fear of the pain involved.

　　[D] Unwillingness to find out about one's disease because of fear.

61. What does Cartmill say about regular check-ups for men?

　[A] They may increase public expenses.

　[B] They will save money in the long run.

　[C] They may cause psychological strains on men.

　[D] They will enable men to live as long as women.

Passage Two

Questions 62 to 66 are based on the following passage.

High-quality customer service is *preached*(宣扬) by many, but actually keeping customers happy is easier said than done.

Shoppers seldom complain to the manager or owner of a retail store, but instead will alert their friends, relatives, co-workers, strangers—and anyone who will listen.

Store managers are often the last to hear complaints, and often find out only when their regular customers decide to frequent their competitors, according to a study jointly conducted by Verde Group and Wharton School.

"Storytelling hurts retailers and entertains consumers," said Paula Courtney, President of the Verde group. "The store loses the customer, but the shopper must also find a replacement."

On average, every unhappy customer will complain to at least four others, and will no longer visit the specific store. For every dissatisfied customer, a store will lose up to three more due to negative reviews. The resulting "snowball effect" can be disastrous to retailers.

According to the research, shoppers who purchased clothing encountered the most problems. Ranked second and third were grocery and electronics customers.

The most common complaints include filled parking lots, *cluttered*(塞满了的) shelves, overloaded racks, out-of-stock items, long check-out lines, and rude salespeople.

During peak shopping hours, some retailers solved the parking problems by getting *moonlighting*(业余兼职的) local police to work as parking attendants. Some hired flag wavers to direct customers to empty parking spaces. This guidance eliminated the need for customers to circle the parking lot endlessly, and avoided confrontation between those eyeing the same parking space.

Retailers can relieve the headaches by redesigning store layouts, pre-stocking sales items, hiring speedy and experienced cashiers, and having sales representatives on hand to answer questions.

Most importantly, salespeople should be diplomatic and polite with angry customers.

"Retailers who're responsive and friendly are more likely to smooth over issues than those who aren't so friendly," said Professor Stephen Hoch. "Maybe something as simple as a greeter at the store entrance would help."

Customers can also improve future shopping experiences by filing complaints to the retailer, instead of complaining to the rest of the world. Retailers are hard-pressed to improve when they have no idea what is wrong.

62. Why are store managers often the last to hear complaints?

　　[A] Most customers won't bother to complain even if they have had unhappy experiences.

　　[B] Customers would rather relate their unhappy experiences to people around them.

　　[C] Few customers believe the service will be improved.

　　[D] Customers have no easy access to store managers.

63. What does Paula Courtney imply by saying "...the shopper must also find a replacement" (Lines 2-3, Para. 4)?

　　[A] New customers are bound to replace old ones.

　　[B] It is not likely the shopper can find the same products in other stores.

　　[C] Most stores provide the same kind of service.

　　[D] Not complaining to the manager causes the shopper some trouble too.

64. Shop owners often hire moonlighting police as parking attendants so that shoppers _____.

　　[A] can stay longer browsing in the store

　　[B] won't have trouble parking their cars

　　[C] won't have any worries about security

　　[D] can find their cars easily after shopping

65. What contributes most to smoothing over issues with customers?

　　[A] Manners of the salespeople.　　　　[C] Huge supply of goods for sale.

　　[B] Hiring of efficient employees.　　　[D] Design of the store layout.

66. To achieve better shopping experiences, customers are advised to _____.

   [A] exert pressure on stores to improve their service

   [B] settle their disputes with stores in a diplomatic way

   [C] voice their dissatisfaction to store managers directly

   [D] shop around and make comparisons between stores

试题详解

Section A

本文是一篇议论文，介绍了书籍对于人类的意义，强调没有书籍的人生不是完整的人生，书籍影响着人生的广度和深度。

	characters	角色	desire	愿望, 需要
名词(6个)	diversity	多样化	escape	逃避
	personnel	人员	respect	尊敬
	communicating	沟通, 交流	derive	获得
动词(8个)	desire	希望	escape	逃离
	establishing	建立	narrow	变狭窄
	respect	尊敬	widen	拓宽
形容词(2个)	abundant	充足的	narrow	狭窄的
副词(3个)	completely	完全地	naturally	自然地
	properly	恰当地		

47. [F] desire   48. [K] naturally

49. [H] escape   50. [G] diversity

51. [N] respect   52. [I] establishing

53. [B] characters   54. [A] abundant

55. [O] widen   56. [M] properly

Section B

Passage One

本文是一篇问题解决型的议论文，讨论男性健康问题。首先指出男性更容易死于重大疾病，平均寿命短于女性；其次通过举例和引用数据说明男性很少去看医生；接着分析男性不常去看病的两点原因：男性自认为强壮及鸵鸟心态；最后指出男性应该关注健康、定期检查。

57. A　推理题。根据题干，定位到首段前两句：If you're a male and you're reading this, congratulations: you're a survivor. According to statistics, you're more than twice as likely to die of skin cancer than a woman, and nine times more likely to die of AIDS，故选A。B、D选项文中未提及，C选项没有深入理解作者意图。

58. B　细节题。根据题干中的关键词the most important reason定位到第二段后半部分：but perhaps more importantly, men don't go to the doctor，故选B。D选项与题干并非因果关系，而是并列关系。

59. A　推理题。根据题干，定位到第八段尾句。显而易见，省略号后的部分应与前面对应，故选A"也能在我身上发生"。本题考查对句子隐含意思的理解。

60. D　语义题。根据题干中的关键词ostrich approach定位到第九段尾句：Some men are scared of what might be there and would rather not know.（有些男人害怕自己有问题，宁愿不知道），故选D。选项中的fear替换原文中的scared of，unwillingness to find out替换would rather not know。

61. B　细节题。根据题干中的关键词regular check-ups for men定位到尾段前两句：Regular check-ups for men would inevitably place strain on the public purse, Cartmill says. "But prevention is cheaper in the long run than having to treat the diseases..."（卡特米尔说，男性定期体检不可避免地会增加公众钱包的压力，但从长远的角度来看，预防的费用要低于治疗的费用），故选B。选项中的save money替换cheaper。A选项与原文意思相反；C选项中的psychological原文未提及；D选项根据原文无法推出。

参考译文

　　如果正在阅读本文的你是一位男性，那么恭喜你：你是幸存者。根据统计，你死于皮肤癌的可能性比女性高两倍，而死与艾滋病的可能性比女性高九倍。假如你可以活到自然死亡，澳大利亚男性的平均寿命是78岁左右，平均而论，你要比女性早死五年。

　　很多原因可以解释这一现象——典型的原因是男性比女性冒的风险更大，喝酒更多，吸烟更多——但或许更为重要的是，男性不看医生。

　　"男性看病的次数远远不及他们应该达到的次数，"古洛塔医生说。"40岁以上的男性尤其如此，这个年龄更容易生病。"

　　古洛塔认为一位健康的男性应该每一到两年就看一次医生。45岁以上的男性，至少应该每年看一次。

两个月前，古洛塔见到一位50岁的男性，他患有吸烟过多引发的咳嗽，但拖了一年才来看病。

"当我最后一次见到他时，病情已经蔓延了，后来他死于肺癌，"古洛塔说。"早点发现或治疗也许不能痊愈，但至少能够延长他的生命。"

根据最近一项调查，15至40岁之间的女性有95%每年看一次医生，而只有70%的同年龄段男性如此。

"很多男性认为他们是不可战胜的，"古洛塔说。"只有看到朋友在高尔夫球场上猝死之后，他们才会想到'天啊，如果会发生在他身上……'，才会来看医生。"

此外还有鸵鸟心态。"有些男性害怕自己有问题，宁愿不知道。"罗斯·卡特米尔医生说。

"大部分男性检修车辆的频率要高于检查自己身体的频率，"卡特米尔说。他认为大多数经常侵袭男性的疾病通过预防性体检均可发现。

男性定期体检不可避免地会增加公众钱包的压力，卡特米尔说。"但从长远角度来看，预防的费用要低于治疗的费用。此外，最终的代价更大，那就是英年早逝。"

Passage Two

本文是一篇问题解决型的议论文，主要讨论顾客的投诉问题。首先指出顾客很少直接向零售商投诉，而是向周围的人诉说自己糟糕的购物经历；其次分析顾客这种行为的影响并列举了顾客购物时经常遇到的问题；最后给出商家的应对策略和顾客的正确做法。

62. B 细节题。根据题干定位到第三段第一句，原因出现在第二段：Shoppers seldom complain to the manager or owner of a retail store, but instead will alert their friends, relatives, co-workers, strangers—and anyone who will listen, 故选B"顾客宁愿向他们身边的人提及他们不愉快的经历"。A选项与原文第二段意思相反；C选项与文章意思相悖；D选项文中未提及。

63. D 推理题。根据题干定位到第四段第二句："The store loses the customer, but the shopper must also find a replacement."（商店失去了顾客，而顾客也必须去寻找相应的替代），故选D "不向零售商投诉也会给顾客带来一些麻烦"。A选项文中未提及；B选项与原文意思不符且不合常理；C选项与but之前的"商店会失去顾客"无法形成转折关系。

64. B 细节题。根据题干中的关键词moonlighting police as parking attendants定位到第八段首句：During peak shopping hours, some retailers solved the parking

problems by getting moonlighting local police to work as parking attendants,
故选B"不再有停车的麻烦"。A选项与雇用兼职警察无关；C选项是对文中
警察的作用的错误理解；D选项文中未提及。

65. A　细节题。根据题干中的关键词most和customers定位到倒数第三段：Most
importantly, salespeople should be diplomatic and polite with angry
customers，故选A"销售人员的态度"。B、C、D均在倒数第四段提到，但并
非最重要的因素，故排除。

66. C　细节题。根据题干中的关键词shopping experience，定位到尾段首句：
Customers can also improve future shopping experiences by filing complaints
to the retailer, instead of complaining to the rest of the world，故选C "直接向
商店经理表达不满"。A、D选项文中未提及；B选项中的diplomatic应为
销售人员所为，而非顾客。

参考译文

许多人宣扬优质的客户服务，但事实上，要让客户满意说起来容易做起来难。

顾客很少会向商店的经理或老板直接投诉，相反，他们会提醒自己的朋友、
亲戚、同事，甚至任何愿意听信他们的陌生人不去光顾这家商店。

维德咨询公司和沃顿商学院的联合调查表明，商店经理往往是最后一个听
到抱怨的人，并且经常到了他们的常客频繁光顾竞争对手的店面时才发觉。

"传言损害了零售商的利益，娱乐了消费者。"维德公司总经理保拉·考特尼
说，"商店失去了顾客，顾客也必须去寻找相应的替代。"

一般来说，每位不满意的顾客至少会向四个人抱怨，并且不再光顾那家商
店。而商店会因每位不快顾客的负面评价损失三位以上的顾客。这种滚雪球效应
会给零售商带来灾难性的影响。

该调查显示，购买服装的顾客遇到的问题最多，其后依次是购买杂货和电子
商品的顾客。最常见的抱怨包括爆满的停车场、拥挤的货架、超载的物架、脱销
的商品、付账的长队和粗鲁的销售人员。

在购物高峰期，有的零售商雇用当地警察兼职协助停车的工作。有的则雇用
挥旗者把顾客引到空车位。此类引导使顾客不必再没完没了地绕着停车场寻找空
位，并且避免了不同顾客盯住同一车位而引发的冲突。

通过重新设计店面布局，预先储存在售的货物，雇用高效且经验丰富的收银
员，以及让销售代表在现场回答问题，零售商可以摆脱那些投诉带来的难题。

更为重要的是,对待那些恼羞成怒的顾客,销售人员应该表现得老练并彬彬有礼。

"那些能够及时作出反应并且态度良好的零售商,比那些不那么友好的零售商更容易顺利解决矛盾。"斯蒂芬·霍克教授说,"也许一些诸如在商店门口安排一个接待员的简单方式会有所裨益。"

客户也可以通过直接向零售商投诉而非向其他人抱怨的方式来改善未来的购物经历。因为当零售商根本不知道他们做错了什么的时候,是很难去进行改善的。

二、经典真题二

Section A

Directions: *In this section, there is a passage with ten blanks. You are required to select one word for each blank from a list of choices given in a word bank following the passage. Read the passage through carefully before making your choices. Each choice in the bank is identified by a letter. Please mark the corresponding letter for each item on* **Answer Sheet 2** *with a single line through the centre.* **You may not use any of the words in the bank more than once.**

Questions 47 to 56 are based on the following passage.

Every year in the first week of my English class, some students inform me that writing is too hard. They never write, unless assignments   47   it. They find the writing process   48   and difficult.

How awful to be able to speak in a language but not to write in it—   49   English, with its rich vocabulary. Being able to speak but not write is like living in an   50   mansion (豪宅) and never leaving one small room. When I meet students who think they can't write, I know as a teacher my   51   is to show them the rest of the rooms. My task is to build fluency while providing the opportunity inherent in any writing activity to   52   the moral and emotional development of my students. One great way to do this is by having students write in a journal in class every day.

Writing ability is like strength training. Writing needs to be done   53 , just like exercise; just as muscles grow stronger with exercise, writing skills improve quickly with writing practice. I often see a rise in student confidence and   54   after only a few weeks of journal writing.

Expressing oneself in writing is one of the most important skills I teach to strengthen the whole student. When my students practice journal writing, they are practicing for their future academic, political, and __55__ lives. They build skills so that some day they might write a great novel, a piece of sorely needed legislation, or the perfect love letter. Every day that they write in their journals puts them a step __56__ to fluency, *eloquence*（雄辩）, and command of language.

注意：此部分试题请在**答题卡2**上作答。

[A] closer	[I] painful
[B] daily	[J] performance
[C] emotional	[K] profession
[D] enhance	[L] remarkably
[E] enormous	[M] require
[F] especially	[N] sensitive
[G] hinder	[O] urge
[H] mission	

Section B

Directions: *There are 2 passages in this section. Each passage is followed by some questions or unfinished statements. For each of them there are four choices marked* [A], [B], [C] *and* [D]. *You should decide on the best choice and mark the corresponding letter on* **Answer Sheet 2** *with a single line through the centre.*

Passage One

Questions 57 to 61 are based on the following passage.

The January fashion show, called FutureFashion, exemplified how far green design has come. Organized by the New York-based nonprofit Earth Pledge, the show inspired many top designers to work with sustainable fabrics for the first time. Several have since made pledges to include organic fabrics in their lines.

The designers who undertake green fashion still face many challenges. Scott Hahn, cofounder with Gregory of Rogan and Loomstate, which uses all-organic cotton, says high-quality sustainable materials can still be tough to find. "Most designers with existing labels are finding there aren't comparable fabrics that can just replace what you're doing and what your customers are used to," he says. For example, organic cotton and non-organic cotton are virtually indistinguishable once woven into a dress. But some popular synthetics, like stretch nylon, still have few eco-friendly equivalents.

Those who do make the switch are finding they have more support. Last year the influential trade show Designers & Agents stopped charging its participation fee for young green *entrepreneurs*（企业家） who attend its two springtime shows in Los Angeles and New York and gave special recognition to designers whose collections are at least 25% sustainable. It now counts more than 50 green designers, up from fewer than a dozen two years ago. This week Wal-Mart is set to announce a major initiative aimed at helping cotton farmers go organic: it will buy *transitional*（过渡型的） cotton at higher prices, thus helping to expand the supply of a key sustainable material. "Mainstream is about to occur," says Hahn.

Some *analysts*（分析师） are less sure. Among consumers, only 18% are even aware that ecofashion exists, up from 6% four years ago. Natalie Hormilla, a fashion writer, is an example of the unconverted consumer. When asked if she owned any sustainable clothes, she replied: "Not that I'm aware of." Like most consumers, she finds little time to shop, and when she does, she's on the hunt for "cute stuff that isn't too expensive." By her own admission, green just isn't yet on her mind. But—thanks to the combined efforts of designers, retailers and suppliers—one day it will be.

注意：此部分试题请在**答题卡2**上作答。

57. What is said about FutureFashion?

　　[A] It inspired many leading designers to start going green.

　　[B] It showed that designers using organic fabrics would go far.

　　[C] It served as an example of how fashion shows should be organized.

　　[D] It convinced the public that fashionable clothes should be made durable.

58. According to Scott Hahn, one big challenge to designers who will go organic is that _____.

　　[A] much more time is needed to finish a dress using sustainable materials

　　[B] they have to create new brands for clothes made of organic materials

　　[C] customers have difficulty telling organic from non-organic materials

　　[D] quality organic replacements for synthetics are not readily available

59. We learn from Paragraph 3 that designers who undertake green fashion _____.

   [A] can attend various trade shows free

   [B] are readily recognized by the fashion world

   [C] can buy organic cotton at favorable prices

   [D] are gaining more and more support

60. What is Natalie Hormilla's attitude toward ecofashion?

   [A] She doesn't seem to care about it.

   [B] She doesn't think it is sustainable.

   [C] She is doubtful of its practical value.

   [D] She is very much opposed to the idea.

61. What does the author think of green fashion?

   [A] Green products will soon go mainstream.

   [B] It has a very promising future.

   [C] Consumers have the final say.

   [D] It will appeal more to young people.

Passage Two

Questions 62 to 66 are based on the following passage.

Scientists have devised a way to determine roughly where a person has lived using a *strand* (缕) of hair, a technique that could help track the movements of criminal suspects or unidentified murder victims.

The method relies on measuring how chemical variations in drinking water show up in people's hair.

"You're what you eat and drink, and that's recorded in your hair," said Thure Cerling, a geologist at the University of Utah.

While U.S. diet is relatively identical, water supplies vary. The differences result from weather patterns. The chemical composition of rainfall changes slightly as rain clouds move.

Most hydrogen and oxygen atoms in water are stable, but traces of both elements are also present as heavier *isotopes* (同位素). The heaviest rain falls first. As a result, storms that form over the Pacific deliver heavier water to California than to Utah.

Similar patterns exist throughout the U.S. By measuring the proportion of heavier hydrogen and oxygen isotopes along a strand of hair, scientists can construct a geographic timeline. Each inch of hair corresponds to about two months.

Cerling's team collected tap water samples from 600 cities and constructed a map of the regional differences. They checked the accuracy of the map by testing 200 hair samples collected from 65 barber shops.

They were able to accurately place the hair samples in broad regions roughly corresponding to the movement of rain systems.

"It's not good for *pinpointing* (精确定位)," Cerling said. "It's good for eliminating many possibilities."

Todd Park, a local detective, said the method has helped him learn more about an unidentified woman whose skeleton was found near Great Salt Lake.

The woman was 5 feet tall. Police recovered 26 bones, a T-shirt and several strands of hair.

When Park heard about the research, he gave the hair samples to the researchers. Chemical testing showed that over the two years before her death, she moved about every two months.

She stayed in the Northwest, although the test could not be more specific than somewhere between eastern Oregon and western Wyoming.

"It's still a substantial area," Park said. "But it narrows it way down for me."

注意：此部分试题请在**答题卡2**上作答。

62. What is the scientists' new discovery?

　　[A] One's hair growth has to do with the amount of water they drink.

　　[B] A person's hair may reveal where they have lived.

　　[C] Hair analysis accurately identifies criminal suspects.

　　[D] The chemical composition of hair varies from person to person.

63. What does the author mean by "You're what you eat and drink" (Line 1, Para. 3)?

　　[A] Food and drink affect one's personality development.

　　[B] Food and drink preferences vary with individuals.

　　[C] Food and drink leave traces in one's body tissues.

　　[D] Food and drink are indispensable to one's existence.

64. What is said about the rainfall in America's West?

    [A] There is much more rainfall in California than in Utah.

    [B] The water it delivers becomes lighter when it moves inland.

    [C] Its chemical composition is less stable than in other areas.

    [D] It gathers more light isotopes as it moves eastward.

65. What did Cerling's team produce in their research?

    [A] A map showing the regional differences of tap water.

    [B] A collection of hair samples from various barber shops.

    [C] A method to measure the amount of water in human hair.

    [D] A chart illustrating the movement of the rain system.

66. What is the practical value of Cerling's research?

    [A] It helps analyze the quality of water in different regions.

    [B] It helps the police determine where a crime is committed.

    [C] It helps the police narrow down possibilities in detective work.

    [D] It helps identify the drinking habits of the person under investigation.

试题详解

Section A

    本文是一篇议论文，介绍了书籍对于人类的意义，强调没有书籍的人生是不完整的，书籍影响着人生的广度和深度。

名词(4个)	mission	使命，任务	performance	表现；性能
	profession	职业，专业	urge	冲动
动词(4个)	enhance	加强，提高	hinder	阻碍，打扰
	require	要求，需要	urge	催促，鞭策
形容词(6个)	closer	更近的	daily	每天的
	emotional	感情的，情绪的	enormous	巨大的，庞大的
	painful	痛苦的	sensitive	敏感的
副词(3个)	daily	每天	especially	特别，尤其
	remarkably	显著地，非常		

47. [M] require   48. [I] painful

49. [F] especially   50. [E] enormous

51. [H] mission
52. [D] enhance
53. [B] daily
54. [J] performance
55. [C] emotional
56. [A] closer

Section B

Passage One

　　本文是一篇议论文,"总—分"结构,讨论了环保时尚问题。文章首先提出很多设计师开始走环保时尚路线,接着指出他们所面临的挑战以及获得的支持,最后展望环保时尚的发展前景。

57. A　细节题。根据关键词FutureFashion定位到首段前两句。首句提出FutureFashion向人们展示了环保设计发展到何种程度,第二句指出,此次展览首次鼓励众多顶级设计师使用环保布料,故选A"它鼓励很多顶级设计师开始走环保路线"。原文中的top被替换为leading,work with sustainable fabrics被替换为going green。

58. D　细节题。根据关键词Scott Hahn和challenge to designers定位到第二段。该段指出,Scott Hahn认为高质量的环保面料很难找到,没有匹配的面料替代设计师和顾客已经适应的面料,很难找到与合成材料相媲美的环保面料,故选D"没有合成面料的高质量有机替代品"。

59. D　细节题。根据关键词Paragraph 3定位到第三段首句,即该段主题句。结合第二段首句可知,原文中的make the switch被替换为题干中的undertake green fashion(进行环保时尚),第三段说明走环保路线的设计师获得越来越多的支持,故选D"获得越来越多的支持"。

60. A　细节题。根据关键词Natalie Hormilla定位到尾段第二至四句。第二句提到,只有18%的消费者知道ecofashion(生态时尚),Natalie就是没有转变的消费者之一。第四句提到,当被问到是否有环保服装时,Natalie答道:"我不知道有这种服装",故选A"她似乎并不关心它(生态时尚)"。原文中的sustainable clothes被替换为题干中的ecofashion。

61. B　推理题。根据关键词green定位到末段最后两句。原文提及,Natalie这样的消费者脑中还没有绿色时尚的概念,但是在设计师、零售商和供应商的共同努力下,终有一天绿色时尚会进入消费者脑中。由此推断,作者认为绿色环保服装前景光明,故选B"它(绿色时尚)拥有非常光明的未来"。文中的one day被替换为选项中的future。

参考译文

一月举行的被称为"未来时尚"的服装展向人们展示了环保设计已经发展到何种程度。此次展览由纽约当地的非营利性机构"地球宣言"主办,首次鼓励众多顶级设计师使用可持续环保材料。一些设计师已经承诺,将把有机布料纳入他们的选材。

走环保时尚路线的设计师仍然面对诸多挑战。Scott Hahn和Gregory同是使用全有机棉的Rogan and Loomstate公司的创始人。前者声称,高质量的可持续性面料还是很难找到。他说:"现有品牌的大多数设计师发现,并没有可相媲美的面料可以取代你正在使用的和顾客们已经适应的。"例如,有机棉与非有机棉一旦制成衣服后,其实是很难区分的。但是对一些流行的合成面料,如有弹性的尼龙面料,几乎没有与之匹配的环保面料。

那些作出转变的设计师发现他们正在获得更多支持。去年,颇具影响的Designers & Agents贸易展对参加其在洛杉矶和纽约举办的两次春季展览的年轻环保企业家实行免票入场,同时特别表彰了那些作品中包含至少四分之一可持续性产品的设计师。环保设计师已经由两年前的不足12人增加到现在的50多人。本周,沃尔玛计划宣布一项重大措施,目的是帮助种植棉花的农民走上有机种植之路。它将以略高的价格收购过渡型棉花,这有助于扩大一种主要的可持续性面料的供应量。Hahn认为:"(新的)主流即将出现。"

有分析家对此并不十分肯定。只有18%的消费者认识到存在环保时尚,比四年前的6%有所提高。时尚作家Natalie Homilla就是尚未转变观念的消费者之一。当问到她是否有环保服装时,她答道:"我并没有意识到还有这种服装。"像大多数消费者一样,她很少有时间购物。等到有时间购物时,她也是在寻找那些"不太贵的漂亮服装"。她自己承认,她的头脑中还没有"绿色"这一概念。但是,在设计师、零售商和供应商的共同努力之下,终有一天,它会存在于大家的头脑之中。

Passage Two

本文是一篇说明文,"总—分"结构,介绍了一种通过头发判断人居住地点的新方法。文章首先介绍了这种方法,接着说明其原理,最后阐述此方法的应用价值。

62. B　细节题。根据关键词scientists定位到首段。文章指出,科学家设计出一种方法,通过一缕头发就能大致确定人曾经居住过的地方,故选B"人们的头发可以揭示出他们在哪里居住过"。文中的determine roughly被替换为选项中的may reveal, 文中的where a person has lived被替换为where they have lived。

63. C 细节题。根据题干定位到第三段。文中that's recorded in your hair中的that指代and之前提到的what you eat and drink, 故选C"食物和饮品在人体组织中留下痕迹"。文中的what you eat and drink被替换为选项中的food and drink, recorded in被替换为leave traces in, hair被替换为body tissues。

64. B 细节题。根据关键词rainfall in America's West定位到第五段。文章指出, 含有最重同位素的雨先降落, 所以, 形成于太平洋表面的暴风雨带到美国西海岸加州的雨水比带到美国内陆犹他州的雨水要重, 故选B"当雨水向内陆移动时, 其所带的水变得越来越轻"。

65. A 细节题。根据关键词Cerling's team定位到第七段首句: Cerling的团队采集了来自600个城市的自来水样本, 并制出了关于自来水区域差异性的地图, 故选A"一张显示自来水区域差异的地图"。

66. C 推理题。由倒数第六段Cerling所说的it's good for eliminating many possibilities.(它对排除很多可能性有帮助)和尾段侦探Todd Park所说的But it narrows it way down for me.(但它为我缩小了范围), 故选C"它帮助警方在侦察工作中缩小可能性"。

参考译文

科学家已经设计出一种方法, 凭借人的一缕头发就能大致确定他曾经住过的地方。此项技术可以帮助跟踪锁定嫌犯或不明身份的案件受害者的活动场所。

这种方法靠的是测量饮用水中的化学成分在人的发丝中的显示变化。

"你吃喝过的东西都能通过你的身体体现出来, 这些都在你的头发上留下了记录,"犹他大学的地质学家Thure Cerling说。

虽然美国的饮食习惯相对来说比较类似, 但是供水却有差异。这些差异是气候类型导致的。雨水的化学成分随着云的移动会略有变化。

水里大部分的氢氧原子都很稳定, 但这两种化学元素留下的痕迹也以较重的同位素的形式出现。最重的雨最先落下, 所以, 形成于太平洋表面的暴风雨带给加州的雨水比带给犹他州的雨水要重。

类似的形式存在于整个美国。科学家通过测量一缕头发中氢和氧同位素所占的比例, 就能构建出一个地理时间表。每英寸头发对应大约两个月的时间。

Cerling的小组采集了来自600个城市的自来水样本，并且制作了关于自来水区域差异性的地图。他们对从65家理发店搜集的200人的头发样本进行检测，以检验地图的准确性。

他们能够将头发样本准确地定位到与雨水系统的移动粗略对应的地区。

Cerling说："这种方法并不适于进行精确定位，但是对排除很多可能性有帮助。"

当地的侦探Todd Park说这个方法帮助他了解了更多关于一具在大盐湖附近发现的不明身份的女尸的情况。

这位女士身高五英尺。警察找到她的26块骨头、一件T恤和几缕头发。

当Park听到这项研究时，他就把其头发样本交给了研究人员。化学检验表明，在死前的两年中，她每两个月就搬一次家。

她在西北待过，尽管这项检验只能指出大概是在俄勒冈州东部和怀俄明州西部的某个地方。

Park说："这仍然是个大致区域，但是对我来说，已经缩小了范围。"

三、经典真题三

Section A

Directions: *In this section, there is a passage with ten blanks. You are required to select one word for each blank from a list of choices given in a word bank following the passage. Read the passage through carefully before making your choices. Each choice in the bank is identified by a letter. Please mark the corresponding letter for each item on* **Answer Sheet 2** *with a single line through the centre.* ***You may not use any of the words in the bank more than once.***

Questions 47 to 56 are based on the following passage.

In families with two working parents, fathers may have more impact on a child's language development than mothers, a new study suggests.

Researchers __47__ 92 families from 11 child care centers before their children were a year old, interviewing each to establish income, level of education and child care arrangements. Overall, it was a group of well-educated middle-class families, with married parents both living in the home.

When the children were 2, researchers videotaped them at home in free-play sessions with both parents, __48__ all of their speech. The study will appear in the November issue of *The Journal of Applied Developmental Psychology*.

The scientists measured the __49__ number of *utterances*（话语）of the parents, the number of different words they used, the complexity of their sentences and other __50__ of their speech. On average, fathers spoke less than mothers did, but they did not differ in the length of utterances or proportion of questions asked.

Finally, the researchers __51__ the children's speech at age 3, using a standardized language test. The only predictors of high scores on the test were the mother's level of education, the __52__ of child care and the number of different words the father used.

The researchers are __53__ why the father's speech, and not the mother's, had an effect.

"It's well __54__ that the mother's language does have an impact," said Nadya Pancsofar, the lead author of the study. It could be that the high-functioning mothers in the study had __55__ had a strong influence on their children's speech development, Ms. Pancsofar said, "or it may be that mothers are __56__ in a way we didn't measure in the study."

注意：此部分试题请在**答题卡2**上作答。

[A] already	[I] quoted
[B] analyzed	[J] recording
[C] aspects	[K] recruited
[D] characters	[L] total
[E] contributing	[M] unconscious
[F] describing	[N] unsure
[G] established	[O] yet
[H] quality	

Section B

Directions: *There are 2 passages in this section. Each passage is followed by some questions or unfinished statements. For each of them there are four choices marked [A], [B], [C] and [D]. You should decide on the best choice and mark the corresponding letter on **Answer Sheet 2** with a single line through the centre.*

Passage One

Questions 57 to 61 are based on the following passage.

Throughout this long, tense election, everyone has focused on the presidential candidates and how they'll change America. Rightly so. But selfishly, I'm more fascinated by Michelle Obama and what she might be able to do, not just for this country, but for me as an African-American woman. As the potential First Lady, she would have the world's attention. And that means that for the first time people will have a chance to get up close and personal with the type of African-American woman they so rarely see.

Usually, the lives of black women go largely unexamined. The prevailing theory seems to be that we're all hot-tempered single mothers who can't keep a man. Even in the world of make-believe, black women still can't escape the stereotype of being eye-rolling, oversexed females raised by our never-married, *alcoholic*(酗酒的) mothers.

These images have helped define the way all black women are viewed, including Michelle Obama. Before she ever gets the chance to commit to a cause, charity or foundation as First Lady, her most urgent and perhaps most complicated duty may be simply to be herself.

It won't be easy. Because few mainstream publications have done in-depth features on regular African-American women, little is known about who we are, what we think and what we face on a regular basis. For better or worse, Michelle will represent us all.

Just as she will have her critics, she will also have millions of fans who usually have little interest in the First Lady. Many African-American blogs have written about what they'd like to see Michelle bring to the White House—mainly showing the world that a black woman can support her man and raise a strong black family. Michelle will have to work to please everyone—an impossible task. But for many African-American women like me, just a little of her *poise*(沉着), confidence and intelligence will go a long way in changing an image that's been around for far too long.

注意:此部分试题请在**答题卡2**上作答。

57. Why does Michelle Obama hold a strong fascination for the author?

　　[A] She serves as a role model for African-American women.

　　[B] She possesses many admirable qualities becoming a First Lady.

[C] She will present to the world a new image of African-American women.

[D] She will pay closer attention to the interests of African-American women.

58. What is the common stereotype of African-American women according to the author?

[A] They are victims of family violence.

[B] They are of an inferior social group.

[C] They use quite a lot of body language.

[D] They live on charity and social welfare.

59. What do many African-Americans write about in their blogs?

[A] Whether Michelle can live up to the high expectations of her fans.

[B] How Michelle should behave as a public figure.

[C] How proud they are to have a black woman in the White House.

[D] What Michelle should do as wife and mother in the White House.

60. What does the author say about Michelle Obama as a First Lady?

[A] However many fans she has, she should remain modest.

[B] She shouldn't disappoint the African-American community.

[C] However hard she tries, she can't expect to please everybody.

[D] She will give priority to African-American women's concerns.

61. What do many African-American women hope Michelle Obama will do?

[A] Help change the prevailing view about black women.

[B] Help her husband in the task of changing America.

[C] Outshine previous First Ladies.

[D] Fully display her fine qualities.

Passage Two

Questions 62 to 66 are based on the following passage.

When next year's crop of high-school graduates arrive at Oxford University in the fall of 2009, they'll be joined by a new face: Andrew Hamilton, the 55-year-old *provost* (教务长) of Yale, who'll become Oxford's vice-chancellor—a position equivalent to university president in America.

Hamilton isn't the only educator crossing the Atlantic. Schools in France, Egypt, Singapore, etc. have also recently made top-level hires from abroad. Higher education has become a big and competitive business nowadays, and like so many businesses, it's gone global. Yet the talent flow isn't universal. High-level personnel tend to head in only one direction: outward from America.

The chief reason is that American schools don't tend to seriously consider looking abroad. For example, when the board of the University of Colorado searched for new president, it wanted a leader familiar with the state government, a major source of the university's budget. "We didn't do any global consideration," says Patricia Hayes, the board's chair. The board ultimately picked Bruce Benson, a 69-year-old Colorado businessman and political *activist*(活动家) who is likely to do well in the main task of modern university presidents: fund-raising. Fund-raising is a distinctively American thing, since U.S. schools rely heavily on donations. The fund-raising ability is largely a product of experience and necessity.

Many European universities, meanwhile, are still mostly dependent on government funding. But government support has failed to keep pace with rising student numbers. The decline in government support has made fund-raising an increasingly necessary ability among administrators, and has hiring committees hungry for Americans.

In the past few years, prominent schools around the world have joined the trend. In 2003, when Cambridge University appointed Alison Richard, another former Yale provost, as its vice-chancellor, the university publicly stressed that in her previous job she had *overseen*(监督) "a major strengthening of Yale's financial position."

Of course, fund-raising isn't the only skill outsiders offer. The globalization of education means more universities will be seeking heads with international experience of some kind to promote international programs and attract a global student body. Foreigners can offer a fresh perspective on established practices.

注意：此部分试题请在**答题卡2**上作答。

62. What is the current trend in higher education discussed in the passage?

　[A] Institutions worldwide are hiring administrators from the U.S.

　[B] A lot of political activists are being recruited as administrators.

　[C] American universities are enrolling more international students.

　[D] University presidents are paying more attention to fund-raising.

63. What is the chief consideration of American universities when hiring top-level administrators?

　　[A] Their political correctness.　　[C] Their fame in academic circles.

　　[B] Their ability to raise funds.　　[D] Their administrative experience.

64. What do we learn about European universities from the passage?

　　[A] The tuitions they charge have been rising considerably.

　　[B] Their operation is under strict government supervision.

　　[C] They are strengthening their position by globalization.

　　[D] Most of their revenues come from the government.

65. Cambridge University appointed Alison Richard as its vice-chancellor chiefly because_____.

　　[A] she was known to be good at raising money

　　[B] she could help strengthen its ties with Yale

　　[C] she knew how to attract students overseas

　　[D] she had boosted Yale's academic status

66. In what way do top-level administrators from abroad contribute to university development?

　　[A] They can enhance the university's image.

　　[B] They will bring with them more international faculty.

　　[C] They will view a lot of things from a new perspective.

　　[D] They can set up new academic disciplines.

试题详解

Section A

　　本文是一篇说明文，"总—分"结构，介绍了一个实验，实验的结果证明父亲在孩子的语言发展方面所起的作用似乎超过母亲。

名词(4个)	aspects	方面	characters	人物；字
	quality	质量；性质	recording	录音
动词(7个)	analyzed	分析	contributing	贡献，起作用
	describing	描述	established	建立，制定
	quoted	引用	recruited	招募，吸纳
	total	总计，共计		

形容词(6个)	contributing	贡献的, 起作用的	established	确定的
	recording	记录的	total	总的, 全体的
	unconscious	无意识的; 无知觉的	unsure	不确定的, 不肯定的
副词(2个)	already	已经	yet	还, 仍然

47. [K] recruited   48. [J] recording

49. [L] total   50. [C] aspects

51. [B] analyzed   52. [H] quality

53. [N] unsure   54. [G] established

55. [A] already   56. [E] contributing

Section B

Passage One

    本文是一篇议论文, 介绍了作者对美国第一夫人米歇尔·奥巴马的看法。文章首先表明作者对她的关注, 接着阐述了人们对非裔女性的看法, 最后指出人们期待第一夫人能帮助改善人们对非裔女性的看法。

57. B   细节题。根据关键词fascination定位到首段第二句: But selfishly, I'm more fascinated by Michelle Obama and what she might be able to do, not just for this country, but for me as an African-American woman.(但平心而论, 我对米歇尔·奥巴马以及她能做些什么更加着迷, 不仅对她能为美国做什么着迷, 更对她能为同为非裔女性的我做什么着迷), 以及首段尾句: And that means that for the first time people will have a chance to get up close and personal with the type of African-American woman they so rarely see.(这就意味着人们将有机会靠近并接触他们极少见到的这一类非裔美国女性)。故选B"她将向世界展示非裔美国女性的崭新形象"。

58. B   细节题。根据关键词stereotype定位到第二段尾句: Even in the world of make-believe, black women still can't escape the stereotype of being eye-rolling, oversexed females raised by our never-married, alcoholic mothers.(甚至在这个擅长伪装的世界里, 黑人女性仍然无法摆脱人们的思维定势——被未婚且酗酒的母亲带大的翻着白眼、纵欲无度的女人), 故选B"她们属于低下的社会群体"。

59. D 　细节题。根据关键词write about 和blogs定位到末段第二句：Many African-American blogs have written about what they'd like to see Michelle bring to the White House—mainly showing the world that a black woman can support her man and raise a strong black family.(很多非裔美国人在博客中写出他们希望看到米歇尔带给白宫的东西—— 主要是向世界展示一位黑人女性能够支持她的丈夫，并且支撑一个稳固的黑人家庭)，故选D"作为妻子和母亲，米歇尔在白宫应该做什么"。原文破折号后的 support her man被替换为as wife，raise a strong black family被替换为(as) mother。

60. C 　细节题。四级阅读命题一般依照文章顺序，故将答案定位到59题出处(末段第二句) 之后的末段第三句：Michelle will have to work to please everyone—an impossible task.(米歇尔必须努力取悦每个人——这是不可能完成的任务)，故选C"无论她如何努力，她也不可能指望取悦每个人"。四个选项中，只有C是原文的同义转述。

61. A 　细节题。根据关键词many African-American women定位到文章尾句：But for many African-American women like me, just a little of her poise, confidence and intelligence will go a long way in changing an image that's been around for far too long.(但对许多像我这样的非裔美国女性而言，她的些许沉着、自信和智慧都将对帮助改善那些存在已久的印象有长远的影响)，故选A"帮助改变对于黑人女性的流行看法"。

参考译文

在漫长而紧张的选举期间，大家都将注意力集中在总统候选人以及他们将如何改变美国上面。这很正常。但平心而论，我对米歇尔·奥巴马以及她能做些什么更加着迷，不仅对她能为美国做什么着迷，更对她能为同为非裔女性的我做什么着迷。由于可能成为第一夫人，她将被世界关注。这就意味着人们将有机会靠近并接触他们极少见到的这一类非裔美国女性。

通常，黑人女性的生活在很大程度上并未经过考察。主流看法认为，我们都是脾气暴躁、留不住男人的单身母亲。甚而在想象中，黑人女性仍然无法摆脱人们的思维定势——被未婚且酗酒的母亲带大的翻着白眼、纵欲无度的女人。

这些形象限定了人们对所有黑人女性的看法，包括对米歇尔·奥巴马的看法。在她赢得机会可以以第一夫人的身份做一番事业、发起慈善事业或基金之前，她最急迫、或许也是最复杂的任务可能就是做她自己。

　　这谈何容易。由于一直以来都没有什么主流宣传深入关注普通非裔美国女性，人们对我们是谁、在想什么以及平时面对什么几乎一无所知。无论如何，她都将代表我们所有的非裔美国女性。

　　正如她将有众多批评者一样，她也会拥有数百万平素对第一夫人毫无兴趣的狂热追随者。很多非裔美国人在博客中写出他们希望看到米歇尔带给白宫的东西——主要是向世界展示一位黑人女性能够支持她的丈夫，并且支撑一个稳固的黑人家庭。米歇尔必须努力取悦每个人——这是不可能完成的任务。但对像我这样的非裔美国女性而言，她的些许沉着、自信和智慧都将对帮助改善那些存在已久的印象有长远的影响。

Passage Two

　　本文是一篇夹叙夹议的议论文，文章首先在前两段介绍了当今世界上很多大学都乐于从美国招聘校长的现象，接着在最后四段分析了其原因。

62. A　主旨题。根据关键词discussed in the passage可知，本题考查全文主旨，故应在理解全文大意的基础上作答。文章前两段指出世界上很多大学都倾向于从美国聘请校长，然后分析了其原因，故选A"世界上的大学正在从美国聘请校长"。

63. B　推理题。根据关键词American universities和hiring top-level administrators定位到第三段，该段倒数第三句指出：The board ultimately picked Bruce Benson, a 69-year-old Colorado businessman and political activist who is likely to do well in the main task of modern university presidents: fund-raising.（董事会最终选取中了69岁的科罗拉多州商人兼政治活动家Bruce Benson，这是因为他可以圆满完成现代大学校长的主要任务——筹募资金），故选B"他们筹集资金的能力"。

64. D　细节题。根据关键词European universities定位到第四段首句：Many European universities, meanwhile, are still mostly dependent on government funding.（与此同时，很多欧洲大学仍然主要依赖政府拨款），故选D"他们的大部分资金来自政府"。

65. A　推理题。根据关键词Cambridge University和Alison Richard定位到第五段第二句：In 2003, when Cambridge University appointed Alison Richard, another former Yale provost, as its vice-chancellor, the university publicly stressed that in her previous job she had overseen "a major strengthening of Yale's financial position".（2003年，英国剑桥大学任命另一位美国耶鲁大学前教务长

Alison Richard为副校长时曾公开声称：在之前的职位上，她的监管使得"耶鲁的财政地位得到了极大的巩固"），故选A"她因擅长筹集资金而闻名"。选项中的"擅长筹集资金"是对原文"使财政地位得到了极大的巩固"的提炼和同义转述。

66. C　细节题。根据命题与文章顺序基本一致原则，定位到末段。末段尾句提到：Foreigners can offer a fresh perspective on established practices.（这些外国人能为已有的习惯做法带来全新的视角），故选C"他们将从一个崭新的角度看待很多事情"。

参考译文

当2009年秋季新一届高中毕业生来到牛津大学之时，他们将迎来一位新人：55岁的美国耶鲁大学教务长Andrew Hamilton。他将成为牛津大学的新任副校长——这一职位与美国的大学校长比肩。

Hamilton并非唯一一位飘扬过海的教育家。近年来，法国、埃及、新加坡等国的大学也均从海外聘请高端英才。如今，高等教育业已成为一项规模巨大且竞争惨烈的产业。与其他诸多产业一样，它已经全球化。但人才流动却不是世界性的，高端人才通常只倾向于一个方向：从美国去海外。

这其中的主要原因是美国的大学从未认真考虑过从海外引进人才。例如，当科罗拉多大学董事会开始寻找一位新任校长时，他们希望这位新领导能熟知州政府，这是因为州政府是大学预算的主要来源。董事会主席Patricia Hayes说："我们不考虑任何海外人选。"董事会最终选中了69岁的科罗拉多州商人兼政治活动家Bruce Benson，这是因为他可以圆满完成现代大学校长的主要任务：筹募资金。由于美国大学在很大程度上依靠捐款，所以筹资是美国大学特有的现象。筹资能力在很大程度上是经验和需求的产物。

与此同时，很多欧洲大学仍然主要依赖政府拨款。但政府给予的支持已无法跟上不断增长的学生数量。政府支持的不足使得筹募资金逐渐成为大学管理者必备的能力，这也使得众多委员会希望聘请精于此道的美国人。

在过去几年中，全世界的著名大学都卷入了这场浪潮。2003年，英国剑桥大学任命另一位美国耶鲁大学前教务长Alison Richard为副校长时曾公开声称：在之前的职位上，她的监管使得"耶鲁的财政地位得到了极大的巩固"。

当然，筹资能力并非这些外来领导者所展示的唯一能力。教育全球化意味着大学要寻觅具有某种国际经验的领导者，以此推进国际项目并吸引全世界的优秀学生。这些外国人能为已有的习惯做法带来全新的视角。

第三节 强化训练

强化训练一

Section A

Directions: *In this section, there is a passage with ten blanks. You are required to select one word for each blank from a list of choices given in a word bank following the passage. Read the passage through carefully before making your choices. Each choice in the bank is identified by a letter. Please mark the corresponding letter for each item on **Answer Sheet 2** with a single line through the centre. **You may not use any of the words in the bank more than once.***

Questions 47 to 56 are based on the following passage.

An investigator into the drug *overdose*（服药过量）death of *Marilyn Monroe*（玛丽莲·梦露）43 years ago Friday still is not convinced she killed herself. John W. Miner, who investigated Monroe's death as a Los Angeles County prosecutor, claims Monroe's psychologist, Dr. Ralph Greenson, played him secret audiotapes made by the star during one of her therapy sessions __47__ before her death. A key __48__ of the *alleged*（所谓的）tapes, according to Miner, is that Monroe was not __49__ and was actively planning to become a serious Shakespearean actress. Miner says he took careful, handwritten notes of the tapes and later produced a near-exact transcript. There is no __50__ Miner's claims are true, since Dr. Greenson is now dead and no one else claims to have heard the tape.

"You are the only person who will ever know the most __51__ thoughts of Marilyn Monroe," she allegedly told her doctor. In Miner's transcript, Monroe discussed her plans to __52__ Shakespeare. "No __53__ person could possibly think that the person who made those tapes killed herself," Miner said. She also may have recorded her feelings about having to __54__ off her *romance*（罗曼史）with Robert Kennedy. "There is no room in my life for him," she allegedly said. "I guess I don't have the __55__ to face up to it and hurt him. I want someone else to tell him it's over. I tried to get the President to do it, but I couldn't __56__ him."

[A] proof	[I] revelation
[B] reasonable	[J] pursue
[C] postpone	[K] courage
[D] secret	[L] constantly
[E] bold	[M] depressed
[F] break	[N] assignment
[G] optimistic	[O] reach
[H] shortly	

Section B

Directions: *There are 2 passages in this section. Each passage is followed by some questions or unfinished statements. For each of them there are four choices marked* [A], [B], [C] *and* [D]. *You should decide on the best choice and mark the corresponding letter on* **Answer Sheet 2** *with a single line through the centre.*

Passage One

Question 57 to 61 are based on the following passage.

Only special plants can survive the terrible climate of a desert, for these are regions where the annual range of the soil temperature can be over 75℃. Furthermore, during the summer there are few clouds in the sky to protect plants from the sun's ray. Another problem is the fact that there are frequently strong winds which drive small, sharp particles of sand into the plants, tearing and damaging them. The most difficult problem for all forms of plant life, however, is the fact that the entire annual rainfall occurs during a few days or weeks in spring.

Grasses and flowers in desert survive from one year to the next by existing through the long, hot, dry season in the form of seeds. These seeds remain inactive unless the right amount of rain falls. If no rain falls, or if insufficient rain falls, they wait until the next year, or even still the next. Another factor that helps these plants to survive is the fact that their life cycles are short. By the time that the water from the spring rains disappears—just a few weeks after it falls—such plants no longer need any.

The *perennials*(多年生植物) have special features which enable them to survive as plants for several years. Thus, nearly all desert perennials have extensive root systems below ground and a small shoot system above ground. The large root network enables the plant to absorb as much water as possible in a short time. The small shoot system, on the other hand, considerably limits water loss by *evaporation*(蒸发).

Another feature of many desert perennials is that after the rainy season they lose their leaves in preparation for the long, dry season, just as trees in wetter climates lose theirs in preparation for the winter. This reduces their water loss by evaporation during the dry season. Then, in the next rainy season, they come fully alive once more, and grow new branches, leaves and flowers, just as the grasses and flowers in desert do.

57. Ordinary plants cannot survive the desert weather as a result of the following EXCEPT for _____.

[A] the strong winds   [C] the long summer days

[B] the strong sun's ray   [D] the high soil temperature

58. Some grasses and flowers can survive in the desert because _____.

[A] they need little water for their survival

[B] they bear long roots and the seeds are fit for dry weather

[C] they stay in the form of seeds to wait for the right amount of water

[D] with long roots, they do not depend on the shoot system to get enough water

59. We can learn from the passage that the shoot system of the perennials _____.

[A] can help the perennials absorb less of the sun's ray

[B] decides the appearance of the perennials in desert

[C] limits the function of the perennials' branches

[D] may prevent the perennials from losing much water

60. According to the passage, spring is the best time for plants in desert _____.

[A] to find a shady place   [C] to reduce water loss

[B] to get water from their growth   [D] to enjoy the sunshine

61. The last paragraph is mainly about _____.

[A] the comparison between plants in different areas

[B] the growth of new leaves in the rainy season

[C] water loss by evaporation in the dry season

[D] the changes in the leaves of the perennials

Passage Two

Questions 62 to 66 are based on the following passage.

El Nino is a disturbance of the world's normal climate pattern. During El Nino events, the westerly trade winds become slower and the warmer water in the western Pacific moves towards South America. This huge increase in ocean temperatures—as much as eight degrees centigrade—and the change in atmospheric conditions bring rain to the deserts of South America and the rainforests of south-east Asia, with drought conditions throughout eastern and southern Africa. There are many knock-on effects all over the world.

The home of El Nino is Peru. El Nino, "the Christ Child", was first named by Peruvian fishermen one Christmas when they noticed unusual warm currents affecting the Pacific coast of South America. Up and down the country, from desert to highlands, El Nino weather phenomena have brought destructive floods, costing £200 million in immediate and long-term damage, and undoing the work of many development projects.

"The destruction is near total," Dominic Brain, a worker for Christian Aid reported. "Few of the houses could withstand the floodwater. Today I visited Acomayo, a *shantytown*(贫民区) where 17,500 people once lived. Now only ten percent of the houses are still standing. The bulk of the population has lost all their possessions.

The town of Ica seldom sees rain. Houses for the poor are built of adobe—sun-baked mud standing side by side in long terraces. When the River Ica burst its banks in late January, 15,000 houses were swiftly flooded. Up to 5,000 houses were destroyed—a sign not only of the force of the river, which loosened huge rocks and swept them falling down from the Andean mountains, but of the vulnerability of the homes which hardly ever face rain. "They melted like chocolate," exclaimed an eye witness. "The extent of the damage was terrible!"

Almost immediately health became a problem. Without proper *plumbing*(排水), waste matter rose to the surface of the floodwaters. People received cuts walking through the floodwater and mud Cholera—epidemic in Peru in the early nineties—returned, with 90 reported cases in Ica province alone. The entire city seems to have drowned—first in floodwaters 1.5 meters high, and then in mud. Sadly, three people lost their lives, sucked into the floodwaters, but it was a miracle that there were not more *casualties*(伤亡者).

62. El Nino is a warm ocean current _____.

　　[A] which centers on America and Africa

　　[B] which kills many people ever time

　　[C] which was named by an American

　　[D] which has side-effects all over the world

63. It can be inferred from the passage that El Nino first appeared in _____.

　　[A] Pacific　　　　　　　　　　[C] South America

　　[B] Africa　　　　　　　　　　[D] Peru

64. Houses in Ica experienced terrible destruction during the El Nino event because _____.

　　[A] the El Nino event was the strongest

　　[B] it seldom rained there

　　[C] the houses couldn't stand the flood

　　[D] El Nino was unexpected

65. How did the three people in Ica lose their lives?

　　[A] They died in the collapsed houses.

　　[B] They died of an epidemic.

　　[C] They were carried away by the flood.

　　[D] They tried to walk in the floodwater.

66. This passage is devoted to introduction to _____.

　　[A] the causes and effects of El Nino weather phenomena

　　[B] the worldwide monitoring network set up to predict El Nino

　　[C] the relationship between the ocean temperatures and climate patterns

　　[D] El Nino phenomena and destructive effects of one El Nino event on Ica

试题详解

Section A

名词	proof	证据	secret	秘密
	break	休息；破裂	revelation	揭示
	courage	勇气	assignment	任务，分派
	reach	能到达的范围		

动词	postpone	推迟，延期	break	打破，损坏
	pursue	从事，追求	reach	到达，达成
形容词	reasonable	讲道理的，合理的	secret	秘密的
	bold	大胆的	optimistic	乐观的
	depressed	沮丧的		
副词	shortly	立刻，不久	constantly	经常地

47. [H] shortly   48. [I] revelation

49. [M] depressed   50. [A] proof

51. [D] secret   52. [J] pursue

53. [B] reasonable   54. [F] break

55. [K] courage   56. [O] reach

Section B

57. C 细节题。本题考查列举处。第一段前三句分别列举了影响植物在沙漠生长的三个因素：soil temperature(选项D)，sun's rays(选项B)，strong winds(选项A)，只有选项C未提及。

58. C 推理题。根据第二段前三句可推出答案。选项A无原文依据，选项B前半句错误，选项D违背常理。

59. D 细节题。本题提问的是shoot system，而非root system，在第三段末句可找到相关信息，由此确定D为正确答案。

60. B 推理题。第一段末句提到沙漠中的降雨集中在春天，第二段第二句提及种子在下雨季节才发芽生长，由此推出正确答案为B。其他三项均无原文依据。

61. D 主旨题。第四段第一句通过another feature引出本段主题句，本句中心词为perennials和leaves，据此推断答案为D。

62. D 细节题。题中提到的warm ocean currents 和第一段中所说的huge increase in ocean temperatures 是同一回事。第一段倒数第二句话提到了海洋水温的升高影响了很多地方，比如South America, south-east Asia, eastern and southern Africa, 最后一句话又指出There are many knock-on effects all over the world, 因此D为正确答案。

63. D 推理题。题干问的是厄尔尼诺现象最初的发生地点，即第二段第一句话所说的the home of El Nino，因此D是正确答案。

64. C 细节题。文章第四段提到了当地很多房屋都是用adobe(泥砖)建造的，经不住洪水的冲击。倒数第三句中再次提到了the vulnerability of the homes。因此答案为C。

65. C 细节题。根据题中的关键词three people可以在文章最后一段最后一句话找到相关介绍。该句中的sucked into the floodwater作为原因状语，解释了three people lost their lives的原因。因此答案为C。

66. D 主旨题。整篇文章主要分为两个部分，前三段介绍了E1 Nino的形成及影响，后两段介绍了它对秘鲁小镇Ica的破坏作用。

强化训练二

Section A

Directions: *In this section, there is a passage with ten blanks. You are required to select one word for each blank from a list of choices given in a word bank following the passage. Read the passage through carefully before making your choices. Each choice in the bank is identified by a letter. Please mark the corresponding letter for each item on* **Answer Sheet 2** *with a single line through the centre.* **You may not use any of the words in the bank more than once.**

Questions 47 to 56 are based on the following passage.

An international committee of doctors says that the number of cases of brain diseases in developing countries is rising. The doctors were reporting the __47__ for the United States National Academy of Sciences. They say that brain diseases __48__ at least 250 million people in the developing world. These diseases include *strokes*(中风), *epilepsy*(癫痫) and __49__ sickness such as *schizophrenia*(精神分裂症) and *depression*(抑郁症). They also include __50__ development of the nervous system, which causes mental slowness and *cerebral palsy*(脑瘫).

Doctor Murthy says there are two reasons for this. One is a lack of money. The other is a lack of human __51__. For example, a recent study shows that doctors who __52__ mental sicknesses are not enough in most developing countries. Another __53__ to action against brain diseases is the unfair way in which the public acts toward victims. Many victims of brain diseases are treated __54__.

The committee says there are effective and __55__ cost medical treatments for these diseases. Yet these treatments are not often provided in developing countries. The committee says more treatments should be offered to poor countries. It says health care systems in developing countries should provide mental health services for their people. The committee says efforts should be made to increase public __56__ of brain diseases. Finally, the committee says national research programs should be established to study brain diseases.

[A] understanding	[I] physical
[B] treat	[J] barrier
[C] resume	[K] mental
[D] poorly	[L] richly
[E] affect	[M] low
[F] promotion	[N] information
[G] abnormal	[O] resources
[H] interest	

Section B

Directions: *There are 2 passages in this section. Each passage is followed by some questions or unfinished statements. For each of them there are four choices marked* [A], [B], [C] *and* [D]. *You should decide on the best choice and mark the corresponding letter on* **Answer Sheet 2** *with a single line through the centre.*

Passage One

Question 57 to 61 are based on the following passage.

Cheating is nothing new. But today, education and administrations are finding that instances of academic dishonesty on the part of students have become more frequent—and are less likely to be punished—than in the past. Cheating appears to have gained acceptance among good and poor students alike.

Why is student cheating on the rise? No one really knows. Some blame the trend on a general loosening of moral values among today's youth. Others have attributed increased cheating to the fact that today's youth are far more *pragmatic*(实际的) than their idealistic predecessors. Whereas in the late sixties and early seventies, students were filled with visions about changing the world, today's students feel great pressure to conform and succeed. In interviews with students at high schools and colleges around the country, both young men and women said that cheating had become easy. Some suggested they did it out of spite for teachers they did not respect. Others looked at it as a game. Only if they were caught, some said, would they feel guilty. "People are competitive," said a second-year college student named Anna, from Chicago. "There's an underlying fear. If you don't do well, your life is going to be ruined. The pressure is not only from parents and friends but from yourself. To achieve. To succeed. It's almost as though we have to outdo other people to achieve our own goals."

Edward Wynne, editor of a magazine, blames the rise in academic dishonesty on the schools. He claims that administrators and teachers have been too hesitant to take action. Dwight Huber, chairman of the English Department at Amarillo, sees the matter differently, blaming the rise in cheating on the way students evaluated. "I would cheat if I felt I was being cheated," Mr. Huber said. He feels that as long as teachers give short-answer tests rather than essay questions and rate students by the number of facts they can memorize rather than by how well they can synthesize information, students will try to beat the system. "The concept of cheating is based on the false assumption that the system is legitimate and there is something wrong with the individuals who's doing it," he said. "That's too easy an answer. We've got to start looking at the system."

57. Educators are finding that students who cheat _____.

[A] have poor academic records

[B] use the information in late years

[C] are more likely to be punished than before

[D] can be academically weak or strong

58. According to the passage, which of the following statements is true?

[A] Punishment is an effective method of stopping cheating.

[B] A change in the educational system will eliminate the need to cheat.

[C] Students do not cheat on essay tests.

[D] The problem of student cheating has its roots in deeper problems.

59. Which of the following statements reflects information in the passage?

[A] The student who cheats must be at fault because the system is correct.

[B] The 1960's vision of changing the world led students to conform.

[C] Punishment for cheaters has always been severe in this country.

[D] The educational system and its administrators are partly to blame for the rise in the cheating.

60. The phrase "the individuals" in Line 9, Para.3 refers to "_____".

　　[A] teachers who are too hesitant to take actions against cheating

　　[B] students who practice cheating

　　[C] parents who put pressure on their children

　　[D] school administrators who approve of short-answer tests

61. The author probably would agree with the point of view that _____.

　　[A] parents alone must take responsibility for the rise in student cheating

　　[B] the educational system is sound, and students must follow every rule

　　[C] the educational system in this country would benefit from a thorough
　　　　evaluation

　　[D] students who cheat should be expelled from school

Passage Two

Questions 62 to 66 are based on the following passage.

　　Time and how we experience it have puzzled physicists who have created fascinating theories. But their time is measured by a *pendulum*(钟摆) and is not psychological time, which leaps with little regard to the clock or calendar. As someone who understood the distinction observed, "When you sit with a girl for two hours, it seems like a minute, but when you sit on hot stove, a minute seems like two hours."

　　Psychologists have noticed that larger units of time, such as months and years, fly on swifter wings as we age.

　　They also note that the more time is structured with schedule and appointments, the more rapidly it seems to pass. For example, a day at the beach. Since most of us spend fewer days at the beach and more at the office, an increase in structured time could well be to blame why time seems to speed up as we grow older.

　　Expectation and familiarity also make time seem to flow more rapidly. Almost all of us have had the experience of driving somewhere we've never been before. Surrounded by unfamiliar scenery, with no real notion of when we'll arrive, we experience the trip as lasting a long time. But the return trip, although exactly as long, seems to take far less time. The novelty of the outward journey has become routine. Thus taking a different route on occasions can often help slow the clock.

　　When days become as identical as *beads*(珠子) on a string, they blend together, and even months become a single day. To counter this, try to find ways to interrupt the structure of your day—to stop time, so to speak.

Learning something new is another way to slow the passage of time. One of the reasons the days of our youth seem so full and long is that these are the days of learning and discovery.

62. The purpose of this passage is to _____.

[A] show the different ideas of physicists and psychologists on time

[B] state the principles of time

[C] describe various notions about time

[D] explain why time flies and how to slow it down

63. The quotation in the first paragraph is used to indicate that _____.

[A] physical time and psychological time are quite different

[B] with little regard of a clock or calendar, psychological time is quite puzzling

[C] time should not be measured by a pendulum

[D] physical theory has nothing to do with the true sense of time

64. According to the passage, when people live an identical and routine life, time seems to _____.

[A] stop   [C] slow down

[B] speed up   [D] be in a psychological sense

65. What makes time seem to flow more rapidly?

[A] An excursion to an unfamiliar place.

[B] Office work structured with schedules.

[C] Life of a businessman filled with new appointments.

[D] The learning of something difficult and interesting.

66. The word "novelty" (Line 5, Para. 4) means _____.

[A] unfamiliarity   [C] excitement

[B] amusement   [D] distinction

试题详解

Section A

名词	understanding	理解	promotion	促进，提升
	interest	兴趣	barrier	障碍
	information	信息	resources	资源

动词	treat	对待，治疗	resume	重新开始
	affect	影响	interest	使产生兴趣
形容词	abnormal	反常的，变态的	physical	身体的；物质的
	mental	心理的，精神的	low	低的；消沉的
副词	poorly	差地	richly	富裕地，丰富地

47. [N] information

48. [E] affect

49. [K] mental

50. [G] abnormal

51. [O] resources

52. [B] treat

53. [J] barrier

54. [D] poorly

55. [M] low

56. [A] understanding

Section B

57. D 细节题。文章第一段最后一句提到，学习差和学习好的学生都会作弊，D 是对该句话的同义转述，所以选D。A、B在原文没有提及。第一段第二句 指出，作弊的学生比以前更少受到惩罚(less likely to be punished)，C项与 此意相反。

58. D 细节题。文章第二段前两句指出，作弊现象严重的原因目前尚无定论。后 文进一步分析，并给出了两种可能的原因。由此可知学生作弊的原因很复 杂，所以D是正确的。文章第三段只是提到学生作弊很可能是因为教育体 制不合理，但并没有说教育体制的变化就一定能消除作弊现象，所以B是 错的。C的表达过于绝对，A在文中没有提及。

59. D 细节题。文章第三段中Edward Wynne认为学校应该对学生的作弊现象负 责，而管理人员却没有采取果断措施；Dwight Huber则认为教育体制是问 题的根源。D正好符合以上两个人的观点。Dwight Huber认为教育体制是不 合理的，所以A不正确；根据第二段第五句可以排除B；根据文章第一段 第二句可以排除C。

60. B 细节题。the individuals 出现在文章的倒数第三句，是Dwight Huber 所说的 话。这句话的意思是"作弊的概念是建立在一种错误的假设上的：教育体制 是正确的，而那些作弊的人是不对的"。由此可知the individuals是指作弊的 人，所以B正确。

61. C 推理题。原文最后一段提到，教育制度存在问题，需要重新审视，因此C为 作者的观点，而B项中的"教育制度健全"与原文不符合，A、D两项的表述过于 绝对。

62. D 推理题。文章首先指出人在心理上感受的时间与客观上的时间是不一样的。之后列举了令人感觉时光飞逝的原因，最后作者介绍了怎样可以使人感觉时间过得不那么快。B和C在文章开头部分提到，但不全面；A文中没有涉及。

63. A 细节题。文章第一段后半部分举例说：和一位漂亮姑娘一起坐两小时，你感觉似乎才过了一分钟；但坐在一个热火炉上，你却感觉一分钟是两个小时。从这个例子可以看出，作者想告诉我们心理时间和客观上的时间是有差异的。干扰项C中提到的time概念过于宽泛，应该确切地指出是physical time。选项D观点太绝对，而选项B文中没有涉及。

64. B 细节题。文章第三段第一句...the more time is structured with schedule and appointments, the more rapidly it seems to pass（日程安排得越紧凑，约会越多，人们就感觉时间过得越快），意思和B很接近，故选B。

65. B 细节题。文章第三段第一句...the more time is structured with schedule and appointments, the more rapidly it seems to pass，因此选B，同时排除C。根据文章最后一段第一句：Learning something new is another way to slow the passage of time（学习新东西是使时间变慢的另一种方法），可以排除A和D。

66. A 语义题。第四段举了个例子：当你去了个不熟悉的、没去过的地方时，你似乎觉得旅途花了很长时间；但当你原路返回的时候，车外不熟悉的景物已经变得熟悉起来了，你就觉得一会儿就到了。因此novelty的意思应该和routine相反，即"不熟悉"。

强化训练三

Section A

Directions: *In this section, there is a passage with ten blanks. You are required to select one word for each blank from a list of choices given in a word bank following the passage. Read the passage through carefully before making your choices. Each choice in the bank is identified by a letter. Please mark the corresponding letter for each item on **Answer Sheet 2** with a single line through the centre. **You may not use any of the words in the bank more than once.**

Questions 47 to 56 are based on the following passage.

Japan has reached an important 47 point. After World War II, the miracle of Japan's economic growth was achieved through technological 48 and a cheap, well-trained laboratorian. This innovation, however, was based on 49 basic technologies or concepts from the United States and Europe and improving them. The economic success of this 50 approach ended about a decade ago because of the 51 of the Japanese yen, an increase in labor costs and the 52 of other countries in East and Southeast Asia. To achieve further economic development, Japan must develop 53 technologies that promise benefits. This change is not easy, however, because all 54 of Japanese society—including political circles, administration, industry, and education—have 55 been oriented to catching up 56 .

[A] innovation	[I] growth
[B] strength	[J] economically
[C] sectors	[K] catch-up
[D] turning	[L] decreasing
[E] creativity	[M] introducing
[F] breakthrough	[N] previously
[G] stretch	[O] invention
[H] exhaustion	

Section B

Directions: *There are 2 passages in this section. Each passage is followed by some questions or unfinished statements. For each of them there are four choices marked* [A], [B], [C] *and* [D]. *You should decide on the best choice and mark the corresponding letter on* **Answer Sheet 2** *with a single line through the centre.*

Passage One

Question 57 to 61 are based on the following passage.

Some people believe that international sports creates goodwill between the nations and that if countries play games together they will learn to live together. Others say that the opposite is true: that international contests encourage false national pride and lead to misunderstanding and hatred. There is probably some truth in both arguments, but in recent years the Olympic Games have done little to support the view that sports encourage international brotherhood. Not only was there the tragic incident involving the murder of athletes, but the games were also ruined by lesser incidents caused principally by minor national contests.

One country received its second-place medals with visible anger after the volleyball final. There had been noisy scenes at the end of the match, the loser objecting to the final decisions. They were convinced that one of their goals should not have been disallowed and that their opponent's victory was unfair. Their manager was in a rage when he said, "This wasn't volleyball and the International Volleyball Federation is finished." The president of the Federation said later that such behavior could result in the *suspension*(禁赛) of the team for at least three years.

The American basketball team announced that they would not yield first place to Russia after a disputable end to their contest. The game had ended in disorder. It was thought at first that the United States had won, by a single point, but it was announced that there were three seconds still to play. A Russian player then threw the ball into the basket. It was the first time the U.S.A. had ever lost an Olympic basketball match. An appeal jury debated the matter for four and a half hours before announcing that the result would stand. The American players then voted not to receive the silver medals.

Incidents of this kind will continue as long as sport is played competitively rather than for the love of the game. The suggestion that athletes should compete as individuals, or in non-national teams, might be too much to hope for. But in the present organization of the Olympic there is far too much that encourages aggressive patriotism.

57. According to the passage, recent Olympic Games have _____.

　　[A] created goodwill between the nations

　　[B] bred only false national pride

　　[C] led to more and more misunderstanding and hatred

　　[D] barely showed any international friendship

58. What can be inferred from the words of the manager of silver-medalist?

　　[A] There should be no more volleyball matches organized by the Federation.

　　[B] His team will not be allowed to take part in international games in the future.

　　[C] Volleyball and International Volleyball Federation are both ruined by that unfair decisions.

　　[D] The International Volleyball Federation should be dismissed.

59. The basketball example given in the third paragraph implies that _____.

　　[A] too much emphasis on the result of game was displayed in the incident

　　[B] the American team was right in rejecting the silver medals

　　[C] the announcement to prolong the match was wrong

　　[D] the appeal jury was too hesitant in making the decision

60. What can we conclude from the passage?

　　[A] International contests are liable for misunderstanding between nations.

　　[B] Athletes should compete as individuals in the Olympic Games.

　　[C] Sport should be played competitively rather than for the love of Olympic Games.

　　[D] The organization of the Olympic Games has room for improvement.

61. The word "patriotism" (Line 5, Para. 4) is closest in meaning to _____.

　　[A] fierce competition

　　[B] love for one's country

　　[C] challenge to the judge's decision

　　[D] thirst for prizes in international contests

Passage Two

Questions 62 to 66 are based on the following passage.

　　When anti-globalization protesters took to the streets of Washington last weekend, they blamed globalization for everything from hunger to the destruction of home-grown cultures. And globalization meant the United States. The critics call it Coca-Colonization, and French sheep farmer Jose Bove has become a *cult*（狂热分子）figure since destroying a McDonald's restaurant in 1999. Contrary to conventional wisdom, however, globalization is neither *homogenizing*（使同化）nor Americanizing the cultures of the world.

　　To understand why not, we have to step back and put the current period in a larger historical perspective. Although they are related, the long-term historical trends of globalization and modernization are not the same. While modernization has produced some common traits, such as large cities, factories and mass communications, local cultures have by no means been erased. The appearance of similar institutions in response to similar problems is not surprising, but it does not lead to homogeneity. In the first half of the 20th century, for example, there were some similarities among the industrial societies of Britain, Germany, America and Japan, but there were even more important differences. When China, India and Brazil complete their current processes of industrialization and modernization, we should not expect them to be exact copies of Japan, Germany or the United States.

Take the current information revolution. The United States is at the forefront of this great movement of change, so the uniform social and cultural habits produced by television viewing or Internet use, for instance, are often attributed to Americanization. But correlation is not cause. Since the United States does exist and is at the leading edge of the information revolution, there is a degree of Americanization at present, but it's likely to decrease over the course of the 21st century as technology spreads and local cultures modernize in their own ways.

Historical proof that globalization does not necessarily mean homogenization can be seen in the case of Japan. In the mid-19th century, it became the first Asian country to embrace globalization and to borrow successfully from the world without losing its uniqueness. Following the Meiji Restoration of 1868, Japan searched broadly for tools and innovations that would allow it to become a major power rather than a victim of Western imperialism. The lesson that Japan has to teach the rest of the world is that even a century and a half of openness to global trends does not necessarily assure destruction of a country's cultural identity.

62. The author's main purpose in writing this passage is to _____.

　　[A] criticize extreme and violent actions

　　[B] report the progress of some new events

　　[C] tell his readers not to be afraid of globalization

　　[D] recall a certain period of American history

63. The author mentions world history to prove that modernization _____.

　　[A] is one of the long-term historical trends

　　[B] does not result in homogeneity of local cultures

　　[C] is somewhat related to globalization

　　[D] has shaped different traits in industrial countries

64. The author admits that a degree of Americanization does exist because _____.

　　[A] local cultures are gradually weakened over the course of the 21st century

　　[B] it's a long-term historical trend of the world

[C] the Internet and TV promote the spread of American social and cultural habits

[D] industrial societies are almost exact copies of the United States

65. Japan is mentioned in the passage to show that _____.

[A] openness to globalization will not cost a nation's cultural identity

[B] the Meiji Restoration of 1868 was crucial in Japan's history

[C] it was the first Asian country to develop successfully

[D] tools and innovations would allow a country to become a major power

66. From the passage we can conclude that the author is strongly in defense of _____.

[A] modernization   [C] information revolution

[B] Americanization   [D] globalization

试题详解

Section A

名词	innovation	改革,创新	strength	力量,实力,强度
	sectors	部分	turning	弯处;转向
	creativity	创造力	breakthrough	突破
	exhaustion	筋疲力尽	growth	发展
	catch-up	追上	invention	发明,创造
动词	stretch	伸展,伸长	introducing	介绍
形容词	decreasing	减少的		
副词	economically	在经济上	previously	先前,以前

47. [D] turning   48. [A] innovation

49. [M] introducing   50. [K] catch-up

51. [B] strength   52. [I] growth

53. [F] breakthrough   54. [C] sectors

55. [N] previously   56. [J] economically

Section B

57. D 细节题。由题干中的recent Olympic Games定位到第一段...in recent years the Olympic Games have done little to support the view that sports encourage international brotherhood(近年来,奥运会在促进国际友谊方面的工作成效甚微),选项D恰恰表达了这个意思,故为正确答案。

58. C　推理题。由题干中的words of the manager of silver-medalist定位到第二段。
在一次排球决赛中，该球队经理认为裁判不公正，盛怒之下用言语对国际
排联进行攻击：This wasn't volleyball and the International Volleyball Federation
is finished，这和C"排球运动和国际排联因为不公平的裁决而名誉受损"意
思接近。该段最后提到，这种行为会导致禁赛三年的惩罚，暗示这支队伍
还会参加比赛，故排除B，而A、D在文中没有体现。

59. A　推理题。由题干可知本题应定位到第三段，美国队在仲裁委员会判定比赛
结果有效的情况下拒绝接受银牌，说明美国队在比赛中过分看重比赛的胜
负，而不是出于对篮球运动的热爱。

60. D　推理题。文章最后一句提出：But in the present organization of the Olympic
there is far too much that encourages aggressive patriotism，当今的奥委会过
分鼓励咄咄逼人的爱国主义精神，这说明他们的工作还有待改进，和D选
项内容吻合。对于B选项，文章最后一段指出might be too much to hope
for，故可排除。C、D说法武断，且文章中也没有涉及。

61. B　语义题。patriotism出现在文章的最后一句话中，前面一句提到最好的解决
方法就是鼓励运动员以个人身份参赛，以消除各国之间咄咄逼人的竞争。
而目前奥运会的组织方式仍旧在鼓励aggressive patriotism的路上越走越
远，所以推断patriotism是"爱国主义"的意思，答案选B。

62. C　主旨题。全文的主题是：全球化既不能同化世界文化，也不能使世界文化
美国化。全文都是在论述这一观点，所以其目的也是告诉人们不要惧怕全
球化，即选项C。B是第一段的例子，D是文章中的细节，A则是对第一段中
例子的态度，不是全文的观点。

63. C　细节题。由题干中的modernization定位到第二段，题干中的world history对
应文中的historical trends，第二句的意思是：虽然他们之间有联系，全球化
和现代化的历史趋势是不同的，可见二者还是有一定联系，故选C。另
外，somewhat避免语义绝对化，是正确选项的特征之一。第二段第三句话
指出：虽然现代化已经产生了一些相同特点，但当地文化决不会被消除，
B和该句意思相反。A是文章中的事实而非目的。D的说法不全面，因为现
代化不仅使工业国家形成了不同点，还使其形成了相同特点。

64. C　细节题。由题干Americanization定位到文章第三段第二句话：美国走在这
种变革的前沿，因此由电视和因特网所带来的同一社会和文化习惯是美
国化的原因，所以选C。

65. A 细节题。由题干Japan定位到最后一段，作者举日本为例是为了支持自己的观点。该段第一句：全球化并不意味着同一化，日本就是一例，就是作者的观点，所以应该选A，而其他选项都是事实而非目的。

66. D 推理题。本题问作者在为什么辩护。通读全文，第一段作者提出全球化既不能同化世界文化，也不能使世界文化美国化。第二段指出全球化和现代化的历史趋势是不同的。现代化不能消除当地文化。表面的相似不能导致同一性。第三段以美国为例，由于美国走在这种变革的前沿，所以由电视和因特网所带来的同一社会和文化习惯是美国化的原因，但是随着科技的传播和当地文化以自己的方式实现现代化，美国的影响会减少。第四段以日本为例，说明全球化的趋势不需要破坏一个国家独立的文化个性。综上所述，全文都是在说全球化，因此应该选D。由第二段可知道作者是想通过与现代化进行对比从而说明一个国家文化被同化不是全球化的结果，所以A不对。由第三段可知，美国化是全球化的一个例子，所以其他两项不对。

强化训练四

Section A

Directions: *In this section, there is a passage with ten blanks. You are required to select one word for each blank from a list of choices given in a word bank following the passage. Read the passage through carefully before making your choices. Each choice in the bank is identified by a letter. Please mark the corresponding letter for each item on* **Answer Sheet 2** *with a single line through the centre.* **You may not use any of the words in the bank more than once.**

Questions 47 to 56 are based on the following passage.

While waiting for a friend in a Washington, D.C. hotel lobby and wanting to be both __47__ and alone, I had seated myself in a solitary chair outside the normal stream of traffic. In such a setting most Americans follow a rule, which can be stated as follows: as soon as a person stops or is seated in a public place, there balloons around him a small __48__ of privacy which is considered __49__. Anyone who enters this zone and says there is intruding.

As I waited in the __50__ lobby, a stranger walked up to where I was sitting and stood close enough so that not only could I easily touch him but I could even hear him breathing. If the lobby had been crowed with people, I would have understood his __51__, but in empty lobby his presence made me very uncomfortable. Feeling annoyed by this intrusion, I moved my body in such a way as to communicate __52__. Strangely enough, instead of moving away, my actions seemed to encourage him, because he moved even closer.

Fortunately, a group of people soon arrived whom my tormentor immediately joined. Their __53__ explained his behavior, for I knew from both speech and __54__ that they were Arabs. I have not been able to make this __55__ identification by looking at him when he was alone because he was wearing American clothes.

For the Arab, there is no such thing as __56__ in public. Public means public. If A is standing on a street corner and B wants his spot, B is within his rights if he does what he can to make A uncomfortable enough to move.

[A] mannerism	[I] desert
[B] crucial	[J] deserved
[C] behavior	[K] gestures
[D] intrusion	[L] visible
[E] inviolate	[M] visionary
[F] annoyance	[N] anxiously
[G] specify	[O] interfere
[H] sphere	

Section B

Directions: *There are 2 passages in this section. Each passage is followed by some questions or unfinished statements. For each of them there are four choices marked [A], [B], [C] and [D]. You should decide on the best choice and mark the corresponding letter on* **Answer Sheet 2** *with a single line through the centre.*

Passage One

Question 57 to 61 are based on the following passage.

The predictability of our mortality rates is something that has long puzzled social scientists. After all, there is no natural reason why 2,500 people should accidentally shoot themselves each year or why 7,000 should drown or 55,000 die in their cars. No one establishes a *quota*(配额) for each type of death. It just happens that they follow a consistent pattern year after year.

A few years ago a Canadian psychologist named Gerald Wilde became interested in this phenomenon. He noticed that mortality rates for violent and accidental deaths throughout the Western world have remained oddly static throughout the whole of the century, despite all the technological advances and increases in safety standards that have happened in that time. Wilde developed an interesting theory called "risk *homeostasis*(自我平衡)". According to this theory, people instinctively live with a certain level of risk. When something is made safer, people will get around the measure in some way to reassert the original level of danger. If, for instance, they are required to wear seat belts, they will feel safer and thus will drive a little faster and a little more recklessly, thereby statistically canceling out the benefits that the seat belt confers. Other studies have shown that where an intersection is made safer, the accident rate invariably falls there but rises to a compensating level elsewhere along the same stretch of road. It appears, then, that we have an innate need for danger.

In all events, it is becoming clearer and clearer to scientists that the factors influencing our life span are far more subtle and complex than had been previously thought. It now appears that if you wish to live a long life, it isn't simply a matter of adhering to certain precautions: eating the right foods, not smoking, driving with care. You must also have the right attitude. Scientists at the Duke University Medical Center made a 15-year study of 500 persons' personalities and found, somewhat to their surprise, that people with a suspicious or mistrustful nature die prematurely far more often than people with a sunny disposition. Looking on the bright side, it seems, can add years to your life span.

57. What social scientists have long felt puzzled about is _____.

   [A] why a quota for each type of death has not come into being

   [B] why the mortality rate can not be predicted

   [C] why the death toll remains stable year after year

   [D] why people lose their lives every year for this or that reason

58. In his research, Gerald Wilde finds that technological advances and increases in safety standards _____.

   [A] have achieved no effect in reducing the number of deaths

   [B] have helped to solve the problem of so high death rate

   [C] have oddly accounted for mortality rates in the past century

   [D] have reduced mortality rates for violent and accidental deaths

59. According to the theory of "risk homeostasis", some traffic accidents result from
_____.

[A] our innate desire for risk   [C] our instinctive interest in speeding

[B] our fast and reckless driving   [D] our ignorance of seat belt benefits

60. By saying "...statistically canceling out the benefits that the seat belt confers"
(Line 10, Para. 2), the author means that _____.

[A] deaths from wearing seat belts are the same as those from not wearing them

[B] wearing seat belts does not have any benefits from the statistic point of view

[C] deaths from other reasons counterbalance the benefits of wearing seat belts

[D] wearing seat belts does not necessarily reduce death from traffic accidents

61. Which of the following may contribute to a longer life span?

[A] Eating the food low in fat and driving with great care.

[B] Cultivating an optimistic personality and never losing heart.

[C] Showing adequate suspicion to others.

[D] Looking on the bright side and developing a balanced level of risk.

Passage Two

Questions 62 to 66 are based on the following passage.

In 1997, devotees of home electronics eagerly awaited the DVD player, a new device that could play movies without videotape, and with greater clarity. It caught on even faster than CD music players and within four years, DVD movies surpassed VHS tapes in sales. The DVD's success is just one example of a historic shift from analog to digital technologies. They began with computing and are now spreading to industries from banking to publishing. Products and services are shedding the limits of their physical form to become encoded information that never degrades, can be reproduced perfectly and distributed around the world in minutes, or less.

Another example is photography: by the end of this year, the number of images captured digitally each day is expected to surpass the number of images captured on film. With digital cameras and other devices linked to personal computers, we can collect vast amounts of data, which fortunately takes up little or no closet space. Today's average personal computer has a hard drive that can store 300 times more information than a decade ago. Technologies, such as broadband e-commerce, are expected to be the primary means of delivering entertainment and media by the end of this decade. Even life itself is increasingly digitized. The human *genome*(基因组), the recipe for our genetic makeup, has been mapped and encoded and researchers are harnessing the power of computing to accelerate the development of new, lifesaving drugs.

The implications of this broad, digital revolution are enormous, although they tend to be over-shadowed by the struggles of high-tech industries to recover from the go-go years of the 1990s. Those struggles are real, yet there are reasons for optimism about a return to robust economic growth and job creation in the next several years. The digital *innovations*(创新) of the past two decades continue to bear fruit, so stay tuned for good news—digitally, of course.

62. Digital technologies really began to take form when _____.

　　[A] information was encoded 　　　[C] it was used with photography

　　[B] DVD technology was introduced 　[D] used in computing

63. The example of photography is used to show _____.

　　[A] how digital technology has replaced traditional film

　　[B] how economical it is to use digital technology since it stores so much

　　[C] the enormous storage advantages of digital technology

　　[D] how digital technology has improved the quality of production

64. The author implies that excitement over the digital revolution may be hindered by _____.

　　[A] the economic realities of its practicality

　　[B] robust economic growth

　　[C] economic problems of hi-tech companies

　　[D] ignorance of the technology

65. By using the phrase "stay tuned for good news"(Line 5, Para. 3)the author wants us to _____.

　　[A] hope that the good news won't change

　　[B] expect more positive innovations

　　[C] wait for the situation to change for the better

　　[D] try and be more optimistic

66. The passage is based on the author's _____.

　　[A] experience of the changes　　　　[C] hope for changes

　　[B] admiration of the changes　　　　[D] analysis of the changes

试题详解

Section A

名词	mannerism	怪癖，特殊习惯	behavior	行为
	intrusion	闯入，侵扰	annoyance	烦恼，讨厌
	sphere	领域；球形	gestures	姿势
动词	specify	指定，详细说明		
	interfere	干涉，干预		
形容词	crucial	至关重要的	inviolate	不受侵犯的
	desert	荒芜的，荒废的	deserved	应得的，当然的
	visible	可见的，明显的	visionary	幻想的
副词	anxiously	忧虑地，不安地		

47. [L] visible

48. [H] sphere

49. [E] inviolate

50. [I] desert

51. [C] behavior

52. [F] annoyance

53. [A] mannerism

54. [K] gestures

55. [B] crucial

56. [D] intrusion

Section B

57. C　细节题。由题干关键词social scientists和puzzled定位到第一段。该段开头提出the predictability of our mortality rates 是长期困扰科学家的问题，最后一句指出It just happens that they follow a consistent pattern year after year（死亡人数年复一年保持稳定），故C为正确选项。

58. A　细节题。由题干定位到第二段第二句话：He noticed that mortality rates for violent and accidental deaths throughout the Western world have remained oddly static throughout the whole of the century, despite all the technological advances and increases in safety standards that have happened in that time.（尽管技术在进步，安全标准在提高，但奇怪的是，西方世界的暴力和意外死亡率在整个世纪中都保持着恒定），由此判断，技术进步和安全标准的提高并未降低死亡人数，故A为正确答案。

59. A　细节题。由题干中的关键词risk homeostasis定位到第二段后半部分，作者先列举交通事故的例子，然后在最后一句得出结论：It appears, then, that we have an innate need for danger，符合A的意思。

60. C　语义题。本句大体意思是：从数字统计的角度说，(开快车和开车鲁莽导致的死亡人数的增加)抵消了系保险带带来的好处(引起的死亡人数减少)。cancel out意为"抵消，对消"，所以C"因为其他原因引起的死亡抵消了系保险带的好处"正好符合题意。

61. B　细节题，由题干中的关键词life span定位到最后一段结尾部分，其中提到：真正帮助人长寿的是a sunny disposition。选项B中的an optimistic personality and never losing heart正是a sunny disposition的特征，所以是正确答案。文章倒数第二句指出：疑心重的人比乐观豁达的人早逝，排除C；文中所说的eating the right foods并不等于摄入低脂食物，故排除A。D后半部分developing a balanced level of risk不对。

62. D　细节题。从题干中的take form when"成形于……之时"可以判断，此题考查的是digital technologies的起源。关键词digital technologies首先出现在第一段第三句。第四句中的they指代的就是digital technologies，该句话说明了其起源，即begin with computing，选项D的内容与此相符。第一段第三句和第二段第一句分别指出，DVD和photography只是模拟技术向数字技术转变的例子而已，因此排除选项B和C，根据第一段末句可知道，encoded information that never degrades是数字技术产品的特征，因此排除选项A。

63. C　细节题。题干中的the example of photography出现在第二段第一句。本题考查的是文章以摄影为例的目的是什么。从第二段第二句中的collect vast amounts of data和第三句中的store 300 times more information than a decade ago可知，作者要通过这个例子说明数字技术有信息存储量大的优势，这正是选项C的内容。

64. C　推断题。关键词digital revolution出现在第三段第一句。前半句总结上文，说明了数字技术革命好的一面，后半句用although引出其不好的一面。该句中的over-shadowed与题干中的hindered意思相近，也就是说，是the struggles of high-tech industries对数字技术革命造成了负面影响。而the struggles的目的是recover from the go-go years of the 1990s，也就是下句中的a return to robust economic growth。归根结底，这些高科技企业的经济问题对数字革命的成就产生了负面影响。因此C为正确答案。

65. B 语义题。从第三段最后一句中的so 可以看出，其前后两个分句是因果关系：stay tuned for good news 的原因是，历经了二十年的数字技术革命 continue to bear fruit，该句中的digitally 是指from the digital innovations。stay tuned for…常用于广播节目或电视节目中，意思是"请继续收听或收看……"，这里作者是用展望未来的口吻让读者期待digital innovations 有更多的good news，因此选项B为正确答案。

66. B 观点题。文章第一段以DVD为例，引出对a historic shift from analog to digital technologies 的赞叹；第二段以photography为例，说明了数字产品的优势以及生活数字化的好处；第三段第一句话后半句虽然谈及负面影响，但作者主要强调digital revolution的优势。由此可见，作者在文章中主要表达了自己对数字技术变革的赞赏，因此选B。尽管文章结尾对the digital innovations 寄予了很大期望，但这并不是作者在本文中想要表达的主要态度，因此可以排除干扰选项C。

第五章　完形填空

　　根据《大学英语四级考试大纲》，完形填空（Cloze）测试学生在各个层面上的语言理解及语言运用能力。短文长度为220～250词，内容是学生所熟悉的题材。这部分的分值比例为10%，考试时间15分钟。

　　完形填空部分的短文有20个空白，空白处所删去的词既有实词也有虚词，每个空白为一题，每题有四个选择项。要求考生选择一个最佳答案，使短文的意思和结构恢复完整。

第一节　高分攻略

一、应试技巧

　　四级完形填空文章以论说文为主，记叙文为辅，题材涉及教育、科技、人文，不超过四级考生的理解范围。主要从语篇角度综合测试考生对文章的理解能力和对基础知识的运用能力，重点考查实词（名词、动词、形容词、副词）的辨析，包括同义词、近义词，惯用法和固定搭配。

1. 重视首段及首句

　　一般情况下，完形填空的文章往往开门见山，第一个句子不设空格。应充分重视文章的首段及首句，理解文章的思路，寻找全文的脉络。

2. 重视结构与逻辑

　　只有分析清楚文章的结构，了解段落之间的关系，才能选出正确答案。完形填空的文章逻辑关系包括因果、让步、转折、目的、条件、并列等，应积累完形填空历年常考的短语、搭配、习惯用法等基础知识。

3. 重视衔接

　　1）语义衔接：区分同义词、近义词、反义词、形近词、同形异义词。

　　2）逻辑衔接：关联词、衔接手段、否定、指代关系。常考关联词有and, moreover, furthermore, if, but, though, while, instead of 等。

　　3）惯用衔接：即固定短语，常考介词与动词、名词、形容词的固定搭配，以及动词与副词的搭配。

4)结构衔接： 名词、动词、形容词等实词与其他词的衔接，常考从句、平行结构、倒装句、虚拟语气等语法关系和一些固定句型。

4. 重视排除法

1) 分析空格与前后词的搭配关系、语义联系，排除一些选项。

2) 分析空格的名词单复数、时态、语态等与上下文是否一致，排除部分选项。

3) 分析空格部分的词形与句子成分，排除干扰选项。

5. 重视上下文

完形填空的文章围绕一个话题展开，必然出现关键词语的同现、复现、重复或替代。应重视上下文，寻找空格部分的原词、指代词、同义词、近义词或上义词、下义词，要善于捕捉并记忆重要信息。

二、核心考点

1. 词汇

1) 同现或复现

2) 名词：同义词及反义词的辨析

3) 形容词：作定语和表语的形容词

4) 副词：方式、程度、地点副词及句子引导词（疑问、关系、连接副词）

5) 动词：短语搭配、虚拟语气

2. 固定搭配

1) 名词短语

2) 介词短语

3) 形容词短语

4) 动词短语

3. 语法结构

1) 语法结构关系词：代词、介词、连词、冠词等

2) 从句：状语从句、定语从句

3) 虚拟语气

4) 倒装句

4. 语篇

1) 理解全文及段落的意义

2) 理解上下文中词汇与句子的意义

第二节　真题选析

一、经典真题

Directions: *There are 20 blanks in the following passage. For each blank there are four choices marked [A], [B], [C] and [D] on the right side of the paper. You should choose the ONE that best fits into the passage. Then mark the corresponding letter on Answer Sheet 2 with a single line through the centre.*

Playing organized sports is such a common experience in the United States that many children and teenagers take them for granted. This is especially true __67__ children from families and communities that have the resources needed to organize and __68__ sports programs and make sure that there is easy __69__ to participation opportunities. Children in low-income families and poor communities are __70__ likely to take organized youth sports for granted because they often __71__ the resources

needed to pay for participation __72__, equipment, and transportation to practices and games __73__ their communities do not

have resources to build and __74__ sports fields and facilities.

Organized youth sports __75__ appeared during the early 20th century in the United

67. [A] among　　　[C] on
　　[B] within　　　[D] towards

68. [A] spread　　　[C] spur
　　[B] speed　　　[D] sponsor

69. [A] access　　　[C] chance
　　[B] entrance　　[D] route

70. [A] little　　　[C] more
　　[B] less　　　　[D] much

71. [A] shrink　　　[C] limit
　　[B] tighten　　[D] lack

72. [A] bill　　　　[C] fees
　　[B] accounts　　[D] fare

73. [A] so　　　　　[C] and
　　[B] as　　　　　[D] but

74. [A] maintain　　[C] sustain
　　[B] contain　　[D] entertain

75. [A] last　　　　[C] later
　　[B] first　　　[D] finally

States and other wealthy nations. They were originally developed __76__ some educators

and developmental experts __77__ that the behavior and character of children were __78__ influenced by their social surroundings and everyday experiences. This __79__ many people to believe that if you could organize the experiences of children in __80__ ways, you could influence the kinds of adults that those children would become.

This belief that the social __81__ influenced a person's overall development was very __82__ to people interested in progress and reform in the United States __83__ the beginning of the 20th century. It caused them to think about __84__ they might control the experiences of children to __85__ responsible and productive adults. They believed strongly that democracy depended on responsibility and that a __86__ capitalist economy depended on the productivity of workers.

76. [A] before [C] until
    [B] while [D] when
77. [A] realized [C] expected
    [B] recalled [D] exhibited
78. [A] specifically [C] strongly
    [B] excessively [D] exactly
79. [A] moved [C] put
    [B] conducted [D] led
80. [A] precise [C] particular
    [B] precious [D] peculiar
81. [A] engagement [C] state
    [B] environment [D] status
82. [A] encouraging [C] upsetting
    [B] disappointing [D] surprising
83. [A] for [C] over
    [B] with [D] at
84. [A] what [C] whatever
    [B] how [D] however
85. [A] multiply [C] produce
    [B] manufacture [D] provide
86. [A] growing [C] raising
    [B] breeding [D] flying

试题详解

　　本文是一篇议论文，简要论述了有组织的青年体育运动的产生和发展。题目中包含3个逻辑关系题、1个固定搭配题、16个词义辨析题。这充分表明：词义辨析题已成为新四级完形填空考查的重中之重。若想取得完形填空的高分，关键是扎扎实实提高词汇、语法基本功。

67. A 词义辨析题。among意为"在……中间"，指在一群之中。within意为"在……之内"。

68. D 词义辨析题。spread意为"散布"，speed作动词时意为"迅速前进"，spur意为"激励"，sponsor意为"发起，赞助"。空格与organize是并列关系，句意为：来自拥有资源用以组织和资助体育运动计划的家庭和社区的孩子尤其如此。

69. A 词义辨析题。access to意为"（进入、观看、使用的）权利"；entrance to意为"入口"；chance to意为"机会"，用法为the chance to do sth.；route to意为"路线"。句意为：(这些资源)可以保证更容易拥有参与的机会。

70. B 逻辑关系题。本句与前句进行比较，与富裕家庭的孩子比较起来，贫困家庭的孩子参与有组织的运动的可能性更小。空格后likely意为"很可能的"，空格需填比较级。

71. D 词义辨析题。shrink意为"缩小"，tighten意为"变紧"，limit意为"限制"，lack意为"缺少"。根据句意，与富裕家庭相比，低收入家庭缺乏相应的资源，故选D。

72. C 词义辨析题。bill指账单，accounts指账户，fee指各种费用，fare指车费、路费。句中指参加各种活动的费用，故选C。

73. C 逻辑关系题。空格前说低收入家庭没有足够的资源支持孩子参加有组织的运动，空格后说社区也没有建设和维修体育设施和场地的资源，空格前后为并列关系。

74. A 词义辨析题。maintain意为"维修，保养"，contain意为"包含"，sustain意为"承受"，entertain意为"使娱乐，招待"。句意为：社区也没有建设和维修体育设施和场地的资源。

75. B 逻辑关系题。第二段开始讲述有组织的青年运动的相关历史，本句指出其出现的时间和地点，同时句中出现了during the early 20th century，故选B。

76. D 词义辨析题。根据句意，应填"当……时"。when既可表示一点时间，又可表示一段时间，谓语动词可以是延续性的或非延续性的，可与主句动词同时发生或在其之后发生，引导的从句多用一般时态。而while只能表示一段时间，谓语动词只能是延续性的，只能与主句动词同时发生，引导的从句多用进行时态。故选when。

77. A 词义辨析题。realize意为"意识到"，recall意为"回忆起"，expect意为"期待"，exhibit意为"展示"。句意为：教育学家和发展专家意识到孩子的行为和性格会受到社会环境和日常经历的极大影响。

78. C 词义辨析题。specifically意为"具体地，明确地"，excessively意为"过分地，过度地"，strongly意为"强烈地，强有力地"，exactly意为"恰好地"。句意为：小时候的经历对孩子的成长有很大影响。

79. D 词义辨析题。move意为"推动，促使"，conduct意为"指挥"，put意为"放"，lead意为"引导，导致"。句意为：这导致很多人认为，如果他们可以以这种特别的方式安排孩子的经历，就可以影响孩子变成此类的大人。

80. C 词义辨析题。precise意为"精确的"，precious意为"珍贵的"，particular意为"特别的"，peculiar意为"奇怪的"。

81. B 词义辨析题。engagement意为"订婚；约会"，environment意为"环境"，state意为"状态"，status意为"地位"。此处应填空格后surroundings的同义词。

82. A 词义辨析题。encouraging意为"令人鼓舞的"，disappointing意为"令人失望的"，upsetting意为"令人苦恼的"，surprising意为"令人惊讶的"。空格后说的是对进步和改革有兴趣的美国人，即这一发现对这些人是鼓舞人心的，故选A。

83. D 固定搭配题。at the beginning of为固定搭配，意为"在……之初"。

84. B 词义辨析题。句意为：它(人们发现社会环境对人的全面发展有影响)促使那些人思考如何通过控制孩子的经历去塑造有责任感、有生产力的成年人，故选B。

85. C 词义辨析题。multiply意为"繁殖"，manufacture意为"制造，加工"，produce意为"生产，制造"，provide意为"提供"。只有produce后能接表示人的名词作宾语。

86. A 词义辨析题。growing意为"发展的"，breeding意为"饲养"(名词)，raising意为"养育"(名词)，flying意为"飞行的"。句意为：……不断发展的资本主义经济依靠的是工人的生产力。

二、经典真题二

Directions: *There are 20 blanks in the following passage. For each blank there are four choices marked* [A], [B], [C] *and* [D] *on the right side of the paper. You should choose the ONE that best fits into the passage. Then mark the corresponding letter on **Answer Sheet 2** with a single line through the centre.*

注意：此部分试题请在**答题卡2**上作答。

Kimiyuki Suda should be a perfect customer for Japan's car-makers. He's a young, successful executive at an Internet-services company in Tokyo and has plenty of disposable __67__. He used to own Toyota's Hilux Surf, a sport utility vehicle. But now he uses __68__ subways and trains. "It's not inconvenient at all," he says. __69__, "having a car is so 20th century."

Suda reflects a worrisome __70__ in Japan; the automobile is losing its emotional appeal, __71__ among the young, who prefer to spend their money on the latest electronic devices. __72__ mini-cars and luxury foreign brands are still popular, everything in between is __73__. Last year sales fell 6.7 percent, 7.6 percent __74__ you don't count the mini-car market. There have been __75__ one-year drops in other nations: sales in Germany fell 9 percent in 2007 __76__ a tax increase. But experts say Japan is __77__ in that sales have been decreasing steadily __78__ time. Since 1990, yearly new-car sales have fallen from 7.8 million to 5.4 million units in 2007.

Alarmed by this state of __79__, the Japan Automobile Manufacturers Association

67. [A] profit　　　　[C] income
　　[B] payment　　　[D] budget

68. [A] mostly　　　　[C] occasionally
　　[B] partially　　　[D] rarely

69. [A] Therefore　　　[C] Otherwise
　　[B] Besides　　　　[D] Consequently

70. [A] drift　　　　　[C] current
　　[B] tide　　　　　[D] trend

71. [A] remarkably　　[C] specially
　　[B] essentially　　[D] particularly

72. [A] While　　　　[C] When
　　[B] Because　　　[D] Since

73. [A] surging　　　　[C] slipping
　　[B] stretching　　[D] shaking

74. [A] unless　　　　[C] as
　　[B] if　　　　　　[D] after

75. [A] lower　　　　　[C] broader
　　[B] slighter　　　[D] larger

76. [A] liable to　　　[C] thanks to
　　[B] in terms of　[D] in view of

77. [A] unique　　　　[C] mysterious
　　[B] similar　　　[D] strange

78. [A] over　　　　　[C] on
　　[B] against　　　[D] behind

79. [A] mess　　　　　[C] growth
　　[B] boom　　　　[D] decay

(JAMA) 80 a comprehensive study of the market in 2006. It found that a 81 wealth gap, *demographic* （人口结构的）changes and 82 lack of interest in cars led Japanese to hold their 83 longer, replace their cars with smaller ones 84 give up car ownership altogether. JAMA 85 a further sales decline of 1.2 percent this year. Some experts believe that if the trend continues for much longer, further *consolidation* （合并）in the automotive sector is 86 .	80. ［A］proceeded ［C］launched 　　［B］relieved 　［D］revised 81. ［A］quickening ［C］strengthening 　　［B］widening 　［D］lengthening 82. ［A］average 　［C］abundant 　　［B］massive 　［D］general 83. ［A］labels 　［C］vehicles 　　［B］cycles 　［D］devices 84. ［A］or 　　　［C］but 　　［B］until 　　［D］then 85. ［A］concludes ［C］reckons 　　［B］predicts 　［D］prescribes 86. ［A］distant 　［C］temporary 　　［B］likely 　　［D］immediate

试题详解

本文是一篇议论文，文章首先指出汽车在日本的受欢迎程度逐年下降，并给出具体数据，最后分析了原因并预测了这种现象持续下去的可能后果。

67. C　词义辨析题。income意为"收入"，disposable income为固定短语，意为"可支配收入"；强干扰选项payment意为"付款"，一般只与high或low搭配，不与plenty of搭配；profit意为"利润"；budget意为"预算"。

68. A　词义辨析题。mostly意为"主要地，大部分地"，体现乘坐公共交通工具更频繁；partially意为"部分地"；occasionally意为"偶尔地"；rarely意为"极少地"。

69. B　逻辑关系题。根据上题，此人现在主要乘坐地铁和火车，因此应选besides（此外，而且）来连接他所说的两个原因"地铁和火车并不会不方便"和"拥有汽车是20世纪的事了"。therefore意为"因此"；otherwise意为"否则"；consequently意为"所以，因此"。

70. D　词义辨析题。四个选项均有"趋势"的意思，但用法不同。drift常与to或towards连用，指人的思想或形势缓慢变化；tide多以tide(s) of的形式出现，前面不加冠词；current指人的思想领域或舆论媒体等的变化；trend最常用，指普遍、一般、渐进的变化或发展。根据上文，此人由开车改乘地铁，故选D。

71. D 词义辨析题。particularly意为"特别，尤其"；干扰项specially意为"专门地"，并非especially（尤其）；remarkably意为"显著地，非常"；essentially意为"本质上，本来"。

72. A 逻辑关系题。空格所在段的首句指出，汽车在日本失去了吸引力。空格所在句意为"……微型轿车和国外奢侈品牌在国内仍然很受欢迎，除这两者之外的车……"，可知前后两句为转折关系，故选while（尽管，虽然）。

73. C 词义辨析题。slip意为"跌落"，surge意为"上涨"；stretch意为"伸展"；shake意为"摇动"。

74. B 逻辑关系题。结合上下文可知，"不算迷你轿车市场"是假设条件，逗号后是进一步的解释说明，故选if。本句意为"去年销量下降了6.7%，如果不算迷你轿车市场的话，这个数字是7.6%"。

75. D 词义辨析题。结合上下文，此处将别国下降幅度与日本比较，显然别国的9%比日本的6.7%下降更大，故选larger。lower意为"更低的"；slighter意为"更轻的"；强干扰项broader指程度或范围，不合句意。

76. C 词义辨析题。空格前后为因果关系，果前后因，故选thanks to（原因是，由于）；liable to意为"有……倾向"；in terms of意为"从……角度来讲，关于"；in view of意为"鉴于，考虑到"。

77. A 词义辨析题。根据句意，此处应填unique，意为"独特的"；similar意为"相似的"；mysterious意为"神秘的"，由于数字是公开而不同的，故排除；strange意为"奇怪的"。

78. A 固定搭配题。空格前使用了现在完成进行时，故选over。句意为"随着时间的推移，销量稳步下降"。against time意为"争分夺秒"；on time意为"准时"；behind time意为"迟到"。

79. D 词义辨析题。空格前的this state指上段提到的sales have been decreasing/sales have fallen这一现象，故选decrease和fall的近义词decay（衰退）；mess意为"杂乱"；boom意为"繁荣"；growth意为"增长"。

80. C 固定搭配题。选项中只有launch能与study搭配，意为"展开研究"。proceed意为"继续"；revise意为"修正"；relieve意为"缓和"。

81. B 固定搭配题。选项中能与wealth gap（财富差距）搭配的只有widening，意为"扩大贫富差距"；quicken意为"加快"；strengthen意为"加强"；lengthen意为"变长"。

82. D　词义辨析题。根据第二段提到的日本国内的汽车销量稳步下降，可知人们对汽车兴趣的下降是普遍性的，故选general；强干扰项average意为"普通的，一般的"，一般不修饰lack；massive意为"大量的"；abundant意为"充足的"。

83. C　词义辨析题。根据上下文，空格所在句逗号前后是并列关系，应填car的同义词，故选vehicles（交通工具）；device意为"装置"；label意为"标签"；cycle意为"循环"。

84. A　逻辑关系题。根据上下文，此处应填表示并列关系的连词，故选or。

85. B　词义辨析题。根据时间状语this year，此处的行为应是"预测，估计"，故填predict。强干扰项reckon表"估计"时不能接名词或名词短语，只能接that从句，故排除；conclude意为"下结论"；prescribe意为"指示，规定"。

86. B　词义辨析题。句意为"专家认为，如果这种下降趋势持续时间更长的话，汽车部门间的进一步合并将是……"，选项中能形容这种预测的只有likely（可能的）。干扰项temporary意为"暂时的"，文中没有表明，故排除；immediate意为"立刻的，马上的"；distant意为"遥远的"。

三、经典真题三

Directions: *There are 20 blanks in the following passage. For each blank there are four choices marked* [A], [B], [C] *and* [D] *on the right side of the paper. You should choose the ONE that best fits into the passage. Then mark the corresponding letter on* **Answer Sheet 2** *with a single line through the centre.*

注意：此部分试题请在**答题卡2**上作答。

Older people must be given more chances to learn if they are to contribute to society rather than be a financial burden, according to a new study on population published recently.	
The current approach which __67__ on younger people and on skills for	67. [A] operates　　　[C] counts [B] focuses　　　[D] depends

employment is not __68__ to meet the challenges of *demographic*（人口结构的）change, it says. Only 1% of the education budget is __69__ spent on the oldest third of the population.

　　The __70__ include the fact that most people can expect to spend a third of their lives in __71__ , that there are now more people over 59 than under 16 and that 11.3 million people are __72__ state pension age.

　　" __73__ needs to continue throughout life. Our historic concentration of policy attention and resources __74__ young people cannot meet the new __75__ ," says the report's author, Professor Stephen McNair.

　　The major __76__ of our education budget is spent on people below the age of 25. __77__ people are changing their jobs, __78__ , partners and lifestyles more often than __79__ , they need opportunities to learn at every age. __80__ , some people are starting new careers in their 50s and later.

　　People need opportunities to make a "midlife review" to __81__ to the later stages of employed life, and to plan for the *transition*（过渡） __82__ retirement, which

68. [A] superior　　　[C] essential
　　[B] regular　　　　[D] adequate

69. [A] currently　　　[C] anxiously
　　[B] barely　　　　[D] heavily

70. [A] regulations　　[C] challenges
　　[B] obstacles　　　[D] guidelines

71. [A] enjoyment　　　[C] stability
　　[B] retirement　　　[D] inability

72. [A] over　　　　　[C] across
　　[B] after　　　　　[D] besides

73. [A] Identifying　　[C] Instructing
　　[B] Learning　　　[D] Practicing

74. [A] at　　　　　　[C] in
　　[B] by　　　　　　[D] on

75. [A] desires　　　　[C] needs
　　[B] realms　　　　[D] intentions

76. [A] measure　　　[C] area
　　[B] ratio　　　　　[D] portion

77. [A] When　　　　[C] Whether
　　[B] Until　　　　　[D] Before

78. [A] neighbors　　　[C] homes
　　[B] moods　　　　[D] minds

79. [A] ago　　　　　[C] previously
　　[B] ever　　　　　[D] formerly

80. [A] For example　[C] In particular
　　[B] By contrast　　[D] On average

81. [A] transform　　　[C] adjust
　　[B] yield　　　　　[D] suit

82. [A] within　　　　[C] beyond
　　[B] from　　　　　[D] to

may now happen　83　at any point from 50 to over 90, says McNair.	83. [A] unfairly　　[C] instantly 　　[B] unpredictably [D] indirectly
And there should be more money　84　to support people in establishing a	84. [A] reliable　　[C] available 　　[B] considerable [D] feasible
85　of identity and finding constructive	85. [A] sense　　[C] project 　　[B] conscience [D] definition
86　for the "third age", the 20 or more years they will spend in healthy retired life.	86. [A] ranks　　[C] ideals 　　[B] assets　　[D] roles

试题详解

　　本文是一篇议论文，"总—分"结构，指出应给老人更多学习机会。文章首先点出主题，其次说明现在的政策忽视了老年人的学习问题，最后指出老年是每个人的必经阶段，应该正确认识老年人的潜在贡献及价值。

67. B　词义辨析题。focus on意为"关注"；operate on意为"给……做手术"；count on意为"指望，依靠"；depend on意为"依赖"。句意为：目前关注年轻人与工作技能的做法。

68. D　词义辨析题。superior意为"上好的，出众的"；regular意为"有规律的"；essential意为"重要的"；adequate意为"足够的，适当的"。句意为：不足以应对人口结构变化所带来的挑战。

69. A　词义辨析题。currently意为"现在"；barely意为"仅仅"；anxiously意为"忧虑地，不安地"；heavily意为"沉重地"。句意为：现在只有1%的教育预算花在占人口三分之一的老年人身上。本句是对上句的具体说明，故所填词应与上句的current相呼应。

70. C　词义辨析题。regulation意为"规则，规章"；obstacle意为"障碍"；challenge意为"挑战"；guideline意为"指引"。本段承接上段，所填词应与上段中的challenge前后呼应。

71. B　词义辨析题。enjoyment意为"享受"；retirement意为"退休"；stability意为"稳定性"；inability意为"无能，无力"。由空格后的there are now more people over 59可知，大意是说老年人非常多，选项中与此呼应的只有retirement。

72. A 由空格后的state pension age(国家规定的领取养老金的年龄)可知，本句大意为"有1130万人已经超过了领取国家养老金的年龄"，故选A。此段意为：这一挑战包括如下事实：大多数人将在退休后度过余下三分之一的生命，现在59岁以上的人口数超过了16岁以下的人口数，1130万人已经超过了国家规定的领取养老金的年龄。

73. B 词义辨析题。identify意为"识别，鉴定"；learn意为"学习"；instruct意为"教，指导"；practice意为"练习"。句意为：学习需要持续终生，只有选项B与本文主题相符。

74. D 固定搭配题。所填介词需与前面的concentration搭配，且宾语为young people，只有D选项符合条件。句意为：我们历史上对于年轻人的政策关注与资源倾斜。

75. C 词义辨析题。desire意为"(人的)愿望；欲望"；realm意为"王国；领域"；need意为"需要"；intention意为"意图，目的"。所填词应与空格前的动词meet搭配，并与段首的动词need呼应，故选C。句意为：不能满足新的需要。

76. D 词义辨析题。measure意为"措施，办法"；ratio意为"比率"；area意为"地区，区域"；portion意为"部分"，特指整体中与其他不同的部分。句意为：我们的教育预算大部分都花在了25岁以下的人身上。选项D最符合此处的语境和用法。

77. A 逻辑关系题。本句前半部分为状语从句，主句是they need opportunities to learn at every age，需要选择引导状语从句的从属连词，只有when(当……的时候)符合句意，故选A。

78. C 词义辨析题。neighbor意为"邻居"；mood意为"心情，情绪"；mind意为"思想"。所填词作changing的宾语，与jobs, partners, lifestyles并列且词义相近，故选C。

79. B 固定搭配题。选项中只有B可与more...than搭配，意为"比以前更……"。句意为：当人们比以前更频繁地更换工作、住所、搭档和生活方式时，他们在各个年龄段都需要学习的机会。

80. A 逻辑关系题。by contrast意为"相反，反之"；in particular意为"尤其"，强调特殊性，一般不单独使用，用在此处应改为particularly；on average意为"平均"。结合上下文，后句论证前句，故选A。句意为：例如，有些人在50多岁甚至更老时开始从事新的职业。

81. C 词义辨析题。transform意为"转换；变形"；yield意为"生产；屈服"；adjust意为"调节，适应"；suit意为"适合，满足"。句意为：人们需要机会来进行"中年回顾"，以便适应工作生涯的后半段。所填词应与空格后的to搭配，且与空后的plan意思相近，故选C。

82. D 固定搭配题。所填词应与空前的transition搭配，只能选D。句意为：计划向退休过渡。

83. B 词义辨析题。unfairly意为"不公平地"；unpredictably意为"不可预料地"；instantly意为"立即"；indirectly意为"间接地"。句意为：现在退休可能不可预料地发生在从50岁到90多岁的任何时间。所填词应与空后的at any point from 50 to over 90的任意性相呼应，故选B。

84. C 词义辨析题。reliable意为"可靠的"；considerable意为"相当的，可观的"；available意为"可用的；有效的"；feasible意为"可能的，可行的"。句意为：应该有更多可用的资金来支持人们。所填词应能修饰空前的money且符合语义，只能选C。

85. A 固定搭配题。sense意为"感觉"；conscience意为"良心"；project意为"工程，项目"；definition意为"定义"。句意为：建立一种认同感。只有A选项可与of identity形成固定搭配。

86. D 词义辨析题。rank意为"排名，等级"；asset意为"资产；优点"；ideal意为"理想"；role意为"角色；作用"。句意为：为他们的"第三年龄"，即退休后20年甚至更久的健康生活，找到建设性的角色。所填词应与空格前的a sense of identity(认同感)意思相近，故选D。

第三节 强化训练

强化训练一

Directions: *There are 20 blanks in the following passage. For each blank there are four choices marked* [A], [B], [C] *and* [D] *on the right side of the paper. You should choose the ONE that best fits into the passage. Then mark the corresponding letter on* **Answer Sheet 2** *with a single line through the centre.*

Most worthwhile careers require some kind of specialized training. Ideally, therefore, the choice of an 67 should be made even before choice of a curriculum in high school. Actually, 68 , most people make several job choices during their working lives, 69 because of economic and industrial changes and partly to improve their position. The "one perfect job" does not 70 . Young people should 71 enters into a broad flexible training program that will 72 them for a field of work rather than for a single 73 .

Unfortunately many young people have to make career plans 74 benefit of help from a(n) 75 vocational counselor or psychologist. Knowing 76 about the occupational world, or themselves for that matter, they choose their lifework on a hit-or-miss basis. Some 77 from job to job. Others 78 to work in which they are unhappy and for which they are not fitted.

One common mistake is choosing an occupation for 79 real or imagined prestige. Too many high school students—or their parents for them—choose the

67. [A] identification [C] accommodation
    [B] entertainment [D] occupation
68. [A] however [C] though
    [B] therefore [D] thereby
69. [A] entirely [C] partly
    [B] mainly [D] possibly
70. [A] fade [C] survive
    [B] vanish [D] exist
71. [A] since [C] furthermore
    [B] therefore [D] moreover
72. [A] make [C] take
    [B] fit [D] leave
73. [A] job [C] means
    [B] way [D] company
74. [A] with [C] without
    [B] for [D] to
75. [A] competent [C] aggressive
    [B] competitive [D] effective
76. [A] little [C] much
    [B] few [D] more
77. [A] turn [C] leave
    [B] drift [D] float
78. [A] apply [C] stick
    [B] appeal [D] turn
79. [A] our [C] your
    [B] its [D] their

professional field, _80_ both the relatively small proportion of workers in the professions and the extremely high educational and personal _81_. The imagined or real prestige of a profession or a white-collar job is no good _82_ for	80. [A] concerning [C] considering [B] following [D] disregarding
	81. [A] preferences [C] tendencies [B] requirements [D] ambitions
	82. [A] resource [C] reason [B] background [D] basis
choosing it as life's work. _83_, these occupations are not always well paid, since a large _84_ of jobs are in mechanical and	83. [A] Therefore [C] However [B] Nevertheless [D] Moreover
	84. [A] rate [C] proportion [B] thickness [D] density
manual work, the _85_ of young people should give serious _86_ to these fields.	85. [A] majority [C] minority [B] mass [D] multitude
	86. [A] proposal [C] consideration [B] suggestion [D] appraisal

试题详解

本文说明了世上并不存在完美的工作。年轻人应该参加灵活、广泛的培训项目，同时寻求专业顾问及心理专家的建议，选择工作时避免盲目性。

67. D 名词辨析。根据首句可知，本文的主题是career（职业），此处应选其近义词 occupation。

68. A 连词辨析。前句讲理想状态下应该在中学选课之后就确定职业，空格后的句子讲大多数人一生要择业多次，可见空格前后是转折关系，故选however。

69. C 副词辨析。空格所在的句子讲人们多次择业的原因，由because of...and partly to... 可知and前后是两个并列关系的原因，因此前半部分也应填入 partly，与后半部分出现的partly相呼应，以保证语义和结构的完整。

70. D 动词辨析。前句讲到人一生要换很多份工作，由此可以推断出完美的工作并不存在，因此应在not后填入表示"存在"的词，故选exist。fade意为"凋谢，消失"；vanish意为"消失"；survive意为"幸存"。

71. B 副词辨析。前面讲完美的工作并不存在，本句说人们应该参加一些灵活的培训项目，故此处应选表示因果关系的副词，答案选therefore（因此）。since

意为"由于"，后接原因；furthermore意为"此外，而且"，表递进；more-over意为"些外，而且"。

72. B 动词辨析。that引导的从句修饰training program，根据常识，这种培训应该使人符合某种行业的要求，符合结构与句意的只有fit(适合)，fit sb. for sth.意为"使某人适合某事"。

73. A 名词辨析。本句的rather than表明前后为并列关系，句意为：年轻人应该参加一些广泛而灵活的培训，使他们能胜任某一领域的工作，而不是一项单一的工作。此处job是句中work的近义复现。

74. C 介词辨析。本句讲年轻人的职业规划，根据本句第一个单词unfortunately可判断应填表示否定的单词，故选without，本句意为：他们的职业规划没有得到职业顾问或心理专家的帮助。

75. A 形容词辨析。此处填入的应是vocational counselor or psychologist(职业顾问或心理专家)的定语。对于寻求帮助的年轻人而言，最重要的是专家有无水平，故选competent(有能力的，胜任的)。competitive意为"有竞争力的"；aggressive意为"有进取心的"；effective意为"有效率的"。

76. A 形容词辨析。此处应填know的宾语。根据句尾的hit-or-miss(无计划的，无目的的)可以推断，很多年轻人对occupational world知之甚少，而且occupational world是不可数名词，故选little。

77. B 动词辨析。本句意为：有些人不停地换工作，此处填入的词应与from构成固定搭配，所以只能选drift。drift from work to work意为"不停换工作"。

78. C 动词辨析。本句要结合上句进行判断。这两句使用了"Some.... Others..."句型，句意应该相反。前一句是有些人频繁换工作，后一句应是有些人不换工作，故选stick (to)(坚持)。

79. B 代词辨析。根据后文，此处的prestige指工作特征而非人的特征，因此应填its。

80. D 动词辨析。后面提到很多高中生或者其家长帮他们选择工作领域，空格后说这类职业从业者较少或对个人要求很高，由此可知他们的选择是盲目的，没有从客观实际出发，故选disregarding(忽视，漠视)。

81. B 名词辨析。此处应填可以被high修饰的词，表示专业工作的实际情况，故选requirements(要求)，指胜任这些工作所需的技能要求很高。preferences意为"优先选择"；tendencies意为"倾向"；ambitions意为"雄心"。

82. C　名词辨析。此句表示工作的声望好并不能成为选择作为终身职业的好理由，故选reason。resource意为"来源"；background意为"背景"；basis意为"基础"。

83. D　逻辑关系。本句意为：这些工作不一定报酬都很高，与空格前的句子是递进关系，故选moreover。

84. C　名词辨析。此处所填的词应该能构成"a...of"的结构，表示"一部分"，只有proportion（部分）符合题意。rate意为"速度，比例"；thickness意为"厚度，浓度"；density意为"密度"。

85. A　名词辨析。此处提醒年轻人要认真考虑这类工作，当然提醒的是大多数人，而非少数人，故选majority。

86. C　名词辨析。根据上题，作者提醒年轻人认真考虑此事，故选consideration（考虑，顾虑）。proposal意为"提议，建议"；suggestion意为"建议"；appraisal意为"评价，评估"。

强化训练二

Directions: *There are 20 blanks in the following passage. For each blank there are four choices marked [A], [B], [C] and [D] on the right side of the paper. You should choose the ONE that best fits into the passage. Then mark the corresponding letter on Answer Sheet 2 with a single line through the centre.*

The horse and carriage is a thing of past, but love and marriage are still with us and still closely interrelated. Most American marriages, __67__ first marriage uniting young people, are the result of mutual attraction and affection __68__ than practical considerations.	67. [A] specially　　[C] particularly 　　[B] naturally　　[D] fortunately 68. [A] more　　　　[C] less 　　[B] rather　　　[D] better
In the United States, parents do not __69__ marriages for their children. Teenagers begin __70__ in high school and usually find mates through their own academic and social __71__. Though young people feel free to	69. [A] arrange　　　[C] manage 　　[B] engage　　　[D] propose 70. [A] appointing　　[C] marrying 　　[B] dating　　　[D] playing 71. [A] positions　　[C] contracts 　　[B] associations　[D] contacts

choose their friends from __72__ groups, most choose a mate of similar __73__. This is due in part to parental guidance. Parents cannot __74__ *spouses*（配偶）for their children, but they can usually __75__ choices by voicing disapproval of someone they consider unsuitable.

__76__, marriages between members of different groups（interclass, interfaith, and interracial marriages）are __77__, probably because of the greater mobility of today's youth and the fact that they are __78__ by fewer prejudices than their parents. Many young people leave their hometowns to attend college, serve in the armed forces, __79__ pursue a career in a bigger city. Once away from home and family, they are more __80__ to date and marry outside their own social group.

In mobile American society, interclass marriages are neither __81__ nor astonishing.

Interfaith marriages are __82__ the rise, especially between *Protestants*（基督教徒）and *Catholics*（天主教徒）. On the other hand, interracial marriages are still very __83__. It can be difficult for interracial couples to find a place to live, maintain friendships, and __84__ a family. Marriages between

72. [A] separate [C] independent
    [B] identical [D] different
73. [A] background [C] circumstance
    [B] situation [D] condition
74. [A] object [C] select
    [B] reject [D] approve
75. [A] influence [C] afford
    [B] make [D] provide
76. [A] Therefore [C] Moreover
    [B] However [D] Likewise
77. [A] declining [C] increasing
    [B] prohibiting [D] reducing
78. [A] respected [C] reserved
    [B] retained [D] restricted
79. [A] but [C] so
    [B] or [D] unless
80. [A] likely [C] reluctant
    [B] possible [D] eager
81. [A] scarce [C] rare
    [B] risky [D] rigid
82. [A] in [C] for
    [B] at [D] on
83. [A] normal [C] ordinary
    [B] uncommon [D] usual
84. [A] raise [C] grow
    [B] settle [D] unite

people of different national　85　（but the same race and religion）have been commonplace here　86　colonial times.

85. ［A］source　　　［C］origin
　　［B］convention　［D］immigrant
86. ［A］since　　　　［C］by
　　［B］with　　　　［D］during

试题详解

　　本文主要介绍了美国的婚姻状况，前三段讲美国年轻人的婚姻观及父母对年轻人择偶的影响，后两段讲述了美国不同阶级、不同宗教信仰，甚至是不同民族之间的婚姻。

67. C　副词辨析。first marriage uniting young people是most American marriage中的一部分，由此可见作者在这里是以前者为例，particularly（尤其）多用于举例。specially意为"特别地"，多用于表示不普通、不寻常的特点。naturally（自然地）和fortunately（幸运地）与文意相差太远，可以首先排除。

68. B　固定搭配。空格所在的句子讲的是美国人结婚的原因，practical consideration（现实的考虑）与mutual attraction and affection（互相吸引和爱慕）在广义上是一种对比关系，所以应该选rather，rather than是固定搭配，表示"而不是"，相当于instead of。

69. A　动词辨析。本句的意思是：在美国，父母不_____子女的婚姻，根据常识应该选arrange，arrange marriage意为"包办婚姻"。engage（订婚）和propose（求婚）不能与marriage搭配；manage（经营）与原文不符。

70. B　动词辨析。由and usually find mates可知，空格处应该填入与"交友"有关的词，故选dating（约会，特指异性间）。appointing指用权力或共同约定来决定或安排，不合题意。

71. D　名词辨析。through their own academic and social_____是美国中学生交友的途径，故选contact（接触，交往）。positions意为"地位"，associations意为"联系"，contracts意为"合同"，均不符合文意。

72. D　形容词辨析。空格所在分句的句首出现转折连词though，所以前后分句为转折关系。根据后一句中出现的similar可以推断空格处应该填入一个与之意义相反的词汇，故选different。separate意为"分开的"，identical意为"相同的，同一的"，independent意为"独立的"。

73. A　名词辨析。根据前半句可知,大多数美国年轻人不会选择与自己来自不同groups的人,即两个人要有相似的background(背景)。situation意为"情况,情形",circumstance意为"环境",condition意为"条件"。

74. C　固定搭配。由上文可知,美国年轻人选择和自己背景相似的人,部分的原因是父母的引导。本句说"父母不会……,但是会……",根据常识,父母应该不会为子女选择配偶,故答案为select,select...for... 是固定搭配,意为"为……选择……"。object(to)意为"反对";reject意为"拒绝",不能和for搭配;approve(of)意为"同意"。

75. A　动词辨析。由转折词but可知,本句和前半句"不能为孩子选择配偶"应为转折关系,故选influence(影响)。

76. B　副词辨析。上文讲年轻人喜欢找背景相同的配偶,但下文讲的是不同阶级、信仰、种族之间的婚姻,可见前后是转折关系,故选however(然而)。therefore意为"因此",表因果关系;moreover意为"此外",表递进关系;likewise意为"同样地",表对比关系。

77. C　动词辨析。由空格后的the greater mobility of today's youth(如今年轻人更大的流动性)和_____ by fewer prejudices than their parents(比他们的父母更少受到歧视的_____)可知,不同groups之间的婚姻应该是逐渐增加的,故选increasing。declining意为"下降";prohibiting意为"禁止";reducing"减少",都不符合文意。

78. D　动词辨析。此句意为:年轻人比他们的父母受到更少歧视的,结合上文应选restricted(限制)。respected意为"尊敬";retain意为"保持";reserve意为"预订"。

79. B　逻辑关系。根据上下文逻辑关系,前文的求学(attend college)、参军(serve in the armed forces)与空格后的创业(pursue a career)应是并列关系,故选or。

80. A　形容词辨析。根据上下文逻辑关系,离开家乡和家庭(home and family)之后,年轻人与其他社会群体的人约会及结婚的可能性应该是增加了,故选likely,be likely to意为"可能"。possible也意为"可能",但不用这个结构,且表示的可能性较小;be reluctant to意为"勉强";be eager to意为"渴望"。

81. C　形容词辨析。此句意为:在美国,不同阶级之间的婚姻既不_____,也不奇怪,or连接的是并列结构,故空格处应该填入astonishing的近义词rare(稀少的)。scarce意为"不足的";risky意为"冒险的";rigid意为"严格的"。

82. D　固定搭配。on the rise意为"不断上升",表上升趋势。

83. B　形容词辨析。由句首的on the other hand(另一方面)可知，此处应是转折关系，故此处应该填入与on the rise相反或相对的词，答案是uncommon(不寻常的)。

84. A　固定搭配。raise a family意为"养家"。

85. C　名词辨析。根据括号中的解释，这种婚姻的双方种族和信仰相同，但来自不同国家，故选origin(出身)。source意为"(信息等的)来源"，convention意为"习俗"，是干扰项，相同种族和信仰的人习俗应相同，故可以排除；immigrant意为"移民"，也是干扰项，可数名词应使用复数形式。

86. A　介词辨析。空格所在句子为完成时态，而colonial times表示的是一个时间起点，故选since(自从)。

强化训练三

Directions: *There are 20 blanks in the following passage. For each blank there are four choices marked* [A], [B], [C] *and* [D] *on the right side of the paper. You should choose the ONE that best fits into the passage. Then mark the corresponding letter on* **Answer Sheet 2** *with a single line through the centre.*

Mars is not, it seems, the dry old planet we once believed it to be. Astronauts who are __67__ to go there in the next decade may find plenty __68__ water to *slake*(消除) their thirst.

And with water present the __69__ of finding some sort of life on Mars are __70__ brighter.

This is the view of 40 __71__ all over the world who have been analyzing __72__ of pictures and other scientific __73__ obtained by

67. [A] expected　[C] required
　　[B] hoped　　[D] eager

68. [A] to　　[C] more
　　[B] of　　[D] in

69. [A] chances　　[C] occasions
　　[B] openings　[D] opportunities

70. [A] quite　[C] much
　　[B] very　[D] more

71. [A] biologists　[C] sociologists
　　[B] geologists　[D] psychologists

72. [A] lots　　　[C] thousand
　　[B] quantities　[D] thousands

73. [A] tidings　[C] intelligence
　　[B] news　　[D] information

robot explorers in the sixties and seventies.

To begin with, scientists thought the Red Planet was as __74__ as the Moon with

dust storms swirling over vast sandy __75__. But now the picture is very different with mountains and valleys carved by __76__ glaciers and torrential rivers rushing and rumbling deep underground.

In a report on the __77__ of the Martian pictures Dr. Michael Car of the U.S. Geological Survey comments, "I am __78__ there's lots of water on Mars." Any surface water will be in the __79__ of ice. But it

could __80__ explorers having to take so much fresh __81__ with them.

The report says __82__ Mars probably

had a warmer climate in ages __83__ due to its axis having been more steeply tilted towards the Sun.

__84__ convincing signs of plant or

animal life have been __85__ by instruments

soft landed on Mars, __86__ only the immediate vicinity of landing vehicles could be examined.

74. [A] peaceful   [C] lifeless
    [B] quiet   [D] dead

75. [A] deserts   [C] seas
    [B] mountains   [D] rivers

76. [A] energetic   [C] massive
    [B] great   [D] mighty

77. [A] diagnosis   [C] analysis
    [B] syntheses   [D] analyses

78. [A] convinced   [C] believed
    [B] guaranteed [D] proved

79. [A] appearance [C] form
    [B] mould   [D] shape

80. [A] help   [C] carry
    [B] save   [D] prevent

81. [A] water   [C] food
    [B] ice   [D] vegetable

82. [A] what   [C] how
    [B] if   [D] that

83. [A] pass   [C] ago
    [B] past   [D] before

84. [A] Not   [C] Nor
    [B] No   [D] Never

85. [A] detected   [C] seen
    [B] touched   [D] felt

86. [A] probably   [C] supposed
    [B] perhaps   [D] although

试题详解

火星并非如我们先前想象的那样是一个干燥的古老星球。日后人们可能会发现火星上拥有大量的水资源。

67. A 词义辨析。expect sb. to do sth.意为"期望某人做某事",常用于被动语态。hope意为"希望",不能用于"宾语+宾语补足语"的结构;require意为"命令",其用法为require sb. to do sth.;eager意为"渴望的",是形容词,be eager to do sth.意为"渴望做某事",不符合题意。

68. B 固定搭配。plenty of(许多)是固定搭配,其后可接不可数名词或可数名词复数。

69. A 名词辨析。本句意为:有了水的存在,在火星上发现某种生命的_____更有希望。由于第二个空格要填入的是比较级的修饰词,所以该空格不影响对句子的理解,因此只要集中判断第一个空格即可。chances意为"可能性";opening意为"职位的空缺;有利的环境";occasion意为"合适时机";opportunity意为"机会",侧重指做某事的条件或时机。

70. C 语法结构。四个选项中,只有much可以修饰形容词或副词的比较级,表示比较的程度。

71. B 名词辨析。根据常识,研究火星的应是geologist(地质学家)。biologist意为"生物学家";sociologist意为"社会学家";psychologist意为"心理学家"。

72. D 固定搭配。"_____of pictures"和"other scientific_____"是并列结构,由表被动语态的过去分词短语obtained by robot explorers... 修饰,根据常识,机器人探测器在二十世纪六七十年代获取的照片应该非常多,所以第一个空格处应该填入thousands of(许多的,成千上万的),来表达"极多"的含义。

73. D 名词辨析。由于and连接的是并列结构,所以此处应该填入一个与picture对应的能够用scientific修饰的词,所以答案是information,scientific information表示"科技信息"。intelligence多指市场信息和军事情报。

74. C 形容词辨析。从选项判断空格处要填入一个形容词,来描述科学家们最初认为的火星与月亮的一个共同特点。结合第二段提到的由于水的存在,在火星上寻找某种生命的希望更大了,可知科学家们最初认为火星上是没有生命的,故填lifeless(死气沉沉的,没有生命的)。

75. A 名词辨析。根据空格前的dust storms swirling vast sandy... 可以推断描述的是沙漠的景象,故选deserts。

76. D 形容词辨析。由选项可知，空格处要填入一个形容词来修饰glaciers（冰川）。energetic意为"精力旺盛的，充沛的"；great侧重指数量、尺寸或程度上的"大"；massive侧重指尺寸或数量上的巨大。mighty指力量上的强大。结合文意，正确答案应该是D。

77. C 名词辨析。结合选项和句意分析，空格处应该填入一个名词，并且该名词的动词形式能够与the Martian pictures搭配，故而可以首先排除diagnosis（诊断）。systheses（综合）是指将不同的事物或观点合在一起，使之成为一个新的整体，与文意不符，故也可以排除。此处只能选analysis（分析）。

78. A 动词辨析。I am convinced...意为"我被说服相信……"。guarantee意为"保证"，believe意为"相信"，一般不用于被动语态；proved不合题意，不能说"我被证明……"。

79. C 名词辨析。根据常识，冰是水的一种存在形式，所以选form。appearance意为"外表，外观"；mould意为"铸模，模子"；shape意为"外形，形状"。

80. B 动词辨析。由转折连词but可知，此句是对上文的转折。上文说火星上任何的地表水都是以冰的形式存在的。结合"_____explorers having to take so much fresh _____ with them"可以推断，but后说的应该是"探测者们不必带太多新鲜的水"，故此处应选save（节省），save sb. (from) doing sth.意为"省去（某人的）劳力"。

81. A 名词辨析。由80题解析可知，此处应该选water。ice不与fresh搭配，且与文意不符。C和D在文中没有相关信息支持。

82. D 连词辨析。通过分析句子结构可知，say后接宾语从句，故选that。what不是从属连词；if引导宾语从句时，前面的动词一般是ask, doubt, don't know，不用say；how一般引导主语从句。

83. B 形容词辨析。固定搭配in ages/time past（很久以前，在过去）。

84. B 词义辨析。此空格处应填no，no可以放在单数及复数名词前，也可放在句首。not放在可数名词前；nor是连词，常与neither连用，不能作定语修饰名词；never作副词放在句首时，句子应倒装。

85. A 动词辨析。空格所在的分句是被动语态，意为：在火星上，软着陆的仪器没有_____令人信服的生命存在的迹象，故选detect（发现，察觉）。

86. D 词义辨析。通过分析句子结构可知，空格处需要填入连词来连接前后两个分句，所以可以首先排除A和B。空格所在的分句意为：只有登陆车附近的区域可以检查，说明前半句得出的结论是有前提条件的，所以此处应选although引导让步状语从句。suppose表假设引导句子时，后面需加that。

强化训练四

Directions: *There are 20 blanks in the following passage. For each blank there are four choices marked [A], [B], [C] and [D] on the right side of the paper. You should choose the ONE that best fits into the passage. Then mark the corresponding letter on Answer Sheet 2 with a single line through the centre.*

The Internet has become a commonplace for us. While __67__ the Internet, we should not __68__ the alarm bells sounding in our ears, reminding us of keeping __69__ for on-line crimes. Last year, the Melissa and Explore Zip virus caused chaos __70__ the Internet. Last week the "I love you" bug played havoc __71__ the world. What will be the next? No one knows.

Many on-line crimes are not so different to __72__ seen in real world, the spreading of fake data, cheating and blackmail, __73__ property rights infringements and privacy violations. But computer hackers also create new forms of crime __74__ the Internet changes the world into a "global village".

With the __75__ of e-business, on-line crimes could not only cause great damage to __76__, but could also threaten the __77__ of national political, economic

67.	[A] surfing	[C] reaching
	[B] operating	[D] exploring
68.	[A] neglect	[C] omit
	[B] overlook	[D] ignore
69.	[A] guard	[C] alert
	[B] careful	[D] aware
70.	[A] in	[C] inside
	[B] on	[D] with
71.	[A] over	[C] across
	[B] on	[D] through
72.	[A] which	[C] them
	[B] that	[D] those
73.	[A] intellectual	[C] knowledge
	[B] intelligence	[D] cultural
74.	[A] until	[C] as
	[B] before	[D] after
75.	[A] blossom	[C] blooming
	[B] gloom	[D] booming
76.	[A] persons	[C] country
	[B] individuals	[D] society
77.	[A] equality	[C] security
	[B] peace	[D] safety

| and cultural orders. The <u>78</u> legal system in most countries <u>79</u> weak when dealing with on-line crimes, <u>80</u> to the sophisticated technology involved. For this reason, many countries are considering <u>81</u> Internet laws to curb on-line crimes.

 In China, <u>82</u> there are millions of Internet surfers, it is more important to formulate new laws and rules on network security than to <u>83</u> the existing ones.

 When drafting and <u>84</u> new laws, China should also <u>85</u> the relations between protecting network security <u>86</u> the sound development of Internet. | 78. [A] current   [C] nowadays
      [B] today's   [D] contemporary
 79. [A] proving   [C] prove
      [B] proves   [D] proven
 80. [A] owe   [C] thanks
      [B] as   [D] due
 81. [A] shaping   [C] formulating
      [B] founding   [D] setting
 82. [A] that   [C] where
      [B] which   [D] when
 83. [A] date   [C] upgrade
      [B] accelerate   [D] update
 84. [A] implying   [C] importing
      [B] implementing [D] imposing
 85. [A] manage   [C] process
      [B] establish   [D] arrange
 86. [A] with   [C] and
      [B] or   [D] besides |

试题详解

　　互联网日益盛行,网上犯罪也愈演愈烈。对于中国而言,很有必要制定新的有关网络安全的法律法规,同时还要协调处理网络安全与互联网健康发展的关系。

67. A　固定搭配。surf the Internet意为"上网,网上冲浪"。

68. D　近义辨析。由选项可以推断,本句意为:我们不应置耳畔一再响起的警钟于不顾,故选ignore(不顾,忽视),强调主观上的不听或不注意。neglect意为"忽略,疏忽",强调忘了做,overlook意为"未注意,未考虑",A和B都不强调主观上的故意;omit意为"省略,遗漏"。

69. C　固定搭配。reminding us of keeping _____ for on-line crimes是 alarm bells 的具体内容,故应选alert, be alert for意为"对……保持警觉"。guard 的用法

为 be on guard against(警惕，提防)；be careful 意为"小心，谨慎"；aware 的用法为 be aware of(意识到)。

70. B 介词搭配。on the Internet 意为"在网上"。

71. C 介词搭配。across the world 意为"在世界范围内"。

72. D 语法辨析。根据上下文，空格替代 crimes，故选指示代词的复数形式 those。该句非复合句，故排除关系代词 which；them 是宾格，不能接修饰语，故排除。

73. A 习惯用法。intellectual property rights 意为"知识产权"。

74. C 逻辑判断。本句意为：随着计算机将世界变为地球村，黑客们也在发明新的网上犯罪形式，故选连词 as。

75. D 形近词辨析。booming 意为"迅速发展，繁荣"。blossom 意为"花"；gloom 意为"昏暗，忧郁"；blooming 意为"开花的"。

76. B 词汇复现。由 not only...but also... 可知，前后两个分句是递进关系，后半句讲网上犯罪危及"国家的政治、经济、文化秩序的_____"，因此前半句指对"个人"的危害，故选 individuals。

77. C 词义辨析。根据上下文，此处应选 security(安全，保障)，强调因受到保护而感到安全。equality 意为"平等，相等"；peace 意为"和平"；safety 意为"安全，保险"，强调无危险或损害的状态。

78. A 形容词辨析。根据句意，应选 current(现时的，当前的)。today's 为所有格，前面不应加冠词；nowadays 是副词，不作定语；contemporary 意为"当代的，同时代的"，不合句意。

79. B 语法辨析。通过分析句子结构可知，空格处需要填入的是谓语动词，且主语 system 是单数第三人称，故应选 proves。

80. D 短语搭配。due to 意为"由于，因为"。owe 形式错误，应为 owing；as 引导原因或让步状语从句；thanks 是强干扰选项，thanks to 一般接好的原因，表示"多亏"。

81. C 词汇重现。根据下文 formulate new laws and rules，故选 formulating。

82. C 定语从句。根据句子结构，空格指代地点名词，且在从句中作状语，故选 where。

83. D　词义辨析。根据句意：更重要的是制定新的法律法规而非_____现有的，可以确定答案应选update（更新）。date意为"注明日期"；accelerate意为"加快，加速"；upgrade意为"提升，升级"。

84. B　形近词辨析。根据下文，与the laws搭配应选implement（使生效，履行）。imply意为"暗示"；import意为"进口，输入"；impose意为"强加，征税"。

85. A　动词辨析。根据句意，应选manage（管理）。establish意为"建立"，用于此处句意不通；process意为"加工，处理"；arrange意为"安排，整理"。

86. C　介词搭配。between...and...是固定搭配，意为"在……和……之间"。

第六章 翻 译

最新大纲

翻译部分为汉译英，共5个句子，一句一题，句长为15～30词。句中的一部分已用英文给出，要求考生根据全句意思将汉语部分译成英语。考试时间5分钟。翻译需符合英语的语法结构和表达习惯，要求用词准确。

四级考试中未将翻译作为一个独立的技能进行考核。翻译部分主要考核学生正确运用词汇和语法结构并按英语习惯表达思想的能力。

第一节 高 分 攻 略

一、应试技巧

1. 四级汉译英实际是补全句子，加入3～8个单词即可。
2. 只是简单的短句翻译，一般不会考查文学、新闻、科技翻译。
3. 十大考点：主要考查四级常考词组和语法知识。

1) 词汇

例：大纲样题

88. Not only ＿＿＿＿＿＿ （他向我收费过高），but he didn't do a good repair job either.

解析：考查charge(收费)，overcharge(收费过高)。

2) 分词

例：大纲样题

89. Your losses in trade this year are nothing ＿＿＿＿＿＿ （与我的相比）.

解析：此处"与……相比"与主语losses构成被动关系，应使用过去分词 compared with。

3) 词组

例：大纲样题

89. Your losses in trade this year are nothing ＿＿＿＿＿＿ （与我的相比）.

解析："与……相比"应是compare with或in comparison with，不是compare to (把……比作)。

4）比较结构

例：大纲样题

90. On average, it is said, visitors spend only _____（一半的钱）in a day in Leeds as in London.

解析：后半句中出现了as，应使用词组as much/many as（与……一样多）。

5）时态

例：大纲样题

88. Not only _____（他向我收费过高），but he didn't do a good repair job either.

解析：结合后半句，应使用一般过去时，助动词用did。

6）被动语态

例：大纲样题

87. The substance does not dissolve in water _____（不管是否加热）.

解析：这种物质被加热，应使用被动语态，使用动词heat的过去分词形式heated。

7）句型

例：2006年12月真题

88. Since my childhood I have found that _____（没有什么比读书对我更有吸引力）.

解析：考查句型nothing is more...than（没有什么比……更……）。

8）从句

例：大纲样题

87. The substance does not dissolve in water _____（不管是否加热）.

解析：考查让步状语从句whether... or not（不管是否……）。

9）虚拟语气

例：2006年6月24日真题

89. The professor required that _____（我们交研究报告）by Wednesday.

解析：require that sb.（should）do sth. 是建议句型的变体，其中should可以省略。

10）倒装句

例：大纲样题

88. Not only ＿＿＿＿＿＿＿＿＿＿＿＿＿（他向我收费过高），but he didn't do a good repair job either.

解析：not only放在句首时，句子需使用倒装结构，助动词应提到主语前面。

二、选词技巧

1. 选择简洁词汇，避免重复啰嗦。

2. 选择准确词汇，避免用词不当。

3. 选择规范词汇，避免口语、俚语、俗语、生僻词汇。

三、解题顺序

1. 通读全句。透彻理解句子，分清主干和修饰成分，判断简单句或复杂句。

2. 翻译句子。选择准确的词组和语法结构，符合英文表达习惯。

3. 检查全句。

第二节 真题选析

一、经典真题

Directions: *Complete the sentences by translating into English the Chinese given in brackets. Please write your translation on* ***Answer Sheet 2***.

87. The substance does not dissolve in water ＿＿＿＿＿＿＿＿（不管是否加热）.

88. Not only ＿＿＿＿＿＿＿＿＿ （他向我收费过高）, but he didn't do a good repair job either.

89. Your losses in trade this year are nothing ＿＿＿＿＿＿＿＿（与我的相比）.

90. On average, it is said, visitors spend only ＿＿＿＿＿＿＿＿（一半的钱）in a day in Leeds as in London.

91. By contrast, American mothers were more likely _____ （把孩子的成功归因于）natural talent.

试题详解

87. 答案：whether（it is）heated or not

句意：不管是否加热，这种物质都不会溶于水。

解析：1）从句：让步状语从句whether... or not（不管是否），其中it is可以省略。

2）语态：这种物质被加热，应使用被动语态，使用动词heat的过去分词形式heated。

引申：让步状语从句的引导词还有though, no matter how等。

88. 答案：did he charge me too much或did he overcharge me

句意：他不但向我收费过高，而且修得也不好。

解析：1）词汇：收费（charge），表示金钱过高用too much，表示温度过高用too high，表示收费过高也可使用overcharge。

2）倒装句：not only放在句首时，句子需使用倒装结构，助动词应提到主语前面。

3）时态：结合后半句，应使用一般过去时，助动词用did。

引申：可以放在句首引导倒装句的否定词还有：hardly, scarcely, never, neither等。

89. 答案：compared with mine或in comparison with mine

句意：你今年在生意上的损失和我的相比不值得一提。

解析：1）词组："与……相比"应是compare with或in comparison with，而不是compare to（把……比作）。

2）分词：此处"与……相比"与主语losses构成被动关系，应使用过去分词compared with。

3）词汇：此处"我的"应译为物主代词 mine，如译为my losses则太冗赘。

引申：固定搭配词组中的介词和副词至关重要。

90. 答案：half as much（money）

句意：据说，游客们一天中在利兹的消费一般只有在伦敦的一半。

解析：1）比较结构：后半句中出现了as，应使用词组as much/many as（与……一样多）。

2)搭配：spend后应使用不可数形式，故用as much而非as many。money可以省略。

91. 答案：to attribute their children's success to

句意：比较而言，美国的母亲更可能把孩子的成功归于天赋。

解析：1)词组：attribute to(把……归因于)是四级核心词组，必须熟练掌握。

2)搭配：be likely to(容易，可能)，不能省略to。

引申：1)由于：result from, be responsible for

2)导致：result in, lead to

3)形近词组：contribute to(有助于，对……作出贡献)

二、经典真题二

Directions: *Complete the sentences by translating into English the Chinese given in brackets. Please write your translation on **Answer Sheet 2**.*

87. Having spent some time in the city, he had no trouble ＿＿＿＿＿＿＿＿(找到去历史博物馆的路).

88. ＿＿＿＿＿＿＿＿＿＿(为了挣钱供我上学), mother often takes on more work than is good for her.

89. The professor required that ＿＿＿＿＿＿＿＿＿(我们交研究报告) by Wednesday.

90. The more you explain, ＿＿＿＿＿＿＿＿(我愈糊涂).

91. Though a skilled worker, ＿＿＿＿＿＿＿＿(他被公司解雇了) last week because of the economic crisis.

试题详解

87. 答案：(in) finding the way to the Museum of History

句意：在这个城市住了一段时间之后，他要找到去博物馆的路易如反掌。

解析：1)词组：have (no) trouble (in) doing sth.(做某事有/没有困难)

2)动名词：此处应使用动名词finding。

3)专有名词：历史博物馆前应使用定冠词the，最好译为Museum of History，而不是History Museum，这样更符合英文表达习惯。

引申：同义词组：have (no) difficulty (in) doing sth.

88. 答案: In order to / To earn/raise enough money to afford/support/finance my education

句意: 为了挣钱供我上学, 妈妈经常承担超负荷的工作。

解析: 词组: earn/raise enough money(挣钱); afford/support/finance my education (供我上学)

89. 答案: we hand in the/our research report(s)

句意: 教授要求我们周三前交研究报告。

解析: 1)虚拟语气: require that sb. (should) do sth.(建议句型的变体), 其中 should可以省略。

2)词组: hand in(上交)

3)名词的单复数: 此处"报告"使用单复数均可。

引申: "要求、建议、命令、提议"+that+sb. (should) do sth.

90. 答案: the more confused I get/am

句意: 你愈解释, 我愈糊涂。

解析: 1)比较结构: the more...the more

2)词组: get/be confused(糊涂)

91. 答案: he was fired by the company

句意: 尽管他是一名熟练的工人, 但是因为经济危机, 他还是被公司解雇了。

解析: 1)从句: 让步状语从句前面使用了though, 后面不应出现but。

2)时态: 后半句出现last week, 应使用一般过去时。

3)被动语态: was fired(被解雇)。

三、经典真题三

Directions: *Complete the sentences by translating into English the Chinese given in brackets. Please write your translation on **Answer Sheet 2**.*

87. Specialists in intercultural studies say that it is not easy to _____ (适应不同文化中的生活)。

88. Since my childhood I have found that _____ (没有什么比读书对我更有吸引力)。

89. The victim _____ (本来会有机会活下来) if he had been taken to hospital in time.

90. Some psychologists claim that people _____ (出门在外时可能会感到孤独)。

91. The nation's population continues to rise ＿＿＿＿＿＿＿＿＿＿＿＿＿（以每年1200万人的速度）.

试题详解

87. 答案：adapt oneself to life/living in different cultures

句意：跨文化研究的专家们认为，人们不容易适应不同文化中的生活。

解析：1)词组：adapt oneself to(适应)，后面应使用反身代词oneself，泛指主语。

2)搭配：life/living in different cultures(不同文化中的生活)

88. 答案：nothing is more attractive to me than reading 或 to me, nothing is more important than reading

句意：从童年起，我就发现没有什么比读书对我更有吸引力。

解析：1)句型：nothing is more...than(没有什么比……更……)

2)时态：宾语从句是议论、常识或真理时，即使主句使用过去时，从句也应使用现在时。

89. 答案：would have a chance to survive 或 would have a chance of survival

句意：如果那名遇难者被及时送进医院，他本来会有机会活下来。

解析：1)虚拟语气：表示与过去事实相反时，从句用过去完成时，主句用一般过去时，而不是现在完成时。

2)搭配：have a chance to survive / of survival

90. 答案：might feel lonely when they are far from home / are not in their hometown / traveling.

句意：一些心理学家认为，人们出门在外时可能会感到孤独。

解析：1)虚拟语气：claim that sb. might do sth.(建议句型)

2)从句：时间状语从句when they are far from home / are not in their hometown / traveling

91. 答案：at a speed/rate of 12 million per year 或 at an annual speed of 12 million.

句意：这个国家的人口持续以每年1200万人的速度增长。

解析：1)词组：at a speed of(以……的速度)

2)数字表达：12 million(1200万)

四、经典真题四

Directions: *Complete the sentences by translating into English the Chinese given in brackets. Please write your translation on **Answer Sheet 2**.*

87. The finding of this study failed to _____ （将人们的睡眠质量考虑在内）.

88. The prevention and treatment of AIDS is _____ （我们可以合作的领域）.

89. Because of the leg injury, the athlete _____ （决定退出比赛）.

90. To make donations or for more information, please _____ （按以下地址和我们联系）.

91. Please come here at ten tomorrow morning _____ （如果你方便的话）.

试题详解

87. 答案：take people's sleep quality into account/consideration
解析：从词汇角度来看，本题考查的是固定搭配 take...into account/ consideration。从语法角度来看，考查的是 fail 之后的非谓语动词形式的用法（fail to do）。fail to do 和 take...into account 均为四级老题型词汇与结构单选题反复考查的重点。

88. 答案：the field where/in which we can cooperate
解析：本题考查的是定语从句。此句有两种译法：一是使用 where，限定性定语从句在修饰表示地点的名词（如 field）时，可使用关系副词 where 充当状语；另一种译法是使用 in which，限定性定语从句如果修饰物，且关系代词在从句中作宾语时，在介词后只能使用 which。

89. 答案：decided/decides to quit the match
解析：本题着眼于考查考生灵活使用动词固定搭配的能力。谓语动词形式是汉译英设题以来每次都要考查的基础语法点。因为主语为单数形式 the athlete，谓语"决定"只能选择第三人称单数或者过去时形式。

90. 答案：contact us at the following address
解析：今年的考题首次舍弃了表示建议的句型，转而考查同样要使用动词原形而难度相对较小的祈使句。本题重点考查固定搭配 contact sb. at... address。

91. 答案：at your convenience / if it is convenient for you

解析：本题考查不太常用的固定搭配at your convenience。本次考试的最后两题明显侧重于实际交际中的常用表达。可见，新四级题越来越重视考查考生的英语实际运用能力。

五、经典真题五

Directions: *Complete the sentences by translating into English the Chinese given in brackets. Please write your translation on **Answer Sheet 2**.*

87. _____（多亏了一系列的新发明），doctors can treat this disease successfully.

88. In my sixties, one change I notice is that _____（我比以前更容易累了）.

89. I am going to pursue this course, _____（无论我要作出什么样的牺牲）.

90. I would prefer shopping online to shopping in a department store because _____（它更加方便和省时）.

91. Many Americans live on credit, and their quality of life _____（是用他们能够借到多少来衡量的），not how much they can earn.

试题详解

87. Thanks to a series of new inventions

试题解析：本题主要从词汇角度进行考查，"多亏了"译为thanks to比because of, due to或owing to更为准确；"一系列"应译为a series of；invention应使用复数。

88. I am more inclined to get tired than before

试题解析：本题主要考查四级核心词组be inclined to(倾向于)。这再次提醒广大考生：四级汉译英主要考查四级核心词组和语法，需要平时扎扎实实地进行积累。

89. no matter what kind of sacrifice I will make

试题解析：本题主要考查no matter what句型，意为"无论什么"；同时考查四级核心词汇sacrifice(牺牲)以及定语从句I will make的表达方式。

90. the former is more convenient and time-saving

试题解析：本题主要考查四级核心词汇convenient(方便的)和time-saving(省时的)；同时考查考生对于整句的理解。由于前半句出现了两个名词，此处的"它"如果简单直译为"it"会表达不清，译为"前者"(the former)更准确。

温馨提示："后者"译为the latter。

91. is measured by how much they can borrow

试题解析：本题主要考查四级核心词组be measured by(用……来衡量)。需要注意的是，本句的主语为the quality，谓语动词应使用单数形式is。进行汉译英时，务必重视主谓一致、时态、冠词、名词单复数等基本语法，"细节决定成败"。

六、经典真题六

Directions: *Complete the sentences by translating into English the Chinese given in brackets. Please write your translation on **Answer Sheet 2**.*

87. Our efforts will pay off if the results of this research _____(能应用于新技术的开发).

88. I can't boot my computer now. Something _____(一定出了毛病) with its operation system.

89. Leaving one's job, _____(不管是什么工作), is a difficult change, even for those who look forward to retiring.

90. _____(与我成长的地方相比), this town is more prosperous and exciting.

91. _____(直到他完成使命) did he realize that he was seriously ill.

试题详解

87. can be applied to the development of new technology

试题解析："应用于"有一个固定搭配apply to，此处应使用被动语态be applied to。"开发"应译为development，不能译为exploration(探测)或research(研究)。

88. must be wrong

试题解析："一定"应译为must be，must表示对现在发生的事情进行推测时，其后常接系动词be。"出了毛病"译为wrong即可。

89. no matter what it could be/whatever it could be

试题解析："不管什么"可译为no matter what或whatever,引导让步状语从句时,二者可以替换。job在前半句已出现,此处可以用it进行替换,否则会导致用词冗赘。此处为虚拟情况,使用could be比is更加地道。

温馨提示：2007年12月的四级翻译第89题为：无论我要作出什么样的牺牲(no matter what/whatever kind of sacrifice I will make)。在2008年6月的四级考试中,翻译题再次考查了no matter what/whatever句型,而完形填空第84题再次考查了make sacrifice的固定搭配。提醒广大考生：务必充分重视近年四级真题,再次考查的可能性极大。

90. Compared with the place where/in which I grew up

试题解析："与……相比"应译为be compared with,其逻辑主语为this town,故单独使用过去分词作状语放在句首即可。place为地点名词,后面的定语从句可用where或in which引导。"成长"应使用过去时grew up。

温馨提示：2006年新四级大纲样题翻译第89题为：与我的相比(Compared with mine),2008年6月的四级翻译又考到compared with。2007年6月的四级翻译第88题为：我们可以合作的领域(the field where/in which we can cooperate),2008年6月的四级翻译再次考查了地点名词后使用where或in which引导定语从句,同时完形填空85题再次考查了field(领域)。

91. Not until he had accomplished his mission

试题解析："直到"应译为not until,放在句首时,主句使用倒装结构,从句无需倒装。主句使用了did he realize的一般过去时,从句动作发生在主句之前,所以应使用过去完成时。"完成使命"应译为accomplish mission,不能简单译为finish mission。

温馨提示：accomplish, finish, complete均意为"完成"。accomplish=finish successfully,意为"达到,完成;使完美",是四级核心词汇,与mission, purpose, aim, journey, voyage等词形成固定搭配。finish=complete,但不正式,意为"结束,完成"。complete较具体,一般与building, book, project等词搭配。

七、经典真题七

Directions: *Complete the sentences by translating into English the Chinese given in brackets. Please write your translation on **Answer Sheet 2**.*

87. Medical researchers are painfully aware that there are many problems ＿＿＿＿＿＿＿＿＿
＿＿＿＿＿＿＿＿＿＿＿＿＿＿＿(他们至今还没有答案)。

88. _____（大多数父母所关心的）

is providing the best education possible for their children.

89. You'd better take a sweater with you _____
_____（以防天气变冷）.

90. Through the project, many people have received training and _____
_____（决定自己创业）.

91. The anti-virus agent was not known _____
_____（直到一名医生偶然发现了它）.

试题详解

87. to which they have not found solutions so far

试题解析：本句应译为定语从句，problem之后用which引导，介词to提前。"还没有"应译为现在完成时，增译find。"答案"在此处结合上文并非answers，而是solutions。

88. What most parents concern

试题解析：根据后半句，本句缺少主语，故应译为what引导的主语从句。"关心"应译为concern。

89. in case/lest it turns cold

试题解析：本句应译为in case或lest引导的目的状语从句，"天气变冷"应译为it turns cold。

90. decided /determined/resolved to launch /run their own business

试题解析："决定"与前文的received为并列谓语，应使用过去分词，译为decided, determined, resolved均可。"创业"可译为launch/run one's business。

91. until a doctor discovered/found it by chance/accidentally

试题解析："直到"应译为until引导的状语从句。前半句的was表明本句为一般过去时，"发现"应译为discovered。"偶然"可译为by chance或accidentally。

八、经典真题八

Directions: *Complete the sentences by translating into English the Chinese given in brackets. Please write you translation on **Answer Sheet 2**.*

87. Soon after he transferred to the new school, Ali found that he had _____
    (很难跟上班里的同学) in math and English.

88. If she had returned an hour earlier, Mary _____ (就不会被大雨淋了).

89. It is said that those who are stressed or working overtime are _____ (更有
    可能增加体重).

90. _____ (很多人没有意识到的) is that Simon is a lover of sports, and
    football in particular.

91. The study shows that the poor functioning of the human body is _____
    (与缺乏锻炼密切相关).

试题详解

87. difficulty (in) catching up with his classmates

    试题解析：前半句的soon after表明时间较短，使用catch up with比keep up with
    更准确。

    温馨提示：这是新四级翻译部分第二次考查"很难做某事"这一表达，2006年6
    月24日四级翻译87题考查了have trouble (in) doing sth.。

88. would not have been caught in the heavy rain

    试题解析：虚拟语气中，从句使用"had+过去分词"，主句应使用"would have+
    过去分词"。

    温馨提示：这是新四级翻译部分三次考查虚拟语气这一重要语法现象。
    2006年6月24日89题考查了"require+ (should)+动词原形"；2006年12月
    89题同样考查了表示与过去事实相反时，从句使用过去完成时，主句使
    用一般过去时的用法。

89. more likely to put on weight

    试题解析："更有可能"译为be more likely to do sth., "增加体重"也可译为gain
    weight。

    温馨提示：这是新四级翻译部分第五次考查比较级这一语法现象。2006年6月
    24日90题考查了the more confused I am/get(我愈糊涂)；2006年12月88题考查
    了nothing is more attractive to me than reading(没有什么比读书对我更有吸引
    力)；2007年12月88题考查了I am more inclined to get tired than before (我比以
    前更容易累了)；2007年12月90题还考查了the former is more convenient and
    time-saving(它更加方便和省时)。

90. **What many people didn't realize**

试题解析：空格后是谓语动词is，故此处应填主语从句。根据所给中文，从句应使用what引导。

温馨提示：这是新四级翻译部分第二次考查主语从句这一重要考点。2008年12月88题考查了类似的主语从句：What most parents are concerned about（大多数父母所关心的）。

91. **closely related to the lack of（physical）exercise**

试题解析："与……密切相关"用"be closely related to..."表达。其中to为介词，后面应使用名词或动名词，故使用the lack of（physical）exercise。

九、经典真题九

Directions: *Complete the sentences by translating into English the Chinese given in brackets. Please write your translation on **Answer Sheet 2**.*

87. You would not have failed if you ＿＿＿＿＿＿＿＿＿＿（按照我的指令去做）.

88. Despite the hardship he encountered, Mark never ＿＿＿＿＿＿＿＿＿＿（放弃对知识的追求）.

89. Scientists agree that it will be a long time ＿＿＿＿＿＿＿＿＿＿（我们找到治愈癌症的方法）.

90. Production has to be increased considerably to ＿＿＿＿＿＿＿＿＿＿（与消费者不断增长的需求保持同步）.

91. The more exercise you take, ＿＿＿＿＿＿＿＿＿＿（你越不大可能得感冒）.

试题详解

87. **had followed my instructions**

试题解析：本题考查if引导的虚拟语气：主句用would have done，从句应该是had done。另外，instruction表示"指令"时，一般使用复数形式。

温馨提示：本题已是新四级翻译第四次考查虚拟语气这一重要语法现象。2006年6月24日89题考查了"require + that"引导的虚拟语气we hand in our research report(s)（我们交研究报告）；2006年12月89题考查了would have a chance to survive/of survival（本来有机会活下来）；2009年6月88题考查了

wouldn't have been caught by the heavy rain(就不会被大雨淋了)。此外, 2007年6月90题也考查了follow一词的用法: contact us at the following address（按以下地址和我们联系）。

88. gave up the pursuit of knowledge/pursuing knowledge

试题解析: 考点有两个——"放弃"和"追求"。"放弃做某事"译为give up doing sth.或quit doing sth.; "追求"既可译为动词pursue, 也可译为名词pursuit。根据前半句的he encountered, 应使用过去时态。

温馨提示: "放弃,退出"这一表达在2007年6月89题已考查过: decides/decided to quit the match(决定退出比赛); "追求,跟上"这一表达也在2007年12月89题中出现过: I am going to pursue this course, no matter what kind of sacrifice I will make(无论我要作出什么样的牺牲, 我都要上这门课)。

89. before we find the cures for cancers

试题解析: 空格前的it will be a long time表示"在……之前需要很长时间", 故应使用before, 时态使用一般现在时。"治愈方法"应译为cure, 而非treat(治疗)。

温馨提示: 本题已是新四级翻译第四次考查医学方面的翻译: 2007年6月88题考查了The prevention and treatment of AIDS is the field where/in which we can cooperate（艾滋病的预防和治疗是我们可以合作的领域）; 2007年12月87题考查了Thanks to a series of new inventions, doctors can treat this disease successfully.(多亏了一系列的新发明, 医生才能成功地治疗这一疾病); 2008年12月91题考查了The anti-virus agent was not known until it was accidentally found/discovered by a doctor.(直到一名医生偶然发现了它, 这种抗病毒试剂一直不为人知)。

90. keep pace with the constantly increasing/rising/growing demands of consumers

试题解析: 本题考查四级高频词组keep pace with(与……保持同步), 另外考生应该分析出整个句子中文部分的核心词是"需求", demands和consumers应使用复数。

温馨提示: 2009年6月87题考查了"跟上"的另一表达: difficulty in catching up with his classmates(很难跟上班里的同学)。

91. the less likely you will/are to catch a cold

试题解析: 前半句使用了the more, 后半句也应使用"the + 比较级"结构。前半句相当于条件状语从句, 后半句为主句。另外, 本题还考查"得感冒"的表达: catch a cold。

温馨提示：这已是新四级翻译第六次考查"比较级"这一重要语法现象：2006年6月24日90题考查了the more confused I am/get（我愈糊涂）；2006年12月88题考查了nothing is more attractive to me than reading（没有什么比读书对我更有吸引力），2007年12月88题考查I am more inclined to get tired than before（我比以前更容易累了）；同月90题考查了the former is more convenient and time-saving（它更加方便和省时）；2009年6月89题考查了more likely to put on weight（更有可能增加体重）。

真题总结：2009年12月翻译所考查的诸多词汇和语法现象均是新四级翻译历年反复考查的内容，精研真题必将战无不胜！

十、经典真题十

Directions: *Complete the sentences by translating into English the Chinese given in the brackets. Please write your translation on **Answer Sheet 2**.*

87. Because of the noise outside, Nancy had great difficulty _____ _____（集中注意力在实验上）.

88. The manager never laughed; neither _____ _____（她也从来没有发过脾气）.

89. We look forward to _____ _____（被邀请出席开幕式）.

90. It is suggested that the air conditioner _____ _____（要安装在窗户旁）.

91. The 16-year-old girl decided to travel abroad on her own despite _____ _____（她父母的强烈反对）.

试题详解

87.（in）concentrating/focusing on the experiment

试题解析："集中注意力在……上"可用concentrate on表达，"实验"可用the experiment表达。have difficulty（in）doing sth.是固定用法，因此concentrate应为concentrating。

88. did she ever lose her temper

试题解析：根据分号前的句子可确定分号后句子的谓语动词应使用过去时。neither位于第二个分句句首，其后的句子应采用倒装形式，同时分号前后为并列关系，never=not ever，分号后已出现了否定词neither，故只用ever即可。

89. being invited to（attend）the opening ceremony

　　试题解析：look forward to中的to为介词，其后应接动名词作宾语，因此应用being。

90. （should）be installed/fixed by/next to the window

　　试题解析：注意此处是"被安装"，故应使用被动语态。It is suggested that后加should+动词原形，should可以省略。

91. her parents' strong opposition

　　试题解析："强烈反对"可用the strong/violent opposition/objection表达，"她父母的"可用from her parents或her parents'表达。

第三节　强化训练

强化训练一

87. ＿＿＿＿＿＿＿＿＿＿＿＿＿＿＿＿＿（没有什么可做），we played games.

88. He not only ＿＿＿＿＿＿＿＿＿＿＿＿＿＿＿＿＿（把枯燥的工作强加给我），but also took away all our tips.

89. ＿＿＿＿＿＿＿＿＿＿＿＿＿＿＿＿＿（在这种情况下），I couldn't go away.

90. The population of Africa is growing ＿＿＿＿＿＿＿＿＿＿＿＿＿＿＿（极其迅速）.

91. The girl is too young to ＿＿＿＿＿＿＿＿＿＿＿＿＿＿＿＿＿＿（和她的父母分开）.

试题详解

87. 答案：There being nothing to do

　　解析：独立主格结构：there+being+其他成分，多放在句首。

88. 答案：imposed dull work on me

　　解析：1)词组：impose... on sb.(把……强加给某人)

　　　　　2)时态：根据后半句，前半句也应使用一般过去时。

89. 答案：Under/In the/these circumstances

　　解析：词组：under/in the/these circumstances(在这种情况下)

90. 答案：by/in leaps and bounds

　　解析：词组：by/in leaps and bounds(极其迅速)

91. 答案: be separated from her parents

解析: 1)语态: 主语是the girl, 应使用被动语态。

2)词组: separate sb./sth. from(使某人/某物与……分离)

强化训练二

87. Your care-free nature often _____(遇到钱的问题).

88. _____(如果发生火灾), ring the alarm bell.

89. The proposal _____(建设一座图书馆) is to be discussed at the meeting.

90. _____(要是我们没有花这么多钱该多好) on vacation this year.

91. _____(正如今天报纸上所报道的), the Conference of International Trade Cooperation is also open on Sundays.

试题详解

87. 答案: comes up against the problem of money

解析: 词组: come up against(遇到)

88. 答案: In case of fire

解析: 词组: in case of(如果, 万一)

89. 答案: that we should build a new library

解析: 从句: 同位语从句对the proposal进行具体说明, 应使用引导词that。

90. 答案: If only we hadn't spend so much money

解析: 1)句型: if only(要是……该多好)

2)虚拟语气: 此处应使用一般过去时。

91. 答案: As is announced in today's papers

解析: 1) 从句: as引导方式状语从句, 这是一种复杂的语法现象, 主语在此省略。

2)语态: 此处应使用被动语态is announced。

强化训练三

87. _____(位于波士顿), Harvard University is one of the best universities in the U.S.

88. Please _____(将问题提出来) at the next meeting.

89. It is essential that these application forms _____(尽早寄出去).

90. His tastes are _____(和我的相同).

91. It is high time that we _____(保护濒临灭绝的动物).

试题详解

87. 答案：Located/Situated in Boston

   解析：1)词组：locate/situate in(位于，坐落于)

   2)分词：此处应使用过去分词。

88. 答案：bring the problem forward

   解析：词组：bring forward(提出)

89. 答案：be sent as early as possible

   解析：主句中的表语是essential，谓语动词应使用"(should)+动词原形"的虚拟形式，同时使用被动语态。

90. 答案：in harmony with mine

   解析：词组：in harmony with(和……相同)

91. 答案：protected the endangered animals

   解析：1)虚拟语气：假设性虚拟语气句型it is (high) time (that) we did sth.，that引导的从句中谓语动词应使用过去式。

   2)词汇：endangered(有危险的)

强化训练四

87. Not until the child fell asleep _____·(母亲才离开房间).

88. In the U.S., high school English classes _____ (往往把重点放在) improving writing skills.

89. If I were rich, I _____(买了那栋房子) last year.

90. You should _____(充分利用) this valuable opportunity.

91. Although I haven't met her for only a few months, she treats me _____(好像我是一个陌生人).

试题详解

87. 答案：did the mother leave the room

解析：1)倒装句：not until放在句首表示强调，后面的主从复合句中，主句倒装，从句使用正常语序。

2)时态：fell表示句子应使用一般过去时。

88. 答案：tend to focus on

解析：词组：tend to(往往，易于，通常)；focus on(把重点放在，集中精力)

89. 答案：would have bought that house

解析：虚拟语气：if引导的条件状语从句表示对过去情况的虚拟，主句应是与现在事实相反的虚拟句，应使用"would + have +过去分词"的形式。

90. 答案：make the best of

解析：词组：make the best of(充分利用)

91. 答案：as if I were a stranger

解析：1)虚拟语气：表示与事实不符或相反。

2)句型：as if...(好像……，似乎……)

强化训练五

87. The businessman recently _____(忙于从事) foreign trade.

88. The more images you _____ (与一件事联系起来), the more convinced you are that your memory of it is accurate.

89. Adults should _____(原谅孩子们的无知).

90. Nowhere in the city _____(能找到人帮你).

91. The naughty boy _____(以……为乐) pulling the cat's tail yesterday.

试题详解

87. 答案：has been engaged in

解析：1)时态：由前面的recently决定此处应使用现在完成时。

2)词组：be engaged in(从事于，忙碌于)

88. 答案：associate with an event

解析：词组：associate with(把……联系起来)

89. 答案：make allowances for children's ignorance

解析：1)词组：make allowances for(原谅)

2)词汇：ignorance(无知)

90. 答案：will you find a man to help you

解析：倒装句：否定词nowhere放在句首时，后面的句子应倒装。

91. 答案：took delight in

解析：1)词组：take delight in（以……为乐）

2)时态：一般过去时。

强化训练六

87. Because she knew French, she ＿＿＿＿＿＿＿＿＿＿（比我们有利）.

88. It's important that the librarian ＿＿＿＿＿＿＿＿＿＿（确认图书按时归还）.

89. The regulation doesn't ＿＿＿＿＿＿＿＿（生效）until the first of March.

90. My mother wanted me to ＿＿＿＿＿＿＿＿＿＿（从事教育工作）.

91. After arriving at your new university, the following may assist you in ＿＿＿＿＿＿
＿＿＿＿＿＿＿＿＿＿＿＿（减轻文化冲击所带来的紧张感）.

试题详解

87. 答案：had an advantage over the rest of us

解析：1)词组：have an advantage of（比……有利）

2)时态：根据前半句的knew，此处应使用一般过去时。

88. 答案：make sure the books（should）be returned in time

解析：1)从句：主语从句it is important that...

2)虚拟语气：此处主语从句应使用"should+动词原形"，should可以省略。

3)语态：此处"归还"应使用被动语态be returned。

4)词组：make sure（确认）

89. 答案：come/go into effect

解析：词组：come/go into effect（生效）

90. 答案：go in for teaching

解析：词组：go in for（从事）

91. 答案：reducing the strain of cultural shock

解析：1)动名词：assist sb. in doing sth.

2)词组：cultural shock（文化冲击）

强化训练七

87. We had better _____（趁着天气暖和）by going for a walk this afternoon.

88. It is vital that _____（筹集足够的资金）to fund the project.

89. French people, _____（厌倦了使用刀叉），swarm into Chinese restaurant at the weekends.

90. He finished the job _____（以健康为代价）.

91. I wish I _____（今天早晨多睡一会），but I had to get up and come to class.

试题详解

87. 答案：take advantage of the warm weather
    解析：词组：take advantage of(趁着，利用)

88. 答案：enough money be collected
    解析：1)从句：主语从句it is vital that...
    2)虚拟语气：it is vital that+主语+(should)+动词原形，should可以省略。
    3)语态：资金与筹集之间应使用被动语态。

89. 答案：bored with knife and fork
    解析：1)词组：be bored with(对……感到厌倦)
    2)分词：此处是插入语，主语是French people，应使用过去分词。

90. 答案：at the expense of his health
    解析：词组：at the expense of(以……为代价)

91. 答案：could have slept longer this morning
    解析：虚拟语气：wish引导的宾语从句应使用虚拟语气，当wish对过去的事实表达不可能实现的愿望时，宾语从句谓语应使用"could/would + have +过去分词"。

强化训练八

87. We should pursue economic policies _____（根据国家利益）.

88. International students usually submit transcripts when they _____（申请进入）a U.S. university.

89. _____ (他刚下火车) than his girlfriend ran to him.

90. _____ (要不是你帮忙), I would not have finished the task by myself.

91. The president would rather his son _____ (不在同一间办公室工作).

试题详解

87. 答案：in accord with the national interest

解析：词组：in accord with(根据); national interest(国家利益)

88. 答案：apply for admission to/into

解析：词组：apply for admission to/into(申请进入)

89. 答案：No sooner had he got off the train

解析：1)倒装句：no sooner... than... 引导倒装结构。

2)时态：后半句为一般过去时, 前半句应是过去完成时。

90. 答案：But for your help

解析：句型：but for(如果没有, 要不是), 表示与过去相反的条件状语, 后面使用虚拟语气。

91. 答案：did not work in the same office

解析：虚拟语气：would rather 后的从句使用一般过去时表达个人意愿。

第七章　专家预测试卷

第一节　专家预测试卷一

Part I   **Writing**   **(30 minutes)**

注意：此部分试题在**答题卡1**上。

Directions: *For this part, you are allowed 30 minutes to write a letter applying for a position of a company. You should write at least 120 words according to the outline given below in Chinese:*

     1. 申请职位，

     2. 简要介绍自己的情况，

     3. 期待回信。

Part II   **Reading Comprehension (Skimming and Scanning)**   **(15 minutes)**

Directions: *In this part, you will have 15 minutes to go over the passage quickly and answer the questions on **Answer Sheet 1**. For questions 1-7, choose the best answer from the four choices marked [A], [B], [C] and [D]. For questions 8-10, complete the sentences with the information given in the passage.*

Balance between Work and Your Life

The global market place is putting new pressure on childcare arrangement, marriages, and other aspects of the personal lives of employees. Many of us get so caught up in day-to-day pressures that we often find ourselves reacting to external demands rather than designing lives that really fulfill us. That's according to experts who gathered in New York last month at conference on international efforts to achieve greater balance between work and the rest of life. From Australia to North America to Europe, human resource professionals and academics reported that jobs and companies doing business worldwide are increasingly characterized by intensifying work loads, expanding work hours and more time away from home. The change is producing a variety of responses and results.

Conflicts between Work and Life

Researchers from across the globe report that job stress is increasing, job satisfaction decreasing, and work-life balance is more of a struggle. Even when companies have family-friendly programs, ever-expanding work duties often undercut them. Gram Russell, a psychology professor, says the clock really never stops in some international businesses especially for senior managers.

"I'm a manager in an Australian corporation that works in the global environment. I have to be accessible much more than I was ever before. I might be reporting to the company in a local location as well as reporting to somebody globally. So I have got more responsibility. So the nature of my job is changed."

While leading companies often address the employee time shortage by offering childcare or eldercare assistance, Russell is concerned about another price employees are paying: lack of time to establish and maintain intimate adult relationships.

In Western Europe, the work week is shorter compared to the U.S. Women especially work less, and many family-friendly policies are mandated by the government. The Norwegians, for example, are essentially ignoring pressures from the global market place and expanding their family-friendly policies. For a generation, workers there have received even more generous paid leave when they become parents. Currently a parent can take a year off with 80 percent of their normal salary, plus a guarantee of getting the same job back when they return to work. One drawback thought of these generous policies is that in some countries they tend to discourage women from having full-time careers.

In Germany, the government provides free daycare for children aged three to six. But it only lasts half a day. Mothers of young children who want to work full time have few options, and that's doubly true if the child is an infant or toddler.

"From zero to three, there's very little public care. The younger the child, the harder it becomes to find anything. Even private care cannot be bought. It is too expensive. No one offers this."

Most German mothers don't complain. They like the tax breaks that favor households with a single breadwinner. Only 30 percent of German women work outside the home and half of those are part time. However, a sizable minority of women would like to be able to have children and continue their careers full time.

American companies employing Germans provide an exception to the norm. Many U.S. firms with factories and offices in Germany offer on-site childcare for babies and the youngest toddlers as part of their work life benefits. They are interested in keeping women on a straight career path and promoting them to higher levels. However, the American style of corporate childcare is not purely *altruistic*(利他的，无私心的). "Some big American companies are really introducing those benefits because they are demanding its 7-day, 24-hour schedule from their workers. These companies are really changing the German work culture to become much tougher and rougher and be much less protective time-wise of families and of women." So the American influence is a mixed blessing, expanding childcare while increasing working hours.

While in today's economic environment we face many stresses in our jobs, it is still possible to create balance between our work and personal lives.

Tips to Balance the Conflicts

Most of what has been written about work-life balance over the last few years has offered off-shelf solutions to crack this for you once and for all! But for people who work from home, where work and the rest of their life might just be a door apart, the issue is particularly challenging. You have to get creative and personal, to solve this in a way that works for you. Here are tips to help you find a perfect balance between work and the rest of your life.

1. Write down what the balance would be like if everything was perfect. Don't worry about how you get it, just write. Then write down how it is now. Do you notice a contrast?! Commit yourself to taking a tiny step each day to bring you closer to the compelling picture of how you would like it to be.

2. You only have one life, so you must decide what is important in your life. Write down the words that represent this for you, and start now to use these guide how you work, as well as how you play.

3. It is important to learn from what you do in order to get the balance right for you. And, to make changes based on what works and what doesn't. If you make a "mistake", don't spend hours regretting it, spend minutes asking "What have I learned?" "How will I handle it next time?"

4. In working towards the balance you desire, you know there are things that might stop you, temporarily or permanently. Work out what these are, and prepare your response to these things, or people, now. Then when it does happen you will be ready for it, and armed to overcome the obstacle without thinking twice.

5. Tolerating things about yourself, the way people treat you or use up your time, your environment, and your possessions, uses up time and energy that would be better spent elsewhere. Set these limits selfishly to work with you towards the balance you want.

6. Someone who supports you in working towards the balance you are choosing is essential. They will remind you of your commitment, and help you to get clear on your priorities. Choose a coach, a partner, a friend to keep you on track and encourage you when things get tough.

注意: 此部分试题请在**答题卡1**上作答。

1. The conference in New York was held last month to _____.

　[A] find out scientific ways of taking good care of children

　[B] provide women more full-time job opportunities

　[C] reduce the work pressure of women

　[D] balance work and the rest of life

2. The workers in the companies doing business worldwide _____.

　[A] will have more time to travel with their family

　[B] will suffer from expanding job hours

　[C] will have more opportunities to be promoted

　[D] have to speak fluently one or more foreign languages

3. According to researchers in the whole world, _____.

　[A] workers' salary and welfare are higher than ever before

　[B] workers are less content with their jobs

　[C] workers can easily get a balance between work and life

　[D] workers do not work as hard as they should do any more

4. In Norway, even if a parent takes a year off, he still can get _____.

　[A] 80% of his normal salary

　[B] 30% of his normal salary

[C] 24% of his normal salary

[D] 70% of his normal salary

5. In Germany, the children _____ can enjoy free daycare service provided by the government.

[A] who begin to learn to walk

[B] who are still infants

[C] from three to six years old

[D] who are between one and two years old

6. For mothers of young children in Germany, _____.

[A] it is hard to find full-time jobs

[B] it is difficult to give up their career

[C] it is difficult to be free from work

[D] it is easy to get financial support from the government

7. The American companies in Germany expand childcare, and they also _____.

[A] improve workers' motivation

[B] increase workers' working hours

[C] provide workers with more job opportunities

[D] increase workers' income

8. In Western Europe, many family-friendly policies are commanded by _____.

9. One disadvantage of the family-friendly policies in some Western Europe countries is that they may discourage women from _____.

10. It is important to choose someone who can support you in the process of getting _____.

Part III   **Listening Comprehension**   （**35 minutes**）

Section A

Directions: *In this section, you will hear 8 short conversations and 2 long conversations. At the end of each conversation, one or more questions will be asked about what was said. Both the conversation and the questions will be spoken only once. After each question there will be a pause. During the pause, you must read the four* *choices marked [A], [B], [C] and [D], and decide which is the best answer. Then mark the corresponding letter on **Answer Sheet 2** with a single line through the centre.*

注意：此部分试题请在**答题卡2**上作答。

11. [A] The man should take the stereo back to the store.
    [B] The man should refer to the instruction menu.
    [C] She'll go to the man's house and help him.
    [D] She'll give the man her instruction menu.

12. [A] Go to the exhibit tonight with the man.
    [B] Stay at home and rest.
    [C] Find out what time the exhibit opens.
    [D] Help the man arrange his trip.

13. [A] The woman can take a bus to the museum.
    [B] The woman should wait in front of the museum.
    [C] He doesn't know where the museum is.
    [D] There's only one bus that travels down Main Street.

14. [A] Change his diet.
    [B] Take a different kind of medicine.
    [C] Ask another doctor about the problem.
    [D] Do special knee exercises.

15. [A] His coach didn't help him enough.
    [B] He had no chance of winning.
    [C] He didn't follow his coach's advice.
    [D] His coach didn't listen to him.

16. [A] The man should have offered his assistance earlier.
    [B] She doesn't need the man's help.
    [C] She didn't realize the boxes were empty.
    [D] She wants the man to move the boxes.

17. [A] She's still looking for an apartment.
    [B] She was told the dorm was full.
    [C] She doesn't plan to move.
    [D] She wants to move out of the dorm.

18. [A] Linda didn't like it.　　　[C] It was very expensive.

　　[B] Bill lost it.　　　　　　　[D] It was very small.

Questions 19 to 21 are based on the conversation you have just heard.

19. [A] A student and a teacher.　　[C] Two scientists.

　　[B] A student and a librarian.　[D] Two students.

20. [A] The age of dinosaurs.　　　[C] The evolution of mammals.

　　[B] Why dinosaurs became extinct.　[D] Changes in the earth's climate.

21. [A] Scientists.　　　　　　　　[C] Librarians.

　　[B] Students.　　　　　　　　[D] Artists.

Questions 22 to 25 are based on the conversation you have just heard.

22. [A] Taking a walk.　　　　　　[C] Washing windows.

　　[B] Rowing a boat.　　　　　　[D] Looking at pictures.

23. [A] High local living costs.　　[C] Electrical power failure.

　　[B] Heavy boat traffic.　　　　[D] Dirty windows.

24. [A] She wrote about lighthouses.　[C] She was a skillful sea captain.

　　[B] She built her own lighthouse.　[D] She saved many people.

25. [A] Tired.　　　　　　　　　　[C] Angry.

　　[B] Lonely.　　　　　　　　　[D] Brave.

Section B

Directions: *In this section, you will hear 3 short passages. At the end of each passage, you will hear some questions. Both the passage and the questions will be spoken only once. After you hear a question, you must choose the best answer from the four choices marked* [A], [B], [C] *and* [D]. *Then mark the corresponding letter on* **Answer Sheet 2** *with a single line through the centre.*

注意：此部分试题请在**答题卡2**上作答。

Passage One

Questions 26 to 28 are based on the passage you have just heard.

26. [A] Summer vacation.　　　　　[C] Resident advisors.

　　[B] The housing office.　　　　[D] Check-out procedures.

27. [A] At the beginning of the school year.

[B] On June 3.

[C] Near the end of the school year.

[D] After final exams.

28. [A] Their summer addresses.　　[C] When they plan to leave.

[B] Any damage to their rooms.　　[D] Questions for the housing office.

Passage Two

Questions 29 to 32 are based on the passage you have just heard.

29. [A] A poet.　　[C] A student.

[B] A teacher.　　[D] An artist.

30. [A] New England mystery stories.

[B] Eighteenth-century English criticism.

[C] A comparison of poems by Dickinson and Waltman.

[D] The poems of Walt Whitman.

31. [A] In her twenties.　　[C] In her fifties.

[B] In her thirties.　　[D] In her eighties.

32. [A] Hear another report.

[B] Discuss one of Emily Dickinson's poems.

[C] Hear a lecture by the teacher.

[D] Discuss poems they have written themselves.

Passage Three

Questions 33 to 35 are based on the passage you have just heard.

33. [A] To explain the importance of learning rhythm and harmony in jazz.

[B] To show that jazz is not really music at all.

[C] To point out similarities between jazz and classical music.

[D] To describe what makes a good jazz performance.

34. [A] They memorize their music before performing it.

[B] They are more famous than performers of other kinds of music.

[C] They perform their music as a means of individual self-expression.

[D] They possess detailed knowledge of the rules of jazz performers.

35. [A] Practice various jazz rhythms.

[B] Interview a jazz musician.

［C］Watch a film about jazz performers.

［D］Listen to some recordings of jazz music.

Section C

Directions: *In this section, you will hear a passage three times. When the passage is read for the first time, you should listen carefully for its general idea. When the passage is read for the second time, you are required to fill in the blanks numbered from 36 to 43 with the exact words you have just heard. For blanks numbered from 44 to 46 you are required to fill in the missing information. For these blanks, you can either use the exact words you have just heard or write down the main points in your own words. Finally, when the passage is read for the third time, you should check what you have written.*

注意：此部分试题请在**答题卡2**上作答。

This morning, I'd like to tell you about the structure of the university and about some of the（36）_____ of the degree that you're about to enter. The（37）_____ of Social Science is in one faculty within the university: that is the faculty where I work,（38）_____ as Arts and Social Sciences. Here on this（39）_____ we also have the faculties of（40）_____, Law and Science and Technology among others. It's（41）_____ to know something about the structure of the faculty because, as you go through your（42）_____, you may need to call on members of the staff to help you. At the top of the faculty we have a dean and below the dean we have three divisions. Each division has a divisional head and your degree is（43）_____ in the Division of Social Science. Within each of the divisions, there are departments and each of these offers the different degrees. For instance,（44）_____. Each has a departmental head but for practical purposes, the people you are going to see the most are myself as coordinator of the social sciences degree and the actual lecturers who are teaching the subjects that you are taking. For instance,（45）_____. If you have any problems or difficulties, not that I'm anticipating you will, but you never know, then you should go and see your lecturers. For instance,（46）_____. These seem to be the two most common problems that students face.

Part IV   **Reading Comprehension**（Reading in Depth）   （**25 minutes**）

Section A

Directions: *In this section, there is a passage with ten blanks. You are required to select one word for each blank from a list of choices given in a word bank following the passage. Read the passage through carefully before making your choices. Each choice in the bank is identified by a letter. Please mark the corresponding letter for each item on **Answer Sheet 2** with a single line through the centre. **You may not use any of the words in the bank more than once.***

Questions 47 to 56 are based on the following passage.

Dr. Stefan N. Willich, who along with other researchers determined that heart attacks __47__ to occur more often in the morning, now says that Monday mornings are the riskiest, at least among those who begin their __48__ then. His five-year study of 2,636 Augsburg, Germany __49__ shows that the working population's heart-attack risk was 33% greater on Monday than on other days. There was no such marked peak among the nonworking population.

Willich and __50__ are now studying weekly and daily __51__, hoping to learn what causes heart attacks. Although long-term risk factors for heart disease—smoking, obesity, high blood pressure, high cholesterol and lack of exercise—are well __52__, so far the "acute" risk factors—those that provide the final impetus for heart-attacks—are unknown. Possible Monday-morning culprits could include __53__ or mental stress, hormonal and other body rhythms, behavior __54__ and changes in food and drink.

If his study results are __55__ in other communities, Willich says it could lead to finding ways to prevent heart attacks in high-risk __56__ —by warning them to take it easy on Monday mornings, for example, or by designing drug therapies that provide extra protection at that time.

注意：此部分试题请在**答题卡2**上作答。

［A］pretend	［B］weekend	［C］residents	［D］variation
［E］variety	［F］tend	［G］physical	［H］psychical
［I］patterns	［J］documented	［K］confirmed	［L］workweek
［M］individuals	［N］colleagues	［O］comforted	

Section B

Directions: *There are 2 passages in this section. Each passage is followed by some questions or unfinished statements. For each of them there are four choices marked* [A], [B], [C] *and* [D]. *You should decide on the best choice and mark the corresponding letter on* **Answer Sheet 2** *with a single line through the centre.*

Passage One

Questions 57 to 61 are based on the following passage.

When your family wants to buy or replace a car, a television, or a washing machine, you find the money either from savings or by borrowing from the bank, a hire-purchase company or perhaps a friend. Similarly, a family buying a house for the first time commonly borrows from a building society.

If you own a private business, a garage, a shop, or a farm, you will need, from time to time, to buy new equipment, new furnishings, or, if you are doing well, new premises so that you can expand. Some of the cost you can meet from the profits you have kept in the business, but often you will need help.

You will go to your bank, to a finance house, or perhaps to a relative or friend for finance provided from his savings. When you borrow money or raise money in this way, you pay it back out of future profits.

Many large businesses, however, need cash for new developments or expansion far in excess of what can be provided from their profits or from private sources of capital. A new factory, an oil-well in the North Sea, can cost millions of pounds to construct and bring into production; a new design of car or brand of medicine likewise can cost millions of pounds to design, develop, test and market before it reaches the stage where it earns a profit.

Often these costs can be met from profits earned in other parts of the business or from reserves built up from profits earned in past years. Sometimes, however, it's necessary, and often it may be more advantageous, to raise new money from other sources.

There can be little prospect of raising the sort of sums needed by major businesses from friends or acquaintances, and generally the banks are reluctant to provide sufficient cash on a permanent basis for long-term projects, though they will provide short-term finance. Such companies can sometimes only raise the money they need to stay in the front of industry and develop new products and sources of production by turning to the public at large and inviting it to lend them cash or take a share in the business in exchange for a share in future profits. Thus they can do by offering shares in the business or loan capital through The Stock Exchange.

注意: 此部分试题请在**答题卡2**上作答。

57. When buying a house for the first time, which of the following a family usually does?

　　[A] Take money from your savings.

　　[B] Borrow money from a building society.

　　[C] Borrow money from a bank.

　　[D] Ask a friend to help you.

58. The normal way for a small business financing is to ＿＿＿＿＿.

　　[A] arrange a bank loan

　　[B] use profits from the business

　　[C] borrow from friends

　　[D] borrow from a hire-purchase company

59. Large businesses need to borrow huge amounts of money because ＿＿＿＿＿.

　　[A] they can never make enough profit

　　[B] developing and expanding production costs a lot of money

　　[C] developing and producing a new product takes a long time

　　[D] running something like an oil-well is very expensive

60. Large business gets new money to pay for major development by ＿＿＿＿＿.

　　[A] borrowing from friends

　　[B] borrowing from building societies

　　[C] selling shares of their company

　　[D] involving banks

61. According to the passage, which of the following is true?

　　[A] The bank can provide temporary loan for the large businesses.

　　[B] The small company can only get financial help from the bank.

　　[C] The bank is pleased to provide long-term finance for the large businesses.

　　[D] The bank won't lend money to individuals.

Passage Two

Questions 62 to 66 are based on the following passage.

　　Once it was possible to define male and female roles easily by the division of labor. Men worked outside the home and earned the income to support their families, while women cooked the meals and took care of the home and the children. These roles were firmly fixed for most people, and there was not much opportunity for men or women to exchange their roles. But by the middle of this century, men's and women's roles were becoming less firmly fixed.

In the 1950s, economic and social success was the goal of the typical American. But in the 1960s developed a new force called the counterculture. The people involved in this movement did not value the middle-class American goals. The counterculture presented men and women with new role choices. Taking more interest in childcare, men began to share child-raising tasks with their wives. In fact, some young men and women moved to communal homes or farms where the economic and child care responsibilities were shared equally by both sexes. In addition, many Americans did not value the traditional male role of soldier. Some young men refused to be drafted as soldiers to fight in the war in Vietnam.

In terms of numbers, the counterculture was not a very large group of people. But its influence spread to many parts of American society. Working men of all classes began to change their economic and social patterns. Industrial workers and business executives alike cut down on "overtime" work so that they could spend more leisure time with their families. Some doctors, lawyers, and teachers turned away from high paying situations to practice their professions in poorer neighborhoods.

In the 1970s, the feminist movement, or women's liberation, produced additional economic and social changes. Women of all ages and at all levels of society were entering the work force in greater number. Most of them still took traditional women's jobs such as public school teaching, nursing, and secretarial work. But some women began to enter traditionally male occupations: police work, banking, dentistry, and construction work. Women were asking for equal work.

Today the experts generally agree that important changes are taking place in the roles of men and women. Naturally, there are difficulties in adjusting to these changes.

注意：此部分试题请在**答题卡2**上作答。

62. According to the passage, in the past _____.

　　[A] women usually worked outside the home for wages

　　[B] men's and women's roles were easily exchanged

[C] men's roles at home were more firmly fixed than women's

[D] men and women's roles were usually quite separated

63. Which of the following was the result of counterculture force?

[A] Men were more interested in childcare.

[B] Soldiers refused to fight in the war in Vietnam.

[C] Working men all cut down "overtime" work.

[D] Women asked for equal work with men.

64. In the passage the author suggests that the counterculture _____.

[A] destroyed the United States

[B] changed some Americans' point of value

[C] was not important in the United States

[D] brought people more leisure time with their families

65. It could be inferred from the passage that _____.

[A] men and women will never share the same goals

[B] some men will be willing to change their traditional male roles

[C] most men will be happy to share some of the household responsibilities with their wives

[D] more American householders are headed by women than ever before

66. The best title for the passage may be _____.

[A] Results of Feminist Movement

[B] New Influence on Americans' Life

[C] Counterculture and Its Consequences

[D] Traditional Division of Male and Female Roles

Part V   **Cloze**   **(15 minutes)**

Directions: *There are 20 blanks in the following passage. For each blank there are four choices marked [A], [B], [C] and [D] on the right side of the paper. You should choose the ONE that best fits into the passage. Then mark the corresponding letter on Answer Sheet 2 with a single line through the centre.*

注意：此部分试题请在**答题卡2**上作答。

One day a police officer managed to get some fresh mushrooms. He was so 67 what he had bought that he offered to 68 the mushrooms with his brother officers.

When their breakfast arrived the next day, each officer found some mushrooms on his plate. "Let the dog 69 a piece first," suggested one 70 officer who was afraid that the mushrooms might be poisonous. The dog seemed to 71 his mushrooms, and the officers then began to eat their meal saying that the mushrooms had a very strange 72 quite pleasant taste.

An hour 73 , however, they were all astonished when the gardener rushed on and said 74 the dog was dead. 75 , the officers jumped into their cars and rushed into the nearest hospital. *Pumps*（泵）were used and the officers had a very 76 time getting rid of the mushrooms that 77 in their stomachs.

When they 78 to the police station, they sat down and started to 79 the mushroom poisoning. Each man explained the pains that he had felt and they agreed that 80 had grown worse on

67. [A] sure of   [C] pleased with
    [B] careless about [D] disappointed at
68. [A] share   [C] wash
    [B] grow   [D] cook
69. [A] check   [C] try
    [B] smell   [D] examine
70. [A] frightened   [C] cheerful
    [B] shy   [D] careful
71. [A] refuse   [C] want
    [B] hate   [D] enjoy
72. [A] besides   [C] and
    [B] but   [D] or
73. [A] later   [C] past
    [B] after   [D] over
74. [A] cruelly   [C] seriously
    [B] curiously   [D] finally
75. [A] Immediately   [C] Suddenly
    [B] Carefully   [D] Slowly
76. [A] hard   [C] exciting
    [B] busy   [D] unforgettable
77. [A] stopped   [C] settled
    [B] dropped   [D] remained
78. [A] hurried   [C] went
    [B] drove   [D] returned
79. [A] study   [C] record
    [B] discuss   [D] remember
80. [A] this   [C] it
    [B] these   [D] they

their __81__ to the hospital. The gardener	81. [A] road		[C] way
	[B] street		[D] direction
was called to tell the way __82__ the poor	82. [A] how		[C] which
	[B] in that		[D] in which
dog had died. "Did it __83__ much before	83. [A] suffer		[C] harm
	[B] eat		[D] spit
death?" asked one of the officers, __84__	84. [A] to feel		[C] felt
	[B] feeling		[D] having felt
very pleased that he had escaped a __85__	85. [A] strange		[C] peaceful
death himself. "No", answered the gar-	[B] painful		[D] natural
dener looker rather __86__. "It was killed	86 [A] happy		[C] surprised
the moment a car hit it."	[B] interested		[D] excited

Part VI　　　　　　　　　　　Translation　　　　　　　　　　（5 minutes）

Directions: *Complete the sentences by translating into English the Chinese given in brackets. Please write your translation on **Answer Sheet 2**.*

注意: 此部分试题请在**答题卡2**上作答, 只需写出译文部分。

87. _____（当我们遭遇危险时）, our hearts speed up.

88. Americans eat _____（两倍的蛋白质）as they actually need every day.

89. _____（抽象意义上的语言）is our facility to talk to each other.

90. Never in my lifetime _____（看过这样的演出）.

91. _____（你的梦想将会落空）if you don't work on them.

试卷详解

Part I　　　　　　　　　　　Writing

精彩范文

Dear Sir or Madam,

I am a senior **from the Department of** Business Administration. **I am writing the letter in purpose of** applying for your recently advertised position for a staff member.

I am sure that I am qualified for it. First, enclosed with this letter is my

resume, which further details my previous academic qualifications and work experience. Second, not only do my qualifications and experience make me a perfect candidate for it, my cheerful personality is well suited to working as a staff member. Last, my hobbies include sports and music.

Words fail me when I want to express my sincere gratitude to you. Your prompt and favorable attention to my inquiry would be highly appreciated.

Yours sincerely,

Li Ming

参考译文

尊敬的先生或女士：

我是工商管理系大四的学生。我写这封信是为了申请您最近招聘的职员职位。

我确信自己能胜任此职位。首先，随信附上我的简历，简历中进一步详述了我以前的学历和工作经历。其次，不但我的资历和经历使我成为此职位合适的人选，我令人愉快的个性也使我非常适合做一名职员。最后，我的爱好包括体育和音乐。

感激之情，无以言表。非常感谢您对我的询问的迅速而善意的关注。

您真诚的，

李明

Part II   Reading Comprehension (Skimming and Scanning)

公司经营的全球化打破了职工工作与生活之间的平衡。这增加了职工的工作压力，导致他们对工作的满意度下降。文章分析了这种不平衡的现状，并提出了缓和工作与生活间矛盾的六点建议。

1. D 根据关键词New York定位到首段第三句：That's according to experts who gathered in New York last month at conference on international efforts to achieve greater balance between work and the rest of life.(这依据专家们在上个月赴纽约参加的国际会议上达成的看法，这次会议致力于在工作与生活之间达成更多的平衡)，故选D"平衡工作与生活"。

2. B 根据关键词companies doing business worldwide定位到首段倒数第二句：From Australia to North America to Europe, human resource professionals and academics reported that jobs and companies doing business worldwide are increasingly characterized by intensifying work loads, expanding work hours and

more time away from home.（从澳大利亚、北美一直到欧洲，人力资源专家与研究机构发现业务遍及全球的工作和公司越来越具有如下特点：工作压力加大、工作时间延长、出差时间更多），故选B"将忍受延长的工作时间"。其他三个选项原文均未提及。

3. B 根据关键词researchers in the whole world定位到第一个小标题下的首段首句：Researchers from across the globe report that job stress is increasing, job satisfaction decreasing, and work-life balance is more of a struggle.（世界各地的研究者发现，工作压力正在增大，工作满意度正在下降，工作与生活的平衡更像一场斗争），故选B"工人们对工作的满意度更低"。原文中的from across the globe被替换为题干中的in the whole world，job satisfaction decreasing被替换为选项中的less content with their jobs。选项A、D原文未提及，选项C与原文相反。

4. A 根据关键词Norway及a parent takes a year off定位到第一个小标题下的第四段第三至五句，第五句提到：Currently a parent can take a year off with 80 percent of their normal salary, plus a guarantee of getting the same job back when they return to work.（目前，父母可以离职一年，并领取正常工资的80%，而且确保回来工作时还做相同的工作），故选A"正常工资的80%"。原文第三句的Norwegians(挪威人)被替换为题干中的Norway(挪威)。

5. C 根据关键词Germany及free daycare定位到第一个小标题下的第五段第一句：In Germany, the government provides free daycare for children aged three to six.（在德国，政府为三至六岁的孩子提供免费日托），故选C。原文中的aged three to six被替换为选项中的from three to six years old。

6. A 根据关键词Germany及mothers of young children定位到第一个小标题下的第五段，第三句提到：Mothers of young children who want to work full time have few options, and that's doubly true if the child is an infant or toddler.（孩子年纪还小的母亲找到全职工作的机会不多，如果孩子还是婴儿或是刚学走路，情况更是如此），故选A"很难找到全职工作"。原文中的have few options(机会不多)被替换为选项中的hard to find(很难找到)。

7. B 根据关键词American companies和Germany定位到第一个小标题下第八段的尾句：So the American influence is a mixed blessing, expanding childcare while increasing working hours.（因此美国的影响好坏参半，扩展了托儿服务，但增加了工作时间），故选B"增加了工人的工作时间"。

8. the government

根据关键词Western Europe和family-friendly policies定位到第一个小标题下的第四段前两句：In Western Europe, the work week is shorter compared to the U.S. Women especially work less, and many family-friendly policies are mandated by the government.(在西欧，工作时间比美国更短。女性更少工作，很多重视家庭的政策都是由政府强制执行的)，故填the governments。原文中的mandate(强制执行)被替换为题干中的command(命令)。

9. having full-time careers

根据关键词discourage, disadvantage, family-friendly policies和Western Europe countries定位到第一个小标题下的第四段，该段尾句提到：One drawback thought of these generous policies is that in some countries they tend to discourage women from having full-time careers.(这些慷慨政策的缺点之一是在一些国家，它们往往不提倡女性从事全职工作)，故填having full-time careers。原文中的drawback被替换为题干中的disadvantage。

10. the balance you are choosing

根据关键词choose someone who can support定位到第二个小标题下的末段首句：Someone who supports you in working towards the balance you are choosing is essential.(找到能够帮助你达到你所追求的平衡的人至关重要)，故填the balance you are choosing。原文中的towards被替换为题干中的in the process of getting。

Part III　　　　　Listening Comprehension

Section A

11. B　生活场景

选项分析：选项B为"男士应该参考说明书"，选项D为"女士将给男士她的说明书"二者均提到了说明书，意思相近，故其一可能为正确答案。

听音重点：与instruction menu(说明书)相关的细节，究竟是谁的说明书？

听力原文：M: I've had my new stereo for a whole week. But I haven't yet figured out how to record a cassette.

W: Didn't any instruction menu come with it?

Q: What does the woman imply?

12. B 约会场景

选项分析：选项A为"今晚和男士一起去参观展览"，选项B为"待在家里休息"，二者意思相反，故其一可能为正确答案。

听音重点：女士的具体行为：参观展览还是在家休息。

听力原文：M: I'd like you to come with me to the opening of the photography exhibit.

W: I'm exhausted. You'll have to manage without me tonight.

Q: What will the woman probably do?

13. A 交通场景

选项分析：根据选项A、B、C，对话与博物馆有关，选项D与其他选项明显不同，故排除。选项A、B结构相近，其一可能为答案。

听音重点：女士乘车去博物馆还是在博物馆前面等？

听力原文：W: I wonder if there is a bus that goes by the museum.

M: The History Museum on Main Street? Take one that says 30 on the front.

Q: What does the man mean?

14. C 看病场景

选项分析：选项B为"吃一种不同的药"，选项C为"问另一位医生这个问题"，二者均与看病相关，意思相近，故其一可能是正确答案。

听音重点：关于医生或药物的细节：吃药还是问医生？

听力原文：M: My doctor told me I needed to go for some expensive treatment for my injured knee.

W: Are you sure? Maybe you need a second opinion.

Q: What does the woman suggest the man do?

15. C 比赛场景

选项分析：选项C为"他没有听教练的建议"，选项D为"他的教练没有听他的"，二者意思相反，故其一可能是正确答案。

听音重点：与教练及建议相关的细节，究竟谁没有听谁的建议？

听力原文：W: It's a shame you didn't win your tennis match.

M: I might have won if I'd listened to my coach.

Q: What does the man imply?

16. B 生活场景

选项分析：选项B为"她不需要男士的帮助"，选项D为"她想让男士搬箱子"，二者意思相反，故其一可能是正确答案。

听音重点：女士是否需要男士的帮助?

听力原文：M: Need a hand with those boxes?

W: That's OK. They're empty.

Q: What does the woman mean?

17. C 住宿场景

选项分析：选项C为"她不打算搬走"，选项D为"她想搬出宿舍"，二者意思相反，故其一可能是正确答案。

听音重点：女士是否打算搬家?

听力原文：M: I hear you are thinking about moving back into the dorm next semester.

W: Who told you that? I'd never give up my apartment.

Q: What does the woman mean?

18. C 购物场景

选项分析：选项C为"它很昂贵"，D为"它很小"，二者结构相近，其一可能为答案。

听音重点：有关it的细节：很小还是很贵?

听力原文：M: Did you see the diamond ring Bill gave to Linda?

W: I sure did. It must have cost him an arm and a leg.

Q: What does the woman imply about the ring?

Conversation One(论文场景)

M: **Good morning, Professor Harkens. I hope I am not disturbing you.**(19)

W: Not at all, Tom. Come right in. I'm always in my office in the morning.

M: I thought I'd get an early start on my research paper and would like to discuss my topic with you if you have a moment.

W: Of course. I recommend that all my students discuss their topics with me before they begin their research. What do you want to work on?

M: **I was especially interested in your lecture on dinosaurs and the apparent mystery surrounding their extinction.**(20) I'd like to explore that question, but I'm not too sure how to go about it.

W: Well, according to the most widely held theory, the dinosaurs died out because of the sudden cooling of the earth's temperature. Your textbook summarizes the conclusion of several paleontologists on this point.

M: Didn't you also mention a second theory in your lecture? That dinosaurs may simply have been replaced by mammals gradually and might not die out as a direct response to the cool weather?

W: Yes. **Van Vellen and Sloan are proponents of this theory.**（**21**）And I've put some of their articles on reserve in the library.

M: Van Vellen and Sloan? I'd better write that down.

W: Let me know how your work progresses, Tom. If you should run into any problems, be sure to stop by again.

Questions 19 to 21 are based on the conversation you have just heard.

19. Who are the speakers?

　　正确答案：A

　　选项分析：选项A、B、D均与学生相关，选项C为"两个科学家"，与四级听力校园生活主题不符，故排除。

　　听音重点：根据原文Good morning, Professor Harkens. I hope I am not disturbing you，可知对话者是学生和老师。

20. What is the main focus of the man's research?

　　正确答案：B

　　选项分析：选项A、B均出现恐龙，A为"恐龙的时代"，B为"恐龙为何灭绝"，其一可能为正确答案。

　　听音重点：根据原文I was especially interested in your lecture on dinosaurs and the apparent mystery surrounding their extinction，可知男士关注恐龙的灭绝。

21. Who most likely are Van Vellen and Sloan?

　　正确答案：A

　　选项分析：20题各选项表明对话与科研相关，故A"科学家"可能为正确答案。选项D"艺术家"明显与主题不符，故排除。

　　听音重点：根据原文Van Vellen and Sloan are proponents of this theory，可知二人均为科学家。

Conversation Two（郊游场景）

W: Hew! **This rowing is hard work. Let's have the boat toward the old lighthouse now.**（**22**）

M: Good idea. We can rest there a while and eat our lunch. Then we can climb to the top platform where the light is before we visit the museum at the base of the lighthouse tower.

W: Whenever I came out here, I thought about the family who used to live on the little island and take care of the light every night. What a lonely life that must have been!

M: Yeah, to help ships find their way along shoreline, **at night, they had to constantly make sure that the windows up around the light were clean and free of ice and snow.**（23）

W: Dirty soot must have been a problem. Didn't they burn candles up there?

M: This one used to have a kerosene lamp. But they changed over to electricity around 1920, I think.

W: In New Port, Rode Island, people talked about a woman who was a lighthouse keeper for over 50 years. **Ida Louise was her name. She saved a lot of people from dying in ship wrecks.**（24）

M: Was her lighthouse out on an island like this one?

W: On one even smaller and further from land. In stormy weathers, it was pretty dangerous for small boats.

M: I understand the United States Coast Guard takes care of the most modern lighthouses.

W: Yeah, but the light is automatic nowadays. The lighthouse is still a friendly sight at night though.

M: Here we are. This lighthouse is the friendliest sight I've seen today. **I'm exhausted.**（25）

Questions 22 to 25 are based on the conversation you have just heard.

22. What are the people doing?

正确答案：B

选项分析：根据23、24题选项中大量出现的boat, lighthouse（灯塔），sea captain（海上船长），可知对话与划船及航海相关，选项B"正在划船"可能是正确答案。

听音重点：根据原文This rowing is a hard work. Let's have the boat toward the old lighthouse now，可知他们正在划船。

23. What was a major problem for every lighthouse keeper?

正确答案：D

选项分析：由于在海上，选项A"昂贵的当地生活费用"不合常识，故排除。

听音重点：根据原文they had to constantly make sure that the windows up around the light were clean and free of ice and snow，可知主要问题是保持窗户的清洁。

24. Why was Ida Louise famous?

正确答案：D

选项分析：选项B"她建造了自己的灯塔"不合常识，故排除。

听音重点：根据原文Ida Louise was her name. She saved a lot of people from dying in ship wrecks，可知她挽救了很多人的性命。

25. How does the man feel at the end of the conversation?

正确答案：A

选项分析：选项C"生气的"与D"勇敢的"不合常识，故排除。

听音重点：根据原文I'm exhausted，可知男士非常疲惫，答案为同义替换。

Section B

Passage One(住宿：宿舍的退宿手续)

Good afternoon, I'm Torris Don, housing director here at the university. **I'm visiting all the dormitories this week to inform students about check-out procedures.**(26) **I know you have a lot on your minds with finals coming up, but there are a few things you need to be aware of as you prepare to leave for vacation.** (27) This dormitory will be closed during the summer months and will reopen on September 1st. You must vacate your room by June 3rd. Even if you are registered for classes during the summer, you must leave the dorm by June 3rd. If this poses a problem for you, you should contact my office as soon as possible. You should remember to turn in your room key before you leave. Failure to turn in your key can result in a 25-dollar fine. You must also make sure that all of your personal property has been cleared out of your room. I'll be passing out a form for you to fill out concerning the condition of your room. **You should report on the form any damage to your room which has occurred over the last year, such as holes in the room's** walls, door or windows. (28) That way, our summer maintenance crew will know where to make repairs before the next school year starts. If you have any questions during the next few days, please ask your resident advisors or call my office. Now please take one of the forms as they are passed around.

Questions 26 to 28 are based on the passage you have just heard.

26. What does the speaker mainly discuss?

正确答案：D

答案解析：四级短文听力第一题通常考查开头，根据原文"本周我查看所有宿舍，并通知学生们退宿手续"，故选D"退宿手续"。

27. When does this talk take place?

正确答案：C

答案解析：根据原文"我知道你们马上就要进行期末考试了，愁事很多，但在你们假期离开宿舍前，还需要知道几件事"，故选C"接近学年的结束"。

28. What must students indicate on the forms?

正确答案：B

答案解析：四级短文听力最后一题通常考查结尾，根据原文"你们应该在表格上报告去年房间里发生的任何损坏，例如墙上或门窗的小洞"，故选B"他们房间的任何损坏"。

Passage Two(美国文学家：艾米莉·狄金森)

Today it's my turn to give the weekly oral report and the topic that Professor May has assigned me is the life of the poet Emily Dickinson. (29) Compared to Walt Whitman whom we discussed last week, I found Emily Dickinson strikingly different. (30) She seems, in fact, to be the complete opposite of Whitman in her life and in her work. I would like to share briefly with the class some of the essential facts of her biography. Emily Dickinson was born in 1830 in Amherst, Massachusetts, barely a decade after Whitman. In her early twenties, for reasons which still remain a mystery, she began to withdraw from ordinary contact with the world. For the remaining thirty years of her life she was seldom seen outside her home. In this respect she was quite unlike Whitman, who loved the great outdoors. Emily Dickinson spent her solitary days corresponding with her friends and writing hundreds of remarkable poems, notably "I Heard a Fly Buzz", and the poem we read for today—"I'm Nobody". Although she showed some of her poems to her family and sent some in letters to her friends, only four were published in her lifetime. **Most of them, almost 1,200 poems, were discovered in her room after she died in 1886 at the age of 56.**（31）These poems established her as a major poet. And several modern critics consider her the greatest woman poet in the English language. Ah, that's about all I have. Are there any questions? **If not, we should probably begin talking about Dickinson's "I'm Nobody", the poem Professor May assigned for this week's class discussion.**（32）

Questions 29 to 32 are based on the passage you have just heard.

29. Who is the speaker?

   正确答案：C

   答案解析：四级短文听力第一题通常考查开头，根据原文"今天轮到我做每周的口头报告，May教授分给我的题目是诗人艾米莉·狄金森的生平"，故选C"一名学生"。

30. What had been the discussion topic of the previous class?

   正确答案：D

   答案解析：根据原文"和我们上周讨论的瓦尔特·惠特曼相比，我发现艾米莉·狄金森大不相同"，故选D"瓦尔特·惠特曼的诗歌"。

31. Approximately how old was Emily Dickinson when she died?

   正确答案：C

   答案解析：根据原文"她于1886年去世，享年56岁，之后，人们在她的房间里发现了大约1200首诗"，故选C"在她五十多岁时"。

32. What will the class do now?

   正确答案：B

   答案解析：四级短文听力的最后一题通常考查结尾，根据原文"如果没有的话，我们要开始讨论May教授布置的本周课堂讨论的诗歌，狄金森的*I'm Nobody*"，故选B"讨论艾米莉·狄金森的一首诗"。

Passage Three（音乐：爵士乐）

   To play their music well, jazz musicians don't really need to know a lot about the rules of harmony and rhythm. Of course they might have knowledge of both harmony and rhythm, but that kind of knowledge isn't what makes them jazz musicians. **What does make them good is having an intuitive feeling of how the music works.**（33）For artists in the medium of jazz, the music comes naturally. It flows almost spontaneously through them. Their music performance is not planned in advance. As they play, they don't monitor themselves in terms of a formal theory of performance. **As a result, jazz is a natural expression of the moods and feelings of the artists, a moment-by-moment expression of the self.**(34) Now you are in for a treat. I brought some recordings of my favorite jazz artists. **We'll spend some time listening to some examples of really good jazz.**(35)

Questions 33 to 35 are based on the passage you have just heard.

33. What is the main purpose of the talk?

正确答案：D

答案解析：四级短文听力第一题通常考查开头，根据原文"使他们优秀的正是拥有如何创造音乐的直觉"，故选D"描述如何演奏好的爵士乐"。

34. What does the speaker say is a distinctive characteristic of jazz musicians?

正确答案：C

答案解析：根据原文"结果是，爵士乐是艺术家们的心情与感觉的自然流露，是自我的瞬间表达"，故选C"他们以个人自我表达的方式来演奏音乐"。

35. What will the class do next?

正确答案：D

答案解析：四级短文听力的最后一题通常考查结尾，根据原文"接下来我们将花点儿时间听一些真正优秀的爵士乐"，故选D"听一些爵士乐唱片"。

Section C

36. requirements
37. Bachelor
38. known
39. campus
40. Architecture
41. vital
42. course
43. located

44. two of the departments which offer the major subjects for your award are Sociology and Psychology

45. in the first semester, you'll be doing four subjects: Psychology, Sociology, History and Economics

46. you may find that you can't need a deadline for an essay or perhaps you're having problems with attendance

Part IV　　　　Reading Comprehension（Reading in Depth）

Section A

47. [F] tend

48. [L] workweek

49. [C] residents

50. [N] colleagues

51. [D] variation

52. [J] documented

53. [G] physical

54. [I] patterns

55. [K] confirmed

56. [M] individuals

Section B

57. B　细节题。由题干buy a house 可定位到文章第一段最后一句：第一次买房的家庭通常从住房互助协会那里借钱。B符合文章说法。而其他选项是买车、电视、洗衣机的措施。

58. A　细节题。由题干a small business financing定位到文章第二段结尾和第三段：but often you will need help 和you will go to your bank...or perhaps...，由此可知，小公司的主要做法是向银行贷款。其中，转折句是考点，but后的内容才是句子的中心意思。选项B在but之前，不是句子的重心。由perhaps可知C不是通常的做法。

59. B　细节题。由题干borrow huge amounts of money 定位到第四段第一句：很多大公司需要资金来发展和扩大，而这些资金远远超出了他们的支付能力和私人资金来源。B与此句同义。

60. C　细节题。题干major development 和major businesses同义，由此可定位到文章最后一段：大公司不需要指望从朋友或亲戚那儿筹到足够的钱，而且通常银行也很难为长期的项目提供足够的资金。这些公司有时只能通过出售股份来筹集资金。

61. A　细节题。由四个选项可以判断该题与银行提供资金有关，可在全文查找有关bank的句子。由最后一段第一句though they will provide short-term finance(虽然他们能提供短期的资金)，可知答案为A。B是干扰项，句中的only过于绝对。文章开头说：如果个人想买车、电视、洗衣机，可向银行借款，所以D不对。C与A的意思相反，故排除。

62. D　细节题。文章第一段就提到，过去可以根据男女的分工不同来定义男性和女性，男女做着不同的工作，而且角色没有转换的余地。因此D为正确答案。

63. A 细节题。文章第二段提到：Taking more interest in childcare, men began to share child-raising tasks with their wives（男人照看孩子的兴趣增强，开始与妻子共同承担抚养孩子的任务），故A为正确答案。文中只说美国人拒绝入伍，而没有说正在服役的军人拒绝参加越南战争，所以B错误。C项中all的说法过于绝对。D项中提到的变化是女权运动的结果，而不是反传统文化的结果。

64. B 主旨题。文章第二段说赞同反传统文化的人不再把成为美国中产阶级看作自己的奋斗目标，并且男性对当兵的看法发生了改变。第三段说参与反传统文化的人并不是很多，但它的影响却波及美国社会的很多领域。由此可见，反传统文化改变了一些美国人的价值观，因此B为正确答案。A项夸大了事实，文章中只提到反传统文化改变了一些人的价值观，并没有说它对美国造成破坏性的影响。C项与文章不符，能让美国人的价值观有所转变的事件不可能不重要。

65. B 推理题。文章第二段说，随着反传统文化势力的出现，对抚养孩子有兴趣的丈夫开始与妻子共同承担抚养孩子的任务，而一些年轻男子则拒绝入伍参加越南战争。由此可知，男人愿意改变他们的传统角色，B为正确答案。A项过于绝对，一般而言，含有never, absolute等表示绝对含义的词的选项往往都不是正确答案。C项中的most men夸大了文意，文章中只提到了一部分男人愿意和妻子共同承担家务。D也夸大了事实，文中只提到了男女的社会角色有了很大改变，并没有说女性现在在家庭中占主导地位。

66. B 主旨题。文章主要讲反传统文化势力以及女权运动的出现都对男女角色的变化产生了影响，因此B为正确答案。

Part V   **Cloze**

67. C 短语辨析。根据上文的managed to get some fresh mushrooms（好不容易买到新鲜的蘑菇）和下文的offer to（＝express willingness to）可知，此处应选pleased with（对……感到满意）。sure of 意为"确信"；careless about 意为"对……不小心"；disappointed at 意为"对……失望的"

68. A 动词辨析。由the mushroom with his brother officers可知，此处应选share（分享）。

69. C 动词辨析。根据常识，蘑菇的毒性是无法闻出来的，故排除smell。A和D的动作狗均无法完成，故选C，try a piece=try eating a piece。从下文提到的"狗也吃了蘑菇"，也可以推断答案是C。

70. D　形容词辨析。根据上下文，这位警官担心蘑菇有毒，建议让狗先试吃，可见其细心程度，故选D。

71. D　动词辨析。根据下文the officers began eating their meal可知狗enjoy (eating) his mushroom，故选D。

72. B　词语辨析。修饰名词taste的两个形容词strange和quite pleasant之间存在转折关系，故选but。besides是介词，不能连接形容词，故排除。

73. A　固定搭配。an hour later=after one hour(一小时后)。

74. C　副词辨析。由上文提到的they are all astonished(他们都大吃一惊)可以推断，园丁说话的口气应该是 seriously(严肃地，认真地)。cruelly意为"残酷地"；curiously意为"好奇地"；finally意为"最后，最终"。

75. A　副词辨析。本句意为 "一听到狗死了，警官们立刻跳进车内，驶向医院"，故选immediately。carefully意为"认真地"，suddenly意为"突然"，slowly意为"慢慢地"，均不符合题意。

76. A　形容词辨析。根据常识，洗胃很痛苦，故选hard。

77. D　动词辨析。根据上文可知，此处getting rid of的对象应该是残留在胃里的蘑菇，故选 remained。

78. D　动词辨析。return=go back，表示从医院回到警察局。

79. B　动词辨析。根据下文Each man explained the pains that...，可知警官们回来后开始讨论蘑菇的毒性。故选B。

80. B　代词辨析。these指代前面提到的the pains。

81. C　固定搭配。on one's way to...意为"在去……的路上"。

82. D　定语从句。先行词way(方式)在定语从句中作方式状语，所以引导词不能用how，而要用in which。

83. A　动词辨析。根据上文可知，警官们以为狗是中毒死的，故而问狗死前是不是很痛苦，因此答案选A。

84. B　语法结构。根据下文可知，此处填入的词作谓语动词asked的伴随状语，故选B。to feel可作目的状语，但前面不用逗号；felt缺少连词and构成并列谓语；having felt表示发生在谓语动作之前的动作，作原因或时间状语。

85. B　形容词辨析。根据常识，中毒死亡应该是painful(痛苦的)。

86. C　形容词辨析。根据最后一句可知，狗死于车祸而非中毒，所以园丁对警官的问题应该感到吃惊，故选surprised。

Part VI   Translation

87. 答案：When we are confronted/encountered with danger

    解析：1)从句：此处应使用when引导的时间状语从句。

            2)词组：be confronted/encountered with(遭遇)

88. 答案：twice as much protein

    解析：1)比较结构：倍数+as much/many as+名词+as，蛋白质为不可数名词，故用much。

            2)词汇：protein(蛋白质)

89. 答案：Language in the abstract

    解析：词组：in the abstract(抽象意义上的)

90. 答案：have I seen such a performance

    解析：1)倒装句：否定词never放在句首时，后面的句子应部分倒装。

            2)时态：根据前半句in my lifetime，此处应使用现在完成时。

91. 答案：Your dreams will fall through

    解析：词组：fall through(落空)

第二节　专家预测试卷二

Part I   Writing   (30 minutes)

注意：此部分试题在**答题卡1**上。

Directions: *For this part you are allowed 30 minutes to write a composition on the topic Is Stress a Bad Thing? You should write at least 120 words and base your composition on the outline below:*

    1. 有人害怕压力，

    2. 有人认为压力并不是坏事，

    3. 我的看法。

Part II   Reading Comprehension (Skimming and Scanning)   (15 minutes)

Directions: *In this part, you will have 15 minutes to go over the passage quickly and answer the questions on Answer Sheet 1. For questions 1-7, choose the best answer* *from the four choices marked* [A], [B], [C] *and* [D]. *For questions 8-10, complete the sentences with the information given in the passage.*

Improving Reading Speed

It is safe to say that almost everyone can double his speed of reading while maintaining equal or even higher comprehension. In other words, anyone can improve the speed with which he gets what he wants from his reading.

The average college student reads between 250 and 350 words per minute on fiction and non-technical materials. A "good" reading speed is around 500 to 700 words per minute, but some people can read a thousand words per minute or even faster on these materials. What makes the difference? There are three main factors involved in improving reading speed: (1) the desire to improve, (2) the willingness to try new techniques and (3) the motivation to practice.

Learning to read rapidly and well presupposes that you have the necessary vocabulary and comprehension skills. When you have advanced on the reading comprehension materials to a level which you can understand college-level materials, you will be ready to begin speed reading practice in earnest.

Understanding the role of speed in reading process is essential. Research has shown a close relation between speed and understanding. For example, in checking process charts of thousands of individuals taking reading training, it has been found in most cases that an increase in rate has been paralleled by an increase in comprehension, and that where rate has gone down, comprehension has also decreased. Most adults are able to increase their rate of reading considerably and rather quickly without lowering comprehension.

Some of the facts which reduce reading rate:

(a) limited perceptual span, i.e., word-by-word reading;

(b) slow perceptual reaction time, i.e., slowness of recognition and response to the material;

(c) vocalization, including the need to vocalize in order to achieve comprehension;

(d) faulty eye movements, including inaccuracy in placement of the page, in return sweep, in rhythm and regularity of movements, etc.;

(e) regression, both habitual and as associated with habits of concentration;

(f) lack of practice in reading, due simply to the fact that the person has read very little and has limited reading interests so that very little reading is practiced in the daily or weekly schedule.

Since these conditions act also to reduce comprehension, increasing the reading rate through eliminating them is likely to result in increased comprehension as well. This is an entirely different matter from simply speeding up the rate of reading without reference to the conditions responsible for the slow rate. In fact, simply speeding the rate especially through forced acceleration, may actually result, and often does, in making the real problem more severe. In addition, forced acceleration may even destroy confidence in ability to read. The obvious solution, then is to increase rate as a part of a total improvement of the whole reading process.

A well planned program prepares for maximum increase in rate by establishing the necessary conditions. Three basic conditions include:

1. Eliminate the habit of pronouncing words as you read. If you sound out words in your throat or whisper them, you can read slightly only as fast as you can read aloud. You should be able to read most materials at least two or three times faster silently than orally.

2. Avoid regressing (rereading). The average student reading at 250 words per minute regresses or rereads about 20 times per page. Rereading words and phrases is a habit which will slow your reading speed down to a snail's pace. Furthermore, the slowest reader usually regresses most frequently. Because he reads slowly, his mind has time to wander and his rereading reflects both his inability to concentrate and his lack of confidence in his comprehension skills.

3. Develop a wider eye-span. This will help you read more than one word at a glance. Since written material is less meaningful if read word by word, this will help you learn to read by phrases or through units.

Poor results are inevitable if the reader attempts to use the same rate indiscriminately for all types of materials and for all reading purposes. He must learn to adjust his rate to his purpose in reading and to the difficulty of the material he is reading. This ranges from a maximum rate on easy, familiar, interesting material or in reading to gather information on a particular point, to minimal rate on material which is unfamiliar in content and language structure or which must be thoroughly digested. The effective reader adjusts his rate; the ineffective reader uses the same rate for all types of material.

Rate adjustment may be overall adjustments to the article as a whole, or internal adjustment within the article. Overall adjustment establishes the basic rate at which the total article is read; internal adjustment involves the necessary variations in rate of each varied part of the material; as an analogy, you plan to take a 100-mile mountain trip. Since this will be a relatively hard drive with hills, curves, and mountain pass, you decide to take three hours for the total trip, averaging about 35 miles an hour. This is your overall rate adjustment. However, in actual driving you may slow down to no more than 15 miles per hour on some curves and hills, while speeding up to 50 miles per hour or more on relatively straight and level sections. This is your internal rate adjustment. There is no set rate, therefore, which the good reader follows inflexibly in reading a particular selection, even though he has set himself an overall rate for the total job.

In keeping your reading attack flexible, adjust your rate sensitivity from article to article. It is equally important to adjust your rate within a given article. Practice these techniques until a flexible reading rate becomes second nature to you.

注意: 此部分试题请在**答题卡**1上作答。

1. Which of the following is not a factor in improving your reading speed?

   [A] Willingness to try new techniques.

   [B] Motivation to improve.

   [C] Desire to practice.

   [D] Maximizing reading rate.

2. Understanding college-level materials is a prerequisite for _____.

   [A] beginning speed reading

   [B] learning to comprehend rapidly

   [C] having the necessary vocabulary

   [D] practicing comprehension skills

3. For most people, _____.

   [A] a decrease in comprehension leads to a decrease in rate

   [B] a decrease in rate leads to an increase in comprehension

[C] an increase in rate leads to an increase in comprehension

[D] an increase in rate leads to a decrease in comprehension

4.　Which of the following facts reduce reading rate?

[A] Limiting perceptual span.

[B] Speeding up the rate for reading.

[C] Avoiding regressing or rereading.

[D] Understanding the role of speed in reading process.

5.　Speeding up your reading rate through forced acceleration often results in _____.

[A] reducing comprehension

[B] increasing comprehension

[C] reducing your reading problem

[D] increasing your reading problem

6.　Which of the following factors will help you increase reading rate?

[A] Reading word by word.

[B] Developing a wider eye-span.

[C] Concentrating and being confident.

[D] Developing the habit of pronouncing words as you read.

7.　In order to improve reading speed, you have to _____.

[A] make return sweep inaccurately

[B] establish a flexible reading rate

[C] use the same rate for all types of material

[D] simply accelerate reading speed intentionally

8.　Research has shown that in most cases an increase in rate has been paralleled by

_____.

9.　A poor reader uses _____ when reading different material.

10.　Even though a good reader has set himself _____ for the total

reading, there is no set rate.

Part III　　　　　　　　　**Listening Comprehension**　　　　（**35 minutes**）

Section A

Directions: *In this section, you will hear 8 short conversations and 2 long conversations. At the end of each conversation, one or more questions will be asked* *about what was said. Both the conversation and the questions will be spoken only once. After each question there will be a pause. During the pause, you must read the four choices marked* [A], [B], [C] *and* [D], *and decide which is the best answer. Then mark the corresponding letter on* **Answer Sheet 2** *with a single line through the centre.*

注意: 此部分试题请在**答题卡2**上作答。

11. [A] Disappointed.　　　　　　　　[C] Nervous.

　　[B] Surprised.　　　　　　　　　[D] Uninterested.

12. [A] He didn't get the clothes.

　　[B] The store closed while he was cleaning the car.

　　[C] He'll clean up when he has more time.

　　[D] The clothes aren't ready.

13. [A] He has already finished his assignment.

　　[B] He's bothering the woman.

　　[C] He forgot to attend class.

　　[D] He's willing to help the woman.

14. [A] Ask Joan to recommend a good restaurant.

　　[B] Have dinner at Joan's house.

　　[C] Ask their friends about the restaurant.

　　[D] Go to the restaurant.

15. [A] He has been asked to join the committee.

　　[B] There are several new people on the committee.

　　[C] He'd like to take the woman's place on the committee.

　　[D] The woman should try to join the committee.

16. [A] He watched the television program with his mother.

　　[B] His mother told him his professor was on television.

　　[C] Answering the phone caused him to miss the television program.

　　[D] His mother missed the television program.

17. [A] He plans to get his hair cut.　　　[C] He works in a hair saloon.

　　[B] He has a new hairstyle.　　　　[D] He decides to grow his hair longer.

18. [A] Buy a car from the woman.　　　[C] Buy a new car.

　　[B] Help the woman paint her car.　　[D] Look for a less expensive car.

405

Questions 19 to 21 are based on the conversation you have just heard.

19. [A] A recording artist.   [C] A student.

　　[B] A French teacher.   [D] An engineer.

20. [A] He's having a job interview.

　　[B] He wants to know where the tapes are.

　　[C] He's showing her a new tape recorder.

　　[D] He's recording her voice on a tape.

21. [A] Change her class schedule.   [C] Organize tapes on the shelves.

　　[B] Fill out a job application.   [D] Work on the French lessons.

Questions 22 to 25 are based on the conversation you have just heard.

22. [A] There aren't enough cabinets.

　　[B] There is too much noise.

　　[C] Office supplies are taking up space.

　　[D] Some teaching assistants don't have desks.

23. [A] To chat with Jack socially.   [C] To hand in their assignments.

　　[B] To get help in the course.   [D] To practice giving interviews.

24. [A] Give Jack a different office.

　　[B] Complain to the department head.

　　[C] Move the supplies to the storage room.

　　[D] Try to get a room to use for meetings.

25. [A] They'd have to get permission.

　　[B] Jack wouldn't like it.

　　[C] She thinks it might work.

　　[D] The other assistants should be consulted.

Section B

Directions: *In this section, you will hear 3 short passages. At the end of each passage, you will hear some questions. Both the passage and the questions will be spoken only once. After you hear a question, you must choose the best answer from the four choices marked [A], [B], [C] and [D]. Then mark the corresponding letter on **Answer Sheet 2** with a single line through the centre.*

注意：此部分试题请在**答题卡2**上作答。

Passage One

Questions 26 to 28 are based on the passage you have just heard.

26. [A] On a Tuesday.   [C] On a Thursday.

    [B] On a Wednesday.   [D] On a Friday.

27. [A] There will be only multiple-choice questions.

    [B] The exam will be both multiple-choice and essay questions.

    [C] The exam will have an oral and written section.

    [D] There will be only essay questions.

28. [A] During the first week of class.   [C] On the last day of class.

    [B] During midterm week.   [D] During holiday.

Passage Two

Questions 29 to 32 are based on the passage you have just heard.

29. [A] Energy conservation.

    [B] Transportation of the future.

    [C] Strip cities.

    [D] Advantages of air transportation over railroads.

30. [A] A lack of available flights.   [C] Boredom on long flights.

    [B] Long delays at the airport.   [D] Long trips to and from airports.

31. [A] It is more comfortable than a conventional train.

    [B] It doesn't require very much track maintenance.

    [C] It doesn't remain in any station very long.

    [D] It carries more passengers than a conventional train.

32. [A] They are subject to fires.

    [B] They become less fuel-efficient.

    [C] They produce too much noise.

    [D] They have trouble staying on the tracks.

Passage Three

Questions 33 to 35 are based on the passage you have just heard.

33. [A] A recipe for a soft drink.   [C] The history of Cola.

    [B] The medicinal effects of Cola.   [D] Soft-drink production.

34. [A] As a soft drink.   [C] As flavored hard candy.

    [B] As medicine.   [D] As a cooking oil.

35. [A] By mixing it with special oils.

   [B] By heating it.

   [C] By combining it with different flavors.

   [D] By adding soda water.

Section C

Directions: *In this section, you will hear a passage three times. When the passage is read for the first time, you should listen carefully for its general idea. When the passage is read for the second time, you are required to fill in the blanks numbered from 36 to 43 with the exact words you have just heard. For blanks numbered from 44 to 46 you are required to fill in the missing information. For these blanks, you can either use the exact words you have just heard or write down the main points in your own words. Finally, when the passage is read for the third time, you should check what you have written.*

注意：此部分试题请在**答题卡2**上作答。

Remember that this is a vocational training institute. We train you so that you can take up a （36）_____ kind of job. So it is important that you know the main （37）_____ of the jobs, what the work is like and what kind of qualities you need to （38）_____ at them. A Physical Fitness Instructor works in health and fitness centers preparing （39）_____ programs for ordinary members of the public. Physical Fitness Instructors prepare （40）_____ of exercise to suit the individual （41）_____ age and level of fitness. Sports （42）_____ run clubs and sporting associations. Their duties include such things as booking playing fields with local （43）_____ and organizing the schedule of games or events for the club, so they need good organizational skills. Sports Psychologists spend time with professional athletes helping them （44）_____. They do this by improving motivation and concentration or assisting with stress management. Physical Education or PE teachers （45）_____. PE teachers help the development of coordination, balance, posture, and flexibility with things like simple catching and throwing skills. They are not expected to be excellent in all sports, （46）_____ _____.

Part IV   Reading Comprehension (Reading in Depth)   (25 minutes)
Section A

Directions: *In this section, there is a passage with ten blanks. You are required to select one word for each blank from a list of choices given in a word bank following the passage. Read the passage through carefully before making your choices. Each choice in the bank is identified by a letter. Please mark the corresponding letter for each item on **Answer Sheet 2** with a single line through the centre. **You may not use any of the words in the bank more than once.***

Questions 47 to 56 are based on the following passage.

Recently more and more attention has been focused on the problem of __47__ the environment in the UK.

On the past thirty years or so, the quality of many people's lives has become worse in some __48__ because of technological progress. People living near airports are constantly troubled by the noise of __49__ larger and more powerful airplanes taking off and landing. It is believed that __50__ have been responsible for a lot of damage to the environment. They've led to the construction of increasingly noisy and dangerous roads and have polluted the __51__ with exhaust fumes.

The countryside has been affected by the large-scale use of insecticides. The killing of insects has resulted in a loss of __52__ balance. Insects, although a __53__ to farmers, provide food for birds. Moreover, many people are afraid that fruit and vegetables __54__ with chemicals are harmful to our health. Recently, however, certain measures against environmental destruction have been __55__. One of these measures was the Clean Air Act, which introduced __56__ zones in large towns and cities. Rivers that were polluted with industrial chemical wastes are now being cleaned, and fish that could not live in them a few years ago can now be caught again.

注意：此部分试题请在**答题卡2**上作答。

[A] increasingly	[B] atmosphere	[C] sprayed	[D] invent
[E] introduced	[F] enforce	[G] resulted	[H] automobiles
[I] preserving	[J] respects	[K] climate	[L] environment
[M] smokeless	[N] headache	[O] ecological	

Section B

Directions: *There are 2 passages in this section. Each passage is followed by some questions or unfinished statements. For each of them there are four choices marked* [A], [B], [C] *and* [D]. *You should decide on the best choice and mark the corresponding letter on* **Answer Sheet 2** *with a single line through the centre.*

Passage One

Questions 57 to 61 are based on the following passage.

Hollywood suggests attraction, a place where the young star-struck teenagers could fulfill their dreams. Hollywood suggests luxurious houses. And the big movie stars were millionaires. Many spent their fortunes on *yacht*（游艇）, Rolls Royce and diamonds. A few of them lost their attactions quite suddenly and were left with nothing but emptiness and immense debts.

Movies were first made in Hollywood before World War I. The constant sunshine and mild climate of Southern California made it an ideal site for shooting motion pictures. Hollywood's fame and fortune reached its peak in the 1930s and 1940s, the golden days of the black and white movies. Most of the famous motion picture corporations of those days, Columbia, and Warner Brothers are still very much in business and great star like Clark Gable, and many others besides, have become immortal. In those days Hollywood was like a magnet, drawing ambitious young men and women from all over the world.

Nowhere else in the world has developed so expertly the skill of advertising as the Hollywood. The Hollywood studios by means of advertising, turned starlets into superstars. Many studio chiefs were *tyrants*（暴君）, determined to get their own way at all costs, no matter how *unscrupulous*（不道德的）the means. The stars were held on a tight control by the studio chiefs who could make and break all but stars with really big appeal. The stars were "persuaded" to sign seven-year contracts, during which time the studio saw to their training and packaging. Under their contracts（the stars did not have the rights to choose their parts）, they were often typecast. Their studios decided everything.

Hollywood still remains much of its attraction, crowned with such movie hits as "Gandhi", "Amadeus", "Born on July 4th", "Schindler's List", "Titanic" along with a group of superstars including Mery Streep, Dustin Hoffman, Anthony Hopkins, Al Paccino, etc., all of them together add up to a weighty achievement of Hollywood today. In the recession years of 1992, the movie industry in the U.S. ranked among the brightest spots in the country's balance-of-trade spreadsheet, bringing in more than $1.7 billion in foreign revenue.

The major difference that has occurred to Hollywood studios is that most movies today are filmed on location, that is to say, in any part of the world that the script demands. The Hollywood studios are still standing, but most of them have been leased to television networks. About 80% of all American TV entertainment comes from Hollywood. Nevertheless, Hollywood is a name which always be associated with motion picture-making, and for many years to come Hollywood movies will be shown in movie houses and on TV screens all over the world.

注意：此部分试题请在**答题卡2**上作答。

57. What is the most appropriate title of the passage?

　　[A] Hollywood: Stylish Life Styles

　　[B] Hollywood: a Big Draw for Motion Picture-Making

　　[C] Hollywood: Golden Days of Black-and-White Movies

　　[D] The Attraction of Hollywood: Yesterday and Today

58. It can be inferred from the first paragraph that Hollywood stars _____.

　　[A] are always brilliant　　　　　　[C] are not always secured in position

　　[B] are rich in all their life　　　　　[D] easily get bankruptcy

59. According to the passage, the Hollywood studios can make a star by _____.

　　[A] elaborate packaging

　　[B] controlling the star tightly

　　[C] persuading the star to sign a 7-year contract

　　[D] spending much money shooting a big film

60. According to the passage, in early years, _____.

　　[A] Hollywood was a prime site for TV because of its southern Californian sunshine

　　[B] Hollywood stars didn't have to sign long-term contracts

　　[C] many Hollywood producers handled their businesses without moral integrity

　　[D] Hollywood stars were free to bring their acting talent into full play

61. According to the passage, Hollywood studios are no longer the heart of the world's motion picture production because _____.

[A] stars are not as important as they once were

[B] 80% of all American TV entertainment are made in Hollywood

[C] most movies are now filmed at places outside the studios

[D] the best Hollywood movies are shown on TV screens

Passage Two

Questions 62 to 66 are based on the following passage.

"Family" is surely an elastic word. But when British people say that their society is based on family life, they are thinking of "family" in its narrow, peculiarly European sense of mother, father and children living together alone in their own house as an economic and social unit. Thus, each British marriage suggests the starting of a new and independent family—and then, the tremendous significance of marriage in British life. For both the man and the woman, marriage means going away from one's parents and starting one's own life. From that moment on, the man's first duty will be to his wife, and the same is to the wife. He will have a total responsibility for her financial support, and she for the running of the new home. They together will be responsible for their children as well as alone. Neither the wife's parents nor the husband's, nor their brothers or sisters, aunts or uncles, have any right to interfere with them—they are their own masters.

Readers of novels like Jane Austen's *Pride and Prejudice* know that in the past the girl's parents made arrangements on marriage among wealthy families, that is, it was the parents' duty to find a suitable husband for their daughter, preferably a rich one, and by skillful encouragement to lead him in the end to ask their permission of marrying her. Before that, the girl was protected and maintained in the parent's home, and the relief of getting rid of her in finance could be seen in their giving the newly married couple an amount of money called a *dowry*(嫁妆). Today it's very different. Most girls now get a job when they graduate and before they get married, they are financially independent. This has caused two results. A girl chooses her own husband, and she gets no dowry.

注意：此部分试题请在**答题卡2**上作答。

62. The purpose of the writer saying that "'Family' is surely an elastic word" is to tell
_____.

[A] different families in different time

[B] different countries have different families

[C] different families have different style of life

[D] different definitions could be given to the word "family"

63. The husband's duty in an English family is _____.

    [A] financial while the wife is running the home

    [B] to support the family financially while the wife is raising the children at home

    [C] independent while the wife is dependent

    [D] the only master in the new family

64. In a family everything is decided _____.

    [A] with the help of their parents   [C] by brothers and sisters

    [B] by the couple   [D] by the husband

65. The book *Pride and Prejudice* _____.

    [A] is a handbook of marriage

    [B] provides a great deal of information about wealthy families in the past

    [C] is the most popular book on marriage

    [D] presents some aspects of English social life in former time

66. In the aspect of marriage, in Britain, present day girls differ from past time girls in

    _____.

    [A] choosing husbands   [C] social position

    [B] the right to marry   [D] more parental support

Part V   **Cloze**   **(15 minutes)**

Directions: *There are 20 blanks in the following passage. For each blank there are four choices marked [A], [B], [C] and [D] on the right side of the paper. You should choose the ONE that best fits into the passage. Then mark the corresponding letter on Answer Sheet 2 with a single line through the centre.*

注意：此部分试题请在**答题卡2**上作答。

India has about one billion people and a dozen __67__ languages of its own. One language, and only one, is understood—by the elite—across the country：__68__ of the foreigners who ruled it for less than 200	67. [A] minor [C] major
	     [B] vital [D] crucial
	68. [A] which [C] it
	     [B] what [D] that

years and __69__ 52 years ago.

Today, India. Tomorrow, unofficially, the world. That is well __70__ way; at first, because the British not only built a global empire __71__ settled in America,

and __72__ because the world has acquired

its first truly __73__ medium, the Internet. It

is __74__ that some 350 million people speak English as their first language. Maybe 250 million to 350 million do __75__ can use it as a second language in ex-colonial countries or English-majority ones, __76__ 30 million recent immigrants to the United States, or Canada's 6 million French-speaking Quebeckers. And __77__? The guess is 100 million to 1 billion depending on __78__ you define "can". Let

us be bold: __79__ all, 20-25% of earth's 6 billion people can use English; not the English of England, let alone __80__ Dr. Johnson, but English.

That number is soaring __81__ each year brings new pupils to school and carries off monolingual oldies— __82__ now as the

Internet spreads. And English has __83__

69. [A] left   [C] conquered
    [B] came   [D] entered

70. [A] in   [C] on
    [B] under   [D] by

71. [A] and   [C] even
    [B] or   [D] but

72. [A] now   [C] finally
    [B] still   [D] secondly

73. [A] all-round   [C] global
    [B] widespread   [D] local

74. [A] calculated   [C] summarized
    [B] predicted   [D] estimated

75. [A] and   [C] but
    [B] or   [D] yet

76. [A] as   [C] like
    [B] for   [D] likewise

77. [A] where   [C] anywhere
    [B] elsewhere   [D] somewhere

78. [A] how   [C] what
    [B] that   [D] which

79. [A] for   [C] in
    [B] at   [D] after

80. [A] in   [C] for
    [B] by   [D] of

81. [A] while   [C] with
    [B] as   [D] after

82. [A] and   [C] however
    [B] but   [D] thus

83. [A] ever   [C] long
    [B] never   [D] seldom

dominated learned journals: Germans, Russians or French may be useful to their __84__ readers, but English is essential. __85__, if you want your own work published — and widely read by your peers— __86__ English is the language of choice.

84. ［A］expert ［C］skillful
　　［B］skilled ［D］experienced
85. ［A］Nevertheless ［C］Although
　　［B］So ［D］Moreover
86. ［A］therefore ［C］finally
　　［B］however ［D］then

Part VI **Translation** （**5 minutes**）

Directions: *Complete the sentences by translating into English the Chinese given in brackets. Please write your translation on **Answer Sheet 2**.*

注意: 此部分试题请在**答题卡2**上作答, 只需写出译文部分。

87. He never _____(追名逐利).

88. Just do it _____(尽自己最大努力).

89. Don't let the boy play with knives _____(以防他划伤自己).

90. We burned all the important documents lest they _____(落入对方手中).

91. My eyes, _____ (习惯了黑暗), turned instictively away from the light.

试卷详解

Part I **Writing**

精彩范文

　　In the past few years, quite a number of men and women have chosen to do something less competitive. **They are afraid that** the stress and strains of work will rob them of joy and happiness and do them harm both physically and mentally.

　　In fact, however, stress **isn't the bad thing as it is often supposed to be. Above all, unless it gets out of control, a certain amount of** stress **is vital to** provide motivation and challenge, and to give purpose and significance to an otherwise meaningless, idle life. **Furthermore**, people under stress tend to express their full range of potential and to actualize their own personal worth—the very aim of a human life.

Stress **is a natural part of everyday life and there is no way to avoid it. What we can do is to develop our adaptive abilities to deal with it rather than to escape from it.**

参考译文

在过去几年中,有不少男男女女选择去做竞争不激烈的工作。他们害怕工作的紧张和压力会使他们无法享受快乐和幸福,并伤害他们的身体和精神。

然而,事实上,压力并不像人们认为的那样是一件坏事。首先,除非你控制不了它,否则一定的压力可以为人们提供动力和挑战,使本来没有意义、无所事事的生活变得有目的、有意义,这一点对人们的生活很重要。其次,处于压力下的人容易发挥自己的全部潜力,实现自己的个人价值,这正是人生的目的。

压力是日常生活的一个组成部分,你无法逃避。我们所能做的就是培养自己的适应能力,全力应对它,而不是逃避。

Part II　　　　Reading Comprehension（Skimming and Scanning）

本文是一篇说明文,文章首先在一至四段指出任何人均可在不影响理解的基础上提高阅读速度,之后提出影响阅读速度的六大要素,最后给出提高阅读速度的三种方法。

1. D　根据关键词factor和improving reading speed定位到第二段末句：There are three main factors involved in improving reading speed：（1）the desire to improve,（2）the willingness to try new techniques and（3）the motivation to practice.(提高阅读速度有三个主要因素：1. 对提高阅读速度的渴望,2. 尝试新技巧的愿望,3. 练习的动力),故选D。选项B中的motivation替换了原文中的desire,只有选项D文中没有提到。

2. A　根据关键词understanding college-level materials定位到第三段尾句：When you have advanced on the reading comprehension materials to a level which you can understand college-level materials, you will be ready to begin speed reading practice in earnest.（当你能看懂大学水平的阅读材料时,你就可以认真开始进行阅读速度的练习了）,故选A"开始快速阅读"。题干中的prerequisite意为"必备前提条件",替换了原文中的be ready to。

3. C　根据关键词most people定位到第四段第二、三两句：Research has shown a close relation between speed and understanding. For example, in checking

process charts of thousands of individuals taking reading training, it has been found in most cases that an increase in rate has been paralleled by an increase in comprehension, and that where rate has gone down, comprehension has also decreased.(研究表明，人们的阅读速度和阅读理解水平存在密切联系。例如，从上千人参加的阅读培训的测验进步图表中可以看出，在大多数情况下，阅读速度的提高与理解力的提高同时发生，而阅读速度下降，理解力也下降)，故选C"阅读速度的提高会带来理解力的提高"。

4. A 根据关键词facts reduce reading rate定位到第五段开头：Some of the facts which reduce reading rate: 1. limited perceptual span, i.e., word-by-word reading.(以下几种情况会降低阅读速度：1. 视距受限，即逐词阅读)，故选A"限制视距"。选项C"避免回视"可提高理解力，并非降低，故排除。

5. D 根据关键词speeding up, reading rate, through forced acceleration以及result in定位到第六段第三句：In fact, simply speeding the rate especially through forced acceleration, may actually result, and often does, in making the real problem more severe.(事实上，简单地加快阅读速度，特别是强迫加快阅读速度，确实会使真正的阅读问题更加严重)，故选D"加重你的阅读问题"。D选项中的increasing替换了文中的making... more severe。

6. B 根据关键词increase reading rate定位到第七段，该段提到提高阅读速度的三个条件：改掉读出声的习惯、避免回视、扩大视距。第三点提出：Develop a wider eye-span（扩大视距），故选B。选项C中的confident文中并未提到，故排除。

7. B 本题考查提高阅读速度的方法，原文末段尾句指出：Practice these techniques until a flexible reading rate becomes second nature to you.(不断练习这些技巧，直到弹性阅读速度成为你的第二本能)，故选B"建立弹性阅读速度"。

8. an increase in comprehension
    根据题干in most cases an increase in rate has been paralleled by定位到第四段第三句中间部分：it has been found in most cases that an increase in rate has been paralleled by an increase in comprehension.(在大多数情况下，阅读速度的提高与理解力的提高同时发生)，故填an increase in comprehension。

9. the same rate
    根据关键词a poor reader定位到第八段尾句：The effective reader adjusts his

rate; the ineffective reader uses the same rate for all types of material.（高效的阅读者调整阅读速度，而效率低的阅读者对所有材料都采用相同的阅读速度），故填the same rate。题干中的poor同义替换了原文中的ineffective(效率低的)。

10. an overall rate

根据题干中的关键词even though, good reader, set himself和total定位到倒数第二段尾句：There is no set rate, therefore, which the good reader follows inflexibly in reading a particular selection, even though he has set himself an overall rate for the total job.（因此，成功的阅读者即使已经对整个阅读工作确定了整体速度，但在阅读个别段落时也没有固定的速度），故填an overall rate。

Part III   Listening Comprehension

Section A

11. C 学习场景

选项分析：根据四级听力"积极向上"的原则，故排除选项A"失望的"和D"不感兴趣的"，答案可能在选项B"惊讶的"与C"紧张的"之间。

听音重点：男士究竟是惊讶还是紧张？

听力原文：W: You don't seem to be able to sit still today. What's going on?

M: Today they announce who gets the big scholarship for the next year.

Q: How does the man probably feel?

12. A 洗衣场景

选项分析：选项A"他没有拿到衣服"与D"衣服没有准备好"意思相近，故其一可能为正确选项。

听音重点：男士没有拿到衣服还是衣服没有准备好？

听力原文：W: I hope you remember to pick up my clothes from the cleaners.

M: I couldn't go because the car wouldn't start.

Q: What does the man mean?

13. B 学习场景

选项分析：选项B"他在打扰女士"与D"他愿意帮助女士"意思相反，故其一可能为正确答案。

听音重点：男士打扰女士还是帮助女士？

听力原文：W: John, I really can't afford any more interruptions right now. I've got to finish this assignment.

M: I'm sorry, Cathy. Just one more thing, I forgot to ask you if you could give me a ride to school tomorrow.

Q: What can be inferred about the man?

14. **D 就餐场景**

选项分析：选项B"在Joan的家里吃晚餐"与D"去饭店"意思相反，故其一可能是正确答案。

听音重点：就餐地点是家里还是饭店？

听力原文：W: Joan and her friends went to a new restaurant last night and said that it served the best food they'd ever had.

M: That's quite a recommendation. Maybe we should see for ourselves.

Q: What will the speakers probably do?

15. **C 校园场景**

选项分析：选项A"人们邀请他加入委员会"与C"他希望代替女士在委员会的位置"意思相近，其一可能是正确答案。

听音重点：男士参加委员会还是代替女士的位置？

听力原文：W: I don't think I want to be on the curriculum committee anymore, but I'm not sure how to get out of it.

M: Well, you know there are plenty of people who will be interested. Me, for example.

Q: What does the man imply?

16. **B 生活场景**

选项分析：选项A"他和母亲一起看电视节目"与B"母亲告诉他教授出现在电视上"意思相近，其一可能是正确答案。

听音重点：男士与母亲一起看电视还是只有母亲在看？

听力原文：W: Did you catch our very own Professor Stiller on TV last night?

M: I almost missed it. But my mother just happened to be watching at home and gave me a call.

Q: What does the man mean?

17. **B 理发场景**

选项分析：选项A"他打算去理发"与B"他有了新发型"意思相近，故其一可能为正确选项。

听音重点：男士去理发还是已经有新发型？

听力原文：W: You look different today, but I can't quite put my finger on what it is.

M: I finally got around to trying that new hair saloon in the mall.

Q: What can be inferred about the man?

18. C 购物场景

选项分析：选项A"从女士那里买辆车"与C"买一辆新车"意思相近，故其一可能为正确选项。

听音重点：男士自己去买车还是买女士的车？

听力原文：W: Well, if you are seriously considering buying a car, I'm trying to get rid of mine. All it needs is some new paint.

M: Thanks. But most used cars end up being more trouble than they are worth.

Q: What will the man probably do?

Conversation One(求职场景)

W: **Hello, Professor Dennis, my name is Susan Adams. I read in the university newspaper that you were looking for a student to work as a language laboratory assistant?(19)**

M: Yes, we are. **Are you interested in the job?(20)**

W: I think so. But before I apply, I'd like you to tell me more about the work.

M: Have you worked with tape recorders before?

W: I used cassette recorders a lot when I studied French in high school.

M: Good, there are many different kinds of language labs. Ours is a small one, and it's fairly easy to operate. This is the main control panel. You can set the controls so a lot of students can listen to the lessons they want to hear. If you decide to take the job, I'll explain how the system operates. Most of the lessons are on cassette tapes, but some of them are also on long reel tapes or on records. The cassettes are kept in order on these shelves, and they are clearly marked with the language and the lesson number. For example, the cassettes in the green boxes are French lessons. Records and long tapes are over there.

W: How many hours would I work?

M: We need someone ten hours a week, Monday through Friday from 4 to 6 p.m. That is one of the busiest times for this laboratory.

W: **I'll fill out an application for the job right now.** (21) It would fit into my class schedule nicely.

M: Fine, I'll get back to you in a week or so after we review the applications.

Questions 19 to 21 are based on the conversation you have just heard.

19. Who is the woman?

正确答案：C

选项分析：选项B"一位法语老师"与C"一名学生"意思相反，其一可能是正确答案。

听音重点：根据原文Hello, Professor Dannis, my name is Susan Adams，可知女士为一名学生。

20. Why is the man talking to the woman?

正确答案：A

选项分析：选项A、C、D结构相近，故其一可能为正确答案，选项B结构明显不同，故排除。

听音重点：根据原文Are you interested in the job，可知男士在面试。

21. What will the woman do right now?

正确答案：B

选项分析：四选项均为人物动作，可知本题考查具体动作。

听音重点：根据原文I'll fill out an application for the job right now，可知女士将填写一份工作申请表。

Conversation Two(工作场景)

W: Stan, do you have a minute?

M: Oh, hi, Cathy. Sure. What's up?

W: Well, I've been meaning to talk to you about the situation in the office.

M: I'm not in there very often. **It's so noisy that I can't work.** (22)

W: That's exactly what I'm getting at. We're supposed to be able to do our preparation and marking in that office, but have you noticed? **Jack constantly has students coming in to get help with his course.** (23) A lot of people are going in and out.

M: Has anybody spoken to him about it?

W: No, not yet, but someone's going to have to.

M: We can't really ask him to stop having students come in for help, can we?

W: No, of course not. But I'm not able to do my work and neither are you. I imagine it's the same for the others in the office.

M: **Hmmm, could we ask for a kind of meeting room?（24）** When Jack has to talk with students, they could go to the meeting room and not use the office. You know, there's a room down the hall, a rather small room, that we could ask to use. It's only for storing supplies.

W: You mean that little storage room? Oh, that would be too small.

M: Are you sure? With the cabinets taken out, it might be bigger than it looks.

W: **Come to think of it, you may be on to something.（25）** I'd like to have a look at that room. Can we go there now?

M: Sure, let's go.

Questions 22 to 25 are based on the conversation you have just heard.

22. What problem at the office are Cathy and Stan discussing?

正确答案：B

选项分析：选项A和B结构相近，故其一可能是正确答案。

听音重点：根据原文It's so noisy that I can't work，可知噪音很大。

23. Why do Jack's students come to see him?

正确答案：B

选项分析：选项A"与Jack随便聊天"与常识不符，故排除。正确答案在B、C、D之间。

听音重点：根据原文Jack constantly has students coming in to get help with his course，可知学生在课程上寻求帮助。

24. What does Stan suggest to do?

正确答案：D

选项分析：选项A"给Jack一间不同的办公室"与D"尽力找一个房间用作会议室"意思相近，故其一可能为正确答案。

听音重点：根据原文could we ask for a kind of meeting room，可知Stan建议找一间会议室。

25. What does Cathy say about Stan's suggestion?

正确答案：C

选项分析：选项A"他们必须得到许可"与C"她认为也许可行"意思相近，故其一可能为正确答案。

听音重点：根据原文Come to think of it, you may be on to something, 可知女
士认为也许可行。

Section B

Passage One(考试介绍)

Now I'd like to talk to you about the final exam. **The exam will be held next Thursday, the last day of the exam week.**(26) Remember to bring along two or three pens in case you run out of ink. **Unlike the midterm, this test will not include multiple-choice questions. It'll consist entirely of essays.** (27) You'll have to answer three of the five essay questions. The exam will be comprehensive, which means you'll be responsible for all of the subject matter we've covered in class. I would suggest you review your midterm's as well as the textbook and your class notes. The final will count for 50% of your grade in the course. The research project will count for 20%, and the midterm 30%. I'll be in my office almost all day on Tuesday next week. If you run into any problems, please feel free to stop in. **Good luck with your studying and I'll see you on Thursday.**(28)

Questions 26 to 28 are based on the passage you have just heard.

26. When will the exam take place?

正确答案：C

答案解析：四级短文听力第一题通常考查开头，根据原文"考试将在下周四
举行"，故选C"某个周四"。

27. What will be the format of the exam?

正确答案：D

答案解析：根据原文"与期中考试不同，这次考试不含多项选择题，全是问
答题"，故选D"将只有问答题"。

28. When is this talk most likely being given?

正确答案：C

答案解析：根据原文结尾：Good luck with your studying and I'll see you on
Thursday, 可知这是考试前的最后一堂课，故选C。

Passage Two (美国交通：磁悬浮列车)

Although I think the United States generally has an excellent system of transportation, I do not think it does a good job of transporting people between

cities that are only a few hundred miles apart.（29）**A person commuting between Detroit and Chicago or between San Francisco and Los Angeles, so-called Strip Cities, may spend only a relatively short time in the air while spending several hours getting to and from the airport. This situation makes flying almost as time-consuming as driving.**（30）Moreover, airplanes use a lot of their fuel just getting into the air. They simply are not fuel-efficient on short trips. High speed trains may be an answer. One fairly new proposal of such a train is for something called MAGLEV, meaning a magnetically levitated train. Maglevs will not actually ride on the tracks but will fly above tracks that are magnetically activated. **This will save wear and tear on the tracks.**（31）These trains will be able to go faster than 150 miles per hour. **At that speed, conventional trains have trouble staying on the tracks.**（32）As you can see, Maglevs offer exciting possibilities for the future.

Questions 29 to 32 are based on the passage you have just heard.

29. What is the main topic of the talk?

   正确答案：B

   答案解析：文章开头提到"尽管我认为美国的交通系统相当发达，但对于在两个城市之间通勤的人来说仍然有不足之处"，可知文章与交通状况有关，再根据文章结尾"如你所知，磁悬浮列车给未来提供了激动人心的众多可能"，故选B"未来的交通"。

30. What problems face commuters who travel between Strip Cities?

   正确答案：D

   答案解析：根据原文"来往于底特律和芝加哥或旧金山和洛杉矶等所谓带状城市之间的人们，可能在空中只需要相当短的时间，但往返机场则需要花去几个小时"，故选D"往返机场的长途旅程"。

31. According to the speaker, what is one advantage of the Maglev?

   正确答案：B

   答案解析：根据原文"这将省去轨道磨损"，故选B"它不需要很多轨道养护"。

32. What happens to conventional train that speeds above 150 miles per hour?

   正确答案：D

   答案解析：根据原文"在那个速度上，传统的列车很难停留在轨道上"，故选D"它们很难继续停留在轨道上"。

Passage Three(发明史：可乐)

How many of you drink Cola? Nearly everybody. **Did you know that Cola started out not as a soft drink but as a cure for headaches back in the late 1800's?** (**33, 34**) John S. Pemberton, a druggist from Atlanta, had experimented for many months trying to find a cure for the common headache. He worked in his backyard, mixing and heating different combinations of oils and flavors until he found one that seems promising. Pemberton bottled the mixture and began selling it in drugstores as a concentrated syrup that the customer had to mix with water before drinking. Cola's transformation from a medicinal syrup to a carbonated soft drink came about quite by accident. One day, a customer came into a drugstore complaining of a headache and asked for a bottle of Cola syrup. He wanted to take it right away. So he asked the clerk to mix the medicine while he waited. **The clerk, instead of walking to the other end of the counter to get plain water, suggested mixing the syrup with soda water.** (**35**) The customer agreed, and after drinking it, remarked how good it tasted. The clerk continued offering the mix and carbonated Cola grew in popularity. Today carbonated Colas are sold in most countries around the world. And although they no longer contain the ingredients used to cure headaches, they are still very refreshing.

Questions 33 to 35 are based on the passage you have just heard.

33. What does the speaker mainly discuss?

  正确答案：C

  答案解析：四级短文听力第一题通常考查开头，根据原文"你知道吗？19世纪末，可乐最初出现并非作为一种饮料，而是一种治疗头疼的药剂"，故选C"可乐的历史"。

34. How was Cola originally sold?

  正确答案：B

  答案解析：根据原文可知，可乐从一种药用糖浆转化为一种碳酸饮料纯属偶然，故选B"作为一种药物"。

35. How was Cola syrup made into a soft drink?

  正确答案：D

  答案解析：根据原文"这位职员并未走到柜台的另一头去拿普通的水，而是建议使用苏打水来混合糖浆"，故选D"通过加入苏打水"。

Section C

36. particular

37. roles

38. succeed

39. individual

40. routines

41. chiefly

42. Administrators

43. councils

44. approach competition with a positive mental attitude to enable them to achieve their personal best

45. instruct young students in how to exercise, play sports, and do other recreational activities correctly and safely

46. but must be able to show students the basic techniques involved in a wide range of activities

Part IV　　　　　　　　　Reading Comprehension（Reading in Depth）

Section A

47. [I] preserving

48. [J] respects

49. [A] increasingly

50. [H] automobiles

51. [B] atmosphere

52. [O] ecological

53. [N] headache

54. [C] sprayed

55. [E] introduced

56. [M] smokeless

Section B

Passage One

57. D　主旨题。文章开头对好莱坞进行了总体介绍,随后讲述了好莱坞的发展历史,并描述了现状,展望了未来,故选D。

58. C　推断题。文章第一段展示了好莱坞明星令人羡慕的成就和奢华的生活,但最后一句提到"一些人很快就失去了魅力,并且除了巨额债务之外什么也没留下",说明好莱坞明星的生活并不稳定,故选C。

59. A　细节题。第三段倒数第三句提到"制片厂对明星进行训练和包装",故选A。

60. C　细节题。第三段第三句提到"那些制片人为达到自己的目的不择手段",故选C。

61. C　细节题。文章尾段前两句提到"好莱坞发生的最大变化就是,今天大部分电影都是在所需要的地点拍摄。好莱坞电影制片厂仍然存在,但大部分已经租给电视网络使用",故选C。

Passage Two

62. D 语义题。本题考查对elastic这个词的理解，elastic意为"有弹性的，可以伸缩的，不是固定不变的"，整个句子的意思是"家庭当然不是一个固定不变的概念"。本段的后面也提到不同时期的家庭和婚姻状况，由此亦可知family一词的含义是不同的。故选D。文章第一段描述了英国人对家庭的理解，主要是为了说明英国人对家庭的定义是一种狭义的理解，并不能由此概括出C"不同的家庭有不同的生活方式"或B"不同的国家有着不同的家庭"；文章第二段描写了Pride and Prejudice中的家庭与如今的家庭的区别，也是为主题句"'Family' is surely an elastic word."服务的，并不是说A"不同时期存在着不同的家庭"。

63. A 细节题。文章第一段倒数第三句写到：He will have a total responsibility for her financial support, and she for the running of the new home，由此可知，结婚后丈夫负责家庭经济而妻子负责持家，所以A为正确答案。至于C"（丈夫）是独立的而妻子是不独立的"，虽有这样的可能，但是文章中并没有提到。第一段倒数第二句提到They together will be responsible for their children as well as alone，所以选项B"（丈夫）负责家庭经济而妻子在家照顾孩子"是对文章句子的错误理解。第一段最后一句讲到，不论是双方父母还是兄弟姐妹都不能干涉他们的家庭，they are their own masters，故D"丈夫是新家庭的唯一主人"也应排除。

64. B 细节题。由第一段最后一句neither...nor, nor...have any right to interfere with them可以得出答案。此处的them是指夫妻俩，所以B为正确答案。

65. D 推断题。分析本文第二段可知，《傲慢与偏见》这本书讲述了当时的婚姻状况。当时有钱人之间的婚姻都由女方父母做主，女方父母给新婚夫妇一些钱作为嫁妆之后就不再管他们的经济问题，这是当时英国社会生活的一个方面。所以D为正确答案，即展示了过去英国社会生活的一些方面。

66. C 推断题。由第二段后半部分可知，现在女孩的社会地位比以前有很大的提高，表现在结婚前就获得了经济上的独立，可以自己选择丈夫，可以不要嫁妆。所以C为正确答案，而A和B只是社会地位提高的表现。

Part V　Cloze

67. C 形容词辨析。根据句意，应选major(主要的，重要的，较大的)，意为"主要语言"。minor意为"较小的，较少的，次要的"；vital意为"极重要的，致命的"；crucial意为"至关重要的，决定性的"。

68. D 代词辨析。空格指代language,冒号之后为of短语,强干扰项it不能构成该短语。

69. A 逻辑关系。根据上文的ruled it for less than 200 years和下文的52 years ago,排除B、C、D三个选项。根据常识,印度独立于50多年前,英国殖民者应在那时"离开"印度。

70. B 短语搭配。under way意为"在进行中"。in the way意为"挡道";on the way意为"在路上";by the way意为"顺便问一下"。

71. D 语法结构。根据上文的not only,此处需填but(also)。根据句意"英国不仅曾建立全球性的帝国,而且曾在美洲定居",也应是递进关系。

72. A 逻辑关系。at first表示"最初,开始时",故本句中的两个原因应是时间先后关系,故答案选now。与secondly搭配的应是first(ly)或first of all,故排除强干扰项D。

73. C 形容词辨析。此处指世界已获得第一个全球性的媒介——互联网,这体现了文章主旨:英语正在变为全球性语言,故选global(全球性的)。all-round意为"全面的,全能的";widespread意为"广泛的,普遍的";local意为"当地的"。

74. D 动词辨析。根据句意及常识,3.5亿人把英语作为第一语言并非预测而是事实,故排除predicted,选estimated,表示"据估计"。

75. B 逻辑关系。此句意为:"在前英语殖民地国家或英语占主体地位的国家,可能有2.5至3.5亿人口确实或能够运用英语作为第二语言。"空格前后是选择关系,故选or。

76. C 逻辑关系。逗号之后是对上文的举例说明,故选like。as表示"正如"时引导从句,不适合用于此处。

77. B 逻辑判断。上文数据有关前英国殖民地或英语主体国家的,按照逻辑,下文应为关于其他地方的数据。此句起承上启下的作用。

78. A 宾语从句。此句意为:据猜测,能讲英语的人有1到10亿,而具体数字要看怎么定义"能说英语",此处应选表示方式的how引导宾语从句。

79. C 固定搭配。根据上下文,此处应选in all(总共,合计)。for all意为"尽管;虽然";at all意为"根本,全然";after all意为"毕竟,终究"。

80. D 语法结构。let alone相当于连词,前后是并列结构。上文是the English of England,下文应是(the English)of Dr. Johnson。

81. B 逻辑关系。根据下文的as the Internet spreads, 此处应填"随着", 故选as。

82. A 逻辑关系。根据上下文, 前后分句表示承接关系, 应选and, 而不选表示转折或因果关系的however, but, thus。

83. C 语义理解。根据上下文及常识, 英语长期以来一直是学术期刊使用的语言。

84. A 形容词辨析。根据句意, 此处应选expert(专家的, 内行的)。skilled意为"熟练的, 有技能的"; skillful意为"灵巧的, 娴熟的"; experienced意为"有经验的"。

85. B 逻辑关系。根据上下文, 此句与前句为因果关系, 由于英语长期以来是学术期刊所使用的语言, 所以要想使自己的文章发表并被同行所阅读, 就得用英语来撰写。

86. D 语法结构。if... then... 为同现结构。

Part VI　　　　　　　　　　**Translation**

87. 答案：go after fame and wealth
    解析：词组：go after(追求); fame and wealth(名利)

88. 答案：to the best of your ability
    解析：词组：to the best of your ability(尽自己最大努力)

89. 答案：in case he cuts himself
    解析：从句：in case(以防)引导目的状语从句时, 从句一般不用虚拟语气。

90. 答案：fall into the opponent's hands
    解析：1)虚拟语气：连词lest引导的目的状语从句应使用虚拟语气, 谓语动词应使用should+动词原形, should可以省略。
    　　　2)词组：fall into someone's hand(落入某人手中)

91. 答案：accustomed/used to the darkness
    解析：1)词组：be/get accustomed/used to(习惯于)
    　　　2)分词：此处作插入语, 应使用过去分词形式accustomed/used to。

参考文献

[1] 教育部高等教育司.《大学英语课程教学要求（试行）》.北京：高等教育出版社, 2004.

[2] 全国大学英语四、六级考试委员会.《大学英语四级考试大纲(2006修订版)》.上海：上海外语教育出版社, 2006.

[3] 王江涛.《考研英语高分写作》.北京：群言出版社, 2013.

[4] 王江涛.《大学英语四级710分考试全攻略——写作翻译分册》.北京：中国电力出版社, 2006.

[5] 王江涛.《我的满分考研写作书》.长沙：湖南文艺出版社, 2010.

使用说明

  《大学英语四级考试一本通》(第五版)印刷过程中，全国大学英语四、六级考试委员会于 2013 年 8 月 14 日发布四级考试题型调整说明及新四级考试样题。由于原书已无法重印，故笔者加印《新题型全攻略》供考生参考使用。说明如下：

  1、《大学英语四级考试一本通》第一章"写作"的第三节"强化训练"替换为《新题型全攻略》第三部分"写作新题型十大必背范文及十大万能框架"；

  2、第二章"快速阅读"的第二节"真题选析"及第三节"强化训练"替换为《新题型全攻略》第五部分"快速阅读新题型十大经典模拟题"一至八；

  3、第三章"听力理解"第二节、第三节的"复合式听写"部分替换为《新题型全攻略》第五部分"短文听写新题型十大经典模拟题"一至八；

  4、第四章"仔细阅读"保持不变；

  5、第五章"完形填空"已经无此题型，略去不看；

  6、第六章"翻译"替换为《新题型全攻略》第六部分"翻译新题型十大经典模拟题"一至八；

  7、第七章"专家预测试卷"之写作、快速阅读、复合式听写、翻译部分替换为《新题型全攻略》相应部分"十大经典模拟题"九至十；其他部分保持不变；

  8、《新题型全攻略》第二部分"新大学英语四级考试样题及详解"可供考生考前模拟测试使用。

  新四级并不可怕，祝大家征服四级、笑傲云天！

北京新东方学校 王江涛

2013年 9 月 4 日

目　录

第一章　关于大学英语四、六级考试题型调整的说明

自2013年12月考次起，全国大学英语四、六级考试委员会将对四、六级考试的试卷结构和测试题型作局部调整。调整后，四级和六级的试卷结构和测试题型相同。

一、试卷描述

四级和六级的试卷结构、测试内容、测试题型、分值比例和考试时间如下表所示：

试卷结构	测试内容		测试题型	分值比例	考试时间
写作	写作		短文写作	15%	30分钟
听力理解	听力对话	短对话	多项选择	8%	30分钟
		长对话	多项选择	7%	
	听力短文	短文理解	多项选择	10%	
		短文听写	单词及词组听写	10%	
阅读理解	词汇理解		选词填空	5%	40分钟
	长篇阅读		匹配	10%	
	仔细阅读		多项选择	20%	
翻译	汉译英		段落翻译	15%	30分钟
总计				100%	130分钟

二、新题型说明

1. 单词及词组听写

原复合式听写调整为单词及词组听写，短文长度及难度不变。要求考生在听懂短文的基础上，用所听到的原文填写空缺的单词或词组，共10题。短文播放三遍。

2. 长篇阅读

　　原快速阅读理解调整为长篇阅读理解，篇章长度和难度不变。篇章后附有10个句子，每句一题。每句所含的信息出自篇章的某一段落，要求考生找出与每句所含信息相匹配的段落。有的段落可能对应两题，有的段落可能不对应任何一题。

3. 翻译

　　原单句汉译英调整为段落汉译英。翻译内容涉及中国的历史、文化、经济、社会发展等。四级长度为140-160个汉字；六级长度为180-200个汉字。

三、成绩报道

　　成绩报道分为总分和单项分。单项分包括：1）听力，2）阅读，3）翻译和写作。

全国大学英语四、六级考试委员会
2013年8月14日

一、考试样题

Part I　　　　　　　　　　**Writing**　　　　　　　　**(30 minutes)**

Directions: *For this part, you are allowed 30 minutes to write an essay. You should start your essay with **a brief description** of the picture and then express your views on the importance of learning basic skills. You should write at least **120** words but no more than **180** words. Write your essay on **Answer Sheet 1**.*

注意：此部分试题请在**答题卡1**上作答。

Part II　　　　　　　　　**Listening Comprehension**　　　　　**(30 minutes)**
Section A

Directions: *In this section, you will hear 8 short conversations and 2 long conversations. At the end of each conversation, one or more questions will be asked about what was said. Both the conversation and the questions will be spoken only once. After each question there will be a pause. During the pause, you must read the four choices marked A), B), C) and D), and decide which is the best answer. Then mark the corresponding letter on **Answer Sheet 1** with a single line through the centre.*

注意：此部分试题请在**答题卡1**上作答。

1.　A) The man has left a good impression on her family.
　　B) The man's jeans and T-shirts are stylish.

C）The man should buy himself a new suit.

D）The man can dress casually for the occasion.

2. A）Its price.   C）Its location.

   B）Its comfort.   D）Its facilities.

3. A）It is a routine offer.   C）It is new on the menu.

   B）It is quite healthy.   D）It is a good bargain.

4. A）Read the notice on the window.   C）Go and ask the staff.

   B）Board the bus to Cleveland.   D）Get a new bus schedule.

5. A）He is ashamed of his present condition.

   B）He is careless about his appearance.

   C）He changes jobs frequently.

   D）He shaves every other day.

6. A）The woman had been fined many times before.

   B）The woman knows how to deal with the police.

   C）The woman had violated traffic regulations.

   D）The woman is good at finding excuses.

7. A）She got hurt in an accident yesterday.

   B）She has to go to see a doctor.

   C）She is black and blue all over.

   D）She stayed away from work for a few days.

8. A）She will ask David to talk less.   C）She is sorry the man will not come.

   B）She will meet the man halfway.   D）She has to invite David to the party.

Questions 9 to 11 are based on the conversation you have just heard.

9. A）Beautiful scenery in the countryside. C）Dangers of cross-country skiing.

   B）A sport he participates in.   D）Pain and pleasure in sports.

10. A）He can't find good examples to illustrate his point.

    B）He can't find a peaceful place to do the assignment.

    C）He can't decide whether to include the effort part of skiing.

    D）He doesn't know how to describe the beautiful country scenery.

11. A）New ideas come up as you write.

    B）Much time is spent on collecting data.

C) A lot of effort is made in vain.

D) The writer's point of view often changes.

Questions 12 to 15 are based on the conversation you have just heard.

12. A) Having her bicycle repaired.　　C) Lecturing on business management.

　　B) Hosting an evening TV program.　　D) Conducting a market survey.

13. A) He repaired bicycles.　　C) He worked as a salesman.

　　B) He coached in a racing club.　　D) He served as a consultant.

14. A) He wanted to be his own boss.

　　B) He didn't want to be in too much debt.

　　C) He didn't want to start from scratch.

　　D) He found it more profitable.

15. A) They are all the man's friends.　　C) They are paid by the hour.

　　B) They work five days a week.　　D) They all enjoy gambling.

Section B

Directions: *In this section, you will hear 3 short passages. At the end of each passage, you will hear some questions. Both the passage and the questions will be spoken only once. After you hear a question, you must choose the best answer from the four choices marked A), B), C) and D). Then mark the corresponding letter on **Answer Sheet 1** with a single line through the centre.*

注意：此部分试题请在**答题卡1**上作答。

Passage One

Questions 16 to 18 are based on the passage you have just heard.

16. A) They shared mutual friends in school.

　　B) They had many interests in common.

　　C) They shared many extracurricular activities.

　　D) They had known each other since childhood.

17. A) At a local club.　　C) At the boarding school.

　　B) At Joe's house.　　D) At the sports center.

18. A) Durable friendships can be very difficult to maintain.

　　B) One has to be respectful of other people in order to win respect.

　　C) Social divisions will break down if people get to know each other.

　　D) It is hard for people from different backgrounds to become friends.

Passage Two

Questions 19 to 21 are based on the passage you have just heard.

19. A）The art of Japanese brush painting.　C）Characteristics of Japanese artists.

　　B）Some features of Japanese culture.　D）The uniqueness of Japanese art.

20. A）To calm themselves down.　C）To show their impatience.

　　B）To enhance concentration.　D）To signal lack of interest.

21. A）How speakers can misunderstand the audience.

　　B）How speakers can win approval from the audience.

　　C）How listeners in different cultures show respect.

　　D）How different Western and Eastern art forms are.

Passage Three

Questions 22 to 25 are based on the passage you have just heard.

22. A）They mistake the firefighters for monsters.

　　B）They do not realize the danger they are in.

　　C）They cannot hear the firefighters for the noise.

　　D）They cannot see the firefighters because of the smoke.

23. A）He teaches Spanish in a San Francisco community.

　　B）He often teaches children what to do during a fire.

　　C）He travels all over America to help put out fires.

　　D）He provides oxygen masks to children free of charge.

24. A）He is very good at public speaking.

　　 B）He rescued a student from a big fire.

　　C）He gives informative talks to young children.

　　D）He saved the life of his brother choking on food.

25. A）Kids should learn not to be afraid of monsters.

　　B）Informative speeches can save lives.

　　C）Carelessness can result in tragedies.

　　D）Firefighters play an important role in America.

Section C

Directions: *In this section, you will hear a passage three times. When the passage is read for the first time, you should listen carefully for its general idea. When the* *passage is read for the second time, you are required to fill in the blanks with the exact words you have just heard. Finally, when the passage is read for the third time, you should check what you have written.*

注意：此部分试题请在**答题卡1**上作答。

Almost every child, on the first day he sets foot in a school building, is smarter, more ___26___, less afraid of what he doesn't know, better at finding and ___27___, more confident, *resourceful*（机敏的）, persistent and ___28___ than he will ever be again in his schooling—or, unless he is very unusual and very lucky, for the rest of his life. Already, by paying close attention to and ___29___ the world and people around him, and without any school-type formal instruction, he has done a task far more difficult, complicated and ___30___ than anything he will be asked to do in school, or than any of his teachers has done for years. He has solved the ___31___ of language. He has discovered it—babies don't even know that language exists—and he has found out how it works and learned to use it ___32___. He has done it by exploring, by experimenting, by developing his own model of the grammar of language, by ___33___ and seeing whether it works, by gradually changing it and ___34___ it until it does work. And while he has been doing this, he has been learning other things as well, including many of the " ___35___ " that the schools think only they can teach him, and many that are more complicated than the ones they do try to teach him.

Part III   Reading Comprehension   （40 minutes）

Section A

Directions: *In this section, there is a passage with ten blanks. You are required to select one word for each blank from a list of choices given in a word bank following the passage. Read the passage through carefully before making your choices. Each choice in the bank is identified by a letter. Please mark the corresponding letter for each item on **Answer Sheet 2** with a single line through the centre. You may not use any of the words in the bank more than once.*

Questions 36 to 45 are based on the following passage.

One in six. Believe it or not, that's the number of Americans who struggle with hunger. To make tomorrow a little better, Feeding America, the nation's largest ___36___ hunger-relief organization, has chosen September as Hunger Action Month. As part of its 30 Ways in 30 Days program, it's asking ___37___ across the country to help the more than 200 food banks and 61,000 agencies in its network provide low-income individuals and families with the fuel they need to ___38___.

It's the kind of work that's done every day at St. Andrew's Episcopal Church in San Antonio. People who ___39___ at its front door on the first and third Thursdays of each month aren't looking for God — they're there for something to eat. St. Andrew's runs a *food pantry*（食品室）that ___40___ the city and several of the ___41___ towns. Janet Drane is its manager.

In the wake of the ___42___, the number of families in need of food assistance began to grow. It is ___43___ that 49 million Americans are unsure of where they will find their next meal. What's most surprising is that 36% of them live in ___44___ where at least one adult is working. "It used to be that one job was all you needed," says St. Andrew's Drane. "The people we see now have three or four part-time jobs and they're still right on the edge ___45___."

注意：此部分试题请在**答题卡2**上作答。

A）accumulate	I）households
B）circling	J）recession
C）communities	K）reported
D）competition	L）reviewed
E）domestic	M）serves
F）financially	N）surrounding
G）formally	O）survive
H）gather	

Section B

Directions: *In this section, you are going to read a passage with ten statements attached to it. Each statement contains information given in one of the paragraphs. Identify the paragraph from which the information is derived. You may choose a paragraph more than once. Each paragraph is marked with a letter. Answer the questions by marking the corresponding letter on **Answer Sheet 2**.*

Universities Branch Out

A) As never before in their long history, universities have become instruments of national competition as well as instruments of peace. They are the place of the scientific discoveries that move economies forward, and the primary means of educating the talent required to obtain and maintain competitive advantage. But at the same time, the opening of national borders to the flow of goods, services, information and especially people has made universities a powerful force for global integration, mutual understanding and geopolitical stability.

B) In response to the same forces that have driven the world economy, universities have become more self-consciously global: seeking students from around the world who represent the entire range of cultures and values, sending their own students abroad to prepare them for global careers, offering courses of study that address the challenges of an interconnected world and *collaborative*（合作的）research programs to advance science for the benefit of all humanity.

C) Of the forces shaping higher education none is more sweeping than the movement across borders. Over the past three decades the number of students leaving home each year to study abroad has grown at an annual rate of 3.9 percent, from 800,000 in 1975 to 2.5 million in 2004. Most travel from one developed nation to another, but the flow from developing to developed countries is growing rapidly. The reverse flow, from developed to developing countries, is on the rise, too. Today foreign students earn 30 percent of the doctoral degrees awarded in the United States and 38 percent of those in the United Kingdom. And the number crossing borders for undergraduate study is growing as well, to 8 percent of the undergraduates at America's best institutions and 10 percent of all undergraduates in the U.K. In the United States, 20 percent of the newly hired professors in science and engineering are foreign-born, and in China many newly hired faculty members at the top research universities received their graduate education abroad.

D) Universities are also encouraging students to spend some of their undergraduate years in another country. In Europe, more than 140,000 students participate in the Erasmus program each year, taking courses for credit in one of 2,200 participating institutions across the continent. And in the United States, institutions are helping place students in summer *internships*（实习）abroad to prepare them for global careers. Yale and Harvard have led the way, offering every undergraduate at least one international study or internship opportunity—and providing the financial resources to make it possible.

E）Globalization is also reshaping the way research is done. One new trend involves sourcing portions of a research program to another country. Yale professor and Howard Hughes Medical Institute investigator Tian Xu directs a research center focused on the genetics of human disease at Shanghai's Fudan University, in collaboration with faculty colleagues from both schools. The Shanghai center has 95 employees and graduate students working in a 4,300-square-meter laboratory facility. Yale faculty, postdoctors and graduate students visit regularly and attend videoconference seminars with scientists from both campuses. The arrangement benefits both countries; Xu's Yale lab is more productive, thanks to the lower costs of conducting research in China, and Chinese graduate students, postdoctors and faculty get on-the-job training from a world-class scientist and his U.S. team.

F）As a result of its strength in science, the United States has consistently led the world in the commercialization of major new technologies, from the mainframe computer and integrated circuit of the 1960s to the Internet *infrastructure*（基础设施）and applications software of the 1990s. The link between university-based science and industrial application is often indirect but sometimes highly visible: Silicon Valley was intentionally created by Stanford University, and Route 128 outside Boston has long housed companies spun off from MIT and Harvard. Around the world, governments have encouraged copying of this model, perhaps most successfully in Cambridge, England, where Microsoft and scores of other leading software and biotechnology companies have set up shop around the university.

G）For all its success, the United States remains deeply hesitant about sustaining the research-university model. Most politicians recognize the link between investment in science and national economic strength, but support for research funding has been unsteady. The budget of the National Institutes of Health doubled between 1998 and 2003, but has risen more slowly than inflations since then. Support for the physical sciences and engineering barely kept pace with inflation during that same period. The attempt to make up lost ground is welcome, but the nation would be better served by steady, predictable increases in science funding at the rate of long-term GDP growth, which is on the order of inflation plus 3 percent per year.

H）American politicians have great difficulty recognizing that admitting more foreign students can greatly promote the national interest by increasing international understanding. Adjusted for inflation, public funding for international exchanges and foreign-language study is well below the levels of 40 years ago. In the wake of September 11, changes in the visa process caused a dramatic decline in the number of foreign students seeking admission to U.S. universities, and a corresponding surge in enrollments in Australia, Singapore and the U.K. Objections from American university and business leaders led to improvements in the process and a reversal of the decline, but the United States is still seen by many as unwelcoming to international students.

I）Most Americans recognize that universities contribute to the nation's well-being through their scientific research, but many fear that foreign students threaten American competitiveness by taking their knowledge and skills back home. They fail to grasp that welcoming foreign students to the United States has two important positive effects: first, the very best of them stay in the States and—like immigrants throughout history—strengthen the nation; and second, foreign students who study in the United States become ambassadors for many of its most *cherished*（珍视）values when they return home. Or at least they understand them better. In America as elsewhere, few instruments of foreign policy are as effective in promoting peace and stability as welcoming international university students.

注意：此部分试题请在**答题卡2**上作答。

46. American universities prepare their undergraduates for global careers by giving them chances for international study or internship.

47. Since the mid-1970s, the enrollment of overseas students has increased at an annual rate of 3.9 percent.

48. The enrollment of international students will have a positive impact on America rather than threaten its competitiveness.

49. The way research is carried out in universities has changed as a result of globalization.

50. Of the newly hired professors in science and engineering in the United States, twenty percent come from foreign countries.

51. The number of foreign students applying to U.S. universities decreased sharply after September 11 due to changes in the visa process.

52. The U.S. federal funding for research has been unsteady for years.

53. Around the world, governments encourage the model of linking university-based science and industrial application.

54. Present-day universities have become a powerful force for global integration.

55. When foreign students leave America, they will bring American values back to their home countries.

Section C

Directions: *There are 2 passages in this section. Each passage is followed by some questions or unfinished statements. For each of them there are four choices marked A), B), C) and D). You should decide on the best choice and mark the corresponding letter on Answer Sheet 2 with a single line through the centre.*

Passage One

Questions 56 to 60 are based on the following passage.

Global warming is causing more than 300,000 deaths and about $125 billion in economic losses each year, according to a report by the Global Humanitarian Forum, an organization led by Kofi Annan, the former United Nations secretary general.

The report, to be released Friday, analyzed data and existing studies of health, disaster, population and economic trends. It found that human-influenced climate change was raising the global death rates from illnesses including *malnutrition*（营养不良）and heat-related health problems.

But even before its release, the report drew criticism from some experts on climate and risk, who questioned its methods and conclusions.

Along with the deaths, the report said that the lives of 325 million people, primarily in poor countries, were being seriously affected by climate change. It projected that the number would double by 2030.

Roger Pielke Jr., a political scientist at the University of Colorado, Boulder, who studies disaster trends, said the Forum's report was "a methodological embarrassment" because there was no way to distinguish deaths or economic losses related to human-driven global warming amid the much larger losses resulting from the growth in populations and economic development in *vulnerable*（易受伤害的）regions. Dr. Pielke said that "climate change is an important problem requiring our utmost attention." But the report, he said, "will harm the cause for action on both climate change and disasters because it is so deeply *flawed*（有瑕疵的）."

However, Soren Andreasen, a social scientist at Dalberg Global Development Partners who supervised the writing of the report, defended it, saying that it was clear that the numbers were rough estimates. He said the report was aimed at world leaders, who will meet in Copenhagen in December to negotiate a new international climate treaty.

In a press release describing the report, Mr. Annan stressed the need for the negotiations to focus on increasing the flow of money from rich to poor regions to help reduce their vulnerability to climate hazards while still curbing the emissions of the heat-trapping gases. More than 90% of the human and economic losses from climate change are occurring in poor countries, according to the report.

注意：此部分试题请在**答题卡2**上作答。

56. What is the finding of the Global Humanitarian Forum?

    A）Rates of death from illnesses have risen due to global warming.

    B）Global temperatures affect the rate of economic development.

    C）Malnutrition has caused serious health problems in poor countries.

    D）Economic trends have to do with population and natural disasters.

57. What do we learn about the Forum's report from the passage?

    A）It caused a big stir in developing countries.

    B）It was warmly received by environmentalists.

    C）It aroused a lot of interest in the scientific circles.

    D）It was challenged by some climate and risk experts.

58. What does Dr. Pielke say about the Forum's report?

    A）Its statistics look embarrassing.

    B）It deserves our closest attention.

    C）It is invalid in terms of methodology.

    D）Its conclusion is purposely exaggerated.

59. What is Soren Andreasen's view of the report?

    A）Its conclusions are based on carefully collected data.

    B）It is vulnerable to criticism if the statistics are closely examined.

    C）It will give rise to heated discussions at the Copenhagen conference.

    D）Its rough estimates are meant to draw the attention of world leaders.

60. What does Kofi Annan say should be the focus of the Copenhagen conference?

    A）How human and economic losses from climate change can be reduced.

    B）How rich countries can better help poor regions reduce climate hazards.

    C）How emissions of heat-trapping gases can be reduced on a global scale.

    D）How rich and poor regions can share responsibility in curbing global warming.

Passage Two

Questions 61 to 65 are based on the following passage.

It's an annual argument. Do we or do we not go on holiday? My partner says no because the boiler could go, or the roof fall off, and we have no savings to save us. I say you only live once and we work hard and what's the point if you can't go on holiday. The joy of a recession means no argument next year—we just won't go.

Since money is known to be one of the things most likely to bring a relationship to its knees, we should be grateful. For many families the recession means more than not booking a holiday. A YouGov poll of 2,000 people found 22% said they were arguing more with their partners because of concerns about money. What's less clear is whether divorce and separation rates rise in a recession—financial pressures mean couples argue more but make splitting up less affordable. A recent research shows arguments about money were especially damaging to couples. Disputes were characterised by intense *verbal*（言语上的）aggression, tended to be repeated and not resolved, and made men, more than women, extremely angry.

Kim Stephenson, an occupational psychologist, believes money is such a big deal because of what it symbolises, which may be different things to men and women. "People can say the same things about money but have different ideas of what it's for," he explains. "They'll say it's to save, to spend, for security, for freedom, to show someone you love them." He says men are more likely to see money as a way of buying status and of showing their parents that they've achieved something.

"The biggest problem is that couples assume each other knows what's going on

14

with their finances, but they don't. There seems to be more of a *taboo*（禁忌）about talking about money than about death. But you both need to know what you're doing, who's paying what into the joint account and how much you keep separately. In a healthy relationship, you don't have to agree about money, but you have to talk about it."

注意：此部分试题请在**答题卡2**上作答。

61. What does the author say about vacationing?

   A）People enjoy it all the more during a recession.

   B）Few people can afford it without working hard.

   C）It is the chief cause of family disputes.

   D）It makes all the hard work worthwhile.

62. What does the author mean by saying "money is known ... to bring a relationship to its knees"（Lines 1-2, Para. 2）?

   A）Money is considered to be the root of all evils.

   B）Disputes over money may ruin a relationship.

   C）Few people can resist the temptation of money.

   D）Some people sacrifice their dignity for money.

63. The YouGov poll of 2,000 people indicates that in a recession _____.

   A）couples show more concern for each other

   B）it is more expensive for couples to split up

   C）conflicts between couples tend to rise

   D）divorce and separation rates increase

64. What does Kim Stephenson believe?

   A）Men and women view money in different ways.

   B）Money is often a symbol of a person's status.

   C）Men and women spend money on different things.

   D）Money means a great deal to both men and women.

65. The author suggests at the end of the passage that couples should _____.

   A）put their money together instead of keeping it separately

   B）discuss money matters to maintain a healthy relationship

   C）make efforts to reach agreement on their family budgets

   D）avoid arguing about money matters to remain romantic

Part Ⅳ   **Translation**   (**30 minutes**)

Directions: *For this part, you are allowed 30 minutes to translate a passage from Chinese into English. You should write your answer on **Answer Sheet 2**.*

剪纸(paper cutting)是中国最为流行的传统民间艺术形式之一。中国剪纸有一千五百多年的历史，在明朝和清朝时期（the Ming and Qing Dynasties）特别流行。人们常用剪纸美化居家环境，特别是在春节和婚庆期间，剪纸被用来装饰门窗和房间，以增加喜庆的气氛。剪纸最常用的颜色是红色，象征健康和兴旺。中国剪纸在世界各地很受欢迎，经常被用作馈赠外国友人的礼物。

注意：此部分试题请在**答题卡2**上作答。

二、样题详解

Part Ⅰ   **Writing**
精彩范文

　　It is subtly demonstrated in the portrayal a teacher is teaching multiplication table in a certain classroom. **Unfortunately,** one of her students **holds the opinion that** this basic skill might be outdated by the time they are in the job market. **Currently, students in mounting numbers tend to believe it is unnecessary to** learn basic skills.

　　It is my view that the basic skills college students learn **will not turn old-fashioned. Instead, they will remain as vital as they will ever be. Above all,** though basic skills are often classified as less practical subjects that cannot be applied directly to one's future career, **it is** these basic subjects **that lay a solid foundation for** more advanced skills, preparing us for further studies. **In addition,** most of the basic skills, like calculating and literacy, **are always vital in** a variety of occupations. **Apparently,** no employer is willing to hire a graduate who cannot even fully understand a written contract. **For this reason** a lack of these skills may result in future career failure.

　　To conclude, the basic skills are crucial for our success. The more and better basic skills we master, the more likely we are to find a satisfactory job and live a happy life.

参考译文

如图所示，一名教师正在某个教室教乘法口诀表。然而，她的一名学生认为到他们就业的时候，这些基本技能也许会过时。现在，越来越多的学生倾向于认为没必要学习基本技能。

我认为，大学生所学的基本技能不会过时。相反，这些技能将一如既往地发挥重要作用。首先，尽管它们常被归类为不太实用的学科，不能直接应用到将来的工作中，但正是这些基础学科为学习更高级的技能打下坚实的基础，为深造做准备。此外，大部分的基本技能，如算术和读写能力，在各种职业中一直都是至关重要的。显而易见，没有哪个雇主愿意聘用连书面合同都看不懂的毕业生。因此，缺乏这些技能可能会造成将来职场上的失败。

总之，基本技能对于我们的成功至关重要。我们掌握的基本技能越多、越好，我们就越有可能找到一份满意的工作，并过上幸福的生活。

Part II	Listening Comprehension

Section A

1. D 生活场景

   听力原文：M: Finally I've got the chance to put on my new suit tonight. I hope to make a good impression on your family.

   W: Come on, it's only a family reunion. So jeans and T-shirts are just fine.

   Q: What does the woman mean?

   试题解析：根据女士说的jeans and T-shirts are just fine（牛仔和T恤就很好），可知选D"这位男士在这个场合可以穿着随便"。

2. C 住宿场景

   听力原文：W: From here, the mountains look as if you could just reach out and touch them.

   M: That's why I chose this lodge. It has one of the best views in Switzerland.

   Q: What is the man's chief consideration in choosing the lodge?

   试题解析：根据女士所说的From here, the mountains look as if you could just reach out and touch them（从这儿看，这些山看起来似乎你能伸手摸到它们）和男士所说的It has one of the best views in Switzerland

（它拥有瑞士最好的风景之一），可知选C"它的位置"。

3. D 就餐场景

听力原文：M: Miss, can I interest you in the pork special we're serving tonight? It's only $7.99, half the usual price, and it's very tasty.

W: Oh, really? I'll try it.

Q: What does the man say about the dish?

试题解析：根据男士说的It's only $7.99, half the usual price（它只有7.99美元，是平时价格的一半），可知选D"它很便宜"。

4. C 交通场景

听力原文：W: This crazy bus schedule has got me completely confused. I can't figure out when my bus to Cleveland leaves.

M: Why don't you just go to the ticket window and ask?

Q: What does the man suggest the woman do?

试题解析：根据男士说的Why don't you just go to the ticket window and ask（为什么你不去售票窗口问问呢），可知选C"去问工作人员"。

5. B 生活场景

听力原文：M: Shawn's been trying for months to find a job. But I wonder how he could get a job when he looks like that.

W: Oh, that poor guy! He really should shave himself every other day at least and put on something clean.

Q: What do we learn about Shawn?

试题解析：根据女士说的He really should shave himself every other day at least and put on something clean（他真应该至少每隔一天刮刮胡子而且穿上些干净衣服），可知选B"他对外表不太关心"。

6. C 交通场景

听力原文：M: Why didn't you stop when we first signaled you at the crossroads?

W: Sorry, I was just a bit absent-minded. Anyway, do I have to pay a fine?

Q: What do we learn from the conversation?

试题解析：根据男士说的Why didn't you stop when we first signaled you at the crossroads（我们一开始在十字路口给你做手势时，你为什么不停

下来)和女士说的do I have to pay a fine(我需要付罚款吗),可知选C"这位女士违反了交通法规"。

7. A 生活场景

听力原文:W: My hand still hurts from the fall on the ice yesterday. I wonder if I broke something.

M: I'm no doctor, but it's not black and blue or anything. Maybe you just need to rest it for a few days.

Q: What do we learn about the woman from the conversation?

试题解析:根据女士说的My hand still hurts from the fall on the ice yesterday. I wonder if I broke something(昨天我在冰上摔倒后现在手仍然很疼。我想知道是否我摔断了什么地方),可知选A"她昨天在一次事故中受伤了"。

8. D 生活场景

听力原文:M: I really can't stand the way David controls the conversation all the time. If he's going to be at your Christmas party, I just won't come.

W: I'm sorry you feel that way, but my mother insists that he come.

Q: What does the woman imply?

试题解析:根据女士说的my mother insists that he come(我母亲坚持要他来),可知选D"她不得不邀请David来参加晚会"。

Conversation One(学习场景)

本对话共5个半回合,内容是关于教授与学生就作文所进行的讨论。

M: Hello, Professor Johnson.

W: Hello, Tony. So what shall we work on today?

M: Well, the problem is that this writing assignment isn't coming out right. **(9)What I thought I was writing on was to talk about what a particular sport means to me—one I participate in.**

W: What sport did you choose?

M: I decided to write about cross-country skiing.

W: What are you going to say about skiing?

M: That's the problem. I thought I would write about how peaceful it is to be out in the country.

W: So why is that a problem?

M: As I start describing how quiet it is to be out in the woods, I keep mentioning how much effort it takes to keep going. Cross-country skiing isn't as easy as some people think. It takes a lot of energy. But that's not part of my paper, so I guess I should leave it out. （10）**But now I don't know how to explain that feeling of peacefulness without explaining how hard you have to work for it.** It all fits together. It's not like just sitting down somewhere and watching the clouds roll by. That's different.

W: Then you'll have to include that in your point. The peacefulness of cross-country skiing is the kind you earn by effort. Why leave that out? （11）**Part of your point you knew beforehand, but part you discovered as you wrote. That's common, right?**

M: Yeah, I guess so...

Questions 9 to 11 are based on the conversation you have just heard.

9. What is the topic of the man's writing assignment?

正确答案：B

试题解析：根据长对话"开头必考"原则，对话开头提到：What I thought I was writing on was to talk about what a particular sport means to me—one I participate in（我想写的是谈论一项特殊的运动对我意味着什么——我参与的某项运动），故选B"他参与的一项运动"。

10. What problem does the man have while working on his paper?

正确答案：C

试题解析：根据长对话"听到什么选什么"原则，原文提到But now I don't know how to explain that feeling of peacefulness without explaining how hard you have to work for it(但是现在我不知道在不去解释你必须为了它多么努力的情况下如何解释那种平静的感觉)，故选C"他无法决定是否包括为滑雪所做的努力"。

11. What does the woman say is common in writing papers?

正确答案：A

试题解析：根据长对话"结尾必考"的原则，结尾提到：Part of your point you knew beforehand, but part you discovered as you wrote. That's common, right（你的部分观点你之前就有，但部分观点你写作时才会发现。这是很正常的，对吧），故选A"在你写作的过程中，新的观点会出现"。

Conversation Two（访谈场景）

本对话共3个半回合，内容是关于一位车店老板的访谈。

W:（12）**Good evening, and welcome to this week's "Business World," the program for and about businesspeople.** Tonight we have Mr. Steven Kane who has just taken over an established bicycle shop. Tell us, Mr. Kane, what made you want to run your own store?

M: Well, I've always loved racing bikes and fixing them.（13）**When I was working full-time as a salesman for a big company, I seldom had time to enjoy my hobby.** I knew then that as soon as I had enough money to get my own business going, I'd do it. I had my heart set on it, and I didn't let anything stand in my way. （14）**When I went down to the bank and got a business loan, I knew I'd love being my own boss.** Now my time is my own. I open the store when I want and leave when I want.

W: You mean you don't keep regular hours?

M: Well, the sign on my store says the hours are 10:00 to 6:00, but if business is slower than usual, I can just lock up and take off early.

W: Have you hired any employees to work with you yet?

M: Yeah,（15）**a couple of friends of mine who love biking as much as I do. They help me out a few days a week.** It's great because... we play cards or just sit around and talk when there're no customers.

W: Thank you, Mr. Kane. We wish you success in your new business.

Questions 12 to 15 are based on the conversation you have just heard.

12. What is the woman doing?

正确答案：B

试题解析：根据长对话"开头必考"原则，开头提到：Good evening, and welcome to this week's "Business World," the program for and about businesspeople（晚上好，欢迎来到本周的"商业世界"，一个关于

商务人士并为商务人士提供服务的节目），故选B"主持一个夜间电视节目"。

13. What did Mr. Kane do before he took over the bicycle shop?

正确答案：C

试题解析：根据长对话"听到什么选什么"原则，原文提到：When I was working full-time as a salesman for a big company, I seldom had time to enjoy my hobby(当我在一家大公司做全职销售人员时，我很少有时间享受自己的爱好），故选C"他曾经做过一名销售人员"。

14. Why did the man take over a bicycle shop?

正确答案：A

试题解析：根据长对话"听到什么选什么"原则，原文提到：When I went down to the bank and got a business loan, I knew I'd love being my own boss（当我去银行并得到商业贷款时，我知道我喜欢做自己的老板），故选A"他想做自己的老板"。

15. What do we learn about the people working in the shop?

正确答案：A

试题解析：根据长对话"结尾必考"的原则，结尾提到：a couple of friends of mine who love biking as much as I do. They help me out a few days a week（我的几位朋友像我一样喜欢自行车。他们每周都帮我几天），故选A"他们都是这位男士的朋友"。

Section B

Passage One（故事类：友谊）

本文是一篇记叙文，记叙了作者与一位朋友自小的友谊。出题工整：开头一题、中间一题、结尾一题。

（16）**I first met Joe Gans when we were both nine years old, which is probably the only reason he's one of my best friends.** If I had first met Joe as a freshman in high school, we wouldn't even have had the chance to get to know each other. Joe is a day student, but I am a boarding student. We haven't been in the same classes, sports, or extracurricular activities. （17）**Nonetheless, I spend nearly every weekend at his house,** and we talk on the phone every night. This is not to say that we would not have been compatible if we had first met in our freshman year. Rather, we would not have been likely to spend enough time getting to know each other due to the lack of immediately visible mutual interests. In fact, to be honest, I struggle even now to think of things we have in common. But maybe that's what makes us enjoy each other's company so much. When I look at my friendship with Joe, (**18**) **I wonder how many people I've known whom I never disliked, but simply didn't take the time to get to know. Thanks to Joe, I have realized how little basis there is for the social divisions that exist in every community.** Since this realization, I have begun to make an even more determined effort to find friends in unexpected people and places.

Questions 16 to 18 are based on the passage you have just heard.

16. Why does the speaker say Joe Gans became one of his best friends?

正确答案：D

试题解析：根据"重视开头"原则，开头提到：I first met Joe Gans when we were both nine years old, which is probably the only reason he's one of my best friends（在我们9岁时，我第一次见到Joe Gans，这可能是他成为我一位最好朋友的唯一原因），故选D"他们从童年时就互相认识"。

17. Where does the speaker spend most of his weekends?

正确答案：B

试题解析：根据"听到什么选什么"原则，原文提到：Nonetheless, I spend nearly every weekend at his house（然而，我在他家几乎度过了每一个周末），故选B"在Joe家"。

18. What has the speaker learned from his friendship with Joe?

正确答案：C

试题解析：根据"关注结尾"原则，结尾提到：I wonder how many people I've known whom I never disliked, but simply didn't take the time to get to know. Thanks to Joe, I have realized how little basis there is for the social divisions that exist in every community(我不知道有多少我认识的人，我从未讨厌过，但只是没有时间去了解。多亏Joe，我认识到每个社会群体间都存在社会分化是多么没有道理），故选C"社会分化会通过相互了解来消除"。

Passage Two(社科类：讲座)

本文简要介绍了不同文化的人对待讲座的不同表现方式。出题工整：开头一题、中间一题、结尾一题。

（19）**While Gail Opp-Kemp, an American artist, was giving a speech on the art of Japanese brush painting to an audience that included visitors from Japan,** she was confused to see that many of her Japanese listeners had their eyes closed. Were they turned off because an American had the nerve to instruct Japanese in their own art form? Were they deliberately trying to signal their rejection of her? Opp-Kemp later found out that her listeners were not being disrespectful. （20）**Japanese listeners sometimes close their eyes to enhance concentration.** Her listeners were showing their respect for her by chewing on her words. Someday you may be either a speaker or a listener in a situation involving people from other countries or members of a minority group in North America. （21）**Learning how different cultures signal respect can help you avoid misunderstandings.** Here are some examples: In the deaf culture of North America, many listeners show applause not by clapping their hands but by waving them in the air. In some cultures, both overseas and in some minority groups in North America, listeners are considered disrespectful if they look directly at the speaker. Respect is shown by looking in the general direction but avoiding direct eye contact. In some countries, whistling by listeners is a sign of approval, while in other countries, it is a form of insult.

Questions 19 to 21 are based on the passage you have just heard.

19. What did Opp-Kemp's speech focus on?

　　正确答案：A

　　试题解析：根据"重视开头"原则，开头提到：While Gail Opp-Kemp, an American artist, was giving a speech on the art of Japanese brush painting to an audience that included visitors from Japan（在一位美国画家Gail Opp-Kemp正在为包括日本访客在内的听众进行一场关于日本绘画艺术的讲座时），故选A"日本绘画艺术"。

20. Why do Japanese listeners sometimes close their eyes while listening to a speech?

　　正确答案：B

试题解析：根据"听到什么选什么"原则，原文提到：Japanese listeners sometimes close their eyes to enhance concentration（日本听众有时闭上他们的眼睛来更好地集中注意力），故选B"集中注意力"。

21. What does the speaker try to explain?

正确答案：C

试题解析：根据"关注结尾"原则，结尾提到：Learning how different cultures signal respect can help you avoid misunderstandings（学习不同的文化如何表达尊重能帮助你避免误解），故选C"不同文化的听众如何表达尊重"。

Passage Three（社科类：演讲）

本文以消防队员挽救孩子生命为例，说明了信息量大的演讲对听众的益处。

出题工整：开头一题、中间两题、结尾一题。

One of the greatest heartbreaks for firefighters occurs when they fail to rescue a child from a burning building because the child—frightened by smoke and noise—hides under a bed or in a closet and is later found dead. （22）**Saddest of all is when children catch a glimpse of the masked firefighter but hide because they think they have seen a monster.** （23）**To prevent such tragedies, firefighter Eric Velez gives talks to children in his community, explaining that they should never hide during a fire.** He displays firefighters' equipment, including the oxygen mask, which he encourages his listeners to play with and put on. "If you see us," Velez tells them, "don't hide. We are not monsters. We have come to rescue you." Velez gives his presentations in English and Spanish. Growing up in San Francisco, he learned Spanish from his immigrant parents. Velez—and other firefighters throughout North America who give similar presentations—will never know how many lives they save through their talks, but it's a fact that informative speaking saves lives. For example, several months after listening to an informative speech, （24）**Pete Gentry in North Carolina rescued his brother, who was choking on food,** by using the method taught by student speaker Julie Parris. （25）**In addition to saving lives, informative speakers help people learn new skills, solve problems, and acquire fascinating facts about the exciting world in which they live.**

Questions 22 to 25 are based on the passage you have just heard.

22. Why do some children trapped in a burning building hide from masked firefighters?

正确答案：A

试题解析：根据"重视开头"原则，开头提到：Saddest of all is when children catch a glimpse of the masked firefighter but hide because they think they have seen a monster（最让人难过的是，当孩子们瞥到戴着面具的消防队员时，他们认为自己看到了怪物，藏了起来），故选A "他们误把消防队员当做怪物"。

23. What does the passage tell us about firefighter Eric Velez?

正确答案：B

试题解析：根据"听到什么选什么"原则，原文提到：To prevent such tragedies, firefighter Eric Velez gives talks to children in his community, explaining that they should never hide during a fire（为了防止这种悲剧发生，消防员Eric Velez给他们社区的孩子们进行讲座，告诉他们发生火灾时千万不要藏起来），故选B "他经常教孩子们发生火灾时该如何做"。

24. What do we learn about Pete Gentry?

正确答案：D

试题解析：根据"听到什么选什么"原则，原文提到：Pete Gentry in North Carolina rescued his brother, who was choking on food（北加州的Pete Gentry挽救了他吃东西噎着的弟弟），故选D "他挽救了吃东西噎着的弟弟的生命"。

25. What message is the speaker trying to convey?

正确答案：B

试题解析：根据"关注结尾"原则，结尾提到：In addition to saving lives, informative speakers help people learn new skills, solve problems, and acquire fascinating facts about the exciting world in which they live（除了挽救生命，信息量大的演讲者帮助人们学习新的技能、解决问题，并且了解他们生活的这个精彩世界的一些奇妙的事实），故选B"信息量大的演讲可以挽救生命"。

Section C

26. curious	31. mystery
27. figuring things out	32. appropriately
28. independent	33. trying it out
29. interacting with	34. refining
30. abstract	35. concepts

Part III   Reading Comprehension

Section A

本文介绍了美国最大的饥饿救助组织帮助低收入个人和家庭提供生活所需的情况。

名词(7个):
circling 围绕	communities 团体,社区
competition 竞争	gather 聚集
households 家庭,户	recession 衰退,不景气
surroundings 环境	

动词(7个):
accumulate 积聚,积累	circling 围绕
gather 集合;聚集	reported 报导
reviewed 回顾;评论	serves 服务;供给
survive 幸免,幸存	

形容词(3个):
domestic 国内的;家庭的	reported 据报道的
surrounding 周围的	

副词(2个): financially 财务上,经济上 formally 正式地,形式上

36. E domestic	41. N surrounding
37. C communities	42. J recession
38. O survive	43. K reported
39. H gather	44. I households
40. M serves	45. F financially

Section B

大学已成为国家竞争与保护和平的重要手段,本文详细分析了近年来海外留学生的发展和成就,着重阐述了美国留学政策的变迁以及美国人对于海外留学生观念的转变。

46. D 根据题干中的关键词internship（实习），global careers, undergraduate, international study将本句定位到D段最后两句：And in the United States, institutions are helping place students in summer internships（实习）abroad to prepare them for global careers. Yale and Harvard have led the way, offering every undergraduate at least one international study or internship opportunity—and providing the financial resources to make it possible。故选D。

47. C 根据题干中的关键词3.9, mid-1970s, annual rate定位到C段第二句：Over the past three decades the number of students leaving home each year to study abroad has grown at an annual rate of 3.9 percent, from 800,000 in 1975 to 2.5 million in 2004，故选C。

48. I 根据题干中的关键词threaten, competitiveness, positive impact定位到I段前两句：Most Americans recognize that universities contribute to the nation's well-being through their scientific research, but many fear that foreign students threaten American competitiveness by taking their knowledge and skills back home. They fail to grasp that welcoming foreign students to the United States has two important positive effects，故选I。

49. E 根据题干中的关键词the way, research, globalization定位到E段首句：Globalization is also reshaping the way research is done，故选E。

50. C 根据题干中的关键词twenty percent, the United States, newly hired professors, in science and technology, foreign定位到C段尾句：In the United States, 20 percent of the newly hired professors in science and engineering are foreign-born，故选C。

51. H 根据题干中的关键词September 11, the number of foreign students, U.S. universities, decreased sharply, changes in the visa process定位到H段第三句：In the wake of September 11, changes in the visa process caused a dramatic decline in the number of foreign students seeking admission to U.S. universities，故选H。

52. G 根据题干中的关键词funding, research, unsteady, the United States定位到G段前两句：For all its success, the United States remains deeply hesitant about sustaining the research-university model. Most politicians recognize the link between investment in science and national economic strength, but support for research funding has been unsteady，故选G。

53. F 根据题干中的关键词around the world, governments, encourage the model, linking, university-based science and industrial application定位到F段最后两

句：The link between university-based science and industrial application is often indirect but sometimes highly visible: Silicon Valley was intentionally created by Stanford University, and Route 128 outside Boston has long housed companies spun off from MIT and Harvard. Around the world, governments have encouraged copying of this model，故选F。

54. A 根据题干中的关键词universities, a powerful force, global integration定位到A段尾句：But at the same time, the opening of national borders to the flow of goods, services, information and especially people has made universities a powerful force for global integration, mutual understanding and geopolitical stability.，故选A。

55. I 根据题干中的关键词foreign students, bring American values, back to their home定位到I段第二句：They fail to grasp that welcoming foreign students to the United States has two important positive effects: first, the very best of them stay in the States and—like immigrants throughout history—strengthen the nation; and second, foreign students who study in the United States become ambassadors for many of its most cherished（珍视）values when they return home，故选I。

Section C
Passage One

本文主要围绕一份有关全球变暖影响的报告展开。文章首先说明报告的一些情况，其次说明该报告引起的反应，最后讲述发布报告的机构负责人安南对报告目的的诠释：由于90%以上由气候变化导致的损失发生在贫困地区，因此应加强资金从富裕地区流向贫困地区，提高贫困地区应对自然灾害的能力。

56. A 细节题。根据关键词the Global Humanitarian Forum定位到首段，而第二段是对其报告结果的进一步解释，故将本题定位在前两段。第二段尾句提到：该报告发现，人类影响带来的气候变化导致全球因营养不良等疾病而死亡的比率提高，A选项是对原句的同义转述，global warming对应climate change，故选A。

57. D 细节题。根据关键词the Forum's report定位到第三段，该段提到该报道遭到了气候和风险方面专家的批评，D选项中的some climate and risk experts是原文的some experts on climate and risk的信息复现，was challenged是对drew criticism的同义替换，故选D。

58. C 细节题。根据关键词Pielke和the Forum's report定位到第五段首句。该句提到, Pielke认为该论坛报告是"方法论的尴尬", 后面紧接着对此进行解释: 因为在脆弱地区, 在由人口增长和经济发展所造成的较大损失中, 没有办法区分出由人力驱使的全球变暖造成的死亡和经济损失。由此可见, 他认为就方法论而言, 该论坛的报告是无效的, 故选C。

59. D 细节题。根据关键词Soren Andreasen和the report定位到第6段。该段首先提出, Soren认为, 这些数字很明显只是粗略估计的。接着补充, 该报告的目标是12月要在哥本哈根商讨新国际气候条约的世界领导人。综合可知, 他认为论坛报告里的粗略估计是为了引起世界领导人的注意, 故选D。

60. B 细节题。根据关键词Annan和focus定位到末段首句。该句提到, 安南强调协商的重点是加强资金从富裕地区到贫穷地区的流动, 帮助提高贫困地区应对气候灾害的能力。由此可知, 安南认为怎样使富国更好地帮助贫困地区减少气候灾害是哥本哈根会议的重点, 故选B。

参考译文

据全球人道主义论坛(一个由联合国前秘书长科菲·安南领导的机构)的一份报告显示, 全球变暖每年导致超过30万人死亡, 造成约1250亿美元的经济损失。

周五要发布的这份报告, 分析了数据和现有的对健康、灾害、人口和经济趋势的研究。报告发现, 受到人类影响的气候变化使得全球因疾病(包括营养不良和与高温有关的健康问题)引起的死亡率提高。

但是, 甚至该报告在发布之前, 就遭到了气候和风险方面专家的批评, 他们质疑该报告的方法和结论。

报告称, 气候变化不仅造成了死亡, 而且使得3.25亿人的生命受到了严重影响, 这些人口主要分布在贫困国家。报告预测, 到2030年, 受影响的人口数字会翻倍。

科罗拉多州大学博尔德分校的政治科学家Roger Pielke是研究灾害趋势的, 他说该论坛的报告是"方法论的尴尬", 因为在脆弱地区, 在由人口增长和经济发展所造成的较大损失中, 没有办法区分出由人力驱使的全球变暖造成的死亡和经济损失。Pielke博士说: "气候变化是一个重要的问题, 需引起极大关注。"但是他说, 该报告"会有损对气候变化和灾难采取行为的动机, 因为该报告有重大瑕疵。"

然而, 来自达尔贝全球发展合作机构负责监督该报告撰写工作的一位社会科学家Soren Andreasen为报告进行了辩护。他说, 很明显, 这些数字只是粗略地估计的。他说, 该报告的目标是12月份在哥本哈根商讨新国际气候条约的世界领导人。

在一次描述该报告的新闻发布会上，安南先生强调，协商的重点是加强资金从富裕地区到贫穷地区的流动，以帮助提高贫困地区应对气候灾害的能力，同时控制吸热气体的排放。根据该报告，90%以上的由气候变化导致的人力和经济损失发生在贫困国家。

Passage Two

本文论述了夫妻因为钱的问题而发生的感情冲突，并对此给出了建议。文章首先引出下文"为钱而争吵"的话题，其次说明经济衰退期间夫妻因为钱的问题而吵架的次数增多，指出这种争吵尤其伤害夫妻感情，最后分析夫妻为钱争吵的原因，并对夫妻如何维系健康关系提出建议。

61. D 细节题。根据关键词the author say和vacationing定位到首段第四句。该句提到，我会说生命只有一次，我们工作又很辛苦，如果不能去度假，一切还有什么意义呢？由此可知，作者认为，如果不去度假，辛苦工作就没有意义。换言之，度假让辛苦工作变得有意义，故选D。

62. B 细节题。题干明确标出本题出处位于第二段首句，结合下文提到的"为钱争吵尤其伤害夫妻感情"可知，作者在第二段首句指的是在金钱上的分歧可能会破坏夫妻双方关系，故选B。

63. C 细节题。根据关键词YouGov poll of 2000 people和in a recession定位至第二段第三、四句。这两句提到，调查显示，22%的人表示会因为对钱的担忧而更多地与伴侣发生争执。衰退期间离婚率和分居率是否攀升尚不太明确——经济压力意味着夫妻吵架次数增多。选项C中conflicts between couples tend to rise是对couples argue more的同义转述，故选C。

64. A 细节题。根据关键词Kim Stephen believe定位至第三段首句，该句提到，他认为因为钱对于男人和女人来说象征着不同的东西，所以钱才成了大问题。文中的which指代前面提到的what it symbolizes，其中it指money，选项A是对其同义转述，故选A。

65. B 细节题。根据关键词at the end of the passage和couples should定位至末段最后两句。根据语境可知，这两句中的you指的是couples，作者借Kim Stephen的话对他们提出了建议：夫妻双方需要知道对方在做什么，在一种健康的关系中，夫妻双方不需要对钱有一致看法，但必须得谈论关于钱的事情。由此可知，选项B"为维系健康的关系而谈论钱的事情"是对原文的同义转述，故选B。

参考译文

我们每年都要争论"去不去度假"的问题。我的爱人会说"不去",因为"热水器会坏",或者"屋顶可能坍塌",并且"我们没有积蓄来渡过难关"。我会说"生命只有一次,我们工作又很辛苦,如果不能去度假一切还有什么意义呢?"经济衰退让人高兴之处在于它意味着明年我们将没有争吵——我们是不会去度假了。

既然金钱被公认为是最有可能让婚姻关系难以维系的诸多因素之一,我们应该心怀感激。对许多家庭来说,衰退不仅仅意味着不能预订假期。YouGov针对两千人开展的一项调查显示,有22%的人表示会因为对钱的担忧而更多地与伴侣发生争执。衰退期间分居率和离婚率是否攀升尚不太明确——经济压力意味着夫妻吵架次数增多,但是也使夫妻分离在经济上更难以承受。最近的一项研究显示,为钱争吵尤其伤害夫妻感情。争吵的特点是激烈的言语攻击,争吵往往重演,而且得不到解决,而且,与女人相比,争执更容易使男人愤怒。

职业心理学家Kim Stephenson认为,因为钱对于男人和女人来说象征着不同的东西,所以钱才成了大问题。他解释说:"人们说起钱来可能众口一词,但对钱的用途意见不一。他们会说,钱是用来存的,用来花的,用来获得安全感的,用来获得自由的,用来向某人表明你爱他(她)的。"他说,男人更有可能把钱视作购买地位、向父母显示自己小有成就的一种方式。

"最大的问题是夫妻之间想当然地认为彼此知道对方的财务状况,但事实并非如此。谈论钱比谈论死亡看起来有更多的禁忌。但是夫妻双方需要知道对方在做什么,谁把钱存进联名账户,各自又存有多少钱。在健康的婚姻关系中,夫妻双方不需要对钱有一致看法,但是必须得谈论钱。"

Part IV   Translation

Paper cutting is one of China's most popular traditional folk arts. Chinese paper cutting has a history of more than 1,500 years. It was widespread particularly during the Ming and Qing Dynasties. People often beautify their homes with paper cuttings. During the Spring Festival and wedding celebrations, in particular, paper cuttings are used to decorate doors, windows and rooms in order to enhance the joyous atmosphere. The color most frequently used in paper cutting is red, which symbolizes health and prosperity. Chinese paper cutting is very popular around the world and it is often given as a present to foreign friends.

第三章　写作新题型十大必背范文及十大万能框架

四级考试从1987年开考以来，写作题型多为提纲作文或情景作文，2012年12月突然考查了1991年6月和2002年6月只考查过两次的图表作文，在众多考生以为四级写作将考查图表作文之时，2013年6月四级写作三套真题均突然变为四级从未考查过的图画作文。体现了目前四级写作命题严重的反押题与反模板倾向。虽然新四级写作样题为图画作文，但希望考生务必扎扎实实提高写作实力，全面复习提纲、情景、图表、图画等各种题型以及记叙、描写、说明、议论、应用文等各种文体，做好充分准备。

新题型大纲样题虽然只有两点提纲，但最好写成三段，首段应该简单描述图画，首句进行总体描述，点出图画中的人物+动作+环境，次句进行细节描述，尾句进行小结。第二段应进行图画的意义阐释，挖掘图画深层含义，首句应为主题句，点出图画象征寓意，其次可以用因果、举例、正反等各种手段进行论证，尾句进行小结。尾段可进行归纳结论或提出建议措施，首句应写出结论句，其次提出评论或建议，最后包装结尾，展望未来。

一、新题型十大必背范文

（一）做小事的重要性

Directions: *For this part, you are allowed 30 minutes to write an essay. You should start your essay with a brief description of the picture and then express your views on the importance of doing small things before undertaking something big. You should write at least 120 words but no more than 180 words. Write your essay on Answer Sheet 1.*

If you can empty the dustbin here, you can do anything!

Dad, I'm a bit worried about disposing of nuclear waste.

dustbin

精彩范文

It is subtly revealed in the caricature that a son is expressing his concern about disposing of nuclear waste **to his father, while his father asked him to** empty the dustbin first. **This thought-provoking portrayal illustrates to us the significance of** doing small things before undertaking something big **and reminds us of an old Chinese saying,** "Sweeping your own house before conquering the world."

In the first place, through doing small things, **we accumulate precious experience and essential practical skills, which help us to get better prepared for** any upcoming big things. **In the second place,** doing trivial matters **helps us develop good habits, such as perseverance and patience, with which we won't give up or escape easily when confronted with bigger difficulties.**

Admittedly, it is reasonable for us to aim high and be ambitious, but before we are to undertake something big, we should try hard to fulfill simple tasks such as empty the dustbin.

参考译文

如图所示，儿子对父亲说担心核废料的处理问题，而父亲则对儿子说如果他能先把垃圾倒了，就什么事都能做好。这幅发人深省的漫画向我们揭示了做大事之前先把小事做好的重要性，并且让我们联想到"一屋不扫，何以扫天下"这句中国俗语。

首先，通过做小事，我们能积累宝贵的经验及必要的实用技能，为将来所有可能发生的大事做好准备。其次，做小事有助于我们养成良好的习惯，如坚持和耐心。有了它们，我们在遇到更大的困难时才不会轻易放弃或退缩。

不可否认，我们应该目标高远并且具有雄心壮志，但在我们做大事之前，我们应该努力把像倒垃圾这样的小事做好。

(二)文学

Directions: *For this part, you are allowed 30 minutes to write an essay. You should start your essay with a brief description of the picture and then express your views on the importance of literature. You should write at least **120** words but no more than **180** words. Write your essay on **Answer Sheet 1**.*

LITERATURE

"Just think of it as if you're reading
a long text-message."

精彩范文

As is symbolically portrayed in the cartoon, when a teacher assigns her student to read a literature book, she tells him to think of it as a long text-message. **It reminds us of the significance of** reading literature **while most of the people are spending much more time** reading text-messages than literary works.

Since reading literature **cannot only broaden our horizon but also enrich our mind, it is imperative for us to** read literature. **To be specific,** reading classic works **is a real eye-opener, from which we can acquire theoretical knowledge of different historical events and cultural traditions. In addition, the moral outlooks and views of life revealed** in great works **offer great nourishment and contribute to our growth and wisdom.**

To demonstrate, whenever I am confronted with obstacles, I will reflect on the books I have read, imagining what the heroes would do if they were in my situation. **Then normally I will get the power and overcome any difficulty. To conclude,** reading literature regularly **is crucial to a more colorful and wiser life.**

参考译文

如图所示，当老师在布置文学作品阅读任务时，告诉学生将它当作长篇手机短信对待。这幅图提醒我们，在大多数人阅读手机短信远多于文学作品的当下，阅读文学作品尤为重要。

事实上，由于阅读文学作品不但能拓宽我们的视野，还能充实我们的心智，我们迫切需要阅读文学作品。具体而言，阅读名著能使我们大开眼界，了解到各种重大历史事件以及文化传统。其次，文学作品中传达的道德观和人生观为我们提供了极好的养分，让我们成长并变得睿智。

以我自己为例，每当我遇到困难，我都会想起读过的小说，想象书中的主人公如果处于我的处境会怎么做。然后我通常都会从中获得克服困难的力量。总之，对于更精彩及睿智的人生，经常阅读文学作品至关重要。

（三）流行文化：网络

Directions: *For this part, you are allowed 30 minutes to write an essay. You should start your essay with a brief description of the picture and then express your views on the impact of the Internet on interpersonal relationship. You should write at least **120** words but no more than **180** words. Write your essay on **Answer Sheet 1**.*

网络的"近"与"远"

精彩范文

As is symbolically illustrated in the cartoon, a large number of people are surfing on line within a stretching spider web, either to entertain themselves or to meet the work's needs. **Unfortunately, it seems rather ironic to present people** separated from each other by the spider web when they attempt to communicate.

The metaphorical and impressive portrayal has subtly revealed the duality of the relationship between man and Internet. On the one hand, there is no denying that Internet **is currently one of the most efficient media used for interpersonal communication. But on the other hand, a good many people admit that they are too much addicted to** Internet **to maintain** face-to-face contact with their friends and colleagues. **Once indulged in the fictitious world, people feel reluctant to approach others and to concentrate on real life.**

Hence, it is necessary for us to use Internet **in a reasonable way and restrain from overindulgence. After all,** Internet **is invented to connect you and me, and to bring conveniences to our life rather than set a barrier to keep people beyond reach.**

参考译文

这幅漫画象征性地阐释了无论是为了自我娱乐还是适应工作的需求，很多人在一个拉伸的蜘蛛网之内上网。然而，看来相当讽刺的地方是，这幅图呈现了他们在试图互相交流的同时，却被蜘蛛网彼此隔开。

这幅含有比喻意义并使人印象深刻的图画象征性地揭示了人与互联网之间的双重关系。一方面，不可否认网络目前是用于人际交流的最高效的媒介之一。但另一方面，很多人承认他们太沉迷于网络而不愿与朋友和同事保持面对面接触。一旦沉迷于这种虚幻世界，人们就不愿接近他人并关注现实生活。

因此，我们很有必要合理使用互联网，避免过度沉迷。毕竟，人们发明互联网是为了连接你和我，为我们的生活带来方便，而非设置障碍使人们彼此疏远。

(四)人生哲理：合作

Directions: *For this part, you are allowed 30 minutes to write an essay. You should start your essay with a brief description of the picture and then express your views on the importance of teamwork. You should write at least **120** words but no more than **180** words. Write your essay on **Answer Sheet 1**.*

你一条腿，我一条腿；
你我一起，走南闯北。

精彩范文

As is vividly depicted in the picture, two disabled men are running fast through teamwork although each of them has only one leg. **Obviously, it is** teamwork **that makes it possible for them to** go anywhere they want to.

Simple as it is, what the picture conveys to us is thought-provoking. With the development of economy and society, competition is increasingly fierce. It is impossible for anyone to finish a work all by himself. **Hence, people in mounting numbers put great emphasis on** teamwork. **In fact, it has been universally acknowledged that** the ability of teamwork **is the most essential qualification that anyone who wants to achieve success should possess.**

Accordingly, it is imperative for us to take some measures to enhance the sense of teamwork **in our society. We should bear in mind that** teamwork **is of great significance to both our society and ourselves. Everyone should have the ability of** teamwork. **Only in this way can we achieve success and only in this way can our society become more harmonious to live in.**

参考译文

如图画中所生动描绘的,两个残疾人通过团队合作正在快速奔跑,尽管每人只有一条腿。显而易见,正是合作才使得他们走南闯北成为可能。

尽管这幅图画很简单,但它向我们表达了发人深省的含义。随着经济和社会的发展,竞争日渐激烈。任何人都无法完全独立完成一份工作。因此,越来越多的人开始重视团队合作。事实上,合作的能力是想要获得成功的任何人都应该具备的最重要的素质,这一点已经得到了普遍认可。

因此,我们迫切需要采取措施来提高人们的合作意识。我们应该牢记,合作对于社会和我们自身都非常重要。每个人都应该具备合作的能力。只有这样我们才能获得成功,而且只有这样社会才能变得更加和谐。

(五)社会热点:爱心

Directions: *For this part, you are allowed 30 minutes to write an essay. You should start your essay with a brief description of the picture and then express your views on the importance of love. You should write at least **120** words but no more than **180** words. Write your essay on **Answer Sheet 1**.*

精彩范文

    The picture illustrates the real meaning of love, **by stressing the fact that** love **is emotional strength, which can support us no matter how dark the world around us becomes. As a matter of fact, throughout history people of many different cultures have regarded** love **as the most sublime of human emotions.**

    As an illustration of the power of love, **we should remember how the Chinese people of all nationalities respond to the call to help the victims of the deadly earthquake in Sichuan Province in 2008. Although their incomes are still low by international standards, people all over the country do not hesitate to donate whatever they can—be it money or goods—to help their needy fellow citizens. Furthermore, they do this with no thought of gain for themselves.**

    It is my view that the best way to show love **is to help people who are more unfortunate than we are. Only by doing so can we help to make the world a better place.**

参考译文

    这幅图画诠释了爱的真正含义，它强调了爱心是情感的力量，不论我们周围的世界多么黑暗，爱心都能支撑我们。事实上，历史上处于不同文化中的人们都把爱当作人类最高尚的情感。

    举一个例子证明爱心的力量，我们应该记得2008年中国各族人民如何响应号召去支援四川地震中的遇难同胞。尽管他们的收入按照国际标准衡量还是处于低水平，但是全国人民毫不犹豫地尽其所能捐献——不管是钱，还是物品——去帮助那些受难的同胞们。并且，他们这么做不考虑自己的得失。

我认为，表达爱的最好方式是帮助比我们更加不幸的人。只有这样我们才能把这个世界变成一个更美好的地方。

(六)社会热点：两代关系

Directions: *For this part, you are allowed 30 minutes to write an essay. You should start your essay with a brief description of the picture and then express your views on the importance of self-dependence. You should write at least **120** words but no more than **180** words. Write your essay on **Answer Sheet 1**.*

温室花朵经不起风雨

精彩范文

  The set of drawings above vividly depict the destiny of a flower in different circumstances. **As is shown in the first cartoon,** the flower is growing in full bloom in a comfortable greenhouse that shelters it from the threatening lightning and storm. **On the contrary,** when removed from the greenhouse and exposed to the driving rain, the flower soon fades and withers.

  The delicate flower **is naturally associated with young people, to be specific,** the only children in our current society; the greenhouse epitomizes parents' doting care and abundant material supplies that can shield the children from the storms, or the harsh reality. **Once the young people begin to** seek independence **and accept challenges from the real world, they are found too spoiled to be strong enough in the face of difficulties.**

  Accordingly, it is vital for us to derive positive implications from these thought-provoking drawings. Only by undergoing more challenges and toils in adversity **can young people cultivate strong personality and ability, and only in this way can they become winners in this competitive world.**

参考译文

上述这组图画生动描述了一朵鲜花在不同环境中的命运。如第一幅漫画所示，这朵鲜花正在舒适的温室里绽放，温室保护它免于遭受可怕的闪电和风雨。相反，当被搬出温室并暴露在风雨之下时，鲜花很快就凋谢枯萎了。

这朵娇弱的鲜花自然和我们的年轻人联系起来，具体而言，就是当代社会的独生子女。温室是保护孩子免受风雨的父母溺爱和优越物质条件的缩影，而风雨就是严峻的现实。一旦年轻人开始寻求独立并且接受来自现实世界的挑战，人们发现他们已经被惯坏了，在困难面前无法足够坚强。

总之，我们很有必要从这些发人深省的图画中得出积极的含义。只有经历更多的挑战和磨炼，年轻人才能培养强大的个性和能力，而且只有这样他们才能在这个竞争激烈的世界中成为赢家。

(七)人生哲理：信心

Directions: *For this part, you are allowed 30 minutes to write an essay. You should start your essay with a brief description of the picture and then express your views on the importance of confidence. You should write at least **120** words but no more than **180** words. Write your essay on **Answer Sheet 1**.*

精彩范文

As we can see from the picture, a football match is going on. On guarding the goal, the man on the left seems to be keeping a "huge one" that is easy and inevitable for a goal, while the person on the right hesitates to kick the ball with an illusion about the "huge keeper". **It is obvious that** both of them exaggerate the difficulties in front of them.

When weighing in the mind, we find there is an apparent tendency underlying this phenomenon: the lack of confidence. Firstly, it is well-known that we exist in a dynamic world with various difficulties. We can do nothing but face them. Secondly, attitude is the key point to take the first step. Assuming bravery and confidence to solve the problem, you will find the question is not as "huge" as you imagine. So, with confidence and the right assessment of the difficulties, try and exert our strength, and then we will overcome all the problems.

On the whole, I believe we young people should face the difficulties in right manner.

参考译文

如图所示,一场足球赛正在进行。左边的人似乎在守一个对于射门来说轻而易举、必进不可的"大门",而右边的人由于有"守门员高大无比"的幻觉,踢球很犹豫。显而易见,他们两个人都夸大了面前的困难。

当我们仔细思考时,我们就会发现在这个现象之下有一个明显的趋势:缺乏自信。首先,众所周知,我们生活在一个充满各种困难的多元化世界。我们别无选择,只能面对。其次,态度是采取第一步的关键。拥有勇气和信心来解决问题,你就会发现问题并非你想象的那么"严重"。因此,拥有信心和对困难的正确估计,并且竭尽全力,我们就将解决所有的问题。

总而言之,我认为我们年轻人应该以正确的方式面对困难。

(八)教育文化:教育

Directions: *For this part, you are allowed 30 minutes to write an essay. You should start your essay with a brief description of the picture and then express your views on the importance of choice. You should write at least **120** words but no more than **180** words. Write your essay on **Answer Sheet 1**.*

选择

精彩范文

As is vividly shown in the cartoon, for undergraduate college students, deciding what to do upon graduation **can be a tough decision to say the least. For the vast majority of students, the choice is among** finding a job, pursuing postgraduate studies, going abroad or starting one's own business. **And below the drawing, there is a topic which says:** "choice".

When making this decision, students should consider a variety of factors, including their personal preferences and financial status. **The first factor that they should consider is their own** personal preferences. **Some students may have** entrepreneurial **ambitions and dream of** running their own business. **In addition, some students or their families are able to support** the tuition fees of postgraduate studies or studying overseas, **while for others it would be too much of a financial strain.**

When it comes time for university graduates to decide their next step in life, **there is no one right or wrong choice for everyone. Rather, each student must reach his or her own conclusion.**

参考译文

如图所示,对于本科生来说,决定毕业之后做什么毫不夸张地说是一个艰难的选择。大多数学生都在求职、考研、出国和创业之间徘徊。在漫画下面的话题显示:"选择"。

在做决定的时候,学生应该考虑很多因素,包括个人偏好和经济状况。大学生第一个要考虑的就是自己的个人偏好。有些学生希望成为企业家,梦想拥有自己的公司。其次,有些学生自己或家里可以负担考研或出国的学费,而对有些人来说这些费用是一项沉重的负担。

大学毕业之际,每个人在决定人生中的下一步时无所谓对和错。更恰当地说,每个学生必须给出属于自己的结论。

(九)人生哲理:坚持

Directions: *For this part, you are allowed 30 minutes to write an essay. You should start your essay with a brief description of the picture and then express your views on the importance of making constant efforts. You should write at least **120** words but no more than **180** words. Write your essay on **Answer Sheet 1**.*

终点又是新起点

精彩范文

It is vividly depicted in the cartoon that a boy is running along the racetrack with painstaking efforts, sweat pouring down his face. Straight ahead lies a sign which indicates a new "starting point" and urges him to continue rushing to the next destination.

Undoubtedly, the cartoon conveys the meaning that life is like the process of running **in which one should** make constant efforts and never stop making progress. **Owing to the quickening pace of life, competition goes increasingly fierce in all walks of life, stimulating everyone to** pursue one goal after another. **Once a person** stops making progress, **he can hardly maintain his past glory and survive in this competitive world. Generally speaking, neither a country nor a person can** remain stagnant.

An illustration is closely related to us, the examinees. After we pass this test, we still have to strive for success **in our future academic study, employment and career. On the whole, this example effectively clarifies the saying that** "destination is another starting point."

参考译文

如图生动所示，一个男孩正在沿着跑道跑步。他付出艰苦的努力，汗水淌下脸庞。在他的正前方有标志显示这是一个新的"起点"，激励他继续朝着下一个目标前进。

毫无疑问，这幅漫画显示了如下含义：人生就像跑步的过程一样，人们应该不断努力，绝不停止进步。由于生活节奏的加快，各行各业的竞争变得日益激烈，激励每个人追求一个又一个的目标。一旦一个人不再进步，他很难保持过去的荣誉，在这个竞争激烈的世界中生活下去。总而言之，无论一个国家还是个人都不能停滞不前。

一个例子与我们考生密切相关。在我们通过了这次考试之后，我们仍须在我们未来的学业、职业和事业上为了成功而继续奋斗。总之，这个例子清楚地证明了这一说法："终点又是新起点"。

（十）流行文化：微博、微信

Directions: *For this part, you are allowed 30 minutes to write an essay. You should start your essay with a brief description of the picture and then express your views on the importance of making constant efforts. You should write at least __120__ words but no more than __180__ words. Write your essay on **Answer Sheet 1**.*

精彩范文

    In recent years, Microblog and WeChat have become a kind of fashion and various people, no matter the young or the old, the famous or the ordinary, are in favor of joining in creating their own Microblogs or WeChat and visiting others. As is shown in the pictures, there are symbols of WeChat and Microblog.

    In my opinion, this is the result of social development. To start with, as a convenient means of conveying information, Microblog and WeChat combine the characteristics of web pages and that of forums to enable more people to participate in problem discussion and debate. Besides, they provide modern people a platform, where friends can talk about, exchange, express the emotions and relieve stress.

Although there are a great many benefits of using Microblog and WeChat, **their disadvantages should be taken into consideration. After all,** using them take up time; **if not handled properly, it would** delay the routine work and study. **Moreover, as regards** communication between friends, the manner of expressing views should be polite, avoiding disputes and quarrels.

参考译文

近年来，微博和微信已成为一种时尚，各色人等无论老幼、名人或普通人都喜欢创建他们自己的微博或微信并访问他人的。如图所示，微信和微博有它们的标志。

在我看来，这是社会发展的结果。首先，作为传达信息的一种便利方式，微博和微信结合了网页和论坛的特点，使得更多人可以参与问题讨论和争论。此外，它们给现代人提供了一个平台，在这里朋友们能够讨论、交流、表达情感以及舒缓压力。

尽管使用微博和微信有很多优点，我们也应考虑其缺点。毕竟，使用它们占用很多时间，如果不能适当使用，可能延误日常的工作和生活。此外，至于朋友之间的沟通，表达观点的方式应该礼貌当先，避免争吵。

二、新题型十大万能框架

温馨提示：鉴于目前四级写作存在严重的反模板倾向，本部分仅供参考，切勿照搬原文，如采用也需多加改动，避免留下模板痕迹。如想取得写作高分，考生还需扎扎实实提高写作实力，背诵、默写、仿写经典范文和句型，多读、多背、多写、多改！

框架一：教育文化

It is subtly revealed in the portrayal that _____ Obviously, _____ We are informed that _____

Some driving factors that contribute to the above-mentioned changes may be summarized as follows. First and foremost, China has become particularly active in _____, which leads to the increasing demand of qualified_____ In addition, the development of job market on the whole cannot keep pace with the expansion of college graduates, which obliges a large number of students to stay on campus for another three years to get better prepared for their career.

On the other side of the coin, however, this tendency may bring about a good many problems, such as the waste of talent. It is necessary for us to take effective measures to ensure this situation doesn't get out of hand, and encourage students to choose majors in which theoretical knowledge and practical skills will be demanded in the job market.

参考译文

这幅漫画微妙揭示了……显而易见,……我们得知:……

促成上述变化的一些主要原因可以概括如下。首先,中国在……方面已经变得异常活跃,这导致了高素质……需求的增加。此外,就业市场的总体发展无法跟上大学毕业生的增加,这促使很多学生继续待在校园里三年时间,为就业进行更好的准备。

然而,问题的另一方面是,这种趋势可能带来很多问题,例如人才的浪费。我们必须采取有效措施确保这一状况不会失控,同时鼓励学生们选择那些在就业市场上所需要的既有理论知识又有实践技能的专业。

框架二: 教育文化

The exaggerative and impressive portrayal has subtly revealed the duality of the relationship between adolescents and our society. What the picture conveys goes far beyond merely being ironic. Instead, it carries social meanings as well.

Careful deliberation of this problem has given me several fundamental factors as to why this should be so. Inexperienced and gullible young people plunge into the illusory world of electric games, on-line chat or even pornography. Numerous illustrations can be given, but this will suffice. Looking at this, how can we stay aloof and easy?

It is my view that, first of all, the whole of society should attach utmost significance to the sound growth of the juvenile. In addition, proper guidance and protection of adults and schools are vital to adolescents. Since neither of the suggestions can effectively solve the problem, there is an increased awareness that the two solutions may be combined with other possible solutions to produce the best effect.

参考译文

这幅夸张并且令人印象深刻的图画微妙揭示了年轻人与社会之间的双重关系。这幅图画所表达的远远只是讽刺。相反，它也具有社会内涵。

对这个问题的仔细思考告诉了我这个问题出现的几点根本原因。无知轻信的年轻人陷入电子游戏、网络聊天甚至色情的虚幻世界中不能自拔。可以给出无数的例子，但是这个就足够了。有鉴于此，我们怎能无动于衷？

在我看来，首先，全社会都应该高度重视青少年的健康成长。其次，成人和学校的正确引导和爱护对青少年至关重要。由于这两个措施都不能单独有效地解决这个问题，人们越来越意识到为了达到最佳效果，我们可以把这两个措施和其他可能的措施结合起来。

框架三：教育文化

As is vividly revealed in the portrayal that _____ （人物＋动作＋环境). In the portrayal, there are _____ （挖掘细节词，串连成句). To begin with, the purpose of the picture is to show us that _____ （点出图画的表层含义), yet the symbolic implications subtly conveyed should be taken more seriously.

Superficially, it seems somewhat reasonable, but when weighing in the mind, we find there is an apparent tendency underlying this phenomenon: _____ （点出主题). There are several causes for the significant problem of_____ For one thing, _____ （原因一). For another, _____ （原因二). I can think of no better illustration than the following one _____ （举例论证).

Hence, the thought-provoking social phenomenon is a double-edged sword which can exert profound influence on the sound growth of the juvenile. To begin with, _____ （建议一). Furthermore, we can frequently use these drawings to enlighten adolescents to _____ （建议二).

参考译文

这幅图画生动揭示了……在图画中，……首先，这些图画的目的是告诉我们……，然而我们应该认真对待它们所传达的象征意义。

表面上看，它似乎有一些道理，但当我们仔细思考时，会发现在这个现象之下有一种明显的趋势：……对于这个……的严重问题，有几个原因。首先，……其次，……我想不出什么例子比下面这个更有说服力……

因此，这个发人深省的社会现象其实是把双刃剑，能够深刻影响青年人的健康成长。首先，……其次，我们可以经常利用这些图画来启发年轻人……

框架四：环境保护

As is vividly depicted in the cartoon, with the speedy social and economic development, the number of people who _____ has dramatically increased/shrunk. In the picture, there is/are _____ At the lower part of it, we can see several Chinese characters which read "_____"

The purpose of this picture is to show us that due attention has to be paid to _____. Owing to _____, _____ If we let this situation continue as it is, we do not know where _____ will be in the forthcoming future. By that time, our society will suffer a great destruction.

Accordingly, it is imperative for us to take drastic measures. For one thing, we should appeal to the authorities to make strict laws and regulations to control _____ For another, we should cultivate the awareness of people that _____ is vital to us. Only in this way can we protect our _____ Also I reckon that we humans can surmount this difficulty, and we will have a brighter future.

参考译文

如图所示，随着社会经济的迅速发展，……的人数明显下降。在图画中，有……在图画下方，我们可以看到一些汉字显示："……"

这些图画的目的是告诉我们应该充分重视……。由于……，……的数量明显下降。如果我们对这种情况听之任之，我们不知道……的未来在哪。到那个时候，我们的社会将遭受巨大的破坏。

因此，我们很有必要采取严厉措施。一方面，我们应该呼吁政府制定严格的法律控制……另一方面，我们应该提高人们的意识：……对我们非常重要。只有这样才能保护我们的……同时，我认为我们人类能够克服这个困难，并将拥有更加美好的未来。

框架五：环境保护

The picture indicates that there has been significant changes in _____ in the past _____ years. It can be seen in the picture that _____ The caption reads, "_____"

There is no denying that _____ is the indication of civilization, progress and development. Nevertheless, it causes the serious problem of _____ Scientists have warned that unless effective measures are taken, the problem of _____ will eventually get out of hand. Actually, people are showing a real concern over the problem. For example, people _____ so as to prevent it from happening.

Indeed, the earth is our home and we have the duty to take care of it for ourselves and our descendents. In my opinion, we should work out concrete solutions to the problem of _____ On the one hand, we should _____ On the other hand, it is necessary for us to _____ Only in this way can we really solve the problem of _____.

参考译文

这幅图画揭示了在过去……年在……发生了巨大的变化。从图画中可以看出……文字说明显示：……

不可否认，……是文明、进步和发展的象征。然而，它导致……的严重问题。科学家们已经警告，除非采取有效措施，否则……的问题将最终失控。事实上，人们对于这一问题已经表达了真实的关切。例如，人们……以便阻止它发生。

实际上，地球是我们的家园，我们有责任为了我们自己和后代来照顾它。在我看来，我们应该针对……的问题制定出具体的解决方案。一方面，我们应该……另一方面，我们必须……只有这样我们才能真正解决……的问题。

框架六：教育文化

The past several years have witnessed a phenomenon that a _____ have been arising from all walks of life. Regretfully, quite a lot of _____, just as the man in the given cartoon _____

The first goal of higher education is to accomplish the transition from schools to society. Study is no longer the only purpose for college students in school, and they should learn to deal with a variety of problems, which can be viewed as practice before stepping into real society. The second purpose of college education is to broaden the horizons of university students. There are a good many communities and activities in universities and students are able to acquaint themselves with a large number of aspects which they may have never heard of before entering university.

In accordance with the statements above, the university should cultivate the comprehensive qualities of students. Study is just one of the most important components of college education. As for me, the goal of university education is to endow the students with abilities of mental analysis, study and independence.

参考译文

过去几年发生了一个现象：各行各业开始出现了各种各样的……遗憾的是，相当多的……，正如漫画中的人……

大学教育的第一个目标就是完成从学校向社会的转变。学习不再是大学生在学校的唯一目的，他们应该学会处理各种各样的问题。大学教育的第二个目标是开阔大学生的视野。大学里有很多社团和活动，学生们可以熟悉他们上大学前从未听说的很多方面。

根据上述论证，大学应该培养学生的综合素质。学习只是大学教育中最重要的一个部分。对我而言，大学教育的目标就是赋予学生分析思辨、学习及独立的能力。

框架七：社会热点

As is shown in the caricature, _____ And below the cartoon, there is a topic which says: _____

As the living standard improves, people in mounting numbers are paying attention to their healthy conditions. It is true that physical factors affect one's health conditions a great deal, but at the same time, we should not neglect the mental factors. Many scientific researchers have known that anger, suspicion and anxiety do great harm to human bodies, while being optimistic can cure some small diseases. We have also heard of a great many people who live much longer than doctors' prediction after they have been diagnosed incurable diseases. That is because they keep a good mood and struggle with the difficulties in life.

People use all kinds of methods to keep healthy because they want to live happily. Then in my point of view, there is no other way than keeping a healthy attitude toward life can make people happier and healthier both physically and mentally.

参考译文

如图所示，……漫画下方有个小标题写道：……

随着生活水平的提高，越来越多的人开始关注自身的健康状况。生理因素确实非常影响人的健康，但同时我们不应忽视心理因素。很多科学家已经发现：愤怒、怀疑和焦虑对人体伤害极大，而保持乐观则能治愈一些小的疾病。我们也听说过很多人在诊断出不治之症以后，活得远远超过医生的预期。这是由于他们保持了良好的心态，并与生活中的困难进行斗争。

因为人们想要快乐地生活，所以他们采用各种各样的方法来保持健康。在我看来，最好的方式就是对生活保持一种健康的心态，它能使人们无论在生理上还是在心理上都更加快乐健康。

框架八：图表作文

The chart clearly reveals the statistics of _____ in a certain _____ According to the survey, there has been a steady increase from _____ to _____ for '_____', while the data of _____ jumped markedly to _____

From the table, the writer wants to convey such a message: utmost importance should be attached to _____ Some driving factors that contribute to the above-mentioned issue may be summarized as follows. To begin with, a clear correlation is suggested that _____ has exerted tremendously profound influence on the development of our society. In addition, it is imperative for us to cultivate the awareness of _____ in our society. From what has been discussed so far, it is obvious that _____ is of great concern in our life.

Truly, apart from those benefits, _____ might have its drawbacks. But in my eyes, its negative impacts depend, to a large extent, on how it is used. As a consequence, if we make proper use of it, _____ will never do us more harm than good.

参考译文

这幅图表清晰显示了……的数据。根据调查，从……到……，……从稳步上升到……，而……的数据则急剧上升到……

从图表中，作者想要表达这一信息：我们应该充分重视……造成上述问题的主要原因可以被概括如下。首先，我们可以清楚地看出：……对我们社会的发展产生了非常深远的影响。其次，我们急需培养社会中的……意识。根据上述讨论，显而易见……在我们的生活中值得充分关注。

除了这些优点，……确实也有缺点。但在我看来，它的负面影响在很大程度上取决于人们如何使用。因此，如果我们适当使用，……带给我们的坏处绝不会大于好处。

框架九：书信

Dear Professor _____,

I am very pleased to inform you that Beijing University is organizing an academic conference entitled "_____" on December 8-9 in Beijing.

You are cordially invited to participate in this important Chinese academic event to be our guest speaker. You will be welcome to participate fully in the activities of the conference, including workshops, seminars, and other recreational activities. Your round trip air ticket, accommodation and meal expenses will be subsidized.

We look forward to seeing you in this conference and to having you as a significant part of this event. If you accept this invitation, please advise us of your date of arrival, so that we can make necessary arrangements.

Yours sincerely,

Li Ming

参考译文

尊敬的……教授：

我很荣幸地通知您北京大学将在12月8至9日在北京举办一个名为……的学术会议。

我们诚挚地邀请您参加这次重要的中国学术会议并作为我们的客座发言人。我们将欢迎您全程参与大会的各项活动，包括讨论会、研讨会和其他娱乐活动。我们将负担您的往返机票与食宿费用。

我们期待着您参与会议并作为本次会议的重要一员。如果您接受邀请，请告知到达日期，以便我们进行必要的安排。

您真诚的，

李明

框架十：告示

Notice

December 21, 2013

To improve students' ability and enrich after-class activities, the Students' Union of Department of _____ is organizing a _____ to be held on Saturday next week (12 January) at the Students' Auditorium. Those who are interested in taking part in it may sign up with the monitor of their classes before Tuesday next week. Everybody is welcome to be present at it.

The Students' Union

参考译文

告示

2013年12月21日

为提高同学们的能力并丰富课外活动，……系学生会将于下周六(1月12日)在学生大礼堂组织……有兴趣参加的同学请于下周二之前在本班班长处报名。欢迎大家积极参加。

学生会

第四章　短文听写新题型十大经典模拟题

一、经典模拟题一

Directions: *In this section, you will hear a passage three times. When the passage is read for the first time, you should listen carefully for its general idea. When the passage is read for the second time, you are required to fill in the blanks with the exact words you have just heard. Finally, when the passage is read for the third time, you should check what you have written.*

Around 120 years ago, Ebbinghaus began his study of memory. He ___26___ studying how quickly the human mind can remember ___27___. One result of his research is known as the total time *hypothesis*（假设）, which simply means the amount you learn ___28___ on the time you spend trying to learn it. This can be taken as our first rule of learning. Although it is usually true that studying for four hours is better than studying for one, there is still the question of how we should use the four hours. For example, is it better to study for four hours ___29___ or to study for one hour a day for four days in a ___30___? The answer, as you may have ___31___, is that it is better to spread out the study times. This ___32___, through which we can learn more ___33___ by dividing our practice time, is known as the distribution of practice effect. Thus, our second rule of learning is this: it is better to study fairly briefly but often. But we're not finished yet. We haven't considered how we should study over very short periods of time. Let's say you are trying to learn some new and rather difficult English vocabulary using a stack of cards. Should you look at the same word ___34___, or look at the word and then have some delay before you look at it again? The answer is it is better to ___35___ the presentations of the word you are to learn.

二、经典模拟题二

Directions: *In this section, you will hear a passage three times. When the passage is read for the first time, you should listen carefully for its general idea. When the passage is read for the second time, you are required to fill in the blanks with the exact words* *you have just heard. Finally, when the passage is read for the third time, you should check what you have written.*

In the humanities, authors write to inform you in many ways. These methods can ___26___ three types of informational writing: factual, descriptive, and process.

Factual writing provides ___27___ information on an author, composer, or artist or on a type of music, literature, or art. Examples of factual writing include notes on a book jacket or ___28___ cover and longer pieces, such as an article describing a style of music which you might read in a music ___29___ course. This kind of writing provides a ___30___ for your study of the humanities.

As its name ___31___, descriptive writing simply describes, or provides an ___32___ of, a piece of music, art, or literature. For example, descriptive writing might list the colors an artist used in a painting or the ___33___ a composer included in a musical composition, so as to make pictures or sounds in the reader's mind by calling up specific details of the work. Descriptive writing in the humanities, particularly in literature, ___34___ critical writing.

Process writing explains ___35___ actions that bring about a result. It tells the reader how to do something. For example, explaining the technique used to shoot a film. This kind of writing is often found in art, where understanding how an artist created a certain effect is important.

Authors may actually use more than one type of technique in a given piece of informational writing.

三、经典模拟题三

Directions: *In this section, you will hear a passage three times. When the passage is read for the first time, you should listen carefully for its general idea. When the passage is read for the second time, you are required to fill in the blanks with the exact words you have just heard. Finally, when the passage is read for the third time, you should check what you have written.*

Writing keeps us in touch with other people. We write to ___26___ relatives and friends. We write to preserve our family histories so our children and grandchildren can learn and ___27___ their heritage. With computers and Internet connections in so many <u> 28 </u>, colleges, and businesses, people are e-mailing friends and relatives all the time—or talking to them in writing in online <u> 29 </u> rooms. It is cheaper than calling long distance, and a lot more <u> 30 </u> than waiting until Sunday for the telephone <u> 31 </u> to drop. Students are emailing their professors to <u> 32 </u> and discuss their classroom assignments and to <u> 33 </u> them. They are e-mailing classmates to discuss and collaborate on homework. They are also sharing information about concerts and sports events, as well as jokes and their philosophies of life.

Despite the growing importance of computers, however, there will always be a place and need for the personal letter. A hand-written note to a friend or a family member is the best way to communicate important thoughts. <u> 34 </u> the content of the message, its real point is, "I want you to know that I <u> 35 </u> you." This writing practice brings rewards that can't be seen in bank accounts, but only in the success of human relationships.

四、经典模拟题四

Directions: *In this section, you will hear a passage three times. When the passage is read for the first time, you should listen carefully for its general idea. When the passage is read for the second time, you are required to fill in the blanks with the exact words you have just heard. Finally, when the passage is read for the third time, you should check what you have written.*

<u> 26 </u> the old warning that time waits for no one, time slows down when you are on the move. It also slows down more as you move faster, which means *astronauts* （宇航员）someday may survive so long in space that they would return to an Earth of the <u> 27 </u> future. If you could move at the speed of light, your time would stand still. If you could move faster than light, your time would move <u> 28 </u>.

Although no form of matter yet <u> 29 </u> moves as fast as or faster than light, <u> 30 </u> experiments have already confirmed that accelerated <u> 31 </u> causes a traveler's time to be stretched. Albert Einstein <u> 32 </u> this in1905, when he <u> 33 </u> the concept of relative time as part of his Special Theory of Relativity. A search is now under way to confirm the suspected existence of particles of matter that move at a speed greater than light, and therefore, might serve as our passports to the past.

An *obsession*（沉迷）with time—saving, gaining, wasting, losing, and mastering it—seems to have been part of humanity for as long as humans have existed. Humanity also has __34__ trying to capture the meaning of time. Einstein used a definition of time for experimental purposes, as that which __35__ a clock. Thus, time and time's relativity are measurable by any hourglass, alarm clock, or an atomic clock that can measure a billionth of a second.

五、经典模拟题五

Directions: *In this section, you will hear a passage three times. When the passage is read for the first time, you should listen carefully for its general idea. When the passage is read for the second time, you are required to fill in the blanks with the exact words you have just heard. Finally, when the passage is read for the third time, you should check what you have written.*

Our lives are woven together. As much as I enjoy my own __26__, I no longer imagine I can __27__ a single day, much less all my life, __28__ on my own. Even if I am on __29__ in the mountains, I am eating food someone else has grown, living in a house someone else has built, wearing clothes someone else has __30__ cloth woven by others, using __31__ someone else is distributing to my house. __32__ of interdependence is everywhere. We are on this __33__ together. As I was growing up, I remember being carefully taught that independence, not __34__, was everything. "Make your own way", "Stand on your own two feet", or my mother's favorite remark when I was face-to-face with consequences of some action: "Now that you've made your bed, lie on it!" Total independence is a dominant theme in our culture. I imagine that what my parents were trying to teach me was to __35__ my actions and my choices. But the teaching was shaped by our cultural images, and instead I grew up believing that I was supposed to be totally "independent" and consequently became very reluctant to ask for help. I would do almost anything not to be a burden and not require any help from anybody.

六、经典模拟题六

Directions: *In this section, you will hear a passage three times. When the passage is read for the first time, you should listen carefully for its general idea. When the passage is read for the second time, you are required to fill in the blanks with the exact words you have just heard. Finally, when the passage is read for the third time, you should check what you have written.*

Students have been complaining more and more about stolen property. Radios, cell phones, bicycles, pocket ___26___, and books have all been reported stolen. Are there enough campus police to do the job? There are 20 officers in the Campus Security Division. Their job is to ___27___ crime, accidents, lost and found ___28___, and traffic problems on campus. More than half of their time is spent directing traffic and writing parking tickets. ___29___ accidents and other ___30___ is important, but it is their smallest job.

___31___ crime takes up the rest of their time. Very rarely do any violent crimes actually ___32___. In the last five years there have been no ___33___, seven robberies and about 60 other violent attacks, most of these involving fights at parties. On the other hand, there have been hundreds of thefts and cases of ___34___ damaging of public property, which usually involves breaking windows or lights, or writing on walls. The thefts are not the carefully planned *burglaries*（入室盗窃）that you see in movies. Things get stolen when it is easy to steal them because they are left lying around unwatched. Do we really need more police? Hiring more campus police would cost money, possibly making our tuition go up again. A better way to solve this problem might be for all of us to ___35___ our things.

七、经典模拟题七

Directions: *In this section, you will hear a passage three times. When the passage is read for the first time, you should listen carefully for its general idea. When the passage is read for the second time, you are required to fill in the blanks with the exact words you have just heard. Finally, when the passage is read for the third time, you should check what you have written.*

Americans today have different eating habits than they had in the past. There is a wide ___26___ of food available. They have a broader ___27___ of *nutrition* (营养), so they buy more fresh fruit and vegetables ___28___. At the same time, Americans ___29___ increasing quantities of sweets and sodas. Statistics show that the way people live ___30___ the way they eat. American lifestyles have changed. There are now growing numbers of people who live alone, ___31___ parents and children, and double-income families. These changing lifestyles ___32___ the increasing number of people who must ___33___ meals or sometimes simply go without them. Many Americans have less time than ever before to spend preparing food. Partly ___34___ this limited time, over half of all American homes now have microwave ovens. Moreover, Americans eat out nearly four times a week on average. It is easy to study the amounts and kinds of food that people consume. The United States Department of ___35___ and the food industry collect sales statistics and keep accurate records. This information not only tells us what people are eating, but also tells us about the changes in attitudes and tastes. Red meat, which used to be the most popular choice for dinner, is no longer an American favorite. Instead, chicken, turkey and fish have become more popular. Sales of these foods have greatly increased in recent years.

八、经典模拟题八

Directions: *In this section, you will hear a passage three times. When the passage is read for the first time, you should listen carefully for its general idea. When the passage is read for the second time, you are required to fill in the blanks with the exact words you have just heard. Finally, when the passage is read for the third time, you should check what you have written.*

Time is, for the average American, ___26___. To the foreign visitor, Americans seem to be more concerned with getting things ___27___ on time (according to a predetermined schedule) than they are with developing deep ___28___ relations. Schedules, for the American, are meant to be planned and then followed in the smallest ___29___. It may seem to you that most Americans ___30___ the little machines they wear on their wrists, cutting their discussions off ___31___ to make it to their next appointment on time. American's language is filled with ___32___ to time, giving a clear ___33___ of how much it is valued. Time is something to be "on", to be "kept", "filled", "saved", "wasted", "gained", "planned", "given", "made the most of", even "killed". The international visitor soon learns that it's considered very rude to be late—even by 10 minutes—for an ___34___ in America. Time is so valued in America because by considering time to be important one can clearly achieve more than if one "wastes" time and doesn't keep busy. This philosophy has proven its worth. It has enabled Americans to be extremely productive, and productivity itself ___35___ in America. Many American *proverbs*（谚语）tress the value of guarding time, using it wisely and setting and working toward specific goals. Americans believe in spending their time and energy today so that the fruits of their labor may be enjoyed at a later time.

九、经典模拟题九

Directions: *In this section, you will hear a passage three times. When the passage is read for the first time, you should listen carefully for its general idea. When the passage is read for the second time, you are required to fill in the blanks with the exact words you have just heard. Finally, when the passage is read for the third time, you should check what you have written.*

My favorite T.V. show? "The Twilight Zone." I ___26___ like the episode called "The Printer's Devil." It's about a newspaper editor who's being ___27___ business by a big newspaper syndicate—you know, a group of papers ___28___ by the same people. He's about to ___29___ when he's interrupted by an old man who says his name is Smith. The editor is not only offered $5,000 to pay off his newspaper's ___30___, but this Smith character also offers his ___31___ for free. It turns out that the guy ___32___ the printing machine with amazing speed, and soon he's turning out newspaper with shocking headlines. The small paper is successful again. The editor is amazed at how quickly Smith gets his stories—only minutes after they happen—but soon he's presented with a contract to sign. Mr. Smith, it seems, is really the devil! The editor is frightened by this news, but he ___33___ the idea of losing his newspaper, so he agrees to sign. But soon Smith is reporting the news even before it happens—and it's all terrible—one disaster after another. Anyway, there is little more to tell, but I don't want to __34__ the story for you. I really like these old episodes of "The Twilight Zone" because the stories are fascinating. They are not __35__. But then again, in a way they are, because they deal with human nature.

十、经典模拟题十

Directions: *In this section, you will hear a passage three times. When the passage is read for the first time, you should listen carefully for its general idea. When the passage is read for the second time, you are required to fill in the blanks with the exact words you have just heard. Finally, when the passage is read for the third time, you should check what you have written.*

There was a time when any personal information that was gathered about us was typed on a piece of paper and __26__ in a file cabinet. It could remain there for years and, often __27__, never reach the outside world. Things have done a complete about-face since then. __28__ for the changes has been the astonishingly __29__ development in recent years of the computer. Today, any data that is __30__ about us in one place or another—and for one reason or another—can be stored in a computer bank. It can then be easily passed to other computer banks. They are owned by __31__ and by private businesses and corporations, lending __32__, direct mailing and telemarketing firms, credit bureaus, credit card companies, and government __33__ at the local, state, and federal level. __34__ Americans are seeing the accumulation and distribution of computerized data as a frightening invasion of their privacy. Surveys show that the number of the worrying Americans has been __35__ over the years as the computer becomes increasingly efficient, easier to operate, and less costly to purchase and maintain. In 1970, a national survey showed that 37% of the people questioned felt their privacy was being invaded. Seven years later, 47% percent expressed the same worry. A recent survey by a credit bureau reviewed that the number of alarmed citizens had shot up to 76%.

参考答案

经典模拟题一

26. concentrated on
27. information
28. depends
29. straight
30. row
31. suspected
32. phenomenon
33. efficiently
34. in rapid succession
35. space out

经典模拟题二

26. be classified into
27. background
28. album
29. appreciation
30. context
31. implies
32. image
33. instruments
34. is often mixed with
35. a series of

经典模拟题三

26. communicate with
27. appreciate
28. households
29. chat
30. convenient
31. rates
32. receive
33. submit
34. No matter what
35. care about

经典模拟题四

26. Contrary to
27. distant
28. backward
29. discovered
30. scientific
31. motion
32. predicted
33. introduced
34. been obsessed with
35. is measured by

经典模拟题五

26. company
27. get through
28. completely
29. vacation
30. sewn from
31. electricity
32. Evidence
33. journey
34. interdependence
35. take responsibility for

经典模拟题六

26. calculators
27. handle
28. items
29. Responding promptly to
30. emergencies

31. Dealing with
32. occur
33. murders
34. deliberate
35. be more careful with

经典模拟题七

26. selection
27. knowledge
28. than ever before
29. purchase
30. determines

31. single
32. are responsible for
33. rush
34. as a consequence of
35. Agriculture

经典模拟题八

26. of utmost importance
27. accomplished
28. interpersonal
29. detail
30. are completely controlled by

31. abruptly
32. references
33. indication
34. appointment
35. is highly valued

经典模拟题九

26. especially
27. driven out of
28. owned
29. commit suicide
30. debts

31. services
32. operates
33. is more frightened by
34. ruin
35. realistic

经典模拟题十

26. locked away
27. forgotten
28. Responsible
29. swift
30. collected

31. individuals
32. institutions
33. agencies
34. A growing number of
35. steadily growing

第五章　快速阅读新题型十大经典模拟题

Directions: *In this section, you are going to read a passage with ten statements attached to it. Each statement contains information given in one of the paragraphs. Identify the paragraph from which the information is derived. You may choose a paragraph more than once. Each paragraph is marked with a letter. Answer the questions by marking the corresponding letter on **Answer Sheet 2**.*

Into the Unknown

The world has never seen population ageing before. Can it cope?

A）Until the early 1990s nobody much thought about whole populations getting older. The UN had the foresight to convene a "world assembly on ageing" back in 1982, but that came and went. By 1994 the World Bank had noticed that something big was happening. In a report entitled "Averting the Old Age Crisis", it argued that pension arrangements in most countries were unsustainable.

B）For the next ten years a succession of books, mainly by Americans, sounded the alarm. They had titles like *Young vs Old*, *Gray Dawn* and *The Coming Generational Storm*, and their message was blunt: health-care systems were heading for the rocks, pensioners were taking young people to the cleaners, and soon there would be intergenerational warfare.

C）Since then the debate has become less emotional, not least because a lot more is known about the subject. Books, conferences and research papers have multiplied. International organisations such as the OECD and the EU issue regular reports. Population ageing is on every agenda, from G8 economic conferences to NATO summits. The World Economic Forum plans to consider the future of pensions and health care at its prestigious Davos conference early next year. The media, including this newspaper, are giving the subject extensive coverage.

D）Whether all that attention has translated into sufficient action is another question. Governments in rich countries now accept that their pension and health-care promises will soon become unaffordable, and many of them have embarked on reforms, but so far only timidly. That is not surprising: politicians with an eye on the next election will hardly rush to introduce unpopular measures that may not bear fruit for years, perhaps decades.

E) The outline of the changes needed is clear. To avoid *fiscal*（财政的）meltdown, public pensions and health-care provision will have to be reined back severely and taxes may have to go up. By far the most effective method to restrain pension spending is to give people the opportunity to work longer, because it increases tax revenues and reduces spending on pensions at the same time. It may even keep them alive longer. John Rother, the AARP's head of policy and strategy, points to studies showing that other things being equal, people who remain at work have lower death rates than their retired peers.

F) Younger people today mostly accept that they will have to work for longer and that their pensions will be less generous. Employers still need to be persuaded that older workers are worth holding on to. That may be because they have had plenty of younger ones to choose from, partly thanks to the post-war baby-boom and partly because over the past few decades many more women have entered the labour force, increasing employers' choice. But the reservoir of women able and willing to take up paid work is running low, and the baby-boomers are going grey.

G) In many countries immigrants have been filling such gaps in the labour force as have already emerged（and remember that the real shortage is still around ten years off）. Immigration in the developed world is the highest it has ever been, and it is making a useful difference. In still-fertile America it currently accounts for about 40% of total population growth, and in fast-ageing western Europe for about 90%.

H) On the face of it, it seems the perfect solution. Many developing countries have lots of young people in need of jobs; many rich countries need helping hands that will boost tax revenues and keep up economic growth. But over the next few decades labour forces in rich countries are set to shrink so much that inflows of immigrants would have to increase enormously to compensate: to at least twice their current size in western Europe's most youthful countries, and three times in the older ones. Japan would need a large multiple of the few immigrants it has at present. Public opinion polls show that people in most rich countries already think that immigration is too high. Further big increases would be politically unfeasible.

I) To tackle the problem of ageing populations at its root, "old" countries would have to *rejuvenate*（使年轻）themselves by having more of their own children. A number of them have tried, some more successfully than others. But it is not a simple matter of offering financial incentives or providing more child care. Modern urban life in rich countries is not well adapted to large families. Women find it hard to combine family and career. They often compromise by having just one child.

J) And if fertility in ageing countries does not pick up? It will not be the end of the world, at least not for quite a while yet, but the world will slowly become a different place. Older societies may be less innovative and more strongly disinclined to take risks than younger ones. By 2025 at the latest, about half the voters in America and most of those in western European countries will be over 50—and older people turn out to vote in much greater number than younger ones. Academic studies have found no evidence so far that older voters have used their power at the ballot box to push for policies that specifically benefit them, though if in future there are many more of them they might start doing so.

K) Nor is there any sign of the intergenerational warfare predicted in the 1990s. After all, older people themselves mostly have families. In a recent study of parents and grown-up children in 11 European countries, Karsten Hank of Mannheim University found that 85% of them lived within 25km of each other and the majority of them were in touch at least once a week. Even so, the shift in the centre of gravity to older age groups is bound to have a profound effect on societies, not just economically and politically but in all sorts of other ways too. Richard Jackson and Neil Howe of America's CSIS, in a thoughtful book called *The Graying of the Great Powers*, argue that, among other things, the ageing of the developed countries will have a number of serious security implications.

L) For example, the shortage of young adults is likely to make countries more reluctant to commit the few they have to military service. In the decades to 2050, America will find itself playing an ever-increasing role in the developed world's defence effort. Because America's population will still be growing when that of most other developed countries is shrinking, America will be the only developed country that still matters *geopolitically*（地缘政治上）.

注意：此部分试题请在**答题卡1**上作答。

46. Employers should realize it is important to keep older workers in the workforce.

47. A recent study found that most old people in some European countries had regular weekly contact with their adult children.

48. Few governments in rich countries have launched bold reforms to tackle the problem of population ageing.

49. In a report published some 20 years ago, the sustainability of old age pension systems in most countries was called into doubt.

50. Countries that have a shortage of young adults will be less willing to send them to war.

51. One-child families are more common in ageing societies due to the stress of urban life and the difficulties of balancing family and career.

52. A series of books, mostly authored by Americans, warned of conflicts between the older and younger generations.

53. Compared with younger ones, older societies tend to be less innovative and take fewer risks.

54. The best solution to the pension crisis is to postpone the retirement age.

55. Immigration as a means to boost the shrinking labour force may meet with resistance in some rich countries.

试题解析

本文围绕人口老龄化问题展开。第一至四段引出本文所要讨论的话题——人口老龄化。直到20世纪90年代初期，人口老龄化问题都鲜有人关注。一份题为《避免老龄化危机》的报告指出，大多数国家的养老金系统都无法维持。之后的十年，一系列关于老龄化的书籍为人们敲响了警钟。有些国家目前已经着手改革，但都过于谨慎。文章随后综合阐述了解决人口老龄化问题的办法，以及采取这些办法所面临的现状、结果和困难等。

46. F 根据题干中的关键词employers和older workers定位到F段第二句：Employers still need to be persuaded that older workers are worth holding on to(我们仍需说服雇主们，继续雇用老龄员工是值得的)，故选F。

47. K 根据题干中的关键词a recent study和European countries定位到K段第二句：In a recent study of parents and grown-up children in 11 European countries,

Karsten Hank of Mannheim University found that 85% of them lived within 25km of each other and the majority of them were in touch at least once a week.(在最近一项对11个欧洲国家家长和成年子女的调查中，曼海姆大学的Karsten Hank发现85%的家长和子女居住在离彼此25公里以内的地方，他们中的大多数每周至少会联系一次)，故选K。

48. D 根据题干中的关键词governments in rich countries和reforms定位到D段第二句：Governments in rich countries now accept that their pension and health-care promises will soon become unaffordable, and many of them have embarked on reforms, but so far only timidly.(目前富裕国家的政府承认他们很快就会无法兑现养老和医疗承诺，而且他们当中的很多政府已经着手改革，但到目前为止仍过于谨慎)，故选D。

49. A 根据题干中的关键词in a report, sustainability, old age pension和in most countries定位到A段末句：In a report entitled "Averting the Old Age Crisis", it argued that pension arrangements in most countries were unsustainable(在一篇题为《避免老龄化危机》的报告中，世界银行指出大多数国家的养老金计划都难以为继)，故选A。

50. L 根据题干中的关键词shortage和young adults定位到L段首句：For example, the shortage of young adults is likely to make countries more reluctant to commit the few they have to military service(举例来说，年轻人口的匮乏可能会使国家更不愿意让他们仅有的少量年轻人去服军役)，故选L。

51. I 根据题干中的关键词one-child, urban life和family and career定位到I段最后三句：Modern urban life in rich countries is not well adapted to large families. Women find it hard to combine family and career. They often compromise by having just one child(在富裕国家，现代的城市生活不适合大的家庭。女性认为很难同时兼顾事业和家庭。她们经常通过只要一个孩子来解决这一矛盾)，故选I。

52. B 根据题干中的关键词A series of books, mostly authored by Americans和conflicts between the older and younger generations定位到B段：For the next ten years a succession of books, mainly by Americans, sounded the alarm. They had titles like *Young vs Old*, *Gray Dawn* and *The Coming Generational Storm*, and their message was blunt: health-care systems were heading for the rocks pensioners were taking young people to the cleaners, and soon there

would be intergenerational warfare(在接下来的十年里，一系列主要由美国人撰写的书籍敲响了警钟。在这些标题诸如《年轻人vs老年人》、《灰色拂晓》和《即将到来的代际风暴》的书中，他们直言不讳地传递出这样的信息：医疗保险系统正走向崩溃，领取退休金的老年人将使年轻人一贫如洗，很快就会爆发一场两代人之间的冲突)，故选B。

53. J 根据题干中的关键词 compared with younger ones, older societies, less innovative, take fewer risks定位到J段第三句：Older societies may be less innovative and more strongly disinclined to take risks than younger ones(与年轻化的社会相比，老龄化社会可能没有那么创新，也更加不愿冒险)，故选J。

54. E 根据题干中的关键词 the best solution, pension crisis 和 postpone the retirement age定位到E段第三句：By far the most effective method to restrain pension spending is to give people the opportunity to work longer（到目前为止，控制养老金支出最有效的方法是给予人们延长工作年限的机会)，故选E。

55. H 根据题干中的关键词 immigration, shrinking, labour force 和 in some rich countries定位到H段最后四句：But over the next few decades labour forces in rich countries are set to shrink so much that inflows of immigrants would have to increase enormously to compensate ... Public opinion polls show that people in most rich countries already think that immigration is too high. Further big increases would be politically unfeasible(但是，在未来几十年里，发达国家的劳动力数量必定会减少到只能通过大量引入移民才能弥补……民意调查显示，大多数发达国家的人已经认为移民人数太多。进一步大量移民在政治上将是不可行的)，故选H。

二、经典模拟题二

Directions: *In this section, you are going to read a passage with ten statements attached to it. Each statement contains information given in one of the paragraphs. Identify the paragraph from which the information is derived. You may choose a paragraph more than once. Each paragraph is marked with a letter. Answer the questions by marking the corresponding letter on **Answer Sheet 2**.*

Highways

A) Early in the 20th century, most of the streets and roads in the U.S. were made of dirt, brick, and cedar wood blocks. Built for horse, carriage, and foot traffic, they were usually poorly cared for and too narrow to *accommodate*（容纳）automobiles.

B) With the increase in auto production, private *turnpike*（收费公路）companies under local authorities began to spring up, and by 1921 there were 387,000 miles of paved roads. Many were built using specifications of 19th century Scottish engineers Thomas Telford and John MacAdam（for whom the macadam surface is named）, whose specifications stressed the importance of adequate drainage. Beyond that, there were no national standards for size, weight restrictions, or commercial signs. During World War I, roads throughout the country were nearly destroyed by the weight of trucks. When General Eisenhower returned from Germany in 1919, after serving in the U.S. Army's first transcontinental motor *convoy*（车队）, he noted: "The old convoy had started me thinking about good, two-lane highways, but Germany's Autobahn or motorway had made me see the wisdom of broader ribbons across the land."

C) It would take another war before the federal government would act on a national highway system. During World war II, a tremendous increase in trucks and new roads were required. The war demonstrated how critical highways were to the defense effort. Thirteen per cent of defense plants received all their supplies by truck, and almost all other plants shipped more than half of their products by vehicle. The war also revealed that local control of highways had led to a confusing variety of design standards. Even federal and state highways did not follow basic standards. Some states allowed trucks up to 36,000 pounds, while others restricted anything over 7,000 pounds. A government study recommended a national highway system of 33,920 miles, and Congress soon passed the Federal-Aid Highway Act of 1944, which called for strict, centrally controlled design criteria.

D) The interstate highway system was finally launched in 1956 and has been hailed as one of the greatest public works projects of the century. To build its 44,000-mile web of highways, bridges and tunnels, hundreds of unique engineering designs and solutions had to be worked out. Consider the many geographic features of the country: mountains, steep grades, wetlands, rivers, deserts, and plains. Variables included the slope of the land, the ability of the pavement to support the load, the intensity of road use, and the nature of the underlying soil. Urban areas were another problem. Innovative designs of roadways, tunnels, bridges, overpasses, and interchanges that could run through or bypass urban areas soon began to weave their way across the country, forever altering the face of America.

E) Long-span, segmented-concrete, cable-stayed bridges such as Hale Boggs in Louisiana and the Sunshine Skyway in Florida, and remarkable tunnels like Fort McHenry in Maryland and Mt. Baker in Washington, met many of the nation's physical challenges. Traffic control systems and methods of construction developed under the interstate program soon influenced highway construction around the world, and were invaluable in improving the condition of urban streets and traffic patterns.

F) Today, the interstate system links every major city in the U.S., and the U.S. with Canada and Mexico. Built with safety in mind, the highways have wide lanes and shoulders, dividing medians or barriers, long entry and exit lanes, curves engineered for safe turns, and limited access. The death rate on highways is half that of all other U.S. roads (0.86 deaths per 100 million passenger miles compared to 1.99 deaths per 100 million on all other roads.)

G) By opening the North American continent, highways have enabled consumer goods and services to reach people in remote and rural areas of the country, spurred the growth of suburbs, and provided people with greater options in terms of jobs, access to cultural programs, health care, and other benefits. Above all, the interstate system provides individuals with what they cherish most: personal freedom of mobility.

H) The interstate system has been an essential element of the nation's economic growth in terms of shipping and job creation: more than 75 percent of the nation's freight deliveries arrive by truck; and most products that arrive by rail or air use interstates for the last leg of the journey by vehicle. Not only has the highway system affected the American economy by providing shipping routes, it has led to the growth of spin-off industries like service stations, motels, restaurants, and shopping centers. It has allowed the relocation of manufacturing plants and other industries from urban areas to rural.

I) By the end of the century there was an immense network of paved roads, residential streets, expressways, and freeways built to support millions of vehicles. The highway system was officially renamed for Eisenhower to honor his vision and leadership. The year construction began he said: "Together, the united forces of our communication and transportation systems are dynamic elements in the very name we bear—United States. Without them, we would be a mere alliance of many separate parts."

注意：此部分试题请在**答题卡1**上作答。

46. There were nearly 400,000 miles of paved roads by the early 2020s.

47. General Eisenhower felt that the broad German motorways made more sense than the two-lane highways of America.

48. It was in the 1950s that the American government finally took action to build the interstate highway system.

49. Many of the problems presented by the country's geographical features found solutions in innovative engineering projects.

50. Because of safety considerations, the death rate on interstate highways is half as much as that of all other U.S. roads.

51. The war demonstrated how essential highways were to the defense effort.

52. By providing shipping routes, the highway system has not only affected the American economy, but also contributed to the growth of service stations, motels, restaurants, shopping centers, and so on.

53. The greatest benefit brought about by the interstate system was personal freedom of mobility.

54. More than three-quarter of the nation's freight deliveries arrive by truck.

55. The interstate system was renamed after Eisenhower in recognition of his vision and leadership.

试题解析

　　本文是一篇说明文，文章结构为"提出问题—解决问题—给予评价"。第一至三段提出问题：20世纪初美国原有的不规范公路已不能满足汽车工业和军事的需要，直至二战时期，美国的公路建设仍缺乏统一的国家标准，落后的路况在二战期间呈现出严重弊端，建设全国性的高速公路体系成为当务之急。四、五两段解决问题：1956年开始着手建设州际高速公路，开创性的方案解决了众多地理难题。六至九段给予评价：高速公路给美国经济与人民带来众多好处，它不仅改善了交通状况，降低了事故率，而且还方便居民消费，促进了各地区的融合与统一。

46. **B**　根据题干中的关键词400,000 miles, by the early 2020s定位到B段首句：... by 1921 there were 387,000 miles of paved roads（截止到1921年，一共铺设了38.7万英里的公路），故选B。

47. **B**　根据题干中的General Eisenhower, German motorways, two-lane highways定位到B段末句：The old convoy had started me thinking about good, two-lane highways, but Germany's Autobahn or motorway had made me see the wisdom of broader ribbons across the land（这些破旧的车队让我想起了优质的双车道公路，而德国的高速公路让我见识了贯穿这个国家的这些更宽广纽带所蕴含的智慧），故选B。

48. **D**　根据题干中的关键词in the 1950s, interstate highway system定位到D段首句：The interstate highway system was finally launched in 1956 and has been hailed as one of the greatest public works projects of the century（美国国家公路系统最终于1956年动工，它被誉为那个世纪最伟大的公共建设项目之一），故选D。

49. **D**　根据题干中的关键词geographical features, solutions, innovative定位到D段的第二句和最后一句，第二句指出，要使44000公里的高速公路符合各地的地理特点，就必须想出上百种独特的设计方案；最后一句指出创意性的设计方案已开始在全国实行。故选D。

50. **F**　根据题干中的关键词the death rate on interstate highway定位到F段末句：The death rate on highways is half that of all other U.S. roads（高速公路上的事故死亡率仅为美国其他道路的一半），故选F。

51. **C**　根据题干中的关键词The war, demonstrated, highways, the defense effort定位到C段第三句：The war demonstrated how critical highways were to the

defense effort. (战争证明了高速公路对于防御工作的重要性），故选C。

52. H 根据题干中的关键词providing shipping routes, the highway system, affected the American economy定位到H段倒数第二句：Not only has the highway system affected the American economy by providing shipping routes, it has led to the growth of spin-off industries like service stations, motels, restaurants, and shopping centers （通过提供海运通道，公路系统不但影响了美国的经济，还促进了维修站、汽车旅馆、餐厅以及购物中心等副业的增长），故选H。

53. G 根据题干中的interstate system, personal freedom of mobility 等关键词定位到G段末句：Above all, the interstate system provides individuals with what they cherish most: personal freedom of mobility(最重要的是，州际公路系统提供了个人最为珍视的东西：个人迁移的自由），故选G。

54. H 根据题干中的关键词three-quarter, deliveries arrive by truck定位到H段首句：... more than 75 percent of the nation's freight deliveries arrive by truck(……全国75%以上的货运由卡车完成），故选H。

55. I 根据题干中的关键词renamed, Eisenhower定位到I段第二句：The highway system was officially renamed for Eisenhower to honor his vision and leadership(公路系统被官方更名为艾森豪威尔以纪念其远见卓识和领导才能），故选I。

三、经典模拟题三

Directions: *In this section, you are going to read a passage with ten statements attached to it. Each statement contains information given in one of the paragraphs. Identify the paragraph from which the information is derived. You may choose a paragraph more than once. Each paragraph is marked with a letter. Answer the questions by marking the corresponding letter on Answer Sheet 2.*

Six Secrets of High-Energy People

A) There's an energy crisis in America, and it has nothing to do with fossil fuels. Millions of us get up each morning already weary over the day holds. "I just can't get started." People say. But it's not physical energy that most of us lack. Sure, we could all use extra sleep and a better diet. But in truth, people are healthier today than at any time in history. I can almost guarantee that if you long for more energy, the problem is not with your body.

B) What you're seeking is not physical energy. It's emotional energy. Yet, sad to say life sometimes seems designed to exhaust our supply. We work too hard. We have family obligations. We encounter emergencies and personal crises. No wonder so many of us suffer from emotional fatigue, a kind of utter exhaustion of the spirit.

C) And yet we all know people who are filled with joy, despite the unpleasant circumstances of their lives. Even as a child I observed people who were poor or disabled or ill, but who nonetheless faced life with optimism and vigor. Consider Laura Hillenbrand, who despite an extremely weak body wrote the best-seller *Seabiscuit*. Hillenbrand barely had enough physical energy to drag herself out of bed to write. But she was fueled by having a story she wanted to share. It was emotional energy that helped her succeed. Unlike physical energy, which is finite and diminishes with age, emotional energy is unlimited and has nothing to do with genes or upbringing. So how do you get it? You can't simply tell yourself to be positive. You must take action. Here are six practical strategies that work.

Do something new.

D) Very little that's new occurs in our lives. The impact of this sameness on our emotional energy is gradual, but huge: It's like a tire with a slow leak. You don't notice it at first, but eventually you'll get a flat. It's up to you to plug the leak—even though there are always a dozen reasons to stay stuck in your dull routines of life. That's where Maura, 36, a waitress, found herself a year ago. Fortunately, Maura had a lifeline—a group of women friends who meet regularly to discuss their lives. Their lively discussions spurred Maura to make small but nevertheless life altering changes. She joined a gym in the next town. She changed her look with a short haircut and new black T-shirts. Eventually, Maura gathered the courage to quit her job and start her own business. Here's a challenge: If it's something you wouldn't ordinarily do, do it. Try a dish you've never eaten. Listen to music you'd ordinarily tune out. You'll discover these small things add to your emotional energy.

Reclaim life's meaning.

E) So many of my patients tell me that their lives used to have meaning, but that somewhere along the line things went stale. The first step in solving this meaning shortage is to figure out what you really care about, and then do something about it. A case in point is Ivy, 57, a pioneer in investment banking. "I mistakenly believed that all the money I made would mean something." she says. "But I feel lost, like a 22-year-old wondering what to do with her life." Ivy's solution? She started a program that shows Wall Streeters how to donate time and money to poor children. In the process, Ivy filled her life with meaning.

Put yourself in the fun zone.

F) Most of us grown-ups are seriously fun-deprived. High-energy people have the same day-to-day work as the rest of us, but they manage to find something enjoyable in every situation. A real-estate broker I know keeps herself amused on the job by mentally redecorating the houses she shows to clients. "I love imagining what even the most run-down house could look like with a little tender loving care," she says. "It's a challenge—and the least desirable properties are usually the most fun." We all define fun differently, of course, but I can guarantee this: If you put just a bit of it into your day, your energy will increase quickly.

Bid farewell to guilt and regret.

G) Everyone's past is filled with regrets that still cause pain. But from an emotional energy point of view, they are dead weights that keep us from us from moving forward. While they can't merely be willed away, I do recommend you remind yourself that whatever happened is in the past, and nothing can change that. Holding on to the memory only allows the damage to continue into the present.

Make up your mind.

H) Say you've been thinking about cutting your hair short. Will it look stylish—or too extreme? You endlessly think it over. Having the decision hanging over your head is a huge energy drain. Every time you can't decide, you burden yourself with alternatives. Quit thinking that you have to make the right decision; instead, make a choice and don't look back.

Give to get.

I) Emotional energy has a kind of magical quality: the more you give, the more you get back. This is the difference between emotional and physical energy. With the latter, you have to get it to be able to give it. With the former, however, you get it by giving it. Start by asking everyone you meet, "How are you?" as if you really want to know, then listen to the reply. Be the one who hears. Most of us also need to smile more often. If you don't smile at the person you love first thing in the morning, you're sucking energy out of your relationship. Finally, help another person—and make the help real, concrete. Give a *massage*（按摩）to someone you love, or cook her dinner, Then, expand the circle to work. Try asking yourself what you'd do if your goal were to be helpful rather than efficient. After all, if it's true that what goes around comes around, why not make sure that what's circulating around you is the good stuff?

注意：此部分试题请在**答题卡1**上作答。

46. When it comes to decision-making, one should make a quick choice without looking back.

47. People these days do not tend to lack physical energy.

48. Laura Hillenbrand is an example cited to show how emotional energy can contribute to one's success in life.

49. By mentally redecorating the houses she shows to clients, a real estate broker I know keeps herself amused.

50. Even small changes people make in lives can help increase people's emotional energy.

51. Ivy filled her life with meaning by launching a program to help poor children.

52. Unlike physical energy, emotional energy is without limitation and has nothing to do with genes or upbringing.

53. People holding on to the past will find it difficult to move forward.

54. The energy crisis in America has nothing to do with fossil fuels.

55. Emotional energy is in a way different from physical energy in that the more you give, the more you get back.

试题解析

　　本文首先指出，美国出现了一种能源危机，很多人从早上起床的时候开始就已经觉得疲倦，这不是一种体力的缺乏，而是情感能量的匮乏。后文主要针对美国人出现情感能量匮乏的现状提出了六点建议：尝试做新鲜的事情；重新找回生命的意义；让自己处于快乐地带；告别过去的内疚和遗憾；下定决心；以付出换取收获。

46. **H** 由题干中的关键词decision making定位到H段末句：Quit thinking that you have to make the right decision；instead, make a choice and don't look back（放弃必须做出正确决定的想法；相反，做出选择，并且不要再回头），故选H。

47. **A** 由题干中的关键词physical energy定位到A段第四句：But it's not physical energy that most of us lack（但是我们中大多数人缺乏的并不是身体能量），故选A。

48. **C** 由题干中的关键词Laura Hillenbrand, success定位到C段第六句：It was emotional energy that helped her succeed（是情感能量帮助她取得了成功），故选C。

49. **F** 由题干中的关键词real-estate broker定位到F段第三句：A real-estate broker I know keeps herself amused on the job by mentally redecorating the houses she shows to clients（我认识的一位房产经纪人喜欢在想象中装修她给客户展示的房子，这样使她觉得做这份工作很有趣），故选F。

50. **D** 由题干中的关键词small changes和increase people's emotional energy定位到D段末句：You'll discover these small things add to your emotional energy（你会发现这些小事会增加你的情感能量），此处的small things指的即是作者所鼓励的在生活中做的一些小的改变，故选D。

51. **E** 由题干中的关键词Ivy定位到E段最后两句：She started a program...poor children. In the process, Ivy filled her life with meaning　（Ivy发起了一个项目来告诉华尔街的人如何奉献时间和捐赠金钱给贫困儿童。在这个过程中，Ivy让自己的生活充满了意义），故选E。

52. **C** 由题干中的关键词unlike physical energy, emotional energy, unlimited, genes定位到C段倒数第二句：Unlike physical energy, which is finite and diminishes with age, emotional energy is unlimited and has nothing to do with

genes or upbringing（身体能量是有限的，并且会随着年龄的增长而减少，和身体能量不一样，情感能量是无限的，并且和基因或是教养都没有关系），故选C。

53. G 由题干中的关键词the past, move forward定位到G段第二句：But from an emotional energy point of view, they are dead weights that keep us from us from moving forward （从情感能量的角度来看，充满内疚和悔恨的过去只是阻止我们前行的沉重包袱），故选G。

54. A 由题干中的关键词energy crisis in America 定位到A段首句：There's an energy crisis in America, and it has nothing to do with fossil fuels（美国出现了能源危机，而这与燃料无关），故选A。

55. I 由题干中的关键词different from physical energy, the more you give 定位到I段前两句：Emotional energy has a kind of magical quality; the more you give, the more you get back. This is the difference between emotional and physical energy.（情感能量有一种神奇的特质：你给予的越多，你收获的也越多。这就是情感能量和身体能量的区别），故选I。

四、经典模拟题四

Directions: *In this section, you are going to read a passage with ten statements attached to it. Each statement contains information given in one of the paragraphs. Identify the paragraph from which the information is derived. You may choose a paragraph more than once. Each paragraph is marked with a letter. Answer the questions by marking the corresponding letter on* **Answer Sheet 2.**

Protect Your Privacy When Job-hunting Online

A）Identity theft and identity fraud are terms used to refer to all types of crime in which someone wrongly obtains and uses another person's personal data in some way that involves fraud or deception, typically for economic gain.

B）The numbers associated with identity theft are beginning to add up fast these days. A recent General Accounting Office report estimates that as many as 750,000 Americans are victims of identity theft every year. And that number may be low, as many people choose not to report the crime even if they know they have been victimized. Identity theft is "an absolute epidemic", states Robert Ellis Smith, a respected author and advocate of privacy, "It's certainly picked up in the last four or five years. It's worldwide. It affects everybody, and there's very little you can do to prevent it and, worst of all, you can't detect it until it's probably too late."

C) Unlike your fingerprints, which are unique to you and cannot be given to someone else for their use, your personal data, especially your social security number, your bank account or credit card number, your telephone calling card number, and other valuable identifying data, can be used, if they fall into the wrong hands, to personally profit at your expense. In the United States and Canada, for example, many people have reported that unauthorized persons have taken fund out of their bank or financial accounts, or, in the worst cases, taken over their identities altogether, running up vast debts and committing crimes while using the victim's names. In many cases, a victim's losses may include not only out-of-pocket financial losses, but substantial additional financial costs associated with trying to restore his reputation in the community and correcting erroneous information for which the criminal is responsible.

D) According to the FBI, identity theft is the number one fraud committed on the Internet. So how do job seekers protect themselves while continuing to circulate their resumes online? The key to a successful online job search is learning to manage the risks. Here are some tips for staying safe while conducting a job search on the Internet.

Check for a privacy policy.

E) If you are considering posting your resume online, make sure the job search site you are considering has a privacy policy, like CareerBuilder.com. The policy should spell out how your information will be used, stored and whether or not it will be shared. You may want to think twice about posting your resume on a site that automatically shares your information with others. You could be opening yourself up to unwanted calls from *solicitors* (推销员). When reviewing the site's privacy policy, you'll be able to delete your resume just as easily as you posted it. You won't necessarily want your resume to remain out there on the Internet once you land a job. Remember, the longer your resume remains posted on a job board, the more exposure, both positive and not-so-positive, it will receive.

Take advantages of site features.

F）Lawful job search sites offer levels of privacy protection. Before posting your resume, carefully consider your job search objectives and the level of risk you are willing to assume. CareerBuilder.com, for example, offers three levels of privacy from which job seekers can choose. The first is standard posting. This option gives hob seekers who post their resumes the most visibility to the broadest employer audience possible. The second is *anonymous*（匿名的）posting. This allows job seekers the same visibility as those in the standard posting category without any of their contact information being displayed. Job seekers who wish to remain anonymous but want to share some other information may choose which pieces of contact information to display. The third is private posting. This option allows a job seeker to post a resume without having it searched by employers. Private posting allows a job seeker to quickly and easily apply for jobs that appear on CareerBuilder.com without retyping their information.

Safeguard your identity.

G）Career experts say that one of the ways job seekers can stay safe while using the Internet to search out jobs is to conceal their identities. Replace your name on your resume with a *generic*（泛指的）identifier, such as "Internet Developer Candidate", or "Experience Marketing Representative". You should also consider eliminating the name and location of your current employer. Depending on your title, it may not be all that difficult to determine who you are once the name of your company is provided. Use a general description of the company such as "Major auto manufacturer" or "International packaged goods supplier". If your job title is unique, consider using the generic equivalent instead of the exact title assigned by your employer.

Establish an email address for your search.

H）Another way to protect your privacy while seeking employment online is to open up an email account specifically for your online job search. This will safeguard your existing email box in the event someone you don't know gets hold of your email address and shares it with others. Using an email address specifically for your job search also eliminates the possibility that you will receive unwelcome emails in your primary mailbox. When naming your new email address, be sure that it doesn't contain references to your name or other information that will give away your identity. The best solution is an email address that is relevant to the job you are seeking such as salesmgr2004@provider.com.

Protect your references.

I) If your resume contains a section with the names and contact information of your references, take it out. There's no sense in safeguarding your information while sharing private contact information of your references.

Keep *confidential*（机密的）**information confidential.**

J) Do not, under any circumstances, share your social security, driver's license and bank account numbers or other personal information, such as race or eye color. Honest employers do not need this information with an initial application. Don't provide this even if they say they need it in order to conduct a background check. This is one of the oldest tricks in the book—don't fall for it.

注意：此部分试题请在**答题卡1**上作答。

46. Robert Ellis Smith believes identity theft is difficult to detect and one can hardly do anything to prevent it.

47. Private posting allows a job seeker to post a resume without having it searched by employers.

48. Identity theft is the number one fraud committed on the Internet according to the FBI.

49. Applicants are advised to use generic names for themselves and their current employers when seeking employment online.

50. In many cases, identity theft not only causes the victim' immediate financial losses but also costs him a lot to restore his reputation.

51. Employers do not require applicants to submit very personal information on background checks.

52. Posting your resume longer than necessary will receive both positive and not-so-positive exposure.

53. Using a special email address in the job search can help prevent you from receiving unwelcome emails.

54. To protect your references, you should not post online their names and contact information.

55. According to the passage, identity theft is committed typically for economic gain.

试题解析

　　利用互联网求职在当今非常普遍，但是这也会带来一些潜在的问题。文章首先讲述的便是"身份盗窃"（Identity Theft）问题及其影响，随后针对如何安全地通过网络求职提出了六点建议：查看隐私政策、利用网站特色、捍卫你的身份、建立专门用于搜索的邮箱、保护你的推荐人、不泄露机密信息。

46. B　根据题干中的关键词Robert Ellis Smith和prevent定位到B段末句：...there's very little you can do to prevent it and, worst of all, you can't detect until it's probably too late（我们很难防止身份盗窃，最糟糕的是当你发现身份盗窃时很可能为时已晚），故选B。

47. F　根据题干中的关键词Private posting, job seeker, post a resume定位到F段倒数第三和倒数第二句：The third is private posting. This option allows a job seeker to post a resume without having it searched by employers.（第三个是私下投放。这个选择允许求职者张贴简历而不被雇主搜索到）。CareerBuilder.com给出的三个选择中，第三个选择是private posting，故选F。

48. D　根据题干中的关键词number one fraud和FBI定位到D段首句：According to the FBI, identity theft is the number one fraud committed on the Internet（根据FBI所言，身份盗窃是头号网络诈骗行为），故选D。

49. G　根据题干中的关键词generic names定位到G段第二句：Replace your name on your resume with a generic identifier...（用一个泛指的名称代替你的名字……）和倒数第二句：Use a general description of the company...（笼统地描述你所在的公司……），故选G。

50. C　根据题干中的关键词in many cases, financial loses和restore reputation定位到C段末句：In many cases, a victim's losses may include not only out-of-pocket financial losses, but substantial additional financial costs associated with trying to restore his reputation...（很多情况下，受害者的损失可能不只是包括现金经济损失，还包括大量额外的为了恢复名誉而造成的经济费用），故选C。

51. J　根据题干中的关键词employers, personal information, background check定位到J段第二句：Honest employers do not need this information with an

initial application（真诚的雇主不需要在人们初次申请时知道该信息），此处的this information指的是上一句中提到的较为机密的个人信息，故选J。

52. E　根据题干中的关键词resume, longer, exposure定位到E段末句：Remember, the longer your resume remains posted on a job board, the more exposure, both positive and not-so-positive, it will receive(记住，你把简历张贴在求职网站上的时间越长，你就暴露得越多，不论是积极方面还是不太积极的方面)，故选E。

53. H　根据题干中的关键词Using a special email address和receive unwelcome emails定位到H段第三句：Using an email address specifically for your job search also eliminates the possibility that you will receive unwelcome emails in your primary mailbox（找工作的时候使用一个专门的邮箱地址还可以降低你在平时常用的邮箱中收到垃圾邮件的概率），故选H。

54. I　根据题干中的关键词references定位到I段第二句：There's no sense in safeguarding your information while sharing private contact information of your references（在分享你的推荐人的具体个人信息的同时捍卫自己的信息是毫无意义的），故选I。

55. A　根据题干中的关键词identity theft, typically for和economic gain定位到A段：Identity theft...involves fraud or deception, typically for economic gain（身份盗窃……包含主要为了获取经济利益的诈骗或欺诈），故选A。

五、经典模拟题五

Directions: *In this section, you are going to read a passage with ten statements attached to it. Each statement contains information given in one of the paragraphs. Identify the paragraph from which the information is derived. You may choose a paragraph more than once. Each paragraph is marked with a letter. Answer the questions by marking the corresponding letter on **Answer Sheet 2**.*

Media Selection for Advertisements

A) After determining the target audience for a product or service, advertising agencies must select the appropriate media for the advertisement. We discuss here the major types of media used in advertising. We focus our attention on seven types of advertising: television, newspapers, radio, magazines, out-of-home, Internet, and direct mail.

B) Television is an attractive medium for advertising because it delivers mass audiences to advertisers. When you consider that nearly three out of four Americans have seen the game show *Who Wants to Be a Millionaire?* you can understand the power of television to communicate with a large audience. When advertisers create a brand, for example, they want to impress consumers with the brand and its image. Television provides an ideal vehicle for this type of communication. But television is an expensive medium, and not all advertisers can afford to use it. Television's influence on advertising is fourfold. First, narrowcasting means that television channels are seen by an increasingly narrow segment of the audience. The Golf Channel, for instance, is watched by people who play golf. Home and Garden Television is seen by those interested in household improvement projects. Thus, audiences are smaller and more *homogeneous* (具有共同特点的) than they have been in the past. Second, there is an increase in the number of television channels available to viewers, and thus, advertisers. This has also resulted in an increase in the sheer number of advertisements to which audiences are exposed. Third, digital recording devices allow audience members more control over which commercials they watch. Fourth, control over programming is being passed from the networks to local cable operators and satellite programmers.

C) After television, the medium attracting the next largest annual ad revenue is newspapers. *The New York Times*, which reaches a national audience, accounts for $1 billion in ad revenue annually. It has increased its national *circulation* (发行量) by 40% and is now available for home delivery in 168 cities. Locally, newspapers are the largest advertising medium. Newspapers are a less expensive advertising medium than television and provide a way for advertisers to communicate a longer, more detailed message to their audience than they can through television. Given new production techniques, advertisements can be printed in newspapers in about 48 hours, meaning newspapers are also a quick way of getting the message out. Newspapers are often the most important form of news for a local community, and they develop a high degree of loyalty from local readers.

D) Advertising on radio continues to grow. Radio is often used in conjunction with outdoor *billboards* (广告牌) and the Internet to reach even more customers than television. Advertisers are likely to use radio because it is a less expensive medium than television, which means advertisers can afford to repeat their ads often. Internet companies are also turning to radio advertising. Radio provides a way for advertisers to communicate with audience members all times of the day. Consumers listen to radio on their way to school or work, at work, on the way home, and in the evening hours. Two major changes—satellite and Internet radio—will force radio advertisers to adapt their methods. Both of these radio forms allow listeners to tune in stations that are more distant than the local stations they could receive in the past. As a result, radio will increasingly attract target audiences who live many miles apart.

E) Newsweeklies, women's titles, and business magazines have all seen increases in advertising because they attract the high-end market. Magazines are popular with advertisers because of the narrow market that they deliver. A broadcast medium such as network television attracts all types of audience members, but magazine audiences are more homogeneous. If you read *Sports Illustrated*, for example, you have much in common with the magazine's other readers. Advertisers see magazines as an efficient way of reaching target audience members. Advertisers using the print media—magazines and newspapers—will need to adapt to two main changes. First, the Internet will bring larger audiences to local newspapers. These audiences will be more diverse and geographically *dispersed*（分散）than in the past. Second, advertisers will have to understand how to use an increasing number of magazines for their target audiences. Although some magazines will maintain national audiences, a large number of magazines will entertain narrower audiences.

F) Out-of-home advertising, also called place-based advertising, has become an increasingly effective way of reaching consumers, who are more active than ever before. Many consumers today do not sit at home and watch television. Using billboards, newsstands, and bus shelters for advertising is an effective way of reaching these on-the-go consumers. More consumers travel longer distances to and from work, which also makes out-of-home advertising effective. Technology has changed the nature of the billboard business, making it a more effective medium than in the past. Using digital printing, billboard companies can print a billboard in 2 hours, compared with 6 days previously. This allows advertisers more variety in the types of messages they create because they can change their messages more quickly.

G) As consumers become more comfortable with online shopping, advertisers will seek to reach this market. As consumers get more of their news and information from the Internet, the ability of television and radio to get the word out to consumers will decrease. The challenge to Internet advertisers is to create ads that audience members remember. Internet advertising will play a more prominent role in organizations' advertising in the near future. Internet audiences tend to be quite homogeneous, but small. Advertisers will have to adjust their methods to reach these audiences and will have to adapt their persuasive strategies to the online medium as well.

H) A final advertising medium is direct mail, which uses mailings to consumers to communicate a client's message. Direct mail includes newsletters, postcards, and special promotions. Direct mail is an effective way to build relationships with consumers. For many businesses, direct mail is the most effective form of advertising.

注意：此部分试题请在**答题卡1**上作答。

46. Direct mail is an effective form of advertising for businesses to develop relationships with consumers.

47. Magazines are seen by advertisers as an efficient way to reach target audiences.

48. Television is an attractive advertising medium in that it has large audiences.

49. Advertising on radio is less expensive than on television and this makes advertisers be able to afford to repeat their ads often.

50. With the increase in the number of TV channels, the number of TV ads people can see has also increased.

51. The challenge to Internet advertisers is to create ads that are easy to be remembered by the audience.

52. That more consumers travel longer distances to and from work is one of the reasons why out-of-home advertising has become effective.

53. Compared with television, newspapers as an advertising medium convey more detailed messages.

54. This passage discusses seven major types of media used in advertising.

55. Internet advertisers will have to adjust their methods to reach audiences that tend to be quite homogeneous, but small.

试题解析

　　本文是一篇说明文，采用的是"总—分"的结构，详细介绍了广告商如何选择发布广告的媒体。首段简要介绍背景，接着分别介绍了七种主流广告媒介：电视、报纸、杂志、广播、户外广告、网络、直邮。

46. **H** 根据题干中的关键词direct mail, effective form定位到H段第三句：Direct mail is an effective way to build relationships with consumers（直邮是一种与消费者建立联系的有效手段），故选H。

47. **E** 根据题干中的关键词magazines, reach target audience定位到E段第五句：Advertisers see magazines as an efficient way of reaching target audience members（广告商将杂志视为接触目标读者的一种有效途径），故选E。

48. **B** 根据题干中的关键词television is an attractive advertising medium定位到B段首句：Television is an attractive medium for advertising because it delivers mass audiences to advertisers（对于广告而言，电视是一种极具吸引力的媒介，因为它能为广告商带来大量观众)故选B。

49. **D** 根据题干中的关键词Advertising on radio, afford to repeat their ads often定位到D段第三句：Advertisers are likely to use radio because it is a less expensive medium than television, which means advertisers can afford to repeat their ads often（广告商们倾向于使用广播室，因为它是一个比电视便宜的媒介，这意味着广告商们能够承担起多次反复播放他们的广告的费用），故选D。

50. **B** 根据题干中的关键词increase in the number of TV channels定位到B段倒数三、四句：Second, there is an increase in the number of television channels available to viewers, and thus, advertisers. This has also resulted in an increase in the sheer number of advertisements to which audiences are exposed.（第二，对于观众而言，现在的电视频道越来越多，而对于广告商也是如此。这也使得观众能看到的广告的绝对数量直线上升），故选B。

51. **G** 根据题干中的关键词the challenge to Internet advertisers定位到G段第三句：The challenge to Internet advertisers is to create ads that audience members remember（网络广告商所面临的挑战是创作出让目标受众能够记住的广告），故选G。

52. **F** 根据题干中的关键词 travel longer distances, out-of-home advertising, effective 定位到F段第四句：More consumers travel longer distances to and from work, which also makes out-of-home advertising effective（更多的客户上下班路程增加，这也使得户外广告变得有效），故选F。

53. **C** 根据题干中的关键词 Compared with television, newspapers, more detailed messages 定位到C段第五句：Newspapers are a less expensive advertising medium than television and provide a way for advertisers to communicate a longer, more detailed message to their audience than they can through television.（在报纸上刊登广告，费用没有在电视上那么高，而且与电视相比，广告商可以通过报纸与读者交流更长、更详细的信息），故选C。

54. **A** 根据题干中的关键词 seven 和 major types of media 定位到A段第二句和第三句：We discuss here the major types of media used in advertising. We focus our attention on seven types of advertising...（我们在此讨论广告宣传中用到的主要媒体形式。我们主要关注七种广告宣传形式……），故选A。

55. **G** 根据题干中的关键词 Internet 和 audiences that tend to be 定位到G段最后两句：Internet audiences tend to be quite homogeneous, but small. Advertisers will have to adjust their methods to reach these audiences...（网络受众十分单一，但数量较少。广告商们将不得不调整他们接触到这些受众的方式……），故选G。

六、经典模拟题六

Directions: *In this section, you are going to read a passage with ten statements attached to it. Each statement contains information given in one of the paragraphs. Identify the paragraph from which the information is derived. You may choose a paragraph more than once. Each paragraph is marked with a letter. Answer the questions by marking the corresponding letter on **Answer Sheet 2**.*

That's enough, kids

A）It was a lovely day at the park and Stella Bianchi was enjoying the sunshine with her two children when a young boy, aged about four, approached her two-year-old son and pushed him to the ground. "I'd watched him for a little while and my son was the fourth or fifth child he'd shoved," she says. "I went over to them, picked up my son, turned to the boy and said, firmly, 'No, we don't push.'" What happened next was unexpected.

B) "The boy's mother ran toward me from across the park," Stella says. "I thought she was coming over to apologise, but instead she started shouting at me for 'disciplining her child'. All I did was let him know his behaviour was unacceptable. Was I supposed to sit back while her kid did whatever he wanted, hurting other children in the process?" Getting your own children to play nice is difficult enough. Dealing with other people's children has become a minefield. In my house, jumping on the sofa is not allowed. In my sister's house it's encouraged. For her it's about kids being kids: "If you can't do it at three, when can you do it?" Each of these philosophies is valid and, it has to be said, my son loves visiting his aunt's house. But I find myself saying "no" a lot when her kids are over at mine. That's OK between sisters but becomes dangerous territory when you're talking to the children of friends or acquaintances.

C) "Kids aren't all raised the same," agrees Professor Naomi White of Monash University. "But there's still an idea that they're the property of the parents. We see our children as an extension of ourselves, so if you're saying that my child is behaving inappropriately, then that's somehow a criticism of me." In those circumstances, it's difficult to know whether to approach the child directly or the parent first. There are two schools of thought. "I'd go to the child first," says Andrew Fuller, author of *Tricky Kids*. "Usually a quiet reminder that 'we don't do that here' is enough. Kids have finely tuned *antennae*（直觉）for how to behave in different settings."

D) He points out that bringing it up with the parent first may make them feel neglectful, which could cause problems. Of course, approaching the child first can bring its own headaches, too. This is why White recommends that you approach the parents first. "Raise your concerns with the parents if they're there and ask them to deal with it," she says. Asked how to approach a parent in this situation, psychologist Meredith Fuller answers: "Explain your needs as well as stressing the importance of the friendship. Preface your remarks with something like: 'I know you will think I'm silly but in my house I don't want...'"

E) When it comes to situations where you're caring for another child, White is straightforward: "Common sense must prevail. If things don't go well then have a chat." There're a couple of new grey areas. Physical punishment, once accepted from any adult, is no longer appropriate. "Now you can't do it without feeling uneasy about it," White says. Men might also feel uneasy about dealing with other people's children. "Men feel nervous," White says. "A new set of considerations has come to the fore as part of the debate about how we handle children."

F) For Andrew Fuller, the child-centric nature of our society has affected everyone. "The rules are different now from when today's parents were growing up," he says. "Adults are scared of saying, 'Don't swear', or asking a child to stand up on a bus. They're worried that there will be conflict if they point these things out— either from older children, or their parents." He sees it as a loss of the sense of common public good and public *courtesy*（礼貌）, and says that adults suffer from it as much as children.

G) Meredith Fuller agrees. "A code of conduct is hard to create when you're living in a world in which everyone is exhausted from overwork and lack of sleep, and a world in which nice people are perceived to finish last." "It's about what I'm doing and what I need," Andrew Fuller says. "The days when a kid came home from school and said, 'I got into trouble', and dad said, 'You probably deserved it', are over. Now the parents are charging up to the school to have a go at teachers."

H) This jumping to our children's defence is part of what fuels the "walking on eggshells" feeling that surrounds our dealings with other people's children. You know that if you *remonstrate*（劝诫）with the child, you're going to have to deal with the parent. It's admirable to be protective of our kids, but is it good? "Children have to learn to negotiate the world on their own, within reasonable boundaries," White says. "I suspect that it's only certain sectors of the population doing the running to the school—better-educated parents are probably more likely to be too involved."

I) White believes our notions of a more child-centred society should be challenged. "Today we have a situation where, in many families, both parents work, so the amount of time children get from parents has diminished," she says. "Also, sometimes when we talk about being child-centred, it's a way of talking about treating our children like *commodities*（商品）. We're centred on them but in ways that reflect positively on us. We treat them as objects whose appearance and achievements are something we can be proud of, rather than serve the best interests of the children."

J) One way over-worked, under-resourced parents show commitment to their children is to leap to their defence. Back at the park, Bianchi's *intervention*（干预）on her son's behalf ended in an undignified exchange of insulting words with the other boy's mother. As Bianchi approached the park bench where she'd been sitting, other mums came up to her and congratulated her on taking a stand. "Apparently the boy had a longstanding reputation for bad behaviour and his mum for even worse behaviour if he was challenged."

K) Andrew Fuller doesn't believe that we should be afraid of dealing with other people's kids. "Look at kids that aren't your own as a potential minefield," he says. He recommends that we don't stay silent over inappropriate behaviour, particularly with regular visitors.

注意: 此部分试题请在**答题卡1**上作答。

46. Due to the child-centric nature of our society, people are reluctant to point out kids' wrongdoings.

47. It's more difficult to deal with other people's children than to get your own children to play nice.

48. According to Professor Naomi White of Monash University, when one's kids are criticised, their parents will probably feel the same.

49. White believes that the notions of a more child-centred society should be challenged.

50. Stella Bianchi expected the young boy's mother to make an apology after she talked to the boy.

51. In a world where everyone is exhausted from overwork and lack of sleep, it's difficult to create a code of conduct.

52. According to Professor White, today's parents treat their children as something they can be proud of.

53. Andrew Fuller suggests that, when kids behave inappropriately, people should not stay silent.

54. Nowadays, when kids come home and tell their parents that they get into trouble at

school parents are likely to charge up to the school instead of blaming their own children.

55. According to Andrew Fuller, when seeing other people's kids misbehave, one should talk to them directly in a kind way.

试题解析

本文是一篇问题解决型的议论文，主要讨论管教别人的孩子这一问题。首先叙述了一位家长的经历，说明管教别人的孩子会招来麻烦。其次指出在发现别人的孩子言行不当时，人们对于先找家长还是先找孩子，持有不同看法。接着分析了在对待孩子问题上的一些其他灰色区域和因素。最后指出如何解决这一问题。

46. F 根据题干中的关键词the child-centric nature of our society定位到F段首句："For Andrew Fuller, the child-centric nature of our society has affected everyone（在Andrew Fuller看来，我们社会以小孩为中心的本质影响了每一个人），随后文中指出成年人现在都害怕指出小孩们所犯的错，故选F。

47. B 根据题干中的关键词deal with other people's children定位到B段第五句和第六句：Getting your own children to play nice is difficult enough. Dealing with other people's children has become a minefield(让自己的孩子表现乖巧就已经够难了。管教别人的孩子，就更像是进入了雷区)，言外之意即管教别人的孩子比教育自己的孩子还要难，故选B。

48. C 根据题干中的关键词Professor Naomi White of Monash University定位到C段，其中第三句指出：if you're saying that my child is behaving inappropriately, then that's somehow a criticism of me(如果你说我的孩子表现不好，那么在某种程度上就是在批评我)，故选C。

49. I 根据题干中的关键词notions of a more child-centred society定位到I段首句：White believes our notions of a more child-centred society should be challenged（怀特认为我们更加以孩子为中心的社会这一观点应该受到质疑），故选I。

50. B 根据题干中的关键词Stella Bianchi, young boy's mother和make an apology定位到B段第二句：I thought she was coming over to apologise（我以为她是来道歉的），故选B。

51. G 根据题干中的关键词 exhausted from overwork and lack of sleep和a code of

conduct定位到G段第二句：A code of conduct is hard to create when you're living in a world in which everyone is exhausted from overwork and lack of sleep（当你生活在一个人人都因工作过度和睡眠不足而变得疲惫不堪的世界，就很难建立一种行为准则），故选G。

52. I 根据题干中的关键词treat...as和be proud of定位到I段末句：We treat them as objects whose appearance and achievements are something we can be proud of, rather than serve the best interests of the children（我们把他们看成了物品，以其外表和成就为傲，而不是最大限度地去满足他们的需求），此处的them指的是前文提到的our children，故选I。

53. K 根据题干中的关键词Andrew Fuller和behave inappropriately定位到K段末句：He recommends that we don't stay silent over inappropriate behaviour（他建议我们不要对不恰当的行为坐视不管），故选K。

54. G 根据题干中的关键词kids...get into trouble at school定位到G段末句："The days when a kid came home from school and said, 'I got into trouble', and dad said, 'You probably deserved it', are over. Now the parents are charging up to the school to have a go at teachers."（"孩子放学回家说'我有麻烦了'，而父亲说'你活该'的日子已经结束了。现在家长们会冲到学校去直接找老师"），故选G。

55. C 根据题干中的关键词Andrew Fuller定位到C段倒数第二、三句："I'd go to the child first," says Andrew Fuller, author of *Tricky Kids*. "Usually a quiet reminder that 'we don't do that here' is enough.（"我会先去跟孩子谈"，《棘手的孩子们》一书的作者安德鲁·福勒说。"通常一个温和的提醒'我们不这样做'就足够了"），故选C。

七、经典模拟题七

Directions: *In this section, you are going to read a passage with ten statements attached to it. Each statement contains information given in one of the paragraphs. Identify the paragraph from which the information is derived. You may choose a paragraph more than once. Each paragraph is marked with a letter. Answer the questions by marking the corresponding letter on **Answer Sheet 2**.*

How Do You See Diversity?

A) As a manager, Tiffany is responsible for interviewing applicants for some of the positions with her company. During one interview, she noticed that the candidate never made direct eye contact. She was puzzled and somewhat disappointed because she liked the individual otherwise.

B) He had a perfect résumé and gave good responses to her questions, but the fact that he never looked her in the eye said "untrustworthy," so she decided to offer the job to her second choice. "It wasn't until I attended a diversity workshop that I realized the person we passed over was the perfect person," Tiffany confesses. What she hadn't known at the time of the interview was that the candidate's "different" behavior was simply a cultural misunderstanding. He was an Asian-American raised in a household where respect for those in authority was shown by *averting*（避开）your eyes.

C) "I was just thrown off by the lack of eye contact; not realizing it was cultural," Tiffany says. "I missed out, but will not miss that opportunity again." Many of us have had similar encounters with behaviors we perceive as different. As the world becomes smaller and our workplaces more diverse, it is becoming essential to expand our understanding of others and to reexamine some of our false assumptions.

Hire Advantage

D) At a time when hiring qualified people is becoming more difficult, employers who can eliminate invalid *biases*（偏见）from the process have a distinct advantage. My company, Mindsets LLC, helps organizations and individuals see their own blind spots. A real estate recruiter we worked with illustrates the positive difference such training can make. "During my Mindsets coaching session, I was taught how to recruit a diversified workforce. I recruited people from different cultures and skill sets. The agents were able to utilize their full potential and experiences to build up the company. When the real estate market began to change, it was because we had a diverse agent pool that we were able to stay in the real estate market much longer than others in the same profession."

Blinded by Gender

E) Dale is an account executive who attended one of my workshops on supervising a diverse workforce. "Through one of the sessions, I discovered my personal bias," he recalls. "I learned I had not been looking at a person as a whole person, and being open to differences." In his case, the blindness was not about culture but rather gender.

F) "I had a management position open in my department; and the two finalists were a man and a woman. Had I not attended this workshop, I would have automatically assumed the man was the best candidate because the position required quite a bit of extensive travel. My reasoning would have been that even though both candidates were great and could have been successful in the position, I assumed the woman would have wanted to be home with her children and not travel." Dale's assumptions are another example of the well-intentioned but incorrect thinking that limits an organization's ability to tap into the full potential of a diverse workforce.

G) "I learned from the class that instead of imposing my gender biases into the situation, I needed to present the full range of duties, responsibilities and expectations to all candidates and allow them to make an informed decision." Dale credits the workshop, "because it helped me make decisions based on fairness."

Year of the Know-It-All

H) Doug is another supervisor who attended one of my workshops. He recalls a major lesson learned from his own employee. "One of my most embarrassing moments was when I had a Chinese-American employee put in a request to take time off to celebrate Chinese New Year. In my ignorance, I assumed he had his dates wrong, as the first of January had just passed. When I advised him of this, I gave him a long talking-to about turning in requests early with the proper dates.

I) "He patiently waited, then when I was done, he said he would like Chinese New Year off, not the Western New Year. He explained politely that in his culture the new year did not begin January first, and that Chinese New Year, which is tied to the lunar cycle, is one of the most celebrated holidays on the Chinese calendar. Needless to say, I felt very embarrassed in assuming he had his dates mixed up.

But I learned a great deal about assumptions, and that the timing of holidays varies considerably from culture to culture. "Attending the diversity workshop helped me realize how much I could learn by simply asking questions and creating dialogues with my employees, rather than making assumptions and trying to be a know-it-all," Doug admits. "The biggest thing I took away from the workshop is learning how to be more 'inclusive' to differences."

A Better Bottom Line

J) An open mind about diversity not only improves organizations internally, it is profitable as well. These comments from a customer service representative show how an inclusive attitude can improve sales. "Most of my customers speak English as a second language. One of the best things my company has done is to contract with a language service that offers translations over the phone. It wasn't until my boss received Mindsets' training that she was able to understand how important inclusiveness was to customer service. As a result, our customer base has increased."

K) Once we start to see people as individuals, and discard the stereotypes, we can move positively toward inclusiveness for everyone. Diversity is about coming together and taking advantage of our differences and similarities. It is about building better communities and organizations that enhance us as individuals and reinforce our shared humanity.

L) When we begin to question our assumptions and challenge what we think we have learned from our past, from the media, peers, family, friends, etc., we begin to realize that some of our conclusions are *flawed*（有缺陷的）or contrary to our fundamental values. We need to train ourselves to think differently, shift our mindsets and realize that diversity opens doors for all of us, creating opportunities in organizations and communities that benefit everyone.

注意：此部分试题请在**答题卡1**上作答。

46. Mindsets LLC is a kind of personnel training company.

47. When Doug, a supervisor, respond to a Chinese-American employee's request for leave, he told him to get the dates right.

48. During an interview with her candidate, what bothered Tiffany is that he just wouldn't look her in the eye.

49. After one of the workshops, account executive Dale realized that he must get rid of his gender bias.

50. Tiffany's misjudgment about the candidate stemmed from cultural ignorance.

51. According to the author, in the course of economic globalization, it is becoming essential to increase understanding of people of other cultures.

52. After attending Mindsets' workshops, the participants came to know the importance of inclusiveness to their business.

53. Doug felt very embarrassed when he realized that his assumption was wrong.

54. When we view people as individuals and get rid of stereotypes, we can achieve diversity and benefit from the differences and similarities between us.

55. Dale thinks that Mindsets LLC's workshop helped him make fair decisions.

试题解析

本文是一篇说明文，"分—总"结构，详细介绍了解多元化的好处。首先通过五个案例说明人力资源主管参加思维公司多元化培训的益处，接着总结如何包容多元化。

46. D 根据题干关键词Mindsets LLC定位到D段第二、三两句：My company, Mindsets LLC, helps organizations and individuals see their own blind spots. A real estate recruiter we worked with illustrates the positive difference such training can make.(我的公司，思维定势有限公司，帮助组织和个人看到自身的盲点。一个与我们合作过的地产公司招聘人员举例说明了这种培训能够带来的积极影响)，由此可知，Mindsets是一个人力资源培训公司，故选D。原文中的recruiter替换为题干中的personnel。

47. H 根据关键词Doug和a Chinese-American employee's request定位到H段：道格是参加我们讲习班的另外一位管理人员。他回忆了从自己的员工哪里吸取的一大教训。"让我感到最尴尬的时刻之一就是我的一位美籍华裔员工向我请假去庆祝中国新年的时候。我无知地认为他把日期搞错了，因为一月一日刚刚过去。当我向他提出这点时，我跟他说了半天：应该在正确的日期前递交申请。原文中的request to take time off替换为题干中的request for leave。故选H。

48. A 根据题干关键词during an interview将答案定位到A段第二、三两句：During one interview, she noticed that the candidate never made direct eye

contact. She was puzzled and somewhat disappointed because she liked the individual otherwise.(她觉得十分困惑，甚至有点失望，因为除了这一点之外，她十分喜欢这个人)，原文中的puzzled and somewhat disappointed替换为题干中的bothered，题干wouldn't look her in the eye同义替换原文中的the candidate never made direct eye contact(应试者一直没和她进行直接的目光交流)。故选A。

49. E 根据题干关键词account executive Dale定位到E段：Dale is an account executive who attended one of my workshops on supervising a diverse workforce. "Through one of the sessions, I discovered my personal bias," he recalls...In his case, the blindness was not about culture but rather gender.(戴尔是名业务经理，他参加了我其中一个关于多元化劳动力的讲习班。"通过其中一次课程，我发现了自己的个人偏见"，他回忆说……就他而言，他的盲点不在于文化，而在于性别)。即Dale发现了自己在性别上的偏见，由此推断他认识到自己应该消除性别偏见。故选E。

50. B 根据题干关键词misjudgment和the candidate将答案定位到B段倒数第二句：What she hadn't known at the time of the interview was that the candidate's "different" behavior was simply a cultural misunderstanding.(在面试的时候，她不知道候选人"不同的"行为，其实不过是一种文化误解)，即她对那位候选人的误解是由于她忽视了文化因素，故选B。原文中的hadn't known 替换为题干中的ignorance。

51. C 根据题干关键词 becoming essential定位到C段尾句：As the world becomes smaller and our workplaces more diverse, it is becoming essential to expand our understanding of others and to reexamine some of our false assumptions.(随着世界变小，我们的工作地点变得更为多元化，我们很有必要增加对他人的了解，重新审视我们某些错误的假设)。前文提到的候选人是亚裔美国人，来自不同文化，由此可知此处的"他人"即来自其他文化的人。故选C。原文中的 expand our understanding of替换为题干中的 increasing understanding of, others替换为people of other cultures。

52. J 根据关键词Mindsets和importance定位到J段倒数第二句：It wasn't until my boss received Mindsets' training that she was able to understand how important inclusiveness was to customer service.(我们的老板参加了思维公司的培训之后才认识到包容对于客服的重要性)。文中的It wasn't until...training替换

为题干中的After...workshops，文中的understand how important替换为题干中的know the importance，to customer service替换为题干中的to business，故选J。

53. I 根据关键词Doug, felt和assumption定位到I段第三句：Needless to say, I felt very embarrassed in assuming he had his dates mixed up.（毋庸赘言，我错误地认为他把日期弄混了，这使我感到十分尴尬），故选I。

54. K 根据关键词people as individuals 和stereotypes定位到K段前两句：Once we start to see people as individuals, and discard the stereotypes, we can move positively toward inclusiveness for everyone. Diversity is about coming together and taking advantage of our differences and similarities.（一旦我们把人看作个体，抛弃旧有的思维定式，我们就能逐渐做到对每个人都包容。多元化就是大家聚到一起，充分利用人与人之间的差异和相似之处）。文中的once替换为题干中的when，see替换为view，discard替换为get rid of，move...for everyone 替换为achieve diversity，taking advantage of 替换为benefit from，our替换为between us，differences and similarities原词重现。故选K。

55. G 根据关键词Dale和workshop定位到G段尾句：Dale credits the workshop, "because it helped me make decisions based on fairness." （戴尔把这一点归功于讲习班："因为讲习班有助于我在公平的基础上做出决定"）。原文中的make decisions based on fairness替换为题干中的make fair decisions，故选G。

八、经典模拟题八

Directions: *In this section, you are going to read a passage with ten statements attached to it. Each statement contains information given in one of the paragraphs. Identify the paragraph from which the information is derived. You may choose a paragraph more than once. Each paragraph is marked with a letter. Answer the questions by marking the corresponding letter on* **Answer Sheet 2***.*

Why Integrity Matters

What Is Integrity?

A） The key to integrity is consistency—not only setting high personal standards for oneself （honesty, responsibility, respect for others, fairness） but also living up to those standards each and every day. One who has integrity is bound by and follows moral and *ethical* （道德上的） standards even when making life's hard choices, choices which may be clouded by stress, pressure to succeed, or temptation.

B） What happens if we lie, cheat, steal, or violate other ethical standards? We feel disappointed in ourselves and ashamed. But a *lapse* （缺失） of integrity also affects our relationships with others. Trust is essential in any important relationship, whether personal or professional. Who can trust someone who is dishonest or unfair? Thus, integrity must be one of our most important goals.

Risky Business

C） We are each responsible for our own decisions, even if the decision-making process has been undermined by stress or peer pressure. The real test of character is whether we can learn from our mistake, by understanding why we acted as we did and then exploring ways to avoid similar problems in the future.

D） Making ethical decisions is a critical part of avoiding future problems. We must learn to recognize risks, because if we can't see the risks we're taking, we can't make responsible choices. To identify risks, we need to know the rules and be aware of the facts. For example, one who doesn't know the rules about *plagiarism* （剽窃） may accidentally use words or ideas without giving proper credit, or one who fails to keep careful research notes may unintentionally fail to quote and cite sources as required. But the fact that such a violation is "unintentional" does not excuse the misconduct. Ignorance is not a defense.

"But Everybody Does It"

E） Most people who get in trouble do know the rules and facts but manage to fool themselves about the risks they're taking by using excuses: "Everyone else does it," "I'm not hurting anyone," or "I really need this grade." Excuses can get very elaborate: "I know I'm looking at another's exam, but that's not cheating because I'm just checking my answers, not copying." We must be honest about our actions and avoid excuses. If we fool ourselves into believing we're not doing anything wrong, we can't see the real choice we're making—and that leads to bad decisions.

F) To avoid fooling yourself, watch out for excuses and try this test: Ask how you would feel if your actions were public and anyone could be watching over your shoulder. If you'd rather hide your actions, that's an indication that you're taking a risk and rationalizing it to yourself.

Evaluating Risks

G) To decide whether a risk is worth taking, you must examine the consequences, in the future as well as right now, negative as well as positive, and to others as well as to yourself. Those who take risks they later regret usually focus on immediate benefits and simply haven't considered what might go wrong. The consequences of getting caught are serious and may include a "0" on a test or assignment, an "F" in the class, *suspension*(暂令停学) or dismissal from school and a ruined reputation. In fact, when you break a rule or law, you lose control over your life and give others the power to impose punishment that you have no control over. This is an extremely *vulnerable* (脆弱的) position. There may be some matters of life and death or highest principle, which might justify such a risk, but there aren't many things that fall in this category.

Getting Away With It—Or Not

H) Those who don't get caught pay an even higher price. A cheater doesn't learn from the test, which *deprives*(剥夺) him/her of an education. Cheating undermines confidence and independence; the cheater is a fraud, and knows that without dishonesty, he/she would have failed. Cheating destroys self-respect and integrity, leaving the cheater ashamed, guilty, and afraid of getting caught. Worst of all, a cheater who doesn't get caught the first time usually cheats again, not only because he/she is farther behind, but also because it seems "easier." This slippery slope of eroding ethics and bigger risks leads only to disaster. Eventually, the cheater gets caught, and the later he/she gets caught, the worse the consequences.

Cheating Hurts Others, Too

I) Cheaters often feel invisible, as if their actions "don't count" and don't really hurt anyone. But individual choices have an intense *cumulative* (累积的) effect.

Cheating can spread like a disease. Recent statistics suggest 30% or more of college students cheat. If a class is graded on a curve, cheating hurts others' grades. Even if there is no curve, cheating "poisons" the classroom, and others may feel pressured to join in. ("If I don't cheat, I can't compete with those who do.") Cheating also has a destructive impact on teachers. The real reward of good teaching is seeing students learn, but a cheater says, "I'm not interested in what you're trying to teach; all I care about is stealing a grade, regardless of the effect on others." The end result is a destructive attack on the quality of your education. Finally, cheating can hurt the reputation of the university and harm those who worked hard for their degree.

Why Integrity Matters

J) If cheating becomes the norm, then we are in big trouble. We must rely on the honesty and good faith of others. If not, we couldn't put money in the bank, buy food, clothing or medicine from others, drive across a bridge, get on a plane, go to the dentist—the list is endless. There are many examples of the vast harm that is caused when individuals forget or ignore the effect their dishonesty can have. The Watergate scandal, for example, has undermined the faith of many Americans in the integrity of political and economic leaders and society as a whole.

K) In sum, we all have a common stake in our school, our community, and our society. Our actions do matter. It is essential that we act with integrity in order to build the kind of world in which we want to live.

注意：此部分试题请在**答题卡1**上作答。

46. Integrity matters in that all social activities rely on people's honesty and good faith.

47. If one doesn't wish to fool himself, he should avoid making excuses.

48. A person of integrity not only sets high moral and ethical standards but also sticks to them in their daily life.

49. Violation of a rule is misconduct even if it is claimed to be unintentional.

50. Integrity is the basis of mutual trust in personal and professional relationships.

51. According to the author, a cheater who doesn't get caught right away will pay more dearly.

52. Those who take risks they regret later value immediate benefits most.

53. We must learn to identify the risks we are going to take to ensure we make responsible choices.

54. Many Americans lost faith in the integrity of their political leaders as a result of the Watergate scandal.

55. Cheaters at exam don't care about their education; all they care about is how to steal a grade.

试题解析

本文是一篇议论文，主要论述了诚信的重要性，文章共分七个部分，分别讲述：什么是诚信、要学会识别风险、避免找借口、估量风险、作弊的代价、作弊同样伤害他人、为什么说诚信重要。

46. J　根据题干中的关键词rely on, honesty and good faith定位到J段第二、三句：We must rely on the honesty and good faith of others. If not, we couldn't put money in the bank, buy food, clothing or medicine from others, drive across a bridge, get on a plane, go to the dentist—the list is endless. （我们必须依赖他人的诚实和守信。否则，我们没法把钱存进银行，没法从别人那里购买食物、衣物或者药物，没法开车过一座桥，没法坐上一架飞机或者去看牙医——这类例子数不胜数），故选J。

47. F　根据题干中的关键词fool himself, avoid excuses定位到F段首句：To avoid fooling yourself, watch out for excuses... （为了避免自欺欺人，不要给自己找借口），故选F。

48. A　根据题干中的关键词integrity, not only sets high...standards, but also定位到首段首句：The key to integrity is consistency—not only setting high personal standards for oneself （honesty, responsibility, respect for others, fairness）but also living up to those standards each and every day. ［诚信的关键就是言行一致——不仅要为自己制定高标准（诚实、责任感、尊敬他人、公平），而且每一天都要遵守这些标准］，故选A。

49. D　根据题干中的关键词violation, misconduct, unintentional定位到D段倒数第二句：But the fact that such a violation is "unintentional" does not excuse the misconduct.（但是，这种违规是"非故意的"不能成为不正当行为的借口），故选D。

50. B　根据题干中的关键词integrity, personal and professional relationships, trust定位到B段第三至五句：But a lapse of integrity also affects our relationships

with others. Trust is essential in any important relationship, whether personal or professional. Who can trust someone who is dishonest or unfair? (但是诚信的缺失也会影响我们与他人的关系。信任是任何重要的人际关中必不可缺的部分，无论是私人关系，还是工作关系。如果一个人不诚实或有失公正，谁会信任他呢)，故选B。

51. H 根据题干中的关键词who doesn't get caught, pay定位到H段首句：Those who don't get caught pay an even higher price. （那些没被抓到的人会付出更昂贵的代价），故选H。

52. G 根据题干中的关键词those who take risks they regret later, immediate benefits定位到G段第二句：Those who take risks they later regret usually focus on immediate benefits and simply haven't considered what might go wrong.（那些冒了风险之后又后悔的人，通常只关注眼前利益，完全没有考虑哪里可能会出问题），故选G。

53. D 根据题干中的关键词must learn to, the risks, make responsible choices定位到D段第二句：We must learn to recognize risks, because if we can't see the risks we're taking, we can't make responsible choices. （我们必须学会识别风险，因为如果我们不能看清自己所承担的风险，就不能做出负责任的选择），故选D。

54. J 根据题干中的关键词political leaders, the Watergate scandal定位到J段尾句：The Watergate scandal, for example, has undermined the faith of many Americans in the integrity of political and economic leaders and society as a whole.（比如说水门事件，就已经降低了许多美国民众对政治、经济领导人和整个社会的信任），故选J。

55. I 根据题干中的关键词cheaters, care about, steal a grade定位到I段倒数第三句：but a cheater says, "I'm not interested in what you're trying to teach; all I care about is stealing a grade(但是一个作弊者说："我对你教的东西不感兴趣，我只关心能够窃取到一个成绩"），故选I。

九、经典模拟题九

Directions: *In this section, you are going to read a passage with ten statements attached to it. Each statement contains information given in one of the paragraphs.*

*Identify the paragraph from which the information is derived. You may choose a paragraph more than once. Each paragraph is marked with a letter. Answer the questions by marking the corresponding letter on **Answer Sheet 2**.*

Small Schools Rising

This year's list of the top 100 high schools shows that today, those with fewer students are flourishing.

A) Fifty years ago, they were the latest thing in educational reform: big, modern, suburban high schools with students counted in the thousands. As *baby boomers* (二战后婴儿潮时期出生的人) came of high-school age, big schools promised economic efficiency, a greater choice of courses, and, of course, better football teams. Only years later did we understand the trade-offs this involved: the creation of excessive *bureaucracies* (官僚机构), the difficulty of forging personal connections between teachers and students. SAT scores began dropping in 1963; today, on average, 30% of students do not complete high school in four years, a figure that rises to 50% in poor urban neighborhoods. While the emphasis on teaching to higher, test-driven standards as set in NO Child Left Behind resulted in significantly better performance in elementary (and some middle) schools, high schools for a variety of reasons seemed to have made little progress.

B) Size isn't everything, but it does matter, and the past decade has seen a noticeable countertrend toward smaller schools. This has been due, in part, to the Bill and Melinda Gates Foundation, which has invested $1.8 billion in American high schools, helping to open about 1,000 small schools—most of them with about 400 kids each, with an average enrollment of only 150 per grade. About 500 more are on the drawing board. Districts all over the country are taking notice, along with mayors in cities like New York, Chicago and San Diego. The movement includes independent public charter schools, such as No.1 BASIS in Tucson, with only 120 high-schoolers and 18 graduates this year. It embraces district-sanctioned magnet schools, such as the Talented and Gifted School with 198 students, and the Science and Engineering Magnet, with 383, which share a building in Dallas, as well as the City Honors School in Buffalo, N.Y., which grew out of volunteer evening seminars for students. And it includes alternative schools with students selected by *lottery*（抽签）, such as H-B Woodlawn in Arlington, Va. And most noticeable of all, there is the phenomenon of large urban and suburban high schools that have split up into smaller units of a few hundred, generally housed in the same grounds that once boasted thousands of students all marching to the same band.

C）Hillsdale High School in San Mateo, Calif., is one of those, ranking No. 423—among the top 2% in the country—on *Newsweek*'s annual ranking of America's top high schools. The success of small schools is apparent in the listings. Ten years ago, when the first *Newsweek* list based on college-level test participation was published, only three of the top 100 schools had graduating classes smaller than 100 students. This year there are 22. Nearly 250 schools on the full *Newsweek* list of the top 5% of schools nationally had fewer than 200 graduates in 2007.

D）Although many of Hillsdale's students came from wealthy households, by the late 1990s average test scores were sliding and it had earned the unaffectionate *nickname*（绰号）"Hillsjail." Jeff Gilbert, a Hillsdale teacher who became principal last year, remembers sitting with other teachers watching students file out of a graduation ceremony and asking one another in astonishment, "How did that student graduate?"

E）So in 2003 Hillsdale remade itself into three "houses," romantically named Florence, Marrakech and Kyoto. Each of the 300 arriving ninth graders are *randomly*（随机地）assigned to one of the houses, where they will keep the same four core subject teachers for two years, before moving on to another for 11th and 12th grades. The closeness this system cultivates is reinforced by the institution of "advisory" classes. Teachers meet with students in groups of 25, five mornings a week, for open-ended discussions of everything from homework problems to bad Saturday-night dates. The advisers also meet with students privately and stay in touch with parents, so they are deeply invested in the students' success. "We're constantly talking about one another's advisees," says English teacher Chris Crockett. "If you hear that yours isn't doing well in math, or see them sitting outside the dean's office, it's like a personal failure." Along with the new structure came a more demanding academic program; the percentage of freshmen taking biology jumped from 17 to 95. "It was rough for some, but by senior year, two-thirds have moved up to physics," says Gilbert. "Our kids are coming to school in part because they know there are adults here who know them and care for them." But not all schools show advances after downsizing, and it remains to be seen whether smaller schools will be a cure-all solution.

F) The *Newsweek* list of top U.S. high schools was made this year, as in years past, according to a single metric, the proportion of students taking college-level exams. Over the years this system has come in for its share of criticism for its simplicity. But that is also its strength: it's easy for readers to understand, and to do the arithmetic for their own schools if they'd like.

G) Ranking schools is always controversial, and this year a group of 38 *superintendents*（地区教育主管）from five states wrote to ask that their schools be excluded from the calculation. "It is impossible to know which high schools are 'the best' in the nation," their letter read, in part. "Determining whether different schools do or don't offer a high quality of education requires a look at many different measures, including students' overall academic accomplishments and their subsequent performance in college, and taking into consideration the unique needs of their communities."

H) In the end, the superintendents agreed to provide the data we sought, which is, after all, public information. There is, in our view, no real dispute here; we are all seeking the same thing, which is schools that better serve our children and our nation by encouraging students to tackle tough subjects under the guidance of gifted teachers. And if we keep working toward that goal, someday, perhaps, a list won't be necessary.

注意: 此部分试题请在**答题卡1**上作答。

46. According to the 38 superintendents, to rank schools scientifically, it is necessary to use many different measures.

47. *Newsweek* ranked high schools according to their college-level test participation.

48. Fifty years ago, big, modern, suburban high schools were established in the hope of providing good education for baby boomers.

49. The most noticeable current trend in high school education is that some large schools have split up into smaller ones.

50. As a result of setting up big schools, students' performance declined.

51. According to Jeff Gilbert, the "advisory" classes at Hillsdale were set up so that students could maintain closer relationships with their teachers.

52. We learn about Hillsdale's students in the late 1990s that their school performance was getting worse.

53. The schools funded by the Bill and Melinda Gates Foundation are mostly small in size.

54. To better serve the children and our nation, schools should hire gifted teachers and encourage students to take tough subjects.

55. Simplicity is still considered a strength of *Newsweek*'s school ranking system in spite of the criticism it receives.

试题解析

本文夹叙夹议,讲述在全美高中排名中,小规模学校呈上升趋势,进而引出美国高中学校规模变化趋势及学校排名的依据和目的。

46. G 根据题干中的关键词38 superintendents, many different measures定位到G段第三句: Determining whether different schools do or don't offer a high quality of education requires a look at many different measures (要判断不同学校是否提供高质量的教育需要从许多不同的角度评判),故选G。

47. C 根据题干中的关键词*Newsweek* ranked, according to定位到C段第三句: Ten years ago, when the first *Newsweek* list based on college-level test participation was published, only three of the top 100 schools had graduating classes smaller than 100 students. (十年前,基于高中生参加大学水平测试人数比例的第一份《新闻周刊》学校排名发布时,前100所学校中只有三所学校的毕业生人数少于100),故选C。

48. A 试题解析:根据题干中的关键词Fifty years ago, big, modern, suburban high schools, baby boomers定位到A段前两句: Fifty years ago, they were the latest thing in educational reform: big, modern, suburban high schools with students counted in the thousands. As baby boomers came of high-school age, big schools promised economic efficiency, a greater choice of courses, and, of course, better football teams. (五十年前,大规模的、现代化的、郊区化的高中学校作为教育改革的新生事物出现。当二战后婴儿潮时期出生的孩

子们到了上高中的年龄时，规模大的高中学校承诺更高的经济效益、更多的课程选择，当然，还有更好的足球队），故选A。

49. B　根据题干中的关键词most noticeable, large schools have split up into smaller ones定位到B段尾句：And most noticeable of all, there is the phenomenon of large urban and suburban high schools that have split up into smaller units of a few hundred, generally housed in the same grounds that once boasted thousands of students all marching to the same band（最引人注目的是，一些大规模的市区高中和郊区高中分裂成了有着几百名学生的小分校（单位），这些分校一般仍然在同一校园内，这些校园曾经以有着几千名学生按着统一步调行进而自豪），故选B。

50. A　根据题干中的关键词result, big schools定位到A段第三、四两句：Only years later did we understand the trade-offs this involved: the creation of excessive bureaucracies, the difficulty of forging personal connections between teachers and students. SAT scores began dropping in 1963; today, on average, 30% of students do not complete high school in four years, a figure that rises to 50% in poor urban neighborhoods（多年之后，我们才看到这样的大规模的高中学校引发的问题：臃肿的官僚机构随之产生，师生关系很难建立。1963年，学生SAT分数开始下降；现在，平均30%的学生不能在四年之内完成高中学业，在贫困的地区，这一比例高达50%），故选A。

51. E　根据题干中的关键词Jeff Gilbert, advisory定位到E段倒数第二句："Our kids are coming to school in part because they know there are adults here who know them and care for them."（来我们这里上学的孩子，部分原因是因为他们知道这里的大人了解他们，关心他们），故选E。

52. D　根据题干中的关键词Hillsdale's students, late 1990s定位到D段首句：Although many of Hillsdale's students came from wealthy households, by the late 1990s average test scores were sliding and it had earned the unaffectionate nickname "Hillsjail."（虽然Hillsjail高中很多学生来自富裕家庭，但是在20世纪90年代后期，这所学校平均测试成绩在下滑，让它得到了不受人喜爱的绰号"希尔斯监狱"），故选D。

53. B　根据题干中的关键词the Bill and Melinda Gates Foundation, mostly small in size定位到B段第二句：This has been due, in part, to the Bill and Melinda Gates Foundation, which has invested $1.8 billion in American high schools,

helping to open about 1,000 small schools—most of them with about 400 kids each, with an average enrollment of only 150 per grade. (这要部分归因于比尔和梅琳达·盖茨基金会，该基金会给美国高中投资18亿美元，帮助建立了约1000所小型学校——其中的大多数有约400名学生，平均每个年级仅招收150个学生)，故选B。

54. H 根据题干中的关键词better serve the children and our nation, gifted teachers, encourage students, tough subjects定位到H段第二句：There is, in our view, no real dispute here; we are all seeking the same thing, which is schools that better serve our children and our nation by encouraging students to tackle tough subjects under the guidance of gifted teachers. (在我们看来，并不存在真正的争议，我们都在追求同样的东西——通过鼓励学生在有才能的老师的指导下攻克艰难学科，学校能更好地服务于我们的孩子和国家)，故选H。

55. F 根据题干中的关键词simplicity, strength, system, criticism定位到F段：The *Newsweek* list of top U.S. high schools was made this year, as in years past, according to a single metric, the proportion of students taking college-level exams. Over the years this system has come in for its share of criticism for its simplicity. But that is also its strength: it's easy for readers to understand, and to do the arithmetic for their own schools if they'd like. (今年的《新闻周刊》全美高中排名和往年一样，都是根据一个标准，即高中生参加大学水平测试的人数比例。多年来，该体系由于其标准简单而受到了很多批评。但是，这也正是它的优势：读者更容易理解，而且如果愿意的话，他们能容易地计算出自己学校的排名)，故选F。

十、经典模拟题十

Directions: *In this section, you are going to read a passage with ten statements attached to it. Each statement contains information given in one of the paragraphs. Identify the paragraph from which the information is derived. You may choose a paragraph more than once. Each paragraph is marked with a letter. Answer the questions by marking the corresponding letter on **Answer Sheet 2**.*

The Magician

The revolution that Steve Jobs led is only just beginning

A) When it came to putting on a show, nobody else in the computer industry, or any other industry for that matter, could match Steve Jobs. His product launches, at which he would stand alone on a black stage and produce as if by magic an "incredible" new electronic *gadget* (小器具) in front of an amazed crowd, were the performances of a master showman. All computers do is fetch and work with numbers, he once explained, but do it fast enough and "the results appear to be magic". Mr Jobs, who died recently aged 56, spent his life packaging that magic into elegantly designed, easy-to-use products.

B) The reaction to his death, with people leaving candles and flowers outside Apple stores and politicians singing praises on the internet, is proof that Mr Jobs had become something much more significant than just a clever money-maker. He stood out in three ways—as a technologist, as a *corporate* (公司的) leader and as somebody who was able to make people love what had previously been impersonal, functional gadgets. Strangely, it is this last quality that may have the deepest effect on the way people live. The era of personal technology is in many ways just beginning.

C) As a technologist, Mr Jobs was different because he was not an engineer—and that was his great strength. Instead he was keenly interested in product design and *aesthetics* (美学), and in making advanced technology simple to use. He repeatedly took an existing but half-formed idea—the mouse-driven computer, the digital music player, the smartphone, the *tablet computer* (平板电脑)—and showed the rest of the industry how to do it properly. Rival firms competed with each other to follow where he led. In the process he brought about great changes in computing, music, telecoms and the news business that were painful for existing firms but welcomed by millions of consumers.

D) Within the wider business world, a man who liked to see himself as a *hippy* (嬉皮士), permanently in revolt against big companies, ended up being hailed by many of those corporate giants as one of the greatest chief executives of his time. That was partly due to his talents: showmanship, strategic vision, an astonishing attention to detail and a dictatorial management style which many bosses must have envied. But most of all it was the extraordinary *trajectory* (轨迹) of his life. His fall from grace in the 1980s, followed by his return to Apple in 1996 after a period in the wilderness, is an inspiration to any businessperson whose career has taken a turn for the worse. The way in which Mr Jobs revived the failing company he had co-founded and turned it into the world's biggest tech firm （bigger even than Bill Gates's Microsoft, the company that had outsmarted Apple so dramatically in the 1980s）, sounds like something from a Hollywood movie.

E) But what was perhaps most astonishing about Mr Jobs was the absolute loyalty he managed to inspire in customers. Many Apple users feel themselves to be part of a community, with Mr Jobs as its leader. And there was indeed a personal link. Apple's products were designed to accord with the boss's tastes and to meet his extremely high standards. Every iPhone or MacBook has his fingerprints all over it. His great achievement was to combine an emotional spark with computer technology, and make the resulting product feel personal. And that is what put Mr Jobs on the right side of history, as technological *innovation*（创新） has moved into consumer electronics over the past decade.

F) As our special report in this issue （printed before Mr Jobs's death） explains, innovation used to spill over from military and corporate laboratories to the consumer market, but lately this process has gone into reverse. Many people's homes now have more powerful, and more flexible, devices than their offices do; consumer gadgets and online services are smarter and easier to use than most companies' systems. Familiar consumer products are being adopted by businesses, government and the armed forces. Companies are employing in-house versions of Facebook and creating their own "app stores" to deliver software to employees. Doctors use tablet computers for their work in hospitals. Meanwhile, the number of consumers hungry for such gadgets continues to swell. Apple's products are now being snapped up in Delhi and Dalian just as in Dublin and Dallas.

G) Mr Jobs had a reputation as a control *freak* (怪人), and his critics complained that the products and systems he designed were closed and inflexible, in the name of greater ease of use. Yet he also empowered millions of people by giving them access to cutting-edge technology. His insistence on putting users first, and focusing on elegance and simplicity, has become deep-rooted in his own company, and is spreading to rival firms too. It is no longer just at Apple that designers ask: "What would Steve Jobs do?"

H) The gap between Apple and other tech firms is now likely to narrow. This week's announcement of a new iPhone by a management team led by Tim Cook, who replaced Mr Jobs as chief executive in August, was generally regarded as competent but uninspiring. Without Mr Jobs to shower his star dust on the event, it felt like just another product launch from just another technology firm. At the recent unveiling of a tablet computer by Jeff Bezos of Amazon, whose company is doing the best job of following Apple's lead in combining hardware, software, content and services in an easy-to-use bundle, there were several attacks at Apple. But by doing his best to imitate Mr Jobs, Mr Bezos also *flattered*（抬举）him. With Mr Jobs gone, Apple is just one of many technology firms trying to arouse his uncontrollable spirit in new products.

I) Mr Jobs was said by an engineer in the early years of Apple to emit a "reality" *distortion*（扭曲）field", such were his powers of persuasion. But in the end he created a reality of his own, channeling the magic of computing into products that reshaped entire industries. The man who said in his youth that he wanted to "put a ding in the universe" did just that.

注意：此部分试题请在**答题卡1**上作答。

46. Many corporate giants saw Steve Jobs as one of the greatest chief executives of his time.

47. According to this issue's special report, innovation nowadays originates in the consumer market.

48. Nobody could match Steve Jobs in showmanship.

49. For those who have suffered failures in business, Steve Jobs's life experience serves as an inspiration.

50. Steve Jobs deeply affected people's way of life by starting the era of personal technology.

51. Mr. Jobs's great strength lies in his keen interest in designing elegant and user-friendly gadgets.

52. Amazon, by having hardware, software, content and services combined in an easy-to-use bundle, did the best job in following Apple's lead.

53. In spite of the user-friendliness of Apple products, critics complained that they were closed and inflexible.

54. By channelling the magic of computing into products, Steve Jobs had succeeded in creating a reality of his own.

55. The most astonishing part of Mr Jobs's success is that he inspired absolute loyalty in Apple users.

试题解析

本文是一篇人物传记，首先概括了乔布斯的能力和一生的成就，接着回顾了他一生中的重要事迹并指出他所带来的影响，然后提到没有了乔布斯的苹果公司正在变得平凡，最后对他的一生做了点评。

46. D 根据题干中的关键词 Many corporate giants, one of the greatest chief executives of his time 定位到 D 段首句：ended up being hailed by many of those corporate giants as one of the greatest chief executives of his time（然而正是这样一个人，被那些企业巨擘称为他那个时代最伟大的执行总裁之一），故选 D。

47. F 根据题干中的关键词 in this issue's special report, innovation, consumer market 定位到 F 段首句：As our special report in this issue（printed before Mr Jobs's death）explains, innovation used to spill over from military and corporate laboratories to the consumer market, but lately this process has gone into reverse.（正如印刷于乔布斯先生逝世前的本刊特别报道所指出的那样：从前，科技创新是从军事和企业实验室进入消费市场的，但最近，这一过程恰恰相反），故选 F。

48. A 根据题干中的关键词 nobody could match Steve Jobs 定位到 A 段首句：When it came to putting on a show, nobody else in the computer industry, or any other industry for that matter, could match Steve Jobs.（提到表演艺术，在计算机行业或其他任何行业，没有人可以与史蒂夫·乔布斯相媲美），故选 A。

49. D 根据题干中的关键词 those who have suffered failures in business, an inspiration 定位到 D 段第四句：His fall from grace in the 1980s, followed by

his return to Apple in 1996 after a period in the wilderness, is an inspiration to any businessperson whose career has taken a turn for the worse. （20世纪80年代，他辞职离开苹果公司，事业上遭受重创。数年后，他重振旗鼓，于1996年回到了苹果公司。这段经历，对任何一个事业正处于滑坡阶段的商人而言是莫大的鼓舞），故选D。

50. B 根据题干中的关键词Steve Jobs, deeply affected people's way of life, the era of personal technology定位到B段最后两句：Strangely, it is this last quality that may have the deepest effect on the way people live. The era of personal technology is in many ways just beginning. （令人感到奇怪的是，或许正是他最后的这种品质对人们的生活方式产生了最深远的影响。从许多方面看来，个性化技术时代才刚刚开始），故选B。

51. C 根据题干中的关键词Mr. Jobs's great strength, keen interest in designing, gadgets定位到C段前两句：As a technologist, Mr Jobs was different because he was not an engineer—and that was his great strength. Instead he was keenly interested in product design and aesthetics, and in making advanced technology simple to use.（作为一名技术专家，乔布斯先生是与众不同的，因为他并不是一名工程师，而这正是他的优势所在。相反，他醉心于产品的设计与美观，并且致力于将先进的技术变得简单易用），故选C。

52. H 根据题干中的关键词Amazon, hardware, software, content and services combined in an easy-to-use bundle, did the best job in following Apple's lead定位到H段第四句：At the recent unveiling of a tablet computer by Jeff Bezos of Amazon, whose company is doing the best job of following Apple's lead in combining hardware, software, content and services in an easy-to-use bundle （亚马逊公司是苹果公司最杰出的跟随者，致力于将硬件、软件、内容和服务整合在一起，使之便捷易用），故选H。

53. G 根据题干中的关键词products, critics complained that, closed and inflexible定位到G段首句：Mr Jobs had a reputation as a control freak, and his critics complained that the products and systems he designed were closed and inflexible, in the name of greater ease of use （乔布斯先生素来以控制狂著称。批评家指出，他设计的产品和系统打着更方便使用的幌子，实则是封闭死板的），故选G。

54. I　根据题干中的关键词channelling the magic of computing into products, creating a reality of his own定位到I段第二句：But in the end he created a reality of his own, channeling the magic of computing into products that reshaped entire industries.（最终，乔布斯确实创造了一个属于自己的"现实世界"。他将计算机运作的魔力融入产品中，而这些产品重塑了整个电子行业），故选I。

55. E　根据题干中的关键词most astonishing, absolute loyalty, Apple users定位到E段前两句：But what was perhaps most astonishing about Mr Jobs was the absolute loyalty he managed to inspire in customers. Many Apple users feel themselves to be part of a community, with Mr Jobs as its leader. （但或许乔布斯先生最令人惊奇的是，他能激发消费者的绝对忠诚。许多苹果用户都有一种归属感，而乔布斯先生正是他们的领头人），故选E。

第六章　翻译新题型十大经典模拟题

新题型说明：原单句汉译英调整为段落汉译英。翻译内容涉及中国的历史、文化、经济、社会发展等。四级长度为140-160个汉字。

一、翻译新题型攻略

(一)翻译标准

开始做翻译时，首先想到的两个问题就是：翻译的标准是什么？怎样才算好的译文？

对于四级考生而言，有两点要求：(一)忠实；(二)通顺。"忠实"主要是指内容。翻译是在理解了中文表达的意思之后，把同样的意思用英语表达出来。也就是说，考生的任务是用英语表达指定文字的意思，而不是自己进行创作。因此，就要力求准确地表达原作者的意思。"通顺"指的是语言。在翻译时，要尽量使译文通顺易懂。也许有人会问，只提这样两点要求，标准是否定得太低了呢？事实并非如此。真正做到上述两条，并非易事。

在做汉译英时，要把具有中国特色的人、事、物用英语表达出来，让外国人看懂，并做到语法正确、行文流畅，也不是轻而易举的事。如果我们的译文真能做到既忠实于原文又语句通顺，也就基本上达到了新四级汉译英的要求。

(二)汉译英基本功

汉译英时，理解汉语原文一般来说问题不大。虽然有时原作也不是很容易理解，但这种情况不多。因此，能否攻克汉译英就在于考生驾驭英语的能力。

就英语翻译而言，有以下三个方面值得考生注意：

1.拼写正确

怎样拼写，不可忽视。如不小心，很简单的词也会拼错。比如，occasion一词中包含两个c，一个s。不小心就会误写成一个c，两个s。又如，英语里有很多不规则动词，如come, teach, sit等等，它们的过去式和过去分词有特殊的形式，而不能直接加ed。而welcome是规则动词，其过去式是welcomed，如果仿照come那样去变就不对了。拼写错误的问题好比在汉语短文里写错别字，如果一篇短文有很多错别字，那这篇短文的质量也就可想而知了。

2. 合乎用法

一个词怎样用，和哪个词连用，很有讲究。一不小心，就可能违反其用法。例如，The professor arranged experts from Peking University to give us some up-to-date information we wanted. 汉语中可以说"安排某人做某事"，英语中则要说to arrange for somebody to do something。如果省略介词for，就不合用法了。再如as he welcomed his visitors，这样说是可以的。但汉语常说欢迎某人做某事，英语就不能说welcome somebody to do something，而要说somebody is welcome to do something，需要注意的是，welcome在这里不是动词，而是形容词。

3. 句子平稳

也就是说每个句子都是合乎语法的。比如："在他三岁的时候，父亲去世了，母子无依无靠，处境更加困难，怎么办呢?"如译作：When he was three years old, his father died, mother and son had no support, life become more difficult. What's to be done?"则不妥。第一句译文虽然看上去很接近原文，但这样把几个短句放在一起，结构松散，分句间缺少应有的联系，表达不合乎英语的句法，也不流畅。第二句译文时态不正确，此处讲述的是过去发生的事情，也不属于引用对话，所以不能用现在时。总之，汉译英时必须随时都有自己是在使用英语的意识，要多想想怎样表达才合乎英语的用法规范。

以上三个方面可以说是汉译英的基本功。这三个方面做好了，就可以进一步考虑怎样译得更好一些。如果做到这三个方面还有很多问题，那就还要以练好基本功为重。当然，我们仍在学习的过程之中，在使用英语时可能尚未做到精确表达，但是如果坚持认真对待和不断努力，准确性就一定会得到提高。

二、十大经典模拟题

（一）历史

Directions: *For this part, you are allowed 30 minutes to translate a passage from Chinese into English. You should write your answer on **Answer Sheet 2**.*

秦始皇是秦朝的第一位皇帝。他从公元前230年到公元前221年花了十年的时间逐一消灭了六个不同的国家，并建立了中国历史上第一个中央集权的封建国家(centralized feudal state)。所有重要的中央和地方政府官员都由他任命和免职。

在他统治期间，他制定了一套法律，统一了度量衡，甚至还统一了书面文字。所有这些措施都促进了经济和文化的发展。

Qin Shihuang was the first Emperor of the Qin Dynasty. He spent ten years from 230 to 221 BC to wipe out all the six different states one after another and established the first centralized feudal state in Chinese history. All the important officials of the central and local governments were to be appointed and dismissed by him. During his reign, he worked out a set of laws and fix the standard of weights and measures and even unified the Chinese characters in writing. All these measures promoted the economic and cultural development.

(二)文化

Directions: *For this part, you are allowed 30 minutes to translate a passage from Chinese into English. You should write your answer on **Answer Sheet 2**.*

中国新年是中国最重要的传统节日，在中国也被称为春节。新年的庆祝活动从除夕开始一直延续到元宵节(the Lantern festival)，即从农历(lunar calendar)最后一个月的最后一天至新年第一个月的第十五天。各地欢度春节的习俗和传统有很大差异，但通常每个家庭都会在除夕夜团聚，一起吃年夜饭。其他的活动还有放鞭炮、发红包和探亲访友等。

Chinese New Year is the most important traditional festival in China, which is also known as the Spring Festival. New Year celebrations run from Chinese New Year's Eve to the Lantern Festival, namely, the last day of the last month to the 15th day of the first month of the new year in Chinese lunar calendar. Customs and traditions of celebrating the Spring Festival vary widely from place to place, but generally every family will reunite and have dinner together. Other activities include setting off firecrackers, giving people red envelopes with money in them, visiting relatives and friends and so on.

(三)文化

Directions: *For this part, you are allowed 30 minutes to translate a passage from Chinese into English. You should write your answer on **Answer Sheet 2**.*

昆曲(Kunqu opera)是中国现存最古老的剧种之一，它在艺术、文学、历史方面都有着无可替代的价值。它起源于元朝末年(the late Yuan dynasty)江苏昆山地区，至今已有六百多年的历史。昆曲的表演有它独特的体系和风格，最大的特点是抒情性强、动作细腻(exquisite)，歌唱与舞蹈结合得巧妙而和谐。作为中华文化的代表，昆曲的影响广泛而深远，反映了中国戏剧的鲜明特征。

Kunqu opera is one of the oldest Chinese opera which has irreplaceable value in art, literature and history. It originated from Kunshan, Jiangsu Province at the late Yuan Dynasty and it has a history of more than 600 years. The performance of Kunqu opera has its unique system and styles, among which the most important ones are its lyrical expression and the exquisite movement in it. Songs and dances are combined with each other skillfully and harmoniously. As the representative of Chinese culture, the influence of Kunqu opera, which reflects the distinct characteristics of Chinese operas, is broad and profound.

(四)文化

Directions: *For this part, you are allowed 30 minutes to translate a passage from Chinese into English. You should write your answer on* ***Answer Sheet 2.***

北京大学成立于1898年，以文科和理科闻名，拥有两万多名学生。来自80多个国家的大约两千名留学生正在北京大学学习。这所大学在中国历史上发挥了非常重要的作用。近年来，北京大学在学术研究方面已经经历了恢复和调整的过程。北京大学正在努力成为一所教育中心和科学研究中心，以便为中国转变为一个高度文明的强大现代化国家做出积极的贡献。

Peking University was founded in 1898. It is famous for its liberal arts and sciences, with an enrollment of over 20,000 students. About 2,000 foreign students from more than 80 countries are studying in Peking University. The university has played an extremely important role in Chinese history. In recent years, it has undergone a process of restoration and readjustment in its academic work. Peking University is striving to become a centre both of education and of scientific research so as to contribute positively to the transformation of China into a highly civilized powerful modern country.

(五)文化

Directions: *For this part, you are allowed 30 minutes to translate a passage from Chinese into English. You should write your answer on **Answer Sheet 2**.*

故宫博物院(the Palace Museum),也称紫禁城(the Forbidden City),曾经是明朝和清朝(the Ming and Qing Dynasties)的皇家宫殿。故宫的建设历经14年,于1420年完工。次年,明朝的都城从南京迁到了北京。明朝和清朝24位皇帝曾经在紫禁城进行统治。这座宫殿是仍然屹立的最大的中国古代建筑(architecture)。故宫曾被扩建几次,但原有布局(layout)仍然得以保留。1949年之后,故宫进行了一些修缮(renovations),同时被中国政府列为重要的历史遗迹之一而得到特殊保护。

The Palace Museum, also known as the Forbidden City, was once the royal palaces of the Ming and Qing Dynasties. The construction of the palace took 14 years and was finished in 1420. In the following year, the capital of the Ming Dynasty was moved from Nanjing to Beijing. Twenty-four emperors of the Ming and Qing Dynasties used to rule in the Forbidden City. The palace is the largest piece of ancient Chinese architecture still standing. The palace had been expanded several times, but the original layout was preserved. After 1949, some renovations were done and the Palace Museum is listed as one of the important historical monuments under special preservation by the Chinese government.

(六)文化

Directions: *For this part, you are allowed 30 minutes to translate a passage from Chinese into English. You should write your answer on **Answer Sheet 2**.*

龙对于中国人而言是一个熟悉的动物,但没有人曾经见过一条真实的龙。提到"龙"这个字,中国人民无疑会想到一个巨大(gigantic)的动物,拥有牛头、鹿角、虾眼、鹰爪、蛇身、狮尾,通身被鱼鳞覆盖。在中国传统中,12个动物:鼠、牛、虎、兔、龙、蛇、马、羊、猴、鸡、狗、猪,用于代表人们出生的一个12年的周期。龙是其中唯一虚构(imaginary)的动物。

The dragon is a familiar animal to the Chinese people, but nobody has ever seen a real one. At the mention of the word "dragon", the Chinese people will definitely think of a gigantic animal with the head of an ox, the horns of a deer, the eyes of a shrimp, the claws of a hawk, the body of a snake, the tail of a lion and the whole body is covered by fish scales. In Chinese tradition, 12 animals—rat, ox, tiger, rabbit, dragon, snake, horse, goat, monkey, chicken, dog and pig—are used to represent a cycle of 12 years, during which people are born. Dragon is the only animal which is imaginary.

(七)文化

Directions: *For this part, you are allowed 30 minutes to translate a passage from Chinese into English. You should write your answer on **Answer Sheet 2**.*

　　长城象征着中国的古代文明，是世界上最著名的工程之一。长城的建造始于战国时期（the period of the Warring States）。最初，不同王国在战略地点（strategic points）建造城墙来保护其北方领域。公元前221年在秦代的第一个皇帝统一中国之后，这位皇帝决定将这些城墙连接起来并加以延伸。16世纪明朝时期，长城得以重建。长城是中国古代人民的伟大创造，1987年被联合国教育、科学、文化组织列入世界遗产（heritage）之一。

　　The Great Wall, symbolizing China's ancient civilization, is one of the world's most renowned projects. The construction of the Wall first began during the period of the Warring States. At first, walls were built at strategic points by different kingdoms to protect their northern territories. In 221 BC after the first Emperor of the Qin Dynasty unified China, the Emperor decided to have the walls linked up and extended. The Great Wall was rebuilt during the Ming Dynasty in the 16th century. It is the great creation of ancient Chinese people. In 1987, the Wall was listed by the United Nation's Education, Science and Culture Organization（UNESCO）as one of the World heritages.

(八)经济

Directions: *For this part, you are allowed 30 minutes to translate a passage from Chinese into English. You should write your answer on **Answer Sheet 2**.*

　　今年，全国各地积极推进经济体制和经济增长方式的转变，实施科教兴国（rejuvenate our country）和可持续发展战略，国民经济继续保持良好的发展势头，年初确定的宏观调控目标（macro-regulation targets）可以实现。当前我国经济发展的一个显著特点（salient feature），是既保持了经济的快速增长，又成功地抑制了通货膨胀(inflation)。今年各地都加大了国有企业的改革力度,各项试点工作全面展开,全年对外贸易仍将实现适当增长。

This year, vigorous efforts have been made throughout the country to transform the economic system and the mode of economic growth, to implement the strategy of rejuvenating our country by relying on science and education and achieving sustainable development. The national economy has maintained a good development momentum, and the macro-regulation targets set at the beginning of the year are expected to be met. A salient feature in China's economic development at present is that we have been able to achieve rapid economic growth and successfully kept inflation under control at the same time. State-owned enterprises throughout the country have stepped up reform this year and all pilot work is in full swing. A modest growth of foreign trade is still anticipated for the whole year.

(九)社会发展

Directions: *For this part, you are allowed 30 minutes to translate a passage from Chinese into English. You should write your answer on **Answer Sheet 2**.*

六十四年来,在中国共产党(the Chinese Communist Party)的领导下,各族人民团结奋斗,国家面貌发生了历史性的巨大变化。特别是中国共产党十一届三中全会(the Third Plenary Session of the Eleventh Communist Party Central Committee)以来,在邓小平建设的由中国特色社会主义 (building socialism with Chinese characteristics)理论的指引下,我们找到了适合本国国情的发展道路,我国的各项事业取得了举世瞩目的成就。现在,中国人民正满怀信心地在改革开放和现代化建设的道路上阔步前进。

Over the past sixty-four years, the Chinese people of all ethnic groups led by the Chinese Communist Party have made concerted efforts and brought enormous historic changes to the country. Since the Third Plenary Session of the Eleventh Communist Party Central Committee, in particular, under the guidance of Deng Xiaoping's theory of building socialism with Chinese characteristics, we have found a road to develop suited to our national conditions and scored remarkable achievements in various undertakings. Now, full of confidence, the Chinese people are advancing in giant steps along the road of reform, opening-up and modernization construction.

(十)社会发展

Directions: *For this part, you are allowed 30 minutes to translate a passage from Chinese into English. You should write your answer on **Answer Sheet 2**.*

北京是中华人民共和国的首都,也是全国的政治和文化中心。大约69万年前,北京人(Peking Man)住在北京西南48公里的周口店地区。十世纪初期,北京成为辽代(Liao Dynasty)的第二个都城。从那时起,北京先后成为金代、元代、明代和清代的首都,直至1911年。1949年10月1日,毛主席向全世界宣布了中华人民共和国的成立。北京有超过2000多万人口,大约1000万人住在城里,其他人住在郊区。

Beijing, the capital of the People's Republic of China, is the nation's political and cultural center. Some 690,000 years ago, Peking Man lived at Zhoukoudian, 48 kilometres southwest of Beijing. At the beginning of the 10th century, it was the second capital of the Liao Dynasty. From then on, the city had been the capital of the Jin, Yuan, Ming and Qing Dynasties until 1911. On October 1st, 1949, Chairman Mao proclaimed to the whole world the founding of the People's Republic of China. Beijing has a population of over 20 million; about 10 million live in the city proper and the rest on the outskirts.

三、四级汉译英核心词汇

1. 中国传统文化 traditional Chinese culture
2. 辉煌灿烂的文化遗产 splendid and glorious cultural heritage
3. 春节 Spring Festival
4. 除夕 Chinese New Year's Eve / Eve of the Spring Festival
5. 元宵节 Lantern Festival
6. 清明节 Tomb Sweeping Day
7. 端午节 Dragon Boat Festival
8. 中秋节 Mid-Autumn Festival
9. 重阳节 Double-Ninth Festival
10. 春秋时期 the Spring and Autumn Period
11. 战国时期 the Warring States Period
12. 秦代 the Qin Dynasty

13. 汉代 the Han Dynasty

14. 三国时期 the Three Kingdoms Period

15. 唐代 the Tang Dynasty

16. 宋代 the Song Dynasty

17. 元代 the Yuan Dynasty

18. 明代 the Ming Dynasty

19. 清代 the Qing Dynasty

20. 儒家 Confucianism

21. 佛家 Buddhism

22. 道家 Taoism / Daoism

23. 孔子 Confucius

24. 孟子 Mencius

25. 仁 Goodness / benevolence

26. 义 Righteousness

27. 礼 Ritual / Politeness

28. 智 Wisdom

29. 信 Trust

30. 忠 Loyalty

31. 孝 Filial Piety

32. 廉 Honesty

33. 耻 Honor

34. 《诗经》 *The Book of Songs*

35. 《史记》 *Historical Records*

36. 《西游记》 *The Journey to the West*

37. 《水浒》 *Water Margin / Outlaws of the Marsh*

38. 《红楼梦》 *A Dream of Red Mansions*

39. 《三国演义》 *Romance of the Three Kingdoms*

40. 剪纸 Paper Cutting

41. 火锅 Hot Pot

42. 书法 Calligraphy

43. 对联 Couplets

44. 四合院 Siheyuan / Quadrangle

45. 火药 gunpowder

46. 农历 Lunar Calendar

47. 物质文明 Material Civilization

48. 精神文明 Spiritual Civilization

49. 京剧 Beijing Opera / Peking Opera

50. 功夫 Gong Fu / Kung Fu

51. 太极拳 Tai Chi

52. 天坛 Altar of Heaven in Beijing

53. 故宫博物院 The Palace Museum

54. 相声 Cross-talk / Comic Dialogue

55. 北京烤鸭 Beijing Roast Duck

56. 烟花爆竹 fireworks and firecracker

57. 敦煌莫高窟 Mogao Caves

58. 一国两制 One Country, Two Systems

59. 香港澳门同胞 Compatriots from Hong Kong and Macao

60. 长江中下游地区 The Mid-low Reaches of Yangtze River

61. 中外合资企业 Joint Ventures

62. 大中型国有企业 Large and Medium-sized State-owned Enterprises

63. 文化交流 cultural exchanges

64. 文化融合 cultural blending / integration

65. 京剧 Peking Opera

66. 西方文化 western cultures

67. 多元文化 multi-cultures

68. 文化多元化 cultural diversity

69. 保存珍惜 preserve and cherish

70. 取其精华 absorb it's essence

71. 去其糟粕 resist it's dark side

72. 积极促进文化发展 promote cultural development positively

73. 与时俱进 keeping pace with times

74. 文化传统 cultural traditions

75. 人类文明 human civilization

76. 主流文化 mainstream culture

77. 解读经典 interpretation of classics

78. 市场经济体制 the market economy

79. 经济全球化 economic globalization

80. 科技进步 advancements in science and technology

81. 私营企业 private enterprise

82. 汽车产业 automobile industry

83. 房地产业 real estate industry

84. 电信产业 telecommunication industry

85. 国产品牌 domestic/national/Chinese brand

86. 市场份额 market share/portion

87. 公司 company/corporation

88. 企业 enterprise

89. 吸引外资 attract foreign investment

90. 深远的社会经济影响 profound social and economic consequences

91. 改革开放 the reform and opening-up

92. 社会保障体系 social security system

93. 住房问题 housing problem

94. 公用基础设施 public infrastructure

95. 经济危机 economic crisis

96. 金融危机 financial crisis

97. 经济不景气 economic recession

98. 找工作 seek employment

99. 找工作者 job seeker

100. 应对危机 face the crisis/ meet the crisis/ fight crisis